www.wadsworth.com

wadsworth.com is the World Wide Web site for Wadsworth and is your direct source to dozens of online resources.

At *wadsworth.com* you can find out about supplements, demonstration software, and student resources. You can also send email to many of our authors and preview new publications and exciting new technologies.

wadsworth.com
Changing the way the world learns®

The Practice of Macro Social Work

SECOND EDITION

William G. Brueggemann
Kyushu University of Health and Welfare
Nobeoka, Japan

BROOKS/COLE

THOMSON LEARNING

Australia • Canada • Mexico • Singapore • Spain • United Kingdom • United States

BROOKS/COLE

THOMSON LEARNING

Social Work Executive Editor: Lisa Gebo
Editorial Assistant: Sheila Walsh
Marketing Manager: Caroline Concilla
Project Editor: Tanya Nigh
Print Buyer: Mary Noel
Permissions Editor: Joohee Lee

Production Service: Electronic Publishing Services Inc., N.Y.C.
Photo Researcher: Linda Rill
Copy Editor: Electronic Publishing Services Inc., N.Y.C.
Cover Designer: Bill Stanton
Compositor: Electronic Publishing Services Inc., N.Y.C.
Text and Cover Printer: R. R. donnelley & Sons Company

Wadsworth/Thomson Learning
10 Davis Drive
Belmont, CA 94002-3098
USA

For more information about our products, contact us:
Thomson Learning Academic Resource Center
1-800-423-0563
http://www.wadsworth.com

International Headquarters
Thomson Learning
International Division
290 Harbor Drive, 2nd Floor
Stamford, CT 06902-7477
USA

UK/Europe/Middle East/South Africa
Thomson Learning
Berkshire House
168-173 High Holborn
London WC1V 7AA
United Kingdom

Asia
Thomson Learning
60 Albert Street, #15-01
Albert Complex
Singapore 189969

Canada
Nelson Thomson Learning
1120 Birchmount Road
Toronto, Ontario M1K 5G4
Canada

Library of Congress Cataloging-in-Publication Data
Brueggemann, William G.
      The Practice of Macro Social Work / William G. Brueggemann
            p. cm.
      Includes bibliographical references and index.
      ISBN 0-534-57322-3
        1. Social service. 2. Social service--United States.
3. Social workers--United States. 4. Macrosociology. I Title.

HV41 .B76 2000
      361.3'2'0973--dc21   00-046844

For my children
Jennifer Saeko, William Masato, Sarah Lena Keiko
and others like them whose compassion,
caring, and concern for justice will help
bring about a new post modern social era.

CONTENTS IN BRIEF

PART V
Macro Social Work Resources   427

CONTENTS

Chapter 4   LEADERSHIP: THE HALLMARK OF MACRO SOCIAL WORK   83

PART II
Social Work With Communities   109

Chapter 5   COMMUNITIES   112

PART III
Social Work Practice With Organizations 229

Chapter 9 THE SOCIAL SECTOR AND THE RISE OF THE SOCIAL ORGANIZATION 232

Chapter 10 BECOMING A PROGRAM DEVELOPER 253

Chapter 11 BECOMING A SOCIAL WORK ADMINISTRATOR   **290**

Chapter 12 BECOMING AN ORGANIZATION DEVELOPER   **316**

PART IV
Macro Social Work at the Societal and Global Levels   345

PART V
Macro Social Work Resources 427

LIST OF EXERCISES AND CHECKLISTS

LIST OF FIGURES

PREFACE

*A*t the turn of the 20th century, the field of social work was peopled by leaders of enormous vision and energy whose goal was nothing less than the eradication of the overwhelming social problems of the day—grinding poverty, political corruption, abusive working conditions, exploited women and immigrants, dangerous and unhealthy slums, among many others. These macro social workers wanted to create a wholesome, safe, and equitable social environment in which the American dream would be a promise not only for the rich but for everyone. Jane Addams, Florence Kelly, Rev. Charles Loring Brace, St. Frances Cabrini, Homer Folks, Graham Taylor, Harriet Tubman, Mary Simkhovitch, W.E.B. Du Bois, the Abbott sisters, Clara Barton, Lillian Wald, and many other macro social work heroes displayed boundless altruism and compassion, courage, and character that we rarely see today. The pioneering efforts of macro social workers such as these laid the groundwork for many of the social advances from which we benefit.

But in spite of their effort, social problems continue to plague people of North America and around the world. Many of our cities are in disarray, crime still haunts our neighborhoods, poverty continues to abound, and even after years of legislation, civil rights abuses still occur. Even though our economic and political systems offer opportunity for many, it is becoming increasingly clear that the choices that matter most to us are not made by ordinary citizens, but by a few at the top. Rather than social goods such as social involvement, caring, and commitment, economic and governmental megastructures create alienation, dehumanization, and social passivity.

Not only has the modern project failed to eradicate most of our social problems, but even the social work profession has retreated from whole-hearted engagement in community organization, community development, planning, or other arenas of macro practice. As a result, in the early 1990s, few textbooks existed in the practice of macro social work that helped students grasp its heritage, understand its breadth, realize its possibilities, or capture its vision. The first edition of this book, published in 1996, was intended to fill this gap and assist in inspiring a renewed interest in macro social work.

Since the first edition, however, it has become increasingly clear that we are at the beginning of a new "post-modern era" in which the social will be our most compelling and prominent concern. Even as the ideology of mass-market economy, individualism, and modern functional reason seems to be triumphant, the seeds of its demise are already at work. A new era is emerging that is altering the way we think about social problems, recreating community, providing alternatives to market-centered organizations, and transforming modern politics. These developments are occurring in the least likely places—in the slums and barrios of most poverty-stricken areas of the globe. They are being brought about by the forgotten ones—the members of North America's inner cities, as well as the landless peasants of Guatemala, the homeless beggars of India, the grandmothers of Plaza de Mayo. The poorest people of the earth who bear the brunt of the world's problems are constructing a social revolution, and they are doing it mostly without the help of mainstream North American social work.

It should not be surprising that fundamental social change should arise from those who have been locked out of the benefits of modernity, who experience the violence that sustains it, the poverty that supports it, and the oppression that results from it. Fundamental social change will never come from the powerful who are at the heart and core of the modern project. Rich politicians and influential corporate bosses can do little to change the basic structures on which their power and wealth depend. Social problems will never be solved by clinical social work practice or the individualism on which it is based. Neither will social change come from conventional social work, whose primary energy seems to be committed to maintaining its professional status and authority. This second edition of The Practice of Macro Social Work is intended to help you, the macro social workers at the turn of the 21st century, bring about the new postmodern era, and assist you in creating a profession of authentic social work. This textbook will challenge you to examine your motivation for being a social worker, critique the premises of the social work profession, and help you learn about a world of opportunity and social promise that goes beyond conventional wisdom of the present. You will find generous amounts of history, theory, and practice in this book. I have included many exercises and checklists that I hope will help you think critically about issues, improve your skills, and develop your self understanding. In the appendices you will find listings of social organizations that will help you obtain volunteer experiences, internships, or jobs. You will find other resources and computer ancillaries that will broaden your vision far beyond what this book can accomplish alone.

If you accept the challenge that this book presents, align yourselves with the oppressed, identify with the outcast, the poor, the alienated of this world, and disengage yourselves from modern thinking, you may be among those social workers who will play a crucial role helping the poor people of the earth reshape our global society.

I invite you to let me know how successful this book is in preparing you for the challenges of social work in the new millennium. I will respond to each of your comments and suggestions. My e-mail address is william@phoenix.ac.jp. You can also visit my homepage at the Kyushu University of Health and Welfare. The University's homepage address is http://www.phoenix.ac.jp. When you reach the home page, move your cursor under the caption We Do on the left and scroll down until you come to the highlighted word shakai. Click on it and you will reach the Department of Welfare Administration and Social Planning. Near the bottom of the page you will see three Japanese words in green. Click on the green word at the right. This will bring you to the faculty directory. You will see my name listed. Click on English and you will access my homepage.

ACKNOWLEDGMENTS

Many people have helped me improve this book by their critiques, advice, and friendship. I want to thank Dr. Charles Trent, Wurtzweiler School of Social Work, Yeshiva University, and his class of community social work students; Chris Valley, Associate Executive Director of FamiliesFirst, Atlanta, Georgia; Rev. Bob Linthecum, World Vision International; Paulette Foerster, Executive Director, Lutheran Family and Children's Services, St. Louis; Mike McGarvin, Povarello House, Fresno; Dr. Tom Jones, Worx, Fresno; Shel Trapp and Gordon Mayer, National Training and Information Center, Chicago; Dr. Jim Holm, Director of the Administrative Leadership Program, Fresno Pacific University; David Nelson, Policy Analyst, Family Service America; and his father Dr. Ed Nelson, California State University, Fresno; Barbara Gravin-Wilbur, Center for International Education, University of Massachusetts; and Dr. Mark Hanna, School of Social Work, California State University, Fresno. I also want to thank the Association of Community Organization and Social Administration (ACOSA) and its many members for responding to my requests for assistance and to the social policy office of NASW for their help.

This book could not have been completed without the generous support, assistance, and resources provided by General President Kake of the Kake Educational Institution, Vice Chancellor Miyako Kake, Kyushu University of Health and Welfare, Nobeoka, Japan, and especially Yasuyuki Koseki, Dean of the KUHW School of Social Welfare. I am inordinately grateful to these people of vision and to this university.

The staff of BrooksCole have been particularly helpful and supportive, especially assistant editor Joanne VonZastrow, Annie Berterrechie, production manager Brooks Ellis, and copyeditor Eileen Smith. Finally, my continual gratitude to my wife Lorraine Luri Inaba Brueggemann, who provided constant support and encouragement through both the first and second editions of this book.

1

Overview of the Practice of Macro Social Work

The world is so much larger than I thought. I thought we went along paths—but it seems there are no paths. The going itself is the path.

C. S. Lewis, Perelandra

The dogmas of the quiet past are inadequate to the stormy present. The occasion is piled high with difficulty, and we must rise to the occasion. Just as our case is new, so we must think anew and act anew.

Abraham Lincoln, President of the United States
Annual Message, December, 1862

Ideas in This Chapter

DEATH COMES TO FRANCISCO

Francisco Martinez is dead. One of millions of faceless and insignificant laborers of our country, his passing will scarcely make a ripple in the course of world affairs. But "when his friends chew over the events of that morning, they taste the bile of being strangers in a strange land, the mules pulling agriculture's plow," writes Alex Pulaski. To his friends Francisco's death is symbolic of the hypocrisy of American culture.[1] Searching for a better life, Francisco, a young Triqui Indian, came to America from the state of Oaxaca, Mexico, but as Filemon Lopez, an advocate for the Mixteco Indians said, "the end of all this, for many, is death."

Each year the numbers of Mixteco Indians swell in California when summer farmwork calls. The many who remain in the United States often must live in caves or in the open. Francisco, however, was more fortunate than most. Part of a vine-pruning crew, he was one of 14 men and their wives and children who shared an unheated brick shed owned by rancher Russell Scheidt.

On the morning of January 17, 1993, Francisco's fortune changed. Waking for work at about 5:00 A.M., Augustin Ramirez found Francisco on the floor, his breathing labored, appearing near death. Augustin woke two of Francisco's friends, who ran to the ranch house to ask Scheidt to use the phone. Rousted out of bed, Russell Scheidt was exhausted, having just returned at midnight from a Caribbean vacation in Jamaica. Mario Ramirez told him in Spanish that Francisco was dying and they needed to call the police. Scheidt's response, according to Ramirez, was that they had cars, and they could take him to the hospital if they wished. Then he shut the door in their faces. Later Scheidt said "I can't really remember what I told them…I was kind of incoherent, to tell the truth."

Desperate for help, Francisco's friends sped into Kerman, a nearby town. Stopping at a service station, they talked an attendant into calling the Kerman police. They explained their problem to the officer, who asked several questions and then called the Sheriff's department. The friends waited for twenty-two minutes for the Sheriff's deputies to arrive. Wasting more precious time, the deputies drove to the shed, where they found Francisco at 6:15 A.M. already dead. Finally, they called the ambulance.

Francisco died of acute alcohol poisoning, which caused his brain to shut down his lungs. Tom Stoeckel, manager of the Valley Medical Center's emergency unit in Fresno, said that paramedics can revive victims of alcohol poisoning by simply giving them oxygen. However, death can result if the supply of oxygen to the brain has stopped for even a few minutes. The official report makes no mention of Scheidt or his refusal to allow the workers to call an ambulance. It stated that Francisco was already dead when the workers found him that morning.

The afternoon Francisco died, Scheidt returned with a translator and told the Mixteco men, women, and children to leave. The translator reportedly told them that housing inspectors were coming and the shed was not fit for human habitation. Scheidt said later that the men had finished their work and were basically squatters.

Francisco was buried February 17, 1993, a victim of human indifference, powerlessness, and poverty. His friends, now unemployed and homeless, gave him the best funeral they could buy with the $861 they collected. Four of his friends attended the service. Russell Scheidt did not come.

WHAT YOU WILL LEARN IN THIS CHAPTER

Francisco Martinez died a victim of alcohol poisoning. But more importantly, his death was ultimately brought on by social conditions of poverty, racism, indifference, and exploitation against an entire group of people. Even in America, many are impoverished economically and socially for the benefit of a few. When social abuse occurs in this fashion, our entire society is diminished and degraded.

Macro social workers are professionals who want to make a difference in people's lives where oppression, intolerance, and insensitivity exist. They try to correct social conditions that cause human suffering and misery. They struggle to get at the root of social problems by calling attention to injustice and by discovering where human needs exist. Macro social workers work to strengthen our communities and improve organizational systems. Some macro social workers advocate for better social policies at the national level, and others help resolve social problems in our global society.

Above all, however, macro social workers are active and creative agents in the construction of social reality. They try to see beyond the distortions that those in power sometimes use to justify their positions. They challenge illusions that lead nowhere and contest false answers that only prolong the status quo. They take a fresh look at social conditions and try new ways to resolve old problems.

This overview introduces you to the field of macro social work. You will see how different aspects of macro social work practice are covered in this book. You will begin to discover why the field of macro social work is important, and you will be challenged to consider your own role as a macro social worker. As you read this overview, think about how macro social work and its particular methods could have made a difference to the Triqui Indians and others like them in our world.

WHAT IS MACRO SOCIAL WORK?

Macro social work is the practice of helping people solve social problems and make social change at the community, organizational, societal, and global levels. Let's look at this definition in more detail.

Solving Social Problems

Many social work practitioners help individuals or couples who have been affected by and who bear the scars of *personal problems*. While healing and helping damaged individuals is important, it is its wider social concern that distinguishes social work from other helping professions. This wider concern involves *social problems*—those conditions of society that create personal troubles and are often embedded in the institutions and premises on which our society is based. Among these social problems are racism, sexism, violence, economic inequality, and the maldistribution of political power, to name just a few.

One of the premises that guides this book is that the most effective way of solving social problems is by people who are affected by social problems working together at the local level. Macro social workers believe that when people take charge of their own des-

tinies and become actively involved in the life of their communities, they become empowered to lead fulfilling, meaningful, and productive lives. In Chapter 2 you will look at several theories that have been used to explain why social problems exist. You will be invited to critique these theories and develop your own working definition of social problems. But you will also discover that macro social workers attempt to bring about a better society by means of an asset or strength-based approach.

Macro social workers apply a method called *rational problem-solving* to conditions that cause social problems. Rational problem-solving was conceived as a way of decision-making over 350 years ago and has been gradually applied to economic, political, and organizational problems in modern society. Rational–problem solving was used by macro social workers as early as the turn of the 20th century. Since then it has been adopted by the field of social work as a whole and is now known as the generalist social work method.

In Chapter 3 you'll see how the rational problem-solving process works and learn how to apply it step by step. As important as the rational social work method has been, however, it has limitations, particularly for the helping professions. You'll examine some of those limitations and discover that rational problem-solving needs to be supplemented with thinking *socially*. Social thinking is a method that guides much of the processes in macro social work. It is the means by which social issues become resolved and the way communities generate ideas that are superior to those developed by experts. But more importantly, social thinking is the way that people envision the future, access hope, and escape captivity to present reality. You will learn how to use social thinking to help people engage one another on the common journey of fulfilling meaning and completing the purpose of their lives together.

Making Social Change

People who make social change are change agents. Change agents come from a variety of disciplines and work at resolving different kinds of social issues. Ministers engaged in issues of social justice, for example, or scientists involved in protesting against nuclear war are change agents. Environmentalists are

The heart of social change is leadership. (© Kathy Sloan/Jeroboam, Inc.)

change agents working to save the earth and its ecosystems from destruction. Sociologists who do research on social problems or political scientists who try to improve social policies are change agents, as are public administrators working with or through complex organizations to improve social conditions. Change agents may be ordinary people working voluntarily for change in their own communities.

While change agents may come from many walks of life and any number of professions, there is one profession that claims change agent practice as its own. This is the profession of social work. Social workers need to understand how macro social systems work in order to design systems that are better, fix them when they become dysfunctional, challenge those models that are failing, and infuse with integrity and goodness those that are unethical. No other helping profession claims for itself so broad a social mandate as social work.

The heart of making social change is leadership. To some extent, every macro social worker needs be a social leader. In Chapter 4 you'll explore the most important ideas about leadership and learn how to apply them in macro social work practice. You will be invited to explore your own personal leadership style and how to use it in working with communities and organizations. However, you will find that what is tra-

ditionally described as leadership today is often nothing but a disguised form of paternalism, particularly as leadership has become redefined as management. Macro social workers reject paternalistic leadership. Instead, you will learn how to help people themselves become leaders who take charge of the social, economic, and political conditions that affect their own lives, and which contributes to the process of social betterment.

The Spectrum of Macro Social Work

Solving social problems and engaging in social change by means of macro social work practice is the heritage, the present responsibility, and the future promise of the social work profession. It is social work's commitment to social betterment at all levels that insures its continued impact in our world today. Macro social workers see the spectrum of communities, organizations, society, and global cultures as arenas of their concern and involvement.

Community Social Work   Part Two of this book is devoted to the practice of community social work: helping communities strengthen relationships between people and mediate between individuals and the organizational megastructures of society.[2] Next to our families, communities are our most basic and necessary social systems. We all find our sense of identity and connectedness to others in community. When our communities begin to erode, people's social bonds become weak. People become alienated from one another and from society as a whole. When communities become dysfunctional, people fail economically, emotionally, or socially.

For years, communities in both rich and poor nations have been neglected. Some are in disarray. As a result, many communities are rife with violence, poverty, and exploitation. Instead of oases of hope, enlightenment, and meaning they are deserts of despair, ignorance, and alienation. In Chapter 5 you will examine what community is, why it is so important, and why it may seem to be failing today. You will explore how macro social workers become involved with modern communities, communities of meaning or ontological communities, traditional communities, and communities of color.

Community planners are community social workers who assist local community groups develop plans for their own communities and act those plans. In Chapter 6 you will see how community planners work with locality and nonlocality based communities such as the communities of the aged, developmentally disabled, and others develop and carry out plans for their welfare. You will learn how to do social work community planning and explore a number of planning tools and techniques that you can apply to community projects.

Macro social workers who help make communities better places for individuals and families are called *community developers.* Community developers work in inner city ghettos, slums, barrios, migrant work camps, reservations, and housing projects of America, bringing people together to build strong human relationships and communication between people, and to provide for individual well being and support for family life. You will discover in Chapter 7 how community developers take on economic development projects and create community development corporations that build housing, open banks, form co-ops, and sponsor many community projects bringing new possibilities and opportunity where despair and hopelessxcommunity development corporation. You will also explore how community development and community organization work

together in a double pronged approach to community empowerment and how community developers help ontological communities or communities of meaning become strong and healthy.

Some community social workers help overcome the estrangement imposed by large megastructures of corporate and public life. These social workers are called *community organizers.* Community organization is a process by which neighborhoods and coalitions of neighborhoods work over the long term for community betterment and political empowerment. Community organizers help community members learn how to use their communities as social tools to invent their own futures and control their own destinies. You will see in Chapter 8 how community organizers assist people to overcome the politics of paternalism that keeps them left out, hold officials accountable to the community, create partnerships with government and business, and in the process reestablish democracy as a vital mode of civic life. You will learn how to do community organizing and discover four kinds of community organization practice models from which you can choose to strengthen neighborhoods.

Organizational Social Work   Robert Presthus and others have observed that we live in an organizational society.[3] Almost everyone in our society is intimately connected with and draws his or her sustenance from public sector governmental organizations or from private sector business organizations. You will find that while these organizational systems are by and large the reason for the enormous growth of the economy, at the same time they often allow little existential space for human communities. While community social work, therefore, continues to be a needed arena of macro social work practice, you will see in Part Three why organizational social work is rapidly becoming even more important. In Chapter 9 you will learn about the dynamics of *modern complex organizations*. While organizations and their defects are one reason many of our social problems exist, you will discover that macro social workers and others have been slowly developing a new and unprecedented hybrid form of organization and community by which social problems can be resolved. You will learn how these *social organizations* are structured, and how macro social workers and others have been forging these new social organizations into a third, relatively new *social sector* without which government and the economy could not exist.

In Chapter 10 you will find that some macro social workers, called *program developers*, work full time constructing these social organizations, and that you too can develop one of these new social organizations. You will discover, for example, how to form a community group, help the group become incorporated, form a board, develop funding, and hire staff. Social organizations require skilled social work administrators to implement change over the long haul. *Social work administration*, you'll see in Chapter 11, is a complex arena of macro social work practice including supervision, decision-making, budgeting, personnel, and planning. You will find, however, that social administration is not the management of people. You will explore how macro social workers are redefining administration and returning it to its original meaning of service, and you will learn how to carry out administrative decision-making and administer personnel and finances in organizations.

Sometimes business and governmental organizations become dysfunctional when they fail to adapt to their rapidly changing social environments. When this occurs, corporate and governmental administrators may call upon macro social work consultants called *organization developers* to help bring their systems back to effective functioning. In Chapter 12 you will learn step by step how these management consultants use conventional organization development techniques to bring about organizational change. However, you will also find out how to use a second, partnership approach to organizational development that is more congruent for use with the new social organizations. You will discover how to assist employees and administrators work as partners to develop their agencies into patterns of fulfilling relationships and projects of social betterment that engage clients and community in the process of social change.

Societal Social Work In Part Four, which explores the practice of macro social work at the societal and global levels, you will see how macro social workers get involved in politics, policy, social movements, and international social change. In Chapter 13, for example, you learn about a number of theories from which political scientists claim social policy is derived. You will find that some macro social workers become *professional politicians* by running for elected office. You will read about some of the more prominent social work politicians. Other macro social workers become *professional social policy advocates.* You will explore how they write legislation, lobby, give testimony before state legislative bodies and Congress, and work as watchdogs over regulatory commissions to insure that laws, once enacted, are carried out. You will learn all of the necessary steps to help community members devise their own social policy to control their own communities and engage the political process at the local level, where it really belongs. You will discover how to gather facts, decide among various policy alternatives, choose the best policy, and help your community group implement it.

Yet you will find that, as important as it is, political processes are sometimes ineffective in bringing about social change. When social problems remain unattended for long periods of time, you will see in Chapter 14 how people have organized themselves into mass *social movements* to bring social change. In fact, you will learn that social movements including the abolition, women's suffrage, the labor movement, the disabilities movement, lesbian and gay human rights, the environmental movement, and many others are almost endemic to American culture. Macro social workers who either lead or become involved in these societal movements are called *social activists*. You will examine how macro social work activists organize a modern social movement, and how to use a number of strategies, tactics, and techniques to influence the political process and bring about changes in social policy. You will also find, however, that social movements are not only about changing social policy. We are in the midst of a new social era, even though many are not at all aware of its current existence or its impending impact. Socially aware macro social workers and others, you will discover, are keenly conscious of and are working to move society in a completely new direction. They are involved in what have been called "new postmodern social movements." You will learn about these new movements, how they come about, and how you and other macro social workers can work to bring about a new social order.

International Social Work Macro social workers not only want to make their own societies better, but they reach out to poverty-stricken, war-torn areas of third world and fourth countries in Central and South

One of the most important roles of macro social workers is to build communities of people. (Photo by and courtesy of Earl Dotter and the Center for Community Change)

America, Africa, and Southeast Asia, where hunger, disease, and poverty exist on a scale that is often unknown in the West. In Chapter 15, you will explore how *international macro social workers* assist in community development projects in these often desperate parts of the world. You will discover how indigenous peoples are transforming their own social worlds by means of new international social movements, and how they are becoming involved in developing new social organizations—including *nongovernmental organizations* (NGOs)—to bring about a better, more humane global society. You will learn how to practice international community social work and find out how you too can be a part of this exciting world of global change.

RESOURCES

In Part Five you will find a number of resources that you can use to expand your understanding about macro social work. Many macro social workers have been heroes of social change who not only practiced change but wrote about it. The epilogue of this book

provides you with a list of resources written by and about many of these macro social work heroes.

One way that you can get involved in social change is to volunteer in a social organization. Look at the listings of domestic as well as international volunteer organizations in Appendix A. Then contact them for more information on how you can get valuable experience in macro social work. Another way to gain more understanding is to join a social organization or find out more about what they do. In Appendix B you will find listings of many social organizations in each of the arenas of social work described in this book. Write to them for more information, visit, or invite a macro social worker to your class. As you review the wide variety of social organizations that macro social workers have developed, administer, and serve, you might discover an area to explore for your internship.

A convenient way of accessing information worldwide is by means of your computer. In Appendix C you will learn how to use your computer to access information about macro social work. You will see a listing of user and newsgroups as well as some resources about macro social work issues to contact via the internet. This information can be useful in researching a paper or making a report to your class. Appendix C also contains links to agencies of the federal government others.

A CHALLENGE TO YOU

Modernity has directed the bulk of human intellectual and creative effort at overcoming physical and biological problems that plague humanity. Nearly every day, another medical or physical science breakthrough seems to occur that astounds our imagination. These developments hold the key to extending life and making life more prosperous, comfortable, and enjoyable. Yet in spite of the genuine wonder of these accomplishments, they pale in comparison to the social void that continues to stretch before us. While science and technology promise a world increasingly free of disease and disability, the social professions have abysmally failed to develop a world free of poverty, conflict, violence, hunger, homelessness, crime, oppression, injustice, and ethnic intolerance. Instead of reinvigorating efforts to find new approaches and new solutions to these social problems, most social workers today have retreated entirely from the social arena. They are content to deal with people's personal problems, avoiding the vast social issues under which our global civilization groans.

Many mainstream social workers fail to understand that the genuine technological accomplishments of the modern age do not constitute the real revolution that is occurring around them. They seem unable to recognize that we are living in one of the pivotal moments in history, the hallmark of which is a revitalization of the social. The struggle for authentic social equality, which has eluded mankind for millennia, and the power to construct social reality by the most insignificant is even now being recognized as a major turning point in the human condition. These developments are occurring in the most unsuspected places and by means of the least likely of people: the slums, the jungles, the migrant labor camps; the landless peasant, the homeless refugee, and the exiles who are shut out, left out, and kept out.

The simple quest for their own humanity by the least influential of the world is quietly and unintentionally undermining the foundations of modern instrumental reason, modern complex organization, and the managerial hierarchy of modern corporations and paternalistic governmental bureaucracy. Only the oppressed can save the oppressor and save themselves, and only those who are aligned and identify with the poor can have a part to play in developing new ways of social thinking, new communal forms, new social organizations, and the new social movements of the postmodern social era.

It is not at all remarkable that macro social work may seem an insignificant and undervalued component of the field of social work. In one sense it must be perceived this way. Its power comes from its devalued and seemingly marginalized position, as is true of the people with whom macro social workers most often identify. Social change never comes from the powerful, the influential whose commitments are to the conventionally accepted, the majority, the status quo. Change always comes from a few, the exceptional, those who see farther, those who are not among the mainstream. Because students such as yourselves have a different vision and your hearts are aligned with the least accomplished, you are marked to help bring about the social change that our society needs. If it were not so, you would follow the well-worn path that others follow. But macro social workers, in the main, not only make their own paths but are engaged in helping others make their own as well. You understand what C. S Lewis meant when he said, "It seems there are no paths. The going itself is the path."

If you become a macro social worker, it will be because you already have values and ways of seeing the world that are unique, and that align you with those who seem to be the weakest of the world. Prize this identification. It is your most important ally. This identification will continually help you explore areas of thinking and action that are aimed in the right direction, beckon you to become the person you were meant to become, and help you walk the way you were meant to go.

CONCLUSION

Macro social work is the social work arena committed to making a society that is finally free of social problems the resolution of which has eluded humanity since the dawn of civilization. It is a profession that calls you to think about how your social intelligence, your social ideals, and your social leadership can be brought to bear in constructing a truly humane society. It is the hope and dream of macro social work that a world free of oppression, poverty, and injustice can and will exist.

The practice of macro social work is and ought to be a profession that not only calls forth actions of the greatest humanity of which human beings are capable, but it is also a calling in which you construct yourself and simultaneously build community and build society. Being a macro social worker calls you to engage in the perennial issues of emancipation of the human condition, but in that struggle it challenges you to call forth the excellence in the human character that brings out your most redeeming human qualities. You become a person of character by entering the contest of winning your ideals and testing yourself against the important social problems of our day. You refine your character by standing for justice against all odds, by standing alongside the oppressed, and by holding steadfast against those conditions that degrade the human condition. You test your hope and faith by aligning yourself against the merciless, against those who are consumed by the need to control and oppress, and against those who place ruthless individualism and selfish ambition above human spirit and community service.

Macro social work is a profession whose vision extends to making a world in which redemptive social relationships become the true habitation of people. By encouraging, supporting, and developing community, people can be nurtured, and in such nurture find a milieu that leads to a healthy, free existence in which the human spirit can find its home. As macro social workers engage in community building, humanity can find its source, its inspiration, and its support.

Understanding the workings of our social world and intervening in it, therefore, are crucial to the repertoire of every social worker. While all social workers need to be engaged in macro social work to some extent, there are others for whom macro social work will become a full-time endeavor. I hope that this book may inspire some of you to become interested in macro social work practice as a professional goal in itself. It is probably safe to say that those social workers who engage in macro social work practice will have a lasting impact on our social environment, helping make fundamental changes in the way we live and guiding the future direction of our society.

KEY CONCEPTS

macro social work

social problems

social change

community social work

community

community planning

community development

community organization

organizational social work

modern complex organization

social organization

program development

social administration

organization development

societal social work

social movements

social action

social policy analysis

international social work

nongovernmental organizations

QUESTIONS FOR DISCUSSION

1. What are the characteristics of a good person, a good neighborhood, a good organization, or a good society?
2. Do you think the social has become eroded in today's society? Why or why not?
3. What are some indicators that our society has a strong sense of the social? What are indicators that our society has a weak sense of the social?
4. What do you think is the responsibility of social work for the social good? How do social workers produce the social good?
5. It has been asserted that the trend of the social work profession in the past 30 years has been to concentrate on clinical helping—individual counseling, family therapy, and group work rather than macro level helping.[4] If this is a fair statement, we will tend to serve people who have already been damaged by the effects of social

problems, rather than work toward the eradication of the causes and conditions of social decay itself. In this sense, social work is reactive rather than proactive. Do you believe this assessment is correct? Why or why not? If you believe it is true, comment on the implications of this trend for the practice of social work today.

6. Macro level social workers must often take a moral or ethical stance against people or social systems who perpetrate injustice. In what ways is the stance of a macro social worker similar or different from the ethical stance that micro social workers take in working with individual clients?

EXERCISE 1.1
Developing a Learning Contract

One way of insuring that you learn is to develop a set of learning objectives for yourself. The way to do this is to describe the learning you want to achieve, what you need to do to acquire that learning, and the behaviors from your classmates and instructor that will either enhance or detract from that learning. At home, answer the following questions and bring your lists to class.

1. What are the most important things I want to learn from this course?
2. What are the things that I need to do to achieve this learning?
3. What behaviors or activities of my classmates and the instructor will enhance my learning?
4. What behaviors or activities of my classmates and the instructor will not be conducive to my learning?

In class, form into triads. Your instructor will supply you with newsprint or another method to record your results. First, compare the personal learning you want to achieve. Combine and rank them in order. These become your group learning objectives. Then look at the things you need to do to accomplish your objectives; these are your learning tasks.

Discuss your learning tasks and combine them. Finally, examine the learning behaviors that will help or interfere with your learning. Develop a list of positive behaviors and activities and negative behaviors and activities.

Write your group learning objectives, your group learning tasks, and your positive and negative behaviors on newsprint or some other form and post them so everyone can see them. See how congruent the learning objectives are with the course objectives described by your instructor. Come to a joint agreement about the goals for the class as a whole. These will become your class objectives. Everyone write these down.

Then took at your learning tasks. Come to an agreement on these and record them. These become your individual commitments to the class. Finally, look at both positive and negative class and instructor activities. After discussing them, make an agreement that those positive behaviors will become the rules or norms of behavior in the class. The negative activities or behaviors will become behaviors to be avoided.

These combined lists become your class contract. Each of you should commit to achieving your personal objectives, class goals, learning tasks, and class norms.

The next class period, your instructor will give out class contracts listing the joint course objectives, learning tasks, and course norms. At home, fill in your own personal learning objectives. Sign your contract. Bring it to class and give to your instructor. Your instructor will review your learning objectives and then cosign your contract. Your instructor may even decide to base part of your grade on the extent to which you have met your objectives, course objectives, learning tasks, and course norms.

Learning Contract

Course_____

Date_____

I will work towarrd the following:

1. Individual objectives:
2. Course objectives:
3. Learning tasks: 4. Course norms:

_____
Student's Signature

_____
Instructor's Signature

Midway through the course, your instructor may ask your class to review and renegotiate the course contract. At the end of the course you can also use the contract to assess the extent to which you and your classmates have met your objectives.

EXERCISE 1.2

Solving a Social Problem

Indifference to the plight of others in social pain allows "man's inhumanity to man" to thrive. When we become simple bystanders—spectators not actors in human affairs—we become devoid of social responsibility and retreat into a world of individualism, exploitation, and greed. We become socially and ethically numb, giving tacit assent to a host of social ills that eat at the heart of our social well-being. Macro social workers are people who insert themselves actively in the lives of others, not allowing social ills to go unnoticed or unchallenged.

Imagine for a moment that you are a macro social worker with migrant farm workers in Kerman, California. The news of the death of Francisco Martinez reaches you. The plight of the Mixteco Indians is all too familiar to you: wrenching poverty, oppression, prejudice, powerlessness, miserable living conditions, lack of educational opportunities for children, alcoholism, language barriers, health problems, and long hours of backbreaking labor in fields where temperatures often pass 100 degrees for days on end.

Nine different arenas of macro social work have been briefly described in this overview: community planning, community development, community organization, program development, social administration, organization development, social policy, social action, and international social work.

How would you address the problem of the Triqui Indians? Which method or combination of macro social work methods would you employ? What specific steps would you take?

Outline your methods and then discuss them in class. It is very likely that you already have an intuitive grasp of how to go about social change. Explore your ideas with your instructor and come to some consensus. Keep your answers. When you read Chapter 3, Methods of Solving Social Problems, and later chapters you will discover more completely how they can be brought to bear on social problems.

EXERCISE 1.3

Developing Commitment

There a number of ways that you can individually or as a class confirm you own impressions about

the role of being a macro social worker, find out directly what it is like, and explore questions you might have. Choose one or more activities from the following list and report back to class.

1. Visit some local agencies or investigate nonprofit or governmental organizations that are involved in social problem-solving. Appendices A and B at the end of this book list hundreds of social organizations for you to contact to get more information. Obtain a listing of social agencies from your local United Way, Council of Social Agencies, or County Social Service Department. For example, you might choose Habitat for Humanity, organizations working with the homeless, gay rights groups, political party organizations, human rights commissions, local county boards of supervisors or city councils, action groups, minority rights organizations such as the NAACP, B'nai B'rith Jewish Anti-Defamation League, Mexican American community action groups, or women's rights organizations such as NOW. Bring literature and describe your experience to your classmates.

2. Bring macro social workers to class who can tell you directly about what they are doing. For example, you could invite macro social workers involved in community development or community organization or social work research. You could ask macro social workers who have developed programs, social planners, social administrators, organization development consultants, social activists, social policy analysts, international social workers, or others.

3. Interview a macro social worker who is well known in your community or is doing the kind of work to which you are attracted. In class, share what you have learned about the social worker you interviewed.

4. Read articles in current magazines or watch videos about particular social problems, social policy, and political, community issues.

5. Read a book that has been instrumental in social change. See the Additional Reading section at the end of this chapter for books written by macro social workers, social activists, novelists, journalists, and "muckrakers." In the Epilogue are lists of books by and about the heroes of macro social work. Your instructor may have others to suggest. Choose one to read and report to class.

EXERCISE 1.4
Journey of a Macro Social Worker

Macro social workers are committed to improve society and its defects. I will tell you the story of my own journey into macro social work. After I tell you my story, I would like you to consider your own motivation in the field of macro social work practice by exploring some questions and then filling out a checklist.

Along with her three sisters, my mother, a part Cherokee Native American, was raised in Otterbein Home, an orphanage operated by the Evangelical and Reformed Church in Southern Ohio on property that was originally a Shaker Colony. My father immigrated to this country from Germany in 1929, just before the Great Depression, the same year my mother graduated from the Otterbein Home high school. My mother completed her first year of nursing school but did not have enough money to finish. For nearly ten years, like many Americans, my mother and father existed on jobs wherever they could be found. My mother became a nanny and my father wandered through America as a laborer and cook for a Wild West Show, eventually settling in Cincinnati, Ohio, where he had an aunt and a cousin and a large German population existed. He became a cabinet maker for the Baldwin piano company. He and my mother married in 1939. A year later I was born and shortly afterward America declared War on Japan and Germany. The next five years were difficult for my father and other German Americans. His brothers became soldiers or officers for the Nazis, fighting against my father's adopted country. His German accent, attendance at German gatherings, associations with other German Americans, and activities as a union organizer marked him as a person warranting investigation by the FBI. He never really felt fully integrated into American society.

One day during elementary school, I saw a boy new to the school who appeared very strange looking. In an unthinking and unfeeling way I began to make fun of him. I still remember the look of hurt and confusion on his face. That look made me deeply ashamed of what I had done. He did not attend any of my classes, but sometimes when I saw him on the playground I would talk to him. Over the years, Jackie became one of my closest friends. When I went away to Concordia College in Milwaukee, Wisconsin, and

Concordia Senior College in Fort Wayne, Indiana, to pursue a ministerial career in the Lutheran Church–Missouri Synod, Jackie and I continued to write to one another, and we visited when I came home on vacation. We were both very proud when he graduated from high school, a great achievement for a young man with an intellectual disability.

I became fascinated with group work, partly out of my membership in the Boy Scouts of America and partly as a result of working part-time as a group worker at the Silverspring Neighborhood Center, a program of the Episcopal Church in Milwaukee; as a summer camp counselor at Camp Sidney Cohen, Delafield, Wisconsin, operated by the Jewish Community Center in Milwaukee; as a Training Director for Dan Beard Scout Camp, Cincinnati, Ohio; as a Gray-Y leader for Fort Wayne, YMCA; and as a recreation leader for the Fort Wayne State School for Mentally Retarded.

One of the experiences that helped shape my excitement about being a social group worker was getting to know several social group workers and watching them in action. I decided that this was a career to which I was called. Applying for scholarships and to graduate school, I was accepted at the University of Hawaii, which met my interests in ethnic diversity and social group work.

After graduating with an MSW degree in 1964, I returned home for a visit. Jackie, my friend, was working full-time. If I had not met and been affected by Jackie, it is very possible that I also would not have begun my own first full-time job as a social worker at an institution for persons with intellectual disabilities in Watertown, Wisconsin. Wanting to round out my skills in individual counseling, I attended the University of Wisconsin, Madison, Department of Counseling and Behavioral studies for a year, after which I returned to Hawaii, where I worked as a clinician performing individual, family, and group psychotherapy at Catholic Social Services, Honolulu. After several years of clinical practice, I married and accepted a supervisory position in social group work at a Potrero Hill Neighborhood House in San Francisco. Problems in administration, budgeting, race relations, poverty, housing, drug abuse, and alcoholism impinged on me in ways that clinical practice did not. In addition, the late 1960s and early 1970s was a time of social ferment over the movement to end the war in Vietnam and the Civil Rights Movement. Many social workers, including myself, became engaged in social action, including protest marches and active resistance to the war, as well as advocacy in civil rights demonstrations. I became involved in several community action programs of the "War on Poverty" and worked with neighborhood associations, neighborhood arts and theater groups, and other community groups.

After a number of years as supervisor and director at the Neighborhood House, I decided to begin a small agency for people with developmental disabilities, writing a grant and obtaining funding. As a social administrator for the Potrero Hill Social Development Center, I became actively involved in social planning, serving on several planning boards in health and developmental disabilities and becoming engaged in performing needs assessments for the community of persons with developmental disabilities. Assisting this community expand its services and support systems, I formed a coalition group of four small social development centers, writing and obtaining a federal grant, developing the board, and helping the new organization get on its feet.

I accepted a position at Loma Prieta Regional Center, a small Regional Center for Developmentally Disabled in San Jose, California, beginning as a senior counselor, and as the agency grew larger, becoming its first community resource developer, a position that included social planning, research, and consultation, and program development, helping improve existing programs and work with community groups to develop new ones. Later I became a supervisor managing several different offices.

During this time I became more and more fascinated with wider social problems and began reading widely in the field of political philosophy and social issues. I continued to be concerned with the various discontinuities I saw in our society and became interested in values and value thinking. After taking several courses in administration, the strands of my various interests came together, and I began to pursue doctoral studies at the University of Southern California, School of Public Administration, eventually receiving a master's and doctorate in administration. At the same time, I became involved in practicing organization development with local churches and taught public administration for the University of San Francisco.

I became a full-time faculty member as director of the social work program and teaching administration for Fresno Pacific University in Fresno, California. I joined other faculty members in establishing a small family care home in a residential neighborhood, over strenuous protests of some community members. Several of my social work students, faculty, and I began to work on a plan to include college-age adults with developmental disabilities on our college campus.

Today college-age persons with developmental disabilities attend classes on campus, engage in work-training projects, attend college events, and at graduation walk across the stage in full graduation garb just as any other college student and receive a certificate of completion. Jackie would have been proud. It is one installment on my debt in repayment for that day on the playground in Cincinnati, Ohio.

Like many social workers, I began my professional practice as a clinician. However, I was drawn increasingly to macro social work practice, eventually obtaining experience in many arenas of macro practice. One of the strengths of macro social work is its capacity to accommodate a variety of interests, abilities, and mixes of skills. As I changed and the world about me changed, I was able to find in macro practice a way of using my social work skills to help numbers of people, groups, and communities grow and develop, but it meant I had to learn and grow in different directions as well. Now that you have read my story, let's explore what kinds of patterns you see operating that shaped my interest in social work and in macro social work.

1. My career path in social work began with clinical practice and culminated in teaching and writing. What steps occurred along the way? Was it a straight career path or were a number of factors operating at the same time?

2. My parent's ethnic and cultural backgrounds provided a powerful underlying context that shaped my life, my motivation as a social worker, and my interest in macro social work. Through my mother I learned what it meant to be an orphan at the turn of the 19th century, an experience that connected me to social work and social problems of the Progressive Era. My father's experiences trying to survive as a stranger in a new land during the Great Depression and World War II taught me what it was like to be an immigrant, about poverty, and how it feels to not be a part of the culture in which you live. What backgrounds do your parents and grandparents come from that may have affected your values, what is important to you, and your own interests in social work?

3. For me, religion was always an underlying foundation and motive. Perhaps it is for you as well. What role can religion play in heightening one's sensitivity

to people who are oppressed and for the "orphan and widow and strangers in our midst?"

4. The historical and political situation into which my parents were thrust and which I experienced provided opportunity for me. My parent's coming of age just as the Depression occurred, their marriage on the eve of World War II, my entry into social work in the midst of the Civil Rights Movement, the Great Society, and the War in Vietnam affected my response to the world in relation to the poor and oppressed, social problems, and ethnic diversity. What sorts of historical and political situations have you experienced? Have they affected your views of the world and of the role that social work can play in making it a better one?

5. Sometimes one incident can have a lasting impact in one's life. For me, that incident was my encounter with Jackie. Has there been an incident in your life that may have brought you to an awareness of the kind of person you were meant to be? What kinds of incidents in your life may have affected your interest in social work or in macro social work?

Macro social work is a field in which one can make a real difference. Looking back, I can see programs I began that are still in existence, agency policies and plans on which I had an impact, organizations I helped change for the better, communities that are more healthy, and social organizations that I helped lead. You too may begin your interests in social work at the micro level. However, if you have a larger social concern, the field of macro social work is waiting for you. It is an arena of social work practice that needs committed and dedicated practitioners.

CHECKLIST 1.1

Exploring My Motivation

The following checklist will give you a chance to explore your own motivation to become a macro social worker. Read over each question and circle the number on a range of strongly agree to strongly disagree that reflects your interests.

1. I get concerned when I hear about an injustice perpetrated on others.
   Strongly Agree 1 2 3 4 5 6 7 *Strongly Disagree*

2. I have feelings for people who generally are the underdog or who have been disadvantaged.
   Strongly Agree 1 2 3 4 5 6 7 *Strongly Disagree*

3. I want to take up the cause for people who have been wronged.
   Strongly Agree 1 2 3 4 5 6 7 *Strongly Disagree*

4. I am attracted to particular social issues or problems I feel should be solved.
   Strongly Agree 1 2 3 4 5 6 7 *Strongly Disagree*

5. I feel that everyone ought to try to get involved in his or her community.
   Strongly Agree 1 2 3 4 5 6 7 *Strongly Disagree*

6. I feel particularly hopeful that there is something important for me to do in my neighborhood or community—that I can really make a difference.
   Strongly Agree 1 2 3 4 5 6 7 *Strongly Disagree*

7. I feel I have a role to play in social change, in making life better for others.
   Strongly Agree 1 2 3 4 5 6 7 *Strongly Disagree*

8. I want to become involved in something bigger than myself, larger than my own self-interest.
   Strongly Agree 1 2 3 4 5 6 7 *Strongly Disagree*

9. I get excited about the idea of being engaged in social renewal and transformation.
   Strongly Agree 1 2 3 4 5 6 7 *Strongly Disagree*

10. I feel I have creative ideas and can see possibilities for change that others may miss.
    Strongly Agree 1 2 3 4 5 6 7 *Strongly Disagree*

11. I enjoy working with groups and helping people engage one another.
    Strongly Agree 1 2 3 4 5 6 7 *Strongly Disagree*

12. Sometimes I think about working in a third or fourth world nation.
    Strongly Agree 1 2 3 4 5 6 7 *Strongly Disagree*

Draw a line connecting the numbers. You have a graph that depicts your interests in a very general way. Does the line you have drawn mostly pass through the 5–7 area? Does it hover around the center? Does the line generally pass through numbers 1–3?

What does your graph say about your interests in macro social work? Are there specific areas where you strongly agree and others in which you strongly disagree?

What prime motivators lead you to be interested in social change? What detracts you from interest in being a macro social worker? Your instructor will lead you in sharing both motivators and demotivators.

How will you use macro social work skills in generalist practice? In clinical practice? Do you think you might want to make macro social work a career?

With which arenas of macro practice do you feel most comfortable? Least comfortable?

CHECKLIST 1.2
The Stance of a Macro Social Worker

Within the field of macro social work are a number of particular arenas of practice. This checklist will help you discover where your particular strengths may lie. Look over the following list. On a scale of 1–5 with 1 being the lowest and 5 the highest, mark the ones that are especially meaningful for you, placing them in the columns below. For example, if the statement describes you to a high degree, assign a 5. If it is generally descriptive, assign a 4. If it is sometimes descriptive of you, give it a 3. If it rarely is descriptive of you, give it a 2. If it is not descriptive of you, give it a 1.

It is important for me to:

1. Take part in a movement to bring an end to injustice.

2. Become involved with a community and help mold the destiny of a people.

3. Use my vision to look for possibilities in the future.

4. Shape a system in the here and now over the long term.

5. Gather information and facts to correct dishonesty or deceit.

6. Develop relationships strengthening communities or organizations.

7. Exert my creativity and ability to see the big picture to try out something new.

8. Fix a broken system by applying my technical skills.

9. Help the underdog obtain redress and empower the powerless.

10. Engage others in constructing a social world and forging social bonds.

11. Be a part of something positive that is larger than myself.

12. Make a tangible contribution by implementing concrete decisions today.

13. Get involved in social action and social justice.

14. Get involved in building community or neighborhood.

15. Get involved in developing new programs, plans, or projects.

16. Get involved in making things happen by implementing the details of decisions.

Place your scores for each sentence in the following columns and add up your answers at the bottom:

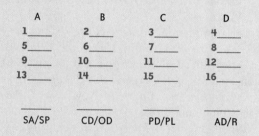

A	B	C	D
1____	2____	3____	4____
5____	6____	7____	8____
9____	10____	11____	12____
13____	14____	15____	16____
_____	_____	_____	_____
SA/SP	CD/OD	PD/PL	AD/R

If you scored highest in column A, you may have more interest in either social action or social policy analysis. If you scored highest in column B, you may have more aptitude in the areas of community or organization development. If you were higher in column C, you might have more interest in either program development or social planning. Those of you who were higher in column D could be better at either administration or social research.

What do your scores say about your motivation and stance as a macro social worker? Compare your rankings with those of others in class. Are there patterns that distinguish you from others?

ADDITIONAL READING

What Motivates Macro Social Workers?

George Bach and Laura Torbet. *A Time for Caring.* New York: Delacourte, 1982.

Allen Luks and Peggy Payne. *The Healing Power of Doing Good.* New York: Fawcett, 1992.

Samuel P. Oliner and Pearl M. Oliner. *The Altruistic Personality: Rescuers of the Jews in Nazi Europe.* New York: Free Press, 1988.

Social Problems

Frantz Fanon. *The Wretched of the Earth.* New York: Evergreen Press, 1969.

Suzanne Pharr. *Homophobia: A Weapon of Sexism.* Inverness, CA: Chardon Press, 1988.

Cary McWilliams. *Brothers Under the Skin.* Boston: Little, Brown, 1951.

———. *Factories in the Field: The Story of Migratory Farm Labor in California.* Santa Barbara: Penguin, 1971.

Jonathan Freedman. *From Cradle to Grave: The Human Face of Poverty.* New York: Atheneum, 1993.

Jeffrey Reiman. *The Rich Get Richer and the Poor Get Prison: Ideology, Crime and Criminal Justice.* 4th ed. Boston: Allyn and Bacon, 1990.

Jonathan Kozol. *Rachel and Her Children: Homeless Families in America.* New York: Fawcett Columbine, 1988.

William Greider *Who Will Tell the People? The Betrayal of the American Democracy.* New York: Simon and Schuster, 1992.

Social Thinking: The Method of Solving Social Problems

E. K. Minnech, *Transforming Knowedge.* Philadelphia: Temple University Press, 1990.

Donald Schon, *The Reflective Practitioner: How Professionals Think in Action.* New York: Basic Books, 1985.

Herbert Marcuse. *One-Dimensional Man: Studies in the Ideology of Advanced Industrial Society.* Boston: Beacon Press, 1964.

Leadership

H. Tichy and M. A. Devanna. *The Transformational Leader.* New York: John Wiley and Sons, 1986.

Peter Block: *Stewardship: Choosing Service Over Self-Interest.* San Francisco: Berrett-Koehler Publishers, 1993.

Edward Oakley and Douglas Krug. *Enlightened Leadership: Getting to the Heart of Change.* New York: Simon and Schuster, 1993.

Community

Harry C. Boyte. *Community Is Possible: Repairing America's Roots.* New York: Harper and Row, 1984.

Howard W. Hallman. *Neighborhoods: Their Place in Urban Life.* Vol. 154, Sage Library of Social Research. Beverly Hills: Sage, 1984.

Community Social Planning

Aaron Wildavsky. *Speaking Truth to Power.* Boston: Little, Brown, 1979.

John Forester, *Planning in the Face of Power.* Berkeley: University of California Press, 1989.

Community Development

Stewart E. Perry, *Communities on the Way.* New York: State University of New York Press, 1987.

John M. Perkins. *Let Justice Roll Down.* Glendale, CA: G/L Books, 1976.

Community Organizing

Saul Alinsky. *Reveille for Radicals.* New York: Vintage, 1969.

———. *Rules for Radicals.* New York: Random House, 1971.

Si Kahn. *How People Get Power: Organizing Oppressed People for Action.* New York: McGraw Hill, 1978.

Steve Burghardt. *Organizing for Community Action.* Beverly Hills: Sage, 1982.

Organization

Franz Kafka. *The Trial.*

———. *Metamorphosis.*

Max Weber. "Bureaucracy." *From Max Weber: Essays in Sociology.* H. H. Gerth and C. Wright Mills, eds. New York: Oxford University Press, 1958.

Alberto Ramos. *Reconceptualization of the Wealth of Nations.* Toronto: University of Toronto Press, 1981.

Ralph Hummel. *The Bureaucratic Experience.* New York: St. Martin's Press, 1977.

Program Development

James L. Heskett, W. Earl Sasser Jr., and Christopher W. L. Hart. *Service Breakthroughs: Changing the Rules of the Game.* New York: Freedom Press, 1990.

Jonathan D. Crane, ed. *Social Programs That Work.* New York: Russell Sage Foundation, 1998.

Social Administration

Carl J. Bellone, *Organization Theory and the New Public Administration.* Boston: Allyn and Bacon, 1980.

Mary Parker Follett. In Elliot M. Fox and L. Urwick, *Dynamic Administration: The Collected Papers of Mary Parker Follett.* New York: Hippocrene Books, 1977.

Michael M. Harmon. *Action Theory for Public Administration.* New York: Longman, 1981.

Organization Development

Anne Wilson Schaef and Diane Fassel. *The Addictive Organization: Why We Overwork, Cover Up, Pick Up the Pieces, Please the Boss, and Perpetuate Sick Organizations.* San Francisco: Harper and Row, 1990.

Social Policy and Politics

M. Abramovitz. "Should all social work students be educated for social change?" *Journal of Social Work Education*, 29(1), 6–11, 1993.

Rachel Carson. *The Silent Spring.* Boston: Houghton Mifflin, 1962.

Richard Cloward and Frances Fox Piven. *The Politics of Turmoil.* New York: Vintage, 1975.

Michael Harrington. *The Other America: Poverty in the United States.* Baltimore: Penguin Books, 1962.

Richard Harris. *A Sacred Trust: The Story of Organized Medicine's Multi-Million Dollar Fight Against Public Health Legislation.* Rev. ed. Baltimore: Penguin Books, 1969.

Ann Withorn. *Serving the People: Social Services and Social Change.* New York: Columbia University Press, 1984.

Social Action and Social Movements

Martin Luther King Jr. *Stride Toward Freedom: The Montgomery Story.* New York: Ballantine, 1958.

Vincent Harding. *There Is a River: The Black Struggle for Freedom in America.* New York: Harcourt Brace Jovanovich, 1981.

Frances Fox Piven and Richard Cloward. *Poor People's Movements: Why They Succeed, How They Fail.* New York: Random House, 1987.

Mary Harris Jones. *The Autobiography of Mother Jones.* Chicago: Charles H. Kerr, 1990.

International Social Work

Rigoberta Menchu. *I, Rigoberta Menchu: An Indian Woman in Guatemala.* Trans. Ann Wright. London: Verso, 1984.

La Pieffe, Dominique. *The City of Joy.* Garden City, NY: Doubleday, 1995.

Social History

Henry Steele Commager. *The American Mind: An Interpretation of American Thought and Character Since the 1880s.* New York: Bantam, 1950.

Richard Hofstadter. *The Age of Reform: From Bryan to F.D.R.* New York: Vintage, 1955.

———. *The American Political Tradition and the Men Who Made It.* New York: Vintage, 1954.

H. Zinn. *A People's History of the United States.* New York: Harper and Row, 1980.

Richard Flacks. *Making History: The American Left and the American Mind.* New York: Columbia University Press, 1990.

S. M. Evans. *Born for Liberty: A History of Women in America.* New York: Free Press, 1989.

G. Lerner. *The Majority Finds Its Past: Placing Women in History.* New York: Oxford University Press, 1979.

Social Critique

Donald Bartlett and James Steele. *America: What Went Wrong.* Kansas City, MO: Andrews and McMeel, 1992.

Albert Memmi. *The Colonizer and the Colonized.* Boston: Beacon Press, 1967.

Paulo Freire. *Pedagogy of the Oppressed.* New York: Herder and Herder, 1970.

Malcolm X. *The Autobiography of Malcolm X.* New York: Ballantine, 1987.

Donna Schaper. *A Book of Common Power: Narratives Against the Current.* San Deigo, CA: Lura Media, 1989.

PART ONE

Solving Social Problems and Making Social Change

Not only man's action towards external objects but also the relations between men and all social institutions can be understood only in terms of what men think about them. Society as we know it, is, as it were, built up from concepts and ideas held by the people; and social phenomena can be recognized by us and have meaning for us only as they are reflected in the minds of men.[1]

Friedreich A. Hayek

Dehumanization, although a concrete historical fact, is *not* a given destiny but the result of an unjust order that engenders violence in the oppressor, which in turn dehumanizes the oppressed.
It is only the oppressed, who, by freeing themselves, can free their oppressors. The latter, as an oppressive class, can free neither others nor themselves. It is therefore essential that the oppressed wage the struggle to resolve the contradiction in which they are caught.[2]

Paulo Freire

The political and economic philosophers of the Enlightenment (1550–1800) who invented the premises of modernity were highly suspicious of the social. They had seen too many instances in which social groups behaved irrationally and violently. They were gravely concerned about institutions that prevented people from thinking for themselves, and they were afraid of the power of tyrannical leaders who used governance for their own personal ends. Enlightenment thinkers staked their hopes on the freedom of the individual, but an individual who operated rationally to pursue his or her interests. This modern rational society and its components would be an artificial construction of men's minds that operated like a mechanical system governed by laws and regulated in such a way that individuals could conduct their lives without fear of disruption by tyrants who would impose their own social designs on them.

19

The modern world, which owes many of its basic assumptions to these thinkers, has been successful in reducing political oppression, emancipating belief, and designing massive economic systems. In many respects, however, it has failed to understand the nature of the social. Rational methods that are useful in calculating how to achieve economic benefits are often useless in solving problems in the social arena. The power orientation of our world is helpless in providing people with meaning or authentic human independence, and leadership has devolved into paternalism.

In spite of its presumption of enlightened action, modernity continues to enforce passivity, compliance, alienation, and lack of autonomy over many important arenas of people's lives. The theories implicit in social systems theory, for example, tend to see people as atomistic rather than as social beings. *Atomistic* means that people are conceived much like atoms, autonomous bits of social matter that interact with other atoms according to physical laws of entropy, inertia, and homeostasis. Humans are treated as parts of social systems just as mechanical components are treated as parts of machines. Motivators are applied to people externally to induce them to greater productivity. People are socialized to function according to the goals of those who control the system. They tend to be acted upon by the huge political and economic megastructures of modern life rather than operate as actors constructing their own social reality. According to Gibson Winter, for example,

> when the subject matter of social science is handled like the subject matter of physical science, knowledge of social laws becomes a knowledge of laws which control man's activity. Knowledge of society reveals man's enslavement to societal forces. Man ceases to be a "subject" and becomes an "object" of calculable forces external to him.[3]

In addition, when the individual is seen as a living unit incorporated into an ecological system people are assumed to be much like other biological organisms that "have no opinion regarding their own survival."[4] Humans are not seen as actors who decide for themselves, but are only capable of adapting in response to changes in their social environment.

According to this kind of social Darwinism, society is not made by man; society develops like any other organic process—evolving according to laws of nature. Society's problem is to recognize the course which nature is taking and to conform to it. Rather than creating and controlling the society of which he or she is a part, a person has little choice but to "discover himself to be the passive object of forces playing upon him." The modern individual, according to systems and social ecological theory, is a "passive, conformed and adapted"[5] atomistic creature acted upon by irresistible biological and mechanical forces who can only respond in predetermined and predictable ways. Under these assumptions,

> the human person is an island unto him or herself and this conclusion of "aloneness" is the natural and preferred state. [Social systems and social ecology] deny and negate the tenacity of

the human community and the inventiveness of people to sustain themselves within social groupings that meet their needs, and they promote the destructiveness of human communities by devaluating all forms that do not meet some traditional norm.[6]

One would expect that social work, which is presumed to be dedicated to and built on a foundation of the social, would explicitly reject the atomistic, deterministic, and passive conception of the self that modernity has fashioned. But social work itself is a "modern" profession. Its presuppositions, its methods, and its conceptions of the human condition are congruent with and largely inseparable from the modern mind. Social work relies heavily on social systems and social ecological models. Many social workers tend to be ambivalent about humans as primarily social creatures. If anything, asserts Hans Falck, the "tendency of individualism to exclude adequate attention to social factors"[7] has been a prevailing tendency in the history of the social work profession.

However, the modern conception of passive atomistic man is giving way to another conception of the human being. This view of the human condition as active-social may become the operative ideal of humans in the coming era. It is the model of humans that informs this book. Active means that individuals engage in and take responsibility for themselves. They are active and creative agents in the construction of social reality, not subject to a deterministic existence ruled by laws derived from physics, biology, or the social sciences. They are not passive creatures who wait to be enlightened by a leader's vision, or who compliantly carry out decisions made by others.

Humans are irrevocably and irrefutably social creatures. The self is a social self, and the world that people construct is a social world. By actively engaging this social world, people become fully human. Social engagement is the essence of humanness, without which people cannot live full, rich lives. "This means that people have a measure of autonomy in determining their actions, which are at the same time bound up by a social context...and focused on subjective meanings that people attach to their own actions and to the actions of others."[8]

People take action together to solve their own social problems and make social change in communities, social organizations, and the world at large, and macro social work is centered in helping people assume that responsibility. Social change does not come from outside, no matter how compelling, or from the top, no matter how powerful, or from experts, no matter how brilliant. It does not happen by professionals acting on people. Change happens when people engage their own visions, carry out their own decisions, exert their own leadership, and bring about the society that they construct themselves. Macro social work is unrelentingly oriented to assisting people identify their own social problems, decide on how to solve those problems, and bring about social change by their own actions.

Social thinking begins in the here and now, in the *we* relation, in the lived experience of the world, and in the vision of macro social workers who not only understand social work techniques and possess knowledge but who are committed to their own growth, openness to change, and to the making of a better world. Social thinking is a process of rebirth in relationship with others who are also on a path of discovering ideas, shaping their values, and applying that learning to constructing a social world.

For macro social workers, to paraphrase John Forester, "it is always better to exert ones own leadership, no matter how poorly, than to be led by others, no matter how well." Authentic leadership is never the prerogative of one or a few at the top, no matter how skilled or well intentioned. It is always the right, the duty, and the privilege of each person to exert leadership in his or her own way. To deny or diminish the leadership potential of even those who seem weakest is to eliminate a human quality that is indispensable.

Social leadership is the capacity of people to have their own ideas, exert their own abilities, and help one another move in a journey of self-discovery to become the people they were meant to become. It does not stress how fast we achieve a goal, how effective or efficient our drive to accomplish our objectives, or how straight the path that leads to the future. What is important is the path that we choose ourselves, no matter how slow, inefficient, or convoluted.

You are at the beginning of a completely new social era whose roots can be seen in the tumultuous struggles of the 1960s. This new social era has the potential for social change as momentous as the scientific revolution of the Enlightenment that brought about our modern era. While the Enlightenment brought about a world of political, economic, and scientific emancipation, the new post-modern world will be a *social revolution*.

We need to look to new ways of solving problems, new ways of thinking, new ways of leading. But most importantly, we need to seek new ways of acting and being. It is my hope for you that you, the macro social workers of the future, will be among the new humans that Paulo Freire describes: neither oppressor nor oppressed, but people in the process of liberation.[9]

Macro social work is *the* arena in social work committed to making a new society that is finally free of oppression, poverty, and injustice. Not only is macro social work committed to eradicating social problems; it is also a profession whose vision extends to making a world in which the social becomes the true habitation of people in whom the human spirit can find its true home.

Part 1 of this book will introduce you to some of the ideas that shape macro social work. The remainder of the book will demonstrate more concretely how our modern world is passing away, how new social forms are emerging, how you can be a part of creating new social structures, bring about solutions to social problems, and make social change. In Chapter 2 you will learn about social problems and how to define them for yourself. In Chapter 3 you will learn about modern reason, and how to devise your own way of thinking socially with others. In Chapter 4 you will learn about a model of leadership that helps everyone take charge of themselves and their own futures.

ADDITIONAL READING

Action Social Model of the Self

William Barrett. *Irrational Man: A Study in Existential Philosophy.* Garden City, NY: Doubleday, 1958.

Nikolai Berdyaev. *Slavery and Freedom.* New York: Scribner, 1944.

Martin Buber. *I and Thou,* 2d. ed. New York: Scribner, 1958.

Viktor E. Frankl. *Man's Search for Meaning: An Introduction to Logotherapy.* New York: Washington Square Press, 1963.

Soren Kierkegaard. *Fear and Trembling and the Sickness Unto Death.* Trans. Walter Lowrie. Garden City, NY: Doubleday, 1954.

Social Critique

Peter Berger and Thomas Luckman. *The Social Construction of Reality.* Garden City, NY: Doubleday, 1967.

Jacques Ellul. *The Technological Society.* New York: Vintage, 1967.

Max Horkheimer. *The Eclipse of Reason.* New York: Oxford University Press, 1947.

Karl Mannheim. *Man and Society in an Age of Reconstruction.* New York: Harcourt, Brace and World, 1940.

Reinhold Niebuhr. *The Children of Light and the Children of Darkness.* New York: Scribner, 1944.

———. *Moral Man and Immoral Society: A Study in Ethics and Politics.* New York: Scribner, 1960.

Karl Polanyi. *The Great Transformation.* Boston: Beacon Press, 1957.

Alberto Guerreiro Ramos. *The New Science of Organization: A Reconceptualization of the Wealth of Nations.* Toronto: University of Toronto Press, 1981.

Walter Rauschenbusch. *A Theology for the Social Gospel.* Nashville: Abingdon, 1945.

Charles A. Reich. *The Greening of America.* New York: Bantam Books, 1970.

Philip Slater. *The Pursuit of Loneliness: American Society at the Breaking Point.* Boston: Beacon Press, 1971.

Alvin Toffler. *The Third Wave.* New York: William Morrow, 1980.

Eric Voegelin. *The New Science of Politics: An Introduction.* Chicago: University of Chicago Press, 1952.

Walter Weisskopf. *Alienation and Economics.* New York: Dell, 1971.

2

Social Problems and Social Change
The Challenge of Being a Macro Social Worker

Let us not forget, when we talk of violence, that the death of a young mother in childbirth is violent; that the slow starvation of the mind and body of a child is violent; let us not forget that hunger is violent, that pain is violent, that oppression is violent, that early death is violent; and that the death of hope is the most violent of all. The organizer brings hope to the people.[1]

Si Kahn

In the final analysis, however, we must realize that social injustice and unjust social structures exist only because individuals and groups of individuals deliberately maintain or tolerate them. It is these personal choices, operating through structures, that breed and propagate situations of poverty, oppression, and misery.[2]

Pope John Paul II

Ideas in This Chapter

OUR MODERN SOCIAL WORLD

Even though the American economy is booming, prosperity has not filtered down to the 36.5 million poor people in the United States, including 4.5 million children. A report by the Children's Defense Fund indicates that the gap between rich and poor is increasing. American corporate CEOs earned 41 times more than their workers in 1960, but by 1995 CEOs were paid 185 times as much. The average CEO in 1995 earned more every two days than the average worker earned in a whole year. Fortune 500 CEOs averaged $7.8 million each in total compensation. This exceeds the average salaries of 226 schoolteachers in a year.[3]

In the 1980s, the salaries of people earning more than $1 million increased by 2,184%; those earning between $200,000 to $1 million saw an increase of almost 700%. Since 1989, the poorest fifth of families in America *lost* $587 each and the richest 5% gained $29,533 each. At the same time that the wealth of the rich grew by staggering proportions, the poorest continued to lose ground. By 1991 the combined wealth of the richest 400 Americans hit $288 billion, an average of $720 million per person, the highest ever recorded in our nation's history.[4] On January 18, 2000, the Economic Policy Institute and the Center on Budget and Policy Priorities revealed that in all but four states "the gap between the average incomes of middle-income families and of the richest 20% of families expanded between the late 1970s and the late 1990s," and for the United States as a whole, the average income of families in the top 20% was more than ten times that of the poorest 20% of families.[5] As the middle class was squeezed and the poor got poorer, "the total amount of dollars in salaries funneled to the rich soared as did the rich themselves." For the twentieth century, "It was a phenomenon unlike any America has seen."[6]

The burden falls most heavily on our children. While millions of stock options helped the earnings of corporate CEOs soar, between 1980 and 1995 those same employers threw millions of children out of health insurance plans at their parent's workplaces. In 1987, 5 million children under the age of six, almost one child out of every four, lived in poverty in the United States, according to the Columbia University National Center for Children in Poverty.[7] Ten years later, the Children's Defense Fund reported that "more than one in five children in America is growing up poor and one in 11 is growing up extremely poor." We have five times more billionaires but 14 million more poor children.[8]

Not only is this pattern commonplace in the United States, but it is occurring with even more ferocity throughout the globe. In 1990 more than three-fourths of the world's population lived in countries in which the per capita gross national product (GNP) is a mere $710. In Switzerland per capita GNP is $32,790, in Japan $25,430, in Sweden $23,860, and in the United States $21,700.[9] According to Ruth Sivard, in the 41 least developed countries of the world, per capita income averaged less than $250 per year and was deteriorating rather than improving. At the extreme, more than 1 billion people had incomes below the poverty line and 1.2 billion people live beneath the threshold of basic needs. The gap dividing the rich from the poor has never been wider: the top fifth of the world's population on the global economic ladder enjoys 60 times the goods and services of the lowest fifth.[10]

While the gap between the rich and poor in North America continues to be a hidden but real social problem, the United States leads in other disparities as well. The United States is number one in real wealth and the number of billionaires, big homes, defense spending and military capability, executive salaries, and physician salaries. At the same time, the United States ranks first in the number of rapes, incarceration rate, drunk-driving fatalities, cocaine use, greenhouse gas emissions contributing to acid rain and forest depletion, hazardous waste per capita, inequality of wealth distribution, bank failures, military aid to developing countries, divorce, single-parent families, reported cases of AIDS, and teenage pregnancy.[11] In Detroit, 72% of all the young employable adults in the city's poorest census tract can't find work—and probably never will hold a job. In New York City, 50,000 homeless people live on the streets. Another 17,000 live in temporary shelters.[12]

As Ronald C. Frederico observes in *Social Welfare in Today's World,* these social problems "take a toll and a dreadful one. People's lives are diminished or destroyed. Society is disrupted by the behavior of those who no longer care, or are so damaged that they cannot function in acceptable ways. Our society continues to suffer from serious problems, some of them longstanding and others more recent."[13]

"Almost everyone agrees today," asserts Anne Schaef, "that American society has reached a critical point." This crisis consists of social problems that "seem well nigh insoluble"[14] and therefore "permanent features of the political landscape." The inability of people to solve many of our most pressing social ills is often because Americans of all social classes have a trained incapacity to understand the causes or conceive solutions to social problems. The result is that people are "unable to identify matters of major social importance or apply available resources to their solution."[15]

If you are like many others, however, you are drawn to the profession of social work by a "passion for social justice and a desire to help those most in need."[16] It is because of such idealism and concern for making our society a better place that macro social work took root. The field of "social work may be thought of as a profession concerned with social problems, their remedy and control,"[17] asserts H. Wayne Johnson. All social workers should be involved in solving social problems such as racism, sexism, economic injustice, urban decay, and dysfunctional political systems. They must have the ability to understand and diagnose social problems and take a stance. More than ever, our society is desperate for people of stature, vision, and resolve who can assist in helping solve our most pressing social problems. It is an endeavor which not only this nation but our entire global society cannot afford to ignore.

WHAT YOU WILL LEARN IN THIS CHAPTER

In this chapter you will explore the difference between personal problems and social problems. You will learn the conventional definitions of social problems, how to critique them, and how to arrive at your own definition. You will discover the most common assumptions that people have about why social problems exist, and you will read about the answers to social problems that don't work. Finally, you will learn about a new social change approach that builds on people's strengths and uses the assets of community. You will be challenged to be among the few social workers to explore this alternative way of looking at the social issues that confront us at the beginning of the new millennium.

DEFINING SOCIAL PROBLEMS

One mark of your skill as a macro social worker will be your ability to understand why social problems exist, critique conventional understandings of social problems, and develop your own working definition of social problems. One place to begin is understanding how social problems differ from personal problems.

Personal Problems and Social Problems

In his book *The Sociological Imagination,* C. Wright Mills comments that "perhaps the most fruitful distinction with which the sociological imagination works is between 'the personal troubles of milieu' and the 'public issues of social structure.' This distinction is an essential tool of the sociological imagination and a feature of all classic work in social science."[18]

The distinction between personal troubles and social problems is an important one. Exercise your own "sociological imagination" and develop your own definition of social problems using your critical thinking skills. Think about what distinguishes personal problems from social problems. For example, purely personal problems usually affect a limited number of people. If you become angry, you may involve others only to the extent that you display anger toward them. Social problems, on the other hand, affect groups of people, ranging from neighborhoods and communities to large segments of the population.

Aiming treatment at the people who have difficulty dealing with the stresses of modern life may sometimes help solve personal problems. If you have trouble managing your anger, for example, curative measures may involve behavior modification, counseling, or training in anger management skills. Can social problems be resolved by aiming treatment at the particular people who are identified as bearing the brunt of social problems? For instance, for years government has tried to eradicate poverty by handing out financial assistance to people. People tended to stay poor. Now government programs are trying to train the poor for jobs and force them to become self-sufficient by cutting off welfare. What do you predict will happen when poor people are forced to depend on the labor market to earn a decent living? Can overcoming a social problem such as poverty occur by training, counseling, coercing, advising, or otherwise applying some kind of external remedy *to* people? Should remedies be developed by politicians, policy makers, or social workers, or should remedies be developed and action taken by people themselves who are affected by social problems? Where, by whom, and how should socially curative measures be directed?

Interventions applied to personal problems are usually limited in scope to a few specific procedures aimed at the locus of the problem. For example, a skilled professional may help a person addicted to tobacco "break the habit" by support, alternative drugs, hypnotism, behavior modification, or avoidance. In the case of social problems, are there a few specific curative procedures that one can apply to resolve a social problem, or must one use many broad-based approaches? What kinds of strategies do you think have been employed in responding to the problems of ethnic intolerance, crime, or poverty? Have they been narrowly focused or broad based? How many of them have been successful?

Often personal problems, particularly drug or alcohol abuse, are met by denial. At these times people exhibiting denial must be confronted with the reality of their behavior. Social problems also result in denial. For many people in America, economic exploitation and ethnic intolerance were not considered social problems. If anything, the exploitation of

Macro social workers help children relate to others, incorporate norms and rules of society, and form themselves into mature human beings. (© Tara C. Patty/Jeroboam, Inc.)

women, children, and immigrants, the extermination of Native Americans, and the enslavement of Africans were seen as necessary to the economic development of America. Can you think of other social problems that people in authority have denied or claimed to be necessary for a higher purpose? What techniques would you recommend when corporate or governmental organizations engage in social denial or rationalize social harm for the common good?

Personal problems may sometimes be resolved fairly quickly. Sometimes just having a talk with a friend may help clear up an interpersonal conflict. Can social problems be solved in a relatively short

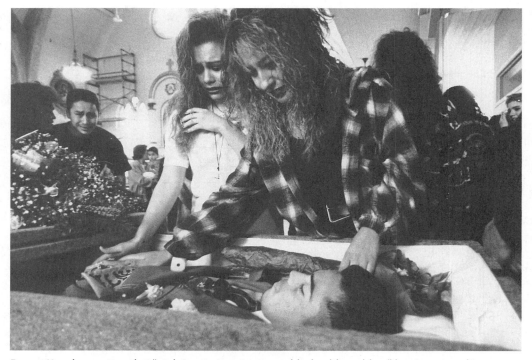

Everett Koop's assertion that "violence in America is a public health problem" becomes a reality as gang members grieve at the funeral of a fellow gang member.(© Kit Hedman/Jeroboam, Inc.)

time? How long have we been trying to resolve problems of ethnic intolerance, crime, violence, or poverty? Do you think we will ever resolve these problems?

Finally, even though individual treatment for personal problems may be expensive, visiting a counselor can often be affordable for people with an average income. Sometimes the costs may be born by insurance or employee assistance programs. The costs incurred by social problems, however, and the issue of who pays for them are a different matter. Try to estimate the costs of ethnic intolerance in America. In your answer, consider the social costs that slavery created in the lives of African Americans and slave owners. Add to this the financial burden of the Civil War. Then calculate the costs of the war in terms of human life lost, families destroyed, and ill will generated. Try to figure the human potential wasted for nearly 100 years after the Civil War by segregating schools and neighborhoods, discrimination in housing and employment, and in many places the restriction of African Americans to vote or participate in the political process. After this, add up costs engendered by

the extermination, forced relocation, and destruction of the culture of Native Americans and Aboriginal Canadians, the forced internment of Japanese Americans during World War II, and the legal prohibition of Japanese immigrants from owning land in California until 1954. Once you have done this, include in your sums the human opportunities lost and burdens that racism perpetrated among Chicanos, Puerto Ricans and other Latin Americans, as well as Chinese, Jewish, Polish, Irish, and Italian Americans. Would you consider these costs affordable? Who bears the costs of ethnic intolerance? Is it born only by the victims? Does everyone in society pay the price?

EXERCISE 2.1

Defining Social Problems

Write out your own definition of social problems. Reflect on who is affected by social problems, their scope, who decides which social problems are important, how long it takes to resolve them, and who should be the focus of resolving them. After you come up with your own definition, compare it with those of your classmates and then to the conventional definitions of social problems presented in the next section.

Critiquing Conventional Definitions

Sullivan and Thompson assert that a "social problem exists when an influential group defines a social condition as threatening its values, the condition affects a large number of people, and it can be remedied by collective action," a definition echoed by Charles Zastrow.[19] Robert K. Merton and Robert Nisbet, two influential sociologists, have defined social problems as "the substantial, unwanted discrepancies between what is in a society and what a functionally significant collectivity within that society seriously…desires to be in it."[20]

Many sociologists tend to agree that social problems have the following components:

1. The problem must have *social* causation rather than be an issue of individual behavior.
2. It must *affect* a large number of people.
3. It must be judged by an *influential* number of people to be undesirable.[21]
4. It must be *collectively* solvable rather than by individual action.

A mark of a good macro social worker is to be responsibly critical of existing knowledge. This means using your own ideas and insights to challenge things that may not seem right. How did your own definition compare with the most common definitions developed by other theorists? How did those of your classmates compare with yours? Were there components that were the same, or did you arrive at some that were different? Can you come up with a composite definition that is even better for macro social work practice than those that are conventionally accepted? Later in this chapter you will return to these definitions and I will give my own definition of social problems. You are invited to compare your definition with this one as well.

ASSUMPTIONS ABOUT SOCIAL PROBLEMS

In addition to a definition of social problems, macro social workers need to have an overall perspective on the causes of social problems. Some people place the locus of social problems in the individual, others in the family or at the neighborhood or intergroup levels of society. Other people see social problems as originating in society's institutions, social systems, or the inherent premises on which society itself is based. Where in society do you assume social problems primarily originate? Are social problems mainly located at one of these levels, in more than one, or can they be located in all of them?

Individualist Model

One of the most cherished ideals of American ideology is self-interested individualism.[22] Individualism is one reason for the creativity of Americans, their energy, and their prosperity.[23] On the other hand, individualism is sometimes seen as a cause of social problems that exist in America. Perhaps the most prevalent way of thinking about social problems begins with the idea that certain individuals fail to take advantage of the opportunities that society makes available. People who disobey the law or enter a life of dependency are said to interfere with the normal workings of society and restrict its progress.[24]

Some among the financially secure or politically powerful like to suggest that it is the fault of the poor that they are poor. They may assert that the poor are lazy, undisciplined, and lack personal initiative. This moral deviance or personal-blame approach assumes that the poor, the marginal, and the criminal are inferior, inadequate, or destructive people.[25] Those holding to this view assert that people whose lives display social problems not only have dysfunctional behavior, but they also are fundamentally different in character from those in the middle or upper economic tiers of society.[26]

Some people may be genetically prone to personal dysfunction. At least 4% of the population, for example, are born with developmental or intellectual disabilities that restrict their ability to live independently in today's highly technological society. There also seem to be genetic linkages to drug and alcohol abuse and mental disorders such as bipolar psychosis, depression, and schizophrenia. Some people may be genetically less able to succeed in modern society. Judith Harris asserts, for example, "Some people are born with characteristics that make them poor fits for most of the honest jobs available in most societies, and so far we haven't learned how to deal with them. We are at risk of becoming their victims but they are victims too—victims of the evolutionary history of our species."[27]

Furthermore, many people who are socialized to rely on face-to-face personal relationships may be unable to succeed in impersonal, functional, technological organizations that require individuals to perform specialized tasks in a highly competitive atmosphere. They may find themselves increasingly on the margins of a world in which opportunities for social communal relationships are reduced.

Many who are unfit or unable to adapt become the pathology of a healthy society. These people are not just incapable of contributing to the welfare of society; they become the causes of societal "illness." According to Soroka and Bryjak, "just as individual humans can be infected and made ill by viruses from outside the body or by diseased cells from the inside,"[28] pathological individuals also act as viruses infecting society, making it sick. In the same way that medical professionals are needed to treat an illness to protect the body, the social pathology assumption requires social professionals to diagnose and apply remediation, education, rehabilitation, or in more serious cases to surgically remove offending pathological elements by institutionalization, incarceration, or even execution.

A PATHOLOGICAL ELEMENT OF SOCIETY

The Alabama legislature declared them "a menace to the happiness...of the community." A Mississippi statute called them "unfit for citizenship." In Pennsylvania, they were officially termed "anti-social beings"; in Washington, "unfitted for companionship with other children"; in Vermont, a "blight on mankind"; in Wisconsin, a "danger to the race"; and in Kansas, "a misfortune both to themselves and to the public." A Utah government report declared them to be a "defect" that "wounds our citizenry a thousand times more than any plague."

A Texas law mandated their segregation to relieve society of the "heavy economic and moral losses aris-

ing from the existence at large of these unfortunate persons." Indiana decided to "segregate from the world" such individuals, and in South Dakota they were determined not to have the "rights and liberties of normal people." An opinion by Justice Oliver Wendell Holmes of the U.S. Supreme Court, upholding the constitutionality of a Virginia law authorizing their involuntary sterilization, ratified the view that they were "a menace...who sap the strength of the state.... It is better," he ruled, to "prevent those who are manifestly unfit from continuing their kind."

In every state of our nation, in nearly every community, the official policy was the exclusion, segregation, defamation, and degradation of people with intellectual disabilities, those who seemed to be among the weakest and most inferior of our citizens.[29]

The social pathology or medical model of social deviance fits within the individualist model. The individualist paradigm tends to maintain loyalty to what people believe are important societal values. Those who define deviancy exact conformity to norms they consider desirable. These social leaders assume individuals will tend to evade personal responsibility for their actions; therefore, they advocate that deviant individuals need to be singled out and held personally accountable for their actions along with everyone else. They assert that professionals do a disservice not only to the individual but to society as a whole if they offer excuses for someone who deviates from the norm. Blaming society, these leaders would maintain, only begs the real question of maintaining individual responsibility. Instead of excusing deviants for their irresponsible choices, they say, the helping professions have an obligation to shape the behavior of these defective individuals so that they conform to society's norms.

Not only are various procedures to reshape individual deviants to be used, but social policies should also be instituted to support the rights of law-abiding citizens and deter dangerous individuals. For example, in America many social leaders assert that it makes no sense to inhibit the constitutionally guaranteed right of all law-abiding citizens to own handguns for their own self-protection while criminals have unlimited access to guns that they use to rob and murder.

While a strong case can be made for the individualist model, critics tend to conclude that blaming the individual is self-defeating. Some of these theorists assert that society can victimize the so-called deviant by making it difficult for that person to enter the mainstream. These critics assert that society *blames the victim* for problems beyond his or her control and then tries to change the deviant person's behavior to conform to social norms.[30] This, they say, misallocates the real locus of the problem. Peter Breggin asserts, for example, that many mental health social workers, "led by psychiatry, have rushed into the void left by default of the family," blaming child victims by diagnosing them as having neglectful or abusive histories, drugging and hospitalizing them, taking "the pressure off the parents, the family, the school, and the society."[31]

Furthermore, critics of the personal-blame approach assert that practitioners of individual treatment may not only misplace social problems by locating them in individuals, but justify the use of a proliferation of psychotherapeutic methods that have not been shown to make any significant difference in changing individual behavior.[32] Professional helpers can harm rather than help if they unnecessarily deprive people of their freedom by confining them in mental hospitals, or undermine their ability to help themselves by claiming only an expert can help. Moreover, irreversible damage can result from psychosurgery or drugs.[33] Ellen Gambrill reports that as a result of professional intervention, presenting complaints may get worse or losses may occur that would not otherwise. A study in *Social Casework,* for example, demonstrated that intensive services provided by social workers to elderly clients resulted in higher mortality than did usual agency procedures.[34]

In spite of these criticisms, however, while counseling may not often "cure" a person who has socially problematic behavior, it may provide assistance for people who are struggling with interpersonal relationship problems. But even in these cases, a study of people who were asked to whom they would turn for help indicated that most people seek out their friends and neighbors and only as a last resort would go to a psychotherapist with their problems. Most people rely on people they trust in their own neighborhoods or communities for assistance. The community of ordinary people is not only the most utilized source of helping but is often just as capable as highly trained clinicians. A study by R. M. Dawes, for example, found that "nonprofessionals are as successful as professionals in helping clients with a variety of problems," and "possession of a degree or 'experience'

does not ensure a unique domain of success in helping people."[35]

Harry Specht, one of the most respected educators and macro social workers of his time, asserts that generations of Americans have been brainwashed with theories that identify the individual as the source of many problems that are social in origin. Psychotherapeutic social work unwittingly reinforces the attitude that the source of social problems is in the individual.[36]

The individualist model actually may contribute to and entrench the very problems it describes. In order to protect society from offenders, for example, we obligate them to carry a label of "criminal" with them as long as they live: when they apply for jobs, are asked to serve on a jury, or join the military. Offenders, who have difficulty fitting into society in the first place, now have to contend with an additional burden that makes it even harder to find employment or become successful citizens. Even if they have been truly rehabilitated, they are branded as misfits, untrustworthy, or dangerous wherever they go and, as a result, may revert to even more criminal behavior than before.[37]

Critics of the individual approach to social problems claim that the more one atomizes social problems to the level of the individual, the less social workers are able to see larger social systems at work. Eitzen and Baca-Zinn, in agreement with Breggin, assert that the personal-blame approach frees government, the economy, the justice system, and the educational system from any blame. This protection of the established order against criticism increases the difficulty of trying to change dominant economic, social, and political institutions.[38]

Rather than look to individuals, therefore, some assert that "it is more effective to reconceive the basic problem."[39] Robert Linthicum suggests that when people are severely limited in what they can do to change their plight, they become impoverished. He suggests that poverty is not so much the absence of goods as it is the absence of power—the capability of being able to change one's situation. Marginalization, incapacity, and lack of opportunity are not the results of poverty, but its primary causes. An effective strategy for breaking up the vicious cycle of mutually reinforcing impoverishment begins by recognizing that poverty is "not a matter of individual or family poverty but the poverty of a way of life."[40] The real cure lies in helping people obtain the power and resources to solve their own social problems, and break the cycle that keeps them trapped.

The solution for helping people with social problems manifested by individual behavioral difficulties does not lie in providing professional therapy to a handful of people. Except in the most serious situations, a more effective strategy is for social workers to develop the community into a therapeutic network of friends who can generate the power and resources by helping one another to change their situation. Skilled social work clinicians could use their skills to train, support, and provide consultation to community members to assist one another so that they receive the support, guidance, and advice they need. Instead of creating dependency on a therapist, the social worker would empower the natural social networks already in place to which most people turn in times of trouble and crisis. Social work will have returned to its true legacy of *social* service, helping people help themselves.

Parent/Family Structures Model

One of the most common taken-for-granted assumptions in psychology and social work is that a child's personality is shaped by the child's parents. When parents are unable to provide positive parenting, where families become dysfunctional, or in more serious cases where child neglect, physical and sexual abuse, domestic violence, or alcohol and drug abuse occurs, we can expect social problems to occur. For example, it has been estimated that a child reared by an alcoholic parent has a 40% chance of becoming an alcoholic. A large percentage of spousal abusers were themselves raised in a home where domestic violence occurred. Many people who end up in prison were abused as children. William Julius Wilson asserts that the cause of poverty among black families is the absence of black males who can serve not only as providers but as role models and provide stability to the family.

The parent/family blame approach is one of the most fundamental assumptions in the field of social work. Almost every social worker is trained to think that the way to break the pernicious cycles of abuse, poverty, and domestic violence is to help families become healthy by education in communication and parenting skills; providing social and financial support to families; providing family counseling when families display dysfunctional behaviors; or in extreme cases of domestic violence or child abuse, protecting children by removing them from the home and placing them in healthier family environments. Most social workers continue to accept the most prized conventional wisdom in psychology reaching back to Sigmund Freud, that parental nurture is the root of the self and that dysfunctional family systems are the cause of personal and social dysfunction.

According to developmental psychologist Judith Rich Harris, "Both the therapist and the patient are participants in a culture that has, as one of its cherished myths, the belief that parents have the power to turn their children into happy and successful adults or to mess up their lives very badly. The belief that if anything goes wrong, it must be the parent's fault."[41] In spite of the conventional wisdom that our personalities, character, and behaviors are molded by our parents and families, Harris maintains that in most homes there is "no relationship between the goodness of the home and the goodness of the offspring. In the formation of an adult, genes matter and peers matter, but parents don't matter."[42] She states, "The assumption that parents have permanent effects on children's behavior is wrong. The *only* parents who do have distinctive effects are the super-bad ones who abuse their kids so severely they wind up in the hospital."[43]

Of course parents do matter. It is mandatory that infants receive nurture, attention, and love from parents for their very survival. "These early relationships are essential not just for normal social development, but even for normal brain development."[44] But as children, even very young children begin to interact with other children, they begin to identify with one another. This social engagement is the universal capacity and necessity of people to take on roles.[45] Role-taking is our ability to place ourselves in the position of others and to act accordingly. We imaginatively construct the attitudes of the other, and thus anticipate the behavior of the other. The capacity of people to take on social roles, is *the* means by which people become social, become engaged in constructing the self and, in large measure it provides them with their ability to become human.[46]

Harris reports that the ability of very young children to assume different roles already occurs in older infants, infants of walking age,[47] and as soon as the child meets other children, the social process of trying on different roles, identifications, attitudes, and self-perceptions expands. According to Lauer and Boardman, role-taking includes an increasingly wider range of the child's behavior, and differentiates the roles that he or she plays in various situations and contexts. Depending on the extent of role involvement with others, even a very young child generates many options for alterations in his or her selfhood, and this occurs "even when the roles are known to be temporary." Whenever we appropriate the attitudes of the other, we modify our "self." Similarly, when we disengage from a role, we also alter the self. Engagement or disengagement can be easy or difficult, exciting or challenging to the individual's self-conception, but the process allows the individual to continually change and modify the self. The self is never static. It is always in a process of change.[48]

The self that a person carries around in adult life is derived, then, from genetic makeup and the person's ability *to choose* from a variety of self-roles to which the person is exposed, beginning with parents or family, but at a very early age expanding beyond the family. As soon as children begin to become social creatures, they no longer "identify with their parents; they identify with other children—others like themselves," Harris states. According to Harris, "it is a mistake to think of children as empty vessels, passively accepting whatever the adults in their lives decide to fill them up with.… Children are not incompetent members of the adult's society; they are competent members of their own society, which has its own standards and its own culture."[49]

In fact, says Harris, "No matter how bad their home environment might be, children will turn into normal adults if the following conditions are met: They do not inherit any pathological characteristics from their parents,… their brains are not damaged by neglect or abuse, and they have normal relationships with their peers.[50] Locating the origin of social problems in the psychological health of the family and the ability of parents to provide the child with adequate modeling is incorrect. Children do not passively and indiscriminately incorporate both healthy and dysfunctional components of parental and family systems into their psyche and are then fated to unconsciously carry those characteristics in their behavior for the rest of their life. The self is a responsible self, choosing the kind of person he or she will become by

means of the quality of the people in his or her social environment. A child's parents and family are not the creator or the cause of social problems, nor are they, except in the most extreme cases, the cause of individual dysfunction.

If we try to cure social problems by focusing on the parents or changing dysfunctional family patterns, therefore, we will be looking at the wrong place. Individual and family psychotherapy are very useful in their own domain—for improving personal *relationships*. Assisting marriages and families that are on the verge of breakdown is an extremely important social work service, without which many people's lives would be in disarray and children would experience psychological trauma. However, "to the extent that these reforms prescribe individualistic remedies for collective grievances"[51] they overlook the general deterioration of social life and are in keeping with American social denial.

Neighborhood Structures Model

An alternate conception of the causes of social problems asserts that if otherwise good people are exposed to "bad influences" in their social environments, they may be prone to adopt the norms of their peers. The idea that bad neighborhoods are the cause of social problems is called *differential association*. Differential association theory was developed by symbolic interaction sociologist Edwin Sutherland, who stressed that "criminal behavior is learned by interacting with others. If people associate with people who break the law, they are more likely to learn to break the law than those who associate with people who don't break the law."[52] Marvin Wolfgang in his "subculture theory" concluded that people who grow up in a subculture that supports certain behaviors will have a high chance of emulating those same behaviors.[53] Judith Harris cites a study of over four thousand adopted children in Denmark that shows that the only increase in criminality among Danish adoptees whose biological parents were criminals was among those who were raised in and around Copenhagen. In small towns and rural areas, an adoptee reared in a criminal home was no more likely to become a criminal than one reared by honest adoptive parents. According to Harris, it wasn't criminal adoptive parents who made the biological offspring of criminals into a criminal; it was the neighborhood in which the child was reared.[54]

Furthermore, Harris asserts, "group socialization theory makes this prediction: that children would develop into the same sort of adults if we switched all the parents around, but left the children's lives outside the home unchanged—left them in their schools and their neighborhoods."[55] These conclusions are supported by Hartshorne and May, who found, for example, the "normal unit for character education is the group or small community."[56] Harris states that the group is the natural environment of the child. "Children identify with a group of others like themselves and take on the norms of the group," and although it may look as though parents are "conveyers of the culture," Harris says they are not: the peer group is.[57] It is the same conclusion that social worker Samuel Slavson arrived at several decades ago in his book *Character Education in a Democracy*,[58] and it is the presumption on which social group work was established as a field.

The implications of the work of Harris, Sutherland, Wolfgang, and Hartshorne and May are vastly important in several ways for macro and micro social workers in trying to deal with social problems. Children's and adolescents' peer groups in their neighborhoods, and the social organizations that support them such as social group work agencies, church youth groups, and organizations such as scouts and boys and girls clubs are *the* most important arenas of human social maturation and character building. They provide the means by which children discover how to relate to others, incorporate norms and rules of society, and in general form themselves into mature human beings.[59] It is the relationships that children find in their own communities and neighborhoods by which the self is born, and by which people grow into healthy social beings. Neighborhoods and social groups are the essential building blocks of the human condition.[60]

If we want to improve children's behavior, we should focus on improving the child's social environment—his or her peer group and neighborhood. If we want to develop a child's character, the best way to do so is by means of character-building peer groups such as scouts, congregational youth groups, and group social service agencies such as the YMCA. If social work is to make any real impact on social problems such as drug abuse, violence, crime, poverty,

or ethnic intolerance, the place to begin is to help people work together to make their communities better places to live.

Macro social workers make extensive use of community planning by which neighbors talk about and devise ways to make their communities better places to live. They assist local groups of people to develop neighborhood social service programs such as group-work services to improve the quality of social relationships among children and teenagers. They help community members build community development corporations to improve the social and economic capacity of their neighborhoods. They assist neighbors to join together into community organizations to "create sufficient power to pressure government, business and values-creating organizations to address issues such as affordable housing, crime, drugs, toxic waste dumps, suburban sprawl, quality of education, public transportation, tax inequities and many others."[61]

Intergroup Conflict Model

The framers of our Constitution were afraid of centralizing all political power in one office. Therefore, they divided power among three branches and, within those branches, divided government between local, regional, state, and national levels. By fragmenting power over a broad spectrum of society, the framers insured that interest groups would compete among themselves and government would play the role of mediator to keep power in check, and at the same time guarantee that everyone would at least have a "piece of the pie."[62] As a result, many powerful organizations and interest groups find access to power at one or another level of government. They press for policy concessions and preferential treatment by which their interests can find a sympathetic voice. This theory of government is called interest-group liberalism. You will read more about this in Chapter 13.

Modern industrialized society has now become so large, Ralf Dahrndorf asserts, that while interest groups continue to manipulate government for preferential treatment, many now carry out economic, political, educational, and other important institutionalized activities themselves. These socially accepted "megastructures" then direct and control the activities of other organized groups and "establish important power differences within and among particular organizations. Since the interests of different authority positions of the organizations in which they are embedded do not normally coincide, established societal authority relations create the bases for conflicts among the groups occupying different levels within the overall hierarchy. They also create the bases for a variety of social problems, as policies enacted to further the interests of some…create effects that work against the interests of others."[63]

When one or another of these organizations achieves power at the expense of another group "the powerful seize as much of society's resources for themselves as they can, and in the process exploit the less powerful and create social problems such as poverty, discrimination, and oppression," Henslin states. "As the exploited react to their oppression, still other problems emerge such as crime, escapist drug abuse, and various forms of violence such as riots and suicide." According to Henslin, "Conflict theorists view the social polices that benefit the less privileged as concessions from the powerful…. They also see them as actions designed to keep the privileged in their positions of power." At the intergroup level, therefore, "social problems occur when powerful groups exploit the less powerful and as the less powerful resist, rebel, or appeal to higher values of justice."[64]

Macro social workers have made extensive use of the intergroup conflict model. Many community developers and community organizers, for example, see in their daily experience how communities and neighborhoods, especially communities of the poor, lack power and are exploited or ignored by the large megastructures of society. One of the goals of these macro social workers is to help communities of people regain control and assert their interests. But macro social workers do not simply attempt to play the game of interest-group politics in a more assertive or shrewder way than corporate or governmental organizations.

Many macro social workers realize that this game of interest-group politics is itself the problem, and to play it better will only further polarize people and entrench power conflicts for limited stakes. A better way is to reconceptualize power and politics. Rather than engage corporate or governmental interests as enemies or competitors in the game of power grabbing, community organizers and community developers invite them as partners in building a better society.

Instead of accepting the idea that power and wealth are scarce and limited commodities over which people must conflict, bargain, and strategize, macro social workers understand that political power and economic prosperity are goods that everyone can share, and that once shared they increase in various ways that can contribute to each other's benefit. In this way not only are the social problems that arise from intergroup conflict dispelled, but various interest groups are transformed into positive assets that can cooperatively work for the good of society as a whole.

Underlying this conciliatory and more positive approach, however, is always the implied if not explicit understanding that communities of people will not let government or corporate "leaders" escape their responsibility. Linthicum asserts that one of the most important tasks "is for people to hold the government, business, educational and social institutions responsible to do what the law requires them to do."[65] By means of community organizations, macro social workers assist people not only to assert their claims for justice and fair treatment in the marketplace and in the court of public opinion, but in direct action if corporate or governmental interests fail to uphold their end of the bargain.

Systems Deviance Model

One of the more popular theories that social workers use is the systems model. The systems perspective is based on a theory of society borrowed from the physical sciences in which society is assumed to be composed of a series of systems and subsystems that work together like a gigantic machine. Each of these systems structures and functions need to be congruent with one another. These systems operate on laws of physical science such as inertia, feedback, entropy, and homeostasis. *Inertia* means that once a system is set in motion it tends to keep going in the same direction. *Entropy* means that every system is prone to eventually wear out or break down.

Social ecology is systems theory derived from biology to describe how people interact in the social environment. In addition to being subject to the laws of physics, biological systems experience growth, adaptation, and interaction with their environment. *Homeostasis,* for example, "suggests that most living systems seek a balance to maintain and preserve the system."[66] Systems and social ecology concepts are useful because they are intended to "give us a method of conceptualizing a great deal of complexity."[67]

Social or ecological systems theorists assume that while society is generally good and healthy, it sometimes develops defects, such as when a system experiences entropy or when one component gets out of sync with other system components and the homeostatic balance is disturbed. Systems theorists tell us that social problems are malfunctions that occur in one part or another of the total system as society adjusts to growth and to changing conditions in its environment. Social problems are to some extent inevitable, but they are also correctable. They are warning signs that tell us where we need to focus our efforts in making society work better.

Social workers want to create social systems that are functional, effective and efficient in carrying out their tasks. If system entropy occurs, macro social workers look for systems dysfunction in the input system, the processing system, or system outputs. Often, the feedback loops break down, or the automatically self-regulating devices in systems cannot respond quickly enough to change. For example, one of the causes of the Great Depression was the belief that it was not the function of government to regulate the economy. When the economy went into a tailspin, government had few tools at its disposal to diagnose and prevent market failure. Since then, the government has changed its philosophy. It continually monitors many economic indicators and regularly adjusts interest rates, tax rates, and money supply to adjust for inflation and recession.

As society progresses, however, it may simultaneously create the conditions of breakdown, the unintended consequences of social decisions. For example, because of improvements in technology, people's job skills become outmoded. This puts pressure on society to continually provide the means for people to upgrade their abilities and adjust to changing job markets. If this does not happen, pools of unemployed and unemployable people will become a drain on the economy.

At other times the rapidity progress on which society depends often outstrips the ability of social systems to adjust and does not allow time to forecast all of the possible outcomes of decisions. Societies that undergo rapid change from the processes of immigration, urbanization, and industrialization may begin to develop social breakdown. Certain areas of cities that experience the most rapid changes, for example, may be found to have disproportionately high rates of vice, crime, family breakdown, and mental disorders.[68]

Social scientists also assert that social problems occur because people simply do not understand the consequences of their decisions. These latent social problems occur because decision-makers lack information, or because they cannot predict all of the possible outcomes of systems processes.[69] Medical science, for example, is increasingly able to decrease infant mortality. Physicians are now able to save premature infants, but at the same time these infants are subject to birth defects and genetic disorders. The medical ability to save lives is paradoxically contributing to an increase in children with birth defects and handicapping conditions.

However, there is another way to look at the systems approach to social problems. Some social theorists propose that what may appear to be mere "latent" or unintended consequences of social systems may actually be *intentionally* constructed components of the system. Charles Perrow, for example, asserts that once a social system is in place, it sustains the values and goals of those in control of that social system. In our society, those in positions of power are rational and goal-maximizing. They mobilize their values and seek advantage by calculating the benefits and costs of achieving their goals. Ecological problems such as air pollution or pesticide poisoning in our water supply, for example, are not merely unintended consequences of technology that have occurred as well-meaning corporate managers provide us with goods and services. Owners and managers spend a great deal of time anticipating all of the possible outcomes of every decision they make. They calculate the financial costs of decisions such as lawsuits, court costs, fines, taxes, and penalties and include them in the costs of doing business. If the projected benefit/cost ratio is favorable to corporate profits, they may continue to pollute even if the decision may be harmful to the public at large. The outputs of the social systems do not occur because owners or managers lack information, are ignorant of the consequences of their decisions, or because they are unable to predict outcomes. Powerful owners and managers are very well aware of the consequences of the social systems they command and intentionally create the conditions under which they operate.[70]

People who are not aware that systems can be and often are used for inhuman purposes will be unable to solve the real social problems that systems create. Social workers, therefore, must not be naive about the systems they are trying to correct. The claim that corporations are beyond reproach because something goes wrong with otherwise well-intentioned decisions or that social problems are the result of the failure of benign social systems in adjusting to social conditions beyond their control is often a mask for simple denial or an attempt to evade responsibility.[71] Owners of large corporations or managers of governmental systems may claim ignorance or blame systems problems for the harm they do, or they may try to justify their actions by saying they are in the interests of those to whom they are beholden, and thus provide a rationalization for the existing status quo. Or, more insidiously, they may hold society hostage to processes that are socially harmful because we are socialized to believe we cannot do without the benefits they provide for us.

On the other hand, the systems approach can alert us to a very real issue in dealing with social problems. When working with social systems, macro social workers must understand that the forces of inertia, homeostasis, and entropy work against systems change. "What makes definitive change so enormously difficult," Perry states, is that "each community, from the richest to the poorest, is constructed out of networks of interlocking forces and institutions that maintain it, and keep it in its recognizable form." A poor community is maintained in its impoverished form by a network of self-reinforcing processes and practices, Perry states, and any attempt to change one part of the network is opposed by the other forces that keep the community the way it is and neutralize the attempted improvement. Not only do social systems resist change, but they are difficult to fix when problems occur. Perry says, for example, "A strategy for change that selects just one part of the community as a focus for improvement…is likely to be neutered in the long run by the rest of the community influences…. Any effective strategy has to consider many parts of the net of interlocking community influences and deal with them more or less simultaneously or at least in interconnected phases so that the different

parts no longer neutralize improvements but actually reinforce the change.[72]

Systems theory, therefore, provides a helpful perspective on the origin of social problems and why social problems are so intractable. But macro social workers also must be aware that at times systems theory also may serve as a disguise for the real causes of social problems, a means to justify the power of the system's owners, an excuse for harmful decisions, and a way of rationalizing the status quo. The challenge for macro social workers using a systems approach to solving social problems is to be sensitive in observing whom the system serves and protects. Is the system serving a latent function which advantages some at the expense of others? Are intentional patterns of exploitation, greed, or injustice masquerading as unintended consequences or as mere ignorance? Is there an implication that the system is its own justification and is beyond criticism?

Institutional Deviance Model

When health care is maldistributed, when poverty persists for millions, "when tax laws permit a business to write off 80% of a $100 luncheon but prohibit a truck driver from writing off a bologna sandwich, when government is run by a few for the profit of the few, when businesses supposedly in competition fix prices to gouge the consumer, then society is permitting what is called *institutional deviance.*"[73]

Institutional deviance occurs when social problems become officially embedded in the major ideologies, the culture, or the structures of society and often become the foundational beliefs, the operating premises on which society is based. Ethnic intolerance in the United States was institutionalized in the social, economic, legal, and governmental structures in this country. Racism was part of the foundational principles that guided many business, governmental, and legal decisions. Bribery, spoils, nepotism, and other forms of corruption were institutionalized in business and politics immediately after the Civil War, until the reforms of Progressive Era social workers such as Florence Kelley, Lillian Wald, Jane Addams, and others. Conceiving of social problems as located in the institutional structures of society permits going beyond explaining social problems exclusively in terms of individual, family, or systems.

Eitzen and Baca-Zinn assert, for example, that "there *are* conditions in society (such as poverty and institutional racism) that induce material or psychic suffering for certain segments of the population; there *are* sociocultural phenomena that prevent a significant numbers of society's participants from developing and using their full potential; there *are* discrepancies between what the United States is supposed to stand for (equality of opportunity, justice, democracy) and the actual conditions in which many people live." According to Eitzen and Baca-Zinn, social workers must keep in mind that powerful agencies of government and business define social reality in a way that often manipulates public opinion and controls behaviors that threaten the status quo and their power. "Slavery on large plantations, for instance, was not a social problem, but slave revolts were. Racism was not a social problem of the Jim Crow South, but pushy blacks were. From the standpoint of U.S. pubic opinion, dispossessing Native Americans of their lands was not a social problem, but the Native Americans who wanted to maintain their native homelands were." When macro social workers look for objective causes of social problems, they state, "we must…guard against the tendency to accept the definitions of social problems provided by those in power."[74]

Macro social workers who get involved in politics and in social policy often struggle against these forces of institutional deviance. Macro social workers understand how social institutions, even those created by well-intentioned people for good purposes, may diverge from their original goals and become deviant. For example, the Second Amendment, which in 1783 permitted states to maintain armed militias to keep order, has become reinterpreted by many today as a license for nearly anyone to own handguns and other weapons, resulting in momentous violence to children and teenagers.

In addition, many macro social workers also understand that some institutions under the guise of noble premises may intentionally serve socially immoral purposes. The defense industry obtains legal sanctions and subsidies from our government to sell weapons to developing countries for profit, ostensibly to promote "a balance of power" or protect our "national interests." In reality, however, selling weapons of war to poor countries steals the sweat of impoverished citizens, often to guarantee that dictators continue to oppress their own people and perpetrate violence against their neighbors, and even war against our own country.

Some businesses do not even have the guise of nobility of purpose behind which to hide their exploitative self-interests. After years of deceit and evasion, for example, the American tobacco industry, having finally been deflected from marketing its products to adolescents in the United States, has now developed the lucrative global market with full realization that it is endangering the health of the world's children and creating enormous health-care costs. Macro social workers who engage in social policy and politics often struggle with how to hold such large institutions accountable and forge social policies that are morally good and socially just.[75]

Social/Cultural Premises Model

Another assumption about social problems is that society can be best understood as a conscious, planned construct. People intentionally create societal structures, laws, and governance out of common understandings about meaning and truth. People are not helpless or determined beings molded by natural societal forces to which they are subject or over which they have little control, as systems or social ecology theorists claim. Rather, as the social pragmatists argue, although a person's "situation confronts him with limitations and problems, he is the one who struggles to understand his situation, to master it, and to utilize it for the realization of his interests."[76] "Human behavior involves the interpretation of events or phenomena and the sharing of those interpretations with others,"[77] and human society "rests upon a basis of consensus, i.e., the sharing of meanings in the form of common understanding and expectation."[78] Society reflects the key ideologies and ways of thinking that were built into it in the first place, and those premises become interpreted and reinterpreted by succeeding generations.

"The cultural perspective assumes that human behavior is guided by patterns of basic assumptions, expectations, and customs that develop over time and slowly drop out of people's conscious awareness," Holland states. These patterns become habits that continue to influence people even when the social environment changes.[79] To fully understand why social problems seem impervious to permanent resolution, therefore, macro social workers must develop an understanding of these patterns. Frank Coleman asserts, for example, that the social failures of American political institutions are "a permanent blindness fixed in the nature of the institutions and the social philosophy used to design them." The social philosophy to which Coleman refers is contained in the heritage of ideas and cherished social ideologies that have shaped "the consciousness of a whole people through our national inheritance" and manifest themselves "in characteristic and unvarying ways related to the American constitutional philosophy." Coleman believes that the powerful legacy of individualism and self-interest and the eradication of the idea of a higher public good in American society formed a "total ideology which could not be challenged or even questioned."[80] Richard Hofstadter adds this observation: "However much at odds on specific issues, the major political traditions have shared a belief in the rights of property, the philosophy of economic individualism, the value of competition… and the natural evolution of self-interest and self-assertion [as] staple tenets of the central faith in American political ideologies."[81]

Individualism   Individualism is the cornerstone of our political and economic systems and determines, to a large extent, the way we conceive our selves. We cherish the individual rights that our Constitution upholds, especially the right to freely express our opinions. The values of dignity, self-reliance, independence, and self-determination are rooted in our tradition of individualism, and our form of government itself is founded "in the principle of liberal democracy…that the sole source of right is the absolute will of the individual."[82] According to Milton Friedman, private enterprise operating in a free market is based on "the individual as the ultimate entity in society." Our economy would not exist if each person did not have the freedom to exert his or her own self-interests and freely pursue them. So crucial is this kind of individual freedom that, according to Friedman, most arguments against the free market seem to reflect "a lack of belief in freedom itself."[83]

While individualism forms the foundation of our culture, Bellah et al. note that "some of our deepest problems, both as individuals and as a society, are closely linked to our individualism." While individualism presupposes autonomy and freedom, in some contexts it also "weakens the very meanings that give content and substance to the ideal of individual dig-

nity." The "immersion in private economic pursuits undermines the person as a citizen," disallowing the person an authentic role in public life.[84]

Individualism claims that "every person should be unencumbered by the rest of society in terms of how he or she conducts behavior within such areas as religion, government, and economy," observe Meenaghan and Washington. If selves are "defined by their preferences, and those preferences are arbitrary, then each self constitutes its own moral universe, and there is no way to reconcile conflicting claims of what is good in itself. All we can do is refer to chains of consequences and ask if our actions prove useful or consistent in the light of our own 'value-systems'" (Bellah et al., p. 80). Without any external guide than one's own internal, subjective perceptions, people become "limited to a language of radical individual autonomy"; they "cannot think about themselves or others except as arbitrary centers of volition." But under these premises society has no natural or organic bases but is "an abstraction," in which "only isolated individuals exist."[85]

Malleable, dependent, and capable of adaptation to almost any kind of circumstance, the docile,[86] valuationally unencumbered self presents exactly the conditions necessary "to succeed in an impersonal world of rationality and competition."[87] Rather than self-reliance, autonomy, and self-direction, the individual becomes passive, socially unengaged, and prone to conformity to the premises and values that social systems select for him or her.

Self-Interest   One of the basic premises of American constitutional philosophy is that everyone should "be committed to the rational pursuit of self-interest."[88] The individual is presumed to have an absolute right to be "his own authority on all points which affect his conscience and self-interest"[89] independent of the restraints of any "higher law." Self-interest has become a dominant motivating force not only in public affairs but in the economy, where acquisitive self-interest is recognized as an innate trait of the American character. It is a "driving force of modern productive work,"[90] a mandatory value on which our market system is based. The market channels self-interest "as the *energy* to thrust the economy forward, to speed up production and generate rapid economic growth."[91] Self-interest is a necessary means of "organizing individual citizens to achieve a high standard of living."[92] Politics is "sustained by the intersection of interests of independently situated political actors," Coleman states. These actors "identify the good for themselves in radically different ways" and then "ruthlessly pursue it."[93]

The intersection of differing interests in the political marketplace automatically gives indicators for the direction of the social order.[94] When aggregated together, these political preferences provide, if not a common good, at least a public interest that is supposed to reflect the desires of the people at any one time. Self-interest enlightened by social concern and altruism also endows society with a means by which social policies can be addressed, and "is viewed as the proper remedy for social ills."[95]

Rejection of Public Good   In spite of its effectiveness and utility, however, self-interest is not socially benign or altruistic, even when aggregated to form the "public interest." At its base it is a pernicious ideology that destroys the public spirit, denies the public good, undermines community, and sets individuals against one another. Reinhold Niebuhr, for example, pulls no punches when he says that "Evil is always the assertion of some self-interest without regard to the whole, whether the whole be conceived as the immediate community, or the total community of mankind, or the total order of the world.[96]

Possessive individualism and radical self-interest ultimately result in "rejecting the notion of conforming private interests to a public purpose," Coleman says, "depriving the populace of an adequate ideal of civilization in terms of which the members of society may be organized."[97] Higher ethical values such as altruism, compassion, or justice become neglected when common or public decisions are at stake. Not only is personal idealism undermined, but according to Means, "the unity of society is destroyed when one does not think of the long-term effects of economic exploitation or of consistently placing private above public interests. If such actions become universal, society would fly apart by centrifugal force."[98]

If the recommendations offered by the social work profession about curing our social ills are to be effective, therefore, they must work to change the ideologies that form the premises of our social order. Social workers must understand that, as Weiskopf states, the ailments of American life "cannot be cured without a profound change in thought and in values."[99]

In spite of the difficulties, macro social workers today are engaged in just such change by means of the creation of new social movements whose purpose is the establishment of new ways of thinking and new social values. They are aligning themselves with a new way of thinking socially, engaged in creating and expanding self-identities, and challenging conventional economic norms such as "more is better," as well as possessive individualism, ruthless self-interest, and the suspension of a public good. Many macro social workers in the United States and Canada, and others as well, are beginning to reject many of the premises on which the Enlightenment project was based and on which modern Western political and economic tradition is founded. They are envisioning a new "postmodern" social environment that will usher in a new *social* era—one that will change the nature of our modern global society. You will read more about how macro social workers are engaged in new social movements in Chapter 14 and how social change is occurring globally in Chapter 15.

ANSWERS THAT WON'T WORK

Just as assumptions that we make can help or hinder us in the resolution of social problems, the range of strategies we use may delude, blind, and prevent us from solving them. Sometimes those mechanisms are so strong that people, especially those in positions of power, condone or perpetuate the very problems they pretend to solve.

Macro social workers must seek answers that work. We must be honest with ourselves and with others when we look for answers. We must be aware that in spite of our good intentions, we may often employ a range of illusions about social problems that exacerbate rather than solve them. We must learn to recognize these escapes to illusion. Among these are denial, avoidance, blaming, moralizing, and the quick fix.

Social Denial

Denial takes many forms. We refuse to acknowledge the existence of social problems. When we do admit their existence, we look at them as "personal" problems instead of "social" problems. We also deny their existence by excluding problem people from our lives, or by rationalizing about our inaction.

Refusing to Admit the Problem Exists

A major form of denial in our society is our refusal to admit that social problems exist. We attribute problems such as welfare, crime, and racism to deviant individuals who refuse to conform to societal norms, who let others carry them or engage in illegal or immoral behavior. Poverty, some argue, is caused by people who are lazy, undisciplined, unmotivated, selfish, immature, and irresponsible.[100] Rather than contribute to society, these deviants restrict social progress.

Personalizing the Problem

Because of our propensity to deny that social problems have a social cause, our treatment generally is individually based. The solution to people who choose not to enter the mainstream of society has been any number of aversive, educative, rehabilitative, reformative, isolative, or curative methods rather than reforming social conditions. Much of our social policy aimed at offenders, drug abusers, the mentally ill, developmentally disabled, and other groups tends to take this approach. By trying to solve problems one person at a time, we create the illusion that we are making social change, while in reality we may only be patching up people so severely damaged that they are beyond repair. We concentrate on the social deviant, but fail to look at the conditions that may cause people to become deviant.

Many social workers fall prey to this illusion. Some may come to believe that individual or family psychotherapy is the major focus and goal of helping. Helping professionals may unconsciously contribute to a mentality that supports a deviance theory of social problems. To the extent that this occurs, social clinicians may actually exacerbate the problems they attempt to cure. By concentrating only on the individual nature of problems, they avoid concerns about wider social causation. In their professional activities, clinicians may sometimes do little to involve themselves in wider social issues or causes.

Excluding Reality

When we personalize social problems, it becomes easy for us to exclude reality by shutting away those with whom we do not want to deal. Excluding reality operates by the maxim "out of sight, out of mind." What we do not see and experience is not part of our reality, and therefore not our problem. We

relocated Native Americans to reservations, Chinese to Chinatowns, Japanese Americans to concentration camps. We effectively banished intellectually, developmentally, and emotionally disabled from our awareness by placing them in large institutions. Segregation in the South before the Civil Rights Act attempted to use this form of denial as a way of dealing with race relations.

Rationalizing

One form of rationalizing is the "yes, but" game. Some rationalizations are: "Yes, gangs are rampant, but more social programs will not make them go away." "Yes, there are few services for children, but throwing more money at social problems is not the answer." "Yes, our cities are deteriorating, but we tried community development in the 1960s and we still have the problem." "Yes, poor people need medical care, but a national health care system will only make the problem worse."

Avoidance

We tend to avoid responsibility for social problems because it may be in our own interests to do so, because they are too difficult to face, or because we are implicated in the social milieu that creates or condones them. Sometimes we avoid social problems by ignoring them, hoping they will go away or waiting until people adjust to their condition.

Avoiding Responsibility

Business corporations tend not to see themselves as a cause of poverty, but rather as a cause of prosperity. In addition, the political system sees itself not as preventing change, but as developing solutions to society's problems. To the contrary, however, as Coleman states, "The political system in America is marvelously well designed to enable actors to evade responsibility for events such as energy waste and widespread pollution, even when these events are the products of decisions they have made."[101]

Society Heal Thyself

One form of avoidance is to insist that if you ignore problems, eventually they will go away. It is easy to delude ourselves that by waiting long enough, social problems will either diminish on their own or become someone else's problem. This laissez-faire approach to social problems expects the powerless to turn down the lamp of reason and rely on the operation of a benevolent social system that will ultimately work things out in their interest.

Time Heals All Wounds   If we give things time, some argue, the naturally self-correcting mechanisms of the social body will cure the problem. While there may be short-term pain or difficulties for certain groups, they say, if we have faith in economic and political systems, everything will work out in the long run.

Social Adaptation   A more subtle variation of he time heals all wounds strategy is the idea that the longer society puts things off, the more people will adapt and accept their lot. They will eventually forget injustices, learning to live with their social condition. As they adjust, however, they form a culture of victimization in which powerlessness becomes part of their milieu. The more people act the role of victims, the more they reinforce their stereotyped roles, becoming unwilling or unable to gain resources for themselves. Delaying and avoiding dealing with social problems always works in favor of those in power.

Blaming

Blaming others is a way of deflecting responsibility from those who create social problems to those who bear their effects. Those in power have often honed this strategy to a fine point. There is no dearth of targets of blame. We can blame the victim, we can blame the providers, we can blame the system, among other targets. This strategy always results in a dead end.

Blaming the Victim   The strategy of blaming the victim, a term popularized by William Ryan, is a way of shifting responsibility and making the victims seem like the perpetrators of problems. The problem of poverty in America is therefore not attributed to an economy that advantages some at the expense of others, but rather to the individual who is laid off and cannot find work, or to a mother who must apply for welfare because her ex-husband refuses to pay child support.

Blaming the Providers   People charged with the responsibility of solving problems are sometimes blamed for their cause. "We have too many bureaucrats." "There is too much inefficiency, too much red tape, too much regulation, too much interference, too much government." All of these games beg the question of the real locus of social problems.

Blaming the Reformers   Sometimes social change agents are blamed for causing social problems. Socialists, pacifists, union organizers, social activists, community organizers, and civil rights activists have all been vilified as malcontents and subversives who tended to disturb social stability and undermine the social order. Many social activists have been harassed, jailed, and even murdered.

Passing the Buck   Sometimes those wanting to exonerate themselves or further their own ambitions use social problems as a means for their ends. Crimes, welfare, or racial intolerance often become the focus of political campaigns. One politician blames another for being "soft on crime" or for the "welfare mess." The President blames Congress or Congress blames the President. One political party blames the other. Social problems become political footballs. After an election has been won, however, and one politician or political party gains power, concern for resolving the social problem often seems to evaporate.

Scapegoating   A social group may be blamed for the existence of a social problem even when they are its victims. The Chinese, for example, were brought to America in the nineteenth century as laborers to blast roads and tunnels for railroads in the high Sierras, and then they were blamed for displacing other workers during recessions. The Chinese laborers, many of whom could not read, write, or speak English, were easy targets of scapegoating and racial hysteria.

Moralizing

Those people who do not meet the moral standards of people in power may be perceived as not deserving help. The poor, for example, are divided into the "deserving" poor and the "undeserving" poor. Those we consider deserving will receive help; those who do not will receive little or nothing. Retribution sometimes follows this way of thinking. In the retribution game, those enmeshed in social problems are made to pay. Punish welfare recipients by reducing payments, passing residency requirements, and increasing restrictions as incentives for people to get off welfare.

Punish criminals by longer, harsher sentences. Once freed, label them so that they will find it even more difficult to find a job.

The Quick Fix

Most social problems are perpetuated by years of reinforcement, neglect, and denial. Those who propose one-shot, short-term, stop-gap solutions and expect an immediate turnaround set up social change efforts for failure. Johnson's War on Poverty, begun in the 1960s, was dismantled by the Nixon Administration after only a few years and is being blamed for problems plaguing our cities 30 years later. The illusion that longstanding social problems can be solved by a quick fix ultimately leads to discouragement and anger.

REDEFINING SOCIAL PROBLEMS

Earlier I asked you to critique the conventional definition of social problems and develop your own definition. Now I will give you my definition of social problems.

> A social problem is experienced collectively by an identifiable group or community of people, caused by a source external to them that harms their welfare in specific ways, and can only be resolved by people themselves in partnership with the public and private sectors of society.

Compare this definition with the conventional definition of social problems and the one you and your classmates came up with. How is it the same? How is it different? Let's look at this definition in more detail and use it to critique the conventional definition. Recall that in the conventional definition, a social problem must have a **social** causation rather than be an issue of individual behavior. It must **affect** a large number of people and be judged by an **influential** number of people to be undesirable. It must be solvable **collectively** rather than by individuals acting alone.

Social Problems Are Experienced Collectively by an Identifiable Group or Community of People

The conventionally accepted definition of a social problem is defective in two ways. First, it is ruled by a quantitative criterion of size. A social problem is presumed to affect a "large" number of people. While it is true that social problems such as poverty, crime, and drug abuse occur "when individual discontent becomes a broadly felt concern,"[102] social problems are not abstractions that occur to people in amorphous mass society. They are experienced directly by smaller community or neighborhood groups as part of their lived reality.

Second, the conventional definition is ruled by a qualitative criterion of influence. An "influential" group of people is required to judge whether an issue is a social problem. In reality, however, social problems interfere, disrupt, or disadvantage people whether those conditions are recognized or acknowledged by those who are influential or powerful, or by anyone else. Social problems, in fact, are most often experienced by people who are not at all influential.

Macro social workers maintain that the essence of being human lies in the ability of people to jointly examine and define the dilemmas of existence for themselves, not accept a definition handed to them by others. People who experience injustice, intolerance, or economic or political oppression need to define their own issues on their own terms, regardless of the size of their group, their influence, their perceptions, or the approval of the majority of the population. When the influential usurp this right, they not only steal people's humanity but assume that people in the mass are incapable of understanding their own social situation; they exclude people from the process of making their own lives better. The presumption that the influential should define and decide for others is the beginning of social problems and the heart of oppression.

Macro social workers accept people's perceptions of social reality as valid, and insist on the right of people to own their feelings and values in relation to those experiences. It is the lived experience which people encounter in their own day-to-day realities that is important, not the experience or perceptions of someone external to them, no matter how powerful. People become empowered when they share experiences with one another, confirm perceptions, reflect on the meaning of those experiences, gain deeper insights into the causes of those conditions, and make decisions about what to do about them. Claiming the right to own one's reality is the first step toward breaking the cycle of oppression. Community organizers, developers, and planners "continually translate personal troubles into public issues and public issues into terms of human meaning."[103]

Social Problems Are Caused by a Source External to People and Harm Their Welfare in Specific Ways

The effects of social problems are often seen in the lives of the people themselves. It may be seen in their attitudes, values, and social behavior. It may be seen in their families, in their ability to raise their children or provide a safe, clean, healthy environment for them. Social problems may be exhibited in communities and in the ability of communities to sustain themselves or provide resources or tools for people to survive. While individuals, groups, or communities often reflect in their behavior the effects of social problems, the source is often, if not entirely, external to them.

It is the role of macro social workers to help those affected recognize the forces in the social environment that have created social problems by placing the locus of the problem where it belongs and identifying its effects. Social problems may be seen in the institutions such as banks, shopping malls, industry, and manufacturing that use the resources of communities and export profits. They may be seen in the unresponsiveness of school systems, police systems, or others to the problems in the community. They may be seen in institutionalized discrimination in housing, loaning practices, and police protection. They may be seen in the attitudes and values of society that keep people poor and excluded for the benefit of others.

Social Problems Can Only Be Resolved by the People Themselves in Partnership with the Public and Private Sectors of Society

Because of modern problems of alienation and apathy, we suffer from the desperation of bearing our problems alone, and from the delusion that the powerful and influential will disentangle the problems in which we are enmeshed. But the solution rarely comes because the problem we experience is our reliance on experts, our separation in apathetic individualism, and our despair in social passivity. We cannot act because we are convinced that our problems are either lodged internally in our psyche or exist externally in social megastructures over which we

have no control. Our malaise is profound and generalized, and our situation seems hopeless. Isolation prevents us from united action with others.

Macro social workers realize that before action can take place, people must be connected into a recognizable group that understands itself as a community in which the "personal troubles of each become public problems of all." Community "is the only possible form of social organization that can meaningfully reconnect people to their world and provide them with some degree of control over its political directions."[104] Only when people refuse to allow themselves to be separated and alone can they break the bonds of individualism. When people bring issues and trouble into the light of mutual communication, they are no longer unsure, or uninformed. When they refuse to allow others to define their social reality for them, they begin to see through the deception that patriarchy fosters. When they confront their common situation together, they not only gain power and mastery, but they begin to become a people.

Communities of people do not rely on the powerful to solve problems for them. They do not ask for permission. They do not wait until the megastructures take notice. People take action on their own behalf, on their own terms, and in their own time. The social environment is theirs to define, shape, and construct.

But they do not have to do this alone. They engage and in fact must connect with other sectors of society in the economy and in government. People who are affected by social problems demand that those in positions of power and responsibility take notice. Once they take notice, community members expect the influential to be accountable and live up to their commitments and responsibilities.

The economic and public sectors of society, therefore, will be compelled to make room for a new, third sector—the voice of communal and social organizations of people united to solve social problems. The community of citizen problem-solvers of the new social sector will be leaders and full partners at the table of decision-making, not invited guests, respectful listeners, or interested spectators. It is the community of citizen problem-solvers who will be the catalysts of change, who will write the agendas, develop solutions, and present them to corporate and governmental leaders, not for permission or approval, but for assistance with action.

Government and business leaders, however, are not used to sharing power or leaving control to others. They are not familiar with agreeing to decisions others make, helping with plans that others create, or following the vision that others see. These "leaders" will need to be resocialized to their new role as partners. It is in this process of helping people redefine and restructure social reality and reformulate the relationship between community, government, and corporate America that macro social workers may make their most substantial contribution toward shaping a new society.

HOW TO SOLVE SOCIAL PROBLEMS

There at least two approaches by which macro social workers can begin to help people solve social problems. One is a contingency approach. A contingency approach is pragmatic and uses any number of ways to solve social problems. The social change approach takes an entirely different perspective on social problems.

Contingency Approach

Social problems manifest themselves in different ways, depending on the situation. No single solution will resolve all social problems, therefore, nor will the application of a solution at one level resolve how that problem affects people at other levels. Social problems have spillover effects. They spill over to different segments and levels of society. A problem at one level will affect other levels. To attribute all social problems exclusively to any one social assumption is to apply an overly simplistic or narrow view to issues that are complex and often interrelated.

A balanced view would require people to assess a social problem at the level in which the problem occurs, examine the particular context of the specific social problem, and choose a solution between alternative courses of action that meets the demands of the particular situation. Such a view is called a contingency approach. For example, macro social workers and neighborhood residents might adopt a posture of

working on several fronts simultaneously, applying different solutions that attack different aspects of a problem at different levels.

Individuals obviously can be malicious and aggressive for purely psychological reasons. Families sometimes become engaged in violent and abusive behaviors. Some people require individual or family therapy, remedial help, or special programs if they are to function normally in society.[105] Child protective social workers, probation officers, and drug counselors would provide assistance to people whose behavior problems have reached the point where they are dangerous to themselves and to others. Counseling and behavioral assistance would be offered to people who have already been damaged by social problems to enable them to develop sufficient inner resources to reengage the struggle for selfhood. In addition, skilled clinicians would train and assist community volunteers to provide help to their friends and neighbors in the form of a therapeutic community.

At the same time, developing better communities, neighborhood social structures, and social peer groups may hold the answer to some social problems. Community social workers would help citizens establish neighborhood planning boards or councils. They would help set up community development corporations and community organizations. Community social workers would assist neighborhood civic associations and churches in partnership with corporate and governmental megastructures to empower local communities and engage local residents to become active in civic and community affairs.

Community social workers would enlist the assistance of social group workers to assist in the provision of neighborhood peer groups, or help neighbors develop an infrastructure of positive peer groups using scouts, YMCAs, Girls and Boys Clubs, church youth groups, and others. They would assist in establishing new community-based social organizations that would provide local social services and programs. A model for such a coordinated community-based system of social care might be similar to that recommended by Specht and Courtney.[106]

Macro social workers would also assist coalitions of neighborhood and social organizations to confront megastructures of society that distort the public good for their own self interests, correct systemic social problems, and develop better social policies. Macro social workers, finally, engage in social movements and social action to shift ideologies and practices that have become oppressive, and they work to bring about a healthier global society.

Social Change: Strength/Assets Approach

Looking at the social world from a "problem" orientation has been the conventional way social workers view the human condition. The roots of this problem-oriented focus are in the Enlightenment tradition on which our modern society is based. The Enlightenment tradition gave rise to science and the scientific method, to modern reason and rational problem-solving. Modern science looks at the world as an aggregation of problems to be solved. Once the laws that govern the physical universe are understood, then little by little the puzzles of how they work can be uncovered. When a problem is solved, it is solved once and for all. The new piece of information can be added to all the others, and gradually the entire universe can be predicted and controlled.

This model has been so powerful that it has brought about the marvels of our modern technological age. So it is no wonder that social workers adopted modern reason and modern rational problem-solving and applied them to trying to solve the problems of the human condition. However, perhaps you have already seen that there are a great many complications with looking at the social world from a problem-oriented perspective. Looking at the world as a problem to be solved often distorts our vision. We see personal problems at the individual level and mistake them for social problems. We see children growing up to become criminals and we believe criminality is lodged in parental upbringing or families. The concepts we adopt from mechanistic science, such as systems theory, presume social problems are due to entropy rather than intentional decisions of social leaders. The ideologies such as individualism and self-interest have been credited for solving many of our economic and political problems, but they may actually have caused many social problems at the same time.

We will probably always look at the human condition from the perspective of problem orientation, but there may be a better way to approach how to achieve a better social world. One way is by looking at society from the perspective of *social change*. Social change is a proactive approach rather than a reactive one. Instead of looking to the past to discover what went wrong, the social change approach looks ahead to see what is possible. Rather than weaknesses, pathologies, and problems, people are seen as having strengths, possibilities, and solutions with which to build their own futures. Instead of assuming communities are arenas of neglect, crime, and poverty, community is perceived as full of resources, assets, and strengths that can be used to make a better society. The social change model utilizes this *assets-based strength approach*.

Ann Weick and Dennis Saleeby assert that "to examine the strengths and resiliencies of people in their everyday lives signals… an important shift in our thinking."[107] When this happens, often with the help of a macro social worker, people begin to gain power. This power comes from a new way of thinking called "*social thinking*" in contrast to "*rational problem-solving*." Thinking socially begins when people apply their common experiences to mutual reflection, thinking through the issues that plague them, and then arrive at a strategy of action. People who felt helpless, separated, and defeated begin to think anew and act anew. They become new people and begin to conceive and construct the world out of those new perceptions of themselves and one another. What began as a problematic and even self-defeating situation becomes transformed into an opportunity for rebirth and renewal. Macro social workers help mobilize people to utilize their assets so they can construct their communities and build their social reality in the way they conceive best. You will find out more about this new approach in the next chapter, and in other chapters that follow.

CONCLUSION

Macro social workers assert that the elimination of many of our social problems requires the active social engagement of people in the processes that contribute to the construction of social reality. Because social problems are part of fundamental principles embedded in the social order, people have a difficult time recognizing and extricating themselves from them. If social problems are to be solved, therefore, macro social workers must have an adequate understanding of society's role in creating social problems, and they must not be naive about the ways that decision-makers justify, minimize, evade, deny, and even perpetuate them.

On the other hand, many macro social workers today are turning on its head the entire way of thinking about social problems. Rather than engage in the debate about why we have social problems, what is their cause, who or what is to blame, or what is the best method of eradicating them, macro social workers today think in terms of social change. They work with communities of people who are building on their hopes and dreams, their visions, and their strengths to make better neighborhoods and a better society. They see communities in terms of their resources and assets rather than in terms of their deficits and weaknesses. People can move ahead and construct a world that is theirs to achieve, and macro social workers stand beside them in the struggle for a better life.

KEY CONCEPTS

social problems

moral deviance

person-blame approach

social pathology

parent/family model

neighborhood group approach

intergroup conflict approach

systems deviance model

institutional deviance model

social/cultural premises model

unintended consequences

refusing to admit problems exist

personalizing problems

excluding reality

rationalizing

avoiding responsibility

society heal thyself

time heals all wounds

social adaptation

blaming the victim

blaming providers

blaming reformers

passing the buck

scapegoating

moralizing

retribution

quick fix

redefining social problems

contingency approach

social change

strength/assets approach

social thinking

QUESTIONS FOR DISCUSSION

1. Why do social problems persist?
2. Ann Schaef says that society is deteriorating at an alarming rate. Do you agree or disagree? If you agree, to what do you attribute this deterioration?
3. Eric Voegelin claims that society is both progressing and regressing at the same time. Do you agree with this assessment? In what areas are we progressing? In what areas are we regressing?
4. Our ways to solve social problems have not progressed a great deal for generations. For example, the most common solutions to crime—incarceration, physical punishment, or execution—have not changed for over 2000 years. Our responses to poverty still rely on principles of the Elizabethan Poor Law enacted 400 years ago. Our responses to drug abuse—incarceration, interdiction, and confiscation—were found unworkable over 70 years ago during Prohibition. Why do people seem so incapable of arriving at better ways of solving the social troubles that have plagued the human condition for millennia?

Exercise 2. 2

Diagnosing Social Problems

Purpose
You will practice diagnosing two social problems and deciding on an approach to them.

Process
Read the vignettes below. Develop a diagnosis of both social problems, then answer the following questions:

1. What role should the profession of social work take in trying to solve each of these social problems?

2. How would clinical social work or casework approach the problem?

3. How would macro social work approach the problem?

4. What implications can you draw for allocating social service resources, training social workers, and strategies that the profession of social work should advocate?

Violence Toward Children

Child physical abuse, sexual abuse, serial murders, and child theft occur with regularity. More than 2 million cases of child abuse were reported in 1986 as compared with 669,000 in 1976. In 1990 over 3,600 children died and 9,000 more were wounded by guns. In 1994 that number reached 5,820, although in 1995 it fell by nearly 10% to 5,277. It is estimated that 375,000 babies were born to mothers who use drugs in 1990.[108]

Racial Discrimination

Nearly 40 years after the Civil Rights Law was passed, and despite affirmative action and equal employment opportunity laws, systemic racial discrimination continues to exist. In 1990 the Urban Institute concluded that when equally qualified for jobs, African Americans were three times less likely to be hired than white candidates.[109]

EXERCISE 2.3

The Illusion Exercise

In class, form into four groups. Each group chooses a different social problem that is current. Ask yourselves what illusions we hold about the problem that prevent us from solving it. Develop a list of potential reasons. Outside of class, each person spends time talking to people, reading newspaper editorials and letters to the editor, listening to talk shows, and watching the news to spot instances of social denial, avoidance, blaming, moralizing, or quick fixes. Make a few notes about your findings.

In class, each group member assumes a role portraying a person who exhibits one or more answers that don't work. Form into a fishbowl with one group's members seated in the center and the other class members seated around the outside. The members of the inner circle discuss the problem that the group studied, with each member role-playing in terms of one of the answers that doesn't work. The outer circle observes the process and gives feedback. The various groups take turns being in the center of the fishbowl and role-playing a discussion of a problem and a set of "answers that don't work." After all groups have had a chance to interact and give feedback, the entire class reassembles and discusses their reactions to the exercise.

EXERCISE 2.4

Using the Contingency Approach

Review the contingency approach. Choose a social problem such as crime or drug abuse. Examine the problem using each of the seven models of analysis described in this chapter. For each level, answer the following questions. After you have answered the questions, develop a solution using the contingency approach.

1. How is the problem currently being perceived using this approach?

2. What treatment methods are being offered?

3. Is the approach effective?

EXERCISE 2.5

Critiquing Assumptions About Social Problems

One of the skills of a macro social worker is the ability to critique models in order to decide which model or which aspect of various models is best and is congruent with your own perspectives. Develop a critique of one of the seven assumptions about social problems. With what parts of the assumption do you agree? With what parts do you disagree? Share your critique with others in class and with that of your instructor.

EXERCISE 2.6

Getting Involved

This exercise is intended to help you begin to get involved in working on a social problem. Think of the kind of issues on which you want to gain experience. For more information about organizations involved in solving social problems, see Appendix B at the end of the book. Make a contract with your instructor to spend an agreed upon amount of time gaining some experience in one of the areas described.

Community Development

There are a number of community development organizations in most communities. One is Habitat for Humanity. Perhaps your local community has organizations aimed at improving neighborhoods through projects such as eradicating graffiti, planting trees, cleaning neighborhoods, or getting better community services. Try to get involved not only in working on the project itself, but in the planning and decision-making processes by which the project is developed. Report on what you discovered.

Community Organization

There are any number of social issues around which people are organizing today. Abortion, gun control, AIDS, women's rights, gay rights, environmental issues, or pollution. You can volunteer in your local political party to work on a local issue of importance to you.

Program Development

Is there an unmet need in your community or at your college or university that needs assistance? Agencies or action groups in your community may be working on developing a shelter for battered women, residence for the homeless, programs to eradicate drug abuse, or centers for runaway teens. Participate in the effort as a small group or as an entire class and then discuss what you learned.

Social Planning

Social planning organizations are active in most communities and deal with mental health, developmental disabilities, aging, and human rights, among other issues. Visit some of these organizations. Visit a local planning commission meeting and report back to class on what happened and what you learned.

Administration

Your college may have a project for which your class could provide administrative assistance. Or you could attend a board meeting of a local social service organization, interview an administrator, or volunteer to carry out an administrative assignment. Tell your class what happened.

Organization Development

Every organization has some problems or dysfunctional areas. What dysfunctions have you observed in your own college community or other organization that you know well? Find a local organization developer or management consultant and interview them.

Social Policy

Social policy issues abound. Abortion, gun control, euthanasia, legalizing drugs, welfare policy, and capital punishment are only a few. Choose one of these or other policy problems and try to come up with a solution.

ADVANCED EXERCISE 2.7
The Purpose of Social Work

This exercise challenges you to come to terms with a crucial issue in social work—to answer the question "What is the chief purpose of the field of social work?" After you have answered that question, decide what kinds of issues social work ought to be addressing. For example, the assumption of this chapter is that social work is concerned with solving problems.

Is this a correct assumption? Consider that a problem orientation assumes that people are basically unable to solve their own problems and are in need of help. Are people generally healthy but live in an unhealthy society, or are people basically unhealthy but live in a healthy society? The way you address this question may reveal whether you are oriented to helping people who experience personal troubles so that they become adjusted to and happy in society. If you see people as basically healthy but influenced by problems in society, then you may see social work as being oriented to helping society become better. On the other hand, perhaps you see both of these alternatives as incorrect.

In your assessment, choose one of the four theorists presented below—Paolo Freire, Clifford Shaw, Saul Alinsky, or C. Wright Mills—and critique that perspective. Reflect on how that perspective agrees or disagrees with your own perspective.

FROM PAULO FREIRE, *PEDAGOGY OF THE OPPRESSED*

The oppressed receive the euphemistic title of "welfare recipients." They are treated as individual cases, as marginal men who deviate from the general configuration of a "good, organized, and just" society. The oppressed are regarded as the pathology of the healthy society, which must therefore adjust these "incompetent and lazy" fold to its own patterns by changing their mentality. These marginals need to be "integrated," "incorporated" into the healthy society that they have "foreseaken." The truth is, however, that the oppressed are not "marginals," not men living "outside" society. They have always been "inside"—inside the structure which made them "beings for others." The solution is not to "integrate" them into the structure of oppression, but to transform that structure so that they can become "beings for themselves."[110]

CLIFFORD SHAW ON GANGS

At a time when most social workers attributed all delinquency to broken homes, Clifford Shaw (1929) focused his attention on the group character of delinquency…. Shaw argues that gang ties and affiliations were the key to delinquency, not broken homes. In a related study Thrasher (1929) studied over 1,300 gangs in Chicago and proposed that gangs are mechanisms whereby slum children achieve satisfaction not otherwise accessible in their underprivileged environments…. Adolescent gangs were part of the institutional configuration of the neighborhood. They influenced and were influenced by family patterns, the church, the rackets, and police.[111]

SAUL ALINSKY ON SOCIAL PROBLEMS

Alinsky's belief in the necessity and desirability of community organization stems from his Chicago School recognition of the social and structural origin of community problems. Private or personal troubles may in fact be shared problems which can become public issues…. One of his goals was to educate and teach people that many of their troubles such as unemployment, poor housing or poor educational opportunities for their children are not isolated and personal matters but concerns shared by others in the community.

Alinsky's social problems orientation also suggests that the most effective and long-term way of dealing with such issues is to attack cooperatively and collectively the general structural sources of the problem. He firmly believed that through the process of coming together in a community organization residents discover that their individual problems are also the problems of others, and that furthermore, the only hope for solving an issue of such titanic proportions is by pooling all their efforts and strengths.[112]

C. WRIGHT MILLS ON SOCIAL PROBLEMS

The knowledgeable man in a genuine public…understands that what he thinks and feels to be personal troubles are very often also problems shared by others, and more importantly, not capable of solution by any one individual but only by modifications of the structure of the groups in which he lives and sometimes the structure of the whole society.[113]

ADDITIONAL READING

Social Problems Textbooks

D. Stanley Eitzen and Maxine Baca-Zinn. *Social Problems,* 6th ed. Boston: Allyn and Bacon, 1994.

William Kornblum and Joseph Julian. *Social Problems,* 9th ed. Saddle River, NJ: Prentice Hall, 1998.

Michael P. Soroka and George J. Brayjak. *Social Problems: A World at Risk.* Boston: Allyn and Bacon, 1995.

James M. Henslin. *Social Problems,* 4th ed. Upper Saddle River, NJ: Prentice Hall, 1996.

Theory of Social Problems

Paulo Freire. *Pedagogy of the Oppressed.* New York: Herder and Herder, 1970.

Paul J. Baker, Louis E. Anderson, and Dean S. Dorn. *Social Problems: A Critical Thinking Approach,* 2d ed. Belmont, CA: Wadsworth, 1993.

Paul G. Horton, Gerald R. Leslie, Richard F. Larson, Robert L. Horton. *The Sociology of Social Problems,* 12th ed. Upper Saddle River, NJ: 1997.

Jerome G. Manis. *Analyzing Social Problems.* New York: Praeger, 1976.

C. Wright Mills. *The Sociological Imagination.* London: Oxford University Press, 1959.

Edward Seidman and Julia Rappaport, eds. *Redefining Social Problem.* New York: Plenum Press, 1986.

David R. Simon and Joel H. Henderson. *Private Troubles and Public Issues: Social Problems in the Postmodern Era.* Fort Worth: Harcourt Brace, 1997.

John Dewey. *The Public and Its Problems: An Essay in Political Inquiry.* Chicago: Gateway Books, 1946.

Individualist Approach

R. M. Dawes. *House of Cards: Psychology and Psychotherapy Built on Myth.* New York: Free Press, 1994.

Richard L. Means. *The Ethical Imperative: The Crisis in American Values.* Garden City, NY: Anchor Books, Doubleday, 1970.

Robert Winslow. *The Emergence of Deviant Minorities, Social Problems and Social Change.* San Ramon, CA: Consensus Publishers, 1972.

William Ryan. *Blaming the Victim.* New York: Vintage Books, 1976.

Social Pathology

Robert K. Merton and Robert Nisbet. *Contemporary Social Problems,* 2d ed. New York: Harcourt, Brace, 1966.

Richard Hofstadter. *Social Darwinism in American Thought, 1860–1915.* Boston: Beacon Press, 1959.

Society as Inherently Defective

Frank M. Coleman. *Hobbes and America: Exploring the Constitutional Foundations.* Toronto: University of Toronto Press, 1977.

Charles A. Reik. *The Greening of America.* New York: Bantam Books, 1970.

Social Systems Approach

Russell L. Ackoff. *Redesigning the Future: A Systems Approach to Societal Problems.* New York: Wiley, 1974.

Special Problems

Gordon Allport. *The Nature of Prejudice.* Reading, MA: Addison-Wesley, 1954.

Carey McWilliams. *Prejudice, Japanese Americans: Symbol of Racial Intolerance.* Hamden, CT: Archon Books, 1971.

Andrew Billingsley and J. Giovannoni. *Children of the Storm: Black Children and American Child Welfare.* New York: Harcourt, Brace and Jovanovich, 1972.

Jacob Riis. *Children of the Tenements.* New York: MacMillan, 1903.

John Steinbeck. *Grapes of Wrath.* New York: Viking, 1939.

Walton Bean. *Boss Reuf's San Francisco: The Story of the Union Labor Party, Big Business and Graft Prosecution.* Berkeley: University of California Press, 1952.

Frank Norris. *The Pit: A Story of Chicago.* New York: Doubleday, 1903.

Gunnar Myrdal. *An American Dilemma.* New York: Harper, 1944.

Research

Ted I. K. Young and William R. A. Freudenburg, eds. *Research in Social Problems and Public Policy,* Vol. 6. Greenwich, CT: JAI Press, 1997.

Journals

Economy and Society. Routledge Subscriptions, ITPS, North Way, Andover, New Hampshire.

Journal of Aging and Social Policy. Hayworth Press.

Social Problems. UC Press for the Society for Study of Social Problems, Journal Dept. UC Press, 2120 Berkeley Way, Berkeley, CA 94720.

Theory and Society: Renewal and Critique in Social Theory. Kluwer Academic Publishers, 3300 Alt Dordrecht, The Netherlands.

The Method of Solving Social Problems

The sum and truth of one, or a few consequences…but to begin at these and proceed from one consequence to another.[1]

Thomas Hobbes

The approach to truth is not easy. There is only one way toward it, the way through error. Only through our errors can we learn; and only he will learn who is ready to appreciate and even to cherish the errors of others as stepping stones toward truth. [Only he will learn] who searches for his own errors, who tries to find them, since only when he has become aware of them can he free himself from them.[2]

Karl R. Popper

Ideas in This Chapter

THOMAS HOBBES AND MODERN REASON

Sitting at his desk in an upper room in Paris in 1650, golden light streaming through a window, Thomas Hobbes contemplated the destructive turmoil of social and political relationships that have occurred since the dawn of history. The natural propensity of people to fight over power, quarrel over religious dogma, and dispute morality, thought Hobbes, had kept humankind in a perpetual "war of all against all" where "every man is enemy to every man… and the life of man, solitary, poor, nasty, brutish and short."[3] Was there some other way political and social relationships could be fashioned that would place society on a less turbulent and more secure foundation?

Galileo, Roger Bacon, and others were engaged in the exciting task of discovering the laws which governed the physical universe. Hobbes's friend Galileo, whom he had visited in 1635, suggested that the physical world, based on Euclidean geometry, was nothing but a set of moving parts. Hobbes reasoned that since society was also nothing more than a system of interrelated components,[4] were there not similar laws by which social and political relationships could be determined? By applying rational calculation, Hobbes thought, could not humankind devise ways of regulating and ordering human relationships?[5]

Published in 1651, Hobbes's *Leviathan* attempted nothing less than to remake the entire world of thinking up to that time. Borrowing from principles of mechanics, Hobbes conceptualized society as an artificially constructed *system* which operated by means of natural physical laws. He believed that humans no longer had to be at the mercy of irrational emotions, religious dogma, or metaphysics; nor did people need to be subject to the whims of fortune or human passions that so often led to turmoil and conflict. Rational science not only would control physical nature, but it would achieve a rational human world whose outcomes

could be predicted and controlled as well. In fact, once a rational framework was established, systems would operate automatically, just as other mechanical devices, because of the principles and rules built into them. In a single stroke was born the idea of modern reason and rational problem-solving systems theory, and the fields of political and social science.

So ubiquitous are the principles of Hobbesian thinking in our day that they have become second nature to us. We accept them because they have become the way we operate, the way we think, the way our society has come to be. We are living in a modern society not only because of the scientific methods devised by the giants of the Enlightenment such as Galileo, Brahe, and Copernicus, but also because of modern instrumental reason devised by Thomas Hobbes along with John Locke, who applied Hobbes's ideas to society,[6] Adam Smith,[7] who applied them to economics, and James Madison,[8] who applied them to politics.

WHAT YOU WILL LEARN IN THIS CHAPTER

Macro social workers help people solve social problems and make social change. In this chapter you will be introduced to two different but related methods of approaching macro social work. You will learn that rational problem-solving is the most well-known method of conventional problem-solving. You will see that rational problem-solving has become *the* way we think about things in our modern world and the form of reasoning used in solving the most complex problems of our day. It has been appropriated by social work as the generalist social work method. You will explore how the rational or generalist social work method works and how to apply it step by step to solving social problems.

Although the generalist social work method is a powerful tool most often used with individuals and organizations, you will find that it has limitations for macro social work. As a result, you will see that it often needs to be supplemented with a method that is more compatible with community building, developing social organizations, and working at the societal and global levels, which I call *social thinking*. Social thinking is a much less recognized or utilized method in social work. You will learn that social thinking uses cognition and practical application as does rational problem-solving, but it adds feeling or valuing, and intuition as well. Instead of focusing on social problems, dysfunctions, or needs, the social change method focuses on the resources, assets, and strengths of people in community. Rather than trying to remediate dysfunctions or discover causes of problems and correct them, social thinking looks ahead to what people can accomplish by using their vision and working together. You will learn how to make social change step by step using the social thinking and the social change approach, and you will be invited to explore their utility in working with groups, building community, and creating a better social world.

MODERN REASON

Reason, says Hobbes, is "nothing but reckoning of consequences." Modern reason is completely limited to quantification. "In any matter whatsoever where there is a place for *addition* and *subtraction*, there is also a place for *reason*; and where they have no place, there *reason* has nothing at all to do." Therefore, "when man reasoneth," Hobbes asserted, "he does nothing else but conceive a sum total."[9]

It was Hobbes's intention to reduce reason to a practical, tangible, and functional role in human affairs by which people can simply calculate the most effective means to attain their goals, interests, or preferences—nothing more complicated or substantive than that. You use modern instrumental solving every day. Whenever you purchase goods, plan a trip, choose a college, or decide on a career, you use modern reason. You compare pros and cons and then calculate which choice meets your goals most effectively.

Individualism and Modern Reason

With modern reason, the ends of choice are intentionally lodged in the subjective values of the deci-

sion-maker. You are the ultimate judge of what is best or good and you are assumed to have full knowledge of your preferences. These ends are generally not open to question. They are inherent in individuals' needs and wants, presupposed by the situation with which a person is confronted, or are given to a person extraneously.[10] According to Rational Choice Theory (RTC), for example, "the unit of analysis is the individual decision made by an individual decision-maker."[11]

It is in this connection that individualism and rational choice become congruent. If you are the supreme arbiter of your own preferences, interests, tastes, and opinions, it follows that it is in your own self-interest to maximize those preferences. The more successfully you do so, the better off you are, and ultimately the happier you become. Rational choice is nothing but a means by which individuals calculate which choices maximize their self-interest.

Politics and Modern Reason

It follows that if individuals are sovereign in their ability and rights to make choices in their own self-interest, government in a democracy has no prerogative or right to impose a set of preference orderings onto people that distorts those self-interests. There are no overarching values to which government owes allegiance, other than those which the populace holds at any one time. Instead, government is established to assist people in achieving their self-interest, and it takes its cues from the individual desires and opinions of people. At regular intervals people are asked to indicate their preferences by voting. By adding up their preferences, the majority of the populace chooses various officials and sometimes even decides on policy issues. This feedback enables government regularly to adjust for shifting values preferences.

While government is prevented from imposing a set of beliefs on the populace, there are imperatives that do operate. Government is obliged by its own self-interest in survival to treat everyone equally and impartially according to a set of rules. These rules provide the boundaries, channels, and networks within which stability, order, and uniformity take place. From this rational perspective, government is little more than a self-regulating mechanism by which rules are carried out, allowing each person a maximum amount of freedom to pursue his or her interests.

Economics and Modern Reason

Rational decision-making in the economy is nothing but getting the best buy. You know what you want to purchase. You have a shopping list, or as economists say, you have full knowledge of your preference schedules. As you look over available items, you choose the one that gives the best quality or amount at the cheapest price. In more technical language, rational consumers purchase the amount of goods, A, B, and C, etc., that maximizes their utility.[12]

Using more economic jargon, you select the alternative on your preference schedule that maximizes your output for a given input or minimizes input for a given output (i.e., more is always better than less). Graham Allison asserts, therefore, that rationality refers to an "essentially Hobbesian notion of consistent, value-maximizing reckoning or adaptation within specified constraints."[13] Just as you vote your preferences in the political marketplace, in the economy you vote by purchasing products which match your preferences at the best price. In this way consumers give signals to the economy about what or what not to produce and about prices people are willing to pay. Rational individuals maximize their self-interest at the least cost to themselves, and the economy has a feedback mechanism that provides an automatically self-regulating system of supply and demand.

RATIONAL PROBLEM-SOLVING

Hobbes was not interested in defining modern reason to set up a system of majority rule, or so that you could get the best deal at a department store. He was interested in developing a way of thinking by which all kinds of decisions, especially political ones, could be made that would provide stability, consistency, and rationality in human affairs. The key to using modern reason, according to Hobbes, was to get a good and orderly *method*. Today we call the method described by Hobbes "rational problem-solving." The theory on which this method is based is called Rational Choice Theory, or RTC, by economists and others.[14] It works best under conditions in which the decision-maker has adequate information and knows all of his or her preferences. According to Zey, each alternative is tested against available information and experience by calculating its benefits and costs, comparing these pros and cons, and ranking alternatives in order. Once an option is chosen, interests are maximized, and the most benefits are obtained at the least cost.[15]

It is not by accident that such problem-solving is called "rational." It is simply a way of computing a *ratio* of benefits/costs or pros and cons.[16] Modern society has adopted instrumental reason as "reason at large" and rational problem-solving as *the* means by which decisions are reached in any number of situations. This rational "economic approach provides a framework applicable to *all* human behavior—to all types of decisions and to persons from all walks of life."[17] Zey, for example, asserts that "Although rational choice models use an economic metaphor, they… explain not only economic behavior, but also the behavior studied by nearly all social science disciplines from political philosophy to psychology. The range of human behavior explained encompasses the entire spectrum including government decision-making, individual consumer decisions, collective economic agents, social institutions such as the criminal justice system or the family; and social behavior in general."[18]

Rational problem-solving was described by John Dewey in his 1933 book *How We Think* as the way people universally make decisions.[19] Politicians use rational problem-solving to make political and public policy decisions. Decision-making tools utilizing complex computers are based on this approach as well as in modern statistical decision theory and game theory.[20] Rational problem-solving is the basis of organization and administrative decision-making.[21] It is called, for good reason, the "systems approach" by Churchman[22] and is the basis for management science in public policy analysis,[23] and social workers have been using it as the "generalist social work method."[24] Rational problem-solving is described in many texts on decision-making.[25] Most social workers agree that rational social work problem-solving involves the following steps:

Deciding on a problem

Gathering information about the problem

Generating a number of alternative solutions

Assessing and comparing alternatives

Selecting the best or most cost-beneficial solution

Developing a strategy or plan of implementation

Carrying out or implementing the solution

Evaluating the results[26]

Rational problem-solving can be used for changing social systems and helping people reach goals effectively. (Courtesy of East Wind Community, Tecumseh, MO)

THE GENERALIST SOCIAL WORK METHOD

Although it has not always been clearly identified and labeled as such, rational problem-solving has been used even before social work as a profession came into existence. As early as 1845, Dorothea Dix, for example, gathered data and made recommendations based on problem-solving research and policy analysis on behalf of persons with intellectual and emotional disabilities. During Reconstruction (1865–1880), Charity Organization Societies (COS) pioneered in placing philanthropy on a rational, efficient, and impartial basis known as "scientific charity." COS workers devised the social casework process aimed at helping people make

the most rational choices for themselves and their families. COS social workers turned their attention to community issues and developed social planning in which charitable organizations would avoid duplication and work together to raise and distribute funding through modern cost-effective service delivery. Settlement House workers of the Progressive Era (1880–1915) and others pressed for "good government," by which they meant placing government on a rational basis to insure fairness, equality, and an end to spoils, bribery, favoritism, nepotism, and amicism (giving preference to one's friends).

EXERCISE 3.1

Critiquing Rational Problem-Solving

Merely because a way of thinking is commonly accepted does not mean that it is good or even correct. Can you think of some reasons to raise suspicions when one universal way of thinking, such as rational problem-solving, is applied to so many different contexts? What objections might you raise? At the end of this chapter you are invited to engage in a critique of rational problem-solving and the generalist social work method. For now, use your own problem-solving skills and list as many concerns as you can. In your reflections, refer back to the introductory story of Thomas Hobbes. Think about what modern reason was meant to accomplish. What was it aiming to eliminate? Practice using your intuition. Does the generalist social work method have utility in resolving social problems? Can modern reason and the generalist social work problem-solving method be applied in the social arena at all? What difficulties might this rational problem-solving method encounter in dealing with values and the ends of decisions? Where can rational problem-solving or the generalist social work method be most useful? Write down as many concerns as you can think of. Then, in class, break into groups of five. Compare your list with others. As a group, come up with as many ideas as you can. Keep both your own list and your group list. Was the group experience helpful in expanding your ideas? Give your instructor a copy of the group list. You will use the list again when the time comes to critique modern reason.

The first person to explicitly link social work with rational problem-solving was Helen Harris Perlman. In 1957 she described the social casework method as a problem-solving process and outlined its steps.[27] Since then, rational problem-solving, or the generalist social work method, has became a conscious part of the core understanding of social work[28] and has been described in many social work texts using various names. Because what is commonly accepted as rational problem-solving is identical to the generalist social work method, I have combined them into the term "rational social work problem-solving" in the description that follows. Today, rational social work problem-solving is systematically used in a number of macro social work contexts[29] such as social work planning, organizational social work, and social policy analysis, and it is synonymous with social work research.[30]

HOW TO USE RATIONAL SOCIAL WORK PROBLEM-SOLVING

Rational social work problem-solving can help you reach a goal efficiently, quickly, and cheaply. Rational social work problem-solving is logical and simple, straightforward and direct. It deals with facts, and as a result, easily lends itself to issues that are clearly defined and can be quantified. It is systematic and sequential. When you use rational social work problem-solving, you are less likely to miss crucial issues or skip over things that need to be considered.(See Figure 3.1.)

Deciding on a Problem

Deciding on a social problem is the most important part of the problem-solving process. It is also the lengthiest. There are two parts to deciding on a social problem: recognizing that a problem exists, and identifying it.

Recognizing the Problem or Issue A social issue, as troublesome as it may be, is not a "problem" until a person or group recognizes and labels it as such. Often social pain and dysfunction exist, but people ignore or deny their existence. Racial discrimination against African Americans, for example, existed since the first slaves were imported to this country. However, racism was accepted as a normal, even necessary, way of life among many members of society and was perpetuated even after the Civil War, until the community of African Americans decided to actively resist. In the same way, the problem of drunken dri-

vers was not a nationally recognized issue until the mother of a child killed by a drunk driver organized MADD—Mothers Against Drunk Drivers.

Identifying the Problem Once your community or organizational group recognizes that a problem exists, the members need to identify what specific problem or issues are important. Make a list of the problems or issues confronting your community or organizational group. Then compare your list with the following guides and narrow your choice to one.

Successful Resolution. Choose an issue that your group has a good chance of resolving successfully. Consider the amount of energy, time, and money you have available. Do not choose a problem that is beyond the resources or the limitations of your group. Rather than a large issue, choose a smaller one that your group has a good chance of solving.

Legitimacy. Select a problem over which your group has some legitimacy. Often community problems are so broad that most community problems can be seen as legitimate ones that you can address. If you are dependent on an agency's financial support, however, make sure that your work falls under the agency's mandate. Otherwise your source of support may disappear or you may be in conflict with the agency. Sometimes the problem being addressed crosses the boundaries of several agencies. In this case it may be helpful to develop a coalition in which agencies and groups from a number of arenas join together in the change effort.

Control. Choose a problem that is potentially under the control of your group or one in which control needs to be established. Consider, for example, a group of low-income residents concerned about the inadequate schooling their children are receiving. They may have little control over the school board or its policies. They may have no input into the amount of funding available for their children. This does not mean, however, that they cannot become empowered to gain control or change school policies. They can strategize to gain seats on the board or put pressure on local governments to make funding more equitable. They can gain control over the forces that affect the lives of their children.

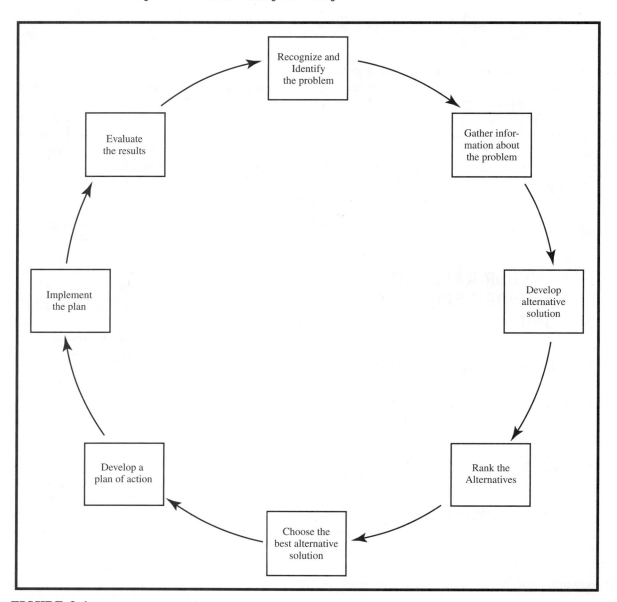

FIGURE 3.1 Rational Problem-Solving Cycle

Meaning. Choose a problem that is pressing and current. It should have meaning to the group members, be deeply felt, and be one that can excite and energize them. Its solution should be important to the community as a whole, and the members should have a vested interest in having the situation resolved.

Beneficial Effects. Select a problem that, when resolved, will have far-reaching beneficial effects. By changing one piece of a problem, your group may begin a process that can bring changes in an entire system. In this way, you can initiate a series of events that can cause an entire facade to crumble. At the very least, your group can prevent future problems from occurring. Make sure that what you are attempting will have a major impact. The effort and energy you and your group expend should pay off in tangible benefits.

A problem-solving group identifies issues by listing the specific problems confronting them.
(© Mark Richards/Photo Edit)

If your group has misgivings about any of these issues, resolve them before you commit yourself to working on the problem. Your group needs to be fully invested in the issue on which it will be working. After you have identified the problem on which you will work, write down a tentative statement of the problem as it appears to your group.

Gathering Information About the Problem

There are a number of ways of gathering data about a problem. The people of the community or organization are the best source of information about what is wrong, and you will spend lots of time talking to them. On a more formal level, however, your group can administer surveys to community or organization members or interview key leaders. The group may also collect information about the problem from agency records, newspapers, or other sources. Macro social workers bring people together in focus groups to discuss the problem from various points of view. Regard-

less of the method you use, your group will need to ask the questions *why, when, who, where,* and *how.*

Asking Why: Observing Patterns   Asking "why" gets at causation, helping you form a social diagnosis of the problem. Once you understand why a social condition exists, you have some control over it. Look at your problem definition and then ask "why" until you can go no farther. Suppose, for example, you are working with a community about lack of police protection. Encourage the group members to ask, "Why is there lack of police involvement?" Because the city's priorities are elsewhere. "Why are they elsewhere?" Because neighborhood residents lack input to decision-making. "Why do they lack input?" Because they have no effective voice in the process. "Why do they have no voice?" Because the system does not provide for citizen input. "Why not?" Because those in power don't want input. They have excluded people from the process. Asking "why" helps your members focus on one possible cause and allows them to see patterns that you can use to correct the problem.

Where: Locating the Pain   While the problem-solving group might want to track down the ultimate cause of a social problem, practically speaking, this may be a waste of time. Like the ripples in a pond, one problem creates multiple effects, each of which spreads out from its source, touching more and more systems in its wake. Furthermore, the ultimate cause of a social problem, even if known, may be irrelevant to its effects. The series of events leading up to the Civil War in the United States, for example, began with the importation of the first slave into this country. Knowing this fact added nothing to resolving the eventual conflict and resultant racial discrimination that this act set in motion.

Causation cannot be undone, but the effects of causation can be understood and dealt with. For the most part, therefore, spend your time understanding the *effects* of social problems and discovering *where* in the system the problem is most acute. The "where" may be a physical location. Where in a city or community do the homeless congregate, for example? Where are the slums developing? These should be the areas to which you are drawn.

The social pain may not be located in a geographical place, however, but with particular groups of people who experience the problem. In the past, for example, very few services nationwide were provided for persons with developmental disabilities. Parents, friends, and professionals joined together, identified themselves as a community, and pressed for changes in education, housing, and access to facilities. Bit by bit, attitudes changed and services improved.

Who: Discovering Victims and Perpetrators

By asking "who," your group pinpoints victims and perpetrators. Victims are those who are damaged by a social problem. For example, a bank may have an unwritten rule to not approve home loans within certain areas of the city that it assesses as risky—usually areas high in minorities or low-income residents. Such policies, called *redlining,* tend to discriminate against minority neighborhoods, making it next to impossible for people to obtain home loans or improve homes, which results in rundown neighborhoods. Redlining makes victims of almost everyone who lives in a targeted neighborhood.

Perpetrators are those who cause, condone, or provide conditions enabling the social problem to exist. The individual acts of specific leaders of businesses or organizations formalize and institutionalize problems

in our social systems. Target the individuals in charge, the leaders, administrators, policy-makers, executives, or others who have control over and can make changes in the system. For example, if redlining policies exist, who are the particular bank owners, officers, and trustees who formulate and carry out those policies? The process of identifying those responsible for instigating, creating, perpetuating, or condoning social problems helps provide the victims of social problems with tangible, personal targets for change.

When: The Time Frame   When did the problem arise and how did it develop over time? Has the problem been increasing over the last six months or year? Answers to these questions help your community or organizational group understand the history, severity, and patterns of the problem. What specific events triggered the problem and when did they occur? Getting a chronology of the problem will also tell you about decisions that were made, who made them, and possibly why they were made.

How the Problem Occurred   If you can understand how a problem developed, you have come a way toward changing it. For instance, you may find out that organizational decisions that once made sense are now outmoded. A system has failed to adjust to changing conditions. Or mistakes were made that have not been corrected and a defective system is being perpetuated. When decision-makers defend the current system by saying "We've always done it this way," or "don't ask questions; these are the rules," there is a good chance that they are allowing system inertia to carry them along. Understanding how organizational or governmental policies and practices came about can help extricate people from dysfunctional patterns in the social system.

On the other hand, you may find that a consciously planned series of events were construed to deprive people of power, control, or resources, keeping them in a position of subservience for the benefit of others. Knowing this history can uncover patterns of systematic abuse and give your members evidence they can use in their struggle to restore justice.

Generating Alternative Solutions

After a problem is selected, defined, and the group members have gathered as much information about it as they can, they are ready to consider potential solutions. If the problem has been well researched, generating solutions should be relatively easy. They should flow naturally from the data. Generate as many alternatives as you can that would legitimately solve the problem.

There are some hazards in developing solutions that you should be aware of, however. For example, there is a tendency for individuals or groups to jump to solutions before they have explored the problem in depth. If your group does this, they may be fitting the problem to their own particular solutions. Sometimes people have pet solutions they use to fit any situation, or they may have a tendency to accept the first solution that occurs to them. Try to avoid these pitfalls, because you will be prematurely limiting your search for the solution that can best remediate the social problem.

One way of opening up the group to consider all possible alternatives is to list every possible aspect of the problem that can be changed, eliminating those that cannot be changed. Then, combine these change variables together into various solutions. Eliminate the ones that do not help accomplish at least some of your goals. Your group should now have several innovative solutions to consider.

Assessing and Comparing Alternatives

After the members have generated several potential alternative solutions, help your group decide which one is best. Assess each alternative in terms of particular criteria that will give some indicator of success. Problem-solving consists "in the right ordering" or assigning weights to various alternative solutions. As Herbert Simon asserts, "rational decision-making always requires the comparison of alternative means in terms of the respective ends to which they will lead."[31]

One way of doing this is by means of a *force field analysis.* Force field analysis was developed by Kurt Lewin and is based on the idea that with every potential solution there are *restraining forces*, also called disadvantages or costs, and *driving forces,* also called advantages or benefits.[32] Restraining and driving forces are constraints; they are conditions or boundaries that your group decides a solution must meet before it can be accepted. For example, the members may decide that the most important constraints are the amount of time, money, or manpower it will take to solve the problem.

Some solutions will be more time consuming, cost more money, or require more manpower than others. Driving forces are the benefits or advantages that an alternative will offer. Decide on a standard set of benefits and costs that your group can use to compare alternatives. You need to estimate the strength of these restraining forces and driving forces on a scale. I have used a scale of 0 to 5. Once you have calculated the strengths of both the restraining and the driving forces for a particular alternative solution, array them on table such as the one in Figure 3.2. Force field analysis is a way of deciding rationally on the best solution.

Choosing the Best Solution

By comparing alternative solutions you can see which will have more potential for success. Add up the benefits and subtract this number from the total costs. The alternative with the highest number will give you an indication of which solution has more power. Another way of calculating is to compute a benefit/cost ratio. The ratio will tell you what chances any one alternative will have of succeeding. A benefit/cost ratio that is equal to or above 1 (B/C=1) will provide your group with at least an even chance of succeeding. The higher the benefit/cost ratio the better.

When calculating benefit/cost ratios, ignore negative numbers. Compute the ratio by dividing total benefits by total costs. In the force field diagram in Figure 3.2, the benefit/cost ratio is B/C=11/12. Would the alternative be one to seriously consider? Why or Why not? What if the benefit/cost ratio were 12/24? What if it were 12/6?

Developing a Change Strategy

Deciding how to implement the solution that your group chooses is called a strategy for change. In many cases the change strategy will flow directly from the problem solution and almost be self-evident. However, there is a more formal way of developing a strategic plan. Here are the various steps that your action group can take to develop your change strategy.

Goals   Planning for action begins with setting goals. Begin with ultimate or long-range goals. More than likely there will be only one or two ultimate goals. On a chalkboard or newsprint, place a long-range goal on the far right. Now work backward, identifying intermediate goals and immediate, short-term goals. List

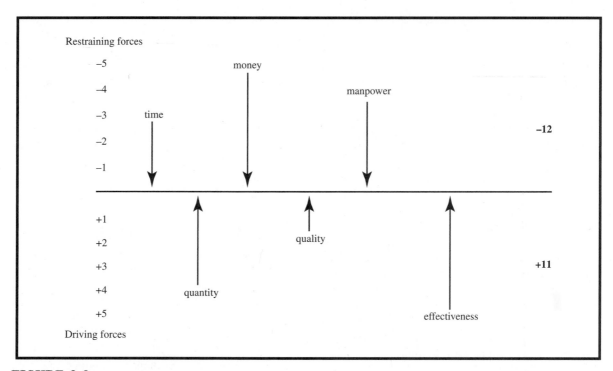

FIGURE 3.2 Force-Field Analysis Alternative I

all of the events that should occur that might precede accomplishing each long-range goal.

Objectives   What specific things need to be accomplished in order to reach the mid-range goals? These become objectives. Each objective should meet three criteria. It should be: (1) time limited, (2) specific, and (3) measurable. For example, "The police department will provide one additional patrol officer on Elm Street by June 1, 2003." Branch these objectives off from the mid-range goals. You may have several objectives preceding each goal.

Tasks   Break down each objective into tasks required. Tasks are specific duties or steps members must take to reach objectives. Tasks may be printing information, calling meetings, contacting the media, meeting with perpetrators, or other actions.

Tactics   Tactics tell you how to carry out tasks, especially activities that are politically sensitive, or that are complex and require coordination of members. Community organization tactics may include holding public hearings, meeting with government or political officials, or lobbying, among others. When deciding on specific tactics, be sure that the group members give thought to the kinds of resistance they might encounter from power figures and how they might overcome resistance.

Targets   Often your tactics will include identifying specific targets. Targets are the key power figures in business, government, or the community that your group wants to influence, change, co-opt, or whose support is crucial to the project.

Reviewing Your Strategy   Review your strategy. There may be duplication. Some issues may be irrelevant or subsidiary. New ideas may have occurred to your group. Revise the plan. Develop a backup or *contingency* plan. Try to anticipate what could go wrong with your strategy. For example, what if you do not meet your objectives? What alternative objectives are there? What if your tactics backfire? What other tactics or targets should be considered? Be prepared to think through these issues so that you will not be caught off guard if things do not go the way you expect.

Finalizing the Plan   After reviewing the strategy, your group is ready to finalize the plan. Decide on the sequence of events that need to be orchestrated in order to accomplish your group's goals. Do certain events, tasks, or activities need to precede others? Which things do the members need to do first, second, or third? Create time-lines. Then assign individuals to those tasks and get commitment from the members to carry them out. Make a list of those assignments and deadlines.

Implementing the Solution

Implementation means carrying out the strategy you have decided on. Members of your group become the nucleus around which the community becomes organized, a program is developed, or a social plan is implemented. Community meetings, for example, inform people about the problem and the proposed solutions. Members also promote community involvement, soliciting help from other community members, and begin organizing the change effort. Your group members may chair committees or lead task forces committed to carrying out the goals of the project. They may even join the board of a social service organization.

Evaluating the Results

Throughout the change process, you need to evaluate its progress. Perhaps the easiest, most useful, and most immediate evaluation is feedback. After meetings, or at least periodically, your group should spend time "debriefing." Debriefing gives members a chance to share stories, let off steam, get recognition, enjoy triumphs, and obtain support when things have not gone well.

Debriefing empowers your group and provides a learning tool for the members. The group has acquired valuable information about resistance, system dynamics, and power structures. Members learn about change and the change process by sharing and involving themselves with one another. Learning takes place as people talk about problems, share perceptions, and wrestle with what to do next. Debriefing helps group members determine whether their predictions about what would happen were correct. Armed with this new information, your group can reassess the situation, modify your strategy, plan, and move ahead.

In addition to debriefing, more formal evaluation processes may be used. For example, keep records of meetings and activities and refer back to them, particularly reviewing progress toward objectives. This will help members shift strategy, keep track of events, and make sense of what has occurred. Writing often helps develop ideas and gain insights. This information also can be helpful in developing a history of the change effort.

EXERCISE 3.2

Critiquing Rational Social Work Problem-Solving

Rational problem-solving is an important key to understanding our modern world and the mechanisms that make it work. It is also a key to understanding why, for all of the ingenuity, effort, and good intentions of the brightest and best of our political, economic, and social leaders, our social problems remain intransigent and impervious to being resolved. Take the critiques you used in Exercise 3.1 and include other ideas that have occurred to you. Critique the rational social work problem-solving method and compare your responses with others in your group. With the help of your instructor, discuss whether or not your criticisms are well founded. Then come to your own conclusions. You are invited to compare your critique with the one that follows.

A CRITIQUE OF RATIONAL SOCIAL WORK PROBLEM-SOLVING

The rational social work problem-solving approach eliminates nonquantifiable values, feelings, or intuition that are not capable of calculation.[33] It is helpless in understanding or developing social goods and fails to assist in overcoming social problems or social "bads."

Values

Social work in general (and macro social work in particular) is a highly value-laden field. Because values are nonquantifiable, they are beyond the realm of rational problem-solving. Rational social work problem-solving cannot evaluate whether the values inherent in decisions are worthwhile or even what constitutes a good or correct decision.[34] Decisions themselves are not judged according to their intrinsic worth, truth, or goodness, but rather in terms of their *utility*. If we accept the ends of those in power as they are given, we are precluded from evaluating the goodness or badness of those goals or ends. Alberto Ramos asserts, for example, that "rational man is unconcerned with the ethical nature of ends per se. He is a calculative being intent only on accurately finding adequate means to accomplish goals." This is why rational problem-solving is "*instrumental*...it functions to map out terrain and achieve goals."[35] It is a purely "technical calculation of means; it contributes nothing substantive to the grasp of ends or values themselves."[36] As a result, you will encounter difficulties where rival ends are in question, where multiple values are involved, or where conflicting values are at stake, such as often occurs in working with communities.

Rational problem-solving is value-skewed. It considers quantification, utilitarian application, facts, and profit as values of the highest order. Other values that escape calculation are simply not recognized. According to Zey, "the values at the basis of preferences do not concern rational choice theorists. What is assumed is that actions are undertaken to achieve objectives that are consistent with the actors preference hierarchy. The substance of these values and their source are irrelevant to RTC."[37] Value or ethically laden issues such as social goods, asserts Ramos, "have no place in the area of rational debate."[38]

The only values that are recognized in rational problem-solving are the pre-given ends, which are inherent in the problem itself. If, for example, the end is to increase the tax base of a deteriorating urban inner city, rational problem-solving can assist in deciding which among such alternatives as building a parking lot, a high-rise office building, a park, or a shopping mall is the most cost beneficial. The issue of whether destroying the neighborhood itself is worthwhile is not open for consideration, nor are the opinions of the residents, the value of the neighborhood that is to be destroyed, or the lives of the people to be removed. It is impossible to use modern reason to decide between the value of a community of people, even those living in a deteriorating slum, and that of a parking lot or shopping mall.

As a result of using modern rational problem-solving for the majority of our decisions, we have emptied decisions of moral content to such an extent that there are no "evil decisions or actions. There are only mistakes."[39] The world is reducible to errors only. Those errors can be discovered, corrected, and eradicated. Morality has become reduced to calculation, and to error reduction.

If social work were to attempt to exempt itself from immersion in the world of human values, it would become wholly inhuman, impersonal, and antithetical to itself. This sometimes happens as social workers, in an attempt to appear objective and impartial, adopt a value-neutral stance in relation to social decisions. Furthermore, a calculative logic can pervade organizations where strict adherence to rules and procedures captures the way people engage one another. When this occurs, we deprive ourselves of the ability to think in valuational terms at all. Values themselves become suspect, and we are persuaded to distance ourselves from them as if they were dangerous. Schimmel, for example, asserts that

> Amoral psychology is uncomfortable with "oughts"—it prefers to think that it can deal with facts about human nature, shunning values. This is neither possible nor desirable for real, living humans, whose lives are an inseparable interweaving of fact and value. As long as secular psychology continues to avoid confronting the role that values play in everyday life—what is right and wrong for us to do to ourselves and others...it will fail to ameliorate our anxieties. We need to reclaim the rich insights into human nature of earlier moral reflection if we want to lead more satisfying lives.[40]

The values implicit in rational problem-solving promote self-interest maximizing behavior. When you selflessly give to overcome misery, poverty, or injustice, you are acting irrationally by standards of modern reason. Modern reason, in fact, is opposed to altruistic, compassionate action, one of the core components of social work.[41]

In addition, if you rely on modern reason you may often tend to abandon thinking critically about social policy and social decisions. Instead, you may uncritically accept the ends and goals of those in authority, the theories of respected academics, and the ideologies of popular politicians, and apply yourself only to the task of how to implement those ideas. To the extent that you adopt the premises of modern reason and embed them in the generalist social work method, therefore, you deprive yourself of the ability to think valuationally, may harden yourself against compassion, and may uncritically adopt morally obtuse solutions to social problems. If you use value-neutral, impersonal reason, you may attach yourself to the application of technical expertise, rather than infuse yourself with altruism and shared meaning. You sit at the conference table of top-down, expert scientific logic rather than in the company of bottom-up social thinking where values are a core component.

Emotions

Emotions suffuse one's existence and are an ineradicable component of the human condition. Feelings of love and compassion when combined with ethical values can call forth acts of the greatest humanity and altruism. Emotions, however, are not compatible with impersonal, objective calculation. Feelings are seen as unreliable and values antithetic to objective fact gathering. As a result, in order to achieve a reliable model that is unbiased and strictly neutral, modern reason was intended to eliminate from decision-making all emotions that "escape calculation."[42] The key to modern problem-solving is its impersonality and strict adherence to calculable rules in which every situation is treated alike. For this reason, modern problem-solving promotes standardization, uniformity, and attention to facts, regardless of one's feelings.

Social workers who are trained as psychotherapists to be sensitive to emotions and understand "unconscious" irrational components of human behavior will face difficulties when the primary social work problem-solving method is completely blind to feelings and denies their utility in decision-making. It also complicates decision-making for macro social workers, whose main role is to develop more human, personal, and fulfilling social relationships.

Private, Public, and Social Goods

Modern reason is overwhelmingly successful and effective for making economic decisions in the private sector based on maximizing the self-interest of an individual or of a firm, the arena for which it was designed. Rational problem-solving is used with somewhat less success in public-sector decision-making, the domain of public goods.[43] On the other hand, rational social work problem-solving is applied with nearly complete failure in the social sector, the arena of social welfare, where *social* goods are produced.

Private Goods Private goods are tangible goods and services that are produced by the private sector of the economy, which is the one sector of society where modern reason can be applied most effectively. Modern reason is meant to calculate how to maximize the private interests of individuals, interest groups, and business corporations in attaining their goals in the most efficient way. Modern reason is exactly compatible in the economy because private goods are easily quantifiable, priceable, and consumable. They can be bought and sold. Rational calculation is *the* means by which decision-makers in the economic sector produce private goods.

Public Goods When issues involving public goods are encountered, rational problem-solving begins to suffer failure. This becomes a serious consideration in the political arena, where questions of value and what is the best use of public goods comes into question. Public goods are things of common value such as the environment, public health, or the people's welfare—goods that cannot be privately produced in the economic sector. Unlike private goods, public goods cannot be possessed by anyone but are "owned" in common. They can only be produced, protected, or regulated by a governance system that is accountable to all. Public goods such as highways, for example, cannot be privately bought or sold. Once they are produced, they become available to all. No one can be excluded from their benefits. They "spill over" to everyone. Neither can public goods be privately consumed. A person cannot own or privately consume his or her share of national defense, for example. Nor can someone purchase more national defense than is commonly available or sell his portion to others.

In the same way, when public "bads" occur, they affect everyone. If a company pollutes the air, everyone who breathes that air is affected. If people plunder a public good such as the ocean for their own benefit, everyone is affected when the ocean becomes depleted of fish.

Because public goods cannot be individually owned, their worth cannot be calculated. Can you put a price on an endangered species, calculate its value if it is saved or the cost if it becomes extinct? It is impossible to calculate the monetary value of enhancing the lives of the poor or the loss when people live in misery. Modern reason cannot answer these questions. Nor can rational problem-solving help calculate among rival public goods. Rational problem-solving cannot help decide whether the benefits of a social program for youth is more important than a home for battered women. It cannot help decide how much of a public good such as child welfare or criminal justice a nation ought to produce. It cannot help decide if child welfare ought to be produced at all. These are questions that only people in community can decide, based on their shared experiences, values, and feelings.

Serious miscalculations may occur when rational problem-solving is used to assess the value of public goods. In deciding on the amount and kind of national defense to be produced from about 1963 to 1974, for example, planners at the U.S. Defense Department, using the most sophisticated computerized decision techniques, completely miscalculated the communal resistance of villagers in the largely rural and undeveloped country of North Vietnam. The result was a war that destroyed human and natural life, and a military defeat for the United States.

Rational, self-interested actors may fail to generate public goods. Even if rational individuals all agree that a particular public good is needed, asserts Mancur Olson, they will not act to produce that good because it is not rational for individuals to sacrifice their own self-interests for the interests of others.[44] In the absence of other ways of thinking, rational individuals will not voluntarily contribute to the provision of public goods. That is why, even though it is in everyone's best interest to pay the costs of government, rational individuals will not voluntarily contribute to its support. Public goods will only be produced by some means of coercion, such as taxes, that obligate people to do so.

Social Goods   Social work is concerned with producing social goods such as honesty and trust, relationship and meaning. Social goods of citizenship, public spirit, truthfulness, integrity, loyalty, social responsibility, and caring are fundamental to any society. It is impossible for the economy to exist, for example, unless people are basically honest, trustworthy, and dependable. Government could not operate without people who have public spirit and display citizenship, courage, integrity, honor, and fairness. Yet social goods such as these cannot be produced by the economic or public sector. They can only be produced in the social arena, in community.

Social goods may be thought of as nearly the opposite of private economic goods. Social goods, for example, are not capable of being priced, privately consumed, or owned. In fact, if a price is attached to a social good, it becomes corrupted. For example, bribery is the purchase of someone's trust. One cannot put a price tag on a person's honor. You cannot buy love or friendship.

In addition, while a private good is only useful to you if you consume it, it is impossible for a social good such as trust or honesty to be privately owned or consumed. Social goods must be shared, externalized, and made available to others in order to exist at all. For example, if you try to privately consume friendship or keep it to yourself, friendship disappears. Friendship can only exist if you are a friend to others. The more you offer friendship to other people, the more friendship will exist. Moreover, the more you freely give friendship away to others, the more friendship you have as well. This same principle applies to all other social goods, such as honor, respect, or justice. The more you treat others honorably, respectfully, or justly, the more of these goods others will have and the more the social good will flow back to you. Conversely, the less these goods are shared, the less they will exist, and the less you will have. It is somewhat of a paradox that the most important goods we have only exist by giving them away freely to others. This, in part, is why such goods are social. They only occur among people when they are shared.

One cannot use rational problem-solving to create social goods, calculate the value of social goods, or decide among rival social goods. If courage or self-sacrifice on behalf of your family or community is required, you do not "count the cost." You give out of love and compassion. Rational methods cannot be used to inspire altruism or caring. Can you calculate the value to a community of the character-building activities of the boy or girl scouts in generating leadership, integrity, and citizenship? Can you place a money value on citizens who act on the basis of honor, trust, and honesty? Rational social work problem-solving is completely helpless in this arena.

Private goods are discrete entities, and deciding among them is easy. On the other hand, it makes no sense at all to try to choose between honor and integrity, justice or mercy. All social goods are related to one another. One social good often cannot be created without others as well. For example, trust is based on honesty, integrity, and honor. If you are not honorable, you will not be trusted, but if you display integrity and honesty, people will tend to trust you.

Social Bads   Modern reason or rational social work problem-solving is just as impotent in resolving issues of social "bads"—social problems. One of the primary reasons we have been singularly unsuccessful in dealing with social problems is because modern thinking and rational problem-solving are universally inappropriate in the social arena. One cannot overcome social problems by rational calculation.

Rational problem-solving tends to look at social issues from the wrong angle. It is oriented toward a needs-centered or deficit approach to the human condition. Poor communities, for example, and the people in them are seen as problematical, weak, helpless, and in need of correction. Rational problem-solving often requires expert city planners, politicians, business professionals, or others who assess problems according to their preference schedules to calculate the costs and impose their solutions from the top down, to maximize their version of the public good in the most efficient way.

Social problems, however, cannot be resolved by applying rational techniques by professional decision-makers from the top down. When the role of creating the public or social good, deciding on what is best, or solving the issues of the human condition is appropriated by experts, social goods lose their substance, what is best is deprived of purpose, and people are disengaged from the very issues whose solutions form the meaning of their existence. The people of a community are placed in a helpless, passive position, unable to use their natural human capabilities on their own behalf. The use of modern rationality by technical experts mistakes the strength of people and of community. It misunderstands the necessity for people to be creative actors in constructing their own social reality.

Rational social work problem-solving tends to maintain the status quo. The system is returned to its stable state, so it operates as before only to become broken again sooner or later. On the other hand, when you are involved in generating social goods, using values, expressing feelings, and engaging in social change by mutual engagement and interaction, a better society can be created that is in a continual process of re-creation.

These limitations in rational problem-solving create enormous problems for social work. While rational problem-solving is very powerful and has a place in social work, it may be accepted only with a number of qualifications. It cannot be welcomed as a universal method of problem-solving, nor can it be wholeheartedly utilized in macro social work by itself. Rational social work problem-solving always needs to be supplemented with other forms of thinking, and it needs to be utilized only in its proper sphere, where calculation and quantification are appropriate and necessary.

SOCIAL THINKING AND SOCIAL CHANGE

Social work is based on an understanding of the dynamics of social relationships, social meaning, and the necessity to construct your own social reality. A kind of thinking and deciding that is congruent with these kinds of tasks is *social thinking*. Social thinking is not a technical, specialized, or abstract way of understanding meant only for highly educated professionals or technical experts. It is a common, ordinary, and simple way of knowing that we use in natural human engagement with one another. Because social thinking is so common, it is barely recognized as a way of thinking at all. But for all of its commonality, it has the power to help people solve some of the most difficult and important issues of the human condition. It begins with and is centered in the mutual interaction of community members as they work out the meaning of events they encounter, arrive at an understanding of themselves and their social world, and devise the social goods and social reality within which their lives take shape. As you engage in these social tasks, you utilize multiple ways of knowing.

Thinking socially is the basis for the social change approach using peoples' strengths and community assets, as described in Chapter 2. The very essence of social change lies in an aggrieved group of people who organize themselves into a community and who collectively engage in political discourse to identify the root causes of their grievances and then strategize together to overcome those conditions.

One way that you can emancipate yourself from the assumption that instrumental reason or empirical investigation is the only correct mode of knowledge is to understand that there are *multiple ways of knowing*. Carl Jung was perhaps the first person who observed that people have four general ways or "functions" of relating to their environment and making decisions. These are sensing, intuiting, thinking, and feeling. According to Jung, sensing and intuiting are ways people have of *perceiving* the world or *obtaining* information. When you obtain information primarily through your senses such as seeing, hearing, touching or tasting, you are using your sensing function. When you relate to the world by means of your imagination, which goes beyond sense perception, you are using your intuition. Thinking and feeling, on the other hand, are ways people have of *making decisions* or *processing* the information with which their senses and intuition provide them. When you process information by means of thinking cognitively, you gather facts and analyze them. On the other hand, when you base your decision-making primarily on emotions and values, you are using your feeling function. (See Figure 3.3.) I will re-label Jung's feeling function as "feeling/valuing" because that term is more descriptive of what this function actually means.

Understanding the human condition in all its complexity is impossible without apprehending feelings and emotions, thinking ethically, or using intuition and imagination along with cognition. Each of these functions, however, is useless without action. You put your feelings/values and cognition to work by doing. Understanding through these four functions is what people mean by "social intelligence." Heus and Pincus call this "whole-mind thinking."[45] Chris Valley, a program development director of Families First, illustrates this kind of whole-mind thinking. He asserts that "my basic professional 'tools' are intellect (thinking) and imagination (intuition). I am a thinker who is also a doer (sensing). Underlying what I 'think' and

'do' is a belief (feeling/valuing) in the capacity of people to address and resolve their problems."[46]

Feeling/Valuing

The feeling/valuing functions of your personality are most closely aligned with the social. They also create the most difficulties with modern reason and have been at the center of controversy in modern science. Emotions have been regarded as untrustworthy and unreliable sources of understanding and deciding. You are cautioned to not allow your personal feelings to intrude on decisions. Value thinking has come under even more criticism. Modern science has rejected values as alien to authentic science. Correct understanding must be "value free" and unbiased. You must not allow your beliefs or prejudgments to interfere with what the data or the facts say about themselves.

This hard line, however, has been softened somewhat in the last few decades. Social science has come to recognize how a person's feelings and values can actually be used in understanding. In the meantime, traditional social work has emulated the scientific approach to understanding. Social work ethos, says Julio Morales, is based on "impartiality, neutrality and objectivity."[47] Thinking socially breaks with this tradition of suspicion and rejection of one's feeling/valuing function in social work.

Value-Centered Thinking

The world of science and technology is consumed with understanding facts. Facts are the raw material out of which we derive understanding about the world. So compelling is the search for empirical truth and the power of predication and control that many people rarely take the time to consider that facts are only part of the real world. There is another way of looking at reality. This is the world of values. Values are not tangible, directly observable, or clearly identifiable. They do not exist in space and time. In spite of this, we all know they are real. They are qualities by which facts are ordered. The meaning that you impose on facts give facts their power. Facts without values are meaningless.

If we were bound by facts alone, we would live a completely determined existence, but because of people's ability to evaluate things and make value choices, we are not completely constrained by facts. When we

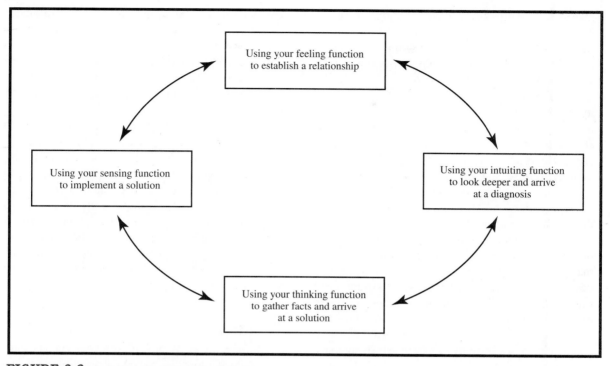

FIGURE 3.3 Social Thinking/Whole-mind thinking

say "ought" to physical phenomena, we are implying that there is more to facts than "is." The human capacity to apprehend values provides people with freedom. Because things are as they are, for example, does not prove that they must be so,[48] nor that they should not be different from what they are. Values, therefore, allow us to impose an "ought" onto factual reality. In the ugliest of conditions, you can find beauty, and in the most desperate of circumstances, hope.

Values are the qualities, meanings, and intentions by which we order our lives. They are premises and assumptions upon which we base our choices, decisions, and ideas. While we construct the content of our choices out of facts, the choices themselves are driven by our values. We are who we are because of our values, and because we are valuing creatures we can create a social world based on those qualities we consider important, such as justice, honor, compassion, integrity, altruism, and others. It is by means of values such as these that our social lives acquire meaning.

Because values and value thinking have become generally discredited as a mode of understanding in modern society, however, people in general tend to give little thought to values or ways of understanding them. In general, modern society operates at the most basic level of "subjective values," and our thinking rarely extends beyond this. Subjective values are the attitudes, opinions, tastes, interests, and preferences that each person subjectively acquires simply by means of life experience. Subjective values are not open to dispute because they are based entirely on one's private perceptions of the world. They are valid for the individual who holds them, although they may not be for anyone else.

Subjective values are most compatible with facts. Social science can add up the aggregated opinions, tastes, or preferences of people and develop theories about the nature of people's attitudes, for example. Politics is nothing else than aggregating the opinions and preferences of people at a particular moment and deciding who will hold positions of power. The economy is based on catering to people's interests and tastes, and government protects the rights of people to hold their own subjective opinions and preferences, and the freedom to pursue their own self-interest.

Subjective values, however, for all of their utility, have no intrinsic ethical content. Ethics attaches itself to values that transcend the individual or society and reach for absolute significance. When a society attempts to do more than simply reach for a majority consensus of subjective opinions and become a society that is good in and of itself, it is infusing ethics into its social values. It is only then that we can talk about social ethics.

The classical Greeks determined that there are only three ultimate ethical values to which all others may be attached: Truth, Good, and Beauty. Ethical values such as these are universal because they transcend time and place and apply to all societies. They are absolutes because they are ends in themselves and cannot be reduced to any other value. An individual, community, or society may attach subjective opinions, preferences, tastes, and interests to ethical absolutes that are true, good, and express beauty, or subjective values may be converted into ones that approach lasting and ultimate worth. Purpose, for example, is a value that may be ethically good, depending on whether it is attached to a value absolute.

At the subjective level, one's purpose is self-interest. There is nothing intrinsically good or necessarily bad about a person's self-interest. Self-interest that does not take into account the interests of others, however, devolves into selfishness. Purposive acts that are selfless, in the interests of others, and aim toward the good are called noble. We recognize that people who act with nobility of purpose put higher values before their own self-interest.

Only when you apprehend shoulds or oughts by means of your feeling/valuing function can you decide what is valuable or worthwhile, what is good or right. The classical Greeks grasped that the epitome of being human lay in understanding the highest and best, and designing community on those values. This way of value thinking is called *substantive or "classical reason*," in contrast with value-empty instrumental or functional modern reason. According to Ramos, classical reason is a force active in the human psyche that "moves the individual toward a continuous, responsible, and arduous effort to subdue his passions and inferior inclinations."[49] Substantive rationality assists the "individual to distinguish between good and evil, false and genuine knowledge," Ramos asserts, and thereby "achieve that excellence of character [moral virtue] which is potential to [his] nature".

Substantive reason, then, is the means by which people attempt to identify the good or truth for themselves using their feeling/valuing function, and to give it a place by which they can order their personal and social lives. Your feeling/valuing function is the means by which social goods are produced. This is why classical reason is irrevocably social. Social goods can occur only when people in community use feeling/valuing or substantive reason in considering what constitutes the "good life" and jointly determine to achieve it in action with others.

Intuition

Intuition is a way of delving into your unconscious, bringing ideas together, making connections, and seeing relationships beyond information from your senses. Your intuition helps you make leaps of insight and seek inspiration. Intuition is the creative side of thinking in which you envision possibilities and opportunities that others may not see. Your intuition enables you to be a visionary, dream about future directions, and be hopeful and forward looking. When you perceive with your intuition, you see with imagination and insight and not with your eyes. People who are highly intuitive usually see numbers of options and ideas. If you have highly developed intuition, you may tend to rely on your hunches and may see beyond empirical facts to gain insight into situations. You can look broadly at things and see the whole situation.

Experience and even values or emotions are useless unless you can reflect upon them and apprehend their meaning. According to Lauer and Handel, intuition helps people reflect on experience and generate a response by attributing meaning to it.[50] Meaning is not inherent, however; nor is meaning an external phenomenon that is imposed upon the individual. "Meaning is created by interaction," Lauer and Handel assert, and meanings that people impute to their experiences are "cooperatively created by many people".

The social worker must, in some ways, help people think like artists, using intuition—people's dreams and visions, hope and faith. While visions and dreams are nonrational and nonquantifiable, they are often the substance on which community is built. The wisdom literature of the Hebrews recognized this truth: "Where there is no vision, the people perish." When people interact together and envision things as they might be, they use their common intuition. Intuition and imagination are the foundation of hope. "It is a common experience that before action, a human being visualizes a desired result. He visualizes the future and undertakes to bring it about."[51]

Cognitive Thinking

Thinking is one way of making decisions using information gathered by your senses or your intuition. Your thinking function helps you decide by looking logically and analytically at things, and using cognition to understand situations. When you use your thinking function, you will be interested in what is objectively right or wrong. You will be critically minded, seeing the consequences of decisions, even when they are unpleasant. Your thinking function helps you to not falter when the facts point to difficult realities, and to stand against opposition. By using logic and analytical skills, you hold to a position that is right, particularly if supported by facts. When you use your thinking function, you are deciding with your head and not your heart. Your thinking function helps develop theories and use ideas to solve problems. If you have a highly developed thinking function, you may tend to be tough minded and firm. You will want to be treated with fairness and honesty and may get particularly concerned when others are dishonest or treat people unfairly.

Sensing/Acting

Your sensing function honors immediate experience as a valid form of knowledge. Your sensing function enables you to see the world realistically and pragmatically. It helps you conceive of solutions to problems and put a plan into action. Your sensing function helps you get beyond concepts or theories. It helps you deal with details of everyday reality, and with how to put together a project or construct a program.

If you have a highly developed sensing function, you tinker with the machinery of life, get immersed in fixing things and working on details, and face present issues realistically. When you perceive with your sensing function, you see the real world as it is with your eyes, not imagine it as it could be with your intuition, or as it should be with your feeling/valuing.

Sensing, however, is more than merely grasping experience in its raw state. Your sensing function helps you move to action to accomplish something, and to see the results of that action in tangible programs and services. Of all the ways of understanding, thinking by doing is among the most important. You learn by doing, by putting your feelings, intuition, and ideas into practice. The more you practice, the more experience you acquire, the more your feelings become useful, the more insights you develop, the more ideas you have, and the more skills you have. The crux of social thinking is putting all of your functions into action.

SOCIAL THINKING AND MACRO SOCIAL WORK

Each of us has the four functions—feeling, intuiting, sensing, and thinking—at our disposal. However, each of us gradually adopts one dominant way of perceiving the world and one way of making decisions with which we are more comfortable. For example, you may grasp information primarily by means of your senses and transform that information into decisions or ideas by means of your value/feelings. Your intuition and thinking are subsidiary functions. You may grasp information by your intuition and make decisions by means of your thinking function supported by sensing and feeling/valuing. The particular functions you choose depend on any number of factors, such as your genetic predisposition, your family upbringing, conditions in your environment, or circumstances that you encounter in your life.

The strength of one or another of these functions determines your own social thinking style. There is no one right or wrong style. All combinations are useful under different circumstances. The more conscious you are of your own social thinking style, the more in control and aware you become in using yourself productively. You can choose to develop your subsidiary functions more fully in order to become a more whole and stronger problem-solver. You can also become more conscious of how you use your functions when you work on solving social problems. In addition, as you grow older, your more dominant functions will tend to give way to those that are only used in a subsidiary way now. The more you are aware of these changes, the more you can guide yourself in gaining strength in the use of all your functions.

Moreover, the more variety of functions that are available, the wider the range of experiences, and the more perspectives you can apply to a social problem, the better chances are that the social problem can reach a satisfactory conclusion. As a macro social worker, you understand that your own perceptions and perspectives are inevitably limited. You understand that the broad combination of functions and perspectives which community members possess will guarantee that the ultimate strategies and processes they adopt will have a greater chance of success. The more you exercise your social thinking functions, the more skill and ability you will acquire. The full range of social thinking functions must be included and engaged by people at the local level. As you engage issues together, the dominant functions of some will complement the dominant functions of others. Even though any one or two people may not be able to completely access the full range of thinking, as more people are engaged, the entire community develops "whole mind" social thinking. (You and your classmates may be interested in exploring your own social thinking functions more in depth. Checklist 3.2 at the end of this chapter will assist you in learning more about our own thinking functions.)

HOW TO ENGAGE THE SOCIAL THINKING PROCESS

Social thinking often occurs as people experience a social situation that may cause dissonance. As people gather together, however, they share their mutual feelings about that experience and filter it through their values to make sense of it. They engage in mutual reflection by means of their intuition and begin to generate common understanding about what that dissonance means. They use cognition to examine the

facts and develop a strategy of action. Once a strategy is in place, people test themselves in the fires of experience, putting their new understandings into action. However, these different steps are not sequential. They are reciprocal and build on one another.

Sensing/Experiencing: Cognitive Dissonance

In many situations of everyday life "action proceeds automatically, without any consciousness of meaning." Only when some difficulty arises in the course of an action or experience will a person be prompted to be "consciousness of meaning, thought, and a disruption of mechanical repetition."[52] The disruption of our normal thoughts when an incident in our social environment becomes incongruent with our ordinary life experiences is called *cognitive dissonance.* Many people, for example, experience something as tragic, wrong, or unjust. A gap exists between what is and what ought to be. People are jolted out of their ordinary activities and are confronted with trying to understand the meaning that the discontinuity creates. They try to cope with their feelings and wrestle with their values, while at the same time they struggle to make sense of what has happened. The result is often a reorientation of consciousness and an attempt to establish a new meaning for the self.

Social workers are very familiar with these experiences. They occur during times of crisis, such as when a loved one dies, a person loses his or her job, or a tragedy suddenly occurs. Social workers apply social thinking to help people cope with these personal crises and wrestle with the inevitable process of working through grieving and putting their life back together.

On the other hand, some people are burdened with an ongoing, chronic sense of dissonance. Their entire existence becomes problematic because of the life situation in which they find themselves. For people who experience social problems such as ethnic intolerance, gender discrimination, prejudice because of sexual orientation, or economic injustice, dissonance is an ongoing, chronic, daily experience that saps their energy, destroys their identity, and injures their spirit. Unlike grieving over a death or a particular injustice, the experience of social difficulties is so generalized that their entire life is experienced as problematical, as tragic, and there is often no one specific incident or experience onto which grieving can be attached.

Such social dissonance throws the meaning of one's entire existence into question. Unlike personal tragedies, the common dissonance that people feel who share injustice and oppression cannot be dealt with individually, but only commonly. Sharing feelings in common becomes the way in which new meaning and new solutions can occur. It is also the way community often comes about. The very experience of common troubles brings people together in community, and community often becomes the means by which those troubles can be overcome.

Shared Interaction: Feelings and Values

The experience of oppression and injustice that megastructures impose on the human condition is inevitably alienating. It creates a sense of isolation, disengagement, and guilt. It drives out the social, destroys the basis of communality, and undermines people's resolve to transcend their distress. However, most macro social workers understand that the way people can begin to reclaim their lives is by rejecting alienation and its effects. When people begin talking together about their mutual experiences, they become connected with one another. The common memories of injustice and oppression become a cohesive force that cements them together. Their mutual history binds them together into a community.

Sharing feelings is therapeutic in another way. As people begin to face their feelings, the depression and hopelessness and guilt that once enveloped them begin to give way to anger. Anger helps people translate their apathy into action.

Intuitive Reflection

Herbert Blumer asserts that a community of persons who are experiencing dissonance must confront a world that they must interpret in order to act. Communities of people use intuition as a means of active reflection to understand the events that confront them. Active reflection means to set yourself aside momentarily to allow new perceptions of reality to enter your consciousness. When this happens, you transcend ordinary reality and open yourself to alternative perceptions of the world. When people in community generate these new ways of looking at things, often assisted by a macro social worker, they provide new perspectives, new alternatives, new ideas, and new ways of becoming and being.

Active intuitive reflection is very different from scientific thinking or rational problem-solving, in which a narrow, highly disciplined method is used to apprehend reality and to see things in a narrow sense. This is one reason social problems cannot be solved by top-down solutions or by experts who provide ready-made solutions to people. Instead, people refuse to accept the conventional or presumed definition of things or to take at face value what those in power assert is true. As your community sees what a situation means for themselves, they begin to understand what may only be implicit in a situation. Their intuitive social consciousness helps them understand the meaning behind the reality that presents itself. When this occurs, your members understand their situation not as tragic, but often as having transcendent importance, and in some cases they are compelled to rise above their own solitary interests and alienation which separates them. As Lauer and Handel point out, meaning is not an external phenomenon imposed on an individual; instead, "meaning emerges from the interaction process."[53] According to Kaufman,

> The values of *human* life never come about automatically. The human being can lose his own being by his own choices; a tree or stone cannot. Affirming one's own being creates the values of life…. Individuality, worth, and dignity are not *gegeben;* given to us as data by nature, but *aufgegeben*—given or assigned to us as a task which we ourselves must solve.[54]

There is no meaning in merely calculating alternative preferences and choosing the best one among them by rational problem-solving. The process of infusing meaningfulness into one's life can occur only in community as people reflect on their common experiences.

Cognitive Thinking: Developing a Strategy

After your community develops a vision of what is possible, along with a shared identity and mutual sense of their own common destiny, they begin to look clearly at the facts that have placed them in the particular situation in which they find themselves. They begin to gather information. Members put facts together to form a pattern. This helps them understand cognitively and empirically what their feelings and intuition have already told them. Unlike emotion and intuition, however, the facts help people deal with the concrete reality. Facts help them identify perpetrators, patterns, and opportunities and make decisions about what kind of action to take.

Cognition in combination with intuition helps communities of the oppressed imagine alternative strategies that they can put into action. Consider, for example, a problematic situation in which several alternatives are suggested for a situation, only one of which can be implemented. As members intuit the various meanings that are implicit in the situation, they can review their joint past experiences with each different type of response and *imagine* the consequences of implementing them, and "new real possibilities emerge in the process of interaction between individuals as they cooperate in a common environment."[55]

Moving to Action: Thinking as Doing

Action is not simply a mechanism of carrying out a strategy, a mechanism of operating that has no other meaning than the final step, like pushing a button to turn on a machine. Instead, meaning is a personal investment of yourself along with others who likewise commit themselves to a cause, a goal, an idea. Blumer states that a community uses meaning as the basis for directing its action.[56] George Herbert Mead asserts that "when we respond to an act, we generate meaning. Meaning is not in the objects or in the event that impinges on us, but in the response that *we* make to the event.…We generate meaning when we take action about an event in our lives. The meaning that the event has for us becomes part of our repertoire of behaviors which we have generated."[57]

Community members use cognition to think through the issues that confront them, but cognition related to the meaning of the situation, not merely to accounting for the least cost or most efficient solution. Community members ascertain the meaning of the actions of others and map out their own line of action

in the light of such interpretation.[58] In social thinking, action itself is just as important as the motives behind it. It is the experience of putting yourself into the arena of action that is crucial.[59]

The power of social thinking does not stand or fall on the selection of the best alternative; nor does it depend on the success of a particular strategy, as it does in rational problem-solving. With social thinking, any number of strategies can be used. If one strategy does not work, community members can try another. In social thinking, the failure of a strategy is just as important as its success. If one "response is unsuccessful, we become consciously concerned with meaning until we arrive at a solution and satisfactory meaning is achieved."[60] It is the meaning of events that is important, not only whether you win the struggle. Learning does not take place in a world where everything goes according to plan. It is in learning how to cope with failure, imperfection, and incompleteness in yourself and in others that you become mature and refine your plan's direction.

The very act of doing is the means by which thought is engaged. Putting values, feelings, intuition, and cognition into action is a rehearsal for testing out new ways of action, which generate new experiences and pave the way for more value generation, intuitive reflection, meaning generation, and more action.

This process of thinking socially is congruent with a "strength perspective" and a proactive model of social change. Ann Weick and Dennis Saleeby assert that, in fundamental ways, "the strength perspective changes the modernist heritage of psychopathology and problem-solving which has permeated social work practice for a significant part of this century."[61] Social thinking focuses on the hopes, meaning, and power of people who want to build a life for themselves and their children. While your community members may begin with few physical resources, when they work together they use their aspirations and strengths to add to the resources they have.

THE SOCIAL EMANCIPATION OF SOCIAL WORKERS

Modernity is dominated by the economy, in which the social is relegated to a restricted and often insignificant and irrelevant enclave. Under conditions of rational choice and its hegemony over all other ways of thinking in modern society, the social is subsumed as a category of the economy. Modern economic society becomes for most people a massive and seemingly impenetrable presence. The meaning that people's lives hold is unimportant compared with inducing them to act as functionaries who carry out tasks and consume products that keep the economic machinery of society operating. Even "social interaction is basically an economic transaction," Zey states, and it "is guided in its course by the actor's rational choices among alternative outcomes."[62]

Modern social work has allowed itself to adopt economic methods that exclude not only the social, but values, meaning, and emotions without which social work is crippled, impotent, and blind. Social work must begin to emancipate itself from its captivity to economic calculative reason and base its methods on the social itself. As Nobel Prize–winning economist Kenneth Arrow asserts, "Rationality gathers not only its forces but its very meaning from the social context in which it is embedded. It is most plausible under very ideal conditions. When these conditions cease to hold, the rationality assumptions become strained and possibly even self-contradictory."[63]

Rational social work problem-solving must be mediated by the social context in which it is used. Where its social application fails, it may need to be discarded. Social workers in general and macro social workers in particular, therefore, must be very careful about uncritically accepting rational economic models and, instead, develop those that emancipate people from the economic society in which they are captive. But first, social work must emancipate itself. Barry Checkoway offers this advice: "I believe that there is no single model that fits all approaches to practice....The key is to formulate your own concepts and to create a framework that fits your particular situation."[64]

CONCLUSION

We use rational social work problem-solving in a context of human needs, interests, and aspirations, within a milieu of the buzzing noise of politics, and in the framework of the pushing and hauling of democracy.

Rational problem-solving tends to be based on objectivity, prediction, and control, which assumes that we can know the real world in its raw and uncontaminated state. If we understand this world, we can make decisions on which we can rely with some confidence that they reflect a measure of truth about the systems we observe. Rational problem-solving, however, is a "thought" process, not a rigid model. As a thought process it is helpful in its own domain. Once you have mastered its steps, you have a tool at your disposal that you can adapt to a number of situations. Process, however, is a tool, not a master. You learn a particular process in order to gain mastery. Like any other tool or process, rational social work problem-solving must be molded, adapted, and modeled to the contours of the people with whom and for whom you are working.

Social thinking, on the other hand, is based on mutual decision making. "The motive or normative expression of our sociality is mutuality in primary face-to-face relationships," Harmon states, and the motives underlying responsible action are "a function of the *commitment* of one person to the other—as persons."[65] Community members who carry out decisions to affect changes in the social environment not only bear responsibility for their own actions, but they benefit from the power of deciding and accepting the consequences of those decisions. By taking charge of their own destiny, by deciding *and* doing, community members actively engage those in power who impose functional and dependency roles upon them. They challenge the assumption that they cannot or ought not decide and act on their own behalf but must leave deciding in the hands of the powerful.

People in a community who visualize the future not only repair a community, but they build it. Building community is a process that people must do together. They do not need to rely on politicians to show them what aspirations to have. They do not require social workers to tell them how to hope. They do not need to ask expert planners to explain how to become a people or how to create social goods. People construct their own social reality by a process of shared meaning and mutual engagement with one another, by envisioning social change, and by thinking socially. Members "must be seen as social creations—as being formed in and arising out of the process of definition and interpretation as this process takes place in the interaction of people.... Human group life is [a social process] in which people are forming, sustaining, and transforming the objects of their world as they come to give meaning to objects."[66]

Macro social work, therefore, is a highly personal venture, one that depends on you and your own mix of perceptions, personality functions, and ability to apply yourself to making a better society. There is no one rigid model, nor is there a right or a wrong way of making social change. While there are skills to be learned, macro social work cannot be reduced to a bag of tricks or techniques. What you decide to do and how you decide to do it are complex matters of immersing yourself into the social environment with which you are working, understanding the social dysfunctions that are occurring, and engaging people to bring about conditions that are just, socially healthy, and empowering.

KEY CONCEPTS

Enlightenment

modern reason

Rational Choice Theory (RTC)

modernity

instrumental reason

rational problem-solving

problem-solving cycle

generalist social work method

deciding on a problem

gathering information

generating alternative solutions

assessing and comparing alternatives

selecting the best solution

developing a change strategy

implementing the solution

evaluating the results

rational problem-solving cycle

force field analysis

goals

objectives

tasks

techniques

contingency plan

substantive reason

social thinking

four functions of social thinking

whole-mind thinking

intuiting

feeling/valuing

sensing

cognition

meaning

QUESTIONS FOR DISCUSSION

1. What are the strengths of rational social work problem-solving? What are its weaknesses?
2. What are the strengths of social thinking? What are its weaknesses?
3. It was asserted that modern reason is value neutral. Why is being value neutral important? Why is it problematic for social workers? Should social workers be value neutral in helping people solve problems? Should social workers understand and be engaged in the values that attend social issues?
4. The idea of "meaning" occurred several times in the description of social thinking. Review the section "How to Engage the Social Thinking Process." See how many times meaning is discussed. Why is meaning a pervasive theme in social thinking? Why is it absent in rational social work problem-solving? Is meaning an important component in thinking and in macro social work?

CHECKLIST 3.1
Group Problem-Solving Skills

The following checklist will help assess your problem-solving skills. For each item, indicate if it is something that applies to you often, sometimes, or never. Is there a pattern in the issues you have marked? What do these patterns say about you and your problem-solving skills? What areas would you like to improve?

1. I am the kind of person who generally can see larger solutions problems quickly.
   Often _____ Sometimes_____ Never _____

2. I like to focus on one aspect of an issue and nail it down.
   Often _____ Sometimes_____ Never _____

3. I get stuck with my own perception of a problem and find it hard to let go of it.
   Often _____ Sometimes_____ Never _____

4. I usually go along when the group moves off in a direction that I feel is wrong or bad.
   Often _____ Sometimes_____ Never _____

5. I am able to present my position clearly and succinctly.
   Often _____ Sometimes_____ Never _____

6. I tend to ramble and talk around subjects.
   Often _____ Sometimes_____ Never _____

7. People usually listen and respond to me when I present my ideas.
   Often _____ Sometimes_____ Never _____

8. When I talk, people simply wait me out until I'm finished and then move on.
   Often _____ Sometimes_____ Never _____

9. I find myself jumping to conclusions before the group is ready.
   Often _____ Sometimes_____ Never _____

10. I find myself looking at details, and sometimes discover that I have missed the larger situation.
    Often _____ Sometimes_____ Never _____

CHECKLIST 3.2

Problem-Solving Inventory

This test, adapted from David Kolb's *Learning Style Inventory* and based on Jungian personality functions, will help you understand how you go about solving problems.

In the following inventory, you will need to complete ten sentences. Each sentence has four endings

intended to help you discover how you go about solving problems. Think of a situation in which you were faced with a problem you had to solve. Then, in the spaces provided, mark with the number 4 the ending that best fits your problem-solving style; mark with a 3 the ending that fits next best, and so on to the one least like your style. Put a different ranking in each space.

For example:

1. I solve problems best when
   _3_ I explore what is good
   _1_ I anticipate options
   _4_ I use logic
   _2_ I engage in practice

   4 = most like you
   3 = second most like you
   2 = third most like you
   1 = least like you

1. I solve problems best when
   _____ I center myself in what is right
   _____ I grasp the future
   _____ I think things through
   _____ I do something tangible

2. I decide by
   _____ using my felt values
   _____ using my intuition
   _____ using my mind
   _____ using my practicality

3. When I problem-solve I consider
   _____ others
   _____ all possibilities
   _____ only the facts
   _____ what is most effective

4. When I decide I pride myself in
   _____ my caring attitude
   _____ my creative insight
   _____ my ability to assess data
   _____ how I get things done

5. The best kind of problem-solvers
   _____ are compassionate
   _____ have vision
   _____ rely on ideas

Each of the four groups gives an indication of one aspect of the personality functions problem-solvers use. These functions are Feeling–group *a* (F); Intuiting–group *b* (N); Thinking–group *c* (T); and Sensing–group *d* (S).

On the diagram below, place a dot on the scale corresponding to your T, N, F, or S scores. Connect the lines. You will get a kite-like shape. The shape and position of your scores will show which of the functions you prefer most and which you prefer least.

Thinking (T)

40
38
36
34
32
30
28
26
24
22
20
18
16
14
12

Sensing (S)   10   **Intuiting (N)**

40 38 36 34 32 30 28 26 24 22 20 18 16 14 12 10   10 12 14 16 18 20 22 24 26 28 30 32 34 36 38 40

10
12
14
16
18
20
22
24
26
28
30
32
34
36
38
40

Feeling (F)

FIGURE 3.4 Understanding Your Personality Functions

_____ have common sense

6. When faced with a problem I rely on
_____ how it affects others
_____ my hunches
_____ logic
_____ what has worked before

7. The best problem-solvers are
_____ enthusiastic
_____ imaginative
_____ analytical
_____ down to earth

8. Problem-solving requires
_____ a warm heart
_____ inventiveness
_____ a touch mind
_____ hands-on action

9. Problem-solvers should depend on
_____ grounded experience
_____ creative insights
_____ empirically proven theories
_____ practical models

10. Problem-solvers should always attempt to discern
_____ the meaning a situation holds
_____ the opportunities a situation presents
_____ what the facts say is correct
_____ what is feasible

Total the scores for all the a answers. Then total the scores for all the b, c, and d answers.

a_____(F)
b_____(N)
c_____(T)
d_____(S)

To interpret your scores in the four categories of feeling, intuiting, thinking, and sensing, see Figure 3.5.

EXERCISE 3.3
Solving a Social Problem

Take one of the problems you have chosen in Chapter 2. Outline how you would use the rational problem-solving process to solve it. Try to be as specific as possible.

1. Give your definition of the problem.
2. What facts would you need to obtain? Where would you get those facts? How would you collect them? Whom would you need to contact?
3. How would you decide on alternative solutions?
4. What kind of criteria would be useful for ranking alternative solutions to your problem?
5. What strategies can you think of?
6. How would you implement your plan?
7. How will you know whether you have achieved success?

ADVANCED EXERCISE 3.4
Examining Modern Reason

Even though rational problem-solving is so much a part of us, it is not without its critics. It is important to understand these criticisms from the outset. Read the following critique of modern reason. Then answer the questions that follow.

Sociological Attack
One stream of criticism comes from a group of sociologists and social philosophers. The problem with modern rational problem-solving is not that it is ineffective, but that it has been overly utilized. The philosophical argument says that acceptance of pure instrumental reason is the "triumph of technique over purpose."[67] It allows one to reach goals faster and more efficiently, but it avoids the issues of what goals and whose goals, and the important question, "Are those the right goals?" Only by infusing modern reason with ethics can we be assured that our social policies are good or proper.

While modern reason "works," it has become so pervasive that it has all but eliminated other ways of thinking that are often more authentic and appropriate. Substantive or classical reason, for example, challenges humans to reach for ethical constructs that are good and true in and of themselves, whether or not they can be empirically demonstrated. Another way of thinking is intuition. Another is spiritual thinking that goes beyond ethics and intuition.

Pragmatic Attack

The second argument against modern reason comes from practical realists. Their argument is not that modern reason doesn't work, but that it doesn't work well enough. This attack comes from various sources, all centering around the role of the individual in problem-solving. Herbert Simon, for example, says that the problem with instrumental reason is that it requires near omniscience,[68] the accumulation of near perfect information, and places nearly impossible demands on the human intellect. As a result, it has "little discernible relation to the actual or possible behavior of flesh and blood human beings." Instead, says Simon, "human behavior is intendedly rational, but only limited" because "administrative man can make his decisions with relatively simple rules of thumb that do not make impossible demands upon his capacity for thought."

Because human beings cannot possibly be fully rational, there needs to be another kind of system into which they can be integrated that allows them to reach full rationality. This system is the organization. According to Simon, the "organization permits the individual to approach reasonably near to objective rationality." This is so because "the behavior patterns we call organizations are fundamental…to the achievement of human rationality in any broad sense. The rational individual is, and must be, an organized and institutionalized individual." Therefore, for Simon, modern reason is no longer a function of the individual but the organizational context in which the individual is embedded. The more integrated the individual in the organizational milieu, the more nearly he or she can attain complete rationality.

Political Attack

The third attack on modern reason is leveled by Aaron Wildavsky and William Morrow, who assess the role of politics in organizational life.[69] The political attack claims that organizational systems are not really rational either. In fact, while organizations pretend to be fully rational, they are highly irrational. Decisions are really made, say these writers, by any number of factors in organizations such as expediency, survival, self-interest, and short-term gains. While calculation occurs, it is often used not for lofty goals or for the achievement of principle, but rather for the specific interests of people who are out to further their own particular agendas.

Therefore, rationality is rarely a smooth process in which agreed-upon goals are easily achieved in a linear fashion. Instead, there is pulling in all sorts of directions as individuals in positions of power seek to have their own preferences ratified by means of the political process. In this game, any number of strategies are employed that will guarantee success. Therefore, there are many political actors, each applying pressure to extract concessions from public organizations in an atmosphere of bargaining and negotiation.

Normative Attack

Formaini employs a normative attack in rejecting rationality in the change process. He says that scientifically based (i.e., justified) public policy is a dream that has grown ever larger since the Enlightenment and that perhaps reached its apogee at the close of the twentieth century. Rational policy-making is a myth, a theoretical illusion.[70] While science can supply information and facts, inevitably those facts are often disputable, subject to distortions, and will always be used by decision-makers who will apply their own norms or values to them. In the last analysis it doesn't matter what the facts are. What really matters is that "eventually someone has to decide the issue on purely normative grounds." In the United States that normative model is the democratic process, a system of checks and balances, combined with adherence to certain rights. In spite of its weaknesses, Formaini says that "there is no better way to decide such issues. Reliance on tradition, whether cultural or legal, is unworkable…. It is the virtue of a democratic political system that its mechanisms for change are available to those who wish to organize and use them."

1. Social work, and society in general, has tended to adopt premises of rational problem-solving as the means by which decisions are made. While this chapter claims that rational problem-solving has considerable utility, it also points out its weaknesses. What is your assessment of the utility and importance of rational problem-solving?

2. The sociological/philosophical attack claims that modern reason is a truncated or partial way of thinking, primarily because it does not allow for ethics and other ways of thinking to emerge in

problem-solving. Is this a fair criticism? Is there a way of overcoming this defect?

3. Herbert A. Simon claims that individuals are not fully rational, but that rationality is provided extraneously to people by organizational systems, without which humans would remain only "intendedly rational." Is Simon right or wrong? What are the implications of his assessment?

4. Aaron Wildavsky and William Morrow attack modern reason because they suggest that decision-making is ultimately "irrational," at least in the political arena. Is political problem-solving ultimately irrational?

5. Formaini asserts that rational problem-solving is a myth. Instead, procedural democracy is the best available system we have for solving our social problems. What is your opinion of this assessment?

6. Can you think of other difficulties in applying modern reason to social issues? For example, modern reason assumes one has complete knowledge of the consequences of alternative decisions. Is this ever possible? How does this assumption relate to Robert Merton's assessment in Chapter 2 that many social problems are the result of unintended consequences of our decisions?

5. Compare rational social work problem-solving with the social change method of social thinking. Is social thinking a viable alternative to rational problem-solving? What are the strengths and weaknesses of social thinking?

6. Should social thinking be abandoned? Should it replace rational problem-solving? Should both be used together? Should each be used but in different situations?

Advanced Exercise 3.5

Rationality and Social Work

Rational social work problem-solving has become so deeply embedded in conventional social work that the Council on Social Work Education (CSWE) now officially recommends that schools of social work teach the following skills to all students: the ability to (1) define issues, (2) collect and assess data, (3) iden-tify alternative interventions, (4) select and (5) implement courses of action and (6) monitor and evaluate outcomes.[71] Not only are these approved and designated social work skills useful in themselves, but Charles Zastrow asserts they also "interestingly provide an excellent framework for conceptualizing the change process in social work."[72] Zastrow's insight should by now be no surprise to you. These skills *are* exactly those that make up the rational or generalist social work problem-solving process.

However, Mary Zey asserts: "We do our students a disservice by teaching them that the rational choice models of decision making are the only acceptable models. Students may perceive rational choice models not only as explanation, but also as justification for making decisions on rational bases only. That is, students make not only economic decisions, but also family and personal relationship decisions on a rational, self-interested, even narcissistic basis…. Carried to its extreme, the rational choice models define *competition* as the core human value, and therefore the higher the level of competition, the better for humans and collectives…. If these are the values we teach, winning is the rational choice for all politics, and maximized wealth is the rational choice of all economic behavior."[73]

Critique the decision of the Council of Social Work Education and its curriculum recommendations to schools of social work to utilize rational social work problem-solving as its primary method. Examine Zey's reasons for not using rational choice as the only or preferred model. What are your opinions about this issue?

Break into triads and discuss the content of what CSWE is intent on teaching you. Reform into class and come to a conclusion.

ADDITIONAL READING

Schon, Donald. *The Reflective Practitioner: How Professionals Think in Action.* New York: Basic Books, 1985.

Learning Theory

Hilda Blanco. *How to Think About Social Problems: American Pragmatism and the Idea of Planning.* New York: Greenwood Press, 1994.

John Dewey. *How We Think.* Chicago: Heath, 1933.

David A. Kolb. *Experiential Learning: Experience as the Source of Learning and Development.* Englewood Cliffs, NJ: Prentice Hall, 1984.

———. *Learning Style Inventory.* Boston: McBer and Company, 1981.

David Kolb and R. Fry. "Toward an applied theory of experiential learning" in *Theories of Group Processes,* ed. C. Cooper. London: Wiley, 1975.

Jungian Personality Theory

Isabel Briggs Myers. *Introduction to Type.* Palo Alto, CA: Consulting Psychologists Press, 1987.

———. *Gifts Differing.* Palo Alto, CA: Consulting Psychologists Press, 1980.

Rational Problem-Solving

Ralph Brody. *Problem-Solving: Concepts and Methods for Community Organizations.* New York: Human Sciences Press, 1982.

Graham T. Allison. *The Essence of Decision: Explaining the Cuban Missile Crisis.* Boston: Little, Brown, 1971.

4

Leadership
The Hallmark
of Macro Social Work

Men who cannot conceive a happiness of their own accept a definition imposed upon them by others.

Earl Shorris, Scenes From Corporate Life

Strong leadership does not have within itself the capability to create the fundamental changes our organizations require. It is not the fault of the people in these positions, it is the fault of the way we have all framed the role. Our search for strong leadership expresses a desire for others to assume ownership and responsibility for our group, our organization, our society. The effect is to localize power, purpose, and privilege in the one we call leader.

Peter Block, Stewardship: Choosing Service Over Self-Interest

Ideas in This Chapter

JANE ADDAMS, SOCIAL LEADER

Year after year during her lifetime, she was voted the greatest woman in the United States, the greatest in the world, and on one occasion, the greatest in history.[1] Even today, in a survey of 100 professors of history she was second only to Eleanor Roosevelt as the most influential woman of our century. Publicist and persuader, social reformer, crusader, and social activist in the causes of progressive education, housing reform, child labor legislation, criminology, labor organizing, recreation, direct democracy, feminism, treatment of the immigrant, pacifism, and more, she was vitally engaged in almost every important issue of her day.[2]

She was Laura Jane Addams, one of the great pioneers of the progressive era in American history, winner of the Nobel Peace Prize, and macro social worker. Born on September 6, 1860, two months before Abraham Lincoln was elected to the presidency, she became valedictorian and president of her senior class at Rockford Female Seminary in an era when there were no clearly defined roles for young college-educated women, most of whom were thought of as being primarily homemakers. Jane Addams was clearly out of the mainstream. Intensely sensitive, wealthy, and a born leader, but with no clear arena in which to expend her gifts, she entered a period of seven years of deep personal suffering, incapacitating back pain, and depression. Except for a brief period in medical school, these apparently fruitless and painful years were a period of gestation in which her character, determination, and sense of mission and purpose were being formed.

Restless and unhappy, Addams had no thought of entering social work when at the age of 27 she landed at Southampton three days before Christmas, 1887. She had, however, come into direct contact with the poor for the first time on an earlier trip to Europe. Now, she and her companion, Ellen Starr, investigated social work in the slums of London and met Canon Samuel A. Barnett, founder of the first Settlement House, Toynbee Hall. For the next six weeks Addams and Starr lived at Toynbee Hall. It was an experience that would change Addams's life forever. Like Barnett, she saw how the absence of leadership in the poorer districts had allowed local government to fall into disrepair. Guilt at the desertion of duty by those who had been trained to lead impelled her to absorb the milieu of Toynbee Hall, its philosophy, ideals of service, leadership, community, and culture in the face of massive urban disorganization and poverty. It was this experience that ended her desperate years of struggle. Jane Addams had finally found her mission in life.

She not only conceptualized a new way of life, but lived it. Upon arriving back in the United States, Addams and Starr bought Hull House, a large mansion on Halstead Street in the middle of a Chicago slum, and turned it into a social settlement. For the next 40 years Addams lived not as an observer of social causes, but as a resident in one of the poorest sections of Chicago. She engaged people where they were, immersing herself in the sorrows, joys, and garbage, the suicides and dirt. Unafraid to get her hands soiled by the squalor around her, she determined to learn from the homeless poor, the immigrants, working-class women, children, and the elderly. But most of all, she learned from experience, from trying things out. Wherever there was a need, she was open to experiment, establishing programs, building relationships, improving neighborhoods, and forging community. "She had the kind of mind which could tolerate and even thrive on uncertainty and new experiences."[3]

Jane Addams was a visionary, a part of the radical tradition in America. Ahead of her time in numerous issues, she planted the seeds of reform, many of which were to bear fruit years later. "The poor were poor," she said, "because of misconstructed social environment, not because of a defect in themselves,"[4] but Americans in general proved resistant to this idea. She advocated for the rights of women and laborers, and was "concerned with the poor, immigrants, and children simultaneously…She seemed to regard all of them as sources of the social salvation which she continuously sought." She was convinced it was the outcasts of society who could "bring to reality the social vision which she had been formulating….She wanted to enfold the poor, immigrants, children, blacks and women to full participation in American life not only because as a matter of right they deserved it, but because all of society would be redeemed by their inclusion."[5]

Concrete experience and envisioning the future, however, were only the beginning. As she reflected on the misery she saw around her she "effectively convinced Americans…of the seriousness of the problems the nation faced, and of the need for change."[6] A publicist for almost every social cause in her time, the author of 12 books and hundreds of articles and speeches, she became a master at persuading people to take up the cause of reform.

But even more than simply reflecting and writing about human misery, Addams put her words into action, clearly pointing the direction these changes should take. As a leader of the settlement house movement, Jane Addams was instrumental in developing day care, kindergartens, adult education, group work and recreation, immigrant education, sanitation, public health and labor research, unions, child welfare and child labor legislation, programs to combat juvenile delinquency, neighborhood playgrounds, probation services, food safety, the eradication of sweatshops, and improvement of sewage disposal. She supported and was active in the Illinois Equal Suffrage Association, Christian Socialists, the Chicago Peace Society, the National Consumer's League, the Legal Aid Society, the Juvenile Protective Association, and many labor unions. She had a vision of an "America in which women not only had the vote but…would aspire and have opportunity to become college professors, legislators, policy makers in the executive departments of government."[7]

Even before World War I, Addams was a fervent advocate for peace, nearly destroying her reputation and credibility. Her unwavering efforts were finally recognized in 1931 when she was awarded the Nobel Peace Prize. She died in 1935 in the midst of the great reforms of Franklin Roosevelt and Harry Hopkins, each of whom followed her legacy—that the role of government in social welfare was not only practical but necessary.[8] Jane Addams, macro social worker, was without doubt one of the great social leaders of our time.

WHAT YOU WILL LEARN IN THIS CHAPTER

The hallmark of macro social work practice is *leadership*.[9] A leader helps people envision a better future for themselves, take risks, and travel a path to accomplish their goals. Leadership comes from your personality functions and social thinking style, but more importantly, in how your abilities are used. Like Jane Addams, each step of a leader's personal journey is a challenge in exercising your thinking, intuiting, feeling/valuing, and sensing functions.

In this chapter you will explore how social leadership differs from management. You will learn that social leadership involves making leaders of others. You will discover how social leadership is based on your four social thinking functions, and how to put your leadership functions into action You will learn about group-centered leadership, how to modify your leadership style depending on the readiness of group members, and how to lead the group through its life cycle.

WHAT IS LEADERSHIP?

We admire the great humanitarians of the past, social leaders like General William Booth, Lord Robert Baden-Powell, and Sir George Williams of Britain; Toyohiko Kagawa of Japan; and St. Elizabeth Anne Seton, Dorothea Dix, Frederick Douglass, Clara Barton, and St. Francesca Cabrini of the United States. Each of these social leaders exemplified courage, persistence, and compassion in the service of others. The heritage of social work is full of people who, in the words of Elenore Brilliant, "manifested leadership both within and outside the profession. We have had leaders of great significance in the development of the [social work] profession and…we have had some who achieved a prominent place in the community at large…. Jane Addams, Edward T. Devine, Florence Kelly, Edith Abbot, and Harry Hopkins…earned reputations beyond the social work community, influencing the course of social welfare and the quality of life in our country in a broader sense."[10]

In spite of this impressive history, however, the "role assigned to leadership by the social work profession, has declined in recent years," reports Burton Gummer.[11] In the main, the de-emphasis of social work leadership has been the result of an intraprofessional "struggle for primacy between individual intervention and social change to improve the quality of life."[12] The resultant retreat of social work leadership is "in sharp contrast to fields like business and public administration, where the preparation of graduates to assume leadership positions is given high priority."[13]

Because social workers have tended to abdicate the powerful and central leadership role in society that we once had, we have developed few leadership theories on which to base social work practice. We have not tended to translate social leadership into explicit

A leader helps people take risks and envision a better future for themselves. Here, Dr. Martin Luther King, Jr. addresses a rally in Washington, D.C., August 1963. (AP/Wide World Photos)

models based on social work principles of self-determination and empowerment. For the most part we have accepted models borrowed from business.

Business Management

Today, *management* is the word used to describe the function of business leaders and has largely come to be synonymous with leadership. Business is almost uniformly based on the idea that management is located at the top of an organization and imposes governance "which can best control costs, deliver quality, adapt quickly to customers, shorten the time cycle, and keep employees driving toward these markets."[14] Most corporations are driven by efficiency and effectiveness. Business corporations, therefore, choose persons for managerial roles who seem most capable of using informational, economic, and material resources, including its human components, to reach its goals effectively. Unlike inanimate resources, however, human beings tend to "track all kinds of mud from the rest of their lives with them into the organization and have all kinds of interests that are independent of the organization."[15] A great deal of effort, therefore, is expended to shape the behavior of employees so they operate smoothly and produce results. This is why the process of utilizing the human resources of the organization is correctly called management.

When you accept an offer to work for a firm, you obligate yourself to the manager to give your best effort in meeting the corporation's goals. You accept the manager's authority[16] to tell you what, how, and when to perform your duties, and to socialize you to the norms and culture of the organization. *Authority* is the power of the manager to impose decisions on employees that guide their behavior. "The superior frames and transmits decisions with the expectation that they will be accepted by the subordinate. The subordinate expects such decisions, and his conduct is determined by them."[17]

Even more importantly, management is best achieved when employees internalize *decision premises* of the organization. According to Simon, management works to establish in the employee "attitudes, habits and a state of mind which lead him to reach decisions advantageous to the organization."[18] You accept the prerogative of the manager to persuade you to accept the plans laid out by the top executive team, to motivate you to give your best efforts to help the firm succeed, and to induce you to identify with the corporate culture. The more you are socialized to think and act as the managers of the organization desire, the more you will make decisions as the organization wants you to decide.

Managers use many techniques to insure that you accept the premises of organizational decisions and behave according to them. Managers offer inducements such as money, advancement, status, power, and other benefits. They set limits and use threats, punishment, and coercion. Managers use personal influence ranging from suggestion and persuasion to commanding compliance.[19] Management exacts conformity by such mechanisms as chain of command, standard procedures, the hierarchical ordering of power relationships, and by training and indoctrination of its functionaries.[20] Management uses unobtrusive controls by shaping what gets communicated to whom, developing the organization's own internal language, and by channels of decision-making.

The way we structure organizations reinforces the view that leadership resides in only a few who dispense opportunity for advancement, benefits, and status. Because command-oriented hierarchical management has become the means by which superior/subordinate relationships are devised, many of us accept as normal the surrender of our autonomy and the prerogative of those in charge to decide for us. Given its premises and its perspective on human character, business management of necessity is paternalistic or patriarchal. Fully functioning adult humans are assumed to be incapable of managing themselves and therefore need to be managed by a boss. We come to depend on those in charge because we are forced to obtain their approval before we can take action.

We expect the manager to tell us what to do, and because power along with the capacity to dispense favors resides at the top, we look for strong leaders to provide what we cannot give ourselves—the capacity to decide our own futures.[21] "The wish for leadership is, in part, our wish to rediscover hope and…have someone else provide it for us….We hold to the belief that hope resides in those with power." Eventually we begin to live the myth that if we do not have sponsorship from the top, we cannot realize our intentions.[22]

Paternalistic management is self-reinforcing. It keeps us in helpless, dependent positions and usurps our capacity to decide for ourselves. Eventually we become convinced of our own inability to take responsibility. Herbert Simon asserts that we accept decisions made by others because of our "simple unwillingness or disinclination to accept responsibility…. If the assigned task is not unduly unpleasant, many individuals would prefer being told what to do to being forced to make the decisions themselves."[23]

Strong leadership is something we desire because we have been socialized to believe we need leaders who are powerful and in control, leaders of vision who can take us to places we have never been before. Paternalistic leadership does not question its own desire for dominance. All that business and political leaders ask is that we trust them and allow them to lead. In return we ask only that dominance be implemented humanely. The handcuffs of control become golden when they are fitted with the promise of protection and satisfaction.[24]

Managerial Leadership

Managers are desperate to win the competitive race by having their companies succeed. They are burdened with the continual task of squeezing more productivity out of their employees. For nearly 100 years beginning with Frederick Winslow Taylor's book *Scientific Management,*[25] managers have struggled with how to motivate workers to accept decisions made by others, assume responsibilities imposed on them, and perform tasks which are boring, physically demanding, distasteful, or even dangerous. One of the more recent variations in this effort has been to redefine management as leadership, as if imputing substantive content onto the managerial role will make a difference. Browsing through the business management section of your local bookstore will reveal how many popular management "gurus" redefine management into "visionary," "enlightened," "empowering" leadership. Yet for all the efforts of managerial theorists to paint paternalism with the glitter of egalitarian, employee-centered, and visionary leadership, instrumental management remains handicapped by its top-down hierarchical premises and a self-interested, privatized, control orientation.

There is a fundamental difference between corporate management by which private firms operate and authentic leadership by which people in community and society find direction. Management is appropriate in command structures of privately owned firms, threat systems such as the military and police, and systems requiring speed and effectiveness such as emergency medical services. Management can be an acceptable means of inducing people to become machinery of productivity, defense, or saving lives so long as we consciously, ethically, and with full information decide to accept a functional role in return for rewards that a job offers. But when management is presumed to be leadership at large, or a means by which we achieve access to authentic direction in life, then management exceeds its boundaries, leads us astray, and becomes deceitful. Moreover, when social workers use instrumental management because we have not conceived of other ways of leading, we deceive ourselves. When social workers adopt hierarchical structures in which people are assumed to be docile, dependent, and irresponsible, we lead ourselves and our clients astray. Today, however, macro social workers are helping us understand the necessity of deciding for ourselves, following our own visions, and looking to a better future. Macro social workers are inviting social workers as a whole to recover their original heritage of social leadership.

Social Leadership

Social leadership is a process of equipping us to shape plans, become the persons we were meant to become, confront mutual problems of meaning, and devise a community culture of collective sharing. Social leadership rejects paternalism, dependency, and conformity. Social leadership is based on social goods, joint enterprise, empowerment, meaning, partnership, and service.

Social Goods   Social leadership encourages us to create social goods of self-direction, personal responsibility, and making use of all of our potential. Leadership itself is a social good "owned by everyone," not a private good that resides in or is owned by one person. Authentic leadership is something that everyone possesses. It exists only to the extent that it becomes available and is utilized by all of us. The more we exert our capacity to lead, the greater the amount of leadership in the community, the more opportunity to seek meaning and shape our common understanding and experience. If leadership is hoarded, it is diminished and degraded, ultimately devolving to command and control.

Joint Enterprise   Social leadership is not a solitary process in which a manager makes decisions for us, but a collective enterprise in which we all engage in deciding and doing. You become a leader as you contribute your perceptions, understanding, intuition, and values to the group. Macro social work is committed to help all engage in leadership, not just "the best and brightest" or those who are most skilled in impersonal rational problem-solving.

Expressing your skills on behalf of others both informs the self and forms community. In the process of reciprocal learning and leading, of following and giving assistance, true community occurs. Each of us contributes our own unique gifts, skills, and insights to the leadership process, unlike paternalistic management where everyone is obliged to follow the lead of the boss. While functional managers attempt to "take people to places they have never been before,"

social leaders help communities move in a direction that its members want to go.

Empowerment   Management hoards power and keeps employees in positions of relative powerlessness. The power of social leadership, however, cannot be hoarded. Power belongs to everyone in the social community. Social leadership, in fact, "leads to a concern with *increasing the power of others*, rather than seeking their submission."[26] Social leadership asserts that we already have authority to act and speak, to think and plan, to decide and do, to share and serve. We do not "need permission from others to have feelings or approval from those in authority to take what matters into our own hands," Peter Block states. It is everybody's right and a duty to create a vision and translate those visions into concrete practices. "We do not need sponsorship from above to do the right thing," says Block. "The only reliable leadership is our own."[27] Social leadership empowers us, stands beside us, and affirms that we can act on our own behalf to create the kind of society we desire.

Meaning   Corporate management carries out organizational premises to implement the owner's goals. Social leadership helps us define the premises that guide us toward our common goals. You come to understand that there is a purpose beyond your existence, something more than your own interests that you can contribute to the cumulative life of others. You grasp meaning and pass it on. In this way the life of the entire community is enhanced. Each person becomes a leader, because every person mutually contributes to the meaning and direction of the community. It is the mutual leading, informing, gathering, seeking, and communicating that give the community its voice, its eyes, and its sense of direction and sense of itself.

Partnership   Social leadership is partnership. Social leadership expects that community members become partners with one another but also partners with people in the corporate world and in government. When we develop social leadership, we achieve joint ownership over the common processes and power in the community. Social leaders never accept corporate or governmental structures as superordinant entities that exist independently of community members. We may treat corporate officials and the companies that operate in our localities as respected guests who may be permitted to use community resources, but with qualifications. Corporate managers may be seen as partners in the joint venture of community prosperity, but not as figures who have peremptory permission that supercedes citizens at large, or proprietary rights to siphon resources out of the community for their own benefit.

In the same way, government officials, agency bureaucrats, and politicians are viewed as partners not bosses. They are welcomed and applauded only when they deliver on their promises. They are expected to be honest, trustworthy, and reliable in carrying out their responsibilities as public *servants*. Partnership between officials of megastructures and community members is not condescension, benevolence, or participation. Partnership is a commitment to a dialogue between equals—community members and managers act in a joint venture of service, through cooperation not concession.

Service   Social leadership provides service to others. This does not mean subservience or servitude. Social leadership serves the community or organization as an ally in accomplishing the purposes for which the community was established not as a vehicle of self-assertion or self-interest.

> For 41 years, Cesar Chavez taught the poorest people in America to stand up for their rights— and to do it without violence. Against tremendous odds he organized the first successful farm workers union in history. He turned compliant and submissive people into courageous champions of their families and communities. His formal education ended after the eighth grade. He never owned a home or earned more than $6,000 a year. He chose a life of self-imposed poverty, grueling hours, and the frequent threat of physical violence and death. Yet his deeds live on in the millions of people he inspired with an unshakable conviction that society can be transformed from within.[28]

Social leaders do not dominate the community but assist each of us to become leaders and use the resources in the community to move it in a better direction. Social leadership upholds our rights to own our own vision, claim our futures, and construct the community of which we are a part. Social leadership facilitates empowerment not patriarchy, meaning not self-interest. Social leadership

acts as a partner, not a boss, and offers encouragement, not control, service not subservience.

HOW TO HELP OTHERS BECOME SOCIAL LEADERS

Understanding Your Leadership Style

Before you can help others become social leaders, you must understand your own leadership style. Exercise 4.1 will help you apply feeling/valuing, intuiting, thinking, and sensing functions to your leadership.

EXERCISE 4.1

Leadership Preferences Inventory

The Leadership Preferences Inventory is based on a Jungian personality typology. Each of us has four different personality functions that we can use and modify to assist us in our leadership. This inventory will help you understand your leadership role and the different mix of your own style preferences. It will help you identify your strengths and be a more effective leader. It will also help you change your leadership style when appropriate.

Instructions

In this exercise, you will complete 16 sentences, each of which has something to do with how you lead. There are four endings for each sentence. Rank each of the endings according to how much it resembles you. Place a 4 next to that ending that most resembles you, a 3 next to the ending that is second most like you, a 2 next to the one is third most like you, and a 1 next to the ending least like you.

Example:

1. I like leaders who are strong in
   - _3_ thinking   (second most like you)
   - _1_ imagining   (least like you)
   - _4_ feeling   (most like you)
   - _2_ observing   (third most like you)

1. I like leaders who are strong in
   - _4_ thinking
   - _1_ imagining
   - _2_ feeling

_3___ observing

2. As a leader I would
____ conduct an impersonal analysis of the situation
____ explore all of the options
____ weigh how deeply I care about the issue
____ dig up the facts

3. I admire a leader who is full of
____ justice
____ hope
____ compassion
____ mercy

4. I like a leader who above all is
____ fair
____ original
____ friendly and kind
____ down to earth

5. If I were a leader, I would focus on
____ reason
____ experience
____ relationships
____ factual observation

6. I appreciate a leader best who is
____ logical and systematic
____ stimulating and creative
____ warm and caring
____ practical and realistic

7. When in doubt as a leader I would
____ stand firm
____ look at the ultimate purpose
____ conciliate
____ et involved in the here and now situation

8. As a leader I would speak from
____ my head
____ my dreams and visions
____ my heart
____ my actions

9. I admire leaders who
____ find flaws in something in advance
____ bring up new possibilities
____ appreciate values such as what is good and right
____ keep track of essentials

10. I believe that the best leaders show interest in
____ rational thought
____ envisioning the future
____ convictions
____ concrete things in the here and now

11. I enjoy leaders who
____ explain things logically
____ stimulate my imagination
____ relate to me personally
____ give a concrete demonstration

12. In my leadership role I like to
____ analyze and predict the logical outcomes of choices
____ conceive of a plan and dream about its future
____ see the effects of choices on people
____ have details of a program and carry them out

13. I relate best to a leader who is
____ analytical
____ imaginative
____ sympathetic
____ sensible

14. I would rather lead
____ a decision-making group solving a problem in a logical way
____ a brainstorming group trying to come up with all of the possibilities
____ a support group that deals with feelings and personal issues
____ a task group dealing with the here and now

15. I work best when I
____ am treated fairly
____ can learn new skills
____ get occasional praise
____ focus on the immediate job

16. What I appreciate about a leader is his or her
____ ideas and theories
____ invention of future possibilities
____ feelings and values
____ ability in practical application

Total the scores in each Column

Column 1   Column 2   Column 3   Column 4

____   ____   ____   ____
(T)   (N)   (F)   (S)

On the diagram in Figure 4.1, place a dot on the scale corresponding to your T, N, F, or S leadership scores from the Leadership Preferences Inventory. Connect the lines. You will get a kite shape. The shape and position of your scores will show which of the four leadership functions you prefer most and which you prefer least.

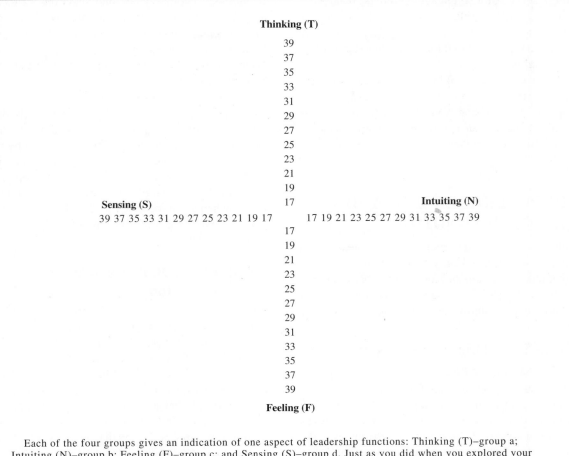

Thinking (T)

39
37
35
33
31
29
27
25
23
21
19

Sensing (S)   **Intuiting (N)**

39 37 35 33 31 29 27 25 23 21 19 17   17 19 21 23 25 27 29 31 33 35 37 39

17
17
19
21
23
25
27
29
31
33
35
37
39

Feeling (F)

Each of the four groups gives an indication of one aspect of leadership functions: Thinking (T)–group a; Intuiting (N)–group b; Feeling (F)–group c; and Sensing (S)–group d. Just as you did when you explored your problem-solving functions, place a dot on the scale corresponding to your T, N, F, and S leadership scores. Connect the lines. You will get a kite-like shape. The shape and position of your scores will show which of the four leadership functions you prefer most and which you prefer least.

By looking at how you score on the four leadership functions, you can get an idea about where your leadership strengths lie. The strongest areas are those that you will tend to use most often and with the most ease. The ones on which you score lowest will be areas that you will need to work harder to use or will use less often.

FIGURE 4.1 Understanding Your Leadership Style

A macro social worker is not the official or designated leader of the group, but a facilitator, adviser, and consultant who helps the members become leaders. You develop an atmosphere in which members are free to express and use their various functions. While you keep in touch with your own leadership functions, you simultaneously engage the group on multiple levels. You attend to the arena of discussion, but you imaginatively place yourself outside of it. For example, you listen to what each member is saying, while looking for patterns of interaction that can help the group as a whole move ahead. You pay attention to the content of discussion but look more deeply into what the members may be implying. You think about the problem at hand but try to understand the meaning behind the issues that the members present. You look for patterns of communication, cohesion, and group spirit, especially as the members exhibit levels of readiness and the group moves through different stages.

You observe but also engage members, make connections, and see relationships and patterns. You reflect back to members the issues they have been describing, picking up themes and messages, ideas and insights.

You use your thinking function to help your members confront the past. You use your intuition to inspire a shared vision. You use your feeling/valuing function to help create community. You use your sensing function to help the community move to action.

SOCIAL LEADERSHIP AND THE FOUR FUNCTIONS

Although the social leadership model is presented as a cycle (see Figure 4.2), you may begin anywhere along this continuum and move either backwards or forwards, depending on the issues that confront you in building community and solving social problems.

Using Your Thinking Skills to Confront the Past

When you use your thinking function, you help your members gain a sense of the injustices that have been perpetrated against them. You confront the way things have been done in the past that create troubles in the present. You challenge the way things are done today, so as to bring about a better tomorrow. You help people develop a sense of mission that can shape and improve their lives. Community members who have a clear sense of direction are best able to lead themselves and help others develop an idea of where they want to go. As Burton Gummer asserts, "People who present clear and convincing arguments for taking action in situations where knowledge is limited or absent will be influential in shaping the thinking and behavior of others."[29]

Your thinking function gives you stability and consistency. "It is consistency between words and actions that build your credibility."[30] Management consultant Edgar Shein says, "I learned that my own consistency sends clear signals to audience about my priorities, values, and beliefs. It is the consistency that is important, not the intensity of attention."[31] You use your thinking to help your members develop a set of

intentions, outcomes, goals, and directions for themselves. Your thinking function helps you and your members become confident in your ability to make things happen,[32] and helps you access members' confidence as well. You know what results you and your members are trying to accomplish.

If you are firm in your thinking function, you stand up for your beliefs and assist members to firm up their beliefs. You practice what you preach and show others by your own example; you live by the values that you profess. You are not simply committed to truth and justice in the abstract; you exemplify the truth in your own life and actions. Your thinking function helps you focus yourself, and your members gather strength and confidence in using their thinking function as well.

Using Intuition to Inspire a Shared Vision

The members of your community must have a vision to effect social change. You help your members generate a shared vision of where they want to go. According to Theodore Hesburgh, president of the University of Notre Dame, "Vision is the key to leadership." Unless your members have a vision of where they are going, they are not going to get there.[33]

Your community members "begin with imagination and with the belief that what is merely an image can one day be made real."[34] You accept your members as they are, damaged and hard pressed on every side, and help them envision themselves as they might be. As you talk with the members and affirm their perceptions, you help members gather their hopes and dreams about what is possible. You help articulate those dreams and assist your members to rekindle inside themselves what is theirs—a future possibility, even though few may see it clearly. You assist your members to envision the outcome and help them head toward it.

"Every organization, every social movement begins with a dream. The dream or vision is the force that invents the future."[35] This dream gives shape and meaning to people's lives. Dr. Martin Luther King Jr. combined his thinking function, challenging injustice with an intuited vision. He "envisioned the future 'gazing across the horizon of time' and imagining that greater things were ahead. [He] foresaw something

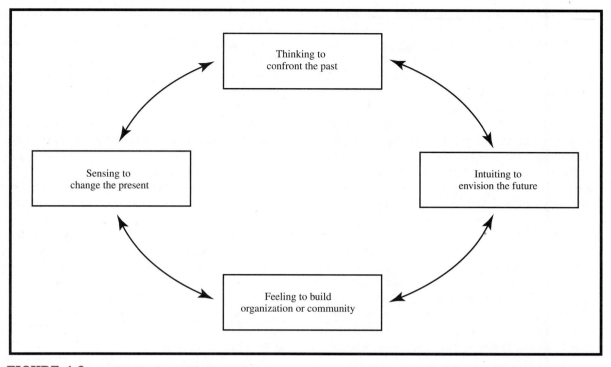

FIGURE 4.2 Social Leadership and the Four Functions

out there, vague as it might appear from the distance, that others did not. [He] imagined that extraordinary feats were possible,...that the ordinary could be transformed into something noble."[36]

You reflect their vision back to your members so that they see themselves and their purposes anew; they see their common future and the possibilities of what they can do and be. The community becomes the vehicle by which the shared vision is transmitted.

Using Your Feeling Function to Create Community

As you hold to your sense of justice and engage in a shared vision with your members, use your feeling function to help members form themselves into community partners in block clubs, neighborhood associations, community organizations, community planning boards, community development corporations, and social organizations. Using your feeling function, you reach out to those who may be alone, alienated, separated, distrustful, and disengaged from one another. You engage others, connect people, and help bind your members together. If you do nothing else, you do this. Going out into the neighborhood, you bring people in. You invite them to share their difficulties and disappointments, successes and failures; you listen as they recount their stories, and you affirm their feelings. You listen to their values and help unite them into a community.

> Leaders find that common thread that weaves together the fabric of human needs into a colorful tapestry. They seek out the brewing consensus among those they would lead. In order to do this, they develop a deep understanding of the collective yearnings. They listen carefully for quiet whisperings in dark corners. They attend to subtle cues. They sniff the air to get the scent. They watch faces. They get a sense of what people want, what they value, what they dream about.[37]

By being fully human, having passion for the cause, and being genuine and real to others, you bring your feeling/valuing function to leadership. You often may feel strongly about the issues that engage your community, and you let your passion show. As you do this, you set a tone of engagement and accessibility, an atmosphere in which your members depend on and reach out to one another.

You enable and encourage members to respond to one another with caring and compassion, with commitment and cohesion. The real flesh and blood encounters with one another and the feelings that are elicited add substance to the dream so that it is not a vision only, but a reality that occurs as people engage one another in mutuality and trust. In doing this you foster collaboration, strengthening, and enlisting others in capturing the future that your members were meant to have.

In forming community you help discover meaning. You "act as a channel of expression between the down-to-earth followers and their other worldly dreams,"[38] not only communicating but *creating* meaning as well. Social work leaders attempt to become the embodiment of the truth of the community, a truth that makes this people unique. This uniqueness gives your people their sense of identity, their own particularity, which sets them apart from all others. This "differentness," cherished and prized among people, fosters pride and self-respect. As you prize your own thinking, intuiting, and feelings/values, you model your differentness and lead others to take pride in theirs.

Using Your Sensing Function to Move to Action

Armed with facts, a vision, and having formed a community of the oppressed, you use your sensing function as one who "commits people to action, who converts followers to leaders, and who converts leaders into agents of change."[39] Delving into the practical everyday life of your members, you assist them to grasp the hands-on realities of shaping and forming a better world for themselves. You work with them as they develop programs, engage in political activities, or work in wider social movements. Your members may have to acquire particular skills such as doing research, leading meetings, speaking at public hearings, organizing committees, writing proposals, seeking funding, hiring staff, training a board, proposing policy, carrying out services. Members may discover talents they did not realize they had, and they put those talents to use in meaningful work that contributes to the common good.

By developing tangible services and programs, community members discover strength in action. Relationships take shape as people become servants to one another and as they meet the real needs of those who are in trouble and in pain. You keep your eye on the larger picture, as your community moves ahead one step at a time. You help break larger problems into small units, and the community gains with small wins. "The magic in small wins is the experimentation process, or setting up little tests that continually help you learn something."[40]

The social leadership process now comes full circle. You help members challenge injustice with their thinking function, apply their intuition to hold onto their dream in the face of challenges, draw on their feeling/valuing function to strengthen the community in times of stress, and use their sensing functions to immerse themselves in strategizing and planning.

GROUP-CENTERED LEADERSHIP

In 1969 Paul Hersey and Kenneth Blanchard, two organizational psychologists, developed a leadership model that they called "3-D Leader Effectiveness Theory,"[41] later termed "situational leadership." Hersey and Blanchard assumed that individuals in groups go through various phases of development. As people develop their abilities, their needs change. As a macro social worker, you adapt your style to these changing situations. Hersey and Blanchard conclude that you modify your guidance and direction and the amount of socio-emotional support you offer, depending on the readiness level of members.

Levels of Member Readiness

Hersey and Blanchard defined four levels of member readiness. Members who are unwilling (lack motivation) and are unable (lack skills) will display low readiness to successfully complete a task, engage in group problem-solving, or work on a community project. For example, if you are working with people with low readiness, you should adopt a high-task/low-relationship (HT/LR) "telling" stance characteristic of a directive leader. As your members become more motivated and skilled, you shift to a high-task/high-relationship style (HT/HR) "selling" stance of a democratic leader. Your members will often experience a stage when their skills have progressed but they still need reassurance and encouragement, or a high-relationship/low-task (HR/LT) "participating" style from you. Finally, when group members are highly capable and self-motivated you take a low-relationship/low-task (LR/LT) "delegating" style similar to that of a laissez-faire leader.[42] (See Figure 4.3.)

Stages of the Group

Not only do your members change and develop as they learn to work with others in a group, but your group itself goes through a cycle of change. The Group-Centered Leadership model shows how you can adapt your style to member needs as the group as a whole moves though its stages of development.[43] There are four stages of the group life-cycle (see Figure 4.4). The Forming stage occurs in the beginning stage of group life, the Norming and Storming stages are middle stages of the group, and the Performing stage occurs when group members are fully functioning.[44]

Groups will not move through these stages in a lockstep fashion. Instead, some groups may skip stages, and others may move through some stages slowly or very quickly. A group may work on issues at several stages at the same time. Other groups may move through issues involving several stages in one meeting. Some groups resolve issues at one stage only to return to those issues again later.

Assessing the Stages of the Group

One way for you to be an effective group leader is to assess the level of readiness and skills of members at each stage of the group's life. Checklist 4.1 will help you make such an assessment.

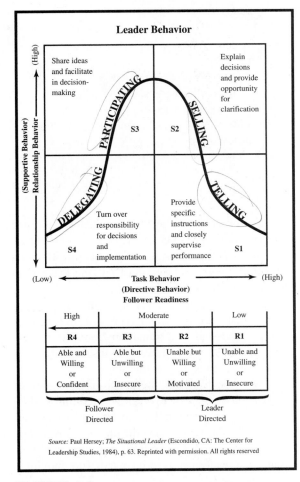

FIGURE 4.3 Group Life Cycle and Leadership Model

Within the figure:

Leader Behavior

(Supportive Behavior) Relationship Behavior (High)

PARTICIPATING — Share ideas and facilitate in decision-making — S3

SELLING — Explain decisions and provide opportunity for clarification — S2

DELEGATING — Turn over responsibility for decisions and implementation — S4

TELLING — Provide specific instructions and closely supervise performance — S1

(Low) ← **Task Behavior** (**Directive Behavior**) → (High)
Follower Readiness

High		Moderate		Low
R4	**R3**	**R2**	**R1**	
Able and Willing or Confident	Able but Unwilling or Insecure	Unable but Willing or Motivated	Unable and Unwilling or Insecure	

Follower Directed   Leader Directed

Source: Paul Hersey; *The Situational Leader* (Escondido, CA: The Center for Leadership Studies, 1984), p. 63. Reprinted with permission. All rights reserved

---

CHECKLIST 4.1

Group Life-Cycle Assessment

This assessment survey will help you identify the stage of the development of a group. Answer as honestly as you can to help the leader and members understand at which level the group is functioning. Circle one of the following that most closely matches your feeling about each statement:

1 *Strongly Disagree* **2** *Disagree* **3** *Agree* **4** *Strongly Agree*

If you agree with only part of a question, mark it disagree. After you have finished one section, add up the points and enter the total next to Score_____.

Section I

a. I need to know what is expected of me in this group.
1 *Strongly Disagree* **2** *Disagree* **3** *Agree* **4** *Strongly Agree*

b. I need to understand what this group is supposed to accomplish.
1 *Strongly Disagree* **2** *Disagree* **3** *Agree* **4** *Strongly Agree*

c. I need to know when the group is supposed to accomplish its goals.
1 *Strongly Disagree* **2** *Disagree* **3** *Agree* **4** *Strongly Agree*

d. I need to get to know members of this group.
1 *Strongly Disagree* **2** *Disagree* **3** *Agree* **4** *Strongly Agree*

e. I need to know what the members of this group are supposed to do.

1 *Strongly Disagree* 2 *Disagree* 3 *Agree* 4 *Strongly Agree*

f. I need to know how to proceed in this group.

1 *Strongly Disagree* 2 *Disagree* 3 *Agree* 4 *Strongly Agree*

g. The leader of this group needs to give us clear directions about how this group is to go about its business.

1 *Strongly Disagree* 2 *Disagree* 3 *Agree* 4 *Strongly Agree*

Score:_____

Section II

a. I know what is expected of me but am not sure how to do it.

1 *Strongly Disagree* 2 *Disagree* 3 *Agree* 4 *Strongly Agree*

b. I am uncomfortable about some of the procedures in this group.

1 *Strongly Disagree* 2 *Disagree* 3 *Agree* 4 *Strongly Agree*

c. I disagree with some of the rules in this group.

1 *Strongly Disagree* 2 *Disagree* 3 *Agree* 4 *Strongly Agree*

d. I am sometimes confused about the direction the group is going.

1 *Strongly Disagree* 2 *Disagree* 3 *Agree* 4 *Strongly Agree*

e. I think we are wasting time in this group.

1 *Strongly Disagree* 2 *Disagree* 3 *Agree* 4 *Strongly Agree*

f. I don't think we are accomplishing everything we could.

1 *Strongly Disagree* 2 *Disagree* 3 *Agree* 4 *Strongly Agree*

g. I have feelings about how the leader is conducting the group.

1 *Strongly Disagree* 2 *Disagree* 3 *Agree* 4 *Strongly Agree*

Score:_____

Section III

a. This group has internal conflicts it needs to work out.

1 *Strongly Disagree* 2 *Disagree* 3 *Agree* 4 *Strongly Agree*

b. I find myself disagreeing with members in this group.

1 *Strongly Disagree* 2 *Disagree* 3 *Agree* 4 *Strongly Agree*

c. Some members in this group need to be more forthright.

1 *Strongly Disagree* 2 *Disagree* 3 *Agree* 4 *Strongly Agree*

d. Some members in this group dominate discussion.

1 *Strongly Disagree* 2 *Disagree* 3 *Agree* 4 *Strongly Agree*

e. Some members in this group tend to get off track.

1 *Strongly Disagree* 2 *Disagree* 3 *Agree* 4 *Strongly Agree*

f. Some members in this group waste too much time.

1 *Strongly Disagree* 2 *Disagree* 3 *Agree* 4 *Strongly Agree*

g. The leader needs to help group members work though interpersonal issues.

1 *Strongly Disagree* 2 *Disagree* 3 *Agree* 4 *Strongly Agree*

Score:_____

Section IV:

a. Members of this group demonstrate that they know what to do and are able to do it.

1 *Strongly Disagree* 2 *Disagree* 3 *Agree* 4 *Strongly Agree*

b. Rules in this group are jointly worked out with everyone.

1 *Strongly Disagree* 2 *Disagree* 3 *Agree* 4 *Strongly Agree*

c. This group is well on its way to accomplishing its goals.

1 *Strongly Disagree* 2 *Disagree* 3 *Agree* 4 *Strongly Agree*

d. The procedures in this group are clear and workable.

1 *Strongly Disagree* 2 *Disagree* 3 *Agree* 4 *Strongly Agree*

e. Leadership in this group is shared by all the members.

1 *Strongly Disagree* 2 *Disagree* 3 *Agree* 4 *Strongly Agree*

f. Conflicts in this group are resolved internally.

1 *Strongly Disagree* 2 *Disagree* 3 *Agree* 4 *Strongly Agree*

g. Members need only occasional assistance from the leader.

1 *Strongly Disagree* 2 *Disagree* 3 *Agree* 4 *Strongly Agree*

Score:_____

Each section in Checklist 4.1 relates to a different stage of the group. Section I is the Forming stage, Section II is the Norming Stage, Section III is the Storming Stage, and Section IV is the Performing Stage. Compare scores from each section. A score of 7–14 indicates that a particular member is not operating at that stage. A medium score of 15–21 indicates that a member is in a transition from one stage to another. A high score of 22–28 indicates that a member is clearly operating at this stage.

When scoring for the group as a whole, ask whether members received low, medium, or high scores for each section. Do most members rank one or two sections higher than the others? This will tell you at what stage the group is operating and what issues the leader needs to resolve before moving to the next stage.

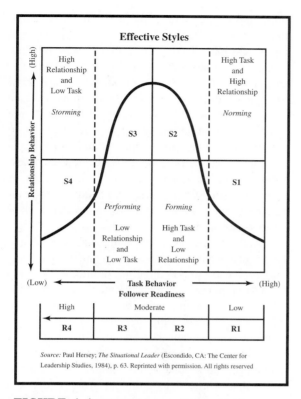

Effective Styles

Task Behavior
Follower Readiness

FIGURE 4.4 Situational Leadership Model

Situational Leadership® is a registered trademark of the Center for Leadership Studies, Escondido, California.

If some members scored high on one section and others scored high on a different section, the group is operating at different levels. This tells you that members are experiencing differing levels of maturity. If members are evenly split, the leader should aim his or her style at the higher level, expecting that the less-ready members will catch up. In fact, it is probably a good idea to have some members at a lower stage and others at a higher stage so that the higher-stage members can assist lower-stage members. However, if several members are two or more stages ahead or behind the others, the higher-stage members may feel bored and out of place, or the lower-stage members may appear to be a drag on the group.

HOW TO USE THE GROUP-CENTERED LEADERSHIP MODEL

Your goal is to help individual members and the group as a whole to move through the different stages.

At the beginning you give direction, but gradually you loosen control as the members mature, until your group members no longer need you.

The Forming Stage

At the beginning of a group, your members may tend to be anxious and uncertain. You may not know your members, and the members may not know one another. Group members may be unsure about whether you or other members will personally accept them, or whether their abilities will be recognized or utilized. Your members may not have a clear understanding of their roles, know the rules or boundaries, or know what behaviors are expected of them. Although your members may come with skills and experiences that are relevant to the group, they may have little understanding about the processes they will be expected to use.

In the forming stage of a group, members do not know what to do or how to do it. They may not be able to take full responsibility for carrying out tasks or directing their own actions. Members generally need a leader on whom they can depend. They will look to you to explain what to do, how to do it, and when and where to do it. Your members will need you to answer questions and provide the structure needed to get the job done. They will expect you to get things started, and to give guidance along the way until they get enough experience to begin functioning on their own. As a result, your most effective stance is to be structured, organized, and directive, using a "telling" low-relationship/high-task (LR/HT) style.

Introduce the general purpose of the group, welcome members, and help members become acquainted with one another. Provide structure, often by handing out an agenda or telling members what the meeting is supposed to accomplish. Explain the purpose of the group, and go over some of the goals that may help the group accomplish its purpose. You want members to feel excited and motivated by the group. Help them see how they can make a real difference in making social change.

Suggest procedures by which the group can accomplish the group's purpose. For example, use brainstorming or round-robin techniques in which you go around the table and ask each one for input on their goals and ideas. Help the group stay focused. If the group gets off track, you redirect the group by restating the purpose and clarifying the direction the group should be going.

Obtain commitment by asking members to structure the agenda for the next meeting, and to decide on the next steps in accomplishing the group's purpose. Ask members to accept assignments to become actively involved in specific tasks, and set up timelines for accomplishing the group's purpose. At the end of the meeting, summarize the meeting's accomplishments, the task assignments, the goals of the next meeting, and its time and place.

The Norming Stage

At the norming stage, your members know the rules, boundaries, and their roles intellectually. However, before members can be fully functioning, they need to make sure the group environment is secure and stable. They need to test the boundaries, rules, norms, and structure of the group for themselves, integrate them into their own experience, and make sure they are practical. The norming stage is one in which members need to "own" the rules and processes and make the group their own. Your members are still dependent on you for direction but are struggling against their own dependency in their desire for mastery. They want to perform but may not know how to do it successfully. Members may know something about what to do but may not be able to do it yet. Your most effective stance at this stage is to remain task-oriented but supportive, characteristic of a "selling" high-relationship/high-task (HT/HR) leadership style.

As members express feelings of being unsure or lacking understanding, respond to their needs for more information, clarity, or structure. Help your members gain greater experiential understanding about the group's task and how they might accomplish those tasks. You assist members to see "the relevance and importance of issues as they are brought before the group."[45]

Don't be surprised when your members test themselves against you to assure themselves that you are firmly in charge. Expect and even welcome this testing because it is an indication that your members are ready to take on ownership of the group. Members need to challenge you before they can make the group their own. The way you respond to group challenges at this stage will set the tone for much of the life of the group. You may even test the members by reversing the challenges and ask them what they

think and begin encouraging them to decide about the rules, roles, goals, and process. Look for verbal and nonverbal cues that indicate misunderstanding, anxiety, or unwillingness on the part of members. Listen carefully for themes or patterns of unclarity. Suggest an exercise to help the group as a whole come to terms with the issues around which they are struggling. Members may ask lots of questions to clarify their roles and to understand the group's boundaries and its procedures. Welcome these questions, affirm them, and validate the importance of openness in questioning. Answer the questions members pose, but at the same time ask members for their suggestions or ideas.

At this stage, members will inevitably make mistakes because they still lack skills and ability. They may go too far in one direction or another. To help keep them on track, give encouragement while at the same time reminding them about the purpose of the group and its goals. Help members critique ideas or suggestions to ensure they are consistent with what the group is to accomplish. As you clarify, explain, encourage, and validate while simultaneously expecting them to work at integrating the group's goals and processes, members will gain confidence as well as skill in discussion, developing understanding, gaining motivation, and generating ideas.

The Storming Stage

Once your members have accepted the tasks, boundaries, and goals of the group, they will tend to work hard at trying themselves out within the group structure. In their efforts to accomplish a group task, they will work to adapt their skills and abilities to the task. Your members will try to find their own style of working, discover how their style fits with others in the group, and accommodate their own personality functions to those of the leader and members of the group. As a result, however, your members may come into conflict with one another as they try to solve mutual problems and as they increasingly become dependent on one another for information, cooperation, and mutual support. The storming stage is one in which you help members' roles become clear and assist the group to resolve internal conflicts and relationship issues. You shift your leadership stance to a "facilitating" high-relationship/low-task (HR/LT) stance.

A leader provides training and information so that group members can understand what is possible. (Courtesy of National Association for Community Leadership)

Members may discover that they have personal differences with one another and with the styles of other group members. Members, for example, who rely mainly on their thinking function and focus on facts may not be comfortable with members who emphasize feelings and want to make decisions based on relationships or meaning behind the facts. Intuiters who look at the big picture may become impatient with sensers who get involved with details of issues. Some members may be overly dominant or subservient. Others may over disclose or withhold information.

You welcome differing learning styles and viewpoints as opportunities for members to gain greater understanding of one another. Validate the importance of various problem-solving functions, and encourage those with different functions to work with one another. Help members share information, thoughts, and feelings with one another.[46]

Ensure that everyone is included in the decision-making process. You help members learn good prob-lem-solving skills and model them for members. One way to do this is to encourage members to keep comments brief, for members to listen attentively to what others are saying, to wait until the speaker is finished, and to always include silent members. Make sure everyone has time to present his or her ideas fully, and that all ideas count. Build on suggestions, affirming individual contributions. Work toward a clear understanding of the topic and that it is relevant to everyone. Frequently summarize progress, check for understanding on issues that need clarification, and review issues that were not fully discussed.

When conflicts occur, you help develop a conflict resolution process. Ask members to elaborate on thinking that led to their positions. Ensure that members listen carefully and ask questions *before* they react. Help members refrain from evaluating ideas or suggestions until all ideas have been generated. As members respond, point out areas of consensus and mutual interest as they arise.[47] Build on agreements, rather than disagreements, promoting consensus rather than discord.

Help members learn good communication skills. Encourage members to use "I" statements in which people assume responsibility for their own ideas and feelings rather than "you" statements which tend to be judgmental, block communication, and often project blame. Assist members to engage in perception checking, in which members ask for clarification about another person's position, paraphrase in their own words what they heard the other person say, and obtain affirmation before they respond.

The result of navigating through the channels of the storming stage will mean that members accept one another's differences and learn to use those differences in problem-solving. They will have developed skills in conflict resolution and communication and have grown in their ability to work independently together.

The Performing Stage

The final stage of the group is the performing stage. Your members are now willing and capable. A formal leader has emerged who facilitates the meetings. Members understand the group's task. They know what to do and how to do it. They have skills, experience, and confidence in their abilities. They own the group and have made its rules and boundaries their own. They have developed working relationships with one another and resolved conflicts that may have gotten in the way of accomplishing their task. They have learned skills in problem-solving, group process, and interpersonal relationships. They are working as a cohesive unit with high motivation.

A good strategy when working with highly independent and motivated members is to take a "hands off" low-relationship/low-task (LR/LT) stance, characteristic of a laissez-faire or "coaching" style of leadership. You encourage, observe, and monitor, but you don't give direction, persuade, or interfere with the group process. Your members should take responsibility and implement decisions on their own.

Attend carefully to the group and its members, listening, often remaining silent but involved with the process. Maintain eye contact, express interest, offer support and encouragement. Give input when asked, and in a way that avoids taking sides. Raise questions, clarify, or summarize. Take notes and keep track of process so that important ideas or decisions are not forgotten.

As the group struggles with communicating openly, resolving conflicts, and working toward shared decision-making and equal participation, however, you may observe dysfunctional patterns emerge. If members avoid issues that they must face, you point this out. If they are reverting to previous behaviors in the struggle for adaptation, explore this pattern and help members deal with it. If members need information, resources, or assistance, help them process how they can obtain it without doing it for them. Give the formal leader support and encouragement. After meetings, meet with the formal leader to review and critique the process so that he or she becomes more effective.

CONCLUSION

Social leadership is a substantive approach to leadership based on respect for the self-determination of the members of the group and the community and on the rights of the members to decide, to have a vision of their future, to act on that vision, and to take responsibility for the outcomes of those actions. It rejects paternalism, unobtrusive controls, and soft colonialism. It rejects implied threats, subtle deceitfulness, and other forms of management in which people are induced to conform or give up their autonomy, self-will, values, or right to construct their own social reality.

Rosabeth Moss Kanter observed that "powerlessness corrupts and absolute powerlessness corrupts absolutely."[48] People who have little power will tend to hoard what little power they do have and lord it over others. Social leaders enrich and empower their followers. They "use their power to transform their followers into leaders."[49] As a social leader, you give of yourself so that your followers move ahead on a journey to find their dreams, so that in struggling and working together, they learn to overcome obstacles, achieve goals, and become the kind of people they want to become.

Macro social work "leaders make heroes of other people."[50] It is the people who hear the call, make the commitment, endure the struggles, face the trials, move through transitions, and engage in a journey that they walk together toward a common goal that they eventually win. Once the goal is won, the community becomes the promise for themselves and their children. It is theirs to own and to possess.

KEY CONCEPTS

leadership

management

paternalism

authoritarianism

patriarchal leadership

social leadership

partnership

task behavior

relationship behavior

situational leadership

member maturity

HT/LR

HT/HR

LT/HR

LT/LR

telling leadership style

selling leadership style

facilitating leadership style

coaching leadership style

group life-cycle leadership

forming stage of the group

norming stage of the group

storming stage of the group

performing stage of the group

QUESTIONS FOR DISCUSSION

1. Have you ever exerted leadership? What did you do? What did you learn about yourself? What did you learn about leadership?

2. What leadership opportunities do you have around you? Have you considered trying to become a leader?

3. Do you have a vision for something that could change—at your school, work, church, or in your community? How would you go about improving it?

4. Look over the story of Jane Addams at the beginning of this chapter.
   a. What leadership preferences did she exhibit?
   b. What does this tell you about macro social work leadership?

5. Kouzas and Posner say that "Leaders take us on journeys where we have never been before."
   a. How does this statement relate to the social leadership?
   b. Does a community go on a journey?
   c. How does that journey inform the individuals who are the community's members?
   d. How do the personal journeys of community members inform the larger community?
   e. Can all members of a community also be its leaders?
   f. Do leaders take people on journeys, or do the people themselves decide on their own journeys and walk their journeys with the help of one another?

6. Burton Gummer, one of the influential writers in macro social work, asserts that social work leadership has declined in recent years.
   a. What is your opinion about this statement?
   b. Is social work leadership on the decline?
   c. If you believe it is, to what do you attribute this?
   d. Is this something about which social work ought to be concerned? Why or why not?

7. Compare the two statements below. What are the strengths and weaknesses of each statement?
   a. "Developing and promulgating …a vision… is the highest calling and truest purpose of leadership."—Burt Nanus
   b. "The purpose of social leadership is to make leaders of others."—The Author

---

CHECKLIST 4.2

Leadership Development Inventory

This inventory will give you a chance to explore more deeply leadership skills connected with your functions and discover which ones you may need to work on. First, read through the following inventory deciding where you are ok, which you need to do more of, and which you need to do less of. Keep in mind that thinking needs to be balanced by feeling, and sensing needs to be balanced by intuition.

	ok	need to do more	need to do less
Thinking Functions			
making up my mind firmly	___	___	___
organizing myself	___	___	___
being consistent	___	___	___
relying on my logic	___	___	___
reaching objectives on schedule	___	___	___
making tough decisions	___	___	___
facing unpleasant tasks	___	___	___
being efficient	___	___	___
living by the rules	___	___	___
holding to my principles	___	___	___
Intuitive Functions			
conceiving new possibilities	___	___	___
using my imagination	___	___	___
enjoying being good in lots of areas	___	___	___
looking to the future	___	___	___
looking forward to challenges	___	___	___
being interested in growth	___	___	___
showing enthusiasm for projects	___	___	___
Feeling Functions			
needing approval	___	___	___
being sensitive to others	___	___	___
being loyal to others	___	___	___
valuing harmonious relations	___	___	___
persevering	___	___	___
being conciliatory	___	___	___
concerned with quality	___	___	___
raising ethical questions	___	___	___
Sensing Functions			
focusing on the here and now	___	___	___
being good at practical application	___	___	___
going step by step	___	___	___
being good at details	___	___	___
dealing with facts	___	___	___
enjoying hands-on work	___	___	___
following plans	___	___	___

After you have finished the inventory, break into groups of 4 or 5 and share what this exercise says about your skills.

CHECKLIST 4.3

Leadership Skills Inventory

Leadership is a learning process that occurs as members interact with one another and with the leader. This checklist will help assess your leadership skills. Mark those items that you do often, sometimes, or never. Is there a pattern in the issues you have marked? What do these patterns say about you? What areas would you like to improve?

Leadership Skills Inventory

1. I seek out the lead in groups or situations.
   Often _____ Sometimes _____ Never _____

2. I wait for others to take over.
   Often _____ Sometimes _____ Never _____

3. People follow my ideas.
   Often _____ Sometimes _____ Never _____

4. People ignore my ideas.
   Often _____ Sometimes _____ Never _____

5. It is easy for me to let others take the lead.
   Often _____ Sometimes _____ Never _____

6. Is it hard to let go of the lead.
   Often _____ Sometimes _____ Never _____

7. It is easy for me to accept responsibility in a group.
   Often _____ Sometimes _____ Never _____

8. I resist doing things in a group.
   Often _____ Sometimes _____ Never _____

10. I have been elected to an office in a group.
    Often _____ Sometimes _____ Never _____

11. I avoid trying out for office.
    Often _____ Sometimes _____ Never _____

12. I end up taking over in groups whether I want to or not.
    Often _____ Sometimes _____ Never _____

13. I do not take over in groups even when I want to.
    Often _____ Sometimes _____ Never _____

14. I need to have others recognize what I am saying.

Often _____ Sometimes_____ Never _____

15. I need to have people like me in a group.
Often _____ Sometimes_____ Never _____

16. I am persistent in getting something done.
Often _____ Sometimes_____ Never _____

17. I tend to let nature take its course.
Often _____ Sometimes_____ Never _____

Look over your lists and choose some areas about which you would like to get feedback. Your instructor will help divide you into dyads. In the dyad, one person shares an item and the partner gives feedback. Reverse roles. Share as many items and give as much feedback to one another as time allows.

CHECKLIST 4.4

Membership Skills Inventory

Through interaction with one another and with a leader, individuals acquire skills in being group members. The following checklist will help assess your membership skills. Mark those items that you do often, sometimes, or never. Is there a pattern in the issues you have marked? What do these patterns say about you? What areas would you like to improve?

Membership Skills Inventory

1. I feel exposed in a group.
Often _____ Sometimes_____ Never _____

2. I am in control of my thoughts and ideas in a group.
Often _____ Sometimes_____ Never _____

3. I am the first person to break a silence in a group.
Often _____ Sometimes_____ Never _____

4. I hold back until everyone else has spoken.
Often _____ Sometimes_____ Never _____

5. I can't wait to get things off my chest in groups.
Often _____ Sometimes_____ Never _____

6. I have difficulty speaking my mind in groups.
Often _____ Sometimes_____ Never _____

7. I over disclose at the beginning of a group.
Often _____ Sometimes_____ Never _____

8. I under disclose in group meetings.
Often _____ Sometimes_____ Never _____

9. I am comfortable fitting in with others.
Often _____ Sometimes_____ Never _____

10. I feel that I compromise myself in group situations.
Often _____ Sometimes_____ Never _____

11. People seem to enjoy me in groups.
Often _____ Sometimes_____ Never _____

12. I seem like a problem to others in groups.
Often _____ Sometimes_____ Never _____

13. I generally include myself in groups.
Often _____ Sometimes_____ Never _____

14. I tend to be on the fringe in groups.
Often _____ Sometimes_____ Never _____

15. I am comfortable with the role that I play in a group.
Often _____ Sometimes_____ Never _____

16. I feel that I get stuck with a role that I don't like.
Often _____ Sometimes_____ Never _____

EXERCISE 4.2

Visionary Leadership

According to leadership theorist Burt Nanus, "The leader selects and articulates the target in the future external environment toward which the organization would direct its energies. This is the meaning of vision."[51] Nanus also asserts:

The forces unleashed by the right vision can be summarized in one word that has become the theme for leadership in the 1990s: empowerment. The vision is the beacon, the sense of destination shared by the people who care most about the organization's future. Once people buy into the vision, they possess the authority, that is, they are empowered to take actions that advance the vision, knowing that such actions will be highly valued and considered legitimate, and productive by all those who share the dream…. Vision is not a luxury but a necessity; without it, workers drift in confusion or, worse, act at cross purposes. As the wise old proverb of Italian sailors states, "Who will not be ruled by the rudder must be ruled by the rock." In the end, therefore, human behavior in organizations is very much shaped by a shared vision of a better tomorrow. Developing and promulgating such a vision is the highest calling and truest purpose of leadership, for people instinctively follow the fellow who follows the dream.[52]

Discuss in class the following questions.

1. Do you agree or disagree with Nanus's assertion that the meaning of vision is when "the leader selects and articulates the target" and that empowerment is "unleashed by the right vision"?

Is empowerment unleashed when the right vision is articulated by a leader? If you disagree, what is unleashed when a leader selects a target?

2. Nanus asserts that when people "buy into the vision, they possess the authority, that is, they are empowered to take actions that advance the vision, knowing that such actions will be highly valued and considered legitimate." Critique this statement. Is it consistent or inconsistent? Do you need someone's authority to advance a vision? What do you think would be the consequences for someone who decided not to "buy into the vision"?

3. If you did not have a leader's vision to guide you, is it inevitable that you will "drift in confusion or, worse, act at cross purposes" with others? What does this statement imply about people's capacity for self-direction, cooperation, and self-motivation?

4. What does the "wise old proverb of Italian sailors" mean? Is being "ruled by a rudder or by a rock" the only two options that people have? What other options are there?

5. Do you agree or disagree that "developing and promulgating…a vision is the highest calling and truest purpose of leadership"? If you disagree, what is the highest calling and truest purpose of leadership?

6. If you were truly empowered, would you "instinctively follow the fellow who follows the dream"? If Nanus was your leader, what would happen if you followed your own dream? Would Nanus applaud your individuality, or would he try all the harder to induce you to conform to his dream?

EXERCISE 4.3
Kissinger on Leadership

Henry Kissinger (former Harvard professor, diplomat, and secretary of state under Richard Nixon) once said, "The task of the leader is to get people from where they are to where they have not been. The public does not fully understand the world into which it is going. Leaders must invoke an alchemy of great vision. Those leaders who do not are ultimately judged failures, even though they may be popular at the time."[53] Exercise your critical skills and critique Kissinger's statement.

1. Do you need a leader to get you from where you are to where you have not been? Why or why not?

2. Do you agree that "the public does not fully understand the world into which it is going"? If you agree, why do you suppose people do not understand, and why is it that only leaders have such understanding? If you disagree, what does this assertion tell you about attitudes of our top leaders?

3. Is a leader who does not invoke an alchemy of great vision ultimately a failure? Why or why not?

EXERCISE 4.4
Qualities of Good Leaders

The following is a list of some qualities of good leaders. Read over this list. Are there qualities missing that you think are important? What do you think are the most important ones? How difficult are these qualities to achieve? In class, spend some time discussing what makes a good leader.

1. Good leaders enable people to become and feel empowered. Members feel significant and are infused with purpose. Each person can make a difference.

2. Good leaders inspire values of shared compassion. In a caring community, each person, no matter how small, has meaning. A community is judged to be good to the extent to which it prizes and values its weakest members.

3. Good leaders insure that learning and competence matter. In communities that prize learning, there is no failure, only mistakes that give us feedback and tell us what to do next so members can learn and grow.

4. Good leaders help people feel a sense of unity. They develop community and cohesion where everyone is welcome and has a role to play. Everyone is wanted and needed.

5. Good leaders help members develop a sense of security and trust not only in the leader but in one another.

6. A good leader will display reliability. Reliability means constancy. You know where you stand.

7. A good leader is honest and trustworthy. Integrity means that the leader has an inner core that commands allegiance to higher values and standards. A good leader does not compromise these values for expediency.

EXERCISE 4.5

What Kind of Leader Am I?: A Feedback Exercise

This exercise will require some self-disclosure, skill in communication, active listening, and feedback.[54] The instructor should review active listening skills and characteristics of how to offer feedback.

First, think of the person who is the most admired leader that you have ever known. Picture that person. Think of all the characteristics you admire most about that leader. Write down at least five of those traits that you admire most.

Next, think of a leader you dislike or think is the worst leader you have ever known. Write down five of the characteristics of that leader.

These lists give a rough idea of the qualities in leaders that you value. What do these lists say about your own leadership values?

The instructor will list the positive and negative characteristics in two columns side by side on a board in rough alphabetical order. You now have a composite of the leadership qualities that this class values and those which are not valued in leaders. What patterns are there? What does this say about the kinds of things this class values and does not value?

The next phase of this exercise involves both positive and negative feedback. Choose someone in class with whom you are comfortable in sharing feedback. Each person should silently write down three items from each list that describe positive and negative leadership traits of their partner.

After each partner has written the traits, one partner solicits feedback. First do the positive characteristics. Spend some time discussing why your partner chose those about you. Then disclose the characteristics that you chose about your partner. How close were the ones you chose and those your partner chose?

Now that you have shared positive characteristics, move on to the negative ones. Share feedback. After you are finished, your instructor will lead a discussion of the entire exercise. What did you learn about your leadership style?

EXERCISE 4.6

Matching Leaders and Macro Social Work Arenas

Listed below are some fields of macro social work practice as well as prominent social leaders and change agents. How many leaders can you associate with a field of macro social work? If these leaders are not immediately recognizable, look them up in the *Encyclopedia of Social Work* or a general encyclopedia. Some leaders may be associated with several fields of macro social work.

1 Community Development
2 Community Organization
3 Program Development
4 Administration
5 Social Policy
6 Politics
7 Social Action

Toyohiko Kagawa ____	Frederick Douglass ____
Jane Addams ____	Florence Kelly ____
Saul Alinsky ____	Homer Folks ____
Sir Robert Baden-Powell ____	Lilian Wald ____
Canon Samuel Barnett ____	Grace Abbott ____
William Booth ____	Mary Simkhovitch ____
Edolphus Townes ____	Clifford Beers ____
Charles Loring Brace ____	St. Frances Cabrini ____
Mary Ann Mikulski ____	Clara Barton ____
Dorothea Dix ____	Whitney M. Young Jr. ____
Michael Harrington ____	Mary Parker Follett ____
Harry Hopkins ____	W.E.B. DuBois ____
Harriet Tubman ____	Booker T. Washington ____
Si Kahn ____	Dorothy Day ____
George Wiley ____	Jeanette Rankin ____
Roy Wilkins ____	Sojourner Truth ____
Sir George Williams ____	St. Elizabeth Ann Seton ____

EXERCISE 4.7

Leaders or Managers

Managers sometimes try to appear as if they are social leaders. The appropriation of management as leadership causes confusion. Stephen Robbins asserts that managers are charged with achieving organizational goals, and power is a means for facilitating that achievement. Managerial power "focuses on tactics for gaining compliance." Exerting power in organizations "does not require goal compatibility, merely dependence." In contrast, leadership, says Robbins, "requires some congruence between the goals of the leader and the led."[55]

Warren Bennis describes the difference between leadership and management this way: "Leaders are people who do the right thing; managers are people who do things right. Both roles are crucial, but they differ profoundly." According to Bennis, American organizations are "underled and overmanaged. They do not pay enough attention to doing the right thing, while they pay too much attention to doing things right." Bennis argues that one antidote for the managerial dilemma is to train individuals to "lead," which means doing the morally right thing, rather than training them to be managers who apply administrative power to exact people's compliance to achieve organizational goals.[56]

Break into small groups and discuss the following questions. After you have come to a conclusion, return to the class as a whole and share with the others.

1. Bennis says, "Leaders are people who do the right thing; managers are people who do things right." What does this statement mean? Do you agree with it or disagree? Can you think of leaders who have done the wrong thing? Can you think of managers who have done the right thing?

2. Are leaders and managers crucial to the operation of our society? Is it crucial for people to be led by others? Why is it crucial that some people be managed? What would happen if people took responsibility for their own leadership and for their own self-management?

3. Do you agree with Bennis's distinction that the roles of leader and manager differ profoundly? For example, Bennis asserts that they are qualitatively different. Peter Block asserts, on the other hand, that they are only different in the extent to which they are paternalistic. Leadership, Block says, is a "soft" form of making decisions for others. Management tends to be autocratic. Who is right, and why?

4. Should social work train selected people to be leaders, or should social work assist as many people as possible to exercise leadership? Why?

5. What is the difference between what Robbins and Bennis mean by being a leader and what is described in this chapter as social leadership?

ADVANCED EXERCISE 4.8
Critical Incidents

The incidents described below are all real-life situations that first-line social work supervisors have faced in their jobs. These incidents will help you apply the group-centered leadership model described in this chapter. Before you decide on a response to each incident, spend some time diagnosing the stage of the group (forming, norming, storming, or performing). Make sure that your decision is not just formed "intuitively." You should be able to point to a specific indicator that tells you what stage the group is operating at. Once you have grasped the level of the group by means of facts, then apply your intuition to think about what processes may be occurring that are not immediately obvious.

Then, try to think about how you can help the group move ahead in resolving the issues that confront it. For example, how would you assist members become more ready or more willing, more self-directing, and more independently operating?

Once you have decided these issues, write down your "verbatim response" to the incident. A verbatim response is the exact words you would say to intervene in the situation.

In class, your instructor may form you into triads and ask that you first discuss your various diagnoses. After the class regroups, the instructor may ask for volunteers to present their diagnoses. After discussing the diagnoses and coming to some consensus, the instructor may ask for responses. Individuals or groups may contribute what they consider their best response given the discussion that has preceded. The instructor can also add comments. Keep in mind that there are no absolutely right or wrong answers, because a response must be based on one's perception of the situation. However, some responses may be more appropriate than others.

Incident 1
Group Complaint The task unit has been in some confusion for a while. The rules in the agency have changed often and roles have become unclear. As a result, performance is down. In the middle of an informational meeting, members begin to voice general complaints about lack of direction and confusion. It is clear that people are frustrated and that your unit is looking to you for direction. Underneath is an implied challenge. The meeting is beginning to get loud. Some members look at you helplessly.

Given what you know about the life cycle of the group, what is your diagnosis about what is occurring in this group at this moment? Based on your understanding of group leadership styles at this stage of the group, what is your verbatim response?

Incident 2

Conflict Decision You have been supervising a unit for more than a year. Most members have been doing well individually, but there are conflicts among members over what you consider to be petty things, such as desk space or having a window. Overall, the unit is doing adequately, but its performance could be improved.

You are trying to figure out whether to deal with the conflicts on an individual basis, with the entire group, or whether you should let the group work the issues out on their own. What reasons could lay behind the conflicts? How would you resolve the conflicts? Would you deal with them individually with group members or with the group as a whole, or would you let the group itself try to work them out?

Incident 3

What Are the Rules? You have taken over a new unit. Although it has been performing fairly well, it has never been one of the high-achieving units. You have met with each one of the members individually and know there is some anxiety about your leadership style. Your first meeting went well. It is your second meeting. You are finishing your agenda when one of the more verbal members, who is one of the lowest achievers in the unit, looks you in the eye and in a challenging voice asks, "What are you going to do about the smoking in this building? I have allergies and the smoke is killing me." The group looks at you expectantly. Some members are nodding their heads in agreement, while others who are smokers avoid eye contact.

The entire group waits for your response. What stage do you think the group is in? What dynamics are occurring in the task group? Is there more going on than a simple request to deal with smoking? Do you respond individually to the staff member about smoke or do you address the issue with the entire group? What stage is the group at, and what is your verbatim response?

Incident 4

The Impossible Task The agency has been poorly managed for some time. Layoffs have occurred. As a result, your unit has been expected to pick up some of the extra work. The entire staff is worried about more layoffs, and many are behind because of the added cases. You have

seen individuals become increasingly tardy and calling in sick, creating even more of a backlog. Morale is at the lowest ebb you have ever seen. Your supervisor has been on your back for accountability. You know that many of your staff are stressed. You call a unit meeting to try to deal with performance and with stress.

Jack says, "I just can't do any more. I don't know what they expect out of us. You can't get blood out of a turnip." The other members of the unit nod their heads. There follows a long period of silence. The unit seems glum.

What is your diagnosis of the situation in the unit? What would you do at this point?

Incident 5

Who Is Responsible? It is the early phase of a participative management project. The task-group members are supposed to be skilled and work independently, and they are expected to develop a new and creative process in their work area. After meeting with them several times to get them started, you have generally let them alone. On one of your visits to the group, you inquire about the status of the project and are surprised to hear Janet say, "I'm getting frustrated. I thought you were supposed to tell us what to do—otherwise how can we know what to do? We're getting nowhere this way." The group turns to observe your reaction.

What is your diagnosis of what has happened in this group? What is your response?

Incident 6

Don't Tell Me What to Do Your unit is composed of highly skilled, technically proficient workers. They are used to working on their own and obtain satisfaction from making their own decisions and following them through. They see themselves as competent professionals. While they have never enjoyed the paperwork end of the job, they have generally managed it satisfactorily. New, more stringent, and time-consuming paperwork requirements, however, have just been developed which require more work and are more complicated. Your efforts at giving information about how to meet the requirements have met with some resistance. As you monitor the unit, you find that the new paperwork is not being done as well as it could be.

In a meeting, you propose additional training. Members look unresponsive, and Henry finally breaks the silence by saying, "We all know how to do our jobs. And we do them pretty well. I don't want anyone telling me what to do." Members nod their heads.

What is the stage of this group and what is your verbatim response?

ADDITIONAL READING

Social Leadership

Peter Block. *Stewardship: Choosing Service Over Self- Interest*. San Francisco: Berrett-Koehler Publishers, 1993.

B. Lakey, G. Lakey, R. Napier, and J. Robinson. *Grassroots and Nonprofit Leadership: A Guide for Organizations in Changing Times*. Philadelphia: New Society Publishers, 1995.

Robert K. Greenleaf. *Servant Leadership: A Journey Into the Nature of Legitimate Power and Greatness*. New York: Paulist Press, 1977.

A Portnoy. *Leadership: What Every Leader Should Know About People*. Englewood Cliffs, NJ: Prentice Hall, 1986.

H. Tichy, and M. A. Devanna. *The Transformational Leader*. New York: John Wiley and Sons, 1986.

Conventional Managerial Leadership

Warren G. Bennis and Burt Nanus. *Leaders: Strategies for Taking Charge*. New York: Harper and Row, 1986.

Sheila Bethel. *Making a Difference: Twelve Qualities That Make You a Leader*. New York: Putnam, 1990.

James MacGregor Burns. *Leadership*. New York: Harper and Row, 1978.

Ernest Flores. *The Nature of Leadership for Hispanics and Other Minorities*. Saratoga, CA: Century Twenty One, 1981.

John Gardner. *On Leadership*. New York: Free Press, 1990.

Paul Hersey. *The Situational Leader: The Other 59 Minutes*. New York: Warner Books, 1985.

William Hitt. *The Model Leader: A Fully Functioning Person*. Columbus, OH: Battelle Press, 1993.

James Kouzes and Barry Posner. *The Leadership Challenge: How to Get Extraordinary Things Done in Organizations*. San Francisco: Jossey Bass, 1987.

James Kouzes and Barry Posner. *Credibility: How Leaders Gain It and Why People Demand It*. San Francisco: Jossey-Bass, 1993.

Followership

Goeffrey Bellman. *Getting Things Done When You Are Not in Charge: How to Succeed From a Support Position*. New York: Simon and Schuster, 1992.

Robert Kelly. *The Power of Followership: How to Create Leaders, People Who Want to Follow and Followers Who Lead Themselves*. New York: Doubleday, 1992.

Small Group Leadership

Dorwin Cartwright and Alvin Zander. *Group Dynamics: Research and Theory*. 3d ed. New York: Harper and Row, 1968.

Donelson R. Forsyth. *Group Dynamics*. 2d ed. Pacific Grove, CA: Brooks/Cole, 1990.

Ronald W. Toseland and Robert F. Rivas. *An Introduction to Group Work Practice*. 2d ed. Boston: Allyn and Bacon, 1995.

Stewart. L. Tubbs. *A Systems Approach to Small Group Interaction*. 4th ed. New York: McGraw-Hill, 1992.

Alvin Zander. *Making Groups Effective*. San Francisco: Jossey-Bass, 1983.

Peter Koestenbaum. *Leadership: The Inner Side of Greatness*. San Francisco: Jossey Bass, 1987.

PART Two

The Practice of Social Work With Communities

Social work's mission should be to build a meaning, a purpose and a sense of obligation for the community. It is only by creating a community that we establish a basis for commitment, obligation, and social support. We must build communities that are excited about their child care systems, that find it exhilarating to care for the mentally ill and the frail aged, and make demands upon people to contribute, and to care for one another.

Psychotherapy will not enable us to do that, and the further down the psychotherapeutic path social workers go, the less effective they will be in achieving their true mission.[1]

Harry Specht and Mark Courtney

Community social work *is* social work[2]

Hans Falck

A quiet revolution is revitalizing neighborhood after neighborhood across the North American continent. Social workers involved in this revolution are promoting civic involvement, exerting leadership to solve some of our most intractable social problems, and working to bring about fundamental social changes in Canada and the United States. The key to this revolution is community.

Community social workers are helping us create social goods, capture a vision of a good society, and stimulate the growth of a new substantive democracy. They are assisting people to develop social thinking, giving substance to the communal social self and a means of escape from apathy, alienation, and paternalism, so common in North American culture.

With the assistance of community social workers, neighborhoods are resisting the powerful cultural tides that threaten to drown their autonomy and overwhelm their uniqueness. Where this resistance is most effective, it helps us find meaningful relationships, a renewed sense of purpose, a center of engagement that binds us more closely to one another. In locations where community has been diminished and degraded by modern megastructures, community social workers are helping to restore the "practices of commitment that still have animating power" in society.[2] When we become a part of these changes, we become empowered to see change as not only permissible but possible. We become determiners of our own future, not passive recipients of a future handed to us by others. We develop the power to critically examine the social world in which we find ourselves. We come to see society not as a static, impenetrable presence, but as a reality in process of transformation.

In Part 2 of this book, The Practice of Social Work With Communities, you will explore how people are mobilizing themselves for action and taking responsibility for the life of their communities. You will learn about the importance of community in constructing the self and shaping the lives of its members, as well as providing a medium for relating to the larger, more impersonal megastructures of society. You will discover how community social workers facilitate this effort by means of community social planning groups in cooperation with local government. You will learn how community development corporations have revolutionized the field of community development. You will find a new and exciting role for social workers who want to use their creative, entrepreneurial skills to help people gain economic independence by developing business-oriented corporations.

You will discover that community organizations, coalitions, and federations are slowly reshaping the social landscape of North America. You will learn how social work community organizers are using faith-based organizations to gain political empowerment and reclaim community after community.

You will discover how you too can become engaged in this quiet community revolution and make a lasting impact on hundreds or thousands of people's lives. You will find that you can become a part of a renewed social work reclaiming its original heritage, building meaning, purpose, and a sense of obligation for the community, and revitalizing the lives of people from the bottom up.

WEB SITES

Alliance for National Renewal
   http://www.ncl.org/anr/index.htm

National Association for Community Leadership
   http://www.communityleadership.org/

National Community Building Network
   http://www.ncbn.org/welcome.html

A good resource for other community-related websites is the Chronicle of Philanthropy, *Non-Profit Handbook,* 1255 23rd St., Washington, DC 20037; Phone: 202-466-1227.

5

Communities

Seek the welfare of the city where I have sent you into exile, and pray to the Lord on its behalf, for in its welfare you will find your welfare.

Letter to the Exiles in Babylon[1]

We must delight in each other, make other's conditions our own, rejoice together, mourn together, labor and suffer together, always having before our eyes our community as members of the same body.[2]

John Winthrop

Ideas in This Chapter

THE MIRACLE
OF LE CHAMBON

A plague was sweeping through the Western world. In the name of progress it produced a holocaust that wiped out one third of the entire Jewish population with the complicity of established religion and occupied governments. In 1940 France fell to Nazi Germany, and by 1941 the puppet Vichy government began the systematic deportation of the Jews. The Nazis appeared triumphant. To the people of the area of Le Chambon Sur Lignon in Southwestern France, however, that was beside the point. Here, in the course of four long years, 5,000 Jews were sheltered by 5,000 Christians.[3]

Outwardly the people of Le Chambon, a poor farming community 350 miles south of Paris, were much like any other small French village. Most were peasants and villagers descended from Huguenots, the first Protestants in Catholic France. Once they too had been persecuted for their beliefs, their rights abolished, their men deported to slave in galleys, and their women imprisoned in towers where they left notes to their families that said "resist." The persecution they called "the wilderness" lasted for 100 years.

In spite of this, the people of Le Chambon clung to their beliefs, their land, and their community. The memory of their past was the key to their survival. In every challenge there would be an echo of their forebears' faith and struggle. It was not only their religious beliefs, it was the persecution they endured that made them different. At the beginning of the twentieth century, when industry exploited women and children in mass numbers, Le Chambon welcomed sickly working-class women and children from neighboring cities and took them in. In the 1930s they sheltered refugees from the Spanish Civil War, and in 1940 they took in "guests," offering them hospitality because "it was only a natural thing to do." Nothing that occurred during war years was unfamiliar to the people of Le Chambon.

In the beginning, only a few Jews made their way to this tiny corner of the world. At great risk to themselves, villagers took in the Jews. The Jews kept coming and the people of Le Chambon kept taking them in: individuals, couples, families, children, the elderly, those who could pay and those who could not—doctors, merchants, intellectuals, and homemakers from Paris and Warsaw, Vienna and Prague.

One day during a church service a man came into the congregation. "I have," said he, "three old testaments" meaning there were three Jews who needed shelter. Without hesitation, an old farmer raised his hand. "I'll take them," he said. Never once did the people of Le Chambon ask if the strangers were Jews, even though they knew that they were. To them it did not matter. They took in the strangers, protected them, and helped them on their way.

The day before the people of Le Chambon were threatened with occupation by the Nazis, Rev. Trocme delivered a sermon that exemplified their resolve and the roots of their resistance. "The duty of Christians is to resist the violence that will be brought to bear on their consciences through the weapons of the spirit. We will resist whatever our adversaries demand of us that are contrary to the orders of the Gospel. We will also fear, but without pride and without hate." It was a conspiracy of compassion.

The people of Le Chambon started schools for the refugees, boarded the Jews, and even helped them observe their own religious services. They began a center for forging documents, identification cards, and passports, giving the Jews false identities. Even when Nazis occupied Le Chambon, they continued to hide the Jews, once in a hotel directly across the street from where soldiers were bivouacked. Le Chambon became a center of the French resistance.

The community of Le Chambon and the Jewish people were anchored in community. The Jews were the people of God, and the Huguenots of Le Chambon were also a people of God. The Nazis, on the other hand, considered themselves the epitome of progress, modernity, and technological efficiency. How they despised and attempted to destroy community! And yet, the community of compassion and resistance survived, while only a few short years later, all that remained of the Third Reich was the memory of appalling death and destruction.

WHAT YOU WILL LEARN
IN THIS CHAPTER

Our society is building a culture in which a sense of community tends to be lacking. For a large number of us, community exists in only marginal ways, in increasingly diminished form, and comprises little existential space in our lives. The result is that many of us live a lonely, isolated, and alienated existence. Children and adolescents have fewer opportunities for healthy social-group engagement. Most adults find their main source of meaning in career-oriented pursuits, often in large impersonal organizational systems.

Yet, as you will discover in this chapter, community is among the more important social structures that we construct, if not our most necessary and vital social form. You will learn how community is the means by which your self comes into being. You will discover how community supports your self in the midst of personal, social, and political crises that megastructures of society impose on it. You will find that community is the way that we are transformed into a people who solve our common problems and generate a culture that is transferred from generation to generation.

You will explore four kinds of communities with which macro social workers become engaged: modern communities, ontological communities or "communities of meaning," traditional communities, and communities of diversity. While community *seems* to be disappearing, you will find that the triumph of rational artificial social systems is an illusory victory. Community is a perennial and universal component of the human condition. Out of the old forms of neighborhood and community the seeds of new communal forms are, even now, beginning to be generated by macro social workers.

WHAT IS COMMUNITY?

Communities are natural human associations based on ties of relationship and shared experiences in which we mutually provide meaning in our lives, meet needs, and accomplish interpersonal goals. Our predisposition to community insures that we become the persons we were meant to become, discover meaning, generate ethical values, and develop a culture which would be impossible for single, isolated individuals to accomplish alone.

When we talk about community, we talk about two things simultaneously. Community is located in space and time and it exists beyond space and time. Community is embodied in a place, structure, and presence, but community transcends location; it cannot be confined by structure or mere history.

Embodied Community

Every one of us needs community. Community arises spontaneously because of an innate sociality of the human condition. With relatively rare exceptions community has been *the* form of human associated life by which people have related throughout history. Your self cannot, in fact, reach its full realization in isolation, but *only* as you are nurtured, guided, and suffused with the life of the community in which you exist.

Localized community needs to be embodied to have existence. In its purest sense, community is an arena of social interaction, a milieu of social relationships in which we engage one another at a time and in a place where we gather together. For many communities to have permanence, they often become identified with physical space that the community claims as its own. This could be a territory or a neighborhood that we identify with a name and includes homes, schools, and shops. Communities such as a local church, neighborhood, or ethnic or civic association often develop a structure or a form of association, infuse it with values, and derive meaning from it. The location or the structure becomes the embodiment of and symbolizes community. Thus it is appropriate to talk about community as a neighborhood or association that exists in space and time, that has permanence and structure.

Transcendent Community

Although a community can be found in a locality or be embodied by a structural form, community is never simply a static physical location that we inhabit, as social ecologists assert; nor is it merely a structure or mechanical process, as systems theorists suggest. Community is the *act* by which we engage one another, experience relationships, and become a people. Wherever humans exist, we spontaneously seek and form community.

Communities are an indelible component of the human condition, not relative to a particular historical era, place, or time. Neither are communities unique to one race, national, or cultural group. Community transcends history and cannot be contained by mere history. Deeply rooted in our nature, community may be said to be a universal human phenomenon, not contingent on circumstances.

Community transcends location. As people in community move from place to place, we carry our community with us. When the nation of Israel was destroyed and most of her people were exiled to Babylon in 597 B.C., they lost their land, but they never lost themselves, their community. They were then, and 2,600 years later remain, a people, a community, regardless of where they are located.

Community transcends its structure. The original group that called themselves "people of the Way" was a small association whose members met in the Temple at Jerusalem and in one another's homes, and who owned everything in common.[4] Christian churches today are far different from those original communities in the way they are structured and governed, and in the manner and language in which worship is conducted. Yet they remain communities united in a common belief and heritage.

Community transcends time. A community exists before we were born and will live on after we die. We develop a shared memory and obtain a sense of ourselves by means of our common history together. The symbols and meaning that community incorporates, while originating in time, become timeless.

There is not just one model of community or one community ideal. Each community is a unique blending of the people of which it is composed. The many good communities that come into being add to the shape and texture of human existence. The more communities that develop, therefore, the more opportunities for us to explore alternative ways of being in the world, and different ways of achieving richness of character.

THE ROLE OF COMMUNITY IN MODERN SOCIETY

Community provides at least three functions whenever or wherever it exits. Community is the source of the self. Community is the bearer of the self. Community is the means by which selves are transformed into humanity, into a people.

Community as a Source of the Self

Community is the means by which solitary, isolated human beings are transformed into persons.[5] Your self is a social self. This social self is the result of a complex process of engagement with particular others, groups, and the community as a whole.

The Social Self Community begins with a conception of the person. Individualism and psychological theory derived from it, for example, assert that you are always a unitary self. The word *individual* shares its derivation with *indivisible.* Our self is a unity that has its own separate existence and integrity. Psychologists understand that this unitary self arises from autonomously generated mechanisms of the mind, and that a troubled mind can be healed through its own self-reflection by means of psychotherapy.

In addition, most systems and social ecological theory are alike in seeing you as a responding organism who adapts to and is determined by natural laws and an ecology of systems processes in its wider social environment. You are perceived to be the product of social stimuli[6] that cause you to react in often predictable ways.

Contrary to popular belief, however, you do not exist as an indivisible unitary self. You do not entirely consist of an "inner" psyche full of perceptions, feelings, attitudes, and behaviors. "The individual is neither the product of impinging stimuli, nor a reflection of an overarching and overwhelming cultural system, nor an organism driven by and essentially determined by internal mechanisms like Freudian instincts."[7]

Neither are you an atomistic bit of social matter embedded in mechanistic systems determined by societal forces to which you must adapt. Nor are you a passive creature who merely responds to impersonal processes in your social environment. Macro social workers tend to resist the implications of social Darwinism, which proposes that the self in society develops like any other organic being—evolving according to laws of nature. We reject conventional wisdom that counsels people to recognize the inevitable course which nature is taking and conform to it.[8] Instead, most macro social workers assert that your "self is always a social self."[9] You consciously choose to become the person to which you aspire, aided by a community of other selves.

Self and the Other "The self arises from and becomes itself in relation with others."[10] This social self exists in what Alfred Schutz called the "we-relation" in which "interdependence rather than dependence characterizes the self's relation to society."[11] As Gibson Winter asserts, "We depend on each other in the 'we-relation' for the confirmation of our being-in-the-world. The possibility of actualization as self-in-the-world depends upon the intersubjective experience of self and other in the 'we-relation.' "[12]

You are an inherently meaning-creating creature who develops social relationships, interacts with others, and actively constructs your self with the help of the others. Your self becomes real as you engage others in mutuality. As you see yourself indirectly through the eyes of another, you become an object to yourself. When another person responds to you, you treat your self as an object[13] responding implicitly to your own behavior.[14] According to David Miller, you see yourself reflected back through the gestures, responses, and engagement of the other. As you observe those responses, you shape your response in terms of the self you intend to become,[15] often incorporating the response of the other within your own response. According to Miller, the attitude of the other is an essential component of your self—the social component. If your self is to form, you must become an object to yourself and at the same time incorporate the attitude of others as a necessary condition of the self you are becoming.[16]

The set of key persons or "significant others" supported by a chorus of less significant others in your community repetitively confirm your identity as a person. Moreover, you choose particular people who continuously affirm the self that you are forming, or you select others who provide responses that conform to the different aspects of the self you are shaping.[17] The quality of responses from others informs you about who you are, gives you opportunity to understand yourself, and provides you with the human material out of which you construct your self. You use your own seeing, reflecting, thinking, and doing as stimuli in creating your self,[18] and in the process you try out new and different behaviors. As you learn more about your self, you refine your choices, placing yourself in situations and among people who will assist you become the person you want to be.

Self and the Group   While you respond individually to others, even more importantly, you engage people in groups. Miller asserts that "no self can emerge apart from the other members of the group, and no self can emerge apart from being a participant

in a social act."[19] The various selves that are available to you in social groups become an integral part of your thinking. In taking the role of many others, and incorporating group attitudes into your self, you learn to take on different roles in different situations. "As individuals participate in group life, each person can represent the activities of the group within his or her own mind and act according to how he or she thinks others will act."[20]

The opportunity to imaginatively place yourself within a group and then directly engage it helps you develop the ability to understand a social situation as a whole. You intuitively assess what kind of role and response is called for and modify your verbal and nonverbal communication depending on the meaning, values, and self-identity that you intend to project into the group. You present your self to others in the group in ways you expect will evoke a response that will reinforce the image of yourself in the eyes of others. The group's response provides you with powerful messages of affirmation or disconfirmation. You learn alternative ways of being that add to your self-understanding. Group members reciprocally confirm their mutual identities. When you respond to the group's response, you increase members' understanding of you as well as their understanding of themselves. In the multiplicity of mutual confirmations, a larger perception of reality occurs. Members see others in ways they had not seen before, realize things about themselves that they had not known, and they begin to see themselves and others differently.

George Herbert Mead states that "what a human being *is* depends upon interaction with others. And what a human being *does* depends not simply upon what kind of person he or she is (personality), but upon the person's interaction with others. At the same time the individual is part of the interaction, acting and not merely reacting, creating and not merely being formed or controlled."[21]

The social group is an integral part of thinking in which we take on the role of others and incorporate the attitudes of those others into the self.[22] Children's groups, for example, provide the content of many selves with which its members can identify and in which children "give themselves to learning and practicing activities that define the self, entering into the shape of its character."[23] George Herbert Mead, in fact, viewed this process as the essence of intelligence, putting ourselves in the place of others, so that we become sensitive to feelings and attitudes toward ourselves and others.[24] This "social intelligence" is an essential component of social work. The more group situations we experience, therefore, the greater the repertoire of options available to us, and the richer and deeper our selves become.

Self and Community   The milieu of others and groups which provide the content of our self depends on the existence of community. Each of us "is rooted in a biological organism," Mead states, that "acquires a self only though its interaction with a community"[25] of other selves. According to Winter, community is *the* means by which "the 'me'—my self as social or seen from the perspective of significant others and the community in general—comes to be."[26] The task of creating our self is fundamentally a communal enterprise and speaks to the essential sociality of the human condition. "No individual exists without participation, and no personal being exists without communal being."[27]

Community does not determine the character of our self, but it offers each of us a variety of meanings, values, and situations which we can accept or reject. Our selves, as objects, decide which aspects of the community we want to identify with and incorporate. Our selves comes into being as a reflection of the attitudes, approvals, and meanings that are inherent in the community.[28] Our "person as a fully developed individual self is impossible without other fully developed selves."[29]

Community as a Bearer of the Self

While community is crucial in the construction of the self, the large impersonal institutions or "megastructures" of our organizational society pose a continuing threat to the integrity and development of the self. These threats create crises at the individual, social, and political levels.

Modernization has brought about a historically unprecedented dichotomy between public and private life in society. The most important large institution ordering public life is the modern state. In addition are the large economic conglomerates of capitalist enterprise, organized labor, public bureaucracies, and the organized professions. These institutions are called megastructures.[30] Their domain includes all of the important mechanisms that produce public and economic goods and services. They maintain the

infrastructures of our social environment. Megastructures dominate almost all of the economic, political, and social space we inhabit today. Social functions such as meaning, intimacy, and decision-making unavailable in the economy and left over from public life are relegated to individuals and families.

Each of us tends to live a split existence in the modern world. We migrate between the megastructures of public life, on the one hand, and microstructures of personal individual and family life on the other. This ongoing migration poses a triple crisis for us. It creates a *personal* crisis because megastructures come to be devoid of meaning and are viewed as artificial, unreal, or even malignant.[31] It imposes a *social* crisis as we carry on a balancing act between meeting our needs for intimacy and the impersonal demands of organizational society. The polarization of the individual and organizational megastructures creates a *political* crisis in which we are distanced from centers of power and are prevented from making decisions which really matter to us.

Personal Crisis   We search for personal meaning and transcendent purpose to which we can attach ourselves. When we look to megastructures, the market society puts us to work producing personal emptiness and then induces us to fill the void with a succession of products whose consumption, manufacturers promise, will give us the happiness we lack. We ultimately discover, however, that the megastructures of society are not intended to provide personal meaning. They do exactly the opposite. The highest "virtue" of these structures is their built-in functional capacity to dehumanize individuals in the interests of efficiency. Deceived by economic corporations, we are thrown back upon our own resources. "Left very much to our own devices, we become uncertain and anxious."[32] We become alienated from our selves and from others as well. Estranged and hungry for meaning, we live in the midst of a population of other likewise disconnected individuals who search for ultimate purpose but often cannot find it.

Social Crisis   The demands that our organizational society imposes on us to master technology, maintain a decent standard of living, and provide advantages to ourselves and our children place increasing burdens on family life and allow decreasing opportunity for meeting our social needs. Family life can go only so far in providing a complete range of relationships, and it is often stretched to the breaking point with the demands placed upon it.

Moreover, the fundamental premises on which North American society is based mitigate against the capacity of society to provide for a full social existence of intimate, close connections with others. While possessive individualism and ruthless self-interest provide us with freedom and opportunity, they leave little space beyond the self by which we can obtain social nurture. We experience an "absence of social life…intimated by a frequently expressed hunger for binding relationships."[33]

Organizational megastructures, furthermore, teach us to think functionally, ignore compassion,[34] and live with impersonality.[35] If we try to find in functional organizational structures a capacity for expressing feelings or values, we quickly discover that there is little place for such expression.

Political Crisis   Conventional wisdom maintains that government is "of the people and by the people," yet people are excluded from decisions that affect their lives on a daily basis. Modern political organizations rarely allow us to inject our common values into the decision-making process, or have a say about the ends of their decisions.[36] To do so would dilute the power of the few who decide for us and impair the ability of megastructures to operate with speed and precision to unambiguously carry out the directives of those in charge.

Without an institutionally reliable process of mediation between the individual and politics, the political order becomes detached from the realities of individual life. We learn to conform to decisions of others as if those decisions were our own and accept as a good bargain the surrender of our involvement in public affairs for the freedom to pursue our own private endeavors. The political megastructures of modern society create apathy, passivity, and disengagement from the political process, leaving us "without any sense of political belonging."[37]

Community Mediating Structures

Community helps obliterate each facet of the triple crisis that modernity imposes on us. Community dissolves the personal crisis of meaninglessness that megastructures create. Community provides an arena of sociality,

restoring intimacy and relationship in our lives. Community, particularly community organizations, reconnect us to political empowerment and decision-making.

Community Mediating Structures and the Personal Crisis   We are meaning-oriented creatures. Communities of meaning help overcome the personal alienation that megastructures create by providing a structure of belief, an opportunity to construct our own meaning, and the means to put our values into practice. Churches and community and ethnic associations provide belief structures and a basis of common understanding that strengthen us to withstand the dehumanization that megastructures impose on us. These belief structures are based on universal truths distilled from community sagas of the past, which provide focus, guidance, and direction as we walk our particular journeys. The truth embodied by the community not only constitutes a way of individual being in the world, of mere existence, but a way of life, of meaningful existence. Communities illuminate our human spirit in its quest for ultimate purpose by the beliefs that bind us together and the truths that they contain.

Not only are meanings shared in community, but community helps us cooperatively create meaning ourselves. When the communal belief structures are tested in new situations and are proved to be reliable and true, new meanings are constructed. As new meanings and shared identities are generalized for the entire community, we generate new understandings, and we take on unity of purpose. Community becomes a social process in which we form, sustain, and transform our world as we give meaning to it.

Managers of megastructures tend to assert that we can attain happiness by pursing our self-interest. Leaders of communities of meaning claim that we attain a meaningful existence by putting our values into practice for others. When members of community engage in action, not only do the values to which we aspire come into clear relief, but we develop commitment to those values and to one another. We generate meaning out of practicing the beliefs that we hold dear and the values we cherish. We make intimacy real by our commitments, caring, and self-sacrifice for the benefit of others. We become jointly oriented to a necessity of centering our lives on something larger than ourselves as the basis of a good life toward which we direct our efforts.[38]

Community resolves the personal crises that megastructures impose on our existence, assisting us to search for meaning and an end to alienation. In community we find a place to engage in truth building, and a way to put our beliefs and values into practice.

Community Mediating Structures and the Social Crisis   Community mediates between our need for intimate, personal connection with others and the emptiness that market structures impose on social life. Community can be a place of refuge from domination of the market society in which everything has a price, buying and selling become the preeminent activity of human beings, and we become commodities in the marketplace. In community we are prized, appreciated, and valued for ourselves, not what we produce. Communities, particularly communities of meaning, become social enclaves in a wider economizing society; they shelter us from the "getting and getting all the more" mode of being.

The more social relationships in community are shared, the more they become available to all. By fostering caring and committed social relationships, communities can become centers of sociality, helping overcome impersonality and loneliness in modern society. Some of the most important "products" of community are friendship, public spirit, social engagement, intimacy, nurture, and support, without which people live a shallow and lonely existence. Settlements, community centers, neighbor houses, churches, and group work agencies such as the Boy and Girl Scouts, YMCA, Jewish Community Centers, Boys and Girls Clubs and others help communities revitalize the social life of their members. They provide a safe and healthy social atmosphere by which we can find many points of access to relate to others.

Community Mediating Structures and the Political Crisis   Community mediates between the need to have our voices heard and the apathy, powerlessness, and lack of decision-making which political megastructures create. As community organizers help form people into coalitions to engage wider issues, we become activated, reconnected, and engaged in those political processes that affect our lives. Community organizations provide empowerment, which reduces political indifference and brings decision-making back to the level of ordinary people, where it counts. Community organizations help reduce the intimidation we

feel when we encounter massive governmental structures. They make megastructures more human, more reachable, more responsive, and therefore less alienating, distant, and oppressive.

Politically engaged community organizations no longer simply accept dominant power arrangements or the existing culture as givens. Community organizations help us shift the balance of power and make megastructures accountable and accessible to people by providing a collective means of engaging in decision-making at the grassroots.[39]

We learn that substantive democracy is "not synonymous with the centralized democratic state apparatus or the structure of mass representative constitutional democracy, nor will those structures be the vehicle of human liberation."[40] We become empowered to challenge social decisions, social structures, economic processes, and political policies that are unjust, and arrive at alternatives that are better.[41] We discover that political processes are not merely for those at the top, but the prerogative of those at the bottom.

Community as a Creator of Humanity

Community transcends the boundaries of social relationships to include broader public concerns. Community inevitably becomes engaged in wider public life when we collectively experience consciousness as having shared issues in common. At times these shared issues are social problems by which we come to believe that what we first may consider personal grievances are in fact socially grounded, that others suffer the same treatment, and that some form of broad-based collective action will result in social change. Social problems will not be solved without their mutual recognition by the community of people that bears them as part of their lived reality, or as John Dewey says, unless "affected aggregates become conscious of themselves as a community.[42]

At other times, however, the shared issue may be a social problem that affects some people, but becomes the concern of other communities. The people of Le Chambon, for example, took in Spanish refugees fleeing the fascist regime of Franco and Jews who sought shelter from the Nazis "because it was the natural thing to do." The memory of their own oppression compelled the Chambonoise to assist the Spanish refugees and Jews because they too were an oppressed people. The struggles of the Chambonoise formed them into a people whose communality connected them to others outside their territory.

In community, we interpret the uncertainties and unknowns of our existence, overcome adversity, and discover meaning. Out of those meanings, individuals can come to see themselves as a people and ultimately as human. The transcendent communal memories of shared suffering, injustice, and oppression, and the struggle to overcome adversity are the material out of which myth is born. Myths are universal truths distilled from stories of our collective endeavors, conflicts, successes and failures, victories and defeats. The collective myth is the truth of a society by which we find common identity, guidance, understanding, and rootedness. These universal truths are often commemorated in rituals of life passages, a coming together in celebrations, and in symbolic acts that have existential meaning for us. They "contain conceptions of character, what a good person is like, the virtues that define such character"[43] and the substance that relates them to other communities.

Community is a recipient of the collective history and culture that has gone before, contributing its own saga to the history of others who follow. We pour our experiences, understanding, and learning back into our community, adding to the cumulative wisdom for others who are passing this same way. Community is *the* means by which our individual selves become transformed into a people, and a people into humanity.[44] It has been and remains the way in which humanity is transferred from generation to generation.

TYPES OF COMMUNITY STRUCTURES

Macro social workers become involved with four types of community structures: modern communities, ontological communities, traditional communities and communities of diversity.

Modern Communities

Modern communities exist in neighborhood districts, ethnic neighborhoods, planned communities, low-income communities, towns, or villages. Some cities have well-defined neighborhoods. In San Francisco, for example, geography and ethnicity play a role in defin-

ing communities. Districts bear names that give these neighborhoods specific identities, such as Mission District, Potrero Hill, Twin Peaks, Noe Valley, The Marina, and Bernal Heights. People identify themselves with their neighborhoods and take pride in them.

Many neighborhoods also have an ethnic distinctiveness. San Francisco's Chinatown, for example, is world famous. Everyone in San Francisco knows Nihon-machi. It is the center of the Japanese-American community. The Mission District has a large percentage of the city's Chicano and Filipino population. Potrero Hill is still the home of San Francisco's Molokon Russians.

In many of our large cities, people sometimes live in planned neighborhoods. One kind of planned community for the affluent are townhouse communities, which often are completely enclosed so that only residents or guests can enter. Another kind of planned community is one consisting of mobile homes.

Increasingly in modern society, neighborhood becomes devoid of community either by choice or by circumstance. Neighborhoods are not always healthy, communally centered, and desirable places in which to live. People on the fringe of today's modern social systems, for example, may exist in remnants of neighborhoods that are weakened enclaves within the wider society. These areas become little islands that lack economic resources, leadership, goals, structure, and purpose. They exist among dispossessed homeless residents of deteriorating inner cities in Washington, D.C., and in the Bronx, New York. They include residents of low-income housing projects, in Cabrini Green, Chicago, and in Hunter's Point, San Francisco. They are neighborhoods of Vietnamese, Laotian, or Hmong immigrants who live crammed together in San Jose, Fresno, and Los Angeles, California.

Modern neighborhoods of the poor exist among migrant workers living in substandard housing with few sanitary facilities along the Rio Grande in Texas and in California's rich Central Valley. They are found in farming or rural areas of Minnesota where the economy has become eroded, in once prosperous mining areas in the hills of Appalachia, or in high-unemployment, steel mill towns like Clairton, Pennsylvania. Dysfunctional modern neighborhoods exist in every state, in every large city, and in every area of this country. Macro social worker Robert Fisher, asserts that many people are trapped in neighborhoods by class barriers and racism;

Community has become vulnerable in today's modern world. In a larger area cleared for urban renewal, a single building remained in Manhattan's TriBeCa district, New York city. (© Spencer Grant/Photo Edit)

others view the neighborhood as only a temporary space, a place to live before moving to a better one.[45]

Wynetta Devore, a community social worker, no longer sees modern communities as places of support for families, but rather as places of danger. "It is difficult for families to feel a sense of community that defines its shared history, mutual expectations, roles, values or norms. The city as a community is no longer a haven for families. They appear to be trapped in a dangerous environment, at significant risk in the economic and social areas of their lives."[46]

Such "neighborhoods are territorial spaces whose values, goals, and activities are not inherent, but rather mirror the class and racial conflicts of the larger system."[47] Just as a lost child in a family system bears the family's pain, even more clearly, many neighborhoods and the kinds of communities that exist within them can be seen as displaying the value dysfunctions of the larger society. They offer negative socialization experiences for children and guarantee a continuation of hopelessness, helplessness, dependency, behavioral acting out, and the creation of dysfunctional selves. People in these dysfunctional modern communities are often oppressed, alienated, anonymous, and depressed.

Oppression   Communities of oppression are dualistic, often divided into "haves and have nots," winners and losers. "Haves," often wealthy and advantaged, may work in sparkling high-rise financial centers and live in lush suburban neighborhoods. The winners not only have their own resources, but they have the influence, capability, and social networks to guarantee that good things flow into their neighborhoods. They are able to provide their children with many opportunities for socialization and personal enrichment. Members of affluent neighborhoods, however, most often express the conservative and protective views of their communities. They may oppose commercial development, organize neighborhood watches, protect real estate values against intruders, and sometimes possess a mentality of being defensive, distrustful, and suspicious of anyone who does not seem to fit in.

Down the street or across the tracks, communities of the poor may exist in squalor, dirt, and desperation. Poor neighborhoods bear the wounds of a society that harbors economic injustice at its core, playing a "zero-sum" scarcity game in which there is never enough to go around. One easily identified group may be scapegoated or systematically oppressed to the advantage of other segments of the population. The "have nots" may bear the pain of the economic injustice of the system and are often subject to the racial prejudice, discrimination, and intolerance of the larger society. When older communities are taxed to fund the massive supporting infrastructure for new, more exclusive development, the poor are further enervated, the process accelerates, and injustice increases. As polarization continues, the concentration of poverty creates waves of socioeconomic decline that roll onward astonishingly fast.[48]

Oppressed neighborhoods will invariably comprised people who seem to be less desirable, less valuable, and less worthwhile. Resources will not flow to these neighborhoods.[49] Unable to provide opportunities for their children, people in these neighborhoods may see themselves as less capable and less powerful. We isolate poor communities so we do not have to see them. When our encounter with them becomes unavoidable, our blinders go up and denial sets in. We pretend that they do not exist.[50]

Alienation   One of the effects of modernity is loss of opportunity for authentic close personal relationships with others outside the home. Many modern neighborhoods are enclaves of separated individuals and families who rarely come together or interact as a whole. Even residents of relatively affluent neighborhoods display alienation and lack community spirit. With the dominance of complex organizations, opportunities for intimate social relationships are reduced to fewer arenas of social space.

Large megastructures of modern society operate impersonally in order to provide for efficiency. Managers involved in the transmission of institutional realities are not so much 'significant others' as functionaries with whom there is little emotional involvement. While this is necessary in government and business, impersonal and impartial treatment tends to reinforce superficial, functional relationships in a world of increasing alienation and loss of meaning. The less we engage one another on a personal level, affirming, validating, and looking beyond surface appearance, the more our sense of selfhood gradually diminishes. Thomas Bender, for example, asserts that "any appraisal of the current condition of community in America must…conclude that a market orientation dominates too much of our lives and that the experience of community does not comprise enough of them. We have acquiesced in a market and competitive model of social relations in areas of our lives in which we can legitimately demand community."[51]

Anonymity   Traditional forms and structures of community may no longer be satisfactory or even possible in today's modern culture, where anonymity seems to rule the day. In modern communities many of us do not even know our own neighbors. Interaction with our neighbors may be limited to nodding acquaintanceship. Many neighborhoods lack even the possibility of developing real community spirit. In our mobile society, people come and go so frequently that they find less time and opportunity for a deepening expression of community spirit. There is no guarantee that we will remain in any of these communities long enough to have a stake in them.

Few ties actually bind us together in these communities. For example, most of us do not work in our neighborhoods, but outside it. We commute from home to work and back. Recreation and social activities are usually conducted outside of the community. If we go to church, more than likely it will be a church located outside our neighborhood. For many, aside from shopping, banking, and a few other incidental services that may be conducted in the neighborhood, the only real center of such modern communities is the local elementary or middle school. We are developing a culture of anonymous selves who have little identification with a place, community, or others.

Many of us have little understanding of our own heritage, where we belong, or where we are going. Many modern people are shadow persons who live ambiguous, pseudo existences in artificial systems. We often lack substance, authenticity, and meaning. The anonymous self breeds loneliness, fear, and lack of identification with others.

Depression   Dysfunctional modern communities are ultimately depressed. Many inner cities, for example, have become communities of hopelessness. Many services and businesses have moved. Those who remain tend to exhibit gross indifference and inattention to people's needs. People are allowed to remain in suffering and are ignored. What remains is social decay. Runaway children and teenagers become preyed upon. Prostitution and drug abuse become rampant. The chronically mentally ill find few services, the homeless wander the streets, and vagrants exist on the fringes of the community. Communities of adolescents develop a culture of violence, hopelessness, and despair. Desperately they protect their own turf from others in a dangerous and often futile effort to find respect, meaning, and identity in a world that offers them little. People feel helpless, out of control, and unable to do anything to change things.

Si Kahn says "the organizer brings hope to the people."[52] Community is always possible, perhaps even because there is nowhere else to go. Community social workers understand that there is always hope when we stand together. Macro social workers assert that once we begin to face our common circumstances, we are on the road to recovery. Community social work planners assist us to decide on goals and work together to make our neighborhoods into authentic communities for the good of all. Community developers use entrepreneurial skills in social enterprise development, helping members use the assets of a modern community to build a strong financial base. Community organizers work to overcome oppression, anonymity, alienation, and depression in a culture in which, Alinsky asserts, people are trained to be apathetic.

Ontological Communities

Community associations, civic associations, and churches are called ontological communities, or communities of meaning. They often symbolize and become the heart and soul of the larger community. The Japanese Cultural Association is a center of meaning for the Japanese community in many cities, often supported by the Buddhist Temple, sponsoring Japanese schools, evening classes, summer youth programs, and cultural events such as Bon dances and Taiko drum and Kendo demonstrations, all of which keep the spirit and culture of the Japanese community alive. The same is true for Chinese and Southeast Asian communities. The Knights of Columbus, founded by Irish Americans in New England in 1882 as a fraternal insurance society, soon spread nationwide and eventually became the largest Catholic layman's group in the world. The Sons of Italy organization provides an arena in which Italian Americans can share and celebrate their culture.

Any discourse on faith starts from and takes its bearings from the life of the community.[53] Such a form of life is one that many people in North America are already aware of as members of religious communities—churches, synagogues, temples, and mosques. For many people, ontological religious communities are among the only arenas in which community survives today. The Jewish synagogue is not only a center of religion and worship, but also a cultural, social, intellectual, and ethnic center of life for the Jewish community. Mosques provide similar identity for Muslim immigrants, as does the Buddhist Temple for many East Asians. For African Americans, Wynetta Devore says that "The church stands out as a center of community life providing spiritual, social, and economic resources."[54]

> The black church...was *ours*. Before the Civil war slave masters appointed white preachers to pastor their slaves, making the church just one more tool of domination.... But with Emancipation, the number of black churches in the South mushroomed. At least we had one social institution that was ours. This newly independent church was the one place where we enjoyed true freedom of speech. It was the one place where, for a few hours a week, we could feel really free. So we often spent the whole day at church.
>
> Naturally, then, the black church came to be not only the center of spiritual life but also the focus of social life and culture for the religious and not-so-religious blacks alike. Because the church provided the only setting where black leadership could arise, the preacher quickly became the central figure in the black community. It was to the church, then, that the black community turned for leadership. If change was to take place, it would start there. The church, and only the church, held within its grasp the means to bring to fruition the hopes and dreams of black America.[55]

Religious institutions form by far the largest network of voluntary associations in North American society. On any given Sunday there are probably more people in churches than the total number of people who attend professional sports events in a whole year. There are close to 500,000 local churches, temples, synagogues, and mosques voluntarily supported by the American people, and many others in Canada.[56] In the public policy areas, the historical development of most health, social welfare, education programs, ideas, and institutions is inseparable from the church. In some parts of North America, notably in the older

Community development aims at the active participation of community members and the fullest reliance on the community's initiative. (© Tom Carter-mga/Photri)

cities of the Northeast, the great bulk of social welfare services function under religious auspices.[57]

Not only are religious institutions significant players in the public realm, but they are singularly important to the way people order their lives and values at the most local and concrete levels of their existence. Thus they are crucial to understanding family, neighborhood, and other mediating structures of empowerment.[58] The faith-based religious community is a primary agent for bearing and transmitting the operative values of our society. This is true not only in the sense that most North Americans identify their most important values as being religious in character, but also in the sense that the values that inform our public discourse are inseparably related to specific religious traditions.[59]

The ontological community is *the* arena that survives today as "concrete communities of discourse about issues of ethics and justice," says theologian Francis Fiorenza. Such communities "exist in a pluralistic society and articulate the potential of its particular tradition in a way that enables it to engage in public discourse within the public realm."[60] In ontological communities, members engage in critiquing

existence as part of ordinary communal experiences. Ontological community members celebrate inquiry into substantive meaning, and their lives revolve around understanding value questions and a commitment to enriching values.

Ontological communities accept the wider culture as a reality, learning and growing from it while maintaining their own particular values and truths. They neither succumb nor become that wider culture, but they do not reject or resist it either. Instead, they are committed to encountering the dilemmas of existence as a perennial reality, and work to strengthen the wider society in which they find themselves. For thousands of years people in religious communities have been conscious of a fundamental split in the human condition and provided a means by which people have born the tension that this existential alienation has caused.[61] A community of meaning is one in which you may find people who offer not only support but guidance, "wise women and men who listen well, who offer advice and support, who help us clarify and recognize our options and make choices, and who seek and find in us the same realities."[62] We find people who share and reflect meaning back to us and help develop our ability to act meaningfully with others.

Religious communities offer historic remembrance that links their members to others who have gone before. "This historical consciousness consists largely in 'stories' from the perspective of the oppressed. Voices of the poor and oppressed provide the means out of which justice must be sought."[63] The church seeks to demonstrate ways in which the weak and strong can be related without paternalism. Ontological communities are often judged by their altruism, compassion, and caring. Many such communities prize justice and develop programs that "take in the stranger, assist the needy, and care for widows and orphans."[64]

Ontological communities supplement components of modern life that are missing. They provide stable values, ritual, substance, and direction to our lives; fulfilling our needs for affiliation, connection, socialization, and ultimate purpose, which our modern society often lacks. Spirituality "is nurtured in community, the oneness with others that springs from shared vision and shared goal, shared memory and shared hope," Kurtz and Ketcham assert. Communities of meaning prize mutuality, the antithesis of the giving/getting mode of being. In mutuality one gets by giving, and by being open to receiving, by shared values and shared experiences in personal, face to face relations.[65]

Ontological communities, particularly religious communities, are united into a communion of communities that embrace and transform humankind, not through domination but through quiet faith, undying hope, and a love that all the hate and indifference in the world cannot extinguish.

Because of the importance of ontological communities, macro social workers become concerned when these primary social systems fail to function. When assisting these communities, macro social workers are interested in their leadership, mission, boundary, organizational and growth problems, intolerance and rigidity.

Leadership Leadership of communities of meaning is particularly difficult in the modern world. The leader must play several often incongruent roles simultaneously. For example, the leader must understand and relate the truths, values, and purposes of the community to the world in which it exists. The leader must also relate the values of the wider society to community members so that they have a means to respond to the external culture. The leader must be skilled as a ceremonial figure capable of symbolizing, articulating, and living the community's ideals. The leader is a bridge between both worlds, a model, and a teacher showing how both worlds can learn and grow from one another.

In addition, the leader of a community of meaning must also be an administrator of the organization. Administration requires skill in carrying out goals, attending to detail, budgeting, working with paid and unpaid staff, relating to a board, leading task groups, and program development.

A leader who is a good administrator, providing efficient organizational structure, but who is ineffective in inspiring and communicating the values of the community will fail to help the community in its basic function. Members may lose their sense of altruism, caring, and compassion. Their values, boundaries, and purpose may become weakened. On the other hand, a leader who is a strong charismatic figure but poor in administration may have an organization that flounders because plans are not developed or are carried out ineffectively, details are not attended to, meetings are poorly run, roles become unclear, communication becomes muddled, or conflicts go unresolved.

CHURCH AS A CENTER OF COMMUNITY

Overall, the organizing effort for self-help and self-development programs in the Chinese-American communities for the past twenty years have been the establishment of hundreds of churches of all denominations in this country.... The congregational development of the church as a strategy and tool of community organization has been considered as a successful event to achieve the concepts of self-help and self-development. It also preserves the ethnic identity of Chinese Americans in a multiethnic cultural society.

Even though the primary purpose of the church is to proclaim the gospel of Christ and to promote spiritual growth, its practical objective is to assist the church members cope with various psycho-social problems and social adaptation as well as to meet their socio-cultural needs in the ethnic community. Each local church can be considered a community service center even though it may not be staffed with professional social workers or community organizers....

The basic reason for the existence of a church as a community agency is that church programs are meeting the various needs of its members.... Most social gospel-oriented churches have developed community service programs for their neighboring communities. They usually provide services to lonely elderly, frustrated women in family crisis, dependent children without parental care and teenagers without proper supervision, such as the Good Shepherd Formosan Presbyterian Church in Monterey Park. It has provided child care and nursery school for children and youth programs for teenagers. The Cameron House of Chinatown in San Francisco, which was set up for girls about a hundred years ago, has become the cradle for training the Protestant pastors, teachers, community organizers, social advocates and youth leaders of Cantonese-speaking Chinese-Americans in this country....

The Protestant churches, Catholic Social Services, and many Buddhist organizations can play a very important role in organizing community resources and providing social services to meet the psycho-social and socio-cultural needs of their followers and the neighboring communities.[66]

Mission   Sometimes problems arise because the mission or purpose of the ontological community is unclear. Is the mission of the community to maintain itself as best it can, serve the needs of its members, or provide services to the culture in which it is embedded? Must that mission remain static, or can the mission of the community change and grow as the needs and requirements of the members change and grow?

Boundaries   When communities of meaning fail to reevaluate their primary mission or become unclear about their purpose, the boundaries of the community become fluid, and the community may lose its strength and firmness. As a result, it may fail to uphold the particular truth that it stands for. When ontological communities succumb to the culture around them and fail to maintain their distinctiveness, they become indistinguishable from the wider social environment.

On the other hand, if boundaries become impermeable, some ontological communities may become so immovable about the truth they represent that they become enclaves unto themselves and refuse to accept truths that exist in the wider culture. If this occurs, they fail to infuse the wider culture with their particular truth, alienating their own members by not helping them understand or see the place of the truth of their community in the wider world. They become isolated and alone.

Intolerance and Rigidity   When boundary problems become severe, ontological communities become inverted, rigid, and intolerant. They lose their true mission. Instead of helping their members bear existential tension, they insulate and defend themselves against it. They isolate themselves and their members by refusing to join with others. They may become dogmatic and legalistic. They confuse morality with moralism, often perpetuating the very conditions that they attempt to solve.

Time Orientation   Communities of meaning are, for the most part, based on long-term relationships, stability, and continuity over time. Because our society is increasingly mobile and operates on shorter time commitments, these communities may find it difficult to adapt quickly to changing circumstances.

Lack of Growth   Communities of meaning begin failing when they experience lack of growth and loss of members. Communities that experience member loss find it difficult to maintain programs and services. Relationships become harder to establish, and there may be a tendency to rely on a few of the "old guard" to carry on the core functions of the community. In Chapter 7 you will discover how community developers assist ontological communities to work though a process of reclaiming their strength and power in helping mediate between the individual and megastructures of society.

Traditional Communities

Traditional communities exist side by side with modern culture but attempt to maintain their separateness, uniqueness, cultural integrity, and historical identity. They exist at variance with "normal" modern society, which operates on values of speed, efficiency, mass production, increasing technological advancement, wealth accumulation, competition, growth, progress, and individualism.

The mutual relationships, commonality, tradition, ritual, and social bonds distinguish traditional communities from modern communities. An African proverb asserts that "It takes a whole village to raise a child." A communal endeavor, child rearing is so important that it cannot be left up to parents entirely. Everyone has responsibility for raising children; the community becomes their parents. The traditional community is the mother and father of its people.

The work and the social relationships of the traditional community tend to be inseparable. Members of traditional communities may interact and relate to society in general, but in a restricted way and often on their own terms. For the most part, traditional values and way of life are seen as more important than the promises of technology, wealth, or prosperity of modern society.

There are probably only a few remnants of authentic traditional community in North America today. Native American and aboriginal Canadian nations and tribes that have survived decimation continue to struggle to maintain their own identity. Of these, the Navajo have been among the most successful, having developed their own system of laws, governance, economy, and social systems within the majority culture in the southwestern United States. While not every Native American would agree with the following assessment, it does describe a common ideological preference. Carter Camp, chairperson of the American Indian Movement (AIM), asserted in an interview in the Akwesasne News:

> We can live by what would be considered a poor standard of life by white standards and still have a good life and be happy. That is one of the differences between us and the struggles of other minority groups. We are not concerned with having a $10,000 median income for our people. We are concerned with our people being free and living the way they want to live....We're not looking for the 9–5 job, a white collar job for all our Indian people. We're not looking for upward mobility in the social structure of the United states. We don't need that. We don't want that, we don't want anything to do with that. We're looking for our sovereignty, our ability to govern ourselves, and for every person to live as a free person. To live the way they want to live.[67]

The most important kinds of traditional communities exist in "Third World" countries in Africa, South America, and Southern Asia, the last remnants of a precolonial and premodern era. Many people in "developing" (third world) or "least developed" (fourth world) nations of Africa and Central and South America are suffering the effects of and have been on the periphery of "development" because their own customs, culture, and attachments are alien to those of Western industrialization. Trying to hold on to customs and a way of life that have sustained them for thousands of years, they find themselves an anomaly in the modern world.

Traditional communities exist where drought, war, famine, disease, poverty, or conflict rage. They are found, for example, in the jungles of Guatemala, drought-ridden regions of Northern Africa, the poverty-stricken City of Joy in Calcutta, and villages of Haiti. The difficulties of community life in the United States are mild compared to those experienced by the people in many of these areas. In barrios, towns, and villages, children with swollen abdomens die of malnutrition or suffer irreparable brain damage. In the garbage dumps of Manila, children forage for food. By drinking water from rivers and streams in African towns, people become infected with parasites and eventually become blind.

Indigenous community developers and community organizers help members of traditional communities resist cultural, economic, and political destruction. International macro social workers are committed to helping traditional communities in the developing and least developed nations survive on their own terms. You will learn more about international community social work in Chapter 15.

Communities of Diversity

Today the majority of white North American citizens aspire to a middle-class existence, live in suburbs, and work in large corporations or public organizations. They drive to work on crowded highways and delight in carrying out professional or technical tasks. Their children often learn that today's modern, rational, highly technological and professionalized existence is the best one, and from an early age they are taught how to master the skills of that world. The majority of North Americans have already given up their ethnic, communal, and cultural roots and are firmly homogenized and acculturated to an organizational societal existence.[68]

There is another group of people, non-white, often living in inner cities, barrios, reservations, and migrant camps, who struggle to adapt to the rational, organizational world of impersonality, calculation, and technology. In addition, many new arrivals to

North America, members of diverse ethnic groups, often must choose between giving up the community and culture that formed the heart of their existence and adapting to the rational, practical existence of modern North American culture, which offers many attractions. They may well have aspirations to abandon the solidarity of their own community and join the march of progress.

However, the strength of the communal life of many of these people can be observed in the histories of those who have refused to surrender them. Many people are no longer willing to give up their heritage and cultural roots in the hopes of security, economic betterment, or becoming "Americanized." They understand that freedom "prescribes not only individual liberty, but also a democratic society, respect for human rights, and a process where citizens effect changes. In a real sense people no longer live by bread alone, they also want to determine their lives and collectively with others, their futures."[69] Many Southeast Asian Americans, for example, have come to the realization that "we could accommodate and acculturate, but we can never assimilate. Thus the ability to retain one's culture and language is fast becoming a source of pride rather than a cause for embarrassment."[70]

Community self-determination means that people ought not be coerced into giving up their central culture as the cost of inclusion, survival, or the hope of material well-being. Macro social work recognizes that all communities, but particularly ethnic communities, need to maintain rights to their own heritage, language, culture, religion, and other expressions of uniqueness, and to engage wider society on their own terms and be guaranteed freedom and independence. Just as government protects individual rights, it is the duty of government to honor, protect, nurture, and support the rights of communities of people to establish themselves, to be free from exploitation, and to have the availability of resources by which they can grow.

Many people of color continue to be close to their communal roots. Their linkages with community are strong and personal. Furthermore, because of stigma and lack of integration into the mainstream, their own communities have provided them with a system of support, nurture, and identity, much of this forced upon them because of necessity. African Americans gathered together in their own communities of Harlem, Central Los Angeles, and Hunters Point. Mexican Americans

gathered in the Mission District of San Francisco, in East Los Angeles, and barrios in other cities. Puerto Ricans gathered in Spanish Harlem, Native Americans and aboriginal Canadians on reservations and rancherias, Chinese Americans in Chinatowns in New York, San Francisco, and other large cities. The same pattern is occurring with newer immigrants from India, Korea, Southeast Asia, and the Middle East.

There is evidence that community is beginning to experience a revival. This is occurring not in spite of but *because* members of ethnically diverse communities have been left out of the modern ideologies and have been excluded from being socialized to their norms. It is occurring because many of these people have had to depend on one another and their communities rather than the privileges of wealth and technology. These people understand, as others do not, the vital necessity, healing power, and strength that community offers.

For people who identify strongly with their ethnic group, community is a place of refuge, a reminder of their roots, and a place where their traditional language is spoken, foods eaten, rituals celebrated, and relationships combined into a milieu suffused with meaning and substance. If community is to survive today, it may be because of the people who have not forgotten and have preserved community against the encroachments of modern life.

The African American community of West Oakland, California, for example, has attacked the drug problem head on, with many community leaders making themselves visible enemies of major dealers. Nearby an African American teacher has promised to pay for the college education of her first-grade class if they maintain a "C" average and go on to college. The teacher annually saves $10,000 from her modest salary for this fund. In the rural mountains of Eastern Puerto Rico there is an exciting revitalization of the community through an energetic community development program. Southeast Asian communities in Boston, New York, Houston, and San Francisco have organized legal immigration and refugee task forces to help fight the arbitrary deportation of undocumented workers. Derelict neighborhoods in New York, Chicago, and Philadelphia are being revitalized through cooperatives and community development activities. Native American tribes are attacking problems of alcoholism through indigenous healing rituals that have the sweat lodge ceremony as its core. Success rates are often dramatic, as in the village of Ahiok, Alaska, where 90% of its adults were chronically drunk and at least 80% were able to sustain sobriety after treatment. The Latino community in Boston has a very successful grassroots health program called "Mujeres Latina en Action," which has successfully integrated Third World health models that include the concept of the extended family in health care delivery systems. A culture- and gender-sensitive model of community organization is used to reach women in the barrios.

North America is more ethnically diverse than any society that has ever existed. In any large city, hundreds of languages are spoken, and representatives from almost every nation of the globe can be found. There is scarcely a middle-size town in most of North America that is not ethnically diverse. We have a unique opportunity to learn from and preserve this multitude of diverse communal forms. But it is a treasure that is often belittled, despised, and ignored. The gift of ethnic community is often seen as an impediment to "acculturation." Their languages, traditions, and social mores are often systematically stripped from these people, as if it is impossible for them to be citizens in America and Canada while retaining this rich heritage, the roots of their past.

Social work, having adopted values of individualism and having been socialized to organizational norms, along with mainstream North American society, has abandoned in large part its understanding of the social and communal.[71] Ethnically diverse communities are a constant reminder of social work's abandoned path, but they are also a signal flag calling us back to our original mission, to demonstrate again the strength of our ideals and commitments. Community work with North America's ethnically diverse populations may be a way of redeeming social work from the direction it has chosen.

As professional social workers identify and link closely with ethnically diverse people and position themselves as champions of the oppressed, they will have an opportunity to learn a wealth of lessons about social and communal relationships. Julio Morales, for example, says that "the collective humanism of Puerto Rican society is…a culturally sanctioned pattern that enhances community organizing. It appeals to a sense of justice and fairness, an important guiding principle for community social work practice."[72]

CONCLUSION

Community is the means by which our selves are formed, by which healthy relationships are developed, and by which larger societal culture is formed. Without healthy communities, we tend to become aimless, vulnerable, displaced persons whose freedom becomes simple emptiness. In order for us to be authentically free, we must experience and have available to us free communities from which we can draw strength and which act as centers of values and character.

Authentic social work is nothing less than assisting people to choose the kind of social world they decide is best, and then helping people struggle, against all odds, to make this world real. Community social workers engage modern communities, ontological communities/communities of meaning, traditional communities, and communities of diversity.

The best use of social workers is often in a supportive, helping role assisting community residents build the infrastructures of their communities, helping utilize the therapeutic potential of friends in developing helping relationships with one another, and in establishing strong, positive peer groups by means of social-group work programs. A fundamental task of social workers is to be partners in the process of bringing about strong communal relationships, and in the process of forming selves who express the values and meanings of their communities.

Social work that recognizes the connection between the self and community is irretrievably committed to and engaged in the process of community building. Macro social workers help design community policies and plans; they become catalysts of empowerment, helping community leaders build community and organizations; and they overcome economic injustice by helping to build community development corporations.

KEY CONCEPTS

community

embodied community

transcendent community

social self

self and the other

self and the group

personal crisis

social crisis

political crisis

community mediating structures

oppression

alienation

anonymity

depression

modern communities

ontological communities

communities of meaning

traditional communities

communities of diversity

QUESTIONS FOR DISCUSSION

1. Le Chambon Sur Lignon is an example of a modern community. Compare it with the components of modern communities described in this chapter. Which components does it have? Which components does it not have?

2. This chapter makes a point that communal social systems are slowly finding themselves being eroded by the encroachment of mega-structures of society. What is your opinion about this observation?

3. Pantoja and Perry assert, "Many traditional sociologists, writers, and social observers will say that communities no longer exist. They characterize communities as inventions of primitive and prehistoric people. We are even taught that a desire to belong to a community is an outdated need not entertained by sophisticated people who are socially or physically mobile."[73] Can a case be made that the phenomenon of community has outlived its usefulness, and that we should allow it to die off as social systems evolve to a new and higher level?

EXERCISE 5.1

The Ideal Community

This exercise gives you a chance to design an ideal community. Think of communities you have known or read about. What qualities constitute a human environment that not only provides for meeting needs but also inspires people to reach excellence as well? After you have thought about the components of your ideal community, consider what it would take to actually implement it.

Compare your vision with those of your classmates. What are the qualities that make up an ideal community? What are the difficulties in constructing such a community?

EXERCISE 5.2

The Future of Community

Social work needs to refine and develop alternative models of community, and to advocate for social policies and programs that support community in the face of increasing anomie, alienation, loneliness, and social despair. The traditional view of community as existing in a particular locale is already becoming an anomaly, and social work viewed as "locality development" is becoming out of step with modern reality. For example, a Census Bureau analysis released in 1994 indicates that "more than 2 in 10 of all the nation's households moved in the 15 months before the 1990 census." Furthermore, the study "found that fewer than 1 in 10 households had been ensconced in the same house since Dwight Eisenhower was President.... Pittsburgh and two New York City suburbs—Long Island and northern New Jersey—were the only major metropolitan areas in the nation where people who moved in the 15 months before the census were outnumbered by people who had lived in the same house since 1959."[74]

Consider the following statement: "Community cannot exist under conditions in which neighborhoods are continually shifting membership and where there is no real central focus that binds people together. Neighborhoods today tend to be simply places people are housed, not where people commune together."

1. Do you agree or disagree with this statement?

2. Should community macro social workers encourage or discourage this trend?

3. What alternative forms of community can you conceive of by which people can retain social relationships but adapt to our highly mobile and technologically sophisticated society?

EXERCISE 5.3

Practicing Focused Interviews

This exercise will give you an opportunity to perform focused interviews, record answers, obtain data on community attitudes, collate and assess data, and come to conclusions about the community.

Pair up in dyads. Each research team will randomly choose a shopping mall or street corner and conduct focused interviews with ten subjects. In each interview, one student is to be the interviewer; the second student the recorder. After each interview, students reverse roles so that each student serves as interviewer for five subjects and as recorder for five subjects. Each research team will complete a total of ten short interviews.

Role of Interviewer: The interviewers strike up a conversation with a random selection of people at a shopping mall or street corner. The interviewers introduce themselves and ask potential respondents if they are willing to engage in a two-minute survey. If a respondent agrees, the interviewer administers the "Community Quality Interview Schedule."

Role of Recorder: While the interviewers are asking questions, the recorders complete the "Community Quality Interview Recorder Form." After the interview, the recorders add the data to the "Supplementary Summary Sheet."

Data Analysis: After the ten interviews have been completed, the dyads collate and assess the data using the "Focused Interview Data Collation and Analysis" form. Using the collated data, each dyad is to write its conclusions about the following.

1. The willingness of people in this community to talk about their community.

2. Their perceptions about the community.

3. Their ideas about how to improve the community.

When the class reassembles, the instructor summarizes the experience by asking the following:

1. Describe your experience of doing focused interviews.

2. When you interviewed, did you stay on track or get off the subject?

3. Did you observe body language and make guesses that led you to progressively get deeper into the subject and get more information?

4. Did the recorder find it easy or hard to collect information?

5. To what conclusions did you come about the willingness of people to be interviewed?

a. Was it easier to interview men or women?

b. What general attitudes prevailed about the community?

c. How many felt the community was a good place to live?

d. How many felt the community was not a good place to live?

e. What things made the community desirable?

f. What things made the community less desirable?

g. What suggestions did people make about improving the community?

Alternative

The instructor can ask the dyads to prepare a written report of their experience and hand in interview schedules along with the "Focused Interview Summary Sheet."

A Community Quality Interview Schedule

Identify yourself as students performing a community survey. State that the survey will take two minutes. Ask if the respondent is willing to be interviewed.

If the respondent agrees, the interviewer asks the following questions:

a. Are you a resident of the community?

_____ yes _____ no

If yes, for how long? _____

b. Is this community a good place to live?

_____ yes   _____ no

If yes, what are the desireable things about this community?

If no, what are the undesireable things about this community?

c. What can be done to improve this community?

Community Quality Interview

Recorder Form

Respondent no. _____

Gender _____

1   Are you a resident of the community?

_____ yes   _____ no

If yes, for how long? _____

2. Is this community a good place to live?

_____ yes   _____ no

If yes, what are the good things about this community?

If no, what are the less desirable things about this community?

3. What can be done to improve this community?

Focused Interview Summary Sheet

Summary Sheet

1. Number of male respondents _____

2. Number of female respondents _____

3. Percentage people are willing to be interviewed: _____

Percentage not willing to be interviewed: _____

4. Characteristics of those who agreed to be interviewed:

5. Characteristics of those who refused to be interviewed:

2. Length of residence in the community:

Range: (Longest minus shortest= range)

Average length of residence:

3. Is this community a good place to live?

_____ yes   _____ no

4. If yes, what are the desirable things about this community?

5. If no,what are the less desirable things about this community?

6. What can be done to improve this community?

ADVANCED EXERCISE 5.4

The Demise of Community

S. K. Khinduka asserts that developing or building communities is a useless endeavor because:

In the first place the local community no longer exercises decisive control over the lives of an increasingly mobile population. Due largely to the population explosion, implosion, and diversification, and the accelerated tempo of social and technological change—factors which constitute the "morphological revolution"—the local community does not offer any realistic possibilities of genuine Gemeinschaft environment dictated by natural will and characterized by intimate, spontaneous, inclusive and enduring personal relationships. Even if the morphological revolution could be halted, it would require all the power and resolution of a sovereign world organization; local communities are too feeble to effect such a reversal.75

Khinduka uses terms that need some clarification. First, he talks about the "morphological revolution." This revolution is similar to what Ferdinand Toennies described as the tendency of Gesellschaft to override Gemeinschaft. Gesellschaft is a form of human association in which artificial, impersonal, technological relationships dominated by complex organizational systems become the way society operates. This is in contrast to Gemeinschaft, which are natural, personal, social relationships characterized in community.

It was Toennies' observation that in society Gesellschaft relationships have become the dominant mode, and society becomes impersonal, artificial, and designed and controlled by others. Max Weber, in his classic article on "Bureaucracy," made exactly the same observation. Weber asserted that modern complex organization is the means by which communal action (Gemeinschaftshandeln) is converted into rationally organized action (Gesellschaftshandeln).

Now, examine Khinduka's statement again.

1. Do you agree that the "morphological revolution" of impersonal, artificial, organizational control is becoming so powerful today that "the local community does not offer any realistic possibilities of genuine communal environment dictated by natural will and characterized by intimate, spontaneous, inclusive and enduring personal relationships?"

2. Khinduka also seems to be saying that community itself has become so eroded that it no longer offers a genuine communal environment, and we can no longer expect to obtain "intimate, spontaneous, inclusive and enduring personal relationships" in community. Do you agree or disagree with Khinduka's assessment?

3. If we cannot find inclusive and enduring relationships in community, where do you think we would be able to find them?

4. Khinduka further asserts that "Even if the morphological revolution could be halted, it would require all the power and resolution of a sovereign world organization; local communities are too feeble to effect such a reversal."76 Can the morphological revolution, characterized by impersonal, technological, artificial systems of domination, be halted by "the power and resolution of a sovereign world organization" which is itself based on impersonal, technological, and artificial domination? Why or why not?

5. Do you agree that community, as feeble as it may appear, is unable to reverse the power and strength of a world dominated by rational, complex, and impersonal organizational systems and ideologies? Why or why not?

6. Are communities impotent in this struggle for ideological world domination and control of social systems?

ADDITIONAL READING

Phillip Fellin. *The Community and the Social Worker.* Itasca, IL: F. E. Peacock, 1987.

John E. Tropman. *Successful Community Leadership: A Skills Guide for Volunteers and Professionals.* Washington, DC: NASW Press, 1997.

Sociology of Community

Robert N. Bellah, Richard Madsen, William M. Sullivan, Ann Swidler, and Steven M. Tipton. *Habits of the Heart: Individualism and Commitment in American Life.* New York: Harper and Row, 1985.

Peter L. Berger. *Facing Up to Modernity: Excursions in Society, Politics and Religion.* New York: Basic Books, 1977.

Peter L. Berger and Richard John Neuhaus. *To Empower People: From State to Civil Society.* 2d ed. Washington, DC: American Enterprise Institute Press, 1997.

Individualism and Commitment in American Life

John Patrick Diggins. *The Promise of Pragmatism.* Chicago: University of Chicago Press, 1994.

Lawrence Haworth. *The Good City.* Indianapolis: Indiana University Press, 1966.

Rene Koenig. *The Community.* London: Routledge and Kegan Paul, 1968.

Alfred Schutz. *Collected Papers.* Arvid Brodersen, ed. The Hague: Martinus Nijhoff, 1962.

Ferdinand Toennies. *Community and Association.* London: Routledge and Kegan Paul, 1955.

Roland L. Warren. *The Community in America.* Chicago: Rand McNally, 1963.

History of Community

Thomas Bender. *Community and Social Change in America.* New Brunswick, NJ: Rutgers University Press, 1978.

Philip Hallie. *Lest Innocent Blood Be Shed: The Story of the Village of Le Chambon and How Goodness Happened There.* New York: Harper and Row, 1979.

Lewis Mumford. *The City in History.* New York: Harcourt Brace Jovanovitch, 1961.

Barry Alan Shain. *The Myth of American Individualism: The Protestant Origins of American Political Thought.* Princeton, NJ: Princeton University Press, 1994.

Ontological Communties

Gustavo Gutierrez. *The Power of the Poor in History.* Maryknoll, NY: Orbis, 1983.

Thomas A. Kleissler, Margo A. LeBert, and Mary C. McGuinness. *Small Christian Communities: A Vision of Hope.* Mahwah, NJ: Paulist Press, 1991.

Sergio Torres and John Eagleson, eds. *The Challenge of Basic Christian Communities.* Trans. John Drury. Maryknoll, NY: Orbis, 1981.

John Paul Vandenakker. *Small Christian Communities and the Parish: An Ecclesiological Analysis of the North American Experience.* Kansas City, MO: Sheed and Ward, 1994.

Community Research

W. Ron Jones. *Finding Community: A Guide to Community Research and Action.* Palo Alto, CA: Freel and Associates, 1971.

6

Becoming a Social Work Planner

It is better to plan for ourselves, no matter how badly, than to be planned for by others no matter how well.[1]

John Forester

Our view can never reach far enough to be certain that any action will produce the best possible effects. Even if we can never settle with certainty how we shall secure the greatest total of good, we at least try to assure ourselves that the probable evil of the future will not be greater than the immediate good.

G. E. Moore, Principia Ethica

Ideas in This Chapter

GRASSROOTS COMMUNITY PLANNING COMES OF AGE

Since the 1960s a clear trend has been emerging in neighborhoods across the nation. In city after city, indigenous community leaders are organizing planning groups in their neighborhoods, and wherever they are found, they increase community awareness and competence. Sometimes leaders are specifically identified and asked to initiate the organizing effort; sometimes indigenous leaders emerge once the program is announced, or existing community organizations are asked to take over a planning role in their communities. But in every instance, communities are bringing about a planning process that meets community needs, and they are doing it on their own. Neighbors are active participants, planning their own communities in every large city and increasingly in middle and smaller ones as well.[2]

Neighborhood planning represents a new wave of federated partnerships in which federal, state, and local governments cooperate with local planning groups at the grassroots level by providing funding and support. It is a process that is revolutionizing democracy and the way that government is being conducted. These partnerships are based not only on idealism, but also on the practical reality that this is the best way to conduct governance. And government is putting its money into the process. More than 80% of the community planning organizations receive federal money, covering most if not all of the administrative costs of operating neighborhood planning councils, supplemented by local planning commissions, community development agencies, and city managers or mayors offices that provide funding directly to neighborhood planning councils. They also hire social work planners to provide staff support. The city of Houston, for example, provides technical assistance through workshops, a newsletter, and consultation. In Atlanta, Raleigh, and Wilmington, local government provides staff assistance to help develop local plans and analyze development proposals. In Cincinnati and St. Paul, funds are provided directly to local groups to hire their own staff and fund projects, as well as for operating expenses and capital improvements in the neighborhood.

These community planning organizations are characterized by a variety of methods to define neighborhoods and to organize groups. Their processes are invariably democratic but express a wide diversity in the way democracy is conducted. All of these organizations and methods emerge out of the ideas of grassroots people themselves. The particular way of organizing is less important than the ability of citizens to decide for themselves. "In Atlanta" said one participant, "you have the whole spectrum of types of participation from New England town meetings to elected councils. If people can't participate in the way they feel comfortable, then the process won't work." In St. Paul, neighborhood group members elect a local council, which selects a chairperson. In other cities, the officers are elected directly by members of the community organization. In some areas, selection processes vary throughout the neighborhoods of a city.

Citizen community planning councils increase leadership. "When we get educated by city government, we learn how to get things done," asserts a Wilmington, Delaware, citizen planner. "The program brought out a whole new leadership in neighborhoods," resulting in increased community awareness and competence, and improved relations between citizens and government. Serving as chairperson of a neighborhood organization provides training in leadership skills. One member said, "I helped meetings get more information. I was asked to help plan the community development budget. Some of my ideas were incorporated into the plan." Supplemented by more formal training offered by the neighborhood planning program, a number of these chairpersons have gone on to hold elected or appointed offices in the city.

As a result, neighborhood-planning groups are acquiring power, and official status. In St. Paul, Raleigh, Wilmington, and Cincinnati, neighborhood planning councils have been authorized by resolution of the city council. In other cites, they are brought into being by executive order of the mayors; and in others they are sanctioned by city charter amendments giving community planning organizations a firm legal basis. These citizen-based planning groups exert their political power by speaking for their neighborhoods at council meetings, through personal contacts with the mayor or members of the council, by seeking out politicians to discuss local issues, and by using the media. When necessary, citizen protests are used, including packing council meetings, forming delegations, and voting as a block to support political candidates or specific referenda or initiatives. When the

Public Works Department in Wilmington wanted to expand a garage for city vehicles with Economic Development Administration funds, the local citizens planning council fought the proposal and was able to stop the project. In East St. Paul, the city wanted to take an old hospital site and put up townhouses. "The city was really pushing saying, 'Hey, we need the tax base!' but the community said, 'No, we don't want that; we want a park,' and they got what they wanted."

Neighborhood citizen planning councils, however, do more than merely block proposals that are not good for the neighborhood. They develop comprehensive social plans for their neighborhoods as well as plans for specific projects. So successful are these plans that in St. Paul, more than 80% of the neighborhood projects were funded. In Cincinnati, community planning groups obtained funding for neighborhood improvement and housing programs. Community plans led to improvement in police services, crime prevention, and witness assistance programs. A district council initiated a neighborhood dispute board to address local conflicts and minor criminal acts such as vandalism, and a youth federation to provide counseling and advocacy. In other communities drug education, and counseling for local youth, day care cooperatives, tutoring, youth recreation, emergency paramedic units, and a multiservice center have emerged out of the community planning process. Neighborhood planning programs have also established many new neighborhood organizations in areas where they did not exist, more equitable distribution of public resources, major improvements for poorer neighborhoods, and increased quality of life in neighborhoods.

The strength of neighborhood citizen planning is the quality and validity of the plans that neighbors develop. They reflect the reality of neighborhood conditions and the involvement of citizens who know their own situations and can make recommendations that will work, unlike plans made by city planners who are not engaged in the local neighborhood. Neighborhood planning groups in Raleigh discovered that undesirable proposals were being submitted to the city and took a stand on nine zoning amendments. The groups appeared eight times before the board of adjustment to voice their opinions. Now "developers have begun to work with the local task forces before submitting proposals to the city." In part this is due to the personal relationships, communication, and trust being developed between neighborhoods and government. "Our credibility came from responsible recommendations and building a rapport with developers and the council," commented one citizen planner. Local planners have "pretty good influence with the council. They have input on the comprehensive plan and have gotten more people involved," one citizen planner asserted.

As a result, neighborhood planning councils are seen as an indispensable way of operating city government. They review and comment on city-initiated proposals, prepare plans for neighborhood development, and hold informal hearings on requests for zoning changes. Mayors and councils rely on these groups to provide necessary linkages with communities to represent the needs and concerns of the area. Neighborhood planning organizations are involved in problem identification, assessing and communicating the needs and problems of their communities by means of systematically surveying existing conditions. A citizen planner asserted, "citizens have tremendous influence. The city is built on neighborhoods. Citizens are running the government." In St. Paul, "city officials have become less formidable to the community. Now the community is not afraid to talk with these people, and city officials come to the community to hold hearings."

Citizens and public officials agree that the money and labor put into city planning projects will go for naught if local residents are not involved in community planning. One citizen representative comments that "comprehensive community plans helped the city accept community groups as partners in the planning process. More citizens are interested in government than before." Citizen engagement is an essential ingredient of government, and neighborhood planning programs are well suited to provide that ingredient.

WHAT YOU WILL LEARN IN THIS CHAPTER

Macro social workers are vitally concerned about preserving and protecting the public good when that good is trampled by private self-interest ruthlessly pursued. It is out of this concern that macro social workers become engaged in the arena of community social planning.

In this chapter, you will learn why people plan and what social work planning includes. You will explore a short history of planning in housing, mental health, and poverty. You will explore approaches to community social work planning. You will learn how to do community planning and specific techniques that social work planners use.

WHY PLAN?

When you think about what you want to do in any one day, you are planning. If you have a goal that you are trying to reach or something that you want to accomplish, you begin to plan for it. Things happen when you plan.

All modern social systems exist by planning. Large and small business organizations expend a great deal of energy developing marketing plans, engaging in strategic planning, and planning new products. City planning departments develop land use plans and plans for municipal services. Regional and state governments develop comprehensive health plans, water resources plans, environmental plans, and mass transportation plans. The federal government plans for national defense and space exploration. Planning also occurs at the international level. The Marshall Plan was a means by which those nations who experienced massive destruction after WW II rebuilt themselves. Today, the European Union develops cooperative economic plans providing fiscal arrangements for its member countries. The members of the world's eight wealthiest nations hold a yearly summit to ratify plans for international economic stability. Planning even occurs at the global level. Through the World Health Organization (WHO) the United Nations develops plans to eradicate disease. The World Bank finances community development plans and projects worldwide.

WHAT IS SOCIAL WORK PLANNING?

Macro social workers engage in the process of social planning to insure that services are provided on behalf of those who are in most need. Social planning is a "process of selecting and designing a rational course of collective action to achieve a future state of affairs"[3] for the social good, including "development,

expansion, and coordination of social services and social policies" at both the local and societal levels.[4]

Social work planners insist that communities of people who have fewer resources, less power, and little influence be given opportunity to develop plans for their welfare which compete on an equal footing, recognition, funding, and entitlement with plans developed by powerful business corporations and governmental bureaucracies. Until recently, however, communities have been completely ignored in planning for their own welfare. Community members were invited to only token membership in the planning process. As a result, entire neighborhoods have been decimated to build highways, corporate office buildings, or housing projects in the name of "redevelopment." Funding has flowed into middle-class and upper-middle-class suburbs, ignoring neighborhoods most in need of support.

The planning process is one of the key means of citizen access to power, where community needs can be met, and plans that destroy the community can be stopped before they are implemented. Community social planning is one way by which macro social workers assist communities of people take charge of their future.

SOCIAL WORK PLANNERS

There are three kinds of social work planners. Some social work planners are staff specialists working in large public and quasi-public direct-service case management and clinical services organizations. Social work planners work closely with the agency executive. They analyze needs, assess services, write grant proposals, conduct research, and make recommendations to help the agency meet the needs of its clientele, adjust agency resources, and adapt services to a changing population.

Social work planners working in direct-service agencies often begin their careers as clinicians or counselors, and they develop an interest in social planning as they become involved in wider social work issues. They may have a variety of titles, such as planning consultant, staff analyst, planning analyst, mental health or developmental disabilities specialist, or resource developer. Some analyst or planner positions require a bachelor's degree. Others require an

Social planners provide expert advice, make assessments, coordinate, and plan new services where existing services are poorly, inequitably or ineffectively provided. (Courtesy of Goodwill Industries)

MSW degree and some experience, particularly in the field in which the agency works.

A second type of social work planner works for an organization that is exclusively dedicated to social welfare planning for a specific population on a regional basis. Social welfare planning agencies assess needs, regulate the amount and kinds of services in their service jurisdiction, review and make recommendations for awarding governmental grants, assist in developing new services, and in some cases maintain quality control over services in their mandated arena. Welfare planning organizations interact with a variety of service providers, agencies, and parent organizations, as well as ancillary service systems such as universities, governmental agencies, businesses, and community groups to develop comprehensive plans for their service area.

Area Developmental Disabilities Boards, for example, gather information and develop comprehensive welfare plans that become the basis for the provision of new services and the awarding of governmental grants. They oversee the provision of services and make funding recommendations. Area Agencies on Aging assess needs, make recommendations, formulate plans, and oversee grants for services to maintain and enhance the welfare of persons who are elderly. Social work planners in these agencies most often have a planning background or degree in planning, policy, or public administration in addition to an MSW degree.

In the last few decades, a new and potentially revolutionary role for social work planners is developing that goes beyond agency or regional planning for specific populations. We are working more and more frequently with local neighborhoods through city planning commissions, mayors offices, or local community organizations. Community social work planners can play one of the most potentially important roles in the field of social work today.

Community social work planners assist neighborhood residents to organize themselves into effective community planning councils. We help form neighborhood planning groups, identify local leaders, and provide assistance to newly formed groups. We assist community members to organize neighborhood leadership training workshops. We help new organizations write bylaws, rules of procedure, and constitutions. Community social work planners train groups in membership recruitment, record keeping, accounting, and fundraising. We assist local planning leaders to develop committees, assist board members to conduct meetings, and aid community planning groups in maintaining their organizations. We help neighborhood groups conduct evaluations of their own organizations or the programs that they initiate, or provide evaluations ourselves to help community groups function more effectively.

Community social work planners consult, train, and give information and technical assistance to neighborhood planning councils as citizens construct their own local plans, budgets, and projects. We assist citizen groups to develop action plans and grant proposals for addressing local problems. When community planning councils are asked to comment on city-initiated plans and public services, we help citizens to develop criteria for evaluation, analyze city plans, write reports to city government, and provide input for comprehensive neighborhood plans.[5]

Community social work planners act as liaisons between city politicians, staff and neighborhood organizations. On the one hand we help community planning councils obtain information about publicly and privately initiated plans that may affect their areas. We teach members about the operation of city government, explain city budgeting procedures and local, state, and federal program requirements, and agency operating procedures. We train citizens to be influential in civic affairs. We assist citizens in obtaining data, maps, regulations, and statistics to develop responsible plans for their neighborhoods. We provide neighborhood planning groups with the contacts to work effectively through governmental administration and city and state bureaucracy.[6]

On the other hand, community social work planners help city planning commissions, city councils, mayors' offices, and other public officials to understand the concerns and desires of neighborhood groups. We provide communication linkages and use our contacts with neighborhoods to keep local government in touch with neighborhood needs. We use our understanding of the neighborhood and its members to act as their advocates and mediators. As advocates, we explain the position of a neighborhood to the mayor or city manager, present a proposal to the city council, or provide input on neighborhood conditions to other public officials. If there is misunderstanding or conflicts, we often bring conflicting parties together to discuss issues and promote compromise and reconciliation.[7]

Community social work planners use a consensual approach to community social work. We not only help community members develop neighborhood planning organizations and assist local residents become effective planners, but when planning points to the need for other ways of empowering the community, we work with citizens to develop social programs, help initiate community development projects, or work with local leaders to develop community organizations.... In the Pendleton area of Cincinnati, for example, community planners helped the existing Thirteenth Street Tenant Organization and a newly formed group unite into a more broadly based community organization council.[8]

SOCIAL WORK PLANNING IN AMERICA

American society is a combination of planning and freedom from planning. The founders were the first people in history to plan a new nation from scratch. They were acutely aware that although plans provide a direction, once they are made and become binding, they tend to prescribe a path that eliminates other options. The social plan we call our Constitution was a way of insuring that choice would not be limited to only a few people who could impose their own plans or ideas onto the populace. It was a social plan that prevented the few who hold power from planning for everyone else. We call this the "balance of power."

In the minds of the planners of our nation, there were three areas where people should be particularly free from oppression. First, people should be free from political oppression. Instead of politics holding a monopoly on power, individual citizens were to hold power, and government was to be subject to the will of the populace. Second, people should have opportunity to pursue their own private economic interests rather than have a centralized authority determine what their interests ought to be. Government was not to regulate or interfere with the free operation of the economy. Instead government was to be a sort of referee ensuring that individuals could carry out their own legitimate economic interests. Third, people should not have a system of belief forced on them. Religion was to be forever separated from the state, preventing government leaders from imposing a belief system on the populace and insuring that small groups would not impose their beliefs on the public at large. Liberty was conceived in political, economic, and religious terms.

As America grew, the social and political environment evolved a new phenomenon unanticipated by the framers of the Constitution—a complex modern system of interlocking corporations. After the Civil War, gigantic corporations acquired enormous wealth and unregulated power, eventually controlling the political process, and dominating local, state, and even the federal government.

During the Progressive Era (1880–1910), macro social workers became concerned that economic freedom had become mere license of the rich and powerful to exploit the poor and powerless. Social problems were unaddressed and social issues unattended. Macro social workers began to press for renewed commitment to America's democratic principles. Progressive social workers advocated and succeeded in changing state constitutions allowing for direct citizen legislation by means of initiatives and referendum. Social workers helped pass laws that provided for the recall of oppressive or corrupt politicians. Social workers successfully worked with others to provide for direct citizen election of U.S. Senators. Progressive social workers also advocated that government develop social plans to organize and place the provision of public services on a more rational and secure basis. They intended to insure that the poor and disadvantaged would not be excluded, and that equity and access to opportunity would be guaranteed.

As a result, social work planning in America developed along two planes. Progressive social workers advocated for a stronger centralized social planning at the federal level, and they also worked for localized planning at the community level. At both levels, they worked to develop plans and policies to assist some of our most vulnerable citizens: women, children, and immigrant laborers.

Early Social Work Planning Organizations

Among the early social work planning organizations were settlement houses (described in Chapter 4), through which social workers engaged in research and reform at the local levels and worked to strengthen government intervention at the federal level. Settlement house members developed the Children's Bureau and advocated for government regulation of big businesses, labor laws, and better wages, hours, and working conditions for men, women, and children. They advocated for women's rights, suffrage, regulation of sweatshops, and labor's right to organize. They also pressed for federal laws in consumer protection and for safe food and drugs.

The Charity Organization Society (COS) movement largely utilized methods and principles of social planning at the local level. Originating in 1877 "in response to rapid urbanization and industrialization and the effects of the Great Depression of 1873,"[9] the COS movement developed a "science of charity" based on "rationality, efficiency, foresight, and planning."[10] Committed to the principle that "poverty could be cured and prevented if its causes could be discovered and removed,"[11] it attempted "to achieve rationality in social welfare by managing the entire voluntary system based on the most respected social science principles of the time."[12] The COS movement affirmed that a collective and cooperative approach to the problems of poverty could be made, avoiding duplication and ensuring collaboration, resource coordination, and efficiency.[13] The early Charity Organizations Societies are "generally credited with being the beginning of modern social work."[14] From its inception, social work and social planning were seen as largely synonymous, having common roots and common methods.

Francis McLean, superintendent of the Brooklyn Bureau of Charities and full-time organizer for the Russell Sage Foundation, served as the executive of the National Association of 62 charity organization societies in 1911. McLean saw the need for a new coordinating device, a citywide "Council of Social Agencies" that brought community agencies together for regular meetings for a collective review and planning of community needs and services[15] as well as coordinating funding of social agencies and the operation of voluntary service agencies.[16] Social services would be organized in an effective and efficient way producing greater centralization of operations and more emphasis on professionalism.[17]

Soon, these councils sprang up in many cities throughout the country, continuing the momentum toward coordination and planning initiated by the COS movement, emphasizing "efficiency, centralization, and specialization in the planning and delivery of services by private agencies within the community." By World War I, centralized fundraising agencies called Community War Chests were developed to "centralize planning and administration and achieve greater efficiency in utilization of community resources."[18] These agencies emphasized rational planning for the use of funds, efficiency, planning, and a willingness to respond to community priorities.[19]

The community chest and council movements were "early attempts to assess community needs and for rational decision-making in projecting the development and location of community agencies"[20] by citizen volunteers and professional social work planners. So important were these councils that the influential 1939 Lane Report cited the Council of Social Agencies as the only urban community organization on the scene that organized resources to meet community needs.[21]

As important as they were in social planning, coordination, and private charity, however, the efforts of Councils of Social Agencies and united fundraising were not sufficient to meet the massive relief needs created by the economic collapse of the nation during the Great Depression. With the New Deal of President Franklin Delano Roosevelt "the federal government assumed a greater role in social planning"[22] and in the provision of relief and in the development of social programs.

Social planning became one of the weapons in the federal government's arsenal of social programs, such as the Social Security system, which "required a projection of the number of and size of beneficiary claims and revenues"[23] and any number of federal social programs involving cooperative and coordinated effort. Since the Depression, social planning assumed an even larger and clearer role in governmental social service provision, with the social planner becoming a more central, if technically oriented, professional.[24]

Housing and Urban Renewal

During the 1930s, under the Works Progress Administration, a national effort was undertaken to attack the problem of growing inner-city slums and a lack of decent housing for low-income people. The Housing Act of 1937 had triple objectives of slum clearance, job creation, and the development of low-rent housing. Spurred by these federal initiatives, community civic organizations in many cities including Philadelphia, Cleveland, and Chicago took the initiative to develop plans for local neighborhood districts. While citizen groups were given a great deal of control, however, the result was always the same: Planning commissions overrode or ignored citizen recommendations and demolished neighborhoods on behalf of large public and private organizations. In Chicago, for example, two large institutions, Michael Reese Hospital and the Illinois Institute of Technology, were able to acquire sizable acreage though wholesale clearance and redevelopment. Chicago adopted redevelopment plans that cleared another area to provide for a large campus for the University of Illinois, Chicago Circle.[25]

Congress gave redevelopment a major boost by authorizing federal support though the Housing Act of 1949, which encouraged community planning by means of a "community master plan," a planning concept that achieved broad public support.[26] As planning was becoming a central tool of government in assessing need and developing social programs, it was seen as too important an endeavor to be left to professionals alone.[27]

After reviewing the neighborhood clearance approach, the Eisenhower administration offered recommendations for greater emphasis on housing rehabilitation. As a result the Housing Act was amended in 1954, calling for a "Seven Point Workable" program that specified seven requirements before funding for redevelopment would be approved, including planning, code enforcement, relocation of displaced residents, financing, and most importantly citizen participation in the planning process.[28] Citizen participation, however, was generally limited to the appointment of a citywide advisory committee composed of civic leaders to work with planners. Representation of the poor who were usually most affected by renewal activities, was neither mandatory nor commonplace,[29] and in practice, strong citizen participation was the exception rather than the rule. In 1959, for example, Gerda Lewis surveyed the first 91 cities with approved workable programs and found that the community advisory committees were composed most often of real estate, construction, downtown business, and civic organizations. Minority groups had limited representation, and project areas almost none. In only a few places were there separate project area committees. Even then, the citywide advisory committees were confined to the review of plans and policy recommendations.[30]

Some localities did more, however. In a special demonstration project, the Housing Association of Metropolitan Boston placed organizers in various neighborhoods to boost resident involvement in urban renewal planning. In Philadelphia's Eastwick project, the Redevelopment Authority contracted with the Citizens Council on City Planning to provide an organizer. In Detroit, staff from the City Planning Commission assisted citizens in the Concord-Mack area, but eventually the strain of working for both the neighborhoods and city hall became too great and the city withdrew its organizer. Likewise in Baltimore, an attempt to build a strong community-organizing component into a consolidated housing and urban renewal agency foundered on the issue of divided allegiance. To be effective from the neighborhood perspective, staff support had to be independent. There were scarcely any sources of funds for neighborhood organizers. The United Funds were too timid or too committed to social services. Not many foundations were interested. Most neighborhoods, especially the poorer ones, didn't have or didn't try to raise the necessary revenues, though a few did.[31]

Community action and Model Cities experiences in the 1960s had an impact on urban renewal. As residents demanded and in many localities achieved greater participation in urban renewal planning, HUD issued a regulation in 1968 mandating project area committees in all renewal projects involving housing rehabilitation and permitted federal funds to be spent for that purpose. Many cities provided staff services to these committees, and some were allowed to hire their own staff.[32]

The Housing and Community Development Act of 1974 continued to encourage social planning at the local level by requiring citizen participation and led to greater efforts to include grassroots citizens in social planning in other social arenas as well. Requirements for citizen participation spread to other federal aid programs: education, social services, health, employment and training, economic development, transportation, water resources management, and many more. In 1978 the Advisory Commission on Intergovernmental Relations (ACIR) tallied 155 federal grant programs with statutes or regulations mandating citizen participation, more than one-fourth of all grant programs, but more significantly they accounted for over 80% of federal grant expenditures. ACIR reported that among the major roles of participation, over one-half of the programs required boards or committees to reflect the public in various ways in their membership. Compared to the degree of neighborhood involvement in public programs in the 1950s, federally mandated citizen participation marked a noteworthy advance. While the requirements fell considerably short of the planning activists aspirations, federal regulations and money significantly aided increased neighborhood participation.[33]

Social Planning for Mental Health

In 1950s and early 1960s, social work planners and community activists engaged in social reform efforts to improve the nation's mental health system. State social welfare planners "tirelessly worked as advocates to provide information about the need for mental health services and the rights of mental patients," Madelene Stoner states. "They were effective campaigners and social activists who viewed their roles as most effective when stimulating the public welfare sector to provide more and better services."[34]

Supported by President John F. Kennedy, these efforts paid off with the passage in 1963 of the Comprehensive Community Health Act, which encouraged planning and development of local community mental health centers, mental health planning boards, and community consultation.[35] More importantly for community-based social work and planning, the Community Mental Health Centers Act of 1963 "made it possible to employ community organizers in service delivery settings," Stoner states, providing the first major impetus for agency-based community social work practice in mental health. The door was opened for transforming hospital-based psychiatric case work into psychotherapeutic social work, paving the way for government reimbursement for treatment, state licensure of clinical social workers, and private social work practice. The Community Mental Health Centers Act expanded the delivery of psychotherapy at the local level.

Implicit in the philosophy of community-based mental health care was the role of advisory councils drawn from the providers and consumers of the services. "Together with the state agency the councils had the responsibility for inventorying state facilities for the mentally ill and developing state-wide plans for the creation of mental health centers," asserts Stoner. As a result, social work community organizers and planners were able to work inside the mental health service delivery system "using a non-medical model that sought to prevent mental illness though non-clinical services that reflected social goals rather than psychiatric ones." According to Stoner, community social workers relied on "community groups to define issues and problems and to participate in developing services. This principle of citizen participation became the rationale and basis for much community social work practice." In addition, community social work planners and organizers helped mental health clients actively engage in planning and organizing services, "buttressed the individual's sense of personal control," and empowered clients by emphasizing "local and democratic control of social institutions."

Just as the number of community mental health centers began to peak, however, newly elected President Richard M. Nixon began to dismantle social service and mental health programs. By the early 1970s, the government's interest in citizen participation began to diminish, and in "1973 the 'drift' became a tiderace."[36] Citizen participation in the mental health movement went into remission and was relegated "toward minimal or token change," Stoner states. Never completely comfortable with citizen participation in mental health planning, powerful psychiatric and managerial professionals used community mental center legislation to consolidate and expand their interests rather than those of the citizenry at large. According to Stoner, mental health became a closed system.

In 1980, at the end of President Carter's administration, the Mental Health Systems Act was passed, which would have provided for more community-based services and community involvement in coordination and development. The act was repealed, however, under the Reagan administration. The initiative for planning was taken away from local communities, and instead, block grants were given to states for mental health, alcohol abuse, and drug abuse programs. In spite of financial reductions, however, community mental health centers continue to provide services, a testimony to advocacy-based social work planning in the field of mental health.

Planning the Great Society

Building on the impetus of citizen participation and community-based social care established by the community mental health movement, "President John F. Kennedy's Council of Economic Advisers began working on antipoverty proposals using recommendations by the President's Committee on Juvenile Delinquency, the Ford Foundation and various cabinet-level departments."[37] Carrying forward the proposals of these groups after President Kennedy's assassination, President Lyndon Johnson undertook one of the most ambitious campaigns of social change since the New Deal of Franklin Roosevelt. The Comprehensive Employment and Training Act, National Health Planning and Resources Development Act, and Economic Opportunity Act, "carved out a role for new quasi-public bodies to assume a planning, coordinating role on municipal or regional basis."[38]

The Economic Opportunity Act (EOA) passed in 1964, often called the War on Poverty, initiated numerous programs with the goal of abolishing poverty. A task force that included leading academics and social scientists came up with what Trattner calls "a make-do, crash program that left a good deal to be desired" and that many critics considered bound to fail, "primarily because it was designed not to change society but to change its victims.... It emphasized not adequate income and job creation... but rather education, manpower training and various social services."[39]

One of the antipoverty programs, however, did involve community organization and planning—the Community Action Program (CAP). Community Action Agencies (CAAs) were created to improve public services, mobilize resources, and ensure the contribution of the poor in planning programs that affected them and their neighborhoods. According to Pine, CAAs provided "advocacy for welfare recipients, establishment of day care and health care, and pressured welfare public housing and other agencies to respond more effectively and equitably to the poor." An important requirement of CAAs in improving inner cities, Pine asserts, was " 'maximum feasible participation' by the poor in planning, development and execution of the programs that the CAAs coordinated or sponsored." While this requirement became highly controversial, the CAAs represented the poor in dealing with bureaucracies, trained individuals for leadership, and "helped institutionalize citizen input concerning federal programs and agencies for all members of society, not just the poor."[40]

In addition to the CAAs, the Demonstration Cities and Metropolitan Development Act of 1966 (the Model Cities Program) was expected to bring "resident groups, business interests, and social welfare agencies together in a planning network for developing the physical and social aspects of the community"[41] as well as increase the supply of housing, enhance the social environment, and improve delivery systems. Cities that qualified for an initial planning project were provided funds to change the social environment of the target area using benefit/cost analysis as well as active engagement of residents in planning and executing the programs.[42]

Planning for Older Americans

The Older Americans Act (OAA) of 1965 and its implementation insured that services to the elderly "became the province of the expert planner," Monk states. State agencies on aging were to design programs, coordinate services, and assess needs. At the local level, the nearly 700 Area Agencies on Aging (AAAs) were required to produce three-year plans, award grants for services, contract with local providers, and monitor the implementation and quality of services. According to Monk, the AAAs were "responsible for mounting a continuous process of planning, including definition of service priorities, and development of a comprehensive system specially designed to improve delivery of services."[43]

Although these administrative responsibilities did not openly encourage planning advocacy, "advisory boards had enough latitude to become interest-group representatives," asserts Monk. "Assisted by planners with a bent toward policy analysis, they took stands on proposed legislation, lobbied on behalf of their constituents, and maintained a constant watch on trends in program funding." These efforts paid off in tangible benefits to the elderly so that by 1971 OAA funding was about $30 million, and by 1980 it exceeded $500 million.

With the 1973 amendments to the Older Americans Act, citizen participation in planning gained ground when the government spearheaded broad citizen participation, but five years later, the 1978 amendment signaled the end of an expansionist era in social planning for the elderly and the beginning of a more cautious managerial mandate. Rather than focusing on advocacy and citizen involvement, says Monk, "social work planners in state agencies and local AAAs became more involved in scrutinizing program compliance, writing contracts in the language of management by objectives, measuring units of service, adjudicating purchase of service agreements, negotiating budgets, establishing quality central and quality assurance procedures and evaluating program efficiency."

GRAHAM R. TAYLOR AND THE SURVEY

Born in Hopewell Junction, New York, on March 17, 1880, Graham R. Taylor was familiar with social planning through the work of his father, who founded Chicago Commons, one of the earliest and best-known social settlements in the country. With an AB degree from Harvard in 1903, Taylor became a reporter in Boston and then an Associated Press correspondent in Albany. In 1904 he joined the editorial staff of The Commons, a periodical established by his father in 1896. The Commons merged in 1905 with Charities, published in New York City. The combined publication took the name of The Survey in 1909 and become one of the most important and well-known journals in social work and social welfare. Taylor was responsible for many of its articles on social issues and social and industrial problems.

A series of articles on planned industrial communities such as Pullman, Illinois, and Gary, Indiana, was published in book form under the title *Satellite Cities: A Study of Industrial Suburbs* (1915). In Chicago and other cities, Taylor was active in movements to integrate public social and recreation facilities and improve living conditions though citywide planning.

In 1916 Graham Taylor traveled to Russia as a special assistant to the U.S. ambassador to investigate the condition of German and Austrian civilian prisoners and was later detailed to the America Consulate General in Moscow when the Russian Revolution broke out in November 1917. He remained in Russia as head of the Leningrad office of President Wilson's committee on public information until May 1918. In April 1919, he traveled through China and India. Upon returning to the United States, Taylor turned his attention to Chicago race relations, and in 1920–1921 he conducted a survey to determine the causes of the Chicago race riots of July 1919. The report, *The Negro and Chicago* (1922), was called one of the important documents in the history of race relation in the United States.

In this period, Taylor became the executive secretary of the American Association of Social Workers. He again went to Russia as a member of the National Information Bureau to investigate famine and recommend relief measures. He then joined the Commonwealth Fund as director of its joint committee on methods of preventing juvenile delinquency.

Taylor directed the Commonwealth Fund's division of publications until his death. In addition, he was director of the Common Council for American Unity and the National Urban League and a member of the Council on Foreign Relations of the National Conferences of Social Work.[44]

Neighborhood Councils

By the late 1950s the idea of planning and political involvement at the neighborhood level began to come of age when the president of Manhattan Borough in New York City appointed advisory community planning boards. A 1961 charter amendment applied this concept citywide, and subsequent amendments have added to their roles, though they have remained appointed bodies. They are now simply called community boards. In 1967 the advisory Commission on Intergovernmental Relations drew up model state legislation authorizing cities and counties to set up neighborhood subunits with advisory powers. During the next several years, bills based on this model were introduced in the legislatures of Oklahoma and Minnesota but not adopted. Among the specific recommendations were neighborhood action task forces, neighborhood city halls, and multiservice centers.[45]

In 1968 the National Commission on Urban Problems appointed by President Johnson recommended decentralization of municipal services to the neighborhood level, and efforts were initiated to establish channels of communication. New city charters in Honolulu, Pittsburgh, the District of Columbia,

New York, and Newton, Massachusetts, authorized neighborhood councils. Similar recommendations were proposed in Los Angeles, Boston, Chicago, Detroit, and Rochester but were defeated over other issues. City councils in Birmingham, St. Paul, Wichita, Anchorage, Eugene, Salem, and Portland, Oregon, passed ordinances creating neighborhood councils or officially recognized existing neighborhood associations. Among the most comprehensive was the plan in Dayton, Ohio, where 149 residents were elected to Dayton's five neighborhood priority boards in 1971. They joined the 21 elected members of the Model Cities Planning Council in being responsible for the allocation of $5.2 million in federal funds under the Model Cities Program.[46]

During the first half of the 1970s, a number of other cities set up neighborhood councils, defined as broad-based organizations of residents, usually elected, with official recognition by city government and assigned advisory roles on matters affecting their neighborhoods. For example, New York City created 62 local planning councils to screen proposals for development in their respective neighborhoods or districts. Cincinnati formally recognized self-generated neighborhood organizations by drawing up official boundaries for its 44 neighborhoods after consulting with them. Washington, Baltimore, and other cities provide money and technical assistance to neighborhood organizations. In other locales, less formal systems developed to give quasi-official recognition to neighborhood associations. In 1971, for example, the California legislature adopted an act authorizing counties to establish municipal advisory councils in unincorporated areas, and by 1977 there were 27 of them in eight counties.[47]

BRADLEY BUELL

Community organizer and planner Bradley Buell (1863–1976) was born in Chicago and educated at Oberlin College and the New York School of Philanthropy, now the Columbia University School of Social Work. He assisted in the development of the American Association of Social Workers, in which he served as secretary and as associate executive.

Buell was the director of the New Orleans Community Chest and Council, field director of Community Chests and Councils, and founder and executive director of Community Research Associates. He wrote about community planning, consulted, and conducted research projects in 156 communities. In 1952 he published *Community Planning for Human Services,* analyzing the work of more than 100 agencies in St. Paul, Minnesota, finding that multiproblem families used almost 50% of all services. He published another book, *Solving Community Problems,* in 1973.

WHAT SOCIAL WORK PLANNERS DO

Committed to finding the most rational and feasible solution to social problems, the social work planner has a complex role, engaging people in the planning process, gathering empirical facts, and engaging in organizational politics and compromise. According to Benveniste, "Effective planning is the management of change." Social work planners are "designers who match technical, rational, aesthetic, and systemic thinking with selected configurations of supporters," Benveniste asserts, and they "exercise choices."[48]

Social work planners provide expert advice, make assessments, coordinate, and plan services. We scan the social environment of the community for gaps in service provision or areas where services are poorly, inequitably, or ineffectively provided. We attempt to discern where new needs may arise, and we work to develop new programs or strengthen existing ones.

Some theorists believe there are four different approaches to social work planning:[49]

1. *Reactive planning: to restore the past.* Reactivists tend to look to a simpler, less complicated past that becomes their operative reality. As a result, they may tune out significant aspects of the causes of social problems, pretending that by holding onto an imaginary past they can exclude the pain of the present and minimize the struggles of the future.

2. *Inactive planning: to preserve the present.* Inactivation does not mean "not acting." To inactivate means to neutralize or stop the action. Inactivists

work hard at keeping things the same and preventing change. A large number of people must be kept busy without actually accomplishing anything or they must be kept busy keeping others from doing something. Inactivist policymakers, for example, set up commissions and committees that study problems, then do nothing, giving the illusion of progress while delaying it at the same time.

3. *Proactive planning: to accelerate the future.* Proactivist planners accelerate movement into the future rather than slow it down, and encourage change instead of resisting it. For them, the future is filled with opportunity. Change is virtually synonymous with progress. Proactive planners attempt to forecast alternative futures and spend considerable time researching and anticipating.

4. *Activist planning: to create a just society for the future.* Activist planners seek to engage community members to eliminate social problems by changing the system that has the problem. Activist social work planning is infused with social thinking. It is community-oriented, future-directed, democratically aimed, and advocacy based.

ACTIVIST PLANNING

Activist planning is infused with social thinking. Activist social work planners use quantification and experimentation, and we use experience and qualitative judgment where quantification and experimentation are impossible or ineffective. We help our members use their intuition to look beyond the present. Activist planning is not bound by constraints of rationality or technology that simply implement goals incrementally and in a linear fashion. Activist planners seek technical solutions where possible, but we infuse rational decision-making with value content, consciously using our feeling/valuing functions. Because activist social work planning is often at the center of competing interests, we aim at equity, justice, fairness, and creating a vision of a good society.

Activist community planners assume that plans, even those based on technology, never work out exactly as expected. There are often unintended consequences of decisions, both good and bad. Activist planning must be morally acute, and the values implicit in planning must be sensitive to system change. Activist social work planning is flexible and innovative. Activist planners continually scan social systems and adapt plans as the situation changes. We adjust to difficulties along the way, often learn a better way to accomplish goals, and even change directions if that is called for.

Community Oriented   Activist community planners not only work to achieve a goal, but we help our members make quality decisions. Activist social work planners use all of our social thinking functions and help community members use and develop theirs as well. While we want our plans to succeed, we understand that "more development takes place by engaging in planning than as a result of the implementation of plans," and that "it is better to plan for ourselves, no matter how badly, than to be planned for by others no matter how well."[50] This is the iron law of activist community planning.

To allow planning professionals, government officials, politicians, and corporate managers to devise and put their plans into action without our involvement means that we are disenfranchised from creating our own dreams, making our own decisions, putting our ideas into action, and developing our own culture. Our lives are not entirely our own. The most important processes at the center of our humanity have been appropriated by others. Planning is a role that is integral with community life. If it is removed from people, the community begins to die. A plan not devised by the people is morally destructive to the people upon whom the plan is imposed.

Activist community social work planners insist that community members are not only capable of planning for our future betterment, but that community social welfare cannot be achieved without our personal engagement and involvement. Where we are deprived of the opportunity to plan for ourselves, activist social work planners assist us reclaim our rights to self-determination. When we are provided only token involvement, activist planners help us press for total inclusion.

Future Directed   Activist social work planners are not bound to the past as are reactivists, or committed to the present as are inactivists; nor do we rush into the future as do proactivists. Activist planners assist community members to learn from the past, reshape the present, and work to transform the future. We utilize our intuition and help community members "try to idealize"[51] the future for themselves. Together with our members "we become credible inventors of the future, designers and analysts who are also involved in selecting supporters and mobilizing the implementation of plans."[52]

Activist community planners help community members control their present, design the most desirable future, and invent ways of approximating it as closely as possible. We learn to calculate what is possible and at the same time nurture emergent ideas. Moving beyond simple prediction and preparation, we assist community members to create and control their future, shaping not only its design but its internal culture and values as well.

Democratically Aimed   Representative politics tends to consist of manipulating self-interested power, resolving conflict, and adding up the sum of individual preferences to arrive at a majority. Activist social work planners believe that democracy also can be a choiceworthy lifestyle in which people shape a social world that aims toward the achievement of a good society. Activist social work planners believe that planning must be carried out by means of a deliberative, substantive, and transformative democratic process.

Advocacy Based   The activist social work planner assists community members by acting as a facilitator of the planning process, helps members gain access to governmental and corporate power structure, provides technical assistance to members in research and in management science techniques, and trains community members in the planning process. Most importantly, activist community planners are supporters and advocates.

Social work planners are always pressured to divert their attention away from addressing the needs and issues of the people whose interests should be their primary concern. Activist community planners resist subordinating social and human systems to economic, utilitarian purposes. Activist planners always advocate for the community and resist the temptation to sacrifice members' interests to expediency, procedural issues, or the self-interest of others. We work to "anticipate and counteract pressures that stifle public voice, that manipulate democratic processes of consensus-building, and that ignore the many in need so that a few may prosper."[53] We use our skills to manipulate influence on behalf of those who have been manipulated by the influential.

Activist planners are concerned about the effectiveness of social programs, but also about welfare of all people, and the eradication of hurt, want, and need. We implement a vision of the public interest and the public good that equalize power and service arrangements for those who are powerless, and speak for and with those who have little voice in speaking for themselves.

HOW TO DO SOCIAL WORK COMMUNITY PLANNING

Planning should make a difference. Making a difference means changing something that would otherwise not have changed. Social work activist planning can be considered effective to the extent that things are changed in a direction that is better. By engaging in a thoughtful and planned process of change, working with and through political, business, and social institutions, citizens can have a substantial impact on the quality of life.

Armand Lauffer asserts that community planners must be "sensitive to and have methods available by which the needs of a community are recognized and resources and services are equitably and fairly distributed.[54] The method many community social work planners use corresponds closely to the rational problem-solving model described in Chapter 3. The community planning model includes (1) Building a structure or network of community and organizational relationships. (2) Developing an action planning group. (3) Defining the problem. (4) Mobilizing guiding values about the problem or issue. (5) Gathering information about the problem. (6) Generating a number of alternative solutions. (7) Assessing and comparing alternatives. (8) Providing feedback. (9) Presenting the solution to the community. (9) Presenting the solution to decision-makers. (10) Implementing the solution. (11) Monitoring and evaluating the plan.

Even though social work planning methods are rational and based on facts, it is important to understand that arriving at a plan to achieve an ideal future state cannot always be routinized. There are too many unknowns, too many variables for planning to be caught in a rigid process or method. Methods themselves need to be contingent on the particular situation that presents itself to the activist planner.

Building a Network of Relationships

One of the key skills of an activist social work planner is the ability to bring people together about a social problem of concern to them and help them seek its resolution. Community social work planners are not mere value-neutral technicians. We plan with people and engage in a number of organizing efforts, including networking, negotiating, coalition creation, and consensus building. We bring people together about difficult social issues for which answers may be unclear, opinions differ, goals may conflict, and interests may clash. Social work planners need to be good listeners and able to relate to a variety of people, many of whom have a vested interest in the issues at stake, and who may want more rather than less while contributing less to the process rather than more.

Forming a Planning Group

The first step in community social work planning is to form a planning group from members of the community. In every community there are numerous actors, vested interests, groups, organizations, and agencies that may be affected by, have information about, and have a stake in the outcomes of the problem. The most important of these stakeholders are interested and involved community members, but other stakeholders may be people in positions of power, such as representatives from governmental agencies and business corporations which operate in the community. Ideally the group should be composed of people with a variety of skills and leadership traits. To be effective, therefore, a social work planner needs to consider the range of inclusion and the kinds of roles that various members ought to play in developing a response to the problem.

A planning group is best if it includes between 15 and 20 members. This is large enough to represent a variety of interests of the community, but small enough for face to face meetings and for getting work accomplished. It is also large enough to break into several smaller groups that can be assigned smaller projects and report to the larger group.

Defining the Problem

Defining a planning problem may occur from two different perspectives. On the one hand, the definition of the problem may come from the social agency responsible for the substantive service arena for whom the action social planner is employed. For example, the Area Agency on Aging (AAA) may define a problem as assessing the needs of Alzheimer's victims over the next five years and developing a comprehensive program for meeting those needs. Under the best circumstances, however, defining a problem comes from community members themselves. A citizen's planning council on developmental disabilities, for example, may define a problem as the lack of day programs for severely disabled adults. A neighborhood planning board may be concerned about the lack of social programs for teenagers.

Mobilizing Guiding Values

One of the crucial issues that the community planning group needs to discuss is its guiding values. These values may be divergent from those of county planning commissions or other governmental agencies, which are often used as tools by developers and corporations to obtain variances, policy concessions, and rulings that benefit them. Community planning groups need to clearly understand what values are most important, why they are important, and how to present the content of those values to others. They must also understand the values that powerful interests represent, and how to counteract them. The community social work planner can be a valuable resource in helping the planning group discuss and articulate the content of the their values and particularly the interests of those in power with which they may conflict.

Gathering Information

Social work planners must be able to assess the strengths as well as social needs of people in order to plan with accuracy. We help community members conduct research about the social problem that we are trying to correct. Activist planners help members of community planning councils perform surveys, collect data, use statistics, analyze information, and prepare reports. Community planners most commonly use three kinds of research in gathering information about social problems: the social indicators approach, focused interviews, and social surveys.

The Social Indicators Approach   Social indicators are "inferences of need drawn from descriptive statistics found in public records and reports."[55] They are markers by which your planning group can spot underlying social issues. Lots of information exists to help your group members discover such indicators of social problems in your community. Health services both locally and nationally collect data on incidence of diseases and health of the population, including disabilities, aging, and specific diseases. The Department of Housing collects information on need for low-income housing. Social workers are interested in and on the alert for these indicators. Appendix C has a listing of websites that you can use to obtain statistical data.

While "using social indicators is unobtrusive and can be done quickly and inexpensively," Rubin and Babbie caution that "this must be weighed against potential problems in the reliability of a particular data base…and the degree to which the existing indicators can be assumed to reflect future service utilization patterns accurately."[56]

Focused Interviews   Focused interviews, or "the key actors approach," can help your planning group understand people's perceptions about their community and its problems. The key actor approach is "a research activity based on information secured from those in the area who are in a position to know the community's needs and utilization patterns."[57] A key actor can provide detailed historical data, knowledge about contemporary interpersonal relationships, and a wealth of information about the nuances of everyday life. In addition to key community members, interview various other stakeholders. For example, a planning group for homeless mentally ill will interview key members of the local mental health association, support groups for mentally ill, psychiatric hospitals and clinics, county mental health departments, and departments of social services.

A focused interview tends to be semi-structured; it "centers on selected topics but specific items are not entirely predetermined."[58] Keep a notebook to jot down names and phone numbers of key people you meet, as well as names of others that may be important to you. It is frustrating to meet key people and not be able to follow up because you can't remember their names or phone numbers. Keep a journal and, as soon after the interview as possible, write down the things you want to keep in mind, questions you want to ask, names and addresses of other people to contact, and issues to track down.

If your group members choose only people who are sympathetic to the issues on which they are working, they may have ignored those antagonistic to the problem. If they only talk to those who reached top positions in agencies, they may leave out important grassroots individuals who can provide your group with a different perspective. If you confine your discussion to those who are affluent or white, you will not hear the views of the poor, people from ethnically diverse communities, or nonvocal groups such as developmentally disabled, elderly in nursing homes, or children.

Make sure, therefore, that your focus interviews include a variety of key individuals, insuring that you have heard all sides of community opinion. One way to do this is to ask for names of people who share opposite points of view, who are leaders of groups who would block or even fight against your efforts. For example, if you discover that unemployment is a problem, you will want to talk to the head of the local chamber of commerce, the heads of large businesses or factories, and union leaders as well as social workers, vocational counselors, equal opportunity agencies, and private industry councils.

If you find that certain groups meet you with skepticism or rejection, try to discover why they feel this way. Talking with these people is crucial because they may give your planning group valuable insights about restraining forces or issues in the community of which the group may have been unaware. This will broaden your perspective and help you get a feeling for the potential opposition the planning group may be facing.

As your planning group members interview people, they will not only get information about the problems that people see, but they will be developing relationships with them and gathering insight into the kinds of services that exist. Let people know that your group will be using information to bring about positive changes and to work on problems in the community that the people being interviewed feel are important. You may want to ask these people to help you later in your change efforts. Key community leaders can be very important in opening doors, and using their influence and power in helping your planning group get goals accom-

plished. Everywhere they go, your group acts as a people who build bridges, make connection, and develop relationships.

Prepare yourself for your interview with a series of questions you want to ask. Try to ask each question the same way each time, so that you can compare answers. If you ask completely different questions with different people, you will get incomplete or fragmented answers. However, while you want to cover the same ground with all your respondents, be flexible enough to go into more depth, drawing people out. An advantage of focused interviews is that you may obtain unanticipated information that interviewees offer that will help you define the problem better.

Tell people about how many questions you have and how long the interview will take. People tend to be busy, and this will give them some assurance that you will not interrupt something important. Let people know that what they tell you will be confidential and that you will not quote them or otherwise misuse their information. This will help them be open and honest with you.

Generally, use a "funneling" technique in going from the general to the specific. For example, ask whether a respondent is aware of the drug problem in the Hillcrest neighborhood. If she or he answers yes, go deeper and ask questions such as whether they have personally been affected by the problem, if it is an important issue to them, and what things they think might help alleviate it. Keep your eyes open for nonverbal cues such as a raised eyebrow, an unexplained smile, a laugh that may seem out of place, the tone of voice, or a hesitation about answering. All of these cues may open up the door to asking for more information.

Social Surveys and Needs Assessments

Surveys give you the opportunity to quantify information and ask specific questions to which you need answers. A survey is a systematic inquiry of perceptions or attitudes about problems affecting an entire population or a sample of that population. Surveys can be used to "explore, describe, or explain respondent's knowledge about a particular subject, their past or current behavior or their attitudes and beliefs concerning a particular subject."[59] Sometimes "for state and national organizations, a survey might be the only practical way of finding out about the feelings of the organization's widely scattered membership."[60]

Because surveys ask specific questions, however, they are limited in the depth of responses you may receive. Therefore, they are best used when you want to narrow down issues, ask respondents to rank the importance of particular concerns, or give you an indicator of a range of preferences among items. This can be very important for a community because it gives specific information members can use in making decisions about the direction in which they should go.

Needs assessments are surveys that focus on gaps in service and unmet needs. In social planning, for example, you may study the lack of services or the needs of people with developmental disabilities, people with AIDS, immigrants, or migrant laborers. Often needs assessments are required if you are going to write a grant to fund a project because the funding source will want to insure that there is a real need that your project will serve.

Performing surveys correctly means that you need to word the questions correctly, field test the questionnaire, and choose your sample carefully if you are only giving your questionnaire to a portion of the population. In addition, if you are going to assess a sample of the population, you will need to analyze your data statistically to insure that the data you develop are statistically significant. All of these components of using surveys may at times be technically complicated.

Three factors are important in designing a survey or needs assessment: When—the time frame; who—the population you wish to survey; and how—how the survey will be accomplished.

When—The Time Frame

The time frame of your research may be important. Your community group may need to meet any number of deadlines. If you are applying for a grant, the foundation or governmental agency may require a needs assessment. These funding sources have deadlines for submitting applications, and if you want to apply you will have had to conduct your needs assessment by that deadline. Community planning groups are often interested in legislation. For example, a bill on gun control about which your community is interested may be scheduled for a public hearing. A survey can provide data to support your community's position, but you need to have it ready in time for the hearing.

A planning commission meeting may soon be held about a proposal to run a highway through a low-income area of your community, and you know that a survey of resident's perceptions could have an important impact on the decision. Your group needs to obtain and analyze the data before the hearing.

Who—The Survey Population

Sometimes you will survey all of the individuals involved in the issue being investigated. Often, however, the numbers of people that live in the area you want to survey are so large that you cannot reach all of them. Your time frame or costs are limited and you need to reduce the number of people you survey. In this case a small number of the population called a "sample" must be used.

If you are surveying a sample of an entire population, it is important to select the subjects using a valid sampling procedure to assure that the sample is representative, accurately reflecting the composition of the population surveyed. You need to decide on the size of the sample that you use. There are statistical formulas that can help you determine a sample size that will give you a level of accuracy, say of 99% or higher. Try to use as large a sample as possible, because the larger the size of your sample, the smaller the error. Guy et al., for example, recommend that "for most research endeavors, samples will be adequate if they are within the limits of 30 and 500. Samples of less than 30 are usually too small, while samples greater than 500 are seldom necessary."[61]

Four kinds of sampling procedures are common. Simple random sampling, systematic sampling, stratified random sampling, and cluster sampling.

Simple Random Sampling   Simple random sampling is the same as putting everyone's name in a hat and picking out every third name, for example, always replacing the names before drawing the next sample. If a computerized listing of an entire population is available, you can have the computer assign random numbers to each person.

Systematic Sampling   An even simpler, and in some ways better, method than simple random sampling is systematic sampling. First, compile a list of the names of all the people in the population you wish to sample. Then, beginning with a name chosen at random, count down every xth name. For example, for a population of 1000 people, you decide that a sample of 100 people or 10% of the population is the number of respondents you have time and resources to survey. You obtain a list of the 1000 people. Randomly choose a place to begin, and count down every 10th name to obtain 100 names.

Stratified Random Sampling   It is important to make sure that your sample is accurate enough to include every subgroup in proportion to its actual representation in your population. For example, in a survey of a college population, there may be a number of Asians, African Americans, and Hispanics. A simple random sample may not give you an accurate representation of them. One way to make sure that your sample is representative is to "stratify" your sample.

First, calculate the percentage of subgroups such as African American, Hispanic, and Asian persons in the population you are sampling. Then sample each of these populations separately by randomly drawing out names until you reach the proportionate amount. For example, assume you are going to take a total sample of 100 people from the total population of 1000. You know that the population is 20% Hispanic, 15% African American, and 5% Asian. Separate the names of all African Americans, Hispanics, and Asians from the total population to be studied. Out of the group of Hispanics you draw 20 random names, from the population of African Americans you draw 15 names, and from the group of Asians 5 names. From the remaining names you draw 60. You now have a representative sample with exactly the same proportion of African Americans, Hispanics, Asians, and Caucasians as in the total population.

Cluster Sampling   Sometimes you have many different groups of people such as families, schools, or businesses from which to obtain a sample. In this case you can do a cluster sample. Assume, for example, you are conducting a survey of religious group members in your town. First, define a "religious group" for your purposes. Then, cluster the groups into categories depending on the purpose of your research. Take a stratified sample of each group to ensure you get an accurate count of both large and small ones. You now have a representative list of the specific religious groups.

Obtain a membership listing from each religious group selected, and take a systematic or simple random sample of names from each of these. In this way your survey will accurately represent the membership of religious groups in your town.

How—Accomplishing the Survey   Surveys use questionnaires. Questionnaires can be administered by means of an interview in person, over the telephone, or by mail. When you decide how you will conduct the survey, your community group will need to consider its resources of time, energy, and money. Interviewing 100 people in person is time consuming and takes a lot of energy, particularly if the people are spread out over a large geographical area. Your group may also have to deal with not finding people home. In addition, face-to-face interviewing requires skill and training of the interviewers.

On the other hand, doing interviews face to face insures that you will get the information you need and often insures accuracy. A good face-to-face interview will often allow you to obtain a completion rate of at least 80–85%, which is usually required if you are conducting a survey funded by the federal government.[62] A face-to-face interview decreases the number of "don't know" answers, and the interviewer can sometimes help clarify survey questions that are vague.

Mailing questionnaires is popular because they reach people living in widely disbursed geographical areas at relatively low costs. However, a major problem with mailed questionnaires is the response rate. Rubin and Babbie state that for mailed questionnaires, "a response rate of at least 50 percent is usually considered adequate for analysis and reporting. A response rate of at least 60 percent is good and a response rate of 70 percent is very good." However, the response rate for mailed questionnaires may be "well below 50 percent." A mailed questionnaire, therefore, may not give you enough data. However, you can overcome this by increasing your sample size, sending out reminders, or making phone calls to nonresponders.[63]

The third method of conducting surveys is by telephone. Telephone interviews can reduce the cost and inconvenience of personally interviewing respondents. Telephone interviewing allows your members to dress as they please without affecting answers the respondents give. Telephone interviews allow workers to operate in comfort and safety, which is particularly important if the survey is being conducted in areas of a city that may offer threats to their safety. A disadvantage of telephone interviewing is the tendency for people to refuse to talk because of the number of calls they get from solicitors. However, if the interviewer introduces the issue as one that is of interest or concern to the respondent and if the questionnaire is short, telephone interviewing can be effective.

Preparing the Questionnaire Whether your survey is face-to-face, mailed out, or by telephone, you need to prepare a questionnaire. It is important that your questionnaire helps get information about the kinds of problems your community wants to resolve. The questionnaire should be clear, easy to administer, and not too long.

Review the information you have already gathered from social indicators or focused interviews. Ask your community planning group what they need to know to decide what direction to take. For example, if your group is working on economic development in a highly industrialized community where there is a large amount of unemployment, you may need to know the numbers of people who are out of work, the kinds of job skills required, and the kinds of training people might need.

Brainstorming can help you elicit the kinds of questions you need to ask. Group members give as many responses as they can without discussion. Write down each of them. When no more questions are forthcoming, your group looks over the responses. Some of them may be redundant, vague, or have more than one idea in them. Refine and add to the responses until you have enough questions to obtain the information you need from your survey.

When you develop questions for your questionnaire, there are a few rules to follow.

1. Don't ask for more information than you need. Keep your questionnaire short and to the point and make sure the answers are necessary in planning action.

2. Aim your questions at the level of education and background of your respondents.

3. Try to avoid jargon. For example, you may talk about "delinquent" while your respondents may talk about "being in trouble."

4. Do not ask two questions at once. Asking a double-barreled question will cause confusion. For example, "Should the government reduce the amount it pays to welfare recipients and spend it on education instead?" is a double-barreled question. One respondent may agree with reducing welfare but not that money should be spent on education. Others may want to increase spending on education but not at the expense of reducing welfare. Another may disagree with both parts of the statement. Whenever the word "and" appears, check if it is a double-barreled question and, if so, break it apart into separate questions.

5. Make sure your questionnaire items are clear. Consider the question "What is your level of education?" and the possible response items: (a) grade school, (b) high school, (c) college, (d) graduate school. A person who has attained all these levels could circle every category. It is also not clear whether "level of education" means that a person graduated or simply attended at that level. A clearer instruction would read: "Circle the highest level of education from which you have graduated."

6. Do not ask leading questions. Leading questions are those that presuppose an answer or skew the answer in a certain direction. For example, "Delinquent teenagers should be placed in institutions. yes no" is leading because it biases the response toward a yes answer and gives only two choices.

7. Avoid long items that may confuse the respondents.

8. Avoid negative terms. In responding to the statement "Carrying guns should not be allowed on our streets," some people may overlook the word "not" and answer on that basis.

9. Try to use a mixture of "closed-ended" and "open-ended" questions. Closed-ended questions are those in which a respondent can answer with a yes or a no. Another kind of closed-ended question is a listing from which a respondent is to choose a response. Closed-ended questions are easy to quantify, but they only repeat your preselected answers. Open-ended questions, on the other hand, allow flexibility in response but are harder to quantify. Often you may follow a closed-ended question with an open-ended one.

For example, "In your opinion, is the President doing a good job? Yes No," is a closed-ended question. If you then ask, "Why or Why not?" you are following it up with an open-ended question that gives you more information.

Scales and Rankings   A common way to get a range of responses is to ask respondents to answer using a scale. One common scale is a Likert scale. A Likert scale looks like this:

1	2	3	4	5
Strongly Agree	Agree	Neutral	Disagree	Strongly Disagree

Ranking asks respondents to make choices among a range of answers. For example:

On a scale of 1 to 5 with 1 being the highest and 5 the lowest, rank the community services that are most important to you.

_____ education

_____ employment

_____ health

_____ police

_____ recreation

Writing a Cover Letter and Introduction   Give your questionnaire a title and write out an opening paragraph or script that your group members will use in describing the purpose of the research. Include a statement on confidentiality. In the case of a mail-out questionnaire, this will take the form of a cover letter. Emphasize the importance of the research and the need for accurate and truthful answers. Assure the respondents that their answers will be anonymous.

Tell how many questions the questionnaire contains and how long it will take to answer them. Explain how the questionnaire is to be filled out. For example, if you are using a scale, explain how it is to be scored.

Pretesting the Questionnaire   It is important to pretest the questionnaire. Select a number of people from your population and try out the questionnaire on them. Pretesting helps you answer the following questions: Does the questionnaire give you the information you need? Are the questions worded correctly? Were they clear and unambiguous? Is the length of the questionnaire appropriate? Was it easy to administer?

After you have pretested your questionnaire, meet with your community group and revise the questionnaire using the information from your pretest.

Analyzing the Data   Count the number of responses to each question and calculate percentages of people responding to each question. If you have a large number of respondents, arrange your data in graphs or tables rather than describing the data in narrative form only. Computer programs are available that can automatically convert raw data into beautifully arrayed graphs and tables. One such program is SPSS. Follow up tables or graphs with a narrative explanation or interpretation highlighting the points that you want to make. Summarize the data as you go along. Be sure that you have fully answered the question you have posed.

Every sample has some built-in error. Formulas exist that can help you determine the degree of confidence that a reader can have in the study and the degree of sampling error that may exist. Computer programs can also be helpful in this area, enabling you to avoid complex mathematics involved in using statistics.

Developing Alternative Solutions

The community planning group needs to look at the variety of alternative solutions and assess their effectiveness in achieving the community's goals. Social work planners use a variety of decision-making and forecasting techniques such as difference equations, Markov models, networks, linear programming, queuing, simulations, benefit/cost analysis, and decision analysis.

Difference Equations   Suppose you are asked to help assess the ability of a mental health system to successfully fund its programs over the next several years. In order to do this you need to project income and expenses over that time to decide what programs to expand or reduce. A public hospital in an inner city is faced with severe overcrowding. One possible solution is to build an additional facility; another is to disperse services into community clinics. A local Area Agency on Aging is asked to fund programs for

Alzheimer's patients over the next ten years. In order to put together a budget, the AAA needs estimates of the number of people in day programs during the first two years.

All of these forecasting problems are issues that rely on difference equations. Difference equations are tools for exploring the way things change over time. They use rates of growth over a specific time period in the past to project growth rates during a specific period in the future.

Markov Models   Suppose you are a social work planner in a low-income community with high unemployment. You want to plan programs to deal with unemployment and you need to know not only how many unemployed people there are now, but how many people will be unemployed at any particular time in the future, and how those numbers will vary given certain conditions. If you can trace employment rates over time and within differing conditions, you can with some assurance develop some solutions to unemployment that can impact the problem effectively.

Markov models can help you trace changes in a system over time. Assume, for example, that you think up four different solutions to the problem of unemployment. One solution is to obtain federal funds to improve the job security of those already employed. Another is to establish a training program for unemployed. A third is to attract new industry through tax concessions, and a fourth solution is to increase unemployment compensation. Which alternative will gain the most employment? Markov models can help you chart how employment and unemployment will vary with each of these different programs, which may help you decide which solution or combination of solutions would be most effective.

Markov models can also help you understand population flows within a system. Imagine, for example, that an institution for the mentally ill in your community is operating at full capacity. The mental health planning board has decided to open a new wing. Should it be a facility for long-term patients or short-term patients? What size facility do they need to build? Markov analysis can help predict how many new persons can be admitted to the facility at three-month intervals, for example, and how many people will be in the facility two years hence. This kind of information can help the board decide whether they need a short-term or long-term facility, and what size the facility should be.

Networks   During World War I, Henry Gantt, a prominent efficiency expert, developed a model called a Gantt chart, by which workflow through various departments in an organizations could be charted. A manager could "tell at a glance the status of both the projects that are under way and activities and performance of the operating departments."[64] Gantt charts were predecessors of the Program Evaluation and Review Technique (PERT) and the Critical Path Method (CPM), which are now used to chart projects that involve many interrelated activities. PERT was the major planning technique used in the Polaris missile program. "To build the Polaris missile, management developed an intricate plan that consisted of a series of interrelated steps, some of which could be implemented simultaneously and some of those had to be finished before others could begin."[65] PERT and CPM are nearly the same; but if time estimates are certain, CPM is used, and if the time estimates are uncertain, PERT is used.

The Critical Path Method consists of "laying out or diagramming the flow of activities in a project to identify all possible sequences of steps from beginning to the end of the project. The longest sequence is the *critical path*, which determines the completion time of the project. Once it is known, managers can focus on those particular activities that are likely to delay the project."[66] In using CPM, first you identify every significant event that must occur to compete the project. These events, called milestones, are arrayed in sequential order and a time is allocated to each event. All milestones are plotted on a chart. The total time is then calculated and a model is created showing all the events with timelines so that each one is performed in order.

Linear Programming   Linear programming is useful when you allocate scarce resources to completing projects or objectives.[67] Because of its power, linear programming is one of the most highly developed and widely used management science techniques. It can be an invaluable aid for making policy choices that range from allocating the budget for a small library to selecting the components of a gigantic hydroelectric plant. A linear programming model of the entire Ganges-Brahmaputra river system, for example, takes into account flood control, power production, irrigation, navigation, and salinity control.

The usefulness of linear programming in many ways occurs because it is an optimizing model. In other words, it is "concerned with choosing the best levels for various activities in situations where these activities compete for scarce resources." Linear programming, for example, is useful if the issues are straightforward, such as when an administrator in a child protective service agency must allocate 450 hours of a caseworker's time among various cases, when a center for disabled must develop a work schedule to use $100,000 of staff time efficiently, or a neighborhood house must determine expenditure level for various activities.[68]

Often, however, the problems are such that inequalities exist. For example, a manager may want to minimize the cost of a job training program, but at the same time she may be willing to go over budget if particularly good jobs can be found or more people placed. Fortunately computer software can be obtained to perform these kinds of calculations.

Queuing   Waiting line analysis, or queuing, uses formulas developed in the early 1900s to reduce time lost by waiting in a line or the costs incurred by having an empty station with no one waiting. This is important particularly in agencies where establishing a waiting line for services is not appropriate or where there are specific time limits, such as in child protective agencies. The goal of queuing is to find an appropriate level of service that reduces the amount of time people wait in line and provides the most efficient utilization of existing resources. By calculating the average arrival time, the average time in the line, and how the lines are arranged, you can decide to either hire more workers, prioritize services such as in a "triage" system used in emergency rooms, or develop strategies to reduce waiting time.

Costs to the agency in operating service stations include construction costs, operations costs, maintenance, insurance, rent, and other fixed costs. The costs to the agency by keeping customers waiting are loss of business, ill will, and potential harm to the client. If the service facility is an emergency room in a hospital, the cost of waiting to the customer could be death. In a child protective service agency, the costs to the client could be the risk of continued child abuse. The larger the facility and the more stations, the higher the agency's cost but the less the cost to customers in time waiting. The fewer the stations, the lower the agency's cost, but the cost to the customer is higher. A queuing analysis is a means of deciding how to balance these costs. Formulas exist to help calculate the most efficient waiting line processes.

Simulations   Sometimes you may be faced with a complex situation, the outcome of which is not predictable by using simple mathematical formulas. In this case you develop a miniature or simulated model and manipulate it to discover how situations would work in the real world. Simulations help you discover flaws in your solution so you can modify the solution before you expend energy and incur any expense. You define the problem and construct the simulated model including all the relevant steps, interactions, and decision rules. Define all of the variables and boundaries within which the model must operate. Finally, run the simulation, evaluate the results, and refine and revise the model.[69] Computers can help develop such simulations and determine the best course of action.

Assessing and Comparing Alternatives

After your planning group has developed two or three alternatives for reaching its goals, your members need to compare them. One way to do this is by force-field analysis (described in Chapter 3) or benefit/cost analysis (described in Chapter 14). Rational decision-making such as benefit/cost analysis will give your planning group an estimated relative cost of various proposals. The least costly option, however, may not be one that the community as a whole would choose. While it is useful to calculate and rank alternatives, the final decision about a community plan should ultimately be decided by the community as a whole.

Providing Feedback

At every step in community planning, feedback to officials in positions of political power is vital. It is politically expedient to insure that those in power who will be asked to support or approve the plan are kept informed and asked for affirmation. If there are questions, issues, conflicts, misunderstandings, or other difficulties, they can be brought into the open and examined rather than allowed to complicate or damage the planning process.

The community as a whole on whose behalf the planning process is being conducted must be apprised about its progress and expected outcomes. Community members from the community at large can give valuable periodic feedback to the community action planning group about the feasibility of the planning objectives and outcomes.

Continually involving community members in the process insures that people who may not have been able or who did not want to become involved in the process initially may see an opportunity or may want to become a part of the planning process. Keeping community members involved and informed provides an army of volunteers to take on various parts of the project where their skills and abilities can provide valuable assistance, such as data collection, making contacts, arranging for meetings, and other tasks. The more the planning process includes and involves members of the community, the greater its impact and success may be.

Presenting the Solution to the Community

As soon as the planning team decides on the several recommended solutions to the problem, they should present the proposal to the wider community to solicit feedback in a series of open community forums. In a forum, the community planning committee should give a short history of the problem and how the committee generated its solutions. Insure that all alternatives are thoroughly presented by debates, focus-group discussions, or panel discussions with audience participation. When the community as a whole has had time to reflect and consider the merits of the various ideas, a general meeting should be called to rank them according to the solution that they think is best. For example, if there are three alternatives, the first choice receives a score of 3, the 2nd a score of 2, and the last a score of 1. The totals are calculated and divided by the number of voters. This gives an accurate assessment of the rankings of each alternative.

Presenting the Solution to Decision-Makers

The community planning group needs to devise its strategy for dealing with political decision-makers. You and your group must not be naive about this political process. There are many interests compet-

ing for attention and for approval. These claimants press for policy and legal concessions to further their own interests and may actively challenge and undermine the planning efforts of your community. The political process can be highly irrational, fraught with emotion, and dependent on compromise, bargaining, and negotiation.

Provide training to your group about the political process. A community planning group that assumes that dominant interests are bound by rules, rational arguments, facts, or figures will miss the point of organizational power and self-interest and be out of touch with the real operating principles of conventional politics. Your group may use forecasting or decision techniques to develop a very rational analysis, but when they present their case to politicians, developers, and citizen groups, they may find that no one seems to be listening.[70] The merits of the case, if they are not in the interests of those in power, are beside the point. Your group must be able to communicate with and present its plans to political leaders who have the power to approve the plan and set it into motion. Help community members develop good communication skills. Assist your members to present proposals and ideas in language that people can understand. An analysis not communicated well, Forester says, is "worse than useless—it can be counterproductive and damaging, just as it might also at other times deliberately serve to obfuscate important issues." Help your planning group get involved, talk, and argue, especially when confronted by misinformation, misrepresentation, disparities in power, and subversion of a process that advantages some and disadvantages others. Help community members "anticipate misinformation in time to use those strategies effectively, rather than looking back and saying, "Well, what we should have done was…." A "good idea presented the week after a crucial meeting (or too late on an agenda, or on the wrong agenda) will no longer do any good."[71]

Assist your planning group and community members to learn how to actively lobby key political decision-makers, network with key leaders, negotiate, build coalitions, and create consensus on behalf of the social plan. We try to even the scales, balancing power misalignments so that truth will win out in the end, encouraging "democratically structured, publicly aired political argument, not covert wheeling and dealing." How do you assist your community engage in such political action? According to Forester, by "informing the 'affected but unorganized' earlier rather than later in the planning process," as well as by helping the community in

> checking, double-checking, testing, consulting experts, seeking third-party counsel, clarifying issues, exposing assumptions, reviewing and citing the record, appealing to precedent, invoking traditional values (democratic participation, for example), spreading questions about unexplored possibilities, spotlighting jargon and revealing meaning, negotiating for clearly specified outcomes and values, working though informal networks to get information, bargaining for information, [and] holding others to public commitments. [72]

Implementing the Solution

A plan, even if it is well thought out and well designed, is of little use unless it can be implemented. You help the planning group itemize the steps by which the plan can be put into action by community members themselves in partnership with governmental and corporate leaders who may have resources that the community needs. For example, the plan may recommend that community members organize a community development corporation. The plan must help community members design and develop the corporation. (You will learn how to do that in Chapter 7). The plan may call for the development of a social program or social agency. You assist the planning group transform itself into a board of directors and form a social organization. (You will learn about doing that in Chapter 10). The plan may call for coordination, funding, and implementation of services by existing social agencies. Social work administrators will need information on how to proceed with such implementation. You may act as a consultant to administrators or help community members facilitate administration of the plan.

Monitoring and Evaluation

The planning process is not complete until a plan for monitoring and evaluation is developed. Often if a private agency is responsible for writing a grant and obtaining funding from a social planning organization, a program evaluation component will have been a part of the grant proposal. You will be active in working with community groups to analyze the consequences of change, monitoring program effectiveness, providing consultation, specifying adjustments needed, and identifying new problems which may call

for action and planning.[73] Program evaluation will be explored in Chapter 11.

SOCIAL WORK PLANNING FOR THE 21ST CENTURY

For much of the last half of the 20th century, a number of theorists and practitioners proposed increased neighborhood government, asserting that neighborhood government, controlled by residents, would provide services more responsive to individual needs.[74] Many cities across America have officially designated neighborhood planning organizations in partnership with city councils, mayors' offices, and planning commissions to take responsibility for developing, monitoring, and carrying out plans in their communities.

Yet, in spite of the importance of community planning, "these programs have had only limited success in meeting their goals. There has been a lack of societal commitment to the goals of these programs." The resources committed to these programs by government have been insufficient. Funding levels typically allow only limited activities in limited geographic areas. Many of the problems that have been addressed by these programs are the result of larger structural problems and are not easily addressed by local action. The unemployment problem, for example, has not been particularly amenable to neighborhood-oriented approaches.[75]

However, coalitions of neighborhood planning organizations could exert power and approach larger planning issues along with community organizations in partnership with government and corporate structures. Local planning efforts could take the lead in recommending structural changes in society as a whole to open up planning and politics to a wide spectrum of society. The emphasis on just one dimension of a neighborhood rather than a coordinated approach including social, political, and physical dimensions may have limited program effects. A comprehensive approach to neighborhood development may meet with greater success. Government at all levels must be convinced that continued support for neighborhood planning is not only necessary for democracy, but for effective government as well.[76]

Community social work planning has not enjoyed a high level of commitment or institutional support by the social work profession. Community social work planning has not generally been the recipient of advocacy, leadership, or foresight by the Council on

Social Work Education. As a result, one of the potentially most important, powerful, and necessary methods by which empowerment, democracy, and human welfare can be furthered languishes as a generally inattentive profession devotes the majority of its resources to individual treatment. While existing community planning efforts have demonstrated their usefulness, social work planning in the 21st century must increasingly be developed as an instrument by which people take charge of their own communities. Macro social work planners have been among the few leaders who have been consistently instrumental in this process.

CONCLUSION

Social work planning is one of the most important and potentially powerful means by which macro social work achieves its goals. It has, from the beginning of the social work profession, been a key player in the inception and implementation of social programs. Social planning has been one of the major points of entry for macro social workers into many social programs such as housing, mental health, poverty, and social services with the elderly. In addition, the organized efforts inherent in social planning provide a role of engaging citizen participation in ways that had not previously occurred. Social planning has resulted in an expansion of effective social programs in many areas of need. Since the Great Society programs, the emphasis on welfare-state planning has declined while the movement toward greater community involvement, citizen participation, and local initiatives has grown. This is a substantive shift in decision-making and politics, indicating a new era of grassroots democracy and local responsibility, in people planning for their own futures with centralized government as partners in the effort.

Social planning has major potential for empowering people in a community to take direction over their lives. Social work community planners, armed with rational planning techniques, mandates for citizen participation written into law, as well as responsibility to control and fund program services may have an impact on economic and governmental systems. But ongoing commitment to community planning must be increased by government and by the profession of social work if neighborhood residents are to achieve greater self-determination.

KEY CONCEPTS

Community social work planners

Charity Organization Society

Community Welfare Council

Councils of Social Agencies

Housing Act, 1949

Housing and Community Development Act, 1974

Comprehensive Community Health Act, 1963

Economic Opportunity Act, 1964

Community Action Program (CAP)

Community Action Agency (CAA)

Demonstration Cities and Metropolitan Development Act, 1966

Older Americans Act, 1965

citizen participation

reactive planning

inactive planning

proactive planning

action planning

planning process

questionnaires

surveys

sampling

simple random sampling

systematic random sampling

stratified random sampling

cluster sampling

difference equations

Markov models

networks

Gantt chart

PERT

Critical Path Method (CPM)

linear programming

optimizing

queuing

simulations

QUESTIONS FOR DISCUSSION

1. If planning is a normal aspect of the human condition, why has there been so much controversy over planning, particularly in the field of social welfare?
2. As you have read in this chapter, because of social planning and community organization, "the door was opened for transforming hospital-based psychiatric case work into psychotherapeutic social work, paving the way for government reimbursement, state licensure of clinical social workers, and private social work practice." It appears ironic that while macro social work was in large part responsible for the development of clinical social work practice, social work planning and other community social work arenas have declined while clinical practice has boomed. If it is true that clinical practice is reactive, dealing with past hurts, rather than activist in nature such as community social work planning, what is your assessment of the ultimate capacity of clinical social work to survive?
3. What do you believe will be the role of activist community social work planning in the future?
4. What role should social work planning take?

EXERCISE 6.1

One Best Way

Social planners advocating one or the other approaches to social planning assume that theirs is the one best way. Read the following excerpt from *The Road to Serfdom* by Friedrich A. Hayek, a Nobel prize–winning economist, and the statement about a contingency approach. Answer the questions that follow.

The dispute between the modern planners and their opponents is *not* a dispute on whether we ought to choose intelligently between the various possible organizations of society; it is not a dispute on whether we ought to employ foresight and systematic thinking in planning our common affairs. It is a dispute about what is the best way of so doing.[77]

Another stance is to assume that there is no one best way, but that each social problem might be addressable by different approaches depending on the situation. Such an approach may be called a "contingency" approach to social planning, which would match the approach with differing conditions or situations. Consider whether a contingency approach to social planning is appropriate or even possible.

1. Do you agree that there is a best way to do social work planning?
2. On what principles do you base your answer?
3. If there is a best way, which approach would you consider the best?
4. If you believe that a contingency approach is best, what "contingencies" or factors would you use to determine which approaches should be used?

EXERCISE 6.2

Presidents and Planning Approaches

Each president has developed a different approach to governmental planning. Review the leadership approaches of the following American presidents. What planning approaches characterize these presidents?

In class, arrange yourselves in triads. Compare your assessments and discuss why you chose the planning approaches you did. After you return to the class as a whole, compare your assessments and your rationales. Which presidents are reactive, inactive, proactive, or activist? Which style do you think has been most effective? With which presidential style do you most identify?

1. Roosevelt (1933–1945)
2. Truman (1945–1953)
3. Eisenhower (1953–1961)
4. Kennedy (1961–1963)
5. Johnson (1963–1969)
6. Nixon (1969–1974)
7. Ford (1974–1977)
8. Carter (1977–1981)
9. Reagan (1981–1989)
10. Bush (1989–1993)
11. Clinton (1993–2001)

EXERCISE 6.3

Social Problems and Planning

The following are examples of solutions to various social problems. Try to characterize which planning approach they exemplify.

1. Controlling the use of handguns.

2. Outlawing abortion.

3. Developing a system of national health insurance.

4. Abolishing slavery.

5. Allowing gays to serve in the military.

6. Landing a man on the moon.

7. Developing the human genome project—the book of life.

8. Interdicting illegal drugs.

9. Mandating English as our official language.

10. Building a fence to prevent illegal aliens from entering the country.

11. Requiring women on welfare who have been convicted of child abuse to wear a birth-control implantation device.

12. Requiring corporations to contribute part of their profits to replenish the resources in the physical or social environment.

13. Developing neighborhood councils with power to develop community plans.

EXERCISE 6.4

The Tragedy of the Commons

Read the following abridged and edited version of Garrett Hardin's article "The Tragedy of the Commons" and answer the questions that follow.

The tragedy of the commons happens in this way. It begins with a pasture open to all. Each herdsman may keep as many cattle on the commons as he wishes. Normally, such an arrangement works when tribal wars, poaching, and disease keep the numbers of cattle and people well below the ability of the land to contain them all. Finally, however, the day comes when modern technology equalizes the ability of the open pasture to carry the burden. Wars are negotiated, disease is cured, and hardier strains of cattle are introduced. At this point, the logic of the commons degenerates into tragedy.

As a rational actor, each herdsman wants to maximize his self-interest and asks, "What is the benefit to me of adding one more animal to my herd?" On the one hand, since the herdsman receives all of the profits from the sale of the additional animal, he will receive a positive utility of +1. On the other hand, adding one more animal will result in the land being overgrazed. Because the effects of overgrazing are shared by all, however, the cost of overgrazing for any herdsman making this decision is only a fraction of -1. Therefore, for a rational decision-maker, it is only sensible to add another animal to his herd, and another, and another.

The same conclusion is reached by each herdsman sharing the commons. Each rational actor is locked into a way of thinking that compels him, in a world that is limited, to add to his herd without limit. Therein lies the tragedy of the commons. "Ruin is the destination toward which all men rush, each pursing his own best interest in a society that believes in the freedom of the commons. Freedom in a commons becomes ruin to all."[78]

The tragedy of the commons is a modern tragedy in which the rational pursuit of private self-interest resists planning and, in a world of high technology, overrides the public good—whether that good is land, the ocean, the air, or even people.

Garrett Hardin asserts some social problems have no technical solution. He defines a technical solution as one that requires a change only in the techniques of the physical or biological sciences, demanding little or nothing in the way of change in human values or ideas of morality. For example, technology cannot solve the tragedy of the commons because technology created the problem in the first place, and technical solutions are immune to changing people's values. Technology, moreover, is based on calculative, self-interested rationality. In fact, for some problems, modern science and technology actually make things worse. One example is the population problem. As science develops techniques for a healthier, longer-lived population, fewer resources will become available to support that population.

Hardin is describing what is known in economy as a "public good" as opposed to private goods. A public good is like the air or the ocean, the common good, political freedom, national security. It is freely available to all. It cannot be divided into pieces and sold. It cannot be priced. Public goods are the purview of government. Private goods, however, are divisible, can be priced, bought, sold. Private goods are the purview of the economy. If the public good is used for the private good of others and these uses have spillovers, then disastrous results may occur. An example of a spillover is pollution. Pollution in the air or the ocean spills over beyond the territorial boundaries of the company or state or nation producing it. If someone contaminates the ocean through private use, the quality of that good is diminished for all. If a person or company releases waste products of production into the air, everyone who breathes the polluted air is paying a price, and in a sense is subsidizing the profit of the manufacturer. The private use of a public good can have public consequences.

1. What is your evaluation of Hardin's assessment?

2. Are there potentially injurious effects of technological advances for which technology itself has no solutions?

3. How can public goods be protected from overconsumption or spillovers?

4. Proactive social planners rely on technology and growth. What are the implications of the "Tragedy of the Commons" for proactivist social planners?

5. What parallels are there between private issues and social problems? For example, how does private greed result in a public or social problem?

EXERCISE 6.5

An Enemy of the People

Read the following summary of part of Henrik Ibsen's play *An Enemy of the People*,[79] or, better yet, read the entire play in its original form. In class, discuss the questions that follow the play's summary.

Great excitement is in the air. Dr. Thomas Stockman, a physician, planned a series of baths that would increase the health of the community and could be used for a profit. While a different model of construction than the one recommended by Dr. Stockman was developed by the town leaders and the baths committee, the town is beginning to anticipate their opening and the prosperity that is on the horizon. Peter Stockman, the doctor's elder brother, is the town mayor and chairperson of the baths. Peter is a man of action who took the doctor's idea and made it into a practical reality. He is an administrator, one who enjoys doing things, turning ideas into tangible results, and manipulating people for power and profit. Dr. Stockman, on the other hand, is an imaginative, creative, and idealistic professional who chafes at the bureaucratic process that seems to contaminate ideas by compromise and hidden agendas.

When the doctor tests the water because of some isolated cases of typhoid and other complaints, he discovers that the water, instead of being pure and healthy, is polluted by tanneries upstream. If the baths open, a serious public health problem would occur,

with a major outbreak of illnesses. Seeking out a sympathetic ear, Dr. Stockman tells the editor of a liberal newspaper, who agrees to print the doctor's findings. Immediately, Dr. Stockman sends a copy to his brother, expecting the mayor to shut down the baths and praise him for saving the lives of people and the reputation of the community.

His realist brother, however, is not at all happy with this news. It would ruin the town's plans as a health resort. Not only that, but the repairs the doctor recommends would take years to accomplish and would be extremely costly. The town has already invested a great deal of money, energy, and expectation on this project. The entire economy of the town is based on the success of the baths. In addition, Peter Stockman rationalizes, there is no proof that people will really become ill, and if they do, it is the doctor's responsibility to treat them. Dr. Stockman, the mayor asserts, has a moral obligation to the town not to attribute any illness to the baths unless it can be definitively proven. Moreover, the doctor himself is an employee of the baths, and frightening people without a clear scientific basis would display disloyalty as an employee. His brother, the mayor, as his boss, orders Dr. Stockman to keep quiet.

Shocked and indignant at his brother's insensitive and authoritarian response, Dr. Stockman refuses to back down. A shrewd strategist, the mayor talks to the leader of the tradespeoples organization, telling them that if Dr. Stockman has his way, the mayor will be forced to raise taxes. Threatened with financial ruin as well, the editor of the newspaper decides not to print the doctor's report.

Seeing his support crumbling about him, the doctor decides to go directly to the citizens themselves. The mayor, however, refuses to allow him to use a public building, so Stockman decides to give his speech at the home of a friend.

The night of the speech, the bureaucracy surreptitiously has stacked the cards against the doctor. A chairperson is put in charge who permits the mayor to speak first. The mayor repeats how the baths are the lifeblood of the community, turning the crowd against the doctor even before he speaks. But Dr. Stockman begins anyway, accusing the people of being poisoned by their own greed. "A community that lives on lies deserves to be destroyed," he says. The crowd shouts, "He is an enemy of the people." The chair of the meeting makes this sentiment official: "I move that we embody this opinion in a resolution." Dr. Stockman, the responsible planner, is now the official enemy of the people.

Read the rest of the play to find out what happens. Here are several questions that will help direct your class discussion of the play.

1. In your opinion, is Dr. Stockman an enemy of the people?

2. Even though the play was written nearly 100 years ago, what parallels can you think of today?

3. How would you characterize the ethical dilemma of planning the baths?

4. We read about "whistleblowers" who expose corruption, waste, and fraud in government or the private sector. What often happens to these whistleblowers?

5. What lessons in social planning does Ibsen's play uncover?

7. What would you have done if you were Dr. Stockman?

EXERCISE 6.6

Planning for the Homeless

Review the planning principles and planning process described in the text. Form into planning task force groups of five members each. Read the case study below, "Planning for the Homeless in Los Padres." Each task force is to develop a process by which social plans for the homeless in Los Padres can be implemented. In the planning process, task force members should consider the following:

1. How would you gather information about the extent of the need?

2. What groups or individuals would you contact?

3. What planning alternatives and courses of action would you consider?

4. How would you implement your plan?

Planning for the Homeless in Los Padres

What may be a charitable response to the poor and homeless may, in the long run, sometimes be an excuse by the larger community to ignore and abdicate its responsibility. Twenty years ago there were no services for homeless men in California's central valley community of Los Padres. Today, only two services exist. One is the Los Padres rescue mission that provides 25 beds and meals for 50 persons. However, the need is much greater than that. Although it cannot expand its ser-

vices without additional funds, the rescue mission has a strong policy against accepting government aid.

The Salvation Army provides a small residential facility for alcoholic men. The quality of services is good, but this facility can only house six men at a time. The problem is exacerbated during the summers, when migrant workers move into the valley to work in the fields. Often the laborers are laid off if the crops are not large. During these periods, many homeless single men end up staying in Los Padres and add to the growing population of the homeless.

Recently a number of muggings have occurred in the downtown area. Homeless, alcoholic men are being preyed on. Furthermore, the police and Department of Social Services have received complaints from businesspeople about vagrants sleeping in alleys and on street corners, as well as approaching customers for money. Ernest Rivera, director of Social Services, has asked you to develop a plan that he can present to the County Board of Supervisors.

ADVANCED EXERCISE 6.7

Deinstitutionalizing Jefferson State

The following is a real-life planning problem. Names of persons, places, and facilities have been changed. This exercise can be used as a final assignment or as a class presentation. It is best if one person is assigned the role of planner and other class members take different roles to assess the situation from their own particular perspective. There are no right or wrong answers to this problem.

The Jefferson State Hospital for developmentally disabled, which is located in Jefferson City, is under court order to deinstitutionalize residents by the year 2012 in order to provide a "least restrictive" environment and more normal life for its current residents. Over 2,000 persons currently reside at the hospital. The court has set strict time-lines by which the deinstitutionalization will occur. The hospital is to release 100 adult residents, 50 adolescents, and 25 children annually beginning in the year 2002.

In addition, except for severely medically fragile, severely autistic, and Praeder-Willi clients, a moratorium on new hospital placements has been imposed. The state office of developmental disabilities appealed this ruling but lost the appeal.

Many of the children and adolescents housed at the hospital will be returned to the county in which their parents have residency, but it is assumed that some, especially teenagers, will remain in Developmental Disabilities Area IV, a four-county area served by the Great Plains Regional Center.

What creates the major stress is the fact that because the hospital is located in Jefferson City, patients over 18 years of age are officially considered residents of Jefferson County. They have a right to remain in the county if they so desire. As a result, state hospital staff see the communities in Jefferson County as well other counties in Area IV as the first option for placement of these adults. There is a high probability that 100 developmentally disabled adults, adolescents, and children will enter Area IV each year for the next ten years.

Workshops and day programs in the counties are currently full. Normally, a workshop or day program operates with about 30 to 40 clients. It takes at least 6 to 12 months to develop a workshop or day program from scratch. Existing workshops or day programs can develop new programs more quickly, but this means existing programs must be willing to expand beyond current limits.

A small family care home can be licensed for up to 6 persons but usually has fewer than that number. Residential housing and day programs are currently operating at near capacity in Jefferson County. Few services, particularly day programs or residential facilities, currently exist in outlying counties. Placing 100 adult hospital residents per year in Jefferson County or even spread throughout Area IV will overly saturate the area in several years, assuming that most facilities would be small group homes that can accept a maximum of 6 residents. This would mean developing 17 homes per year. It takes a minimum of 3 months under good conditions to develop a small group home. This includes finding an operator who has a 4-bedroom home (1 bedroom for the husband/wife operators and 3 bedrooms with 2 clients per room) and going through the paperwork/licensing process. This process could take longer depending on renovations that may need to be made. If an existing operator intends to purchase a home and staff it, the process could take longer, depending on obtaining a loan, licensing, hiring, training, and getting staff approved, and making renovations.

Group homes can accommodate more than 6 residents but require live-in staff. It takes at least 6 to 12 months to develop a residential care home, including forming a board, becoming incorporated, applying for loans, finding an appropriate site, purchasing or renting a home, deciding on level of disability and type of clientele, applying for and obtaining licenses, making physical renovations to the facility, hiring and training staff, and accepting referrals from the Regional Center. A caseload for a residential social worker at the Regional Center is about 40 clients.

The local Area IV Developmental Disabilities Board is charged with planning for the needs of developmentally disabled citizens in the four-county regional area. It is not known what specific needs or levels of service the hundreds of adults who will be released from Jefferson State Hospital over the next few years will have. Neither is it known whether all 100 adults will actually move to Area IV, since some may choose to live elsewhere. At a minimum, however, they will need housing, day programs such as workshops, vocational training services, and probably a variety of specialized dietary, speech, community awareness, recreational, and mental health services. Under the most pessimistic assumptions, however, it is clear that the counties in Area IV do not presently have the capacity to absorb 100 developmentally disabled adults per year without more housing and other services as well as social workers to locate housing and services, and additional funding by the regional centers to pay for the additional housing and service costs.

Further complicating things is that, while the hospital does have information about individual clients, actual release of clients from the hospital will depend on having facilities and services available for them. Obviously, a plan for deciding who will be released and when must be coordinated with developing services.

Any plan must be coordinated with the local Regional Center, which provides case management and residential placement services for developmentally disabled in the Area IV region, the Area Disabilities Board IV, the county school system, and county mental health system.

Class members are to form into groups called the Deinstitutionalization Planning Task Forces. Task force members assume roles of representatives from the state hospital, the Regional Center, the county schools, the mental health system, the local Aid to Retarded Citizens organization, and the Association of Residential Operators. Your task is to develop a plan for deinstitutionalizing the hospital. The planning proposal needs to be presented at the next Area IV Developmental Disabilities Board meeting.

1. Define the planning problem facing the regional area of developmentally disabled.

2. Develop and prioritize a plan for assessing client needs, services, and other data.

3. Assess what other impacts need to be considered, such as number of Regional Center program developers, case managers, and administrative and staff specialist employees, numbers of ancillary services that may need to be developed , and the estimated costs of these additional services.

4. What are the political feasibility and social impact constraints that will need to be considered?

5. Decide on at least two alternative plans. What is the likelihood that the Area Developmental Disabilities Board, the State Hospital, and the Regional Center—the three agencies mandated with responsibility for carrying out the court orders—will not be held in contempt for not complying with the court order?

ADDITIONAL READING

John Forester. *Planning in the Face of Power.* Berkeley: University of California Press, 1989.

Jamshid Gharajedaghi. *A Prologue to National Development Planning.* New York: Greenwood Press, 1986.

Alfred J. Kahn. *Theory and Practice of Social Planning.* New York: Russell Sage Foundation, 1969.

Armand Lauffer. *Social Planning at the Community Level.* Englewood Cliffs, NJ: Prentice-Hall, 1978.

Robert R. Mayer. *Policy and Program Planning: A Developmental Perspective.* Englewood Cliffs, NJ: Prentice-Hall, 1985.

———*Social Planning and Social Change.* Englewood Cliffs, NJ: Prentice-Hall, 1972.

Donald N. Michael. *On Learning to Plan and Planning to Learn.* San Francisco: Jossey-Bass, 1973.

William M. Rohe and L. B. Gates. *Planning With Neighborhoods.* Chapel Hill: University of North Carolina Press, 1985.

Jack Rothman. *Planning and Organizing for Social Change: Action Principles From Social Science Research.* New York: Columbia University Press, 1974.

Alan Walker. *Social Planning: A Strategy for Socialist Welfare.* Oxford: B. Blackwell, 1984.

Aaron Wildavsky. *Speaking Truth to Power.* Boston: Little, Brown, 1979.

Management Science Techniques

E. J. Mishan. *Economics for Social Decisions: Elements of Cost-Benefit Analysis.* New York: Praeger, 1973.

Edith Stokey and Richard Zeckhauser. *A Primer for Policy Analysis.* New York: W. W. Norton, 1978.

Mik Wisniewski. *Quantitative Methods for Decision Makers.* 2d ed. London: Pitman Publishing, 1997.

General Works

Milton Friedman. *Capitalism and Freedom.* Chicago: University of Chicago Press, 1962.

John Kenneth Galbraith. *The New Industrial State.* 2d ed. Boston: Houghton Mifflin, 1971.

Friedrich A. Hayek. *The Road to Serfdom.* Chicago: University of Chicago Press, 1944.

7

Becoming a Community Developer

Social change isn't going to come as quickly as any of us would like it to come. Building a community is a subtle, delicate, long-term process.

Sam Brown, community organizer[1]

Each person in a community must do his part. All have gifts and an area to do. Together we can accomplish great things. Where there is no vision, the people perish. If we don't continue with that vision before us then in essence our community will perish.

Margaret Kinaanen, community leader, Embarrass, Minnesota

Ideas in This Chapter

COMMUNITY DEVELOPMENT FINDS ITSELF

The 1960s was perhaps one of the most turbulent periods in America's history. Between 1962 and 1965, at least twelve major disorders occurred in large metropolitan centers. In 1965 a racial disorder in Los Angeles was the worst that the country had seen since 1943, when massive World War II riots took place in Detroit.[2] In the first nine months of 1967, the nation experienced 167 outbreaks of civil disturbance. In that one year, major riots occurred in eight cities, involving damage to property, violence, and death. In Detroit, 43 people were killed. Thirty-three cities experienced serious disturbances, and lesser disorders occurred in 123 more.[3] Twenty-five cities suffered disorders at least twice, and New York City suffered five times. Major riots in Cleveland and Rochester involved loss of life. In the spring of 1968, the evening of the day that Martin Luther King Jr. was assassinated, cities across the nation again erupted in looting and burning.

Black neighborhoods seemed to hit rock bottom. When the looting and burning stopped, however, a growing black consciousness began to stir. It was, after all, black citizens of all classes who were suffering most from the riots. The urge to burn was destroying their own neighborhoods. The riots mobilized middle-class and working-class blacks into a new and different kind of struggle, joining poorer and more alienated people in reassessing the black agenda. All over the stricken areas, independent neighborhood groups formed to work out the meaning of these events and to light a different beacon.

As neighborhoods in each city puzzled out their local scene, the pieces of the answer began to fall into the same pattern. Whatever was wrong went far beyond the acts of those who set the fires or looted or taunted the police and fire fighters—or shot at them. The community itself had not taken enough responsibility to direct its own destiny or counteract systemic inattention, degradation, or exploitation by the larger society. If their communities had been forgotten by the rest of society, however, it also seemed that they had been forgotten by the residents themselves.

Suddenly it became clear that the stricken neighborhoods would never improve because of natural and spontaneous market forces or because government agencies would eventually do something. If change was going to happen, these neighborhoods would have to consciously take their destinies into their own hands and build all of the necessary resources—the institutions and social tools that make a community work. Community members began to look to themselves and toward local self-determination. Across the country an awareness grew that the community members themselves needed to develop and control the economic institutions in their own black neighborhoods. Communities began to "shift their perspective from an individually based legal conception of black civil rights to the socio-economic concept of black community," asserts Stewart E. Perry. A new social and economic tool, now known as the "community development corporation" or "CDC," was invented in a number of different black ghettos "where desperate need, combined with ingenuity, opportunity, and talent, brought forth this new institution…. In each instance the CDC seemed to have been a direct reaction to the local disasters of an inner-city riot."

The CDC represented a direct community approach to comprehensive revitalization of the neighborhood, including businesses that created jobs and incomes, political networks, housing, schools, recreation facilities, and all of the mediating infrastructures that build a new sense of self-respect and self-determination. A decisive turning point in the life of community had occurred. Members of these communities were committed to their own recovery. They would no longer look to external forces to determine their direction. They would not allow the community's resources to be drained or exploited. They would not be dependent on government or on outside experts. People in poor communities across North America would find in themselves and in one another the power and the resources to revitalize their communities and in the process find themselves as well. Community in America would never be the same again.

WHAT YOU WILL LEARN IN THIS CHAPTER

There is scarcely a modern town or city that does not have pockets of poverty, groups of mentally ill, homeless, immigrants, or others who cry out for community development efforts. Neither corporate nor governmental assistance alone will provide the answer to America's depressed communities. Neither business leaders nor politicians have the will or the ability to solve the problems of inner-city and rural poor. Only the people of a community, in partnership with government and the economy, can solve their common problems. Along with community organization, community development has potential to revitalize community and to remediate social problems that have gone unsolved for generations. Community development is one of the most important arenas of macro social work today.

In this chapter, you will learn what community development is. You will explore a short history of community development. You will learn how macro social workers approach community development in modern communities, how to begin a community development corporation, and how to assist in restoring ontological communities.

WHAT IS COMMUNITY DEVELOPMENT?

The term *community development* came into popular use after World War II. Community development is derived from economic development, from which it takes its surname, and community organization, from which it takes its first name. Economic development has been chiefly concerned with increasing productivity and efficiency by developing businesses that multiply and distribute economic resources to improve the financial situation of a locality. Community organization engages local residents seeking empowerment and self-determination in issues that affect their communities.[4]

Community development is much like grassroots democracy, in which power is shared in an equal and open forum. It encourages values of citizenship and citizen participation in the life of the community, promotes education in civic pride and civic consciousness, and sees in community itself an arena where the public interest can become a living force. Community development is a method by which macro social workers assist community members to develop resources and promote networks that enable a community to become a source of social, economic,

political, and cultural support to its people. Antonia Pantoja and Wilhelmina Perry define community development as a means by which members of an economically dependent and politically disenfranchised community work together to:

1. Understand the forces and processes that have made them and keep them in their state of poverty and dependency.

2. Mobilize and organize their internal strength, as represented in political awareness, a plan of action based on information, knowledge, skills, and financial resources.

3. Eradicate from individuals and from group culture the mythology that makes them participants in their own dependency and powerlessness.

4. Act in restoring or developing new functions that a community performs for the well-being of its members—starting with the economizing function.[5]

Community development aims at the creation "of economic and social progress for the whole community with its active participation and the fullest possible reliance on the community's initiative."[6] Community developers with oppressed, alienated, and depressed modern communities use "democratic procedures, voluntary cooperation, self-help, development of indigenous leadership, and educational opportunities" to cooperatively solve common problems.[7] We assist communities of meaning that experience declining membership, and boundary and leadership problems. We become strengthened with a renewed sense of purpose and mission. We work with traditional communities to

> inculcate among the members of rural communities a sense of citizenship and among the residents of urban areas a spirit of civic consciousness; to introduce and strengthen democracy at the grassroots level through the creation and/or revitalization of institutions designed to serve as instruments of local participation; to initiate a self-generative, self-sustaining, and enduring process of growth; to enable people to establish and maintain cooperative and harmonious relationships; and to bring about gradual and self-chosen changes in the community's life with a minimum of stress and disruption.[8]

A SHORT HISTORY OF COMMUNITY DEVELOPMENT IN NORTH AMERICA

There are two main periods of community development in North America. The period of convergence from 1890 to 1960, and the era of community development corporations from 1960 to the present.

Convergence 1890–1960

In North America, community development did not begin to emerge until the 20th century. It did not burst on the scene suddenly. Instead, a convergence of a number of influences ultimately grew into the field of community development,[9] including Charity Organization Societies, Cooperative Extension Services, universities, and the federal government, all of which took slightly different approaches to community development.

Charity Organization Societies   With their emphasis on public participation and a social planning perspective, Charity Organization Societies encouraged community development and coordination of community-based programs and projects at the beginning of the 20th century. Community development continued to evolve out of the early work of the community chest movement, the United Community Services, and the United Fund.[10]

Cooperative Extension Services   In 1908, rural community development in the United States occurred as a result of President Theodore Roosevelt's Country Life Commission, which encouraged the Department of Agriculture (USDA) and land-grant colleges to take a more active role in the life of rural Americans. This top-down approach resulted in the Cooperative Extension Service, begun in 1914. One of the mechanisms by which the "Cooperative Extension Service assisted rural communities was a series of local clubs that joined with extension agents in developing and working out local programs [of community development] work." Originating in the South in the 1920s, community clubs were widely used in black communities and were based on the principle of developing projects *with* people, rather than *for* people. By 1923, more than 21,000 communities were engaged in cooperative extension community development projects at the grassroots level.[11]

Universities   Educational institutions became involved in training community developers. One of the most influential of these was the National University Extension Association, which began in 1915 and extended through the 1960s. In Canada, cooperative forms of community organizing, community economic development (CED) groups, became a practical alternative for strengthening communities socially as well as economically. Canadian CEDs began in the cooperative movement of the early 20th century, preceding the emergence of the welfare state. One of these movements was the Antigonish Cooperative Movement in Nova Scotia, assisted by St. Francis Xavier University. Xavier has provided distinguished training programs in community development since about 1930. Its cooperative community development programs work within an adult education framework, through group discussions aimed at identifying the causes of economic problems, empowering people, and encouraging them to organize for change.

In the United States, William Biddle, one of the field's most prolific writers, began a community development program at Earlham College in 1947. Since then, universities have continued to provide impetus for community development. The Center for International Education at the University of Massachusetts, for example, provides training and educational materials in international community development.[12]

Federal Government   During the Great Depression, the federal government expanded community development efforts by means of several national initiatives. One of these was the Works Progress Administration (WPA) administered by social worker Harry Hopkins, whose goal was to not only give unemployed people jobs, but to put people to work on projects of community improvement and betterment. In addition, Hopkins pioneered the development of the Civilian Conservation Corps (CCC), through which "young men whose families were on relief" were employed in improving parks and community beautification projects.[13] One of the most famous community development projects of all time was the Tennessee Valley Authority (TVA).

Community Development Corporations 1960–Present

Community development efforts took a leap ahead with President John F. Kennedy in the early 1960s, the era of "big government" spending. Many of the more than 1,000 federal programs provided funding for community programs, and expenditures for housing and community development jumped from $30 million in 1959 to $1.4 billion in 1969—a 466% increase.[14]

President Kennedy captured the imagination of young people with the establishment of the Peace Corps, a volunteer international community development program in which volunteers were assigned to assist third-world communities worldwide. Kennedy also developed the Area Redevelopment Administration, which carried out community and area projects and required that the overall economic development plans be made by local committees of concerned citizens and governmental officials. By the mid-1960s, Rural Area Development committees were active in more than half the counties in the country.[15]

Lyndon Johnson continued and expanded community development efforts in his "Great Society" programs. The Demonstration Cities and Metropolitan Development Act of 1966, better known as the Model Cities program, was the most "ambitious and comprehensive effort by the federal government to aid America's blighted urban areas," according to Pine. The act provided grants and technical assistance to help cities plan, develop and execute programs for enhancing the physical and social environment of neighborhoods.[16]

The Economic Opportunity Act (EOA) passed in 1964, often called the War on Poverty, was aimed at improving and uplifting inner-city neighborhoods. It initiated a series of programs, including Volunteers in Service to America (VISTA), a domestic Peace Corps program; a Job Corps program for school dropouts; a Neighborhood Youth Corps for jobless teenagers; Upward Bound, a program encouraging slum children to go to college; and Operation Head Start, a project of preschool training for children.[17] Community Action Programs (CAP) attempted to engage community residents directly in the development of locally based programs, funding inner-city projects of public and private agencies, such as day care centers, recreation centers, and health centers.[18] The Housing and Urban Development Act of 1968, Pine states, was "the culmination of the federal government's attempts to provide housing and assistance programs for poor and moderate-income families." The act, which Johnson called the "Magna Carta to liberate our cities," affected more than 700 planning grants and funds for water and sewer projects, flood insurance, model cities, and mass transit."[19]

The Origin of Community Development Corporations   In the midst of all of these activities, a fledgling community invention called Community Development Corporations (CDCs) was seeing its first experiments begin in 1967 in the Bedford Stuyvesant community of Brooklyn. Established by Senators Bobby Kennedy and Jacob Javits, the Bedford Stuyvesant Restoration Corporation was probably the biggest and best-known CDC, receiving about $4 million in federal support annually for its multitude of important projects. The Bed-Stuy project was quickly followed by The Woodlawn Organization (TWO) in Chicago, and in 1968 the Hough area project in Cleveland. What followed was a first wave of about 100 CDCs in the 1960s, including North Avondale in Cincinnati, the Hillside Terrace Housing Project in Milwaukee's North Side, the Near Northwest Side of Chicago, the Mission District of San Francisco, the Lower East Side of New York City, Newark, New Jersey; Syracuse, New York; Roxbury, Massachusetts; Austin, Texas, and others. They were an outgrowth of the turbulence of the civil rights and antipoverty movements and an effort by local residents to assert control over their own neighborhoods, funded by a few foundations and Great Society programs.[20]

Expansion and Retrenchment   In the 1970s, the interest in community development encouraged additional neighborhood organizations to spring up in cities such as Birmingham, Brooklyn, Oakland, Stockton, San Diego, Cleveland, and Wichita. The number of Community Development Corporations grew rapidly. "The second wave of CDCs in the 1970s saw a tenfold increase in efforts that began as community residents opposed urban renewal, redlining, factory closings or irresponsible landlords who abused tenant rights.[21] CDCs created partnerships with foundations, particularly the Ford Foundation and the federal government's Community Services

Administration in 1974, and the Office of Neighborhood Development in 1978.[22]

National development organizations were created. The Community Development Society organized in 1969 to exchange ideas and publish community development information through its journal. Neighborhoods U.S.A. (NUSA) began in 1975 and helped develop partnerships among neighborhood residents, elected officials, and professionals by sponsoring conferences on community development issues.[23] The Neighborhood Reinvestment Corporation (NRC) stimulated the creation of local partnership efforts for comprehensive housing rehabilitation services.[24]

In 1973, however, President Nixon declared a moratorium on funding urban development programs, and in 1974 President Gerald Ford signed the Housing and Community Development Act, replacing model cities, urban renewal, and neighborhood facility grants with a single community development block-grant program. "Unlike the Great Society legislation which had forced local officials to share power with neighborhood community organizations, [the act] limited citizen participation to purely an advisory role" and was generally seen as a setback for community development efforts. During the Carter administration, however, the act was amended to allow for more citizen participation and required citizen involvement in planning, execution, and evaluation. As a result, "new community organizations were stimulated and became agents for citizen participation in the local community."[25]

Because of President Carter's commitment to community and neighborhood development, federal interest in neighborhood-based programs grew. The Neighborhood Self-Help Development Act of 1978, for example, recognized "the neighborhood to be a national resource which…deserved to be conserved, revitalized."[26] By the late 1970s, CDCs had become central components of federally assisted neighborhood development programs and by 1980 more than a dozen federal programs provided support for local staff and projects.[27]

With the support of President Carter, "the tireless efforts of those involved in the neighborhood movement to bring the needs and potentialities of the nation's neighborhoods to the attention of federal policymakers" bore fruit with the passage of the National Neighborhood Policy Act of 1977, which created the National Commission on Neighborhoods to investigate the state of the nation's neighborhoods. The commission's report, *People, Building Neighborhoods,* recommended "a system of neighborhood human services, establishment of neighborhood advocacy posts, training and technical assistance" to neighborhoods. While the report was a "well-developed blueprint for improving our communities," it came too late in Jimmy Carter's presidency for implementation, and the Reagan administration ignored the commission's findings.[28]

The Era of Community Development Corporations The third wave of CDCs that developed in the privatization campaigns of the Reagan years were forced to face dramatic cutbacks in governmental funding. The Community Services Administration and Office of Neighborhood Development, for example, were quickly dismantled. In spite of this, however, communities were determined to deal with their own problems to accomplish the goal of building "a non-white middle class by developing highly specific and measurable development projects in which community people could work for their own economic betterment."[29]

CDCs of the 1980s responded by becoming much more businesslike than their predecessors, exhibiting management "talent and development skills once thought to be the exclusive province of the for-profit sector." They produced results. In late 1988, Renee Berger conducted a study of 834 CDCs and found that CDC projects had produced some 125,000 units of owner-occupied and rental housing, and repaired 275,000 additional units. They developed 16.4 million square feet of offices, retail spaces, and industrial parks in poor communities; loaned money to some 2,000 enterprises, mostly for amounts under $25,000; and created or retained nearly 90,000 jobs in the five years prior to the study.[30]

Despite the inadequacy of corporate and federal funding, CDCs continued to spring up, and by the early 1990s the National Congress for Community Economic Development claimed there were at least 2,000 of them.[31] CDCs were increasingly able to attract low-interest loans, loan guarantees, and other financial assistance from private financial institutions and particularly from banks. The main reason for this was the Home Mortgage Disclosure Act of 1975 and the Community Reinvestment Act (CRA) of 1977, both initiated by the community organizing efforts of Gale Cincotta and Shel Trapp of National Peoples Action organization. These acts required banks to disclose how much money they invested in neighborhoods in which they were located. For example, if a bank obtained $1 million in deposits in a poor neighborhood, but loaned only $50,000 to its people, it laid itself open to pressure to lend more money in that neighborhood. By the 1990s many CDCs had developed partnership arrangements with local financial institutions to facilitate CRA lending in deprived communities, and some involved government support in the form of loan guarantees, insurance, and rebate assistance to lessen the risk.

During the Clinton Administration, interest in community development and volunteerism became renewed with the National Service Corps, in which young people were assigned to a variety of community development projects. National neighborhood organizations formed the National Neighborhood Coalition as a vehicle for information sharing and joint action on common concerns, with particular attention to federal legislation and administrative policy. The National Congress for Community Economic Development and the Corporation for Enterprise Development were formed to share information, develop resources for poor and disadvantaged neighborhoods, and analyze proposed federal laws and regulations.[32]

Faith-Based Community Development   Today, faith-based economic development has become the cutting edge of federally assisted community development efforts. In virtually every major American city with a substantial African American population, black churches have undertaken community improvement efforts. Dozens of successful church-based development projects have been carried out in major urban centers such as New York, Detroit, and Kansas City, including the creation of low-income housing development, credit unions, companies, and shopping centers. Through 1993, U.S. community development corporations had created roughly 100,000 jobs, and there are now well over 3,000 CDCs in the United States, two thirds of which have completed at least one concrete development project.[33]

WHAT ARE COMMUNITY DEVELOPMENT CORPORATIONS?

According to Fisher, CDCs "are nonprofit organizations that serve a low income community, are governed by a community based board, and develop commer-

cial/industrial, business enterprise or housing development projects with housing far and away the most prevalent undertaking."[34] Perry defines a CDC as "a coalition organization of neighborhood residents who carry out their own comprehensive program of local renewal activities, especially including business development."[35] Alan Twelvetrees defines CDCs as locally based, community-oriented corporations whose thrust is to develop profitable community resources such as housing, financial institutions and shopping malls, in cooperation with private and government sponsorship for the benefit of the community.[36]

CDCs are organizations focusing on the needs of a specific urban or rural area, usually a deprived or transitional area. They are usually managed by a board of people with allegiances to the neighborhood in the sense that they live, work, or own businesses there, though these boards often include bankers and other people for their expertise. CDCs are usually private nonprofit organizations with some subsidiaries that are intended to make a profit. The main thrust is to increase the economic power of the community and strengthen its leveraging ability by entering into partnerships with business and government. Once the base is established, social services are often delivered as well. Sometimes CDCs spawn other independent companies but keep their own majority representation on their boards.

CDCs serve as vital alternatives to privately owned for-profit businesses whose revenues are almost always siphoned out of the neighborhood. The profit accruing from various CDC ventures is kept in the community and can be used not only for running the CDC and stimulating other businesses but also to provide additional social services.[37] But just as important as the economic projects themselves is the process of neighbors getting together, making decisions, seeing a project through to the finish, and then using their finished products. The CDC builds a sense of community control and enhances individual and collective empowerment.

The well-established CDC knows community needs and can access charitable and private dollars, develop numerous interlocking successful projects, and serve as a financial stimulus for the community. It can become a means by which the community plans and develops its own economic future, rather than leave the local economy dependent on outsiders who have little or no interest in improving the financial strength of the community. CDCs bring new services or goods into the neighborhood, employ local workers, displace higher-cost providers, engage in job training, and make other needed neighborhood improvements.

CDCs vary enormously. Many CDCs engage in constructing or improving housing and commercial or industrial facilities, or creating jobs. Other CDCs establish financial bodies such as revolving loan funds or even savings and loan institutions to try to ensure a supply of finance to home owners and local business people. Many CDCs develop and operate social services and other ventures such as youth training projects.[38]

Some CDCs are basically rather simple, but the biggest and best known are multipurpose organizations that specialize in one kind of business but engage in a number of subsidiary functions. For instance, the primary business of a CDC may be to build and rehabilitate housing for low-income people. The CDC may raise finances from private and governmental sources and act as the developer but contract out the actual building and management to others. Or it may set up its own construction company to actually do the work, and it may set up a management company to manage the property. It may act as a broker to help local businesses and have a small stake in other companies. It may operate a revolving loan fund to assist local businesses, including its own, and it may establish other community-controlled financial institutions. It may also move into real estate and develop shopping centers or industrial parks and use federal or foundation grants to provide job training for minority youth in the projects it runs. It might even set up its own community foundation to serve as a source of funds for community social programs.[39]

The idea is that the various subsidiary activities will feed each other and that the whole will be more than the sum of the parts. For example, if a grant is obtained to rehabilitate housing, by setting up a construction company the CDC can ensure that local people are employed and more money circulates in the neighborhood. This would assist the profitability of the new shopping center that the CDC is also trying to establish. The shopping center would encourage the growth of minority businesses by renting space and creating jobs. Job training programs would ensure a supply of capable and committed local employees in its various projects.[40]

The subsidiaries of multipurpose CDCs are sometimes encouraged to operate in the wider mar-

ketplace. For example, a construction or management company can obtain contracts from other organizations besides its parent body, thus contributing again to the profitability of the main CDC and reversing the normal money flow out of the deprived area.[41] Because of its diversified economic base and governmental support, financial institutions may be more willing to provide a wide range of loan products and guarantees to the CDC that make the market work for the poor in ways that had never been done before.[42]

A multipurpose community-controlled corporation, therefore, can develop a neighborhood area by means of helping residents control their own local economy. CDCs stimulate and operate businesses, provide tangible products and services, and strengthen skills and abilities of residents by job training, employment, and social programs. Not only do CDCs play a major role in improving poor communities in America and Canada, but "CDCs have a significant developmental role to play in the industrialized world and probably in the third world as well, a role which governments seem to have great difficulty playing directly."[43]

BUILDING A COMMUNITY DEVELOPMENT CORPORATION

Building community development corporations is the most important kind of community development work in America today. The goal of a community development corporation is to initiate a strategy to break up the vicious circle of impoverishment in a community.[44]

Deciding on an Approach

There are two approaches to community development with modern communities. One is a conventional problem-oriented or needs-based approach. The second is a resource- or assets-based approach.

The *needs-based approach* is the most common or conventional way most social workers learn to approach clients, whether individuals, families, or communities. The deficit or needs-based approach looks at dysfunctional modern communities from a negative perspective as having needs to be filled, gaps in services to be bridged, and complex problems to be

CDCs serve as vital alternatives to privately owned businesses by constructing or improving housing and creating jobs that make the market work for the poor. (Photo by Marc PoKempner © 1999, courtesy of Neighborhood Housing Service, Chicago, IL.)

corrected, all of which require professional attention. The needs-based approach is problem oriented. Problems are generally the purview of professionals who have the skills to diagnose and treat problems and evaluate the results of their efforts by the use of rational problem-solving. Community professionals are expected to conduct needs assessments, arrive at diagnoses, devise plans, and recommend solutions, such as infusion of capital, developing new programs, reorganizing transportation, or renovating housing and street design. Professionals then work to implement the solutions, most often applying resources from outside the community to resolve the needs, gaps, and issues. The goal of problem remediation is to bring the system back to its original homeostatic balance so that it functions effectively.

An alternative way of seeing impoverished communities is not from the perspective of a lack of money or resources but the poverty of a way of life. Sometimes the trained incapacity of depressed communities will be expressed in a pattern of self-maintaining impoverishment. People may be stuck in an attitude of helplessness or apathy. Community members may lack the human tools and skills to make the changes that they want.[45]

The *resource/asset-based* approach looks at even the most impoverished communities as having capabilities of managing themselves by making use of the wealth of resources available to them. This approach is also known as a *strength approach*. It sees a community as having many assets or strengths on which to draw. Every community has a different pattern of available resources, and these resources can be inventoried and utilized.

Community residents and their allies seek and find the best points of leverage within the community for effective action. They use social thinking to assess the positive aspects on which they want to build, visualize a future for themselves, and develop strategies that can reinforce the strengths of the community and its members. Rather than simply help the community function effectively, the asset-based approach is proactive. It envisions a community as its members want it to be and works to bring about the best social environment that enhances and enriches the lives of all of its members.

Both the needs or deficit as well as the resources/assets or strength approach have value. The needs approach uses rational problem-solving that is useful in examining the economic and organizational complexities of community development corporations. The assets approach is useful in helping with the community and its social aspects.

Choosing a Community

Be as clear as you can about the kind of community in which you want to begin a community development corporation. What size community, ethnic composition, and state of community deterioration are you looking for? The group that developed Chicago's South Shore Bank, for example, was looking for a black community with approximately 75,000 residents and moderate deterioration.

Within your constraints, choose a community in which you have as much in common with the people as possible, so that you can become personally committed to it as well as to particular problems in which you will be involved. This "lived-in-experience" is the most relevant criterion for community development work. Without such experience, a community developer will find it difficult to directly engage a community in all of its history, values, symbols, language, culture, and traditions. This is especially important when working with ethnically diverse communities. "Too often we forget that experiencing racism, economic deprivation and social injustice are the key relevant politicizing forces in most urban areas."[46]

Rivera and Erlich have devised a three-tiered model based on contact intensity and influence that can help determine an appropriate role for community developers with ethnically diverse communities.[47] At the primary level of involvement, the community developer directly, immediately, and personally engages the community. This is the most intense and intimate level of engagement "where the only way of gaining entry into the community is to have full ethnic solidarity with the community…. It is this level that requires racial, cultural, and linguistic identity." Working at the primary level, for example, "would not be possible for a Chinese American in a Vietnamese or African American area."

One step removed from personal identification with the community and its problems would be a Puerto Rican in a Mexican American neighborhood.

At this secondary level of involvement, language identification, although a benefit and a help, is not absolutely mandatory. Community developers at this level of engagement would function as liaisons between the community and outside institutions, and would serve as resources with technical expertise.

The third level of engagement is that of a non-ethnically similar "outsider working for the common interests and concerns of the community. Cultural or racial similarity is not a requirement." Using their technical skills, political connections, and understanding of the outside environment, structures, and systems, non-ethnically similar community developers could play particularly effective roles as advocates and brokers on behalf of the community.

Along with ethnic and cultural identity it is likewise important to remember that "Ultimately in community development work, it is the members of that community who will decide who is with them and who is not. They choose who they will work with and who they want to work with them. Community residents make these choices based on their gut reactions, their ideological views of people, and their demonstrated and informed results of their work together."[48]

Looking and Listening

Before you enter a community, analyze it as well as you can. This is a crucial part of the process. You can learn about the community by gathering census data, crime statistics, and incidents of poverty from local governmental agencies and chambers of commerce. Even the phone book gives you a wealth of information about the population, local businesses, and services.

By walking around, you will easily see particular situations that are in need of remediation. A section of housing may be dilapidated and in need of renovation. Businesses may have moved. An area of the community may be victimized by subtle discrimination and not provided equitable city services. But in addition to deficits, you look for strengths. You look for libraries, schools, churches, community and civic associations, businesses, recreation and community services, parks, and other resources.

Terrence Deal says that you begin at the surface and proceed inward toward the system's "unconscious."[49] Ethnography includes examining the physical character of the setting, what the setting says about itself, its social networks, how the community treats strangers, how people spend their time. Wherever you go, think like a researcher, getting a feeling for the culture, values, beliefs, and meaning of the setting you are in.

Examine the Physical Setting　First, look at the physical setting. The buildings and geography of a community make up the public face that it presents to the world. A community that is proud and confident and has an integrated culture will reflect this pride in the way it appears. What about consistency? Are the streets in affluent sections broad, in good repair, and lined with trees while poorer sections have streets that are narrow, full of holes, and lacking in landscaping? Are people of color clustered in poorer sections of the community? Discrepancies in the quality or quantity of community services and attention for different classes or ethnic groups is a sure sign of a weak or fragmented community culture.

Discover What the Community Reveals About Itself　With what qualities does the community identify itself? Does the community have a motto or logo that portrays its character? Is the motto or logo posted prominently on billboards or signs? Local newspapers describe what is important to community members. Communities with strong cultures recognize and take pride in the diversity of their members and in the accomplishments of their citizens. What stories do the members tell about themselves? If a community is only concerned about its economy, and critical of its less distinguished members, you may have evidence of a community that is fragmented and divided.

Strike up conversations with people you meet on the street corner, in restaurants, or in stores. Ask what kind of a community this is. Is it considered a good place to live? Find out about the qualities of the community that people admire. Ask people about the history of the community and what their role is in it. You will probably find out about important rituals, events, and activities that characterize this people.

Ask about the good things in this community. This will give you a picture of the sorts of things people prize and in what they take pride. Ask what kind of people live there. Who are the heroes? Who has met with success? This will tell you about the values of the community.

Look at Social Networks　What kind of civic organizations exist and what communities of mean-

ing, such as churches and synagogues, have a central place in the community? What is the diversity of these community components? Are the social service networks both public and private? The number and variety of nonprofit social service organizations and agencies will tell you about the civic mindedness of its citizens. Do churches interact and engage one another, or are they insular and disengaged?

How are schools maintained and where are they located? What is the racial and economic balance in the schools? Do some public schools have rich resources and better students while other public schools have fewer resources and poorer students? This will tell you a lot about how resources are allocated, what values are important, and the engagement of citizens in a community.

Are businesses locally owned and operated and is there a variety of them? How engaged are businesses in the community? Do they invest effort in the community or simply take its resources for profit?

Look at How the Community Treats Strangers　Are there social networks for people who are new to the community or those with few connections? Wander into stores and see how you are greeted. Are the clerks friendly or do they ignore you? What is the response if you ask for directions, for change to use a phone, or to use a restroom? Do people pass you by or go out of their way to assist you?

Ask About the Stability of the Population　How long do people stay? A community where people have roots and tend to remain will tell you something about the attachments people have to the neighborhood or if this is a community where people are continually on the move. Is the population rising or falling? What are the opportunities for recreation? How do community members spend their leisure time?

Look for Signs of a Culture in Trouble　Weak cultures have no clear values or beliefs about what is important, or they may have values that are contradictory. Some communities develop subcultures known as lifestyle enclaves, in which people are brought together by insubstantial factors such as appearance, patterns of consumption, or leisure activities. These subcultures tend to be ingrown, have restrictions on memberships, and exclude particular kinds of people.

Weak cultures have few rituals that give meaning and shape to the community or memories of its history. Those rituals which do exist are either disorganized, with everybody doing their own thing, or they are contradictory, with different facets of the community working at cross purposes. Care of strangers, the helpless, and the dependent will be inadequate; people will express indifference to strangers or even resentment of those who are helpless. Cultures in trouble will have members who don't care about the community or act out against it. Extensive behavior problems such as crime, vandalism, and violence are indicators of a culture in trouble. Heroes of a fragmented culture are destructive or disruptive and fail to build a common understanding about what is important. High rates of divorce may indicate lack of support for families, another sign of a culture in trouble.

Focused Interviews and Focus Groups

When you talk to people, try using semi-structured focused interviews (described in Chapter 6). These center on selected topics, but specific items are not entirely predetermined.

Once you have examined the community, you are ready to gather a number of community people together in a focus group to help you identify the opportunities that the members can use to improve their community. Focus groups have three goals: (1) to confirm or elicit new information, (2) to begin generating ideas for change, and most important (3) to begin to engage people in forming a community development task force committed to developing a community development corporation. Ask one of the persons you have met to sponsor the meeting in their home. Generally meet with people who are homogenous in background. For example, hold a focus group for people you have interviewed from the business community. Hold others for members of local neighborhoods. One focus group could be composed of church leaders, social workers, and other community professionals, for example.

Begin by introducing people to one another. As a springboard for discussion, present the findings of your interviews and the comments people have made. Focus on those issues that are of crucial importance to the group. This can be your first opportunity to

begin organizing. When people get together to talk about the issues that they feel are important, they often begin to realize they are not alone. Others also are affected. This understanding helps take away the stigma that social problems such as unemployment or poverty often bring to people. They begin to realize that social or economic forces beyond their control have created the conditions which cause suffering. By helping these people come together to share their perceptions about the problem as well as about the assets and resources that they have to solve them, you begin a process that generates hope. You empower them to begin thinking of ways that they can change things for the better. When people take charge of thinking how to change things for the better, they gain skills in problem-solving and planning, reducing their reliance on technical experts.

Focus groups are one way to begin building community awareness and involvement. Community members begin to see the power that information can give them, and they will have more trust in the outcomes of their effort if they have a hand in framing issues and opportunities.

Make sure everyone understands that the goal is to develop a community development corporation, and that all are invited to participate. Give everyone a chance to speak. After the discussion, engage people for the next step, such as signing up for a community development action group, serving on a subgroup, or helping out in some other way. Remind the group when and where the next steps will occur.

Developing an Action Group

The task of a CDC action group is to select actions that offer the best prospect of reaching the specific goals of the community in general and the community development group in particular. When you begin, the institutions of the community may lack the type, strength, and number of capabilities for building the community and have not yet overcome the vicious cycle of poverty. Even if it is not immediately apparent to them, however, community residents already either have the tools they need to carry out all of the community building functions, or they have the capability to acquire them. It is your role to stimulate, inspire, and assist the action group members to develop those tools so they can organize the corporation.

The first task of community development, therefore, is to build social tools that are under local control. A community-based problem requires a community-based solution, which residents themselves initiate, plan, execute, monitor, and evaluate according to their own priorities. The community development process may include local government, but it will always require the initiative and self-reliance of the community development group. At the same time, you begin to help members become leaders. One place to start is to assess the willingness and ability of members of the group to work together. By doing this you can adapt your leadership style according to the group-centered leadership model described in Chapter 4.

Assessing and Building Community Leadership

Depleted communities, in general, have not had a chance for many of its members to become community leaders. The opportunity to become involved in a community development project offers people not only a chance to improve the conditions in the community, but to develop their own leadership skills as well. Leadership is one of the most important social tools or resources that exists in a community, and once developed it is a key component of the success of community development corporations. One of the more important skills you offer is your assistance in helping community members who seem to be alienated, disengaged, or powerless to become active in solving community problems, and in the process build their skills and leadership abilities.

Situational Leadership With Communities

The place to begin developing community leaders is to diagnose the level of readiness of community members to solve community problems. Checklist 7.1, Community Leadership Analysis, will help you do that as well as determine an appropriate leadership style for yourself.[50]

CHECKLIST 7.1
Community Leadership Analysis

Community Leadership Analysis Checklist

1. To what extent are members aware of community/organizational needs, problems, and issues?

high awareness	moderate awareness	little awareness	no awareness
4 ___	3 ___	2 ___	1 ___

2. To what extent are members aware of available resources, services, or programs that can be used to address community problems?

high awareness	moderate awareness	little awareness	no awareness
4 ___	3 ___	2 ___	1 ___

3. To what extent do people have the capacity or skill to make use of resources, services, or programs that can be used to address community/organizational problems?

high capacity	moderate capacity	little capacity	no capacity
4 ___	3 ___	2 ___	1 ___

4. To what extent do members express interest in mobilizing effort to resolve community/organizational problems?

high interest	moderate interest	little interest	no interest
4 ___	3 ___	2 ___	1 ___

5. To what extent are members willing to act on the problems?

high willingness	moderate willingness	little willingness	no willingness
4 ___	3 ___	2 ___	1 ___

6. To what extent are members able to establish rules, procedures, and assign tasks to resolve community/organizational problems?

high ability	moderate ability	little ability	no ability
4 ___	3 ___	2 ___	1 ___

7. To what extent are members able to resolve conflicts among themselves in setting goals and implementing plans?

high ability	moderate ability	little ability	no ability
4 ___	3 ___	2 ___	1 ___

8. To what extent do members engage one another in mutual problem solving and involvement?

high engagement	moderate engagement	little engagement	no engagement
4 ___	3 ___	2 ___	1 ___

9. To what extent do members coordinate their efforts independently?

high coordination	moderate coordination	little coordination	no coordination
4 _____	3 _____	2 _____	1 _____

10. To what extent do members share leadership and task accomplishment?

high sharing	moderate sharing	little sharing	no sharing
4 _____	3 _____	2 _____	1 _____

Total Score_____

Selling for Low Readiness   Low scores on checklist 7.1, between 10–15 mean that community members are generally not aware of community needs, do not know what services or programs the community offers, do not look to the community as a resource in meeting their needs, and do not see community issues as important to them. Community members at this level will tend to not be highly motivated in becoming involved in making their community a better place or improve its services. Community members who are unwilling and unable may feel helpless to do anything in the face of power or against an overwhelming culture of oppression. They may be so engrossed in their own lives, just trying to survive, that they have little energy or interest in wider community concerns.

Faced with these issues, you should take a high-task/low-relationship (HT/LR) stance. You studiously avoid reinforcing people's expressions of hopelessness, refuse to feed into despair, resist acknowledging helplessness, and do not permit people to indulge in a sense of "victimization." The tendency to dwell on one's misery or to simply complain about personal situations may be strong, but a telling style leader will be actively nonsupportive of members in these kinds of fruitless and self-defeating topics. Instead, you will challenge these attitudes for what they really are—the outcomes of systematically enforced dependency. You help members get beyond these patterns and see themselves differently by focusing on people's strengths and possibilities. You inspire hope, and mobilize people's innate self-interest, pulling them into engagement with one another to make changes on their own behalf. Not only will you refuse to allow members to reinforce their trained helplessness, you give specific direction and information about what is possible.

Your goal at this stage is to help the members think of themselves as a group and function as a group. You begin to specifically train members in communication skills, in the process of conducting meetings, in the way organizations become incorporated, in fund raising, in business management. You help them think of new ideas, visualize options, consider their own strengths, and begin to see a different future for themselves and their families.

Consciousness-raising by appealing to people's sense of pride and justice may be necessary to heighten the sensitivity of those who are most directly affected by the problem.[51] Training them in processes by which they can accomplish their goals together and providing an arena of safety may stimulate otherwise alienated people to become motivated to action and inspire a sense of hope.

Selling for Moderately Low Readiness   If you have helped people deal with their lack of skills and motivation, or if community members score between 16–25 on Checklist 7.1, they are beginning to become stimulated to action. Community members at this stage may be willing to try, but may still be unable. Their lack of experience may keep them from moving. They may still not have a clear idea about what to do or how to do it. They may need help in understanding what they can contribute.

At this stage, you take a high-task/high-relationship (HT/HR) stance. You continue to focus on immediate and specific tasks, and you provide information or help members obtain it. You begin to train members in group process, decision-making, or problem-solving so that members understand what is possible. You bring in experts to give your members mini courses in such topics as obtaining loans, writing business plans, principles of accounting, and organization behavior. Your goal is for your group to become capable of starting and running a business, understand the role of a board of directors, and be able to work together over the long haul. At the same time, you provide encouragement and support in relation to their legitimate uncertainty about task accomplishment. You provide information about what others have done and what is possible. As members begin to try things on their own, you give validation and back far enough away to give them space to try harder. If they try but fail, you acknowledge their efforts, critique what went wrong, and encourage them to try again as soon as they can.

As leaders emerge, you restrain yourself from giving direction or controlling the agenda, but you encourage and support people as they begin to do this on their own. You respect the rights of your community members to make their own decisions, no matter how small and faltering. The more steps they take, the stronger they become. They will begin to generate their own ideas, establish roles and rules, and engage in problem-solving.

You will observe those who have potential to lead the group in problem-solving. You begin to help members individually to maximize their skills. You work individually or in small subgroups of members, actively giving them feedback in how to use their skills effectively, providing resources and information.

Facilitating for Moderately High Readiness

If community members score between 26–35 on Checklist 7.1, they will be motivated, but their skills need to be tested and tried in the fires of experience before they are completely comfortable with their abilities. They need the opportunity to experiment, to try and fail if necessary, knowing that you will be there to help and assist if needed. Community members are ready to put the plans they have generated into action. You understand that the challenge is theirs, just as the risks are theirs, and the victory is theirs as well. As they venture out into the arena of struggle, you wait, watch, encourage, and support, but do not do things for them. You are acting much like a facilitator who takes a high-relationship/low-task orientation (HR/LT), helping and encouraging from the sidelines while the members themselves take control of the action.

When their efforts fail, when they do not accomplish all they have wished, you help them critique what has happened. You give advice, support, strategizing, and help them regroup. You help mediate disputes, assist members to see the larger picture, and assist them in streamlining their roles. You help smooth conflicts generated out of disagreements over strategy or intense feelings members have because of the importance that the cause has taken and the seriousness with which community members have become involved.

Consulting for High Readiness

Community members who score 36 or more on Checklist 7.1 will be those who have experienced struggle together, have claimed some victory and own some defeat. Out of this they have grown in hope, courage, and understanding. They realize that winning a community is often a long and gradual process. At this stage, leaders have emerged. Members have gained skills, capabilities, and techniques. They have learned how to work together, have developed closer relationships, and have worked through differences. They are willing to continue the process on their own and are able to do this independently.

Members only need occasional assistance now. To intervene actively would only defeat people's initiative and diminish their skills. Your role shifts to that of coaching or consultative (LR/LT) style. You consciously do not attend all the meetings, or you tell the members that you will come when invited. You may meet occasionally with leaders to give occasional advice when asked, but gradually and consistently you reduce your presence.

Developing a Resource/Assets Inventory

One of the first tasks that your group will need to accomplish is to develop a resource/assets inventory of the community. Conventionally a resource/assets inventory produces a local review of what the economist calls the factors of production (land, and all the natural resources), labor (people and categories of skills), capital (including dollars and results of previous investments such as buildings, highways, manufacturing), as well as managerial and entrepreneurial resources.[52] To have a grasp of all this information about a local area is to have a powerhouse ready to be put to use in making decisions about local development. But in addition to economic factors, such an inventory also includes social, cultural, and psychological tools that residents of a community already have or must have in order to make things happen. Often these are intangible strengths such as community spirit, indigenous leadership, a desire to improve the community, a history of the community, or sense of shared responsibility and meaning.

The act of jointly inventorying assets is itself a powerful community organizing device that motivates people's collaboration and commitment to action by disclosing opportunities for change.[53] A rural locality may, for example, have significant mineral, land, or forest resources. An inner city may have vacant lots, abandoned buildings, unused office space. The community may have people who have skills in carpentry, masonry, or electronics, or people who are willing to learn those skills. A rural area may have a surplus of people to mine, cultivate, harvest, or manufacture. The community may have access to capital and managerial resources or a ready market for products. But in spite of its factors of production, capital, and managerial resources, a community may still not be prepared to exploit all those factors simply because the social and psychological tools of the community do not permit using the resources or putting all the factors together to develop a plan.[54] Your community development action group must take the information about the resources in the community and put together a plan to use those assets in a positive way. Your community group becomes a catalyst for community engagement.

Deciding on a Set of Actions

There will be a strong incentive for members to jump into deciding on a specific project. However, it is important that the group look at the larger picture at this point. They must begin to devise a set of concrete actions by which they can see their projects to completion.

Always break a set of actions into smaller components. This way you can see all of the parts that need to be done. Breaking things down also helps you chart accomplishment on each piece and makes the entire project manageable.

One way to decide on a set of actions is to visualize the end goal and then work backwards. For example, at this stage the group will probably be interested in devising a project. The end goal is to decide on a project. Ask yourselves what are all the components we need to consider to make a good decision. Some things will become immediately apparent. You have already collected information about the resources and assets in your community. You will also need to gather information about a variety of projects that are possible and feasible. Visiting successful projects will help your group get a tangible idea of things that are possible. Talking to developers of successful community development projects will give you information about pitfalls to avoid. This is a also a good time to use the help of outside business experts who can provide consultation to the group on beginning business ventures and learning the language of entrepreneurial leadership, risks of new ventures, and obtaining capital.

Developing a Project

Once your community action group has processed information from the resources/assets inventory and explored successful community development projects and the process of initiating them, a number of possibilities will occur to members that can be used to help develop the economic resources of your community. Many members will have their own ideas. These need to be validated. But they must also be put into the context of the particular capacity of the community. Your role is to help people think creatively and not jump to solutions or become stuck on one pet project.

Alan Twelvetrees says that many CDCs became involved in housing from the start. The kinds of projects they have undertaken include buying and rehabilitating housing for rent to low-income families, new housing for rent to senior citizens, new housing for sale to low- to moderate-income families, buying and relocating houses displaced by a freeway, and cooperative housing. As Twelvetrees points out, these projects require massive subsidies, and unless construction is completed on time and the management company is effective at collecting rents, the finances will not work out.[55] Choose a project with which you can have a reasonable chance of success.

Try a venture with an assured rather than a speculative return, at least to start with. Identify clearly the various objectives of the proposed venture and distinguish between social and economic objectives— the need to give disadvantaged people jobs and the need to make a profit, for example. If it seems not to be possible to make a profit and meet social objectives at the same time, then social objectives have to take a second place initially. Try to develop a business that "captures the outside market" rather than relying only on money circulating in the local community, especially if it is very poor.

Using rational problem-solving, come up with various possibilities that meet the contingencies that your group has decided upon. Develop pros and cons or benefits and costs of each alternative and try to put the benefits and costs into monetary terms so that your group has a hard-headed financial basis for decision-making. Rank the various possibilities using a quantitative format such as force-field analysis and then present these options to the community in a public forum.

The public forum is a device to give information about what the community development group has done and what projects it is considering, and to solicit input and advice from the community as a whole. Make sure that the constituents at the forum understand that this is not a decision-making meeting, but informational and to solicit input. The public forum should also have a wider purpose of engaging community members to help with the eventual project.

Developing the Corporation

Once your group decides on a project, they will need to form themselves into a corporation in order to do business. This includes developing articles of incorporation, a constitution, and by-laws, filing the necessary papers with state and federal governments, selecting a board of directors, staffing, developing a budget, and structuring the corporation. (All of these topics are covered in Chapter 10.)

Twelvetrees recommends that your group adopt a business model rather than a social services model for the corporation. Undertake a careful feasibility study, and make a good business plan. Hire a skilled executive who can direct the operation, one who can build a cadre of competent middle managers and a strong board familiar with operating a business, and who can oversee the operation, set clear goals, and insure the financial stability of the project. Twelvetrees says, "Try to make sure that the manager of the business has incentives to ensure that the venture is profitable, as well as having the skill to run it. Lack of managerial expertise is one of the main reasons for business failure."[56]

It is not wise to start a business unless there is sufficient capital. A large chunk of that capital needs to be equity rather than a loan, unless it is at a low rate of interest and is to be repaid over a long period. Equity means money or financial resources that you have already acquired. Few businesses make money in the first three years, and loan repayments during that time can be crippling.

Private developers are now joint venturing with CDCs because this is the only way in which they can access public money as well as invest some of their own to redevelop a deprived area. The CDC benefits from the expertise of the developer and, if it has cut a good deal, gets financial payback when the project is running. Some CDCs have used joint-venture arrangements to establish major schemes such as shopping malls.[57] Most successful CDCs have benefited from some form of public assistance such as government contracts, technical advice, a start-up loan, or a block grant.[58]

Developing Relationships With Corporations and Government

Since the 1960s, domestic community development has merged with economic development efforts. "By the 1990s the most enlightened of those in and associated with the CED (Community Economic Development) movement were recognizing that the effective revitalization of deprived areas required a public/private/community partnership or a 'three legged stool.'"[59] Public dollars are needed to provide subsidies, without which most community development projects cannot get off the ground. Corporate assistance in the form of support, expertise, and financial contributions are necessary to assist fledgling community development efforts become successful over the long haul. Finally, community engagement is the crucial link that uses the resources in government and business to revitalize local communities. Without the community engagement and leadership at the local level, business and governmental support will be wasted.

By building community in neighborhoods, neighbors learn to rely on each other, work together on concrete tasks that take advantage of the new awareness of their collective and individual assets, and, in the process, create human, family, and social capital that provides for a more promising future and reconnection to America's mainstream. The primary aim of a community development corporation is not giving money, services, or other material benefits to the poor. The central theme of community building is to obliterate feelings of dependency and to replace them with self-reliance, self-confidence, and responsibility.[60]

Developing Social Programs and Service Delivery

Building a community development corporation is a long-term process the success of which may not become evident for many years. For example, it took eight years before the Chatham-Savannah Youth Futures Authority in Savannah, Georgia, began to see improvement in the neighborhood.[61] Asked how long it took before he knew that the New Community Corporation of Newark, New Jersey, was making a real difference in its target neighborhood, founder Monsignor William Linder answered, "12 years."[62]

Even though social service programs are important, they are not the first priority. The most important goal is to establish the corporation on a firm footing. After the community development corporation develops enough financial stability, however, and has been able to achieve success with one or two projects, the board may consider developing a needed social service program.

Ending the Process

There will come a time when your work as community developer is finished and you move on to other communities, other issues, other problems. The advice that Si Kahn gives to community organizers is equally important for community developers.

> By staying in the community past the time for him to leave, the organizer inhibits the development of community leadership and independence. It is important for poor people in a community to become free not only of their dependence on the power structure but also of their dependence on the organizer. It can be as harmful to a community for an organizer to stay after he has completed his job as for him to leave before he has finished it.[63]

One way of determining whether it is time for you to leave is to assess the extent to which the CDC and the community members have reached their goals.

Members: Do community members continue to identify themselves as victims and play a victim role, or have they gained skills, competencies, confidence, empowerment, and control over their community and the CDC?

Leadership: To what extent have community leaders emerged? Do these leaders act on behalf of the community, or do they use their positions to possess power for themselves? Do the leaders actively train others to take their place? Is leadership broadly shared, or is it hoarded by a few?

Organization: Is the CDC in a strong financial position? Is its board composed mainly of community residents who support and give good direction to the CDC? Do community members identify with the CDC and recognize it as "our organization"? Are community members committed to and engaged in helping the CDC grow and develop? Is the CDC in coordination with business and government capable of eliminating community problems over the long haul?

Accomplishments: Has the CDC established at least one successful, ongoing business project? Has it accomplished at least one of its subsidiary goals?

Politics: How effectively does the CDC work with elected officials? Has the CDC established strong and permanent partnerships with major corporations inside and outside of the community?

Power: Is the community power structure responsive to the CDC and to its political strength? Does the community power structure recognize the CDC as effectively representing the needs of the community?

The CDC may not have achieved all of its goals, but if it has met a number of them in these areas, you can leave knowing that the organization you have helped develop is strong enough to move in a positive direction.

When you feel that the time for you to leave is coming, you need to prepare the community. Just as engaging the community took time and was a systematic process, disengagement should also be done over a period of time and with deliberation. You meet with members, board, and staff of the CDC and explain that you will be leaving and your strategy for disengagement. By this time your leadership style should be a low-task/low-relationship facilitating style. You take less and less active involvement in meetings. You tell your members that you will be absent occasionally, and then more frequently.[64]

You begin to terminate the relationships you have developed. You visit as many people as you can, "attend meetings of block clubs, committees and organizations in the community"[65] to say goodbye. Visit members of the power structure, both those who have supported your efforts and those who have opposed you.

Meet with the CDC board and staff and present your assessment of the organization. In your assessment, explain the condition of the community when you came. Review the history of the CDC, and your evaluation of its condition at present. Affirm their strengths and commend them for their victories. Let them know what areas you think they need to work on in the future to become a stronger organization.

Have a celebration in which you and the CDC can enjoy a closure experience. Members will need to express their feelings toward you, and you will have a chance to say your final goodbyes to them, and share what the organizing experience has meant to you.

When you leave, the community's members should be strengthened and able to carry on its programs, implement the vision, and continue the leadership that they have begun. The community should have a sense of itself, and its members should be walking their way together. There should be a sense of victory and accomplishment, and the vision of the future should be clear and easily seen.

Limitations of Community Development Corporations

Many social workers see community development corporations as superior to centralized government welfare programs and private charity as a way to address rebuilding community infrastructures, reducing poverty, and empowering communities for self-help. However, while CDCs have enormous potential and seem to be heading in the right direction, there are still issues that need to be addressed if CDCs are going to make the kind of impact that their potential suggests is possible. First of all, government and corporate sources need to become active and committed partners with CDCs. Fisher asserts that most funding from private foundations, corporations, and state or local governments is a proverbial drop in the bucket. Such efforts may be useful as a pilot project or good for public relations, but they are not sufficient to "revitalize neighborhoods." Fisher says that "dramatically expanded federal support is essential" if the conditions that oppress so many people in American cities— widespread poverty, crime, substandard housing, ineffective public schools, inadequate health care, and the lack of jobs at a decent wage—are to become the exception rather than the rule. Most proponents now agree that because of the absence of a strong federal presence, CDC efforts continue to "suffer from inadequate coordination and undernourished capacity."[66]

This does not mean that government or corporations should control or "parachute in" assistance as if communities were a devastated war zone. Instead, it means an understanding that top-down decisions don't work. Local communities will be able to resolve local problems, but with federal support. Government richly subsidizes giant private corporations with tax breaks, contracts, subsidies, loans, and bailouts, and other incentives which sustain healthy profits for corporate owners and managers. Even more important than corporate welfare for the rich, the federal government's priorities ought to be redirected to assist CDCs as a first priority in rebuilding the infrastructure of America's communities.

Another issue important to CDC success is that many CDC projects are too small to counteract massive urban problems. Coordination is needed with foundations and corporate interests, who should see CDCs not as competitors but as needed resources to revitalize communities. Cooperation with foundations and corporate structures will assist CDCs as well as community organizations to make strengthening communities and eliminating social problems a first priority.

In this way everyone becomes a winner. Corporations will develop additional markets from increased revenue and purchasing capacities of economically stronger communities. Society as a whole will benefit from reduced crime and welfare, and from a better-educated, more involved citizenry. Communities and citizens benefit from their involvement in revitalizing their communities, from the skills they have learned, the relationships they develop, and the tangible improvements they make in their own lives and the lives of one another.

COMMUNITY DEVELOPMENT WITH COMMUNITIES OF MEANING

In addition to community development corporations, community developers also work with religious communities such as churches, synagogues, mosques, and cultural and civic associations that provide the spiritual, emotional, and existential meaning and support for a neighborhood or community members. Developing communities of meaning, because they already

Communities of meaning often symbolize and become the heart of the larger community. Here, community members march in support of urban peace and justice in Kansas City, Missouri, May 2, 1993. (© Jeffry E. Scott/Impact Visuals)

have an organizational structure, tends to be a more formal process than with modern communities. When you work with an ontological community, you will establish a relationship with its leaders and the community as a whole, work with a task group to develop solutions, present solutions to the community, implement those solutions, and come to closure.

Ideological Identification

Just as when working with an ethnically divided community, community development with communities of meaning will often require ideological identification with that community. For example, in working directly with a Jewish synagogue, it is best if the community worker is Jewish in order to provide value and cultural identification with the community. It would be difficult for a gentile to develop the kind of identification necessary for effective work. The same would be true of a Catholic providing services to members of a Buddhist community, or for a Muslim to provide services to members of a Mormon Church.

Talking With Leaders

At the outset, establish a relationship with the primary "gatekeepers" to the community. These people are the leaders—pastors, priests, rabbis, officers, executive committees, or boards of trustees of the ontological community. Listen actively for areas of dysfunction and pain as you talk with these members. At this point, you are assessing whether the problem is one with which you want to work. If you decide you want to work with this community, you also help the community leaders see that the problems they are experiencing are solvable.

In brief terms describe the process that you will undertake to help resolve the issues. Community development with ontological communities is much like practicing therapy with families or groups. You are going to uncover and break up dysfunctional systems, replacing them with new, hopefully better ones. Make sure that the community leaders understand that the process may take up to six months or more, and require considerable commitment from all of the members of the community. They also need to understand that the process includes taking a hard look at themselves, a willingness to engage in behavioral change, and that things will more than likely become worse before they become better. A commitment to change will often mean at least one weekly meeting of a select committee of community members, individual meetings with community leaders, and other meetings as needed. Explain your fee structure and ancillary costs.

Presentation to the Community

After the community or congregational leaders have "bought into" your process, you will need to present a proposal to the entire community at a special meeting or at the community's annual meeting. Once the entire community agrees to engage in the change process, you either contract for the entire service or for an initial study.

The Problem-Solving Process

The exploration phase begins with gathering information about the community. Read as much as you can about the congregation or community. Find out about its history, its traditions, its values, its culture. Spend time with the community. Attend its functions and gatherings. Talk to its members. Try to discover where the pain and dysfunctions are located. Because ontological communities combine authentic community with aspects of formal organization, you need to discover to what extent the problem lies in the informal communal life of the community, its relationships, and leadership or in its formal organizational structure.

If the problem is in the communal components of the community, you begin where the pain is the greatest. Often this may be centered with the formal or informal leadership of the community. Forming a group of these people, you spend time exploring the pain, working on better communication, and building relationships and conflict resolution. This may take the form of day-long workshops or weekend retreats.

Often problems in community relationships result in organizational problems. When this occurs, you need to look at the fit between what the community wants to do, its goals, and the way it has decided to accomplish them, its structure. You meet with a select committee who have committed themselves to work on the structural/functional fit with you. This becomes your problem-solving team or task force.

Engage your group in an introductory warm-up to develop cohesion with one another and begin a relationship with you. Next, establish the purpose of the group, describe the principles of community growth and process, obtain feedback from the members, and contract with them. Make sure that members understand they will develop solutions and help implement them. Your role is to provide expertise, training, facilitation, and staff support, helping them function as a working group with shared leadership, decision-making, communication, and conflict-resolution skills.

Help members understand the steps of problem-solving and begin a process of problem recognition. First, brainstorm a list of the purposes or mission of the community. List the functions by which the community tries to achieve its purposes and group them in categories. Then make a list of the structures in which the community tries to carry out its functions. There will probably be a number of discrepancies between purpose, functions, and structure. As your group considers the gaps and inconsistencies, help them make a list of all of the problems the members can think of. These might be gaps in service, poor communication, lack of accountability, poor leadership, ineffectiveness in meeting objectives, no objectives at all, or poor motivation.

Assist the team to develop alternative solutions that will help solve the problems and create a better fit between the community's purpose, functions, and structure. At least two and preferably three alternative proposals should be developed—one of which should be the existing structure. Rank each solution according to the pros and cons of each alternative. A force-field analysis process (described in Chapter 3) might be useful to your group.

Presenting Solutions

The team should hold a series of community forum, informational meetings to explain the alternatives, their pros and cons, and to engage the community in obtaining feedback. This input may significantly change some of the alternatives.

After the community forum, the task group should revise and rework their proposals, incorporating the community's suggestions. After this, alternative solutions should be ready to be presented to the community at large. The entire community needs to vote on accepting one of the alternative proposals.

Implementation

The original group which developed the change proposal should be disbanded and a fresh group that has no vested interests in or political aspirations about the project be chosen to help implement the solution. This group can see the proposal from a new and unbiased viewpoint. They may see flaws or faults with the proposal and be valuable in assuring that the proposal actually works.

Assessment and Closure

An evaluation component should be designed before the project is implemented. The project should be evaluated at the end of its first six months or first year to assure that it is functioning properly. As your last effort, organize a community pot luck to give recognition to all those involved, help the community celebrate its success, and give closure to the process. You may also contract with the congregation to revisit them after three months, six months, and a year to consult with the group that is working on implementation or assist with the evaluation process.

COMMUNITY DEVELOPMENT WITH TRADITIONAL COMMUNITIES

Community development has its origins not in the urban ghettos of the United States and Canada, but in the jungles of Africa and the British West Indies in the early 19th century. Even as the major thrust of community development is experiencing renewed vigor in North America, it is even more prominent and important on the parched plains of the Saheil in sub-Saharan Africa, in the rain forests of South America, in the poverty-stricken urban slums of Thailand, Calcutta, and Bangladesh. Today, new forms of community development at the global level have potential to revitalize some of the most desperate conditions that people face. You will learn about international community development with traditional communities in Chapter 15.

NEW DIRECTIONS FOR SOCIAL WORK

Today, community development corporations and community organizations often combine approaches with program development. This blending is called *consensual community social work*. For example, a community organizer working with a community with housing, rent, or job-related issues may help organize a community development corporation, or a community developer may assist the CDC to work on broader political issues. Once solidly established, the corporation that results may expand its effectiveness by developing community social organizations to provide social service programs.

Mike Eichler, a macro social worker, is a community development organizer who uses the consensual community development approach. He helped put together CDC projects in the depressed steel manufacturing area of the Monongahela Valley and established other such projects in Houston, New Orleans, Little Rock, and Palm Beach. With nine full-time community organizers, Eicher helped organize a total of 19 CDCs, most of which produce housing projects. Eichler asserts that by participating in the CDC consensual approach, corporate executives become more active and aware of social problems, city officials see community organizing as valuable instead of threatening, and neighborhood residents feel empowered and obtain more control over community resources.

Consensual community social work tends to see the fundamental goal as rebuilding community, forging a sense of unity among its fragmented elements, and gathering resources to perform specific community tasks. The Association of Community Organizations for Reform Now (ACORN), which began as a community organization in the Welfare Rights Movement, has found itself deeply involved in community development as part of the "fight for democratic control over finance and capital." More recently, ACORN has worked with banks and city officials to turn abandoned dwellings over to "homesteaders." Local homesteading programs have so far been set up in five cities. ACORN helps to do rehabilitation work on these and other sites, setting up "coops" for the new occupants or getting deeds of abandoned housing and doing "sweat equity" projects to put them back into shape for the new homeowners. ACORN also joins in partnerships with mainstream political and corporate funders. In its joint home-acquiring and rehabilitation efforts in Chicago, for example, ACORN works with Citibank, Mayor Richard M. Daley, and the federal government.[67]

In addition to assisting communities with economic development and political advocacy, consensually oriented community developers engage in program development, helping the community develop social organizations and social programs to enhance their communities. The partnership of CDCs along with advocacy-based community organizations and program development provides a triple-pronged approach, strengthening the economic and social base of communities, while at the same time insuring that the public and private sectors do their fair share to promote and enhance the life of the communities. The result is a partnership of public, private, and voluntary or nonprofit arrangements in which all share in the responsibility for revitalizing and restoring communities. (You will learn about community organization in Chapter 8 and program development in Chapter 10.)

Many church-related community development corporations exist in combination with community organizations. These faith-based development organizations are now providing a four-pronged approach to community improvement. They not only combine economic development CDCs with advocacy-oriented community organizations and program development, but they have the additional advantage of a spiritual frame of reference that helps members develop meaning and purpose in their personal lives. Faith-based ontological/CDC/community organizations are mediating institutions that are extremely effective in helping community members support the private life of self and family. At the same time, they relate the members of the community to the larger megastructures of society and make an impact at the local level as well.

There seems to be little doubt that these self-initiated, multifunctional community development organizations have become the most active form of community-based organization and are the most likely to expand in the future.[68] They have the potential to revitalize many of our poorest communities economically, politically, and socially. They are an exciting way for community social workers to combine entrepreneurial business interests and skills in putting together community-owned business projects, empowering communities to develop advocacy-based cooperative relations with corporate financial enterprises and governmental agencies, and help community members develop enhancing social service programs. Macro social work community developers will need to become familiar with both business as well as public sector funding, and entrepreneurial leadership. You will need the ability to work with a broad range of community members and acquire skills in economic and program development. One way that the field of social work can enhance the skills of community developers is to provide education for social workers in the field of business administration so that you can use your business skills on behalf of the community. For example, a joint social work/business administration program aimed at preparing community economic developers skilled in community development corporations would be an important service to many communities in the United States and Canada.

While the field of social work invests its resources training psychotherapists, however, schools of business in the United States and abroad have taken the initiative by creating "Social Entrepreneurship" programs in community development, and they are doing it without help from social work. A program at Harvard Business School called Initiatives in Social Enterprise, for example, "helps give [business majors] who want to do good works the kind of organizational, profit-making and management skills they need to thrive." As a result of such programs, Rodrigo Baggio from Rio de Janeiro brought hi-tech computer teaching schools to slum dwellers in Brazil. Most of the 32,000 young people who have completed the school are employed or are starting their own businesses. In New England, business school graduates established a job training program in a homeless shelter that created a self-sustaining program for the agency rather than relying on grants. A business school student project increased a credit union's membership in a disadvantaged area in London from 200 to 2,000 members in 48 months.[69]

While schools of social work have generally abandoned community, schools of business are reaching out to communities who need assistance. They are doing it without help from social workers, and they are doing it successfully. Social work needs to recapture its commitment to community members, its vision, and its creativity. Community development is one of the places we should start.

CONCLUSION

Community development is much like grassroots democracy, in which power is shared in an equal and open forum. It encourages values of citizenship and citizen participation in the life of the community, promoting education in civic pride and civic consciousness, and sees in the community itself an arena where the public interest can become a living force.

There is need for renewed community development effort. Depressed and impoverished modern communities struggle to maintain themselves. The very concept of community languishes as communities of meaning attempt, often single-handedly, to provide authentic community in today's impersonal and alienated world. If it is true that people cannot exist without authentic community, then our modern society is building a culture in which a sense of community is lacking, one in which we can expect personality dysfunctions, greater alienation, selfishness, lack of identity, and a tendency to ignore those in our communities who are marginal. Community development is a field that aims to change all of that.

Community development is perhaps one of our most urgently needed and yet least recognized arenas of helping in our society today. Community development corporations provide an exciting, fulfilling, and creative arena for macro social work practice. Community development is on the forefront of an entirely new era in the development of human social relationships, one that even schools of business recognize as important. It is a field of endeavor that social work cannot afford to continue to ignore.

KEY CONCEPTS

community development

community development corporation

action model of community development

community self-determination

three-tiered model of intensity and influence

community development process with modern communities

community development process with communities of meaning

consensual community social work

QUESTIONS FOR DISCUSSION

1. One observation about the state of macro social work today is that while it is becoming more generalist, it is at the same time becoming more specialized. For example, because the new wave of community development corporations are occurring in faith-based organizations, a macro social worker interested in community development needs not only general social work skills, but specialized skills in community development, community organization, administration, and business, and an appreciation for religiously oriented communities of meaning. What does this mean for social work education at the BA level? What does it mean for social work education at the MSW level?

2. Another observation about community development is that it draws upon all of one's problem-solving functions, enhancing your growth and mastery by using your skills in a variety of ways. Think about your own needs for professional growth. How well do you think performing community development would assist you in becoming a whole, masterful individual?

3. Comment on this statement: "Becoming skilled in community development allows you to expand your options for the future. For example, a social worker trained to perform psychotherapy will, for the most part, always be a psychotherapist. As a macro social worker skilled in community development, you will not only be able to work with communities, however, but develop new programs and services, become an administrator, a community organizer, a management consultant, and engage in planning as your interests, skills, and capabilities change and develop." Do you agree or disagree with this statement? What is your perspective on the utility of becoming a community developer?

EXERCISE 7.1

Choosing a Community Development Problem

Jane Addams, upon visiting Toynbee Hall in England, caught the vision of a way to revitalize communities in Chicago. Today, many of our communities are faced with problems similar to those Addams confronted. We have many communities of immigrants, deteriorating inner cities, increased violence, racial turmoil, and gangs. As you consider the kinds of social problems facing our cities and rural areas, think of what kinds of community development programs or solutions might work. Write an essay on ways that a community developer might improve them.

EXERCISE 7.2

Critiquing Community-Based Social Care

Harry Specht and Mark Courtney have proposed an alternative way of revitalizing not only our communities but also the social work profession. If possible, obtain a copy of their book *Unfaithful Angels: How Social Work Has Abandoned Its Mission*. Critique their proposal for a Community-Based System of Social Care. Would this alternative work? What are its benefits? What are its costs? What forces of resistance would have to be overcome? What political issues would it encounter? Would it solve the problem of the demise of community in our modern age? Can you think of ways to improve this model, or can you come up with a model of your own?

EXERCISE 7.3

Critiquing Principles of Community Development

The following principles on which community development models might be based are offered for your analysis. What do you think of these principles? Are any of them ones you would not choose? Are any principles left out? How would you prioritize these principles?

1. Shared leadership—everyone participates to the extent they are able and interested. Followership is as important as leadership.

2. Shared information—no secrets here.

3. Shared power—no one lords it over others. Those who have positions of power are seen as servants of others, not their masters.

4. Shared learning and growth—if members "miss" the mark, make a "mis-take," take a "mis-step," or become "mis-placed," the "misses" are acknowledged, owned, and the group goes on from there.

5. Shared experiences and shared joys, shared sorrows and shared memories—everyone is on the road together. Everyone becomes a hero, and each person's journey is a heroic one.

6. Shared meanings. Everyone celebrates and participates in the shared rewards.

EXERCISE 7.4

Researching Community Development Models

The Settlement House movement, the YMCA movement, the Salvation Army of the 1880 and 1890s, the Civilian Conservation Corps of the 1930s, the War on Poverty of the 1960s, the wide variety of self-help groups, the civil rights movement, the Peace Corps, and President Clinton's National Service Corps are all models by which we can build communities that change people, give purpose and meaning to people's lives, and enable us to care about and love one another.[70]

Research these models and compare them. What were they trying to accomplish? Is there anything we can learn from them about adding purpose and meaning to people's lives, and enabling us to care about and love one another? Would you recommend reviving or expanding any of these models today?

EXERCISE 7.5

Community Development Using the Church as a Base

Read the following vignette. Then respond to the questions at the end.

"I knew that I needed to get people to trust and like me and my singing and playing my guitar at the services helped a lot," said Ada Suarez, a young and dedicated second-year community organization student at the University of Connecticut School of Social Work.... Ada had been raised as a Pentecostal in Puerto Rico and was convinced that organizers can tap into the spiritual mandate that Pentecostals have to do "God's work" and enable the "brothers" and "sisters" to be more effective with their goals for church and community improvements. . . .

The church's pastor welcomed Ada's help, seeing her as a nonpaid staff member who also brought University resources. In addition to singing and helping the pastor with clerical duties, Ada visited the homes of people she identified as having leadership potential, met with the church's elders, and played big sister to some of the church's youth. She also distributed questionnaires to members, asking them to provide information about what they felt their needs were. She did this data gathering at youth meetings, meetings of the women volunteers, prison visiting committees, etc. She then shared with the congregation what they had identified as problems and recommendations for addressing them. "Some brothers and sisters want to read and write better in Spanish, some want to learn English, and others want help in finding work or better jobs. . . . Some committees want help in functioning better at meetings and others want to know more about how to help people. . . . The youth want to discuss school issues and some church elders wish to learn how to be better leaders in and out of the church."

Ada brought the public school system into the church to teach literacy (in Spanish) and English classes for non-English speakers. She organized leadership training workshops and called on Puerto Rican Studies faculty, community organization students, and community leaders for help. Wherever possible, church members themselves introduced speakers and planned gatherings. Workshops on job training, resume writing, interviewing skills, and on eligibility for food stamps were conducted at least twice in one year.

Ada also chose to work on some more controversial projects. For example, she organized workshops on AIDS. . . . Ada encouraged young people to talk about their feelings of isolation in school and in the community due to the strict moral codes of the church (no hard rock music, makeup, movies, smoking, etc.) and some parents were less than comfortable with that. In addition, she facilitated and encouraged the women of the congregation to become more assertive and to be more represented on the Board of Elders.

With sensitivity she explained to the church members that since they welcomed drug addicts and worked with prisoners, some had expressed interest in knowing more about the AIDS epidemic. . . . She imparted community organization skills to elders and had them prepare flyers, lead discussions on setting agendas, form committees, and select strategies. She utilized videos, films, and other visuals effects when talking about conserving energy, applying for a job, presenting information on AIDS, etc.[71]

Reflect on the following questions:

1. What kind of process did Ada use?
2. What kinds of qualities did you observe in Ada?
3. Was she successful? Why or why not?
4. Is there anything you would have done differently? Why or why not?

ADVANCED EXERCISE 7.6

Deinstitutionalizing Jefferson State Hospital

Community Consultants, Inc., is a community development organization sponsored by the local United Way. It also receives some additional income from consulting fees, conducts some fund-raising benefits, and applies for grants. Recently, Community Consultants has been working on revitalizing the South Central section of Jefferson City. South Central is the oldest and once one of the most affluent sections. But as residents moved out of the central part of the city to the suburbs, many old and stately homes were left to deteriorate and several of them had been taken over by drug abusers and turned into crack houses.

A number of residents, however, led by Josiah Warner, began to press to save South Central. Warner invited Community Consultants, Inc., to assist. Community Consultants assigned John Heiligman to the project. With John's assistance, the South Central Community Association was formed. The result has been renewed community spirit and Pride. A Neighborhood Watch program was initiated. Pressure was put on police to eliminate drug abuse in the community. Efforts were made to renovate the old Victorian homes. Community consultants has been instrumental in applying for and receiving community improvement funds and in having two homes listed as historical landmarks.

One of John Heiligman's former classmates is Sam Fontaine, Community Resource Developer at the Great Plains Regional Center. For the past six months Sam has been working with a group of parents of developmentally disabled adults who were interested in establishing a residential care facility for their adult children. Such a facility has become even more urgently needed because the Jefferson State Hospital is planning on releasing at least 100 adult developmentally disabled persons into the community in the next year.

One of the older homes in South Central had recently come on the market, and the group of parents was very interested in becoming incorporated as a nonprofit organization, buying the home, and operating it for their own and other developmentally disabled adults.

John Heiligman was enthusiastic about the idea. This would be not only a service to the community but also a source of income to the neighborhood. Before he could bring the idea up at the next meeting of the South Central Residents Association, however, John was shocked to hear Josiah Warner report on the plan and denounce it vehemently. After a short discussion, one of the members made a motion to oppose the plan. In a moment the motion was passed, and Josiah was assigned to write a letter of protest to the mayor, the city planning board, and the city council, objecting to "mental defectives" living in the neighborhood.

Josiah Warner and the South Central Residents Association have asked John's help in drafting this letter. It is clear that they expect him and Community Consultants, Inc., to support them against what they consider a threat to their community, its values, and the property values they have worked hard to improve.

After the meeting, John Heiligman is in a dilemma. On the one hand, he is an advocate for the residents of South Central and is committed to helping improve the community. On the other hand, he understands the need for quality housing for developmentally disabled. The Regional Center's Client's Rights Advocate, Shirley Jenkins, has informed John that the city legally has no jurisdiction over small family-care homes. The state, whose laws supersede those of the city, has determined that a home of six unrelated adults or less is considered a family. No one can prevent six unrelated adults from residing in a neighborhood of their choice, even if they are disabled, as long as the facility meets state licensing requirements.

From his conversation with Sam Fontaine, John also knows that this is probably the first of many attempts by groups to secure housing in the older, less expensive areas of the city like South Central. In fact,

Sam mentioned to him that he is also working with several of the caregivers at Jefferson State Hospital, who will probably be laid off, on a plan for them to use their skills in caring for the disabled by opening their own facilities. Several of these caregivers have their eye on older homes in South Central. This is not a problem that will go away.

Sam calls a meeting of the other community development staff at Community Consultants, Inc. He asks them to help clarify the problem. As he considers the range of problems confronting him, he makes the following list:

1. What are the ethical issues involved here?

2. What does this dilemma say about the potential of a community that acts out of the self-interest of its members?

3. Whose rights should prevail—the rights of disabled to live where they choose, or the rights of residents to protect their community against a perceived threat?

4. What strategies are available to resolve this potential conflict?

5. What alternatives are available to Sam?

a. Should Sam help draft the letter and advocate for the community against the disabled?

b. Should Sam align himself with the disabled against the community?

c. Should Sam voice his personal views that a home for the disabled would actually be an asset to the community?

d. If a public hearing is held and Community Consultants are asked to voice an opinion, should Community Consultants abstain from voicing an opinion or not? What should their stance be?

e. Should Community Consultants be a mediator or should they bring in an outside consultant?

Sam asks the community development staff to help him resolve these questions, develop several alternative strategies, and develop a plan that will help resolve the ethical dilemma he is facing as well as help the community and the disabled resolve the potential conflict. Sam intends to present the plan to the Executive Committee of Community Consultants, Inc., at its next meeting.

ADDITIONAL READING

Community Development Prior to Community Development Corporations

William W. Biddle and Loureide Biddle. *The Community Development Process: The Recovery of Local Initiative.* New York: Holt, Rinehart and Winston, 1965.

Frank Farrington. *Community Development: Making the Small Town a Better Place to Live and a Better Place in Which to Do Business* (1915). The first book on community development published in the United States.

Marshall B. Clinard. *Slums and Community Development.* Glencoe, IL: Free Press, 1966.

Jack D. Mezilrow. *The Dynamics of Community Development.* New York: Scarecrow Press, 1962.

Phillips Ruopp, ed. *Approaches to Community Development.* The Hague: W. Van Hoeve, 1953.

Irwin T. Sanders. *The Community: An Introduction to a Social System.* New York: Ronald Press, 1958.

Community and Economic Development Corporations

Donald F. Kettl. *Managing Community Development in the New Federalism.* New York: Praeger, 1980.

Richard P. Taub. *Community Capitalism.* Boston: Harvard Business School Press, 1988.

E. Shragge. *Community Economic Development: In Search for Empowerment and Alternatives.* Montreal: Black Rose Books, 1993.

Renee Berger. *Against All Odds: The Achievement of Community-Based Development Organizations.* Washington, DC: National Congress for Community Economic Development, 1989.

Harry P. Hatry, Elaine Morell, George P. Barbour Jr., and Steven M. Pajunen. *Excellence in Managing: Practical Experiences From Community Development Agencies.* New York: Urban Institute, 1991.

Alan C. Twelvetrees. *Organizing for Neighbourhood Development: A Comparative Study of Community Based Development Organizations.* 2d ed. Aldershot, Eng.: Avebury Press, 1996.

Paul Mico. *Developing Your Community Based Organization With Special Emphasis on Community Economic Development Organizations and Community Action Agencies.* Oakland, CA: Third Party Publishing, 1981.

Neil R. Peirce and Carol F. Steinbach. *Enterprising Communities: Community-Based Development in America.* Washington, DC : Council for Community Based Development, 1990.

Michael H. Schill and Richard P. Nation. *Revitalizing America's Cities: Neighborhood Reinvestment and Displacement.* Albany: State University of New York Press, 1983.

Stephen J. Fitzsimmons and Abby J. Freedman. *Rural Community Development: A Program, Policy and Research Model.* Cambridge, MA: Abt Books, 1981.

Hubert Campfens. *Community Development Around the World.* Toronto: University of Toronto Press, 1997.

Stewart E. Perry. *Communities on the Way.* Albany: State University of New York Press, 1987.

Twentieth Century Fund. *CDCs: New Hope for the Inner City. Report of the Twentieth Century Fund Task Force on Community Development Corporations.* New York: author, 1971.

Howard W. Hallman. *Neighborhoods: Their Place in Urban Life.* Volume 154, Sage Library of Social Research. Beverly Hills, CA: Sage Publications, 1984.

——— *Neighborhood Control of Public Programs: Case Studies of Community Corporations and Neighborhood Boards.* New York: Praeger, 1970.

Faith-Based Community Development

John M. Perkins, ed. *Restoring At-Risk Communities: Doing It Together and Doing It Right.* Grand Rapids, MI: Baker Books, 1995.

———. *Beyond Charity: The Call to Christian Community Development.* Grand Rapids, MI: Baker Books, 1993.

Robert C. Linthecum. *City of God, City of Satan: A Biblical Theology of the Urban Church.* Grand Rapids, MI: Zondervan Publishing House, 1991.

History of Community Development

Patricia Mooney Melvin. *American Community Organizations: A Historical Dictionary.* New York: Greenwood Press, 1986.

Robert Fisher. *Let the People Decide: Neighborhood Organizing in America.* Twayne Publications, 1994.

Robert Halpern. *Rebuilding the Inner City: A History of Neighborhood Initiatives to Address Poverty in the U.S.* New York: Columbia University Press, 1995.

Community Development With Specific Communities

William Ellish. *White Ethnics and Black Power: The Emergence of the West Side Organization.* Chicago: Aldine, 1969.

Mary H. Manoni. *Bedford-Stuyvesant: The Anatomy of a Central City Community.* New York: Quadrangle/New York Times Book Co., 1973.

Related Works

Paul S. Denise and Ian M. Harris. *Experiential Education for Community Development.* New York: Greenwood Press, 1989.

Journals

Journal of the Community Development Society
International Community Development Journal
Community Development Journal: An International Forum, Oxford University Press, Oxford, England
Human Relations, Plenum Press, New York
Economy and Society, Routledge Subscription Dept., Andover, Hants, United Kingdom

8

Becoming a Community Organizer

In order for this struggle to have meaning, the oppressed must not, in seeking to regain their humanity,...become in turn oppressors of the oppressors, but rather restorers of the humanity of both. This then is the great humanistic and historical task of the oppressed; to liberate themselves and their oppressors as well. The oppressors, who oppress, exploit and rape by virtue of their power, cannot find in this power the strength to liberate either the oppressed or themselves. Only power that springs from the weakness of the oppressed will be sufficiently strong to free both.[1]

Paulo Freire

Dependency, no matter how luxurious, is a form of slavery.[2]

Joan Lancourt

Ideas in This Chapter

WHEN YOU HAVE TROUBLE IN SAN ANTONIO, CALL THE COPS

Mayor Henry Cisneros called the faith-based Communities Organized for Public Service (COPS) "the voice of 150,000 families."[3] Sonia Hernandez, however, often remains skeptical about claims of politicians. "We reject expansion based on boosterism," as she put it. She defined the relationship in a different way: "We rather call upon our public officials to challenge us as well as challenge them to be reciprocal, collaborative, and consultative as we cooperatively forge a new vision and a new consensus for San Antonio." Behind this kind of exchange is a specific organizational philosophy: "Politicians' work is to do our work," Hernandez explained. "When you've got somebody working for you, you don't bow and scrape. It's not meant to show disrespect. When politicians deliver, we applaud them. Not until then."

The point of COPS, she continued, was not politics as usual. "COPS is about people, mainly poor people, who have decided to do something about their lives. There isn't anyone around—not a mayor or a governor—who is going to come in and do anything for us. We are going to do it for ourselves. If we ever lost that touch, we would cease to be COPS." Explained one leader, "If one of our members is thinking of running for office, he will be asked to resign. We will never divide or dilute our numbers by endorsing particular candidates, but we will hold all elected officials responsible for their actions. We will be the conscience of public servants."

In 1973 Father Edmundo Rodriguez invited community organizer Ernesto Cortes and the Industrial Areas Foundation (IAF) to help the Mexican American community in San Antonio try to get itself together. Cortes, who grew up in San Antonio in the 1940s and 1950s, brought back with him the organizing skills he had learned at the Industrial Areas Foundation and a great zeal to see his own people gain power and new

dignity. Prior efforts had failed. A variety of advocacy groups had formed around specific issues like school reform or the environment. But these issue-oriented groups often ignored communities. It wasn't that people were unconcerned; it was that they had rarely been asked what they were most concerned about.

Cortes's basic approach was to listen. "I began to interview pastors and from them got the names of lay leaders in the parishes," he remembers. "I kept records and tapes of each conversation." Through the course of perhaps a thousand interviews during the first year, Cortes gained a detailed sense of what mattered most to people in the neighborhoods. It didn't turn out to be the more visible issues that politicians or Chicano militants usually talked about—things like police brutality or racial discrimination. Instead it was the problems close to families and neighborhoods, such as housing, utility rates, and drainage. It "was like one of those lightbulbs that suddenly appears in cartoons."

The issues that COPS initially addressed broke the mold. So too did those who became the leadership. COPS built around the moderates, not the activists on the Left or the conservatives on the Right. It didn't begin with people who were the politicos or who were in public life, the people who wheeled and dealed. It grew from the people who run the festivals, who lead the PTAs, whose lives have been wrapped up with their children, their parishes, and their jobs. "What COPS has been able to do is give them a public life, the tools whereby they can participate," observes Sister Christine Stephes, the staff director of the organization. Furthermore, Cortes sought an entirely different base of organizing. For Ernie Cortes, however, it was hard to imagine effectively organizing the Mexican American community in San Antonio without drawing explicitly on the religious language and stories of the people, or building on the Catholic Church as an institution. Cortes saw the church as the center of strength in the community.

But this did not mean that the church doled out service to people. "Our iron rule of organizing is 'never do anything for people that they can do for themselves,' asserted Cortes. In San Antonio such an approach meant that Cortes conducted dozens of training workshops on subjects like doing research, chairing meetings, keeping leadership accountable, dealing with the press, breaking down problems into manageable parts, and others.

COPS did not seek funds from any government or foundation or corporate agency. Combining several principles of financial independence by charging dues supplemented with funds from a grant, the remaining budget was raised through sales for an ad book. In addition, COPS stressed the development of new leadership. Every individual organization is free to take on local neighborhood issues it chooses. On larger issues it can ask for aid from the whole organization. Leadership is elected at every level, and top leaders and staff directors alike must regularly change.

COPS held its first annual convention in the auditorium of Jefferson High School on November 23, 1974. Over 1,000 delegates jammed the auditorium, adopting a constitution and a plan for seeking $100 million in city improvements in sidewalks, libraries, and parks, and strategies for fighting problems such as air pollution. To an outside observer, such meetings may have seemed spontaneous and unruly at the least. But behind the events were weeks of planning, discussion, research, and role-playing that taught people to express themselves in a new way, simultaneously articulating and controlling the buried anger.

The previous year the organization had drawn up a Texas-wide plan with planks such as increased aid for school districts with low student achievement scores, state money to help schools cope with immigrant students, and increased funds for bilingual education. A number of organizing efforts around the state also backed the plan, and the Democratic gubernatorial candidate pledged his support. But before the education effort was ever formulated, extensive discussion had occurred in each parish of the organization.

COPS had an educational process all its own. "It's like a university where people go to school to learn about public policy, learn about public discourse, and about public life," described Ernesto Cortes. People reflected on what schools were like in biblical times. They looked at how schools had changed and at the needs of poor people for education today. Behind such discussion is a particular approach to the organization members. "Each person is an individual and you address people as individu-

als. You make sure each person has an understanding of what we are going to do and why and what his or her role is." Treating each member as an individual, capable of making a contribution, soon generated the reputation that the organization was amazingly well prepared. People gained detailed knowledge about the educational system and its problems. As reporter Paul Burke put it in the *Texas Monthly*, it soon became apparent that the COPS rank and file knew more about the issues than did supposedly expert public officials: "The authorities weren't so smart after all."

The stage was now set for COPS intervention in the political process. All during this time, COPS had been evolving a positive understanding of itself as a political alternative to "politics as usual" in America. COPS began to encourage businesses coming into the community to pay a decent wage. Comments Beatrice Cortez, an organization leader, "We realized that you could only do so much with neighborhood improvement. We did research and found out San Antonio paid the poorest wages of any major city." Indeed, according to the *Commercial Reporter*, San Antonio wages were between 20–40% lower than those in other areas of the country. The city establishment's protestation of innocence turned sour when COPS released a copy of the secret study it had somehow obtained called the Fantus Report commissioned by the city's Economic Development Foundation (EDF). The Fantus Report applauded the city's "relatively unorganized" labor force and concluded that San Antonio's corporate and political leaders "must be careful not to attract industries that would upset the existing wage ladder. This would tend to dissipate the cooperative and competitive advantages enjoyed by existing manufacturers."

After COPS exposed this secret citywide collusion to keep the working-class Mexican American community impoverished, their plan for inner-city economic and residential development eventually proved successful, obtaining $46 million in drainage bonds and another $8 million in neighborhood improvements. Over the past two decades COPS has won more than $750 million in new streets, parks, libraries, and other services.[4]

COPS is an organization of organizations, which gives it a certain solidity: parish clubs, church societies, parent groups, youth clubs, senior citizen groups, neighborhood associations, block clubs, and any others interested in seeing nonviolent change for the betterment of their neglected neighborhoods. Pablo

Eisenberg described COPS as the most effective community group in this country. A federal study of American Communities commissioned by the National Commission on Neighborhoods detailed the hundreds of millions of dollars worth of improvements in streets, drainage, public facilities, and cleanup that COPS won for poorer neighborhoods in San Antonio. It described the five, six, or seven thousand delegates who come each year to the COPS annual convention, and it concluded: "There has been a major shift in power from the wealthy blueblooded Anglos to the poor and working Mexican American families of San Antonio. COPS has been at the center of this shift."

WHAT YOU WILL LEARN IN THIS CHAPTER

There is a quiet revolution sweeping the country. Born in the ferment of the Depression, it waxed and waned though the 1940s and 1950s, and the turbulent 1960s gave it a new push. Since the 1960s it has refined its methods and become a groundswell of positive action in small and large communities from Orlando, Florida, to Anchorage, Alaska, from Bangor, Maine, to Honolulu. Less flamboyant, less confrontive, and more permanent, community organizing today most often works through existing faith-based social networks by which people become involved in political and economic action to create a better life for their children, their neighbors, and themselves.

In this chapter you will explore why community organizing is important and learn what community organizers do. You will review a short history of community organizing and learn about four contemporary models of community organizing. You will explore the partnership model of community organizing. You will discover that community organizing is a fundamental part of a new wave of societal change that is gradually reordering the postmodern era. Community is being reborn, the social is being regenerated, and politics is being reshaped. Locality based community organizing is at the forefront of those changes.

WHAT IS COMMUNITY ORGANIZING?

Ordinary people in communities have always suspected something that government officials and politicians are only now beginning to realize— "Those macro, top-down solutions don't work."[5] Powerful government redevelopment agencies that tear down the slums and build high-rise corporate offices will not solve our social problems. The solution to urban social problems does not lie in destroying neighborhoods but in empowering them. Politicians passing laws will not solve them. If politics is expected to work, democracy can no longer be the privilege of a few wealthy politicians at the top but must be the concern of ordinary people at the bottom. Trickle-down economics will not solve social problems. We will wait forever before wealthy corporations trickle good jobs, good pay, or employment benefits down to us.

It is becoming increasingly clear that politics in the White House or Congress, in governor's mansions or state legislatures across the country are often helpless in dealing with issues that matter most to us. "The *only* thing that really works," says Harry Boyte, "is local initiative."[6] Social change happens only when ordinary people working with others make it happen.

Community organizing is a process by which people in neighborhood organizations, associations and churches join together to form strong local organizations to address social problems in their communities, develop their own solutions, and in partnership with government and corporations implement those solutions over the long term.[7]

Community organizing breaks the bonds of depression, helplessness, and hopelessness by bringing community members together to gain empowerment and justice. People who were formerly alienated, apathetic, and uninvolved take responsibility for themselves to ensure that government or the private sector delivers something in deprived neighborhoods.[8] These neighborhood action organizations begin with community issues: municipal services, jobs, health care, housing finance, parent-school problems, consumer action, insurance rates, police protection—all the things that touch us where we live. Each victory strengthens our hope, and hope builds up organizational membership. Gradually we develop the power and skills needed to deal collectively with a variety of local needs and problems.[9] Community organizing transforms powerlessness into empowerment, dependency into interdependence, dehumanization into human dignity.

WHAT ARE COMMUNITY ORGANIZATIONS?

Community organizations provide mutual strength and cohesion in which people decide for themselves what issues are important and systematically engage megastructures in an equal forum to pursue those issues. They help connect people to corporate power structures and governmental agencies and teach people how to use the power of the community to make their common voices heard.

Community organizations exist in nearly every middle to large metropolis in America, most often in poorer neighborhoods but increasingly in middle working-class neighborhoods as well. Today's community organizations (one of which celebrated its 60th birthday in 2000) are becoming increasingly permanent structures on the social landscape. They include millions of people nationwide in thousands of block clubs, churches, neighborhood associations, coalitions, and federations. Perlman wrote in 1976 that New York City alone had 10,000 black neighborhood associations.[10] In 1978 Stuart Langton cited a National Commission on Neighborhoods study that put the figure at 8,000 nationally.[11] Around 1980, some 20 million Americans belonged to voluntary neighborhood-based organizations,[12] and 60,000 organizations existed across the land.[13] Karen Paget estimated in 1990 that 2 million citizen action groups exist in the United States alone.[14]

Michael Williams asserts that although discrepancies in these various estimates appear to be considerable, all are probably right according to their own definitions. In any given city one would expect to find many more small informal block clubs than formal organizations with paid organizers. Small organizations must exist before they can coalesce with each other into federations.[15]

Community organizations are mediating structures that stand with the individual and the neighborhood, between the neighborhood and organizational megastructures, and between the larger community and society as a whole.[16] (See Figure 8.1)

With the Individual and Neighborhood

Community organizations stand *with* the individual, providing an environment in which socially healthy selves are created. Community organizations pro-

FIGURE 8.1 Community Organizations as Mediating Structures

vide individuals with a milieu of support, and are agents of restoration and remembrance as they assist people in social thinking and social learning. Community organizations are a therapeutic environment.

Milieu of Support   Community organizations provide a milieu of support for people who have few support systems, few resources, and even fewer opportunities on their own. Community organizations generate opportunities for action as well as tangible programs and services that help us obtain resources we need to live healthy lives, supporting the whole. Community organizations help rebuild the social infrastructure of neighborhoods from the ground up, not one person at a time, but in entire neighborhoods. Communities become revitalized with social values and social goods, shaping the character and personalities of the people who inhabit them.

Agents of Restoration and Remembrance   Learned apathy, alienation, and anonymity are the major social problems of a free society. They result in social amnesia. We forget who we are and we forget what happened that made this happen. Social amnesia is the result of institutional reification,[17] which views social artifacts such as corporations or bureaucratic structures as superior to the people who constructed them. We often feel obliged to defer to these human tools. When we surrender our own decision-making capability to the systems that we have created, we collude in the belief that we are helpless and dependent. We falsely attribute to organizational systems qualities that are exclusively human, and then operate on the basis of those assumptions. Herbert Simon, a Nobel Prize–winning economist, for example, asserts that we are not inherently rational. Only organization "permits the individual to approach reasonably near to objective rationality."[18] We forget our authorship of the social world.[19] Those who own and operate complex organizations are generally pleased with social amnesia because it permits them to remain in control of the machinery of social life.

Community organizations, however, challenge social amnesia, passivity, and apathy. Community organizations encourage us to remember that we are owners of our social environment, thinkers who construct our own reality. "The struggle for authorship [of social reality] brings us into an active, intimate relationship with our world, resulting in altered perceptions of our selves."[20] These new interpretations are a prerequisite for organizational action, and action is an essential step in eradicating mistaken definitions of our self and social world. We devise new definitions, take part in demolishing the deceitful illusions that keep us in chains, and assert the right to enter the arena of social reconstruction. We shake off illusions of helplessness and powerlessness and discard the false promises of reification. When the pattern of apathy and resignation is broken, we begin to achieve freedom.

Community organizations are agents of restoration and remembrance. Those of us who are alone and separated become restored to one another, and in finding one another, we find ourselves. We remember the past that we have forgotten, rediscover who we are, and imagine ourselves as we could become. As we share our common memories, we discover our common bonds. Those common bonds help us expose the deceit that we have been trained to accept—that we can only make it by our own effort, we must compete to succeed, and if we fail it is our own fault.

Social Thinking and Social Learning
Community organizations are tools of active social learning that assist people in restoration and remembrance. In community organizations we use our intuition to grasp our own reality, our feeling/valuing to gain dignity and moral goodness, our thinking to understand justice, and our sensing to move to action. Social thinking becomes an upward spiral of learning. As each turn is completed, the process begins again, but at higher and higher levels.

Using Intuition to Grasp Reality
In a process of *conscientization,* or consciousness raising, community organizers help us reflect together on the meaning of the experiences we have had. We begin to experience cognitive dissonance, the experience in which reality fails to match expressed belief. Cognitive dissonance is the window of opportunity for social learning, in which we ask the question, "What is wrong here?" It is the deadly enemy of the imposed status quo of forgetfulness and denial that demands, "Don't ask, don't see, don't tell." As we name discontinuities between what we have experienced and what our lives ought to have been like, we begin to remember. Our shared memories give us power.

While society may blame us for our situation, our intuition speaks to us at a deeper level. Community members of poor neighborhoods know that they have as many inherent skills, abilities, and potential as anyone else. We begin to understand that we have not created the conditions that keep us subservient. We realize that we have been subjected to subtle, long-term education in dehumanization, and we call upon our intuition to visualize ourselves as we could be.

Feeling/Valuing to Gain Dignity and Moral Justice
The neighborhood organization is a means of moral education in which we exercise our feeling/valuing functions. We reassert our rights to have feelings other than depression, alienation, hopelessness, or apathy. We exhibit a sense of justice and moral indignation. We feel anger and outrage. We reject the unidimensionality of social life we been forced to assume. We reclaim our ability to feel, to believe, to have hope, and to see ourselves in an entirely different way.

We understand that there is a deeper moral dimension to the issues that confront us: that basic values have been distorted, injustice has become a way of life, honesty is rarely found. Our rights as well as our selves have been violated. The community organization becomes an arena of public and moral discourse in which members of community organizations reassert a sense of ethics into social life, allowing for the reflection of diverse opinion, while always engaging in dialogue with one another about the best course of action.

Thinking to Understand Justice
Using determination, community members begin to exercise their cognitive thinking to gather information and facts. Empirical data give community members evidence that confirm their feelings and intuition. Facts become weapons against injustice that protestations of innocence cannot hide. Information helps us understand "not only what can or cannot be done but more importantly, what ought to be done."[21]

Community organizations help neighbors gain strength in unified engagement as we encounter forces that have kept us down. (Courtesy of Gordon Mayer, National Training and Information Center, Chicago, IL.)

Sensing to Move to Action   Members of community organizations exercise their sensing functions, grasp practical solutions, and experience the empowerment that comes from collective action. We feel strength and release of unified engagement as we encounter forces that have kept us down. We devise strategies, plan actions, and carry them out.

Each turn of the spiral adds more self-understanding, stronger collective identity, greater resolve and deeper insights, consciously controlled emotions, better ideas, and more competent action and skills. As citizen participants, we grow in understanding of ourselves, the political process, and our own inherent power in working collectively on the resolution of neighborhood issues.[22]

Therapeutic Environment   Community organizations provide a therapeutic environment for healing the self. Discouraged individuals find a way to become encouraged as they meet people of valor and vision and begin to discover valor and vision in themselves. People who are distressed find those who face similar problems as well as those who have sur-

mounted the difficulties with which they are surrounded. We affirm our dreams and gain substance for the hope inside us as we talk with one another, sharing our feelings, aspirations, and hopes. Neighbors gain strength, and together we begin to search for common solutions. Community organizations are oases of hope and healing.

Between the Neighborhood and Organizations

Community organizations stand between neighborhood members and the megastructures of the social environment. They help engage individuals in the political process. They counteract governmental or economic social failures of modern society.

Saul Alinsky, the father of modern community organization, was the "sworn enmity of deadly institutionalization and routinization that afflicts social structures."[23] Alinsky's message is a call for people to shake off their lethargy and actively participate in the economic, social, and political life of society. The failure of existing institutions to generate social change or stimulate citizen participation, asserted Alinsky, is one of the major crises facing authentic democracy.

> Even when a person may have a sudden desire to take a hand, he lacks the means by which to translate his desire into active participation. And so the local citizen sinks further into apathy, anonymity, and depersonalization. The result is his complete dependence on public authority and the state of civic sclerosis.[24]

Community organizations help members conjointly articulate grievances against groups responsible for social problems, especially business and governmental organizations.[25] They provide a means by which we mobilize ourselves for action in such issues as public housing, urban renewal, unemployment, and public education.[26] Corporate and governmental structures are held accountable to the neighborhoods and the citizens who comprise them. Where government or business collude to undermine the social or economic capacity of neighborhoods, community organizations work to expose these practices. Where large corporations and governmental bureaucracies ignore, bypass, or exploit inner-city neighborhoods, community organizations become systems of political empowerment.

Community organizations counteract the failure of mass governmental systems to create a society that is truly democratic.[27] They are a forum by which we discuss issues, take a position, and shape our concerns into tangible recommendations, programs, and actions. Community organizations foster grassroots democracy at the level where people's vital concerns are located.

Community organizations counteract the failure of the market system to provide economic justice, economic access, and equal economic opportunity for all citizens. In their role of inventing community development corporations (CDCs), community organizations provide alternatives to community dependence on large corporate structures for financial autonomy, and engage community members to consider ways in which we can work together to support and create a better economic climate for all.

Community organizations alleviate social failures of modern life. While corporate America and big government are helpless in combating drug abuse, neighborhood deterioration, crime, and violence, community organizations forge alliances of neighbors working together to make our neighborhoods socially healthy, positive, safe, and humane social environments.

They overcome the inability of megastructures to provide the social goods without which our society could not exist. Community organizations help produce people who are actively engaged in making trust, honesty, and cooperation living realities. By supporting and developing community pride, involvement, caring, and a consciousness of community as the central means of character building, community organizations help children and youth honor duty, service, and perseverance, qualities on which the self but also the larger structures of society are founded.

Between the Larger Community and Society

Community organizations help people conceive of new social movements. Community organizers promote the active critical assessment of current reality and call for suspension of belief in modern social practices that discourage, defeat, and disillusion people. They provide a means by which personal and social redefinitions of reality are disseminated to the larger social world, reshaping the way we see ourselves and others. When those redefinitions of individual identity and social reality become widespread, the result is a social movement of society-wide proportions. In Chapter 14 you will explore how these larger social movements occur and how they generate new configurations of personal and societal identity.

A SHORT HISTORY OF COMMUNITY ORGANIZING IN AMERICA

Although community organization is a relatively new and modern mode of social work practice, Americans have been organizing and developing community based associations and organizations since at least the 19th century. During the Progressive Era, macro social workers were already organizing communities on their own behalf. Community organizing as a distinct method of insurgent struggle came into its own in the 1940s with the work of Saul Alinsky.[28] During the 1950s and 60s community organizing was often identified with the use of confrontational tactics for limited objectives. Since then community organizing has broadened its aims, often working in partnership with corporations and government, while expecting them to be accountable and responsive to citizens needs and local neighborhoods.

The Progressive Era (1880–1915)

Communitarian social organizers of the Progressive Era worked in Charity Organization Societies, social settlements, and school community centers often located in or near neighborhood slums.[29]

As the Charity Organization Societies (COS) movement evolved, it concerned itself not only with individuals but paid increasing attention to "pauperism," the basic social condition that seemed to keep some people poor. With their concern for the poor, it was natural for charity organizations to focus their services in neighborhoods where poor people lived. They changed the structure of COS to engage communities directly, dividing their operation into districts corresponding to police precincts to get charitable services closer to the people.[30] This locality approach to poverty encouraged many Charity Organization Societies to establish new community services such as anti-tuberculosis committees, housing committees, child labor committees, and remedial loan committees, resulting in the "earliest professional community organization in social work."[31]

Community organization was one of the major characteristics of *settlement* programs. The settlement assumed a "special responsibility for all families living within the radius of a few blocks of the settlement house [and] it sustained a general relationship to the larger district encircling the neighborhood."[32] Settlement workers assisted in the self-organization of community residents to bring about needed changes through direct efforts, mobilization of local resources, and democratic social action.[33] They developed institutional resources suited to the needs of a working-class community, including relief of distress, and development of neglected recreation. They engaged in legislation attempting to improve slums. Pushing for municipal reforms, they worked to improve sanitation, sewage disposal, and clean water. They advocated for regulation and inspection of food to prevent disease and illness.

As settlement workers got to know their neighborhoods and the needs of residents, many of them were drawn into social reform. Some sought to mobilize neighborhood forces, and a few tried to help residents develop self-directed organizations. In Boston, for example, settlements helped organize 16 district improvement societies, which chose delegates to the citywide United Improvement Associations. Settlements formed their own federations. "They played a positive role in delivering needed services, raising public consciousness about slum conditions, and called for collective action to ameliorate problems." Robert Fisher asserts that "there is no question about the sincerity or commitment to social reform of those who made the settlement their life's work"[34]

Social reformers active in settlements, recreation, and adult education banded together as early as 1907 to lobby for the after-school use of school buildings as neighborhood social centers. The Rochester Board of Education appropriated funds to use 16 school buildings for civic and social purposes serving both youth and adults. It worked so well that in 1908 a citywide federation of school-based civic clubs was formed. They were used as "centers for voting, employment information, recreation, education, health services, and Americanization programs."[35] In 1909, however, ward politicians, fearful of competition, cut off funds for the school centers.[36]

In spite of its short existence, however, the Rochester experience attracted wide attention. By 1911, 48 cities were using 248 school buildings as community centers,[37] and by 1919 these community centers were operating in 197 cities. In 1930, New York City alone had almost 500 centers, with an annual aggregate attendance of more than 4 million.[38]

The school community center was "an organizing center for the life of the neighborhood." Community center workers were regarded as neighborhood leaders. They were on the job continuously, stimulating the community to develop its own activities, and showed how they could pay their way. After a while some centers developed self-governing committees consisting of a representative from each member club. In New York, through the influence of the People's Institute, for example, school centers were used as a base for forming neighborhood organizations.[39]

Although community centers were supposed to be governed from the bottom up, throughout the liberal reform movement of the early 20th century, there existed a tendency toward professionalization, bureaucratization, and centralization.[40] "Citizen involvement became limited to membership in clubs and participation in center activities," while planning was left primarily to professionals, who made all the important decisions.[41] Gradually the centers came to belong to the professionals who ran them, not to the neighborhood residents. They evolved into "professionalized forms of neighborhood service delivery that characterized much social work community organization before and since that time."[42] The school center movement peaked in the mid-1920s. The ideal of self-governing school centers never gained widespread application, and other methods developed to organize city neighborhoods.[43]

Saul Alinsky and Community Organizing (1940–1960)

Saul Alinsky (1909–1972) is America's best known community organizer.[44] Although he was not the first to combine political activism with an emphasis on rebuilding a specific community, he was the first to do it in a number of neighborhoods across the nation by organizing existing groups into federated coalitions. He is the main bridge between the past and future of organizing, primarily because of the extent of his work and the number of his students currently influencing the movement. His work is central to a comprehensive understanding of current organizing.

Saul David Alinsky was born in Chicago on January 30, 1909. After receiving his BA degree from the University of Chicago, he accepted a fellowship in the university's graduate program in criminology. He studied the gang of notorious "Scarface" Al Capone, and later Italian street gangs, and he was a research sociologist at the Illinois State Penitentiary at Jolliet.

In 1935, in the middle of the Depression, Alinsky ended his three-year program at Jolliet and joined Clifford Shaw's Chicago Area Project to investigate the feasibility of establishing a juvenile delinquency prevention program in the Back of the Yards neighborhood, a working-class area behind Chicago's stockyards and meat-packing plants. Alinsky became fascinated with the Back of the Yards area as a laboratory for testing his emerging community organization orientation. "I knew that once they were provided with a real positive program to change their miserable conditions they wouldn't need scapegoats anymore. Probably my prime consideration in moving into Back of the Yards, though, was because if it could be done there, it could be done anywhere."[45]

In the meantime, John L. Lewis, president of the CIO labor union, had begun a campaign to organize Chicago's meat-packing industry, the largest employer in Back of the Yards. Alinsky became intrigued by the dedication, conviction, skill, and expertise of the union organizers, who were involved in all the important social and political issues of the day: They entered into the lives of the stockyard workers, convincing people that their problems were not unique but connected with the problems of poor and exploited people everywhere. They preached unity, solidarity, action, and reform.

After three years of learning how to organize mass meetings, identify and develop issues, raise money, and recruit members, Alinsky decided to put his community organizing ideas into practice. He and a group of local residents decided to form a coalition of neighborhood organizations.

On July 14, 1939, the indigenous leaders of the Back of the Yards Neighborhood Council held their constitutional convention, attended by 350 delegates, representing 109 local organizations. Two days later a large delegation from the council marched to a CIO rally as a show of solidarity with meat-packing workers. The rally convinced the company of the grassroots strength of the union and they reluctantly decided to negotiate a CIO contract. Saul Alinsky the social researcher had become a community organizer.

The Back of the Yards council launched new programs, including a well baby clinic, neighborhood job fairs, a credit union, and a lunch program for school children in which 1,400 kids were fed hot lunches. But Alinsky wanted the residents to understand that the real objective of the council was to build collective power so that the Back of the Yards residents could really run their neighborhood and make it the kind of community they wanted.[46]

Alinsky believed that organizational megastructures induce people to accept powerlessness in exchange for security and being taken care of by those in control.[47] Organized apathy, he asserted, is what keeps people from getting involved with one another, keeps them in a state of helplessness and hopelessness, and prevents them from taking action. The hopelessness and alienation people feel may turn them against one another in destructive ways. Describing the Back of the Yards district, Alinsky said:

> The area was a cesspool of hate: the Poles, Slovaks, Germans, Negroes, Mexicans and Lithuanians. Fascist groups like the German-American Bund, Father Coughlin's National Union for Social Justice and William Dudley Pelley's Silver Shirts were moving to exploit the…. It wasn't because the people had any real sympathy for fascism; it was just that they were so desperate that they grabbed onto anything that offered them a glimmer of hope and Coughlin and Pelley gave them scapegoats in the Jews and the international bankers.[48]

Alinsky's strategy was to break the structure of apathy by stirring up dissatisfaction and discontent,[49] disrupt existing, complacent expectations; fragmented and partial loyalties of local groups, and the individualistic orientations of community residents. After every action, Alinsky made the leaders take the time to talk about what had happened. They dissected, analyzed, and criticized each event until they understood why they won or lost. Each victory was celebrated with speeches and impromptu parties. Alinsky's careful organizing paid off. The Back of the Yards Neighborhood Council grew into a vigorous organization.

Later Alinsky reflected on the lessons he had learned from the Back of the Yards experience:

1. To hell with charity. The only thing you get is what you are strong enough to get—so you had better organize.

2. You prove to people they can do something, show them how to have a way of life where they can make their own decisions, then you get out. They don't need a father who stands over them.

3. It comes down to the basic argument of the Federalist papers. Either you believe in people, like James Madison and James Monroe, or you don't…. I do.[50]

In August, 1940, Marshall Field III, who was to become one of Alinsky's closest friends, joined with Alinsky and Bishop Bernard J. Shiel in establishing the Industrial Areas Foundation (IAF). The IAF board of trustees voted to raise $15,000 a year for five years to support Alinsky's organizing efforts, launching his career as a full-time professional community organizer.

Alinsky began sending organizers to other working-class neighborhoods in northern industrial cites, to Mexican American communities in the Southwest, to Kansas City and South St. Paul in America's heartland. Established community leaders didn't always welcome them. Sometimes they were arrested or thrown out of town. As a consequence of his vigorous organizing, Alinsky spent some time in jail, during which he began writing his best-selling *Reveille for Radicals,* published in 1946, and *John L. Lewis: An Unauthorized Biography,* published in 1949.

Community Organizing in the 1950s

By 1950, the slashing of expressways through residential areas, the razing of thousands of slum buildings, and the refurbishing of central business districts produced resentment among the city residents whose neighborhoods were being wrecked. As early as 1953 the idea of mobilizing public opinion for more responsible urban renewal found fertile ground at the local level. Citizen participation began to be the watchword in renewal activities.

Under Alinsky's direction the IAF organization established the Chelsea Community Council (CCC), a coalition of 77 organizations in 1957, the Citizens Federation of Lackawanna (CFL) in New York in 1958, the Butte Citizens Project (BCP) in Montana in 1959, and the Organization for the Southwest Council (OSC) in Chicago in 1959. By 1963 the Northwest Community Organization (NCO) was in operation, and the Woodlawn Organization (TWO) in Chicago, one of the most famous and important of Alinsky's organizations.[51]

On June 12, 1972, Alinsky died in Carmel, California, leaving behind a rich legacy of local, broad-based community organizations. He had organized, in one way or another, a couple of million men and women to take control of their lives, and he made many more Americans aware of the power of organized citizen participation to make needed changes in social institutions and government regulations. The large-scale citizen mobilizations of our time—women, anti-war and antinuclear activists, consumers, environmentalists—whether they know it or not, owe most of their bottom-up organizational strategy and effective nonviolent tactics to Saul Alinsky. "Along with the Rev. Martin Luther King Jr., Alinsky deserves credit for freeing American churches from suburban captivity as ghetto sanctuaries and bringing church people into the city streets and village roads where people were struggling with problems and possibilities of everyday life."[52]

The Turbulent 1960s and Their Aftermath

Primarily because of the work of Alinsky, grassroots, self-initiated organizations emerged full blown from the civil rights struggles of the 1950s and 1960s, providing the first widespread encouragement for the development of community organizations for lower-income and minority populations. With the aid of foundations and federal funding, the motivation for changing the low level of political participation and political organization of the poor took hold. Reformers of the 1960s directed their energies to community participation and organization as a means of gaining access to the system for the poor, and in a short period of time a number of organizations grew in minority and lower-class neighborhoods. Unlike their middle-class counterparts, these organizations were concerned with the need to change the system, redistribute power, and provide access to public resources.[53]

With the inauguration of President John F. Kennedy, the national government became more assertive in promoting and supporting new approaches to old problems and in fostering community change. Federal agencies, national organizations, and some foundations actively pushed the application of new ideas. These national entities began funding local organizers, sometimes sending them in from the outside.[54] Government called for participation of the poor and developed programs to increase it. Pressure for access was a priority, and participation became the byword.[55]

The Great Society programs under Lyndon Johnson added a new dimension to urban community organization. The Economic Opportunity Act of 1964 included Community Action Programs (CAPs) and Community Action Agencies (CAAs), which incorporated citizen participation as part of their processes. On November 23, 1964, Sargent Shriver, director of the new Office of Economic Opportunity, signed the first Community Action Program (CAP) grants, including Head Start, the Neighborhood Youth Corps, and Legal Services. It was the biggest infusion of money ever to initiate neighborhood-based services and community organizing. Community Action Agencies (CAAs) were set up to operate and oversee the various community action programs in local neighborhoods. As they shaped up around the nation in 1965, 90% took the form of private nonprofit organizations, while local government operated the rest. Most CAAs set up neighborhood units as well as resident advisory committees for programs such as Head Start. [56]

The Economic Opportunity Act of 1964 required "maximum feasible participation" of residents in areas served, which initially was interpreted to mean at least one-third representation of the poor on CAA governing boards. Congress made this part of the law in 1966. Most of the representatives of the poor were selected by neighborhood committees or area councils, which themselves were chosen by residents, usually in open meetings but occasionally by ballot. Hiring organizers with public funds became commonplace, and most of the urban CAAs developed neighborhood-based programs.[57]

Community Action Programs constituted a sufficient challenge to existing ways of doing things, however, so that forces of reaction set in almost immediately. A 1967 amendment required that one-third of the local community action boards must be local governmental officials, and allowed local government to take over the programs. While not many governments did, the threat to do so, combined with tightened OEO regulations, constrained the more militant activities of CAAs, and after an initial thrust of organizing, many settled mainly into social service operations. They spent the bulk of their funds trying to remedy perceived defects of individuals rather than changing institutions or social systems.[58]

Community Organizing in the 1970s and 1980s

Gale Cincotta was a community leader who emerged from the Organization for a Better Austin, an Alinsky-style organization. She joined with Shel Trapp and others to convene a National Housing Conference in Chicago in March 1972 that drew 2,000 delegates from 74 cities in 36 states. Out of this conference came a national membership association,

Jack Conway (left) Executive Director of Center for Community change discussed a project
with Walter Reuther, President of AFL-CIO (2nd from right) and community leaders.
(© Gene Daniels/Black Star, print courtesy of National Training and Information Center
and Watts Community Action Committee)

National Peoples Action (NPA) on housing and a
support organization, the National Training and
Information Center (NTIC). [59]

The NPA assisted 13 community groups form
the metropolitan Area Housing Alliance, which led
a campaign that succeeded in getting the Commission of Savings and Loan Association of Illinois to
adopt an anti-redlining regulation in 1974. Turning
their attention nationally, this force, supported by
grassroots organizations in many other cities and
some Washington-based national organizations,
pushed until they got Congress to adopt the Federal
Home Mortgage Disclosure Act of 1975, (which
gave grassroots groups a tool for uncovering redlining practices), the Community Reinvestment Act of
1977 (resulting in more than $100 billion being
invested in neighborhoods), and legislation authorizing a presidentially appointed National Commission on Neighborhoods.[60]

The NPA fought for and won the passage of 14
pieces of national legislation, including the 518(b)
HUD payback program, which returned money to
FHA homeowners when they were defrauded by

sleazy realtors and mortgage bankers. The NPA won
a massive reinvestment program for targeted neighborhoods by Aetna Insurance company and by Mar-
riott International, which established school-to-work
programs for youth.[61]

The growth of National Peoples Action and
other national neighborhood organizations was
greatly facilitated by the staff and network connections of national and regional technical assistance
organizations that came into being in the late 1960s
and 1970s. Jack Conway had moved from the AFL-
CIO to head the OEO Community Action Program
and organized the Center for Community Change in
1968 to provide technical assistance to community
development corporations. In 1969, Howard Hallman organized the Center for Governmental Studies (later renamed Civic Action Institute), which
conducted research on neighborhood decentralization and provided technical assistance to the
National Council of La Raza, the National Urban
League, and the National Urban Coalition, among
many others. Working from a base in the U.S.
Catholic Conference, Monsignor Geno Aaroni, who

had close ties with Gale Cincotta and NTIC, set up the National Center for Urban Ethnic Affairs (NCUEA) in 1970 to provide assistance to business people and residents of predominately white ethnic neighborhoods.

Various training centers dispatched community organizers throughout the country, including the New England Training Center for Community Organizers in Providence, the Industrial Areas Foundation (IAF), Heather Booth's Midwest Academy, Gale Cincotta and Shel Trapp's National Training and Information Center (NTIC) in Chicago, Mike Miller's Organize Training Center (OTC) in San Francisco, Fr. John Bauman's Pacific Institute of Community Organizing (PICO) and the Center for Third World Organizing, both in Oakland, California.[62]

By 1981 the number of national training centers and national support networks and associations expanded to two dozen, including Grassroots Leadership, begun by social worker Si Kahn, Direct Action and Research Training (DART), and the Gamaliel Foundation. Three hundred newsletters and periodicals that focused extensively on community organizations existed in 1985.[63]

Community Organizing Since the 1990s

Today community organizing is more widespread and has more impact than ever before. NTIC, for example, has been instrumental in working with groups such as ADAPT, which made important contributions to passage of the Americans With Disabilities Act. Since 1995 NTIC has collaborated with departments of labor and justice and ten community groups, including the Michigan Organizing Project church-based approach and Action Through Churches Together in Virginia, and Cincinnati's Working in Neighborhoods (WIN), exploring ways to put unemployed people back to work. NTIC continues to work with organizations such as Chicago's West Humboldt Park neighborhood and the Northwest Neighborhood Federation and the Narcotics Nuisance Abatement Partnership, among others.

Organizers must now be more "proactive," linking community organizing with community development. Neo-Alinsky organizer Shel Trapp sees that change as a natural progression.[64] Most community organizations of the 1990s and early 21st century are congregation-based organizations modeled after the social network process developed by the Industrial Areas Foundation (IAF), Pacific Institute of Community Organizing (PICO), Direct Action Research and Training (DART), and the Gamaliel Foundation.[65]

HOW TO DO COMMUNITY ORGANIZING

Community organizing is a creative process that will never be completely perfected, but it calls forth the imagination, ingenuity, compassion, and mutual engagement of the organizer and the people. You begin by seeking to understand the people and helping them define the problem that you will work with them to address. You engage the community, empower forces of change, and build an organization.

SI KAHN

Si Kahn is one of social work's premier community organizers. He was raised in a small college town in the Pennsylvania mountains, where his father was a rabbi and his mother was an artist. He first began organizing as a volunteer with the Student Nonviolent Coordinating Committee (SNCC). He moved on to Georgia, working with African American farmers cooperatives and voter registration, and he became a labor organizer in the North Georgia mountains. Kahn worked with the United Mine Workers as a coordinator during the Brookside strike in Harlan County, Kentucky, and then with the Amalgamated Clothing and Textile Workers Union (ACTWU). His books *How People Get Power* and *Organizing: A Guide for Grassroots Leaders,* both published by NASW Press, are classics in the field of community organizing. Kahn is also a folksinger and songwriter. He has recorded nine albums, plus a double album of protest folksongs with Pete Seeger and Jane Sapp. In 1980, he founded Grassroots Leadership to continue building a multiracial movement in the South.[66] (You can read more about Grassroots Leadership in Appendix B.)

Understanding the People

While you accept the people with whom you work, you must not have illusions about their ability or their dysfunctions. Paulo Freire says that the oppressed sometimes behave in ways that "reflect the structure of domination." Freire notes the "existential duality of the oppressed, who are at the same time themselves and the oppressor whose image they have internalized."[67]

People who are abused and victimized are often unwilling participants in an unequal and hurtful system in which they are powerless. They may feel that they cannot change the system and react to their abuse by adopting any number of mechanisms that enable them to survive often brutal life circumstances. Some may *act out* their pain, turning to a life of crime or gangs. People who have been forced to live in abysmal conditions sometimes develop negative attitudes and behaviors. When this occurs, Saul Alinsky reminds us, that "the organizer's affection for people is not lessened nor is he hardened against them even when masses of them demonstrate a capacity for brutality, selfishness, hate, greed, avarice, and disloyalty. He is convinced that these attitudes and actions are the result of evil conditions. It is not the people who must be judged but the circumstances that made them that way. The organizer's desire to change society then becomes that much firmer."[68]

Others may *get out*—escaping the community and going to a better environment. A very few may *opt out*—rising above poverty and oppression to become successful professionals, actors, businesspeople. There are even a few who *flake out*. Flake outs become comedians who bring the pain out into the open by focusing it on themselves so people can laugh about it. They play a therapeutic role by helping people release the pain they feel.

For the overwhelming majority of people who live with cultural abuse, economic discrimination, victimization, and racism, however, these survival mechanisms are neither available nor appropriate. Many cannot get out, and acting out only adds to their problems. Neither can everyone opt out or even flake out. Instead, most victims of oppression *cop out*. Like adult survivors of abuse, they bury their pain and learn to live with an oppressive situation until they become themselves part of the cycle. They perpetuate, unwillingly and often unwittingly, the cycle of victimization because they have few choices.

Julio Morales calls this "self oppression," or a "colonized mentality," a condition Puerto Ricans have experienced as a result of centuries of oppression and colonization. "Many Puerto Ricans have internalized stereotypes," Morales asserts, and "blame themselves for their fate, not understanding that their poverty is responsible for their alienation and feelings of helplessness or that their poverty is a function of a macro process over which they have little, if any control." Conditioned to accept their situation, they may think they are not as capable, as competent, or as good as others. Some may even believe they deserve poor services and shoddy living arrangements, and that they should be grateful for anything they get. Some express "dependency or unwarranted respect for authority and authority figures, making it difficult, at times, to organize" them. They may hold an expectation that leaders and experts will solve their problems.[69]

As a means of survival, victims of oppression will often repress, minimize, ignore, or deny the circumstances that they have had to endure. When you begin to encounter the oppressed, therefore, some may not want to admit the seriousness of their problems, recognize that their condition is as bad as it is, or believe that things can ever change. They may not be willing to look clearly at the pain they are experiencing.

Rather than give in to this cycle of hopelessness, work to help the oppressed face issues that they would rather avoid. Recognizing and accepting the reality of the situation is the first step in recovery. The problems of the community will not be solved until and unless community members recognize them, take a stand, and resist those who exploit them.

In addition to overcoming denial, you understand that poor people, just like anyone else, are consumed with their own private affairs, personal survival, raising families, making it on the job, and getting along until the next paycheck. Many people in poor, oppressed communities do not have the resources, support systems, education, or influence of more affluent members of society, especially the powerful whom they will be confronting. Moreover, they are made even more helpless by the poverty and stress with which they live. Julio Morales calls this the "full plate" syndrome, in which problem after problem is compounded so that the poor and oppressed have little time or energy to confront their situation. For example,

> racism, violence, AIDS, drugs, crime, homelessness, alienation from the judicial system, massive underemployment or unemployment, high levels of school dropouts, rivalry among adult leadership etc. are common ingredients on that crowded

plate. Insufficient services to families, inappropriate foster care for Puerto Rican children, lack of school curriculum on the Puerto Rican experience, lack of curriculum aimed at building the self-esteem of Puerto Rican youngsters, and the competing and clashing of cultural values within the larger society add to the full plate. The needs leading to the migration [of many families] to and from Puerto Rico, the different perspectives and levels of acclimating to U.S. society that [people] experience, and intra-community issues such as competition for resources…at times fragmentize community efforts.[70]

In spite of all of this, however, the oppressed have their innate dignity, and moral justice on their side. You bring people together, fire up their energies, and mobilize the "rightness" of their cause.

Defining the Problem

As a community organizer, you try to pinpoint and expose areas of oppression, intentionally focusing on one or more problem situations that are clearly visible. The problem must be important to the welfare of the community, and one around which people can be mobilized to action. Begin where people are and help them raise issues of acute concern—lack of police protection, crime, gangs that hang out on street corners, drug abuse, poor maintenance of a housing project, or violence that creates an atmosphere of fear in the neighborhood. You place yourself clearly on the side of the people, and you clearly state your purpose in the neighborhood, but you do not define their problems for them or provide the solutions.[71] Even though you may think that other issues are more important and could be addressed more effectively, if the people in a low-income housing project want to begin getting their housing project repaired or welfare checks increased, you help them act on these issues.

Engaging the Community

As you engage the community and its people, you obtain an understanding of the community that you will be organizing. You gain a feeling for their issues and their plight. This must be done carefully. Social worker Si Kahn explains,

Everything the organizer does after he arrives in a community will be influenced by the initial impression he makes and by how the community reacts to him. During the entry period, the organizer must make such basic decisions as who his first contacts in the community will be; which parts of the community he will try to communicate with and which, if any, he will try to avoid; where he will live and how he will dress; how he will talk and how he will explain to people in the community what he is trying to do.

He may later change his mind about the way he wants to do some of these things, but for the most part, as far as people in the community are concerned, he will continue to be seen in terms of the initial impression he makes. An organizer has the chance to enter a particular community for the first time only once, and the mistakes he makes will stay with him as long as he is there.[72]

Empowering Forces of Change

You provide people with experiences that appeal to their innate dignity. Warren Haggstrom, for example, tells of a group of residents who, with the help of organizers, went to a district sanitation inspector to appeal for better street cleaning. During the meeting the inspector claimed that there was no point in putting more equipment into such neighborhoods because the residents didn't care whether their streets were dirty or not. When the community heard of the report, they became angry at this affront to their dignity. Their anger mobilized them to fight the issue.[73]

Building an Organization

When enough people in the community are concerned about the problem, schedule a series of preliminary meetings to build an organizational structure. Make sure that people remember the meeting day and time. You may have to arrange transportation and continue to encourage people to come. Once at the meeting, "concentrate on moving those attending into decision and action." In principle, a community organization is "always the expression of power through the greatest number of members acting together to resolve the central problems of their lives."[74]

Once the structure becomes clear and a decision is made to organize, help the community members elect officers and develop preliminary committees, role assignments, strategies, and time-lines. Your goal is to build a democratic community-based organization in which ordinary people make the decisions about things that affect them. A series of successful specific and localized confrontations may be one way to achieve your goals, build confidence among leaders and members, and demonstrate the organization's ability to improve the quality of neighborhood life.[75]

During this process, build and train leaders, review and evaluate your strategies, celebrate victories, regroup, and move on to other issues. You solidify the changes you have made. Your organization may develop social service programs or a community development corporation. The aim of community organizing is to develop a community power base capable of broad local political participation.[76]

The Role of the Organizer

Never impose yourself on the community or manipulate the community, Si Kahn says. Always present yourself clearly on a basis "that you help build an organization that belongs and will belong to the members."[77] You do not build an organization to achieve your goals. The organization always exists for the people.

Your leadership style must fit the situation, changing according to the particular readiness levels of the members (described in Chapters 4 and 7). Balance the depth and amount of your interventions so as to continually enable community members to learn skills and assume more and more responsibility. In principle, rarely intervene in the organization directly unless it is absolutely necessary, otherwise members will not see the victories as their victories, acquire knowledge and skills, or develop an effective organization. Continually "ally yourself with the long-term objective self-interest of the people, building an organization through which they can act effectively."[78] You work behind the scenes and work yourself out of a job by training community members to be skilled community organizers.[79]

Evaluation and Termination

Just as you must spend time getting to know the community and its people and developing relationships, you must likewise spend a lot of time disengaging and helping the organization assess itself. The description of assessment and closure in Chapter 7 for how a community developer disengages from a community is essentially the same as the way in which a community organizer exists from a community organization.

HOW TO USE FOUR MODELS OF COMMUNITY ORGANIZING

At least four different ways of doing community organizing have been developed by community organizers. It is important to understand that while models can give you some basic ideas, community organizing is not a static process. It emerges out of the needs of the people and out of the particular situation with which they are confronted. When deciding among these models, assess your situation based on differences between two variables: (1) the number of local associations in the community, and (2) the amount of social cohesion that exists between these organizations (see Figure 8.2).

For example, if there are few if any existing associations in your community and if a sense of locality, cohesion, or commitment to locality is lacking, Cesar Chavez's Linking model may work best. On the other hand, Fred Ross's House Meeting model is useful if there are few if any existing associations in your community but social cohesion and commitment to the locality is high. If there are many existing associations but little cohesion among them, the Alinsky Coalition model tends to be useful. Finally, if there are many existing associations in your community and there is strong cohesion among them, the IAF/PICO Social Networks model might be the best model to consider.

Chavez Organizational Linking Model

Sometimes alienation, commitment, lack of social cohesion, and few associations exist in areas dominated by large business enterprises.[80] Dominant corporate cultures often promote these conditions to keep people in subservience so that they can be exploited. When you work to organize people in these communities, the amount of resistance your community will face will often be high. In Califor-

<table>
<tr><td>

Ross House Meeting Model
Few organizations
High commitment
  and cohesion

</td><td>

Social Networks Model
Many organizations
High cohesion

</td></tr>
<tr><td>

Chavez Linking Model
Few organizations
Low cohesion

</td><td>

Alinsky Coalition Model
Many organizations
Low cohesion

</td></tr>
</table>

FIGURE 8.2   Four Models of Community Organizing

nia, for example, migrant farm laborers have been exploited by large agribusiness interests since the Depression. Many are Mexican nationals who are not citizens and possess few legal rights, or Mexican Americans who possess little education and may not speak English. They work long hours in fields where temperatures reach 110 degrees in the shade for weeks on end, with little pay, poor housing, often no medical care, and only intermittent education for their children. They move seasonally with the crops. Beginning with oranges and avocados in the San Fernando Valley, they move north to California's great Central Valley, picking lettuce in Delano, grapes in San Benito, artichokes in Castroville, strawberries in Watsonville, and almonds in Ukiah. They often have developed little attachment or commitment to the land or to the communities where they work and, aside from the Catholic Church, have few if any associations to which they belong.

These are the conditions that Caesar Chavez found in California's migrant work camps in the 1960s. Chavez realized that in order to organize the farm workers, he would first have to provide a struc-

ture to which the laborers would feel attachment and some commitment. The workers had to be convinced that they actually had an interest in the locality and power to approach growers. Chavez began to help build trust and a sense of community, creating farmworker food and gas buying clubs. These clubs were nonthreatening to agribusiness, but once a number of clubs were organized they became the basis for organizing the workers. The clubs built social cohesion in the farm-worker community. They gave the people a sense of solidarity, commitment to locality, and attachment to one another. They helped develop leadership around common issues. The clubs became a source of community strength.

Once the laborers realized that by working together they could improve their situation, Chavez linked their new associations with existing, legitimizing institutions such as the church and labor unions. They began to assert themselves over issues of low wages, long hours, and abysmal working conditions. Chavez built even more cohesion by direct confrontation methods including picketing, marches, and boycotts, along with intensive negotiation.

Migrant farm workers no longer saw themselves as expendable laborers who could be easily displaced or threatened with deportation. The process was neither easy nor quick. Chavez invested himself for years in a protracted struggle to help the migrant laborers in California's Central Valley become organized.[81]

Ross House Meeting Model

Arguing that many poor people did not already have organizations representing their interests, Fred Ross of the Community Services Organization in California developed a new form of organizing in the 1960s: the House Meeting Model.[82] This model was perfected by the Association of Community Organizations for Reform Now (ACORN), which organized around southern blacks who, like the California farm workers, had few existing organizations, but did have a sense of place and commitment to a particular locality.

House meetings are evening sessions held in poor communities where six to 20 people focus on specific problems and develop a pre-organizational infrastructure. Sometimes house meetings are held in a series that leads to significant growth by expanding membership into new social circles. House meetings are critical for developing group solidarity and leadership skills, instilling confidence, and heightening people's spirit and willingness to struggle. Meeting in a member's home is an ideal forum for getting to know people, listening to what they have to say, talking to them about issues, and encouraging them to become involved.

The First Meeting   Develop as many community contacts as you can, getting people's names, and talking with them in their homes until you find someone who is willing to sponsor the first house meeting. Make sure that first house meeting is representative of the community but limited to less than a dozen people. Meetings usually last no more than an hour and a half. As guests arrive, greet the members and introduce them to each other. Once everyone has arrived, lead a short "icebreaker" to help people get to know each other and feel more comfortable. Then, describe the purpose of the meeting and let people know when the meeting will end. Engage people in identifying issues.

Let people talk about their own personal and local concerns. Your goal is to encourage group members to continue the process and perhaps become part of the organizing committee. Draft a document detailing the concerns of the group. It should include something that the members can do to get involved right away. For example, they might go with you to talk to their friends about their concerns or host another house meeting.

Door Knocking   During the next month or so, go door to door with members of your organizing committee and talk to as many people as you can. "Door knocking" is perhaps the most important activity in which you will engage. It enables you to engage people and draw them out, learn about them as they learn about you, and give them a better sense of their collective power. As does no other method, talking directly with people in the informal, intimate atmosphere of their homes helps you reach them in a personal way. People may get involved not only because they are frustrated and angry over local problems that they feel powerless to correct, but because they like you, trust you, or are looking for something meaningful to do.

Form an Organizing Committee   Invite people to join the organizing committee group and hold more house meetings. After talking with nearly everyone in the community, you and the organizing committee have collected a great deal of information about the community, its people, and its problems.

The issues that initially concerned the organizing committee may no longer be the dominant ones. Hold a meeting to help your organizing committee identify the issues that community members have described as most important and pressing. Members should organize and lead the meeting, and they should decide what issues to attack. Your role is to help generate discussion, keep the discussion on track, and help the group identify criteria for deciding on issues. The issues should galvanize people and be ones that they can win if they organize and work together.

Hold a Public Forum   After the organizing committee has identified two or three key issues that are most important, they should set up a community-wide public meeting or forum. This is the meeting at which the organization will be born. Four important things should occur at this meeting. Your members inform the entire community about the organization and its purposes. The community chooses the most important of the two or three issues to work on. The new organization is officially founded. Community members are involved in the process.

Make this founding meeting as important an event in the neighborhood as you can. Spend a lot of time carefully planning the meeting with the organizing committee. Develop a temporary name and mission statement. Agree on who will lead the founding meeting and the agenda. Get your committee to nominate one another for the election of temporary officers. Develop lots of publicity with telephone calls, flyers, and press releases.

At the meeting, an organizing committee member should explain the purpose of the organization and its temporary mission. Have community members rank the two or three issues that the committee has decided on and add others that they think are relevant. Make sure that everyone who attends gets a chance to speak. People have come to have their say. Make a list of their comments.

Hold an election for temporary offices that will provide an ongoing structure for the organization. Have a committee member explain the next community-wide action steps that were planned roughly by the organizing committee beforehand. Get people to sign up for different jobs or roles such as writing letters or attending a city council meeting or a training session. Have people at the meeting officially join the organization by filling out a membership application form and becoming dues-paying members ($1 a month). Give out membership cards. Dues are significant not only because they provide some funding, but more important, because people relate differently to an organization that they own. Make sure everyone knows when and where the next actions will take place.

Alinsky Coalition Model

The coalition model assumes that a number of associations in the community can be used for organizing, but commitment and social engagement among them is lacking. Through the process of coming together, residents discover that their individual problems are also the problems of others and the only hope for solving an issue is by pooling their efforts.

Learn About the Community　　The organizer's task is to identify natural community leaders, talk to them, get them interested in working together, and

help them develop their native abilities. You immerse yourself in community life, gain an understanding of their experiences, customs, and values, and identify their self-interests and concerns. Alinsky asserts that you must often be like a salesperson trying to convince people to do something. "You pull and jolt them into the public arena," he says. "You listen and appeal to people's self-interest, build anger, work along friendship and relationship networks, as well as other formal and informal social structures."[83]

Identify existing patterns of social structures, community customs and values, formal and informal community leaders. Develop relationships with all the organizations in a community: unions, neighborhood associations, ethnic associations, congregations, civil rights organizations, business associations, and individuals. A people's organization is open to all members of the community—workers, merchants, union and church leaders. The broader and more representative the neighborhood coalition, the stronger the organization.[84] Any organization, group, or individual who is concerned about community issues such as fair housing, decent wages, schools, neighborhood services, quality of neighborhood life, crime, drugs, and jobs should be within your realm of interest.

Develop a Sponsoring Committee　　In Alinsky-style coalition building, you develop a sponsoring committee composed of leaders of major organizations within the community. This sponsoring committee becomes the basis for building a coalition of existing organizations as well as raising money. The sponsoring committee gets leading groups to buy in to the organizing effort and neutralizes political opponents.[85]

Organize Block Clubs　　While you are organizing the sponsoring committee, you may also want to spend time establishing block clubs to ensure that as many parts of the community as possible are represented.[86] A network of block clubs provides a broad foundation for organization on the community level. If people on the block are already acquainted with each other, they can experience a higher level of interactive problem-solving and become open to new views and one another's concerns.[87] As soon as you get to know enough people, invite them to an informal meeting in someone's home. Serve refreshments and allow plenty of time for socializing. Start off with an enjoyable activity that is appropriate to the culture or population that you are organizing and develop a spirit of camaraderie, intimacy, and mutual trust. Encourage members to speak their minds with a spirit of acceptance and listen carefully to their ideas, concerns, questions, and issues. Listen for patterns that you can use in helping organize members into a group that will work toward a common goal.

At the end of the meeting or meetings, help the group come to some sort of decision, with each person saying his or her piece. "The key value in decision making within a poor people's organization is not efficiency, but participation," Si Kahn asserts. "The time required to reach a decision should not be the shortest time required or for a small, select group to make the decision, but the amount of time it takes to educate all the members in the meaning of the decision and to involve them in understanding the decision-making process."[88]

Give everyone a chance to gain leadership experience and status by rotating leadership of meetings. You should play the role of an enabler or facilitator. "The enabler role is one of facilitating a process of problem-solving and includes such actions as helping people express their discontents, encouraging organization, nourishing good interpersonal relationships, and emphasizing common objectives."[89]

In addition to block clubs, wherever possible engage existing associations, particularly church groups, to demonstrate that the community-wide organization is compatible with local interests.[90]

Form an Organizing Committee   When there are enough block clubs or other neighborhood associations concerned about the problem, hold a series of preliminary meetings with their representatives to build an organizational structure. Make sure people remember when and where the meeting will be held. Once at the meeting, "concentrate on moving those attending into decision and action." In principle, the "basic orientation has always to be the expression of power through the greatest possible number of members acting together to resolve the central problems of their lives."[91]

Establish a Community-wide Organization
Assist community members to develop a constitution and plan a founding meeting or constitutional convention to ratify the constitution. At the founding

meeting, the coalition organization becomes officially established. The coalition transforms neighborhood associations and block clubs into a broad-based, multiple-issue, permanent community organization.

Help the members elect officers and develop preliminary committees, role assignments, strategies, and time-lines. Having many standing committees dealing with salient activities is an important aspect of the coalition's structure. A committee structure permits the coalition organization to pursue multiple issues simultaneously and to mobilize the interests of many groups and segments of the community.

Help members develop a mission statement and slogans. A mission statement expresses in one sentence the purpose of the organization. The mission statement of ACORN, for example, is "To advocate a stronger local neighborhood voice in and power over the economic, political, and social institutions that dominate the lives of families of low and moderate income."

Slogans are short: one word or one phrase that sums up the organization. The slogan of the Industrial Areas Foundation (IAF) is "Power, Action, Justice."

After the first congress has ratified the coalition constitution, approved the budget, and elected representatives and executive officers, succeeding annual congresses keep the community up to date on the activities of the organization.

Develop Strategies, Tactics and Move to Action
The first set of issues your group tackles is particularly important when your organization and its leaders are inexperienced, members are tentative in the commitment, and acceptance of the organization and organizers are still in question. Alinsky urges organizations to select initial issues that are highly visible, important to local residents, and easy to win but not divisive or antagonistic to other local groups.[92] Alinsky advocated the use of nonviolent confrontation tactics to achieve the organization's objectives. These tactics are used often by issue-oriented activist social movements. You will find a description of many of these tactics in Chapter 14.

Social Networks Model

The most recent variation of Alinsky's work is the Social Networks Model carried on by his training school for organizers, the Industrial Areas Foundation

(IAF) founded in 1940, the Pacific Institute for Community Organization (PICO), Direct Action and Research Training (DART), and the Gamaliel Foundation. The social networks approach builds on existing congregational relationships, the core Judeo-Christian belief in fellowship (*koinonia*), and biblical ethics of concern for one's neighbor. Community members draw together to care for the poor, the hungry, and the homeless among them, and to rebuild their neighborhoods.

Today's clergy and lay leaders of local synagogues and churches see part of their social mission as helping members organize themselves to provide safe, clean neighborhoods, good schools, more responsive government, and improved relationships with neighboring communities. Local clergy are more outspoken as they see the anguish of their people, and many church people today seem to understand better than their parents that a little community controversy is often a necessary price in the beginning to bring about neighborhood health and stability. "Hundreds of local faith-based coalitions across the country are now reaching out to organize millions of middle class and poorer people who are frustrated by the economy, government paralysis, and anti-community corporate policies."[93]

The social networks, faith-based model promotes the expectation that governmental America will act justly by refusing to give preferential treatment to middle- and upper-class suburbs, and instead recognize the importance of inner cities and working-class neighborhoods. They expect corporations will no longer drain money from poor communities without reinvesting an equal amount in them.

The Industrial Areas Foundation   IAF opted for a strategy of social network organizing rooted in the idea that institutions such as synagogues and churches can be transformed into agents of social change. In the 1970s, IAF organizers depended on social networks of local churches as the backbone of the local organizations they put together.[94] The Industrial Areas Foundation mobilized large numbers of people and brought about significant improvements in marginalized communities.[95]

When a local community asked for assistance in organizing, IAF staff asked them to form a sponsoring committee that would raise initial funds and guarantee legitimacy for the organizing effort. As the community organizations grew, IAF continued to provide leadership training, not only in local communities but also in regular ten-day sessions in different parts of the country. Community leaders would meet leaders engaged in similar efforts, often with similar problems,[96] and share experiences, information, and resources.

In the 1980s and early 1990s, confronting government officials became less and less productive, according to IAF. Local government officials argued that they, too, were sympathetic to the issues but did not have the resources to address them. Beginning in the early 1990s, IAF has been creating working relationships between those with and without power, promoting the interests of its members by creating selective partnerships with government leaders, organizing around a "Standing for the Whole" idea. To "stand for the whole" helps restore public life by redefining politics, getting citizens to become activists, and politicians to become public servants. It now includes developing working relationships with both corporate and government leaders to further the goals of both IAF constituents and the larger community. You share action with a wide variety of people and come to see power as the craft of arguing, listening, revising views, and compromising "in exchange for respect and a willingness to compromise from those who now hold power. What matters to us is not consensus, but a stake in the ongoing dynamic of controversy, resolution and change."[97]

IAF organizers now build almost exclusively on the faith-based social networks already existing in church groups. In 1990 there were 28 IAF-affiliated coalition organizations, and their numbers have grown rapidly. They are having significant impact on a statewide basis. In 1987 pressure from three IAF organizations in California was effective in bringing the state minimum wage to 4.25 per hour.[98] There have been many similar achievements in other states.

The Direct Action and Research Training (DART) Network   In June 1996, DART founded the Federation of DART Organizations, which works with nearly 20 faith-based community organizations to promote justice and equality of opportunity through the empowerment of people with low to moderate incomes. The federation is rooted in an understanding that religious congregations have a role to play in accountability of political and economic systems.

The Pacific Institute for Community Organization (PICO)

In 1972 two young Roman Catholic priests, John Bauman and Jerry Helfrich, fresh out of an organizer training program, moved to the West Coast. The success of their Oakland Training Institute brought inquiries from other clients, and the institute quickly grew. It changed its name to the Pacific Institute for Community Organization (PICO) in 1976. By 1984, PICO had affiliated organizations in Oakland, San Diego, and Orange County, California, and in Kansas City, Missouri. The group decided to use a social network congregation-based approach for community organizing. In October 1997, the Pacific Institute for Community Organization (PICO) celebrated its 25th anniversary, gathering over 400 grassroots leaders, organizers, friends, and supporters from around the country.[99] Today PICO serves a national network of 22 faith-based community organizations in eight states. Over 350 Christian, Jewish, and non-denominational congregations containing about 300,000 families are part of the PICO network.

PICO goes into an area only after being asked by local pastors or congregations. It helps people form a sponsoring committee, raise seed money from local sources, and go through the legal process of being incorporated. The network assists the congregations to select and hire a PICO-trained organizer. This initial process usually takes between one and three years.

PICO helps train pastors, staff, and congregation members in organization techniques. Bauman says, "Our style of organizing is to get into community and listen, and to train people to listen." After an affiliate becomes more established, PICO continues to provide backup support. Twice a year, it holds six-day leadership training sessions to teach principles of the congregation-based model.

Other Faith-Based Groups

The number of faith-based coalitions based on the social networks model increases yearly. For example, Metropolitan Organizations for People (MOP) in December 1994 held its first organizing meeting with the entire coalition of churches and leaders. Says one leader, "We were about 1,000 strong. It was on NBC news. We got together with groups of business people, city council members and members of the school board. We petitioned business for summer jobs for our youth and we got 250 jobs."[100]

In November 1997, a delegate assembly of the Bay Area Organizing Committee (BAOC), a coalition of parishes, congregations, unions, and neighborhood associations, met and formally ratified representatives of a leadership team of over 100 community leaders. Each representative is selected by a member organization. Leaders give at least one or two hours a week, and many give up to 15.

Controlling urban sprawl is the goal of the American Metropolitan Equities Network (AMEN), an umbrella organization of 60 churches. Another group, Faith in Action for Community Equity (FACE), obtained more than $7 million in federal money for repairs, another $200,000 for road work and $500,000 for renovation design, a major victory for the Kalihi Valley Homes Residents Association in Honolulu in their effort to improve living conditions.[101]

In March 1998, more than 1,000 residents of Dorchester, South Boston, and Quincy, Massachusetts, gathered for the first public meeting of the Greater Boston Interfaith Organization (GBIO), a faith-based organization for addressing the community's needs, including safer streets, better schools, and higher-paying jobs.[102] Spearheaded by the Association of Community Organizations for Reform Now (ACORN), a coalition of labor and community groups and churches, the Oakland, California, city council voted unanimously to adopt the Jobs and Living Wage law, requiring companies doing business with the city to pay a living wage, and on March 26, 1998, a new coalition of churches and labor organizations in Contra Costa County, California, met for the first time, bringing the living wage legislation to that region.

The faith-based Queens Citizen Organization (QCO) in New York City is fighting professional arsonists who have burned down much of the Bronx. In California, Oakland Community Organizations (OCO) is developing a citywide campaign to gain control of its neighborhoods. The OCO has reduced truancy in the city schools, developed jobs for unemployed youth, controlled prostitution in residential areas, and set up neighborhood citizen-police cooperation.[103] At the start of the 21st century, these and many other faith-based community organizations continue their efforts to improve low- and middle-income communities across the nation.

COMMUNITY ORGANIZING FOR THE 21ST CENTURY

In the new millennium, community organizing is stronger than ever. Regional and national coalitions, many of them faith based, have brought renewed interest in the restoration of community. Rather than being adversarial, community organization now is based on the *partnership approach*, but without ceding political pressure. Community organizations in the 21st century will press for creative partnerships in service delivery, social impact reviews, federal subsidies and allocation of capital, development of social policy, and renewed cooperation with the social work profession.[104]

Service Delivery

Instead of expecting that recreation, youth building, counseling, and other social services be "parachuted in" to poor and working-class communities, the partnership approach expects governments and corporations to help communities provide their own service delivery programs or else contract for them with private firms. Such services could include some forms of health care, garbage collection, day care, building inspection, housing rehabilitation, property management, crime surveillance, recreation, and employment counseling. Not only could local provision of services increase local employment, but they would improve the neighborhood's desirability in the eyes of its residents, a major factor in neighborhood stability and revitalization. They would help a neighborhood become self-sufficient and increase its importance and meaning for residents.

Different social services require different combinations of centralization and decentralization. Inequities of levels of service may demand changes in state law. Neighborhood service areas could be mandated, but citywide taxation may need to be used to balance differences between need and ability to pay. For example, residents could be given vouchers to pay directly for services. Neighborhood corporations formed by neighborhood organizations might compete for vouchers with private suppliers. Variations on these themes are beginning to surface. Kansas City, for example, has contracts with three neighborhood organizations. In Portland neighborhood groups are repairing streets, and they are constructing sidewalks in Louisville. In Boulder they operate shelters for the poor. In Baltimore and Grand Rapids they maintain parks. In Woodbury a group has contracted to rehabilitate housing. In New York groups from the neighborhood help children and the disabled. Such increased citizen involvement and subsequent commitment of residents to their neighborhoods cannot but help stave off area decline or move it toward rejuvenation.

Social Impact Reviews

The partnership approach calls for legal and material support for locally based "impact reviews," on the model of the California Environmental Impact Review. For example, community standards would be established for any business that operates in a community. Businesses would need to demonstrate that they would make a positive social impact in the community, building resources rather than taking them out. Government decisions likewise would be required not to have adverse impacts on communities. Communities would require a wide range of social accounting. Federal programs, technical expertise, and research support would be provided to assist community-based groups.

Federal Subsidies and Allocations

In the partnership approach, federal subsidies in the form of block grants of unencumbered funds would be provided to communities on need-based formulas. The use of these funds would be decided at community or regional levels, and they would be administered by community residents, with city or county-wide accountability systems.

Community empowerment requires the ability to create community-owned, locally based enterprises. In this sense, community development corporations become an outgrowth of community organization where private market-based investments do not meet community defined needs. For example, community development corporations or community ownership of public utilities could support local autonomy, provide an infrastructure of "soft" energy alternatives, and generate revenues for local use. Community investment in job-creating enterprises could respond to the loss of private investment. Community owned cooperatives, employee-owned businesses, and community sponsored and operated services could offset the loss of services from cost-cutting private firms. The federal government would be a necessary source for capital and expertise for the initiation of such enterprises. A national public bank could be such a mechanism for social investments.

Partnerships in Policy-Making

Formal geographical designation of neighborhoods is an idea whose time has arrived. In the partnership approach, neighborhoods would be official jurisdictions for their own political decision-making processes. Democratically elected neighborhood organizations would become official representatives of these communities. Theoretically, neighborhood associations might become legal and formal partners in developing and passing city budgets and creating or adapting ordinances for their areas. In practice, some neighborhood organizations already do these things, although no city government has yet granted them veto power in such matters.

Partnership With Social Work

The profession of social work is not the primary institution where community organization is taught or where methods are refined. Community organizing does not look to social work to provide leadership. Instead, the center of education and action for community organizing lies with independent training centers such as Jack Conway's Center for Community Change, the Midwest Academy, IAF, PICO, NTIC, DART, and others. If the profession of social work is to be considered a profession of the social, helping restore and rebuild community in North America, it must reenter the field of community organization as a full partner.

CONCLUSION

Community organizing, particularly by means of faith-based organizations, is restoring America's communities, providing a socially healthy milieu in which the personalities and characters of our children and adolescents are formed, as well as a means by which adults who are alienated, discouraged, and apathetic can be restored to active and involved lives. They are creating communities of caring and concern in which neighbors reach out to neighbor, offering friendship, relationship, and help in times of stress and difficulty. Community organization is helping neighborhoods become therapeutic communities in which healthy social selves are not only formed but restored.

Community organization offers people a way of political involvement and a way to express their hopes and dreams, and make those dreams real in tangible policies and programs. It is fundamentally reshaping the way politics is practiced at the local level. When poor and middle-class people work together, their communities become a means by which they can become directly engaged in making political change. When community interests are joined in partnership with government and corporate interests, the results are impressive not only because of the community improvements that are accomplished, but also because of the success that people achieve and in making democracy work. Community organizing enables people to actively take control of their lives, claim their own futures, and assert their own values, while at the same time concretely demonstrating their commitment to a democratic way of life.

In cooperation with social planning and community development, community organization in the last decade has acquired power, influence, and the potential for solving social problems that are beyond the capability of the welfare state and huge corporate America. If America's social problems are to be solved, they will only be solved in the social sector, by the collective effort of local people working through their own neighborhood organizations, associations, and religious centers such as synagogues and churches. Without strong communities, healthy social selves may fail to be developed adequately and massive bureaucratic and corporate organizations may continue to dominate the social landscape, adding to alienation, apathy, and human disengagement.

Social work as a profession needs to reclaim community social work as its mandate and its foundation. Only then will social work be capable of making a lasting contribution to a better social world for ourselves and for our children.

KEY CONCEPTS

community organization

megastructure

Saul Alinsky

Si Kahn

Shel Trapp

Gail Cincotta

social learning

conscientization

charity organization societies

social settlements

school community centers

area coordinating committees

Chicago Area Project

Back of the Yards Neighborhood Council

Community Action Programs

Economic Opportunity Act of 1964

Federal Home Disclosure Act of 1975

Community Reinvestment Act of 1977

full plate syndrome

act out

get out

opt out

flake out

cop out

National People's Action (NPA)

Industrial Areas Foundation (IAF)

Pacific Institute for Community Organizing (PICO)

Direct Action Research Training (DART)

Association of Community Organizations for Reform Now (ACORN)

block club

faith-based community organizations

house meeting model

social networks model

linking model

coalition model

partnership approach

social impact reviews

QUESTIONS FOR DISCUSSION

1. In Saul Alinsky's essay " Of Means and Ends," he said, "the fourth rule of ethics of means and ends is that judgment must be made in the contest of the times in which the action occurred and not from any other chronological vantage point."[105] This seems to imply that morality is fluid and that there are no value absolutes that govern action. On the other hand, it presupposes an objective viewpoint that action must be evaluated in terms of the values, culture, and historical context in which the action occurred and not by standards or values external to that action. What are the implications of Alinsky's fourth rule of ethics for community organization?
2. What are the implications of Alinsky's fourth rule of ethics for ethical macro social work practice?
3. Does Alinsky's fourth rule of ethics allow us freedom to change the context of action?
4. Does Alinsky's fourth rule of ethics imply that action can change the morality by which that action is viewed?

EXERCISE 8.1
Community Organization Projects

1. Look for a neighborhood organization that started during the past ten years. Who organized it? Why? What does it do? What has it accomplished?

2. Is there a neighborhood coalition in your community? Is it citywide or does it exist in only a few neighborhoods? Who are its members? What are its main issues? How does it pursue those issues? Does it put aside any issues because they could cause disunity? What difficulties does it encounter in staying together?

3. Find a neighborhood organization and a neighborhood institution in your city that originated before 1960. Describe the social and political context of its origins, who the initiators were, why they acted, what the organization or institution did initially.

4. Describe how the organization and institution have changed through the years.

5. Read more about earlier neighborhood efforts such as those referred to earlier, especially Jane Addams, or Saul Alinsky.

6. For a more ambitious project, write a history of your neighborhood or a history of a neighborhood organization.

EXERCISE 8.2

Social Work and Community Organization

R ead the following overview of the relationship between social work and community organization.

The professionalization of social work, which began in the early days of the 20th century, was complete by the 1950s. The profession had three major divisions: casework, group work, and community organization. The latter was considered a process used by professional workers engaged in health and welfare planning. It was viewed as a field of activity occupied by agencies whose primary function is social planning, coordination, interpretation, or the financing of direct service agencies.

Very few social workers engaged in grassroots neighborhood organizing. The main exceptions were settlement houses and neighborhood centers. They, too, had become professional organizations and their boards were composed mostly of nonresidents. Their programs had a heavy emphasis on group work through building-centered activities, and they also provided casework services to individual and multi-problem families. But they also studied neighborhood problems, helped organize block associations, neighborhood organizations, and tenant councils, and got involved in social action.

Many school community centers continued to conduct after-hours programs, mainly recreation and adult education. But the zeal to serve as a focus for neighborhood organizations and to reach out to the surrounding community to encourage neighborhood action had long since disappeared.[106]

1. Comment on the term "community organization" as it was used by social work in the 1950s.

2. How has community organization changed since the 1950s?

3. Is community organization a viable specialty within social work today?

4. What role do you believe the profession of social work should take in working with communities?

5. Should community organizing be a major focus or social work? Why or why not?

6. What should the field of social work do to engage, promote, and develop community organization as a field of practice?

EXERCISE 8.3

Leadership Functions and Saul Alinsky

S aul Alinsky called for a practical or applied social science.... He advocated using the social sciences as a tool to generate social change rather than just as a way to study social conditions. Alinsky raised the promise and potential of social science activists using their skill and training to foster grassroots citizen democracy and community initiated social change. Alinsky presents community organization as a way of carrying on the tradition and believed that community organization enables people actively to take control of their lives and fate, while at the same time concretely demonstrating their commitment to a democratic way of life.... [He]stressed active participation in local community organizations as a way of attacking a sense of alienation, powerlessness, and preventing injustices by neglect.[107]

1. What are Alinsky's leadership characteristics?

2. Is he a feeler senser, a feeler intuiter, a thinker senser, or a thinker intuiter?

3. What kind of characteristics do you think make the best combination for a community organizer?

EXERCISE 8.4

Social Surplus

A n environment that supports neighborhood organizations extends well beyond that neighborhood. There are enough dollars to revitalize neighborhoods; the social surplus of the United States is staggering. Cultural values, however, have supported gross inequities in its distribution. If we invest money in our cities, then we will reap rewards of social capital, of good citizens and good will and less crime and leadership, productive lives instead of wasted lives, college graduates instead of ex convicts.[108]

1. What are the implications of the preceding statement for community social work?

2. What should the field of social work do if this statement is true?

3. If this statement is true, why has the American governance system allowed many of our cities to deteriorate?

EXERCISE 8.5

Shel Trapp: Models Just Don't Work

R ead the following excerpt from an essay by Shel Trapp. In class, your instructor will lead a discussion based on the questions that follow.

The model is not the important thing. The important thing is that an organization is being built and the people are winning. [There is] an emerging organization in a small city….[In] their eight months of existence, this organization has gotten the city manager to resign; the police department restructured; a toxic dump removed; improvements made at the local park; eight bad houses fixed up; three houses of prostitution and a porn shop closed; several stop signs put in; and a variety of city services improved. They are quickly moving toward their founding convention. This has not been accomplished by holding hands and passing out bouquets. It has happened because of hard organizing.

The reality is that it is not the model but the organizing which has brought victories and is bringing this community more self-respect, dignity, power, with each passing month. With another six months of hard organizing, they may even be ready to move out of the age of confrontation and into the age of partnerships as their current opponents come to understand that they are not going to go away.

Every local organization that we have assisted in getting started has developed in a different manner and ends up looking a little different. Like human beings, all community organizations resemble one another in certain respects, but each organization is a little different and the steps used to being it into being were a little different. Yet in each case, the organizations have gained local victories and developed local leadership. That is the important thing, not what model was used.

I remember Saul Alinsky once saying, "there is only one rule in organizing. and that is that there are no rules." He would find all the discussion about models pretty amusing, perhaps pathetic, given all the human need waiting to be organized.[109]

On the other hand, Sandra M. O'Donnell and Sokoni Karanja assert that "models can increase our consciousness about what we are doing and why. Models are simplified articulations of the purposes and processes of intervening in and with communities to effect desired change. Models give us the maps necessary to navigate complex community practice environments."[110]

1. This text has described four current models of community organizing. Is Shel Trapp correct when he says, "It is not the model, but the organizing which has brought about the victories"? Are O'Donnel, and Karanja correct? Why or why not?

2. What is the purpose of learning about such models?

3. Can you begin organizing without a model?

4. Of what use can you put a model or framework for organizing?

5. What would you do if you began to use a model and found that it wasn't working the way you thought it should?

EXERCISE 8.6

Midcourse Correction: Mutual Problem-Solving

S tudents will have an opportunity to correct behaviors, which can improve learning. Students will learn how to give feedback, engage in mutual problem-solving, and negotiate solutions. Students will also have an opportunity to give feedback to the instructor about the course as a whole and negotiate with the instructor to change the course objectives or procedures.

The instructor provides a lecturette on "Feedback and Learning" or provides it as a handout. The instructor asks the class to think about the following points.

1. Things that members like about the class. These are things that are positive and have helped enhance learning. These are items either about individuals or the class as a whole that members want to keep on doing or do more of.

2. Things that are getting in the way of learning or impeding members from reaching their goals. These are things that individuals can do differently or do less of. They can also be things that the class as a whole can change or do less of.

3. Which persons would have to do what specific things to make these changes?

Written Assessment

Outside class, each class member and the instructor writes down specific things that each person in the class does that affects him or her:

1. Things that the person should do more of or do better.

2. Things that the person should do less of.

3. Things that the person should continue doing.

4. On a separate piece of paper, each person writes recommendations for the class as a whole. This will go to the instructor.

The instructor collects the recommendation sheets for the class as a whole. Each person, including the instructor, tapes his or her sheets to a piece of newsprint and these are fixed to the walls of the classroom. Some time is spent by class members reviewing the sheets.

Feedback

Class reassembles and a time of feedback occurs. This is a time for clarification and understanding. Members may try to paraphrase what others have said to make sure that they accurately heard the message. The instructor asks for clarification and feedback about the overall course. After everyone is satisfied that they understand their messages, each member reviews his or her list.

Deciding on Issues

Each member chooses one or more specific issues that he or she is willing to change. Each member reviews the lists of other class members and chooses and initials items that he or she feels are important for class members to change. These issues become ones that are negotiable.

Negotiating Rounds

Each person collects his or her statements. Depending on the size of the class and the amount of time available, students may choose one or more issues to negotiate. The negotiation phase begins. Students pair up into dyads with others who have initialed their lists and negotiate for changes. The bargaining consists of statements such as "I will do X if you do Y." For example, one student may ask another to participate more. The student may agree if the first student agrees to stop interrupting when he talks. Achieve a balance of mutual responsibility in which each person receives as well as gives something up.

After each class member has found a satisfactory balance, the instructor negotiates changes in the course as a whole in the same way. For example, students may request shorter lectures. The instructor may agree if students come better prepared to engage in discussion.

Contracts are written up and signed with a mutual agreement as to what consequences will occur if the agreements are not kept. Set a date for a follow-up to determine if contracts are being kept. If time is available, a follow-up meeting can be held to review contracts. Assess items that were met and those not met. Give recognition for progress and renegotiate contracts if necessary.

ADDITIONAL READING

Modern Classics in Neighborhood and Community Organizing

Roger Ahlbrandt and Paul Brophy. *Neighborhood Revitalization.* Lexington, 1975.

Saul Alinsky. *Reveille for Radicals.* New York: Random House, 1989.

———. *Rules for Radicals: A Pragmatic Primer for Realistic Radicals.* New York: Random House, 1989.

Howard Hallman. *The Organization and Operation of Neighborhood Councils.* Westport, CT: Praeger. 1977.

Jane Jacobs. *The Death and Life of Great American Cities.* New York: Vintage, 1963.

Si Kahn. *How People Get Power: Organizing Oppressed Communities for Action.* Washington, DC: National Association of Social Workers, 1991.

———. *Organizing: A Guide for Grassroots Leaders.* Washington, DC: National Association of Social Workers, 1991.

Suzanne Keller. *The Urban Neighborhood.* New York: Random House, 1968.

Milton Kotler. *Neighborhood Government.* New York: Bobbs-Merrill, 1969.

David Morris and Carl Hess. *Neighborhood Power.* Boston: Beacon, 1975.

National Commission on Neighborhoods. *People, Building Neighborhoods.* Washington, DC: U.S. Government Printing Office, 1979.

David O'Brien. *Neighborhood Organization and Interest Group Processes*. Princeton, NJ: Princeton University Press, 1976.

Rachelle Warren and Donald Warren. *Neighborhood Organizers Handbook*. Notre Dame, IN: University of Notre Dame Press, 1977.

History of Community Organizing

Madeleine Adamson and Seth Burgos. *This Mighty Dream*. Boston: Routledge and Kegan Paul, 1984.

Neil Betten and Michael J. Austin. *The Roots of Community Organizing, 1917–1939*. Philadelphia: Temple University Press, 1990.

Harry Boyte. *The Backyard Revolution*. Philadelphia: Temple University Press, 1980.

Robert Fisher. *Let the People Decide: A History of Neighborhood Organizing*. Boston: G. K. Hall, 1984.

Robert Fisher and Peter Romanofsky, eds. *Community Organization for Urban Social Change: A Historical Perspective*. Westport, CT: Greenwood Press, 1981.

Community Organizing: Books by Macro Social Workers

George Brager, Harry Specht, and James L. Torczyner. *Community Organizing*. 2d ed. New York: Columbia University Press, 1987.

Steve Burghardt. *Organizing for Community Action*. Beverly Hills, CA: Sage, 1982.

———. *The Other Side of Organizing*. Cambridge, MA: Schenkman, 1982.

Arthur Dunham. *The New Community Organization*. New York: Thomas Crowell, 1970.

Joan Ecklein. *Community Organizing*. New York: Free Press, 1984.

Robert Fisher and Joseph Kling. *Mobilizing the Community: Local Politics in the Era of the Global City*, Newbury Park, CA: Sage, 1993.

Robert Fisher. *Let the People Decide: A History of Neighborhood Organizing*. Boston: G. K. Hall, 1984.

Robert Fisher and Peter Romanofsky, eds. *Community Organization for Urban Social Change: A Historical Perspective*. Westport, CT: Greenwood Press, 1981.

Si Kahn. *How People Get Power: Organizing Oppressed Communities for Action*. Washington, DC: National Association of Social Workers, 1991.

———. *Organizing: A Guide for Grassroots Leaders*. Washington, DC: National Association of Social Workers, 1991.

Lee Staples. *Roots to Power: A Manual for Grassroots Organizing*. Westport, CT: Praeger, 1984.

Books by Professional Community Organizers and Others

Harry C. Boyte. *Community Is Possible: Repairing America's Roots*. New York: Harper and Row, 1984.

James V. Cunningham and Milton Kotler. *Building Neighborhood Organizations*. Notre Dame, IN: University of Notre Dame Press, 1983.

J. Dahir. *The Neighborhood Unit Plan: Its Spread and Acceptance: A Selected Bibliography With Interpretive Comments*. New York: Russell Sage Foundation, 1947.

Gary Delgado. *Beyond the Politics of Place: New Directions in Community Organizing in the 1990s*. Oakland, CA: Applied Research Center n. d.

Sydney Dillick. *Community Organization for Neighborhood Development: Past and Present*. New York: Woman's Press and William Morrow, 1953.

Howard W. Hallman. *Neighborhoods: Their Place in Urban Life*. Vol. 154, Sage Library of Social Research. Beverly Hills, CA: Sage, 1984.

———. *Small and Large Together: Governing the Metropolis*. Beverly Hills, CA: Sage, 1977.

M. Brinton Lykies, Alli Banuazizi, Ramsay Liem, and Michael Morris, eds. *Myths About the Powerless: Contesting Social Inequalities* Philadelphia: Temple University Press, 1996.

John P. Kretzman and John L. McKnight. *Building Communities From Inside Out*. Evanston, IL: Northwestern University, Center for Urban Affairs and Policy Research, n. d.

Joseph M. Kling and Prudence S. Posner, eds. *Dilemmas of Activism: Class, Community, and the Politics of Local Mobilization*. Philadelphia: Temple University Press, 1990.

Stewart E. Perry. *Communities on the Way: Rebuilding Local Economies in the United States and*

Canada. Albany: State University of New York Press, 1987.

Charles A. Reich. *Opposing the System*. New York: Crown, 1995.

Mary I. Wachter with Cynthia Tinsley. *Taking Back Our Neighborhoods: Building Communities That Work*. Minneapolis: Fairview Press, 1996.

Michael R. Williams. *Neighborhood Organization: Seeds of a New Urban Life*. Contributions in Political Science #131. Westport, CT: Greenwood Press, 1985.

The Alinsky Approach

Robert Bailey. *Radicals in Urban Politics: The Alinsky Approach*. Chicago: University of Chicago Press, 1972.

Bernard Doering, ed. *The Philosopher and the Provocateur: The Correspondence of Jacques Maritain and Saul Alinsky*. Notre Dame, IN: University of Notre Dame Press, 1994.

David Finks. *The Radical Vision of Saul Alinsky*. Mahwah, NJ: Paulist Press, 1984.

Sanford Horwitt. *Let Them Call Me Rebel: Saul Alinsky: His life and Legacy*. New York: Alfred Knopf, 1989.

Joan E. Lancourt. *Confront or Concede: The Alinsky Citizen-Action Organizations*. Lexington, MA: Lexington Books, D. C. Heath, 1979.

Donald C. Reitzes and Dietrich C. Reitzes. *The Alinsky Legacy Alive and Kicking*. Greenwich, CT: JAI Press, 1987.

Michael R. Williams. "Saul D. Alinsky, The War on Poverty: Political Pornography," *Journal of Social Issues,* 21 (Jan. 1965): p. 53.

Community Organization With Specific Communities

Harry C. Boyte. *Commonwealth: A Return to Citizen Action*. New York: Free Press, 1989.

Gary Delgado, *Organizing the Movement: The Roots and Growth of ACORN*. Philadelphia: Temple University Press, 1986.

Paul Kurzman, ed. *The Mississippi Experience: Strategies for Welfare Rights Action*. New York: Association Press, 1971.

Peter Medoff and Holly Sklar. *Streets of Hope: The Fall and Rise of an Urban Neighborhood*. Boston: South End Press, 1994.

Gordana Rabrenovic. *Community Builders: A Tale of Neighborhood Mobilization in Two Cities*. Philadelphia: Temple University Press, 1996.

Jim Rooney. *Organizing in the South Bronx*. Albany: State University of New York Press, 1995.

Peter Skerry. *Mexican Americans: The Ambivalent Minority*. New York: Free Press, 1993.

Faith-Based Community Organizing

Kimberly Bobo. *Lives Matter: A Handbook for Christian Organizing*. Midwest Academy, 1986.

John Coleman, ed., *One Hundred Years of Catholic Social Thought: Celebration and Challenge*. Maryknoll, NY: Orbis Books, 1991.

Harry Fagan. *Empowerment: Skills for Parish Social Action*. Ramsey, NJ: Paulist Press, 1979.

Samuel Freeman. *Upon This Rock: The Miracles of a Black Church*. New York: HarperCollins, 1993.

Robert C. Linthicum. *Empowering the Poor: Community Organizing Among the City's "Rag, Tag and Bobtail."* Monrovia, CA: MARC, 1991.

Harold McDougall. *Black Baltimore: A New Theory of Community*. Philadelphia: Temple University Press, 1993.

Eileen McMahon. *What Parish Are You From? A Chicago Irish Community and Race Relations*. Louisville: University Press of Kentucky, 1995.

Philip Murnion and Anne Wenzel. *The Crisis of the Church in the Inner City: Pastoral Options for Inner City Parishes*. New York: National Pastoral Life Center, 1990.

John M. Perkins. *Let Justice Roll Down*. Glendale, CA: Regal Books, 1976.

Cynthia Perry, ed. *IAF: 50 Years: Organizing for Change*. Chicago: Industrial Areas Foundation, 1990.

Gregory Pierce. *Activism That Makes Sense: Congregations and Community Organization.* Chicago: ACTA Publishers, 1984.

Mary Beth Rogers. *Cold Anger: A Story of Faith and Power Politics.* Denton: University of North Texas Press, 1990.

Rabbi David Saperstein, ed. *Social Action Manual: A Practical Guide for Organizing and Programming Social Action in the Synagogue.* New York: Union of American Hebrew Congregations, 1983.

Jim Sleeper. *The Closest of Strangers: Liberalism and the Politics of Race in New York.* New York: Norton Paperbacks, 1991.

Related Works

Cherie R. Brown. *The Art of Coalition Building: A Guide for Community Leaders.* New York: American Jewish Committee, 1990.

Curtis Lamb. *Political Power in Poor Neighborhoods.* New York: Schenkman, 1975.

Manuel Castells. *The City and the Grassroots.* Berkeley: University of California Press, 1983.

Judith A. B. Lee. *The Empowerment Approach to Social Work Practice.* New York: Columbia University Press, 1994.

Three

Social Work Practice With Organizations

Bureaucracy is *the* means of transforming social action into rationally organized action.[1]

Max Weber

We live in a society that is an organizational society.[2]

Robert Presthus

O ver 100 years ago Max Weber, the foremost and most brilliant sociologist of our time, observed that complex organization was not simply a benign social tool for accomplishing work efficiently and effectively. Modern rational organization is *the* means by which communal society is transformed into a rational society and social relationships into functional, instrumental relationships. Once initiated, Weber asserted, the process of the rationalization of social relations cannot be diverted from its path until it reaches its inevitable conclusion. Today, as Robert Presthus and others have observed, that process is nearly complete. The United States along with other modern developed nations have, by and large, become converted into an "organizational society." The developing nations are not far behind.

Modern organizational society is unlike any that has preceded it. Organizations have provided many of the developed nations with economic prosperity and technological growth that outstrips the imagination. But for all of their productivity and power, modern organizations are a limited social structure. While their rational premises make them unparalleled economic tools, they are less useful in the social arena, where personal relationships, compassion, and altruism are necessary. In fact, while social work has used complex organizations to build the modern welfare state, these systems have not only failed to solve our social problems but tended to create them. Complex organizations are alienating, dehumanizing, and depersonalizing control systems. They foster dependency and subservience. They fail to provide safety and security for people who are unable to adapt to their premises or who do not have the skills to contribute to their power arrangements.

Macro social workers recognize the limitations of hierarchically structured organizational systems, and we have struggled against their defects. Community planners help communities reclaim power that has been appropriated by large political power structures. Community developers work to devise economic systems that contravene large corporate structures that colonize our communities, draining them of their resources. For over 60 years, community organizers have challenged corporate and governmental organizations when they become oppressive and act unjustly. However, while it is imperative that community social workers continue the struggle to help community survive, they cannot overcome the strength of organizational megastructures single-handedly.

Other macro social workers whose skills and personality functions are more attuned to the demands of complex organizations have risen to the challenge. These organizational social workers use a different approach for the social problems that organizations create. Instead of trying to create oases of community betterment in the desert of organizational alienation, organizational social workers have altered the nature of organization itself. Organizational social workers, in partnership with community social workers, have developed a new social form called *social organizations*. They are working to construct an entirely new "social" sector of society.

In Chapter 9 you will learn more about these new social organizations and how organizational macro social workers are using them to reassert the social in a world of impersonality, alienation, and dehumanization. You will find that the emergence of the social sector is another indication of a vast social revolution that is accumulating strength and power in our society to usher in the postmodern era of the 21st century.

In Chapter 10 you will learn how to assist individuals and community groups create one of these new social organizations, including assessing the need for a program, developing a constitution and by-laws, organizing a board of directors, hiring staff, creating a budget, and developing funding. Once a social organization or agency is established, it needs to be administered by skilled, energetic macro social workers. In Chapter 11, you will learn how to translate your social leadership skills into helping operate an organization as a supervisor or departmental or chief social administrator. You will learn how to share the process of taking responsibility for the social organization with social work staff and the community in which it resides. You will learn how to make administrative decisions and engage in personnel administration, budgeting, and agency planning.

Sometimes, macro social workers consult with administrators of social organizations to strengthen or improve their programs. The work of consulting with established social organizations is called *organization development*. In Chapter 13, you will learn how to help employees take ownership of the organization change process and make the social organization a more responsive system for serving its clients and the community. Organizational social work is a process of developing, administering, and improving social organizations as tools for social betterment.

All social workers need to be prepared to relate to our impersonal, complex, inter-related organizational society. Every social worker needs to understand how organizational systems work, design systems that are better, infuse those which are unethical with integrity, and fix them when they become dysfunctional. For a few of you, organizational social work will become a professional goal in and of itself. Those of you who are skilled in organizational leadership, who have the ability to diagnose organizational problems and solve them, will be among the more valued and capable members of our profession. The key to social work in the future will be your ability to work in, understand, and apply your problem-solving skills to complex bureaucratic organizations, but also to bring into existence other forms of human association that preserve and extend social relationships. As North America enters the 21st century, you have a great challenge and opportunity to help rebuild the social framework of our organizational society and create space for an authentically *social* environment.

9

The Social Sector and the Rise of the Social Organization

Man can only create himself through his freedom; otherwise he is created, an object, without dignity. Yet those who would aid him in his life and his productivity are often willing to sacrifice his autonomy, which is his essential well-being, on behalf of his physical or social-well being.[1]

Ed Shorris

When fully developed, bureaucracy also stands, in a specific sense, under the principle of *sine ira ac studio* [without sympathy or compassion]. Its nature, which is welcomed by capitalism, develops the more perfectly the more the bureaucracy is "dehumanized," the more perfectly it succeeds in eliminating from official business love, hatred, and all purely personal, irrational, and emotional elements which escape calculation. This is the specific nature of bureaucracy and it is appraised as its special virtue.[2]

Max Weber

Ideas in This Chapter

232

THE NEW SOCIAL ORGANIZATION

Despite a drop of almost one-fifth the number of girls of high school age between 1978 and 1988, the Girl Scouts of the USA, the world's largest women's organization managed to maintain a membership of 3.5 million, thus significantly increasing its market penetration.[3] In the state of Florida, thousands of criminal offenders sentenced to jail for the first time are paroled into the custody of the Salvation Army. These convicts are poor risks, many of them poor blacks or Hispanics, and three out of every four would become habitual criminals if actually sent to jail. The Salvation Army, however, rehabilitates three out of four of the parolees. Church membership and attendance have been going down quite sharply in all denominations, but membership and attendance is growing fast in those pastoral churches, Protestant and Catholic, mainstream and evangelical, that concentrate on serving the needs, problems, and families of their parishioners. Around 1970 there were no more than 5,000 pastoral churches with a membership of 2,000 parishioners or more. By the late 1980s their numbers had grown fourfold to 20,000, and they employ probably more than a million volunteers as unpaid staff.

Drucker says that these successes are based on greatly increased productivity. Public benefit organizations, or at least a large number of them, get more results out of their resources. The Girl Scouts saw their opportunity in demographic change. They adapted their programs and activities to the married women with children who are now in the labor force. Recognizing that the career aspirations of girls are changing fast in America, they converted those changes into opportunities. They began to recruit aggressively among minorities, offering children and their mothers an opportunity to participate in what had up to then been considered a white, middle-class organization. By 1987 the proportion of African American girls of elementary school age enrolled in the Girl Scouts matched that of white girls. "In the war on drug abuse, the Boy Scouts and Girl Scouts of America have taken the lead. In their work with elementary school children—and one out of every four elementary school children in the United States is a scout—the two organizations try hard, with considerable success, to inculcate resistances to drugs well before the children are actually exposed to the menace."

The Salvation Army used an organizational tool, organized abandonment. They assessed their efforts in crime prevention in the slums and realized that they were ineffective. The return on their investment of time and energy was close to zero. Once they examined the problem, it became clear why they were not effective. Before being caught and convicted, endangered young people in the slums are not receptive to the Salvation Army's message. Each of them thinks he or she will beat the odds. Being arrested but released on probation only confirms this belief. After young people have served even a short term in jail, it is too late. They are traumatized by their experience and corrupted by it. However, the Salvation Army staff realized that for a very short period of time there is a window of opportunity in which pre-convicts (those who have been caught and sentenced to jail, but who have not yet actually been sent to prison) are susceptible to change. They are sufficiently frightened but not yet corrupted by the prison system. Now the Salvation Army contracts with government to keep these young people out of further trouble, and they are doing it with considerable success.

Human sector organizations work at making their governing boards effective. Many have work programs against which they regularly evaluate their boards. In the well-run third-sector organization, there are no more "volunteers." There is only unpaid staff. Third-sector organizations have gone heavily into training. Staff members, whether paid or unpaid, are expected in the Girl Scouts or the Salvation Army to define clearly the performances and contribution for which they are to be held accountable. They are then regularly appraised against these performance objectives. A large pastoral church runs a dozen ministries, both for its 13,000 members and in its community. Yet it has a paid staff of only 160. New members of the congregation are asked after a few months to become unpaid staff. They are thoroughly trained and given a specific assignment with performance goals. Their performance is regularly reviewed, and if it does not come up to high expectations, the volunteer is either shifted to another, less demanding assignment or asked to resign.

The Salvation Army keeps a tight reign on its 25,000 parolees in Florida. About 160 paid staffers supervise and train volunteers and take care of crises while 250 to 300 unpaid people do the work itself. What enabled the Girl Scouts to maintain enrollment in a shrinking market was a substantial increase in the number of volunteers: from 600,000 to 730,000. Many of the new volunteers are young professional women without children of their own, but with a need to be a woman in a feminine environment a few evenings a week and on weekends, and to be with children. They are attracted precisely because the job is professional; they are required to spend several hours a week being trained or work as trainers for newcomers.

One Midwestern diocese doubled its community service even though it had barely half the number of priests it had twenty years before. Its 140 priests preach, say mass, hear confession, baptize, confirm, marry, and bury people. Everything else is done by 2,000 lay people, each of whom is expected to work at least three hours a week and to spend an additional two or three hours in training sessions. Each lay person's performance is appraised twice a year. "It's worse than Marine boot camp," one of these unpaid staffers said. Yet there is a long waiting list of potential volunteers. America's third-sector organizations are rapidly becoming creators of new bonds of community. They create a sphere of effective citizenship and involvement.

Retired working-class and young professionals work side by side in the Salvation Army's efforts with young convicts, in designing programs and training leaders in a local chapter of the YMCA, and helping disaster victims with the Red Cross. What the Girl Scouts contribute to inner-city women may be more important than what they contribute to children. These women are becoming leaders in their communities, learning skills, setting examples, and gaining recognition and status. There are now more African Americans in leadership positions in the two U.S. scouting organizations than anywhere else except in black churches. In the Scouts they are leaders in racially integrated organizations. Human service organizations are creating for their volunteers a sphere of meaningful citizenship.

WHAT YOU WILL LEARN IN THIS CHAPTER

Modern complex organizations are all around us and most of us take them for granted. They are the most beneficial as well as the most powerful social systems ever devised. We owe the enormous prosperity and productivity of our world to the advancement of complex organizations, and the day is not far off when organizational linkages may very well connect international megastructures into one huge global organizational society. It is a development of momentous importance.

However, even as modern organization appears to be triumphant, another kind of social form is beginning to appear. It is an entirely unprecedented phenomenon. This is a hybrid structure, one that combines the efficiency and rationality of modern organization with the relational nature of community. Compared with the size and power of modern organizations, it is a small and insignificant social form that does not yet even have an adequate name. But many believe that its arrival is one indicator that we are living at the beginning of a completely new social period, one that sociologists call the "postmodern era."

In this chapter you will learn about the phenomenon of complex organization, the symbol and bearer of modernity. You will discover its strengths and its limitations. You will find that while modern complex organizations will continue to dominate the economic and political landscapes for a long time, they will become increasingly helpless in reaching into the personal, communal arena where social relationships are so important. You will discover that for all of the genuine concern of social workers who use them, the capability, skill, and determination of administrators who direct them, and the good will and ideals of politicians who establish policies that guide them, we will be unable to use their strength, size, or influence to solve the great social problems of the day. In spite of all of our efforts, social workers will be unable to integrate a multitude of the poor, the marginalized, and alienated into their organizational systems and processes.

You will also explore the new organizational form, the symbol and bearer of the postmodern era, the period in which we are now living. You will learn what this social structure is, why it is important for macro social work, and its potential for social change. You will be challenged to consider the implications of these pivotal developments for yourself and for the field of social work.

WHAT ARE MODERN COMPLEX ORGANIZATIONS?

For the past 100 years, Western society has been dominated by modern complex organization. This social system is the representative of modernity, and its greatest invention. Instrumental formal organizations have been universally adopted as *the* structure by which people are engaged in productive activities. They are extremely useful tools by which we achieve the advancements of science and technology, cure disease, feed the world's population, expand our horizons into outer space, and explore the intricacies of the atom and the genetic code of life. They are the defining characteristic of our age.

So marvelous are these organizational systems in helping us achieve our goals, we use them in almost every sphere of life. You engage modern organizations when you get a driver's license, sign up for social security, vote, pay your taxes, or send a letter. You use other organizations when you watch a baseball game, go to a concert, rent a video, or watch a movie. The clothes you wear, the cars you drive, the housing that provides you shelter, the electricity that powers our society are all manufactured by complex organizations. We are born in organizations, educated in organizations, eat food that was grown, processed, packaged, transported, and sold by organizations, find our livelihood working in organizations, and when we die we will be buried by still other organizations.

Organizations have helped us achieve a level of prosperity unmatched in any other period of history. The reason for this prosperity is the capacity of people using science and modern reason by means of modern organizational tools to calculate how to reach goals efficiently and effectively and to put those decisions into action. Modern corporate organizations are among the largest and richest economies on the globe, outstripping the wealth of most of the world's nations. In 1995 more than half of the top 100 richest economies in the world were companies such as General Motors, Ford, Wal-Mart, General Electric, and IBM. If the gross product of the four wealthiest orga-

nizations were combined, they would comprise the seventh largest economy in the world, richer than Brazil, China, Canada, India, or Russia.[4] We owe our material wealth to organizations and the technologies they support, and because organizations are powerful systems for economic progress and governance, we have come to depend on them.

MODERN ORGANIZATIONS AND SOCIAL WORK

After the American Civil War and into the 20th century, large monopolies threatened to usurp the political process, undermine the nation's economic health for their own interests, and institutionalize injustice and oppression in nearly every arena of public life. Social workers were concerned that massive corporate structures would swallow up the individual, destroy democracy, and create grave disparities in wealth and power. They sought solutions on many fronts, but one of their most creative was to use organization to counteract organization. Progressive social workers struggled to develop a strong, countervailing centralized governmental bureaucracy that could limit the influence of large economic organizations, remove public civil service from bribery, favoritism, and corruption, but most importantly provide a system of justice and opportunity for our most vulnerable citizens. Government would use its power to control monopolies, and it would use the principles of bureaucratic administration to control itself.

Progressive social workers lobbied government to protect the public interest by creating regulatory commissions to oversee safety of food and drugs, inspect factories for unsafe working conditions, and operate in many ways to insure that consumers would no longer be exploited. Progressive social workers helped create the Civil Service Commission in 1883 that would guarantee government operate fairly, impartially, according to rules and procedures by which the most qualified people would be hired. Welfare organizations would be used to insure an end to oppression of women, ethnic groups, and children. Progressive social workers, established the Children's Bureau to prevent children from being exploited and helped put the juvenile court system into place to provide humane treatment of child offenders. They envisioned the organization of government to be a means by which all of those who were oppressed, including laborers, indigenous Americans, African Americans, and immigrants, would find equality, opportunity, and a level playing field.

When the Great Depression crippled the nation in the decade of the 1930s, social workers including Harry Hopkins worked to change laissez-faire government and establish powerful agencies that would provide for people's welfare. Social workers were successful in helping institute the Social Security Act, creating a welfare state apparatus of governmental organizations that committed the federal government to help individuals and families who had fallen into poverty. Social workers stimulated national, state, and local government to guarantee that citizens would never again be at the mercy of an unregulated economy.

In the 1960s, social workers again pressed for large public agencies of the welfare state to insure that economic justice and social progress would be applied on an equal basis to those most in need. Challenged by domestic upheaval and by social work policy analyst Michael Harrington's book *The Other America,* government responded with the "Great Society," a massive network of organizations and social programs designed to eliminate poverty, assist people in helping themselves, develop communities, give toddlers a "head start," and give youth an opportunity to find jobs or go to college.

Each of these organizations, agencies, and programs were the result of hard-fought battles for progressive social welfare legislation and resulted in improving government, reducing economic exploitation, preventing market failure, and helping millions of people over the century obtain equal opportunity, better working conditions, a hand up from poverty and a better life for children, women, and other oppressed groups. Not only did they benefit the marginal, the poor, and exploited, but the entire nation benefited in increased prosperity and the institutionalization of justice and equal opportunity as basic rights in the land.

However, by the beginning of the 21st century, the capacity of the welfare state bureaucracy and the corporate sector of America to solve our social problems and infuse society with social goods seems in doubt. While large federal bureaucracies, regulatory commissions, bureaus, and departments that eventually resulted from the efforts of progressive social work at the turn of the 20th century were innovative for their time and changed American society for the better, and the welfare state apparatus is generally seen today as ineffective in eradicating social problems. Instead of innovation, the top-down hierarchical structures of welfare bureaucracy have nearly become synonymous with inefficiency. Social welfare organizations often become bogged down in red tape and burdened with rigid rules and uniform procedures. Clients are treated impersonally as "cases" rather than as individuals, and governmental officials and citizens alike are critical about the ineffectiveness of the welfare bureaucracy in reducing poverty.

In spite of these criticisms, it is important to understand, that the failure we attribute to social service bureaucracy is is not due to our inability to organize properly. Nor is the inadequacy that organizations display in the social arena due "to personalities, poor leadership, lack of interpersonal skills, or administrative incompetence. It is due to their nature."[5]

Social workers are discovering that organizations are not multipurpose tools that can be applied unilaterally across the board to solving the social problems of the human condition, useful under all conditions and in every circumstance. Modern organizations, instead, are unitary, unidimensional, unipurpose functional *economizing* tools guided by one kind of reason and devised to accomplish one set of norms and goals. Instead of supporting the social, enhancing the human condition, providing for compassion, empowerment, and independent judgment, modern formal organizations destroy the social, create "inhuman human beings;" obliterate compassion, create dependency, and induce us to think as the organization wishes us to think.

Destruction of the Social

Many modern theorists lead us to believe that our modern rational society is "historically typical,"[6] that is, human associated life has always been organized and rationalized. As a result people often do not understand that "it is only our Western societies that quite recently turned man into an economic animal."[7] In all social systems preceding our own, according to Karl Polanyi, "the economic order [was] merely a function of the social order in which it was contained. Neither under tribal, or feudal or mercantile conditions was there…a separate economic system in society."[8] Our modern society is unprecedented because "no other society uses the criterion of economizing as the standard of human existence."[9] The reason for the rise of the economy and its dominance over all other societal functions is the invention of modern economizing organizations.

Modern organizations are not natural human associations. They were not designed to provide social goods, implement social values, or include social thinking as part of their mechanisms. They are artificial economizing tools used to maximize the goals of their owners, whether the owner is a group of stockholders, an interest group, a legislature, or the Congress. Unidimensional organizations operate most effectively when processing data or mass producing automobiles, tools, computer parts, or any other product that requires uniformity, speed, and precision, according to specified procedures and design. They are far less effective when they encounter human beings, each of whom comes with a unique set of issues, ideas, values, and needs.

Many of us have been socialized in caring social milieus where we expect to relate to others on a personal level and where our feelings, needs, ideas, and values are taken into consideration. These qualities, however, are problematic to modern complex organizations because they interfere with the ability of organizations to accomplish the purposes built into them. Wherever complex organizations appear, they become tools for eradicating communal social ways of thinking and transform humans into "functionaries, people who do their organizational duty and do what they are told in the interest of the owner's goal for the organization."[10] If we bring social values, altruistic attitudes, or relationally oriented behaviors into the organization, we must be induced to give them up and accept efficiency, productivity, and task behaviors instead.[11] We are required to treat ourselves, associates and clients, objectively, impartially, neutrally, and impersonally. "Objective" discharge of business primarily means a discharge

of business according to calculable rules and "without regard for persons."[12]

Where we have not been socialized to adopt such an organizational orientation to life, Thompson asserts we must be resocialized to surrender our expectations of personal treatment and become objects who "not only want more things, but have the skills necessary to produce them."[13]

Complex organizations are specifically aimed at destroying social and human elements at every point of social contact. They deny us opportunities for engaging in full social relationships, in we-relationships, and in the mutual construction of new solutions to individual problems.[14] They were explicitly created to drive out natural social relationships and transform them into impersonal, artificial, instrumental relationships. Organizations are unable to produce room for the social goods, solve social problems, enhance social relationships, or provide room for the social needs of people.

The New Inhuman Being

Over 100 years ago, existentialist philosophers looked at the specter of complex rational organization and recoiled with horror at what they saw. Soren Kierkegaard realized that the chief social product of complex organization, alienation, and the inability of people to impute meaning into their lives, is individual and social sickness.[15] Friedrich Nietzsche saw in modern organization only "nihilism," the nothingness and depersonalization of mass technological society which "destroys the creative power in life. Man becomes…a cog in the all embracing machine of production and consumption." The common enemy of the integrity of the human person, these existentialist philosophers claimed, "is the objectifying, depersonalizing power of technical society." They warned us about a society that steals our humanity and turns us into objects, components, tools, or means to carry out the purposes of others even when we have no say in the decisions that affect our lives. Existentialists urged people "to resist a world in which everything was transformed into a thing, a means, an object of scientific calculation, psychological and political management."[16]

Organizations induce humans to become factors of production,[17] "commodities" that behave according to utilitarian constraints of the marketplace. "Students become the 'products' of universities. Workers become the 'tools' of management, and individuals holding roles within an institution become subsystems performing function within a system—functionaries."[18] Atomistic individuals are treated as if they are interchangeable parts in the overall social mechanism, making it possible to construct all the systems society needs.[19] Machinelike qualities become part of the human psyche, and those actions that personalize individual action contrary to calculations that maximize the owner's goals become devalued and discarded. This "structure of objectivation" (transforming life and person partly into a thing, partly into a calculating machine) penetrates all realms of life and all spiritual functions."[20] People are taught to "live comfortably within a contrived reality"[21] as if that reality were authentic and meaningful for human life.

This new inhuman personality is without values, feelings, or independent action unless officially approved and recognized by the organizational processing system.[22] The organizational individual tends to be *unable* to function as a full-fledged human being. Max Weber, the most perceptive analyst of complex organization, put the matter in the clearest and starkest terms. "Bureaucracy develops the more perfectly, the more it is 'dehumanized,' the more completely it succeeds in eliminating from official business love, hatred, and all personal, irrational, and emotional elements which escape calculation...and this is apprised as its special virtue."[23]

What was once considered horrific, the process of making a person into an object, an empty thing devoid of humanity, has become inverted into a social good.[24] In modern self-interested, individualistic society, "each person treats the other primarily as a means to his or her end...to seek to make him or her an instrument of one's purposes by adducing whatever influences or considerations will in fact be effective."[25] Complex organization steals our humanity, turns us into objects, and destroys the most precious elements that make us human. They dehumanize, isolate, and alienate us from our clients, and alienate us from ourselves.

The Demise of Compassion

While the heart of social work is compassion, all relationships in artificial organizational systems are impersonal and abstract.[26] Complex organizations eliminate personal, compassionate, altruistic treatment of individuals. If you press for personalistic, compassionate treatment, even in social service organizations, you may find the "need for compassion is immature, and in the most highly developed bureaucracies, compassion is illegal." According to Thompson, "Compassion, as exceptional, special, non-legitimate treatment is irrational, in relation to the owner's goal, and it is also illegitimate—a form of theft or personal appropriation of administrative resources."

Clients are "cases," not persons, and workers must conform their behavior as well as that of clients to the expectations required by the organization, often in rigidly programmed ways. Social workers are constrained from expressing or acting on altruistic feelings in making decisions for clients if those decisions contradict prescribed agency mandates. "In fact," asserts Thompson, "a caring relationship between the incumbent in a role in a modern organization and a client is regarded as *unethical*."[27]

Even administrators who attempt to "humanize" relationships within their organization's hierarchy will be seen as subverting the basic structure of the organization. They are questioning the taken for granted value systems of the organization and engaging in "corruption" in the true sense of the word by propagating relationships "that threaten death to rationalistically legitimated ones."[28] The most important and valuable qualities that social workers offer, our concern and caring, are eliminated in rational/legal bureaucracy. Even in many social welfare bureaucracies, compassion has become theft.

Disempowerment

We have given organizations and their owners responsibility for shaping and coordinating goals and the direction of our society, says Peter Block. It is a system "based on sovereignty and a form of intimate colonialism" governed above all else by consistency, control, and predictability, and these systems become the means of dominance by which colonialism and sovereignty are enacted. Complex organizations are "consciously designed control machines"[29] that exact conforming behavior in every area of organizational life."[30] According to Block, "We have implemented and perpetuated work structures, financial control systems, information systems, performance appraisal and reward systems, and other management practices that reinforce the class system and reenact in a thousand ways the primacy of consistency, control and predictability. These practices keep ownership and responsibility focused at the top." Patriarchal governance in organizations is taken for granted, and top-down decisions are accepted as the way things operate. Organizational megastructures decide what is in our own best interests, and remove the focus of decisions far from those affected by them. Complex organizations intentionally keep us captured by dependency, chained to helplessness and disempowered by their command and control systems.[31]

Standardization

Organizations as instrumentally rational systems are synoptic. They "see with one eye." They have only one vision, that of the owner, and everyone is trained to envision the organizational environment through that perspective. Once provided with the organizational premises and goals, modern reason is the means by which people implement this singular vision. Once the ends are presupposed and the method of rational problem solving is in place, the decisions become inevitable and predictable. In this way organized individuals will, as closely as possible, always think alike, behave in the same way, communicate with the same technical language, and reach the same decisions as everyone else.

Modern reason operating in and through complex organization, therefore, imposes standardization, routinization, and uniformity over all its components, clients, social workers, and administrators alike. Unidimensional thinking is necessary for organization, so that all of its components think and behave in programmed ways, not only in complex

organizations but also in politics, economics, and nearly every facet of social life.

Implications for Social Work

Because we endow organizations with attributes more compelling and powerful than the human beings who compose them, Alberto Ramos asserts that "organizations in today's market society are necessarily deceitful." They "deceive both their members and their clients, inducing them to believe not only that what they produce is desirable, but also that their existence is vital to the interest of the society at large."[32]

If the field of social work has become ideologically and culturally captive to organizational mechanisms, it is because we have allowed ourselves to be deceived by organizational systems. We have allowed ourselves to accept them with few reservations, welcomed these market-centered tools in spite of their defects, and adopted them for purposes for which they were not intended. We accept their roles, values, and the way they structure relations as if these are only natural and the way things ought to be. We allow them to induce us to give up our sociality, our selves, our compassion, and our ability to use our own thinking. We rarely question them because they appear as massive systems over which we have little control and because we have been socialized to depend on them.

In spite of our acceptance, it is important for us to realize that it is nearly impossible to use modern complex organizations for most social purposes. They cannot be used for infusing people with meaning, or providing personal or compassionate treatment. Complex modern organizations are not created to provide those qualities. They are intended to create private goods, not social goods. To expect a market-centered organization to solve social problems, improve the social infrastructure of community, or become invested in the greater social good of the nation is to ask something for which it was not designed and which it is unable to do.

Complex organization creates problems for our clients. It may be confusing for clients who expect to be treated personally, with caring and compassion, and instead presented with impersonal rules, procedures, and policies. It may be threatening or intimidating for clients to be confronted with persons in authority who have the power to give or withhold needed services, expected to fill out forms, understand organizational jargon, and conform to unclear bureaucratic processes.

Social workers are not immune to the impersonality, uniformity, and dehumanization that complex organization imposes on human life. We may find ourselves changing in the organizational environment. Our compassion may become hardened, our relationships impersonal. We gradually adopt organizational values and language. We discover that we must play the game of organizational politics to survive.

We should not be surprised, therefore, when we encounter social workers who think in stereotyped, control-oriented, impersonal, and authoritarian ways. They have learned to adapt to the milieu of complex organizations and have allowed the premises and ways of thinking of complex organizations to be inserted into their psyches as a normal way of behaving. They have forgotten that social work is personal, social, and service oriented. This is not always the fault of social workers themselves. It is exactly what complex organizations are intended to do.

If social work clinicians were to adopt treatment methods that intentionally dehumanize, alienate, disempower, and damage their clients, we would disown those methods. It is not only ironic but tragic, therefore, that social workers have adopted as our most pervasive system of service delivery an organizational structure that is not only incapable of enhancing the human condition, but actually undermines it, prevents us from providing personal, compassionate services to our clients, and steals empowerment from social workers and clients alike.

COPING WITH DILEMMAS OF MODERN ORGANIZATIONS

Everyone in an organization is affected by the dilemmas of dehumanization, disempowerment, dependency, and control as well as the threats that organizations create. Discrepancies between the role of the social worker and demands of the organization, especially when the organization itself becomes a barrier to obtaining assistance for clients,

inevitably create stress. We may respond in a number of ways to the stress of organizational demands. If we try to cope on our own, our efforts, while well intentioned, may lead to even more stress and even to burnout. Group strategies can lead to conflict and confrontation. It is important for you to understand how to cope with dilemmas that organizations create.

Individual Strategies

Among the strategies that you can use to cope with modern organizations are direct change efforts, blaming the system, taking the blame, or identifying with the organization.

Direct Change Efforts   Often the first response of social workers when exposed to problems in organizational power, communication, politics, rules, roles, or procedures that interfere with assisting clients is to "fire off memos, raise the issue at meetings, or discuss it with their superiors." If you usually face problems directly and quickly seek resolution to discontinuities, you may be confused when your observations and suggestions are met not only with indifference but even with disdain by administrators or coworkers. Given the repeated failure of such direct efforts at problem-solving, you may soon realize "the extent to which organizational problems are endemic to professional life." When you attempt to directly change the way an organization operates, you pit yourself against an entire organization of interlocking subsystems, all of which contribute to keeping the system going. Furthermore, you may not often understand that your role is not to change the system but simply to do your job. Taking time away from clients to solve organizational problems, even when those problems create difficulties for you, may not be rewarded but summarily discouraged.[33]

Blaming the System   If administrators are unresponsive and do not assist in helping resolve the discrepancies you feel, you may begin to blame the system, its policies, or administrators. You may question why administrators support, condone, or develop the policies and procedures that you perceive as not in the interests of your clients, or antithetical to good social work practice. If the situation continues and your administrators ignore, become resistant to, or even punish you, you may begin to feel alienated, resentful, and forced to condone a system that you may view as inherently oppressive. You might seek relief by pressing harder for organizational change or the removal of a particularly oppressive and unresponsive administrator. Blaming the system vindicates the worker who feels forced into complicity with an organization's "corrupt practices."

Taking the Blame   At this point you must not only deal with the original problem, but with your feelings toward the agency. The focus of attention may shift from the issue at hand to your attitude, which your supervisor may believe is negative. Feeling victimized, you may perceive that your only option is to take the blame. You become disenchanted or demoralized or feel defeated. You adopt one of several solutions.

Accommodation—Realizing that you are being blamed for a situation beyond your control, you give up trying to resolve the issue, and instead recoup your losses. You accept that you are the problem, consciously change your attitude, and accommodate to a system you cannot change. You adapt to the organizational culture, accepting its limitations in order to keep your job. This accommodation solution can have payoffs for you, because you demonstrate to your supervisor that you are adaptable, and "mature." You show that you are malleable, nonthreatening, and have potential to "fit in" to the organization.

Alienation—You appear to accommodate to the organization, while you inwardly refuse to adapt to the norms of the organization. You separate yourself psychologically from the "dissonance" you feel, performing your work, but alienated from it at the same time. If you adopt an alienation stance, you maintain your integrity and keep your job, but you become passive, involve yourself in paperwork, and do as your are told.[34] This solution buys time for you. If you can bear the tension that working in an alienating environment causes, you may be able to survive. The issue that brought on the alienation may even be resolved over time. On the other hand, your supervisor may begin to document your mistakes to build a case to eventually move you out of the agency.

Avoidance—If you are alienated, you may try to insulate and isolate yourself from the dissonance you feel. You reduce engagement with others, particularly those who remind you of the dissonance. You may try to avoid sitting on committees because they are not only a waste of time but also a painful reminder of the futility of organizational change. The ultimate result of avoidance is that you may give up and leave the agency.

Identification—Realizing that the way to succeed is not to buck the system, you give up your values in favor of those of the organization. You identify with the oppressor, in this case with the organization or its administrators. You adopt the culture, rules, procedures, and values of the organization as your own. You may even become a protégé of your supervisor, take the agency's side on issues, and be seen by the agency executives as someone who may be "management material."

Group Strategies

Group strategies for coping with organizational dilemmas allow social workers to band together to work for common solutions to organizational problems. An advantage of group strategies is that there is strength in numbers and less likelihood that any one individual will be blamed. On the other hand, group strategies may lead to increased conflict and confrontation. Among group strategies are networking, organizational politics, group confrontation, and as a last resort, collective bargaining.

Networking   As a social worker, when you perceive problems, you begin to talk about them with your coworkers. This informal sharing can help you let off steam in a friendly, nonthreatening way. Your coworkers may have different perspectives on the problem and provide reality testing. If you are naive, misperceive the situation, or have misguided information, you will be able to obtain a clearer picture of the situation from others.

On the other hand, if your coworkers share your perceptions, you may expand your consultation to informally include your entire unit. You and your unit members use social thinking to solve your common grievances. As you share your perceptions and express feelings, reality becomes clarified, misperceptions are avoided, and the group begins to envision possibilities, gather facts, and develop strategies. No single individual can be blamed or scapegoated. Your members feel empowered by one another, and you begin to reconstruct the reality with which you are confronted. Your group arrives at several possible solutions and decides on a joint strategy. When your group presents the issue to the administration, you do it as a whole. You offer solutions to administration as a way of helping the organization change for the better, improve morale, and solve a legitimate agency issue.

Organizational Politics   If your group sees your problem as either too trivial or too threatening to administration, you may decide that direct group action is not workable. Organizational skeptics avoid direct group action by "greasing the wheel" or "sliding around the issue." For example, a particular work procedure may be getting in the way of getting work accomplished or a rule may be outmoded, overly rigid, or inappropriate. The group members jointly decide to ignore the procedure or bend the rule and accomplish their tasks in a way that they view as more effective. Although your group is technically violating agency procedure, you are using your initiative to jointly resolve your common problem. You do not ask permission to change the work environment; you simply begin to change it for the better.

An advantage of organizational politics is that it resolves worker problems without bothering administration. If administration eventually raises a question, you can ask forgiveness for breaking the rule, but point out that you solved a common problem independently. If effectiveness has not been sacrificed or if service has improved, the administration may agree to the change and even commend workers for their initiative. This strategy uses the maxim of proaction, which states, "it is better to ask forgiveness than ask permission."

Confrontation   If administration is intractable, your group may ask for an exception. In return for a promise to accomplish or even exceed your individual and group goals, your unit might ask to be excused from the normal operating procedures that are at issue. You ask only that administration not interfere as the unit structures its work or solves its joint problems. If administration is unwilling to grant an exception or to listen to your group, lines may be drawn and confrontation may take place. In this situation an organization developer may be helpful to workers and administration by using conflict resolution strategies. You will learn more about asking for exceptions and about conflict resolution in Chapter 12.

Collective Bargaining   If problems are long standing or are so great that conflict resolution has not been successful, your unit may have little choice but to formally organize into a collective bargaining unit or union. There are advantages and disadvantages in forming a union. On the one hand, unions provide legal power to employees. Negotiations are conducted openly, formally, and with an agreement that no reprisals will be taken. Contracts with management are binding on both parties. Often a formal grievance process is included in union contracts to insure employee rights. Unions can obtain concessions from management in the form of wages, benefits, and working conditions.

On the other hand, the process of unionization polarizes administrators and workers. In one sense, unions represent a defeat for social workers and administrators alike. Unions mean that relationships have broken and a "cold war" exists between line social workers and administrators. In addition, unions are costly. While you gain benefits, you must also support the union financially. If you go on strike, you may suffer financial losses, at least temporarily. Sometimes union contracts become so rigid by prescribing working hours or worker roles that they interfere with the process of providing services to clients. However, in oppressive agencies, many social workers may feel that the benefits of collective bargaining outweigh their costs.

NEW SOCIAL ORGANIZATIONS

While the preceding strategies may assist social workers in coping with organizational systems, they are often not available for clients or communities who are dependent upon bureaucracy for service. Those who are on the margins of the organizational society become more and more excluded from organizational systems and unable to adapt or accommodate themselves to them. If alternative social forms were available that would allow for personalized social service delivery, communal decision-making, and the development of trust, openness, and respect between administration and workers; the rigidities, dehumanization, and alienation that modern organizations create might be avoided.

Today, macro social workers are engaging in a revolution in thinking, in government, and in the way we understand the social. At the center of this revolution is the meteoric rise of completely new and unprecedented social forms.[35] These alternative forms of social organizations are uniquely suited to promoting components of social life that economizing organizations have been unable to provide, and organizational macro social workers are at the center of bringing these new forms into being.

So new are these social organizational forms that they do not even have a commonly accepted name. They have been variously called nonprofit, nonbusiness, or nongovernmental organizations. But as Peter Drucker says, these are negatives and one cannot define something by what it is not.[36] They have also been called mediating structures, third-sector organizations, human service organizations, and public benefit organizations. The name I have chosen for these new social forms is *social organization*s.

Just as many people have not been aware of the existence or strength of these new social organizations, they have also failed to clearly see the new sector in which they are developing. According to Peter Drucker, "few people realize the size, let alone the importance of the third social sector. In fact, few people are even aware of its existence."[37] This new social sector also suffers from a confusing array of names. It has been variously called the independent sector, voluntary sector, third sector, human services sector, and nonprofit sector. The name that seems to define this sector most broadly, however, is the *social sector.*

New social organizations are neighborhood associations, religious organizations, community organizations, social planning councils, economic development corporations, and community development corporations. They comprise social support organizations including foundations, training organizations, and networks that provide assistance to social organizations. They include many social services, group services, counseling, mental health services, services to intellectually, emotionally, and physically disabled, and a wide range of social enhancement and human service organizations. Advocacy, social justice, human rights, and social policy groups are structured as social organizations. Social organizations comprise the literally hundreds of thousands of nongovernmental, grassroots organizations

and support organizations that exist globally in every nation of the world.

Social organizations are revolutionary not only because they constitute a completely new social form, or because of their amazing diversity, their growth, or even their social purposes. They are revolutionary because they are bringing about a major shift in the way the economy and government are conducted that constitutes a completely new and unprecedented era in American history. The social revolution that social organizations constitute is often unobtrusive. Their emergence as a central feature in society represents a new configuration of public and private power[38] and a necessary force in American society. These social organizations help overcome the existing deficiencies of the market-centered organizations and public-centered bureaucracies in modern society, providing stability and completeness to the existing private economic sector and public governmental sectors of society.

In the United States, social organizations are ubiquitous, and they fulfill an ever larger and highly unique social function. According to Drucker, more social functions are being discharged in and by the local community and, in the great majority of cases, by autonomous, self-governing local social organizations in North America than anywhere else in the world.[39]

Nonprofit social organizations are the fastest growing category of organizations in America. More than 90% of social organizations currently in existence were established since World War II, numbering only 12,500 in 1940, and by 1989 just under a million in the United States, an eighty fold increase.[40] There are hundreds of thousands more in developing countries, with a collective membership of hundreds of millions of people.[41] By contrast the number of business corporations during the same period exhibited a mere sevenfold increase.[42] In the 1980s, social organizations finally achieved the centrality they had always claimed, and as the nation's fastest growing organizational domain,[43] they touched the lives of almost all Americans as donors, board members, employees, clients, consumers, and citizens.[44]

Diversity of Scope and Activities

While economic and governmental bureaucracies are highly uniform in structure, purpose, and ways of

The Salvation Army keeps young people out of further trouble and they are doing it with considerable success. (© Tara C. Patty/Jeroboam)

thinking, the new social sector organizations offer at first glance a bewildering array of diversity[45] both in scope and activities. These organizations come in all shapes and sizes, ranging from small locality-based community and neighborhood associations with no assets and no employees to multibillion-dollar foundations. Most are relatively recently organized and virtually unknown except in the communities in which they operate. Others, including the Boy Scouts, Girl Scouts, Salvation Army, YMCA, and Red Cross are among the oldest and most respected organizations in America, operating in nearly every country on the globe.

Social organizations vary enormously in what they do, from offering traditional charitable assistance to the needy to carrying out advanced research. They supply a considerable portion of the social services, health care, education, research, culture, community improvement, and public advocacy that occurs in this country. Nonprofit social organizations are engaged in activities that reflect the diversity of human interests and full scope of community life. Far from focusing exclusively on the poor or needy, they serve a broad cross-section of the population and respond to a wide variety of needs. They deliver a larger share of publicly funded social services, as well as employment, training, housing, and community development than do government agencies.[46]

Nonprofit social organizations not only provide social and human services, but they also offer culture, arts, recreational activities, education, research, health-related services, and a host of other activities that address a range of community needs and serve a broad cross-section of community members. They include an indescribable variety of cultural enterprises, from neighborhood arts programs and community theaters to hundreds of symphony orchestras, and any number of museums. They include the majority of America's hospitals, as well as large national health care groups such as the American Heart Association, the American Lung Association, the American Mental Health Association and a great many community service groups, including B'nai B'rith, Rotary, and Urban League.[47] They include a very large part of our schools, and an even larger percentage of colleges and universities. Social organizations include the enormous diversity of religious organizations in the United States, ranging from those with more than 10,000 parishioners to conventicles with 25 members. They include large international philanthropic organizations and smaller community foundations and community chests that support local charities.[48]

Social organizations are the most ethnically diverse and pluralistic social systems in America. Administrators of social organizations celebrate new arrivals to the table of equality, actively support their rights to full expression of ideas and perspectives, facilitate their access to all needed resources, and most important, ensure equity power in the pluralistic organization.[49] Bailey says many social organizations are moving in the direction of genuine pluralism. For example, Big Brothers, Big Sisters, and Girl Scouts are designated as "pluralistic organizations," the highest form of organizational evolution in ethnic diversity. According to the Equity Institute pluralistic organization prohibits all forms of discrimination, prescribes governance and management policies and practices that support the value of pluralism, and develops a workforce composed of individuals and groups who subscribe to multiple cultural perspectives.[50]

New Structure

Peter Hall asserts that social organizations are a new institutional form.[51] Social organizations are governed by their own locally elected volunteer boards. In the United States they are mostly run autonomously. They have their own budgets and are operated by administrators chosen by the board.[52] What is unique about many of the newer social organizations is that they are hybrids, combinations of social community *and* an organizational tool. A community is a form of social relationship in which members meet common needs. The structure is the means by which the community attains its ends. The structure, however, is not the community. The structure is the organization. Communities of members have goals. Structures, however, do not have goals. Neither are the structures empowered to conceive the ends that the community members seek.

It is because of this unique combination that I call them social organizations. A social organization is composed of *social* relationships, the community of people who voluntarily associate together for their mutual benefit, and the *organization* that carries out the community's goals. The community reflects on and decides on the goals or ends that their association is to achieve. They develop a structure or organizational tool to carry out the purposes of the community. The community is the "owner" of the organizational tool. Social organizations are, therefore, sometimes called social agencies. The organizational tool is the agent of the community members, who have created it to carry out the community's purposes, express its ends, and represent it to the external world.

Because often the members of the community are also the staff of the organization, it is sometimes difficult to distinguish between the community and the organization. Unpaid staff or volunteers who operate the organization are also members of the community. Members are mutually engaged as partners with one another not only as community, but in the tasks of making the social organization work. The life of the organization and the community tend to be indivisible.

In some social organizations, there may be no paid professional staff at all but many unpaid community staff. In a community organization, for example, there may be only one paid community organizer but hundreds of unpaid staff—the members of the community organization who carry out the work of reconstructing the community. In a faith-based social organization such as a synagogue, church, or mosque, the paid staff may consist of a single rabbi, priest, or mullah. The members of congregations perform the majority of the teaching, maintenance, and secretarial services, leading youth groups, organizing retreats, and assisting in worship. Most importantly, they make the decisions and establish the policies that guide the social organization.

Because the community and organization operate inseparably, hierarchy, control, impersonality, artificiality, uniformity, and unidimensionality have little place in social organizations. Social organizations, however, comprise a multiplicity of social system designs that provide for authenticity, human actualization, meaning creation, and self-expression. In fact, the great diversity of social organizations—including community associations, community organizations, ethnic associations, community development corporations, neighborhood arts and theater groups, cultural associations, cooperative organizations, self-help groups, and religious communities—all provide models of differing arrangements to be considered as potential models. For example, in one model, groups exist in parallel with each other and connect with other functions as the task requires. Structure is formed around the flow of the work process. The Girl Scouts is structured as a series of concentric circles. Information and ideas begin with the local units and pass through the circles toward the central executive group in the middle circle. The circles give emphasis to dialogue and exchange and the idea that everyone is equally important in the operation of the whole system.[53]

New Social Purpose

The new social organizations are a counterculture, different and separate from governmental and business sectors and their respective values and cultures. Instead of self-interest, they are dedicated to service, especially social service. Instead of economic or public goods, these new social forms are established to provide social goods such as citizenship, responsibility, commitment, perseverance, public spirit, and a host of character-building qualities on which the other sectors depend for their existence. Instead of institution building, erecting gigantic economic enterprises or huge governmental structures, they are dedicated to community building and to the social health of the people in whose communities they operate. They are meaning-creating institutions whose purpose is the enhancement of the lives of those who compose it. They are also tools for reinventing society, a means for the social construction of reality. Social organization may be seen as a social form of human enhancement.

The services and structures of social organizations reflect the community, and they are dedicated to building healthy social and physical environments, meaning creating, political awareness, and engagement at the grassroots level. They attempt to orient themselves to community values, especially those values that include compassion, caring, and the value of personal social relationships. Social organizations mediate between the individual and the megastructures of society, helping reduce alienation, and provide a space where people can bear the stresses that organizational dehumanization imposes on modern life. They are dedicated to reconstructing the social infrastructures of society neglected by corporations and governmental bureaucracies alike.

But of equal importance with all of these purposes, social organizations are dedicated to recreating the social as a necessary component of society. As Peter Drucker asserts, "they all have in common, and this is a recent realization, that their purpose is to change human beings." The product of a hospital is a cured patient. The product of a church is a changed life. The product of the Salvation Army, one social organization that reaches the poorest of the poor regardless of race or religion, is that the derelict become a citizen. The product of the Girl Scouts is a mature young woman who has values, skills, and respect for herself. The purpose of the Red Cross in peacetime is to enable a community hit by natural disaster to regain its capacity to look after itself, to create human competence. The product of the American Heart Association is middle-aged people who look after their own health and practice preventative cardiac maintenance in the way they live. The successful resettlement of more than 100,000 Vietnam refugees in 1975 was accomplished not by setting up a government agency, but by working though voluntary social agencies, mainly faith-based social organizations.[54]

Along with community organizations and community development corporations, new social organizations are a means of revolutionizing the construction of social selves, counteracting the depersonalization of the organizational self, providing a means for renewed character development, the infusion of society with social goods, the refreshment of compassion, the realization of social justice, and rejuvenation of the *social* environment.

Clients and Staff

Modern hierarchial organizations have little use for people who are unable to compete, think rationally, engage in highly technical tasks, or contribute to organizational profit. These people are relegated to the margins of society. Social organizations, on the other hand, are meant for all people in society, but they are particularly concerned with those people who are unable to compete in today's utilitarian, technological society, those who "subsist at the fringe of a social system. These citizens are often normless, rootless, unable to shape their lives according to a personal project."[55] They are the indigent, the mentally incapacitated, homeless, homebound elderly, and criminal offenders.

While the doors of modern complex organizations are generally closed to these people, the gates of social organizations not only open, but social workers go into their communities to meet them and welcome them to come in. While modern complex organizations exclude altruism, service, and personalized treatment, the central value and most important feature of the new social organization is compassion, caring, and service. Each person, no matter how damaged or devalued, is treated as a valued individual with dignity, respect, and hospitality and who deserves inclusion. People who seem the least valuable members of modern organizational society become partners with one another and with social workers in the process of constructing society and constructing themselves.

Social organizations provide an important mechanism by which groups of citizens voluntarily band together in support of a wide variety of community purposes.[56] Social organizations not only assist others, but they provide the members who staff these organizations with a means of direct involvement in citizenship that is impossible in large governmental organizations. The human change organizations of the social sector offer us a sphere of personal achievement in which we can exercise influence, discharge responsibility, and make decisions.[57] This may be the most important contribution of the social sector.

The social sector is actually the country's largest employer, though neither its workforce nor the output it produces shows up in the statistics. One out of every two adult Americans, a total of 90 million people, are estimated to work as volunteers in social organizations, most of them in addition to holding a paid job. If volunteers in the social sector were paid, their wages would amount to $150 billion a year.[58]

New Means of Funding

Social organizations draw their resources from an array of sources.[59] Their sources of revenue follow no clear pattern. Some receive all of their funds from

charitable donations while others receive all their funds from government.

Fee income is the most widely used source of agency support, with nearly seven out of ten nonprofit agencies collecting this type of revenue. Private charitable giving ranks third among all major funding sources and accounts for only 21% of the social organization income. What is most surprising, however, is the relatively small proportion of agencies that actually receive private philanthropic support. About 38% of agencies receive foundation grants, 34% corporate gifts, and 23% United Way funding. Direct individual giving is more prevalent but benefits a smaller proportion of agencies than do government and fee income.

Social organizations have developed a variety of sources of financial support and formed supportive links with other sectors of American society. One of these routes of evolution has been the increasingly cooperative and helpful social investment by major corporations. For example, many companies work closely with social organizations that serve persons with disabilities by providing training and employment opportunities. Ben and Jerry's ice cream and other companies invest time and funding in the communities in which they operate. Even more traditional corporate organizations heavily invest in social organizations of their communities by active participation in United Way campaigns and by making direct contributions, lending staff to these organizations, providing consultation, and giving time to such efforts as "Days of Caring." Many social organizations have moved in the direction of increased reliance on self-generated income form dues, fees, and sales.

Human service nonprofit organizations receive more of their income from government than from any other single source. Government support reaches social organizations in a variety of forms and through numerous routes. Assistance sometimes takes the form of outright cash grants. Other social organizations obtain purchase of service contracts, and in still others government provides loans or loan guarantees. Two forms of finance, however, constitute a revolution in government and economics. One of these is the emergence of a grants economy. The other is the subsidy that social organizations receive by virtue of their status as nonprofit corporations.

Capitalist economics is based on two-way exchange in which money is exchanged for something of equal value. A person exchanges money for a product, a commodity, or a service, for example. Social organizations, instead, are based on one-way transfers or a "grants economy." Grants are one-way economic transfers. A grant is a gift offered freely with no expectation of a return by the recipient of the gift. A scholarship, for example, is a grant. Social organizations are based on an economic principle of gifts. From its meager beginnings in the 19th century, Salamon says, the grant-in-aid program has mushroomed into a massive system of interorganizational action. More than 500 grant-in-aid programs exist, making federal resources available to state and local governments for everything from emergency medical services to the construction of the interstate highway system. Since 1955, grant-in-aid funding has grown three times faster than the budget as a whole and by 1979 accounted for over 40% of all domestic federal budget outlays, and about 17% of the total federal budget.

A second and even more important method of funding social organizations is by means of tax subsidy. By exempting individual and corporate charitable contributions from taxation, the federal government delivers an implicit subsidy to the social sector. This subsidy was estimated to be worth $13.4 billion in 1985. About 78% of this subsidy flows to human service organizations, including churches.

The federal government has emerged as a partner of these organizations, linking government and the social sector. The elaborate network of partnership arrangements includes financing nonprofit operations, encouraging nonprofit involvement in new fields, and often helping to create new types of nonprofit entities. The federal government, for example, has turned to a host of social organizations to help it carry out its expanded responsibility rather than expand the federal bureaucracy, and in recent years this partnership has expanded in scope and scale. So extensive are these arrangements that government in the United States today relies more heavily on nonprofit social organizations than on its government agencies to deliver government-funded human services. In some cases, government has created new nonprofit social organizations where none existed before. The result is an elaborate pattern of nonprofit federalism linking government at all levels to nonprofit organizations across a broad front.

The widespread adoption of new tools such as purchase of service contracts, tax subsidies, grants-in-aid, and federal-social organization partnerships has reshaped the public sector in the United States. The characteristic feature of many of these new tools is that they involve the sharing of a far more basic governmental function: the exercise of discretion over the spending of federal funds and the use of federal authority. The $6–8 billion that Congress annually appropriates for employment and training assistance, for example, does not go to the Department of Labor but automatically to more than 450 locally organized prime sponsors. They enjoy substantial discretion in selecting the training and the trainees, and the Labor Department has only limited control.

Restructuring the federal/social organization relationship has been so substantial, Salamon asserts, it constitutes a qualitative not just a quantitative change in economics. Social organizations constitute a "third-party government." The result is a diverse and varied set of institutions connected to government at all levels through a rich network of interactions that differ markedly from place to place in response to local circumstances, traditions, and needs. In fact, in economic terms, the nonprofit sector equals or surpasses the role played by local government. In the Pittsburgh metropolitan area, the expenditures of private, nonprofit organizations exceed the total budget of the county government by a factor of six to one. In the Twin Cities area of Minnesota, the expenditures of the local nonprofit sector are as large as the combined budgets of Minneapolis, St. Paul, Hennepin County, and Ramsey County. In other local areas as well, the nonprofit sector is as significant an economic force as local government. Cooperation between government and the voluntary social sector has become the backbone of this country's human services delivery system, and the central financial fact of life of the country's nonprofit social sector.

CONCLUSION

For all of their power, wealth, and size, the gigantic organizational megastructures in the economy and in the public sector are helpless in resolving the major social dilemmas of our day. They are unable to reach into communal and social relationships or provide hope for the poor, powerless, and marginal who cannot be accommodated into fast-paced profit-making corporations or into the gigantic public bureaucracies. Modern organizations are not neutral, benign social instruments that are controlled by social workers who use and inhabit them. They are systems in which we become totally embedded, and from which we take our higher norms and values. So overwhelming is the influence, power, and control inherent in complex organizational systems that ultimately they swallow up the individual, client and social worker alike.

Modern complex organization is a tool that has become the master of its owner. It is an entirely enclosed social structure in which we obey its demands, operate by means of its imperatives, obey its rules, conform to the roles it demands, operate by its communication systems, think by means of its logic, and adhere to its norms and values. We often do this willingly, out of a sense of obligation to an artificial and abstract system as if this system were a person and not a thing.

Modern complex organizations intentionally are designed to destroy the social and to turn personal, communal social relationships into impersonal, rationally organized relationships. They work against the expression of compassion, are agents for the facilitation of dehumanization, create dependency, and disempower employees and clients alike. They tend to be deceitful enterprises, presuming that humans cannot do without the advantages they provide, and transforming the more prized human values into their opposites. They have generally failed to deliver successful solutions to social problems, but instead often create problems for communities as well as individuals.

While social work has generally utilized and depended on modern organizations, macro social workers are in the process of creating new social forms that are more congruent with the social and have the potential of revitalizing the social and for solving some of our most persistent social problems. These social organizations already play a vital role in American life. They are our fastest growing form of organization and represent an amazing diversity of sizes, structures, purposes, programs, and financial arrangements. In partnership with the federal government, they are reshaping the way social services are delivered and funded.

Just as modern bureaucracy was the structure that brought about the transformation of the modern rational world, it is very possible that, within its boundaries, the social organization will become the midwife of the coming postmodern era. While complex organizations, market-centered, and public organizations have squeezed communal, social relationships into narrower and narrower arenas, the new social organization is in the process of opening more room for the social.

If you accept the challenging opportunity to become involved in organizational macro social work, you will have the opportunity to engage, refine, and participate in the process of using these new social forms in developing social programs, in social administration, and in organization development. You will join with other social workers in experimenting with these new social forms and in partnership with your colleagues, clients, and members of your community to help bring about the new postmodern era.

KEY CONCEPTS

complex organization
social tools
organizational society
social organization
social sector
multidimensionality
unidimensionality

QUESTIONS FOR DISCUSSION

1. To what extent do you think we control organizations? To what extent do they control us?
2. In the process of helping us achieve our goals, is there a danger that organizations will reduce our humanity?
3. While organizations have enabled our society to become massive and complex, to what extent will artificial, contrived social relationships become important in human life in the future?
4. What responsibility has an organization and those who own and operate it to those who work for it, to the community in which it resides, and to society at large?
5. Forester says that we can "generally expect that organizational actors will deter cooperative, well-organized community-based organizations

that might press to meet social needs to the detriment of concentrations of private capital. They distract public attention from social needs and instead focus on the promotion of individual consumption."[60] What does this statement mean? What are its implications for macro social work practice?

6. Social work is a field that prizes altruism, compassion, self-actualization, authentic personal relationships, and two-way communication. Organizations, on the other hand, tend to eliminate altruism and compassion, require impersonal relationships, and use one-way communication. What dilemmas occur as social workers insert personal feelings and values into an impersonal organizational system? How would you cope with these dilemmas?

7. Presthus claims we live in an "organizational society." What is your understanding of that term? What are the implications of organizational society for social work as a whole and macro social work in particular?

8. Some theorists claim that our society is largely an artificial one, in contrast to premodern societies that may be considered "natural." What is the difference between an artificial and a natural society? Is this difference a real one? Why or why not? What are the implications of this for social work today?

EXERCISE 9.1

The Airline Dilemma

George Williams, a pilot for a major airline, will turn 60 this month. He has been a senior pilot for the past 12 years and is in excellent physical health. Remarkably, his eyesight is still sharp and he feels at the height of his ability. Several times he has averted disaster that a younger, less experienced pilot might not have. He loves to fly and wants to continue to do the job that he is best at doing and one which he does well.

Yet Williams is being forced to end his job as a pilot. He has appealed the ruling, but rules are rules. He must retire, even though he has many good years left, has logged thousands of flying hours, and has an impeccable record, better than the younger pilot who will replace him.

Williams must retire because on October 31, 1990, a three-judge federal appeals court upheld a 30-year-old Federal Aviation Administration rule that forces commercial airline pilots to retire at age 60, in spite of the federal government's stance against age discrimination. The agency contends that older pilots face "skill deterioration" and greater risk of "physical incapacitation." Consequently they are more likely to be involved in accidents, even though this may not be true in individual cases.

Many older pilots, and an increasing number of medical experts, on the other hand, maintain that aging pilots in their 60s often are in better physical and mental condition than some in their 30s, 40s, or 50s.

However, the rules must be applied uniformly and impersonally across the board. Captain Williams will retire, not because he has become incompetent, but because the rules say so. While the FCC allows for exceptions, the agency has never granted one.

1. Is it appropriate to bar airline pilots from flying a large commercial airplane just because they have reached the age of 60?

2. What is more important, the even application of rules that apply to all, or taking individual differences into account?

3. Is the real issue passenger safety, or can you think of other reasons for requiring airline pilots to retire at 60?

EXERCISE 9.2

Alternative Solutions

The following four theorists propose solutions to the problem of organization in our modern mass society. Examine each of these positions and answer the questions that follow.

Charles Perrow

Charles Perrow gives us a choice between either changing an economic system in whose service complex organizations operate, or dealing with the issue of who controls the organization.

> Critics, then, of our organizational society, whether they are radicals of the Left emphasizing spontaneity and freedom, the new radical Right demanding their own form of radical decentralization, or the liberal in-between speaking of the inability of organizations to be responsive to community values, had best turn to the key issue of who controls the varied

forms of power generated by organizations rather than flail away at the windmills of bureaucracy. If we want our material civilization to continue as it is, and are not ready to change the economic system along the drastic ways of, say, China, we will have to have large-scale bureaucratic enterprises in the economic, social, and governmental areas.[61]

Alberto Guerreiro Ramos

Alberto Ramos promotes a theory of "organizational delimitation." Recognizing that organizations are a permanent institution on our social landscape, and that our civilization cannot do without them, his solution is to restrict them to specific roles and arenas where they are appropriate and not let them encroach on the rest of society, thereby leaving space for authentic community, social action, and ethical reason in human life. Rather than allow this one overarching social system to dominate every aspect of our existence, he recommends that we develop several different forms of human associated life.

We must learn to develop many kinds of microsocial systems within the overall social fabric. We must limit the role of conventional organization in our lives so as to leave room for authentic interpersonal transactions.[62]

Donald Shon

Donald Shon takes a systems approach to the problem of organizations. He assumes that every system is composed of various parts. When one component part is changed, the rest of the system will, of necessity, also change. The most important components of any system are its underlying premises, or its theory base. If one changes the theory base of the system, then one can change the system itself. Based on Shon's recommendation, social workers would need to develop an alternative theory of social systems design more congruent with the realities and needs of the human condition.

The theory is a core dimension. When the theory is changed, the organization may be critically disrupted in four ways. The change may affect (1) its self-interpretation, (2) its goals, (3) the nature and scope of its operations, and (4) its transactions with its environment.[63]

Victor A. Thompson

Victor A. Thompson asserts that organization is a necessary human tool that we cannot do without. In fact, modern civilization is based on and is better off with organizations and the premises on which they are founded. In Thompson's view, we should not attempt to disrupt or change organizations. Rather, the solution to the problem of impersonality and dehumanization is for people to give up their fantasy of "personal relations" and instead adopt the new, modern organizational system and all the benefits it offers.

The individual needs to be socialized to adopt the collective orientation in all his dealings with economic and governmental organizations…. Modern man needs to learn to be comfortable with impersonality. All this amounts to is giving a high value to instrumentalism, to the achievement of established goals…. I expect abstract systems (impersonal systems of rules, artificial systems) to become more acceptable. They will be the source of more reinforcements, comparatively, than the favors of families and other natural systems…. Man and his institutions will fit one another better. A perfect fit we can never expect short of genetic or behavioral engineering. Such engineering is a long way off. We have not yet decided how to select either the engineers or the designs.[64]

1. With which of these positions do you agree?

2. With which do you disagree?

3. What are the underlying premises of each alternative solution?

4. Where do you think each solution will lead us in the future?

5. What alternative solution can you think of that is better than those presented here?

6. Might a combination of these or other ideas provide a solution?

ADDITIONAL READING

The Social Sector

Lester M. Salamon. *Partners in Public Service: Government-Nonprofit Relations in the Modern Welfare State.* Baltimore: Johns Hopkins University Press, 1995.

Waldemar A. Nielsen. *The Endangered Sector.* New York: Columbia University Press, 1979.

John McKnight. *The Professional Service Business.* Evanston, IL: Center for Urban Affairs and Policy Research, Northwestern University, 1976.

David Osborne and Ted Gaebler. *Reinventing Government: How the Entrepreneurial Spirit Is Transforming the Public Sector.* New York: Addison-Wesley, 1992.

Social Organizations

Peter Dobkin Hall. "Historical Perspectives on Non-profit Organizations," in *Jossey-Bass Handbook of Nonprofit Leadership and Management,* ed. Robert D. Herman and Associates. San Francisco: Jossey-Bass, 1994.

Peter F. Drucker. "Lessons for Successful Nonprofit Governance," *Nonprofit Management and Leadership,* 1(1) (1990): pp. 7–14.

———. "What Business Can Learn From Nonprofits," *Harvard Business Review,* Oct. 1989, pp. 818–893.

———. *The New Realities: In Government and Politics, in Economics and Business, in Society and World View.* New York: Harper and Row, 1989.

Yeheskel Hasenfeld. *Human Services as Complex Organizations.* Newbury Park, CA: Sage, 1992.

Robert D. Herman and Associates. *The Jossey-Bass Handbook of Nonprofit Leadership and Management.* San Francisco: Jossey-Bass, 1994.

Theory of Modern Complex Organizations

Chester I. Barnard. *The Functions of the Executive.* Cambridge, MA: Harvard University Press, 1938.

Amitai Etzioni. *Modern Organizations.* Englewood Cliffs, NJ: Prentice-Hall, 1964.

David Katz and Robert L. Kahn. *The Social Psychology of Organizations.* New York: John Wiley, 1978.

J. Steven Ott. *The Organizational Culture Perspective.* Homewood, IL: Irwin, 1989.

Herbert Simon. *Administrative Behavior: A Study of Decision-Making Processes in Administrative Organizations.* 4th ed. New York: Free Press, 1997.

Frederick Winslow Taylor. *The Principles of Scientific Management.* New York: W. W. Norton, 1947.

James D. Thompson. *Organizations in Action: Social Science Base of Administrative Theory.* New York: McGraw-Hill, 1967.

Victor A. Thompson. *Bureaucracy in the Modern World.* Morristown, NJ: General Learning Press, 1976.

———. *Without Sympathy or Enthusiasm: The Problem of Administrative Compassion.* University: University of Alabama Press, 1975.

Norman Weiner. *Human Use of Human Beings: Cybernetics.* New York: Avon Books, 1967.

J. R. Kimberly. "The Life Cycle Analogy and the Study of Organizations," in *The Organizational Life Cycle: Issues in the Creation, Transformation and Decline of Organizations,* ed. J. R. Kimberly, R. H. Miles, and Associates. San Francisco: Jossey-Bass, 1980.

Critique of Modern Complex Organization

Jacques Ellul. *The Technological Society.* New York: Vintage, 1967.

Ralph Hummel. *The Bureaucratic Experience.* New York: St. Martin's, 1977.

C. H. Parkinson. *Parkinson's Law.* London: Oxford, 1985.

Charles Perrow. *Complex Organizations: A Critical Essay.* 2d ed. Glenview, IL: Scott Foresman, 1979.

Robert Presthus. *The Organizational Society.* Rev. ed. New York: St. Martin's, 1978.

Alberto Guerreiro Ramos. *The New Science of Organizations: A Reconceptualization of the Wealth of Nations.* Toronto: University of Toronto Press, 1981.

Hendrik M. Ruitenbeek, ed. *The Dilemma of Organizational Society.* New York: E. P. Dutton, 1963.

Max Weber. "Bureaucracy," in *From Max Weber: Essays in Sociology,* ed. H. H. Gerth and C. Wright Mills. New York: Oxford University Press, 1958.

———. *Economy and Society: An Outline of Interpretive Sociology,* 3 vols. Ed. Guenther Roth and Claus Wittich. Trans. Elphraim Fischoff et al. New York: Bedminster Press, 1968.

William H. Whyte Jr. *The Organization Man.* New York: Doubleday Anchor, 1958.

Social Critique

Paulo Freire. *Pedagogy of the Oppressed.* New York: Continuum, 1992.

Philip Slater. *The Pursuit of Loneliness: American Culture at the Breaking Point.* Boston: Beacon Press, 1971.

Karl Polanyi. *The Great Transformation: The Political and Economic Origins of Our Time.* Boston: Beacon Press, 1944.

Journals

Non-profit and Voluntary Sector Quarterly

10

Becoming a Program Developer

What would he say, that famous poor man the leaders of this country so often talk about,
and so rarely talk with, if he were given a chance to speak?
That I needed a home, and you gave me food stamps
That I needed a job, and you got me on welfare
That my family was sick, and you gave us used clothes
That I needed my pride and dignity as a man, and you gave me surplus beans.

Si Kahn[1]

Ideas in This Chapter

CLARA BARTON, ANGEL OF THE BATTLEFIELD[2]

Clarissa Harlowe Barton was born in North Oxford, Massachusetts, on December 25, 1821. At 18 years old, Clara Barton displayed the talents that would later distinguish her as a premier community developer by establishing one of the first public schools in the state at Bordentown, New York, and afterwards developing a number of others in New Jersey. Never in robust heath, Barton went to Washington, D.C. to recuperate. There the Commissioner of Patents appointed her to the first independent clerkship ever held by a woman in the United States. She overcame opposition and antagonism that her appointment aroused by means of her tact, faithfulness, and remarkable executive ability. Newly elected President Buchanan relieved her of her position, however, and withheld a large part of her salary because of her Republican and anti-slavery sentiments.

Shortly after the election of Lincoln, Barton was recalled to the patent office, but when the Civil War began, she refused to draw her salary from an already overtaxed treasury. Believing that service to her country lay on the battlefield rather than an office in Washington, she resigned her position and requested permission to nurse wounded soldiers. No woman had ever been permitted in a military hospital or on battlefields, and both military and civil officials declined her services. In her own unequaled manner, however, she succeeded in gaining their confidence and finally made her way to the front. Barton never engaged in hospital service, but from the beginning she remained on the battlefield with the wounded and dying. Side by side with field surgeons, Barton was under fire in some of the most severe engagements of the war—at Cedar Mountain, the Second Battle of Bull Run, Chantilly, Antietam, Fallmouth, Fredericksburg, the Wilderness, Spotsylvania, and the sieges of Charleston, Petersburg, and Richmond. During the four years of the war, she endured the rigors of a soldier's life in action. She was exposed at all times, her clothing was pierced with bullets and torn by shot, but miraculously she was never wounded.

Supplies sent for her work poured into Washington, and at her own expense she had them forwarded to the battlefield. By her quiet self-reliance and prompt decision, Barton obtained such complete recognition that the surgeon general placed hospital supplies, a corps of assistants, and military railways at her disposal. In a short time her courageous work, under the most distressing conditions, gained her the name "Angel of the Battlefield." Barton knew no north or south and bestowed her care indiscriminately on any wounded soldier, whether Union or Confederate. She was a great commander in army camps and on a battlefield, and she never asked for favor or aid because she was a woman.

While the Civil War was still raging in America, Jean Henri Dulant began heading a movement in Europe for relief of wounded soldiers. In 1864 a convention was held in Geneva, Switzerland, at which almost every major nation was present except the United States. Ten articles of agreement were adopted, known as the Treaty of Geneva of the Relief of Sick and Wounded Soldiers, providing that all wounded or sick soldiers and the surgeons and nurses attending them would be held neutral in time of war and not captured by either army. Twenty governments affixed their signatures on August 22, 1864. As a compliment to Switzerland, the Swiss Flag with colors reversed was adopted as the organization's insignia, and with it, the Red Cross, the world's greatest humanitarian movement was born.

After the war, while Barton was visiting Switzerland, war was declared between France and Germany. She immediately offered her services under the Red Cross of Geneva and was present during nearly every battle of the Franco-Prussian war. During the war she helped establish hospitals, organize assistance for women and child refugees, and distribute money and clothing to over 30,000 destitute people. Germany awarded her the Iron Cross for her services.

When Barton returned to America she pledged to devote the rest of her life to introducing the Red Cross to America, and in 1882 President Chester V. Arthur signed the Geneva Treaty. Barton founded the American National Committee of the Red Cross (later the American National Red Cross) and was its president from 1881 to 1905. She extended the scope of the Red Cross in America to provide aid in any great national calamity. As the U.S. delegate to the Red Cross Conference in Geneva, she successfully proposed that the Red Cross provide relief in peace as well as in war. Known as "the American Amendment," this helped distinguish the United States as "a Good Samaritan of Nations."

During her presidency, Barton and the Red Cross engaged every major calamity that occurred in the country, assisting victims of forest fires in Michigan in 1881, floods of the Mississippi and Ohio rivers in 1882, the Louisiana cyclone of 1883, the Ohio river flood in 1884, the Charleston earthquake and the Texas Famine of 1886. When most people were enjoying retirement, at age 66, Clara Barton supervised relief work during the Florida yellow fever epidemic of 1887, the great Johnstown flood of 1889, the Galveston hurricane and tidal wave of 1900, and the San Francisco Earthquake of 1906.

Twice she carried relief to Russia during the Russian Famine of 1891, and she was present during the Armenian massacres in Turkey in 1896, assisting homeless and wounded. Barton was again on the battlefield in Cuba during the Spanish-American War of 1889. During the Boer War in South Africa (1899–1902), she commanded the relief ship *Clinton,* for which the whole American navy made way. To insure immediate action in any emergency, Barton placed $3,000 of her own money at the disposal of the American Committee of the Red Cross.

Throughout her long career of developing and providing relief services throughout the United States and the world, Barton's moral courage, energy, diplomacy, and unwavering integrity were her chief characteristics. She had two rules of action: unconcern for what cannot be helped, and control under pressure. Her career teaches that the meaning of human life lies not in what we get, but what we give. American history has no more eloquent record of self-sacrifice, courage, and devoted service to humanity than that of Clara Barton, one of America's social heroes and great program developers. She died on April 12, 1912, at age 91.

WHAT YOU WILL LEARN IN THIS CHAPTER

Every facility for elder persons, day care program for children, sheltered workshop for adults with intellectual disabilities, treatment program for people with emotional disabilities, socialization program for youth, or shelter for battered women has been developed by a group of people who had a vision about helping their neighbors in a new way or saw an unmet need and worked to meet that need. Social workers who help build such social organizations are program developers.

In this chapter you will learn how you too can assist people develop a social organization. You will explore how to form an organization action group, assess social needs, set up a formal corporation, establish a board, recruit and hire staff, and obtain funding. You will discover that social work program developers are more than mere social entrepreneurs who put together social agencies in the same way that business people develop businesses. Social work program developers are engaged in the task of helping people construct their own social reality and meet their own social needs.

WHO ARE SOCIAL WORK PROGRAM DEVELOPERS?

Program developers are often employed by social agencies serving a particular population, such as persons with intellectual, emotional, physical, or behavioral disabilities. We help insure that social welfare services are in place to meet a range of needs for that population.[3] We meet with various public and private agency staff to assess where gaps in services are occurring and assist parent groups, agency staff, and interested community leaders who want to establish a new social organization from scratch. We assess the changing needs of a community and work with social organizations to improve or expand services that already exist.

Social work program developers are often creative and insightful social workers who can observe needs and quickly conceive programmatic solutions to them. There is a danger if you are an agency program developer, however, and attempt to develop a program or construct a social organization singlehandedly. Robert Linthicum observes, "a problem with professionals is that they are the perceived experts because of their degrees and body of knowledge." They "know what is best" for the individual or for the community. This is the great weakness of outsiders such as legislators or city council persons who want to start programs for others. They look at social problems and come up with ideas that are intended to fix them as if they are social mechanics fixing a broken engine. One group may see the problem of drugs, for example, and say "Let's hire more police officers." Others may read about teenage delinquency in a poor, rundown neighborhood and advise, "Those people need a youth program to get the teenagers off the streets." Some people see homeless mentally ill and alcoholics wandering the streets and they ask, " Why don't they develop a soup kitchen or a shelter?" People become concerned about children running around the vacant lots. "That neighborhood needs a playground," they offer.

While these well-intentioned and concerned people may have many worthwhile ideas, the common element with these solutions is that someone else, often a person from outside the community, sees the community or its people as a problem that needs to be fixed. The assumption is that the people who have the problem are not as capable as others of seeing what needs to be done, do not have the imagination to conceive of solutions that are obvious to others, and furthermore, do not have the capacity to do it themselves. They assert, for example, that if the alcoholics, the homeless, the poor had the ability, wouldn't they have solved their problems long ago? Experts, on the other hand, who have the knowledge, skills, resources, and political connections ought to be the ones who can solve these problems. So social workers and a host of public health, mental health, recreation, and other professionals are called in to make recommendations. Politicians pass legislation and appropriate money, new programs are initiated, and well-intentioned criminal justice or social welfare professionals are hired. All of this ignores one of the primary assumptions of social work. According to Linthicum, "the people best able to deal with a problem are the people most affected by the problem. The people best able to deal with teenagers who are running amok in their neighborhood are the people who live in that neighborhood."

The concept of client self-determination "is one of the most difficult insights" for social workers to apply in their own professional lives. We want to get results, and because of our expertise we may think we know what is best for the community. We unwittingly teach people to be passive recipients and beneficiaries of charity. We train community members to be ancillary spectators and nonparticipants in the vital and necessary forces that shape their social worlds. We expect them to remain socially unresponsive and disengaged from the problems that affect their lives. As a result, members may often feel victimized and demeaned by our benevolence. They may resent social agencies deeply for making them feel so helpless.

Sometimes social work agencies try to set up processes to encourage a sense of ownership of the community's social services. They invite two or three community residents to sit on the agency's board, set up a women's auxiliary, or develop a community advisory committee. But community members normally won't accept that offer of participation because it is not their project or even their idea. They may refuse to get involved, and the burden of leadership continues with the social agency.

The agency becomes cynical about the lack of community involvement, and community members continue to feel no ownership in the project. Eventually social workers and community members burn out on the project. The fate of any program developed under such conditions is inevitable. It will function successfully only as long as others commit people, money, and materials to the program. When the well-intentioned executive can no longer raise sufficient resources, it will die. It will die because it has never been a project of the people.

HOW TO DEVELOP A SOCIAL ORGANIZATION

Community social planning councils may often recommend development of a social program that meets people's needs in some way. Sometimes ideas for social programs come out of the involvement of ordinary citizens who are concerned about social problems in their communities. They meet with their neighbors informally and begin to envision a social program. Many social agencies have been formed in this way. George Williams, for example, was concerned about the spiritual and social needs of young men who recently arrived in London in 1859. He began to form Bible study and socialization groups whose members eventually formed the YMCA. In 1853, citizens concerned with homeless children wandering the streets of New York City organized the Children's Aid Society, the beginning of the foster home and adoption movement in America. Many women's shelters have become established because the experience of domestic violence and rape has moved a citizens group to try to help women escape from a brutal situation.

Whether the concern for developing a social program comes from a planning group, community members, or elsewhere, the process will generally be the same. You assist the community in forming a program development group, identifying a need, incorporating as a formal social organization, forming a board of directors, developing the structure of the organization, obtaining initial funding, and recruiting staff and clients.

Forming a Program Development Group

You help establish the program development group that will carry out the work of developing the social organization. The social organization that results belongs to the community members. Your role is to assist group members by serving as group facilitator, trainer, technical advisor, or management consultant. While developing a social organization is the concrete task around which your group members form, they also develop themselves and learn leadership skills, technical skills, group skills, and skills in planning and administration. They develop primary social relationships and engage in a larger process of community building. You help community members add social meaning to their lives, gain control over the formation of their social world, and learn the skills to make the social program a strong and lasting one.

If a community planning council or team has already identified an idea for a social program, they may decide to reform themselves into a program development group to implement the program. You become involved with a group of neighbors already concerned about a common problem, or you form a group of people to help you work on community-wide issues.

Your group should consist of at least five key community people who will assess needs and, if necessary, put the organization and its programs together. Try to involve members who are heterogeneous in terms of skills, personality, and personal history, but who are homogenous in terms of community membership, who desire to see the program succeed, and who have time and commitment to offer the program development process.

Above all, find people who represent the particular community that the program will serve. Perhaps your community is interested in establishing a social program for youth or a day program for the elderly. These programs will primarily serve the people in a specific geographic location. Community members whose children, adolescents, or elderly parents or grandparents will use the services are the best choices for the program development group. They know the people in the community, its culture, its needs.

On the other hand, communities that some social programs serve may not be locality based. Specialized residential care treatment centers for youth who are disabled emotionally, for example, may serve the needs of parents and their children from different areas of a region. Facilities for children who have severe developmental or physical handicaps may serve families from many localities. While these families may live in dispersed areas, their common problems and needs bring them together to consider ways of providing safe, well-managed facilities for the welfare of their children. Together they can form a group committed to developing a social organization that will not only meet their own needs, but also the needs of many others who live in different geographic localities. Try to find key people who can bring awareness of the culture of that community to the new program or agency.

If possible, locate people who know something about program development. For example, members who have served on boards of social organizations, who have worked as staff members for social agencies, or who have familiarity with budgeting or fundraising, recruiting, or selecting staff would be ideal members.

After your program development group is established, its first task is to verify the need for a social program. After they verify the need, members develop and process documents to create a formal corporation. They will recruit and form a board of directors.

Identifying and Verifying the Need

Help your group develop a list of problem areas that it intends to address. Explore your group members' perceptions and personal experiences about the need for this particular program and develop an objective assessment of the need for the program. Performing a needs assessment is a critical first step in the development of any social program. "The purpose of a needs assessment is to verify that a problem exists within a client population to an extent that warrants the existing or proposed service."[4] Often social planning agencies will not validate or assist in funding programs for which an assessment has not been performed to verify the need.

There are two different kinds of needs. You may define need in normative terms or in terms of demand. Rubin and Babbie state that "if needs are defined normatively, then a needs assessment would focus on comparing the objective living conditions of the target population with what society, or at least that segment of society concerned with helping the target population, deems acceptable or desirable."[5] For example, evaluating services for persons who are developmentally disabled may lead your group to conclude that persons with disabilities lack equal access to educational services afforded others in a particular geographical area. The same may be true of dental care, medical care, or housing for the homeless. These populations may be in need of services whether or not they express the need or claim dissatisfaction with their current conditions. In this case, your group members may advocate for such "underserved" populations by means of developing "precise estimates of the number and distribution of individuals or social units exhibiting the problem."[6]

Your group may define needs normatively by using existing data. For example, the numbers of children who are developmentally disabled who actually attend school may be compared with the number of disabled children in the population. If there is a significant difference, your members might conclude that more school programs need to be established.

When needs are defined in terms of demand, "only those individuals who indicate that they feel or perceive the need themselves would be considered to be in need of a particular program or intervention."[7] Demand data are helpful when mobilizing community support for a program. If need is defined solely in terms of the number of individuals who press for a service or who express an interest in it, however, those who do not understand the service, are not aware of its benefits, or actively resist it will not be included in determining the extent of need. Demand data, therefore, should often be combined with normative data to determine the extent to which those eligible for a particular program would actually use it. Normative data may show that there is a need for additional shelters for persons who are homeless, for example, while demand data would give an indication of the numbers who would actually use them.

Needs Assessments   Involve as many stakeholders as you can in understanding and verifying the need. There are five approaches to performing needs assessments: (1) social indicators, (2) rates under treatment, (3) focused interview or key informant, (4) focus groups or community forum, and (5) survey.

Social Indicators   While you may wish to develop your own needs assessment, many times you'll find that a needs assessment has already been performed by a social service or planning agency. Social indicators such as data on crime, abuse, housing, and health, for example, can be gathered from public and private agencies concerned with these problems.

Rates Under Treatment   The rates under treatment approach is one way of obtaining demand data. Your group assesses the extent to which people utilize particular services within a community over a period of time. For example, if your group is interested in developing a shelter for battered women, the group can study the utilization of shelters in communities of similar size and demographics. This will help determine if such a facility would be used and the amount and kinds of services that the facility should offer.

Key Informants   Key Informants are people knowledgeable about the needs of a particular problem area. Invite potential clients to help define problem areas more specifically. Talk to people with professional, governmental, or other expertise about the need in your intended service area. Meet with people operating similar or existing programs. Ask people who have been identified as community leaders. Rubin and Babbie state, however, that while the key informant approach is easy and quick, and can help build connections with key community resources, the information does not come directly from representatives of the entire community. The quality of information depends on the objectivity and depth of knowledge of the informants.

Community Forums and Focus Groups   Community forums and focus groups give an indication of demand data, but they are suspect from a scientific perspective. Those with vested interests or with a particular ax to grind, or who feel negative about or threatened by a proposed need, may be overly represented in forums or focus groups. For example, when attempting to establish the need for a home for people with emotional, behavioral, or developmental disabilities, your group may find that community members may oppose the idea because they do not want such a facility in their neighborhood—the phenomenon of NIMBY, "not in my backyard." Strong social pressures may prevent some people from speaking or from expressing minority viewpoints at community forums. While forums or focus groups will help you assess the political climate that a program may face, therefore, they may not always assist in demonstrating need. "One way to overcome these threats to the validity of data is to hold closed meetings, one for each preselected homogenous group of people."[8]

Community Surveys   A representative random sample of a community or a sample of the target group can also give an indication of need. If you use mail-out questionnaires, however, you must weigh the advantages and disadvantages of this method, given the problems in accuracy associated with low response rates. Making person to person contacts, on the other hand, will often give you ideas for resources, help you recruit potential board members, and obtain information from key community leaders and groups who can be of assistance to you.

After the Needs Assessment   As a result of their research, your group members may discover that the needs or problems they intend to address may be on target, or they may find them not to be what they originally thought. If your group cannot verify the need, help your members explore their initial impressions and look again at what prompted them to want to develop a particular program. Help your group review the problems it wants to address and select one or two issues that the program realistically can work on in its first years. Ask yourselves, "Over what situations can we have a significant impact?" There may be some aspects of a problem over which you can have no control or influence. If the program can make no difference over certain social problems, or will have little significant impact, it is not worthwhile to choose those problems, at least at the beginning of the group's efforts.

Be specific in selecting and defining the target population for whom the program can make a signif-

icant impact. For example, in 1972 a community program development group in Oakland, California, targeted the neighborhood of West Oakland and issues such as vacant housing, zoning, prostitution, and junkyards. However, it was the specific issue of 1,100 vacant houses that brought leaders from the neighborhoods together and planted the seeds of the Oakland Community Organizations (OCO). In the next five years, OCO staff targeted four more Oakland neighborhoods, and one by one, they developed other community organizations: SAFO, 50th to 80th, and Elmhurst. Today, nearly 30 years later, by targeting a specific community and clearly identified important issues in that community, OCO has developed a federation of over 32 church and community organizations directly involving more than 32,000 families in East, West, and North Oakland, and affecting the lives of 300,000 families.[9]

The better you are able to define the target audiences, the more likely your program will be effective in meeting the needs of your members. Have your group develop a statement of the problem and the defined client population. Such a statement might look like this:

> *Needs:* There are over 1,000 homeless men, women, and children in West Oakland, California. There are also over 1,100 rundown, vacant houses that need to be renovated to make them livable.
> *Problem:* How can the needs of the homeless be met while at the same time utilizing the 1,100 vacant houses that exist?
> *Client Population:* Over 1,000 homeless citizens and 60,000 residents of West Oakland.

Establishing the Legal Corporation

After your program development group has verified the need and identified the problem and the target population, it needs to establish a legal corporation. Although most social organizations become incorporated as nonprofit corporations, it is always a good idea to consider whether to establish a for-profit enterprise or a not-for-profit organization. Once this decision is made, the group must develop a constitution, articles of incorporation, and by-laws and file these with the state secretary general. If members choose to become a nonprofit entity, they must apply for nonprofit status with the federal government. After the formal paperwork is processed and the corporation is legally formed, the team must recruit board members, and the board members must be trained and organized so that they can begin to do the work of establishing the social organization or program.

For-Profit Agencies   Income from a profit-making enterprise becomes the property of the owners to dispose of as they wish and is taxable. If the income earned by the enterprise (minus taxes, interest on loans, salaries, and overhead) will provide profit, then it may be to the advantage of the board to incorporate as a small business enterprise. Many board and care homes, institutions for elderly, hospitals, foster homes, small care facilities, as well as counseling clinics incorporate as profit-making agencies.

Chris Valley, Assoc. Exec. Director for Program Development, Families First, and his staff develop new social programs in Atlanta. (Courtesy of Families First)

To become a business, the board must file a "fictitious name" (the name of the business), obtain a tax number, and apply for licenses required to operate in the city or county. Profit-making enterprises often obtain start-up money by taking out small-business loans, repaying them from income generated by the service.

Not-for-Profit Organizations   The federal government allows most social organizations to apply for tax-exempt status as nonprofit organizations. Among the kinds of organizations that are usually tax-exempt are churches, labor unions, benevolent associations, foundations, private schools, and social welfare organizations. These not-for-profit corporations do not pay taxes on income, property, or other assets as for-profit businesses must. However, just as any other organization, they can acquire assets, own property, and pay staff a reasonable salary. Social organizations that incorporate as not-for-profit agencies must meet requirements of federal and state laws for exemption from taxation. Any surplus income that the agency makes must be used for the charitable purposes for which the organization has been formed and not for the personal profit of its owners, and no substantial part of the corporation's assets may be used for partisan political purposes.

In addition to exemption from taxes, there are a number of other incentives for social organizations to acquire not-for-profit status. Nonprofit organizations can charge fees for services and obtain loans, as do for-profit organizations, and they can contract for services with the government. They also have sources of funding not available to profit-making businesses. Your organization can accept charitable contributions from individuals or corporations which can be deducted from the donor's taxes, providing an incentive for donors to contribute to your organization. Your organization can apply for government and charitable foundation grants. Tax-exempt social organizations may become a member of joint fundraising campaigns such as the United Way.

JANIE PORTER BARRETT

Janie Porter Barrett (1865–1948) was a program developer and activist during one of the most important periods of program building in America.[10] She made her home into a place for needy people. Using her savings and contacts from the Hampton Institute, her alma mater, Barrett led a successful fundraising campaign to develop the Locust Street Social Settlement. She provided job training for people of all ages who learned to sew, care for children, raise livestock, and cook.

In 1915, convinced that the state needed a rehabilitation center for African American girls in legal difficulties, she became superintendent at the Virginia Industrial School for Colored Girls, near Richmond. Barrett obtained regular state and philanthropic subsidies and increased the school's enrollment to 100. By the mid 1920s, the Russell Sage Foundation ranked the center among the country's five best institutions of its type. As a resident among the center's girls, Barrett fostered an atmosphere of community. The center was without locks, bars, or physical punishment, reflecting the ideals of progressive reform, and it set the standard for treatment in which humane social work was becoming increasingly important. Barrett received the William E. Harmon Award for Distinguished Achievement Among Negroes in 1920, and she participated in the White House Conference on Child Health and Protection in 1930.

Incorporation   If your program development group decides to become a not-for-profit organization, it must be incorporated at the state level and apply for not-for-profit status with the federal government, as well as meet local or state licensing requirements. Incorporation means that your organization is officially listed and legally recognized as a corporation. This is important for several reasons. Many agencies are subject to licensing requirements, particularly day programs, residential facilities, food service programs, health or medical treatment programs, and others that provide direct care to clients. A board that attempts to provide such services without formal approval is operating illegally. Incorporation is necessary if your organization wants to apply for governmental grants or contract with public agencies for fees.

The process for becoming incorporated is straightforward. First, write to the secretary of state in the state in which you wish to incorporate. The secretary of state will send you forms that can be filled out by anyone familiar with the organization. Usually, two separate documents are required: the articles of incorporation and the organization's constitution and by-laws.

For the articles of incorporation, the group may use stock paragraphs that apply to any corporation.

These usually include the name of the corporation, date of incorporation, names of officers, and a statement of purpose. Often the secretary of state provides samples of acceptable incorporation language that can be adopted by your organization. You may be tempted to hire a lawyer to draft the articles of incorporation. This is not necessary, and it is expensive. By following the instructions from the secretary of state, you and your program development group can devise an acceptable set of articles for your organization. See Figure 10.1 for a sample of Articles of Incorporation from the state of California.

Standard language also exists for constitutions and by-laws of not-for-profit organizations. The constitution and by-laws usually contain information about the purpose of the organization, its structure, the kinds of officers and their roles, the manner in which officers are elected, the place and times of board meetings, the mechanisms by which meetings are to be conducted, and rules for making decisions. Working on articles of incorporation, a constitution, and by-laws can be a helpful process in thinking through the details of the new organization.

By-laws of the Organization[11]   By-laws are the general rules that govern the organization and the board's composition and structure. The board is an association of volunteers that has legal responsibility and ownership over the organization. The board defines the purposes of the agency, sets policy, owns the assets of the program, and has ultimate authority to make decisions about services, structure, personnel, and the budget. By-laws outline how your board of directors will operate, its size, the selection and tenure of board members, the number of board meetings, the number of officers and committees, the financial and legal procedures, and the purpose of the organization. By-laws should be tailored to meet the needs of your organization.

Because these rules may not be appropriate forever, the by-laws should also outline the steps by which they can be revised when it becomes necessary. Your organization may use the following format to write your by-laws, unless your state requires a different one.

I.   What is the purpose of the organization?
A typical statement of purpose is as follows.

The primary purpose of this organization is exclusively religious, charitable scientific, literary, or educational within the meaning of Section

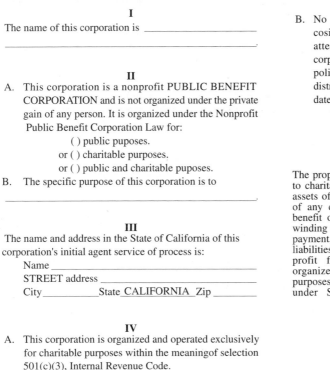

I

The name of this corporation is _____

_____ .

II

A. This corporation is a nonprofit PUBLIC BENEFIT
   CORPORATION and is not organized under the private
   gain of any person. It is organized under the Nonprofit
   Public Benefit Corporation Law for:
   ( ) public puposes.
   or ( ) charitable purposes.
   or ( ) public and charitable puposes.
B. The specific purpose of this corporation is to

   _____ .

III

The name and address in the State of California of this
corporation's initial agent service of process is:
   Name _____
   STREET address _____
   City_____State_CALIFORNIA_Zip _____

IV

A. This corporation is organized and operated exclusively
   for charitable purposes within the meaningof selection
   501(c)(3), Internal Revenue Code.

B. No substantial activities of this corporation shall
   cosist of carrying on propaganda, or otherwise
   attempting to influence legislation, and the
   corporation shall not participate or intervene in any
   political campaign (including the publishing or
   distribution of statements) on behalf of any candidate for public office.

V

The property of this corporation is irrevocably dedicated
to charitable purposes and no part of the net income or
assets of this corporation shall ever inure to the benefit
of any director, officer or member thereof or to the
benefit of any private person. Upon the dissolution or
winding up of the corporation, its assets remaining after
payment, or provision for payment, of all its debts and
liabilities of this corporation shall be distributed to a nonprofit fund, foundation or corporation which is
organized and operated exclusively for charitable
purposes and which has established its tax exempt status
under Section 501(c)(3), Internal Revenue Code.

_____
(Signature of Incorporator)

_____
(Typed Name of Incorporator)

FIGURE 10.1 Articles of Incorporation, California

501(c)(3) of Internal Revenue Code of 1986 or
such other provisions of state or federal laws
may from time to time be applicable. The specific purposes are:

II. Where will be the location of the organization?
State the address of the registered office of the
organization.

The registered office shall be located at
(address) unless otherwise established by the
board of directors.

III. Will the organization have members?
There is a distinction between members of an
organization and members of a board of directors. If
your organization has members, they generally meet
only once a year. Some nonprofits provide for the
members to elect the board of directors, adopt or
revise by-laws, and approve merges, dissolution, and
the sale of assets. In other nonprofits, members are
simply people who make annual contributions. If your

organization will not have members, the by-laws
should specifically state that there are no members. If
the founders of a nonprofit conclude that there is a
value to having members, the following questions
should be addressed:

1. *What are qualifications for membership?*   The
   membership of this corporation shall be open to
   all individuals, persons, corporations, propri-
   etorships, associations, partnerships and clubs
   interested in the promotion of the objectives and
   purposes of this corporation and who are
   deemed qualified for membership under the
   terms established by the board of directors and
   shall have met all condition for membership
   (such as paying dues).

   You may also establish classes of membership,
   such as *individual persons and families* and *corporate members*, each paying different dues or
   fees or having different rights and duties.

2. *What is the length of membership?*   Membership shall terminate at the end of the term as established by the board of directors and may not otherwise be terminated or suspended other than for nonpayment of dues or fees fixed by the board of directors except where the member is given not less than fifteen days written notice and reasons and the member is given an opportunity to be heard orally or in writing. A terminated or suspended member may be reinstated by action of the board of directors.

3. *Powers. What can the members decide, if anything?* Members are not entitled to vote.
Or:
Members shall approve any changes to the by-laws and all mergers.

4. *Meetings.   What is the least number of meetings that will be held during a year; who can call the meeting; what advance notice is required; how many members must be present to conduct business; will Robert's Rules of Order or Sturgis parliamentary rules prevail; can members vote by proxy?*   You should meet at least once a year. Don't set a quorum that will be difficult to reach without extraordinary efforts.

An annual meeting shall be held at a date, time, and place determined by the board of directors, with written notices to each member provided at least fifteen days in advance of the meetings. An officer of the organization shall chair the meeting. A quorum shall consist of (number) members. Proxy votes are (are not) permitted. Roberts Rules of Order shall govern motions, voting, and other conduct of the meeting.

IV.   What will be the structure of the board of directors?

1. *What will be the size of the board?*   The business and charitable affairs of the corporation will be managed under the direction of a board of directors, comprising not fewer than six persons and not more than fifteen, as determined by the board.

2. *Who is eligible to be a member of the board of directors?*   Indicate criteria for membership. For example, explain if any organization staff will be

ex officio members of the board. Ex officio board members, such as the chief staff officer or others, serve because of their office and usually have all of the rights of the other directors. Some nonprofits decide that the executive director should be a member ex officio, but some do not. Since the board hires and oversees the director, a director who is a board member ex officio becomes a member of the group that evaluates his or her performance. Granting the executive the right to vote on policy matters may create a potential conflict of interest as well, and gives the executive disproportional power because the executive controls the information the board needs to do its job.

At all times not less than 25 percent of the directors shall be persons who represent (organization or group). The executive director shall be a member of the board ex officio.

3. *How long do board members serve, and can they serve more than one term?*   The incorporators named in the articles of incorporation can serve as the initial directors, who then elect the additional beginning directors.

Directors shall be elected by the affirmative vote of a majority of the directors present at a duly held meeting of the board, except that no director shall vote for his/her own election, and shall serve for a term of three years each, but shall be so elected that approximately one third are elected each year. A director may serve no more than two consecutive three-year terms.

4. *How are board members who resign during their terms replaced?*   Typically, the board elects replacements, unless it chooses to leave any positions vacant.

Should a director die, resign, or be removed, the board may elect a director to serve for the duration of the unexpired term.

5. *Will board members be compensated for time, services, transportation, or other expenses?*   Generally board members are not compensated.

V.   How are the meetings of the board of directors structured?

1. *What is the minimum number of times the board must meet during a one-year period?* A board meets at least quarterly, preferably bimonthly, and possibly monthly.

2. *Who may call a special meeting of the board?* The chair, executive director, or a certain number of directors may have the authority to call special meetings of the board.

3. *What are the notification requirements regarding meetings?* Generally, written notice regarding the time and place of regular and special meetings must be sent to all board members a certain number of days prior to the meting.

4. *What is the quorum for a board meeting?* Stipulate how many board members must be present in order to proceed with a meeting.

5. *Is a simple majority sufficient to pass a motion at a meeting of the board?* A simple majority is the votes of half of the board members present plus one. A group may decide that two-thirds of the board must approve a motion for it to pass.

6. *Will actions in writing be authorized?* An "action in writing" involves preparing a written motion or resolution and sending it to each director for his or her signature. This procedure makes it convenient to approve a required action against a deadline, especially when the action wouldn't generate much discussion.

7. *What rules or procedures will be used to conduct meetings?* Roberts Rules of Order are generally used. Copies of Roberts Rules are available at most bookstores and libraries.

VI. What shall be the duties of officers?

1. *What officers shall the corporation have?* Officers designated in the by-laws include a chairperson, vice chair, a treasurer perhaps, and sometimes a secretary.

2. *What are the specific powers and duties of each officer?* The board selects one of its members to be the *chair*. The chair presides at meetings, keeps the group directed toward its goals, delegates responsibility for tasks to other members or com-

mittees, and serves as the primary contact between the board and executive director and other staff. The chair is responsible for keeping the group of directors functioning effectively and efficiently. The chair of the board should meet regularly with the executive director. The chair should ensure that (1) board members clearly understand the strategies and goals of the social organization and their roles in the organization's governance; (2) meetings that are called are truly necessary and deal with important matters; (3) agendas and meeting notices are sent well in advance of the meetings, accurate minutes are prepared soon after meetings occur, and these minutes are included in materials sent to the board; (4) staff and board have an opportunity to interact.

The *vice chair* presides at board meetings in the absence of the chair. The *treasurer* reports on condition of the budget and presents the financial statements to the board and is often authorized to co-sign checks on behalf of the corporation. The *secretary* keeps minutes of board meetings, prepares copies of minutes, and sometimes also handles the correspondence of the board.

3. *Which officers are members of the board?* Sometimes the secretary or treasurer may be staff positions.

VII. What will be the structure of committees?

Usually a young agency may start with no committee structure or only one or two committees and add more committees as it develops. Dividing board work by committees is the most effective means of governance for many organizations as well as a way to make sure board members feel well utilized. Committees have only the authority that is specifically given to them by the by-laws or the board. If your board is small, it may prefer to deal as a body with the business of the corporation with no need for committee work. But if your board has a dozen or more members, it may choose to divide its major responsibilities among standing (ongoing) committees that report to the board as a whole.

Board members with interest and expertise in specific areas are appointed generally by the board's chair to serve on standing committees. In some states, all committee members must be members of the board. In other states, the board is permitted to appoint other people to committees, which it may want to do to acquire special expertise. Boards often use several basic kinds of committees.

The *executive committee* is composed of officers of the board and chairs of the key board committees. An executive committee could be given decision-making authority in by-laws to act on urgent business that arises during the periods between board meetings. Sometimes the duties of the executive committee are subject to the approval of the board and the executive committee is only advisory.

The *finance committee* monitors fiscal operations, assists the executive director in developing an annual budget, and ensures that an audit is performed annually. It may also be responsible for developing and overseeing fundraising campaigns.

The *nominating committee* recommends individuals to serve as board members. It may also recommend the criteria for selecting new board members, provide orientation to new members, and review the participation and performance of current members.

The *personnel committee* reviews your organization's personnel needs, determines schedules of salaries and benefits, and develops personnel policies or grievance policies.

The *community relations committee* works with staff in disseminating information about the organization through the media.

The *program committee* advises staff in service delivery, recommends service delivery policies, monitors the agency's services, and provides the board with detailed information regarding the effectiveness of services.

Ad hoc committees are temporary committees that carry out one project and are then disbanded. For example, a special committee may be formed to search for an executive director and be disbanded after that position is filled.

VIII. What special rules will apply to the corporation?

1. *Will the corporation indemnify its board members?* The corporation may decide to protect board members from the financial consequences of liability lawsuits and judgments.

2. *What is the fiscal year of the corporation?* Many for-profit organizations develop their fiscal years around the tax season and so begin their fiscal years in April. Many educational institutions

begin their fiscal year on July 1 to prepare for the coming school year.

IV. What are the provisions for amendment of the by-laws?

The by-laws should indicate the procedure by which they can be changed or added to.

Ending the Program Development Group

With the incorporation of the new organization, the work of your program development group is at an end. It is possible that many of the original members may be willing to carry on as members of the board. If so, they take charge of recruiting and training new board members and helping them become oriented to their new roles. However, some of your team members may decide to end their involvement at this point. This is a good time to have a party celebrating the accomplishment and the hard work of your program development team, giving recognition to its members and welcoming those who will continue as board members of the new corporation.

WORKING WITH THE BOARD OF DIRECTORS

Your role as program developer will change from working with a team to working with the new board of directors. You will meet frequently with the board members, helping them recruit additional board members, train them in the role and function of the board, assist them in leadership processes, help them understand how committee structures work, and familiarize them with parliamentary procedures, as well as with the next steps of establishing the agency.

Recruiting the Board Members

Members of your original program development group should seek out other people to make a full complement of board members who have the interests and skills necessary to help translate ideas into functioning services.[12] Board members must have the time, interest, and willingness to be of service to the agency. Individuals who serve on the board should be able to work cooperatively and tactfully with one

The board defines the purpose of the agency, sets policy, and makes decisions about services, structure, personnel, and the budget. (© Cleo Freelance/Jeroboam)

another. They should be recognized as credible and responsible individuals.

Most boards probably function best with a dozen or so members but new ones might function better with only a half dozen or so. Ideally members of the board should include varied areas of expertise and perspectives and reflect the gender, age, and ethnic diversity of your community. They should be selected according to qualities they can offer your organization, especially in the following areas.

1. Competence: Board members should be capable of making sound governance decisions and, if possible, have special competencies in fundraising, budgeting, law, public relations, personnel, or social work skills.

2. Bridge to constituents: The board should include members of the target population of the program and other stakeholders.

3. Community leadership: Leaders in the community have access to resources or possess affiliations with organizations of importance to yours.

4. Shared goals: Board members should share the mission and vision of the agency and bring a commitment to see the organization succeed.

Board members should have a sincere interest in the work of the organization, a commitment to its goals, a willingness to ask questions, and the ability to offer constructive criticism. They should also have an understanding of the difference between making suggestions to staff and taking over their management prerogatives. Board members should have enough expertise, experience, and good judgment to help keep the organization's mission and strategic decisions consistent with its charitable purpose.

After your team members choose potential board members, help explain to potential board members clearly why they were selected, in what capacity they will serve, what skills you want them to contribute, and committee work they will be expected to do. Potential members need to know how much time they will need to give to meetings and other activities, the length of their terms on the board, possible costs to them such as lunches, travel, time away from work, and any expectations of personal financial contributions. Discuss whether there are any conflicts of interest, such as business or other relationships that could affect their ability to serve the program's interests.

Ask what they want to contribute and how their participation can be easily and best utilized. Explain the rewards members will receive by being on the board—for example, the satisfaction of serving the community, social contacts, and experience in policy-making, fundraising, and other aspects of the agency.

After your group has explored all these issues with potential board members, encourage them to think about their invitation. New board members who are well informed about the organization, its problems and opportunities, and their expected role are more likely to participate well and be effective board members.

CHARLES LORING BRACE, CHILD SAVER

Writer, minister, free thinker, program developer, and social reformer, Charles Loring Brace may be said to be the originator of the child welfare movement in the United States, as well as foster care and placement services. He was one of the primary organizers of the Children's Aid Society of New York City. As its executive director for almost 40 years, Brace chronicled the problems of destitute, vagrant, and homeless children and initiated many child welfare services.

Brace was born in Litchfield, Connecticut, June 19, 1826. He graduated from Yale University in 1846 with honors and entered Yale Divinity School, finishing his course at Union Theological Seminary in New York City. After traveling through Europe in 1850–1851, the Rev. Brace attended lectures at the University of Berlin and visited Hungary out of sympathy with the revolution in that country. The Austrian government suspected him of being in league with Hungarian refugees, and he was imprisoned for a month but released through the efforts of the U.S. Consul.

Brace settled in New York City and began missionary work in the notorious Five Points area and with the prisoners of Blackwells Island. Serving as a city missionary, he became aware of the many homeless children roaming the streets and made a study of the "ragged schools" and prisons, becoming convinced that reformation of the poor must begin with children.

In 1853 the chief of police issued a report calling attention to the multitude of vagrant children who almost of necessity became criminals. A number of citizens, including Brace, began the needed work of reform by organizing the Children's Aid society in 1853. After much hesitation, Brace, who had wanted to continue his ministry, accepted the position of executive officer. "He had every quality for philanthropic work" wrote one who knew him well; "clear insight, perfect sanity of judgment, supreme diligence and indomitable patience."

Under Brace's leadership the Children's Aid Society developed industrial schools, reading rooms, penny savings banks, newsboy lodging houses, night schools, summer camps, sanatoriums, children's shelters, special classes for children with disabilities, and dental clinics. The first newsboy lodging house was founded in 1854, and during the first year 408 boys used its services. Brace pioneered in placing homeless children in families settling in the West. In his last report to the society in 1889, Brace stated that since 1853 over 70,000 children had been transplanted from the slums to good homes and that through the lodging houses probably 200,000 had been helped to improve their condition. Rev. Charles Loring Brace, saver of children, died in Campofer, Switzerland, August 11, 1890.[13]

Training and Orienting the Board

As a program developer, you will help train and orient the board members. Orientation should include information about the needs assessment and the original vision of the group. Give a copy of the organization's constitution and by-laws to each member. Explain the purpose of the new organization and the roles that the board members and its officers will play. For example, all board members should know that the board of directors is the policy-making body of the organization with a legal duty to ensure that the organization's actions are consistent with its goals. Explain that members of the board give general direction and control and that they share collective responsibility for the fiscal and programmatic aspects of the organization's performance.

Board members should be told that boards typically fulfill the following six functions.

1. Maintaining general direction and control of the agency (policy development).
2. Directing short-term and long-term planning (program development).
3. Hiring competent administrative staff (personnel).
4. Facilitating access to necessary resources (finances).
5. Interpreting the organization to the community (public relations).
6. Evaluating operations (accountability).

The First Board Meeting

After the board is trained and oriented, members hold their first meeting to organize themselves to conduct business. One of the members of the original program development group should begin the first meeting and ask for nominations for president or chairperson of the board. The board selects one of its members to be the chair, usually by secret ballot. As soon as the chairperson is elected, the chair presides over the rest of the election process. Other officers such as a vice chair, treasurer, and secretary may be elected.[14]

Following this, the board decides if it will divide its work among committees or if the board will work as a committee of the whole. If the board decides to have a committee structure, the membership of these committees is decided. Usually each committee will select its own chairperson and decide how often it will meet.

The board members decide on the time and place of board meetings. Small, active boards tend to have monthly meetings. Larger boards may meet only quarterly to deal with major issues, while committees of board members work on organizational concerns between the quarterly board meetings.[15]

ESTABLISHING THE SOCIAL ORGANIZATION

After the board has organized itself, it is ready to get down to the business for which it was formed: establishing the new social organization's mission, vision, values, and goals. The board then develops a plan for the agency's structure, staffing, finances, and recruiting clients.

The Mission, Vision, Values, and Goals

The mission statement of the social organization describes the purpose of the organization, the reason it exists. The statement generally identifies its target population and the geographic area of operation. The statement should be short enough that staff, board, and volunteers can recite it from memory.[16] For example, the mission statement of the Pacific Institute for Community Organizations (PICO) is "to assist families build community organizations."[17] The mission of the National Training and Information Center (NTIC) is to "build grassroots leadership and strengthen neighborhoods through issue-based community organizing."[18]

The vision statement sets forth the expected future of the social organization. Your community should understand what is expected over the long term so they can focus on that desired outcome. Keep the vision statement as short as possible.[19] The vision statement of PICO is "Through effective community organization, to empower poor and moderate income families to participate effectively in our democratic system and to enable them to address the issues affecting their lives."[20]

The program's values or guiding principles spell out the ethical framework of how things get done. They tell your stakeholders what kind of organization you are. For example, the Pacific Institute for Community Organization states

Over the years the following beliefs have guided and shaped all our decisions and actions. PICO believes (1) people are precious. (2) Because they are precious, they deserve to live in a world that is just. (3) Justice is a product of the interaction of the spiritual and social dimensions of our lives. (4) Organizing is a tool to integrate these two pieces: the spiritual and social, and create a world of dignity and justice for all the families of our community.[21]

The goals describe the purposes for which the community established the organization, the intended outcomes of what you intend to do. Goals are usually long-term aims driven by the community's mission and vision. A goal statement would not necessarily describe your year to year objectives or program's activities but would set forth what will result from them. Be sure your goal/objective statements describe measurable outcomes. These outcome statements should refer specifically to those who will be affected, describe what these people are expected to do, under what conditions, and how well or to what extent. They should include a time factor.[22]

Once board members have a clear idea of the mission of the program, its vision, guiding values, and goals, they develop a plan for the agency's structure, staffing, finances, and client recruitment.

The Organizational Structure

There is a range of structural models from which you can choose for your social organization. The most common are the whole group, team, and hierarchical models.

Whole Group Model   The board may decide that the organization should be a loosely structured group in which all members have equal roles. This model is particularly useful for small organizations. The entire organization may operate as a single unit or consist of several subgroups. There may be no traditional supervision, leader, or coordinator; instead such roles may be rotated among some or all members of the group. The emphasis is on group decision-making.[23]

Leadership may be based on a partnership or collaborative model in which the ad hoc administrator facilitates the carrying out of tasks of the group. The administrator makes sure that everything necessary is available so that the group can get its business done. The administrator may assume facilitative roles, schedule meetings, make sure everyone has a chance to contribute and between meetings makes sure tasks are accomplished. Instead of commanding or controlling, the leader assists and pitches in to fill in gaps and supports the group and its goals.

Team Model   In a social organization structured according to the team model, the staff may be broken into subgroups by program or by major organizational functions.[24] Senior staff members coordinate the work of the various teams, making sure communication between them is effective, relationships are smooth, they have the resources to get their tasks accomplished, and problems between team members or at the interface between teams are resolved.

Hierarchical Model   Businesses and government organizations concerned with efficiency allow their organizations to become large to decrease overhead costs. As these organizations become larger, however, relationships between units and departments become more complex, need for communication among different groups increases, and coordination is more crucial. With increased size and complexity comes a need for more centralization, standardization, routinization, and control, resulting in hierarchical organization structures (see Figure 10.2). There is little need for social organizations to develop massive hierarchical organizational structures. Most social organizations are most effective when they are small and community based. If social organizations are part of a large organizational network, they operate best when dispersed into smaller units that can reflect and relate to the individual communities in which they reside, rather than to a superordinant centralized control center.

Deciding on the Best Model   How do board members decide on the best model? Think of the experience, age, and maturity of your members. At the beginning some members may need considerable direction, training, support. Smaller organizations may benefit from more intimate, personal, and collegial orientations.

Staffing the Social Organization

Community members often identify the quality of your program by the ability of your paid employees and volunteers.[25] The community looks at the staff and sees your social organization. It is important, therefore, for you to help the board take the time and energy to carefully consider staffing needs of the organization. It is more useful to work from the tasks to be performed and find the kind of people needed than to arbitrarily name a position and then assign responsibilities to people.

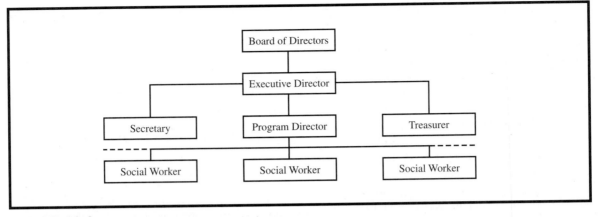

FIGURE 10.2 Organizational Chart for XYZ Social Agency

The Administrator Usually the first person the board hires is the executive director, the chief administrative officer of the organization. The administrator serves as long as the board has confidence that he or she is accomplishing the purposes for which he or she was hired. The executive implements board policy and guides the staff in formulating strategies designed to achieve organizational objectives. The executive draws on the energy, expertise and resources of the board members by involving them and keeping them informed.[26] Staff who report to the chief administrator generally should be hired and evaluated by the administrator, who should also determine their individual compensation within the overall compensation policy approved by the board.

Fair Employment Practices Equal employment practices are not only simple common sense; they are a responsibility that every organization owes to society as a whole. There are certain restrictions on your freedom to hire, promote, pay, and fire people under federal and state law and often under a city's human rights statutes. Call the agencies of your state and city responsible for human rights. They will be able to provide your group with appropriate material specifying your legal responsibilities. Use caution to protect the rights of applicants during all phases of hiring. Be careful not to place unjust or unsupportable demands on applicants. Ask for the knowledge, skills, abilities, and experiences that you are confident are necessary for effective job performance.[27]

The following should never be included as questions on applications, in resume reviews, or in interviews because they may result in illegal discrimination: birthplace, age, height and weight, race, gender, marital status, number and age of children, child care arrangements, weekend working capacity (unless part of regular work week), credit records, public assistance status, medical history, worker's compensation history, arrest and conviction records, military service record, disability, or foreign language proficiency if not required by the job.[28]

Valuing diversity or creating a pluralistic organization has increasingly become a focus of all types of employers. Many businesses, educational institutions, government agencies, and nonprofits have adopted statements similar to the following.

> We will not discriminate against any employee or applicant for employment because of race, color, creed, religion, national origin, ancestry, gender, sexual orientation, age, disability, marital status, or status with regard to public assistance. We take affirmative action to ensure that employment practices are free of such discrimination....We affirm the value of human diversity and seek to manage all aspects of our agency so that every individual has the opportunity to achieve his or her fullest potential.[29]

While the Americans with Disabilities Act applies to employers with 15 or more paid employees, its provisions reflect responsible treatment of people with disabilities, and some state and local laws may apply similar provisions to all organizations. Under ADA an employer must make reasonable accommodations to the known disability of an otherwise qualified employee or applicant, unless the employer can show that the accommodation will impose undue hardship.

For equal employment opportunity or affirmative action purposes, use an applicant register to document the pertinent ethnic and general information of all applicants. (You can get a sample applicant register from your Equal Employment Opportunity office.) Carefully document all aspects of your recruitment and hiring practices as a safeguard against allegations of discrimination. The dates and texts of ads and the publications in which the ads were placed should be recorded, and the hiring procedures should be outlined in writing.[30]

SAINT FRANCES XAVIER CABRINI

Born in Italy on July 15, 1850, Maria Cabrini studied at the Convent of the Sacred Heart, and between 1868 and 1872 she ministered to the poor and sick, taught in a public school, and took charge of a home for orphans. In 1880 she founded the Institute of the Missionary Sisters of the Sacred Heart of Jesus and became the mother general of this group of young women dedicating their lives to missions. In 1889, at the direction of Pope Leo XIII, Mother Cabrini continued her work among Italian immigrants in New York City and established an orphanage and school. Two years later, she founded Columbus Hospital. Gradually her activities expanded to other cities and other countries, resulting in the opening of schools, hospitals, and orphanages in Italy, France, Spain, England, and North and South America. Over 4,000 sisters were engaged in these services. Difficulties were always overcome by her faith, abilities, and courage. In recognition of her exceptional virtues, Mother Cabrini eventually was granted sainthood by the Catholic Church. As a naturalized citizen of the United States, Mother Cabrini became the first American saint.

Positions, Salary, and Benefits

The board should use the social organization's goals and objectives to determine the staffing pattern, salary scales, and benefits for the staff. You can be of assistance to the board as you help members accomplish the following.

1. Determine the skills needed for each task. Task functions or responsibilities should be clustered by skill areas such as administration, clerical support, counseling, education, lobbying, community relations, and fundraising.

2. Determine the length of time required for completing each task. How often must this activity be carried out? How much time will it require? Based on these skills, task, and time estimates, the board develops a list of the staff positions necessary to carry out the organization's program.

3. Develop task assignments for each position.

4. Think about various ways to obtain people to perform the tasks. There may be many possible options besides having full-time paid staff. Alternatives include part-time paid positions, temporary paid staff, paid consultants, unpaid staff (volunteers) including senior citizens, social work interns, and college and high school students.

5. Consider various staffing patterns to determine which is most workable for the organization.

Determine the salary ranges for each of the paid positions. Contact other nonprofit agencies with similar staff positions to find out their salaries. Develop salary ranges (e.g., $21,000–$25,000) rather than a specific salary ($23,000). This allows you to use some discretion when hiring staff so that you can pay each individual according to his or her relevant education and experience. The result should be a list of staff positions and task assignments that indicates the type of employees you need: full or part time, regular or temporary, paid or unpaid, professional or intern.

Job Descriptions

Job descriptions define staff positions and outline their tasks and the experience, education, and personality characteristics of the people needed to perform them. Job descriptions should be developed for each staff position, including volunteer and intern positions. Developing job descriptions forces your board to explain each position in objective, measurable terms. They help potential applicants to decide whether to apply and they are a means for recruiting, screening, and selecting staff. Job descriptions provide guidelines for job performance and employee evaluation.

Decide the primary responsibilities or major tasks that each employee must perform. Develop a statement of one to three sentences that answers the question:

What is the primary reason this position exists? Outline the specific tasks that are *essential* to the job. Give each major responsibility a distinct one-sentence statement. If there are other, secondary activities, list these also.

Decide the education and experience requirements for each position. What must a person know or what skills and abilities must he or she have in order to do those tasks? If the applicants don't have this particular knowledge or skill, will they still be able to do the job while they are acquiring the knowledge and skill?

SAMPLE JOB DESCRIPTION

Agency: Prairie Community Organization Network (PCON)

Job Title: Community Developer

Reports to: Executive Director

Supervises: Community Development Intern

Primary Responsibilities

1. Provides community development services to the Lawndale Community
2. Assists citizens in development of a Lawndale community-based grassroots organization including:

   Assists forming community development task force

   Assists task force conduct needs assessments

   Assists task force develop idea and mission statements

   Assists task force develop nonprofit corporation

   Assists task force develop, train, and organize board of directors
3. Acts as staff to the organization until board and staff are fully functioning
4. Assists board develop organizational structure
5. Assists board recruit and hire director and staff
6. Assists board obtain initial funding
7. Helps introduce new organization to business, political, educational, religious community in Lawndale
8. Provides orientation to director and staff to the board and Lawndale community

Other Activities

1. Serves as member of PCON staff development team
2. Assists in coordination and overall planning for PCON
3. Meets with PCON staff and reports on work in Lawndale community
4. Fills out financial reports, and helps prepare PCON budget
5. Gives input to other staff about Lawndale community project
6. Provides consultation to other staff
7. Provides supervision to community development interns

Skills and Knowledge

Ability to conduct needs assessments

Skill in developing program development team

Ability to assist team members form nonprofit corporation

Ability to form and train a board of directors

Skill in writing grant applications, contract with government, and fundraising

Ability to write job descriptions, recruit, and hire staff

Skill in providing consultation to staff and community members

Ability to relate to various segments of Lawndale community

Education

BA degree in social work, human services, community development or community organization required, MSW preferred with specialization in community organization or community development

Experience

At least 2 years experience in community organization, community development, and/or community planning, up to 1 year of which can be in community practice internship

Other

Ethnic sensitivity and compatibility with Lawndale Community

Desired but not required:

> Ability to speak Spanish
>
> Ethnic identification with Hispanic or Filipino culture
>
> Knowledge of Lawndale community
>
> Ethnic, women, handicapped, etc., welcome

Recruiting and Screening Candidates

Once the positions have been identified and preliminary job descriptions written, your board can begin deciding how to recruit people for paid and voluntary positions.[31] Think about the various means available to reach your target audience: ads in the local papers (daily, weekly, business, minority, suburban), notices in college, university, and technical school placement centers, and state unemployment offices. Include in your thinking public and private retraining centers, job clubs (where job seekers meet in support groups), and business and personal acquaintances via networking. You can also use employment agencies. If you know the agency or know people who have had continued success with them, you may be able to save yourself time and effort. But check out an agency's reputation carefully. Do as much as you can to acquaint the representative with your organization and the job. Sturgeon says, "We give a reputable employment agency an exclusive for a limited period of time (two to three weeks) to see if they were able to produce a match. If they did, fine; if not we did our own recruiting by means of ads and other postings."

Whether your board members do recruiting themselves or work with professionals, the next steps are pretty much the same: read applicants' resumes or employment applications, select the most likely persons for initial interviews, interview these applicants, and narrow your field down to two to five final candidates for a second interview. It reflects well on your organization if, as you weed out applicants, you send them a turn down letter. Its tough to receive one, but even tougher to never hear back at all.

In the personnel world, people are applicants until they have gone through the first screening; those who pass it become candidates. Candidates are different from applicants because any one of them could be hired. Each serious candidate should receive a packet of information about your organization that includes a summary of benefits, vacation policy, relo-

cation policy, and other relevant information. Add informative literature such as a copy of your organization's newsletter, the annual report, and any marketing material that describes your organization.

This is a "courtship" stage during which sloppy communications, neglecting to communicate with candidates for weeks at a time, giving misinformation, or not responding to their questions can lead to losing the person your organization needs. Ensure that whoever is in contact with them treats them with courtesy and care. Candidates are forming an impression of your organization at this time, and communication and interaction are important.

Gather together everyone who interviewed the candidates to make the final selection. Once you have the candidates ordered by preference, it is the time to check references. Try to speak to people who have supervised, been peers of, or worked for the person. Describe the key elements of your job. Ask open-ended questions about the candidate's ability to perform the skills you require. Be sure to cover any important areas about which you have doubts or insufficient or ambiguous information.

Your board or administrator is now ready to select the top person for the position. It is time to focus on your information and your instincts about each of the candidates. In some cases the top choice will be clear, but quite often it is not. Even if you know which candidate you want, remember, it's never over till it's over. Do not turn loose an acceptable runner-up candidate until you've received a firm acceptance from your first choice. Hiring an employee is a little like getting married. If you suddenly feel that what you are getting is not what you think, it is better to back off than to jump in and live for a long time with the consequences. Follow up on a successful offer. Be sure a sign-up and benefits orientation session is scheduled with the personnel or payroll person. Inform the unsuccessful final candidates.[32]

Finding the right person for a position requires objectivity, clarity of thought, application of energy, and steady nerves. A well-written and objective job description that sets forth the basic requirements for the job is essential for legal, ethical, and practical management reasons. Narrowing the field, selecting final interviewees, discussing salary expectations, handling competing offers, checking references, and handling various employment arrangements are important as your board moves toward offering the position to the right person.

SAINT ELIZABETH ANN SETON

Elizabeth Ann Bayley was born into an Episcopalian family in New York City on August 23, 1774, during the Revolutionary War. When she was 20 years old she married William Seton, a prominent banker and descendent of Lord Seton of England. Elizabeth Ann Seton was a very religious woman. Even though she traveled primarily in social circles, she devoted much of her time to the poor. In 1803 her husband's health began failing. After his death, she became involved in the Roman Catholic Church and became a member. Having little property, she opened a school in New York City to support herself and her five children, but the venture was unsuccessful. With the encouragement of Catholic Church officials, she and her three daughters moved to Baltimore, where Seton opened a boarding school for girls, the Paca Street School, the first Catholic elementary school in the United States. In 1809, however, she felt the calling to a religious vocation in the Church. Shortly thereafter, she took religious vows and, with four others, founded the Sisters of Charity, modeled after the Children of Charity founded by St. Vincent De Paul in France. The Sisters of Charity became the first Catholic religious community originating in the United States.

In that same year the sisters founded a school on a farm at Emmittsburg, Maryland, where six other women soon joined them. The sisters suffered much poverty and illness during the winter but in the spring received several boarding and day pupils and by June the school was flourishing. In 1814 they established the Orphan Asylum of Philadelphia, the nation's first Catholic child care institution. Seton established more than 20 communities of the Sisters of Charity, and many orphanages, free schools for the poor, boarding schools, and hospitals in the United States. She died in Emmittsburg in 1821. Canonized in 1975, Elizabeth Ann Seton was the first person born in the United States recognized as a saint by the Roman Catholic Church.

FINANCING THE AGENCY

The Budget

When your board has determined your goals, outlined your programs, considered funding sources, and planned your staffing pattern, you are ready to develop the budget.[33] While the agency's chief administrator ultimately has responsibility for the budget, it is very important to use the skills and experience of staff and board members throughout the process. Such participation can gain a broader perspective, greater knowledge, and stronger staff commitment for the organization. Final approval of the budget is the responsibility of the board of directors as a whole.

Developing the Budget   Begin developing the budget three to six months before the onset of the new fiscal year and get it approved by the beginning of the year. The budget should clearly establish what should happen in revenues and expenditures as a result of your service programs. Income includes *earned income* for which a service must be performed, such as ticket sales and fees for services, and *contributed revenues*, such as governmental or foundation grants and individuals' contributions, including equipment, other goods, and services that are donated. Expenditures include all of the costs of purchasing the services, space, and supplies necessary to operate the social agency.

Developing an Expense Budget   Because fledgling organizations will find it more difficult to project future expenses without financial records and past experience it is helpful to talk to administrators and review the budgets of programs similar to yours. An *expense* budget includes fixed and variable costs. *Fixed costs* including most salaries, insurance, and rent occur regardless of the level of activity or service. *Variable costs* such as postage, printing, and publication costs change directly with the level of use or activity. Telephone expenses are both fixed and variable. Monthly phone service charges are fixed, while the cost of long-distance calling varies depending on the number of calls you make.

Fixed costs are easier to determine than variable ones, although your board should try to anticipate changes such as rent increases and salary increases. Estimate variable costs as best you can. Include seasonal as well as average monthly costs. For instance, postage estimates should include the cost of postage used each month as well as the annual bulk mail permit fee and the cost of the several bulk-mailings that may be planned for the coming year.

Include salaries for each regular, paid staff person, health and life insurance, retirement plans, staff development costs, rent, utilities, telephone, janitorial services, purchased equipment, leased equipment, insurance (fire, automobile, theft, workers compensation, disability, bonding, general liability, and directors and officers liability), loan repayment, supplies, postage, subscriptions, services (consultants, bookkeeper, secretarial), printing, conferences, travel, advertising, licensing, membership fees, and petty cash.

Determining the Income Budget   A social organization rarely has total commitment for funding for an upcoming year at the time it begins budgeting, so it is necessary to estimate as accurately as possible income from those sources upon which you depend for funds. Among the sources of income to include or to generate are fees, contributions from individuals, income from special events, earnings on endowment investments, and anticipated grants.

Many nonprofits obtain a significant percentage of revenues from fees for services. If you intend to collect fees, determine what kind of fees and an appropriate fee structure. Determine direct costs necessary to provide the service, such as staff costs and overhead costs, including rent, supplies, phones, and other costs. Will you have a sliding fee schedule based on income? What do other providers charge? Estimate how many participants you will serve in each of your programs and calculate your anticipated fee income.

Your board members may have pledged to make contributions of a certain amount, or you may have gotten pledges from other individuals, groups, organizations, or businesses. Include in your income budget only amounts for which you have a firm pledge.

Estimate income generated from special events and benefits. Add expected earnings on endowment investments, if you have any. Estimate all the grants you anticipate receiving. Ask the grant sources you are most sure of to confirm their interest in the program, and include the amounts of their grants in the income budget.

Calculate the differences between your anticipated income minus your expenses. The amount left over is the figure you still need to raise. If this figure is a large portion of your budget, your board may have set unrealistically high income goals. You should consider either trimming back expenses or rethink what you will receive from undetermined sources of income. These sources may be individuals, groups, foundations, or corporations you have not yet approached or about whom you are not yet sure.

Calling on potential funders to share your vision and financial needs before you make a formal request from them could help you estimate more objectively the likelihood of obtaining income grants. Engage staff in contingency planning. Think through what you will do if revenues do not develop month to month as you have planned or if some unusual expense occurs.

Be prepared to outline prioritized spending decreases or increases from initial budget plans, depending on the progress you make with your funding sources. Your board can be of significant help in reflecting on the budget and in assisting the administrator and staff with fundraising ideas, with persons to contact, committing themselves to fundraising programs, or making contacts to try to meet your anticipated budget goals.

Accounting

All organizations need workable systems for recording what they do with their money, keeping track of where it comes from and where it goes. When the board sets up its organization, help them do everything possible to commandeer the services of a willing and able accountant to set up the organization's bookkeeping system, teach them or the administrator how to use it, and advise them about the most appropriate type of financial reporting for their organization.

After the board has the books set up with the help of an accountant, they will need a bookkeeper. You may be able to depend on the treasurer, who is usually a member of the board, to fulfill this role on an unpaid basis. Medium-size staffed organizations often rely on paid, specially trained secretaries to do the bookkeeping. Larger agencies sometimes hire part-time or full-time bookkeepers.

A good bookkeeping system provides the means for documenting, recording, summarizing, and reporting the financial transactions of your organization. It will tell where your revenues came from and where they have been spent, and it will assist you with budgeting and calculating fundraising needs. It will also help prevent misuses of funds, save money by identifying wasteful spending, and provide information to construct financial statements. Funders, government bodies, clients, and consumer groups will ask for this information, and the organization's board or administrator must have the means of providing it. The future of the program may depend on the quality of the financial information generated by your organization.

Obtaining Funding

One of the more difficult aspects of beginning a new program is obtaining funding. It needn't be, however. Joan Flanagan, a skilled fundraiser, says that people can "learn to raise money by doing it; they don't need any particular educational background, economic status, or writing skills. The only thing necessary to be a good fund raiser is the desire or will to raise money."[34] You can obtain funding in several ways. Your board may take out a loan, solicit contributions from interested people or businesses, or assess membership dues. Members may hold fundraising benefits or other events, or charge fees for service. If your board operates on a nonprofit basis, you may apply for a grant. Grants are available from private foundations or from the government. Your board may contract with the government.

Independent Solicitation   There are several advantages to approaching individuals for money. It is quick. Unlike asking for money from foundations or the government, if you can sell someone on your program, you obtain funding immediately. You may be able to enlist wealthy individuals in your cause. In addition to money, they may give you services, advice, other assistance or provide you with contacts. A potential drawback in asking individuals for money, however, is that, at times, money comes with "strings attached." It is one thing if the individual wants only recognition but quite another if the donor wants to dictate policy. You need to decide what you are willing to give up in return for the money.

In addition to asking a few wealthy individuals for contributions, you can also ask many less wealthy persons for money. This often requires a well-thought-out campaign. Professional fundraising organizations carry out these campaigns for a percentage of funds raised. Such fundraising can be very sophisticated, with slick brochures, telephone solicitations, and television advertisements.

Other sources of contributions are businesses and corporations. Businesses obtain tax write-offs for making charitable contributions and are sometimes willing to make cash donations to worthy causes, particularly if they can obtain some publicity in return. A business may get behind a worthy project, involving its employees in fundraising efforts and providing donations of material or support services. A grocery store, for example, may donate food, and a building supply company may donate lumber. Many business people are willing to serve on committees, give advice, or even donate services of staff to a worthy project.

Cooperative Solicitation   So many charitable organizations exist today that people become overwhelmed with requests for money. As a result, social agencies make fundraising more efficient, effective, and equitable by means of organized, cooperative solicitation. At the turn of the century, macro social workers organized "councils of social agencies" such as United Way and United Charities. Organizations participating in United Way are released from the burden of spending their own staff time on fundraising and can devote their energy to providing services. More money is raised collectively than if agencies competed with one another.

However, because United Way usually does not fund pilot projects or new, untested programs, they tend to include only a limited number of new programs each year, often those with an established track record. In addition, most United Way organizations have commitments to certain priorities or needs. If your agency does not meet these priorities, you may have difficulty obtaining this funding. Many United Way organizations do not guarantee funding from year to year, nor do they guarantee a given amount of funding. If a program cannot show its effectiveness or is inefficient, its funding may be reduced or eliminated entirely.

Membership Dues   Membership dues are an important part of an organization or project. Churches, YMCA, YWCA, Boy Scouts, Girl Scouts, as well as many neighborhood associations depend primarily on membership dues and member contributions. Dues are not only a source of funds, but a way of developing commitment from your community. As you engage in a membership drive, your members will build support for the program. From your constituency, you can involve people on the board. When community members join and pay membership dues, they "own shares" in the project and have a stake in its outcome.

You can use membership as a gauge of community support. A demographic assessment of membership lists can tell you where your primary support and involvement is coming from, where it is weakest or nonexistent, and where you need to improve community relationships. By means of regular meetings with your members, social activities, and using members as volunteers, you build community spirit, cooperation, and cohesion. Members of your social organization can become involved in fundraising efforts such as organizing benefits.

Fundraising Benefits   Many organizations depend on fundraisers or benefits. Dinners, entertainment, dances, fairs, cook-outs, raffles, auctions, theater productions, walk-a-thons, telethons, car washes, and yard sales are all ways that social organizations make money for worthy projects. The Mennonite Central Committee raises most of its budget by means of an annual auction. The American Cancer Society and the Heart Association sponsor walk-a-thons. Lutheran Social Services sponsors boutiques and dinner dances. The Jerry Lewis Annual Telethon for Muscular Dystrophy is a national event, and the Girl Scouts are known for their annual cookie sales.

A number of side benefits attend such fundraisers. You obtain publicity, develop community awareness, and can engage in community education about your programs. Even the wider community becomes mobilized and involved in the project. Many times people not connected directly with the organization will help out with a benefit. The benefit provides opportunity for the project staff, membership, and board to provide a service for the community. People who hate meetings will often show up at a benefit where they can meet one another, engage in social activities, and develop relationships.

Benefits, however, are time consuming and involve a lot of hard, detailed work. They require skill in organization and often divert staff time to the benefit. There are people, however, who are good at these kinds of projects and who enjoy organizing them. If you are lucky enough to have some of these people on your board or as members, they can make a real contribution to your organization.

Fees for Service   Encourage your board to consider charging a fee for the services you provide. Fees can

be a significant source of funding. Counseling agencies typically charge a fee to help bear the cost of the service. Group work agencies charge fees, as do day care services, alcohol and drug treatment programs, and recovery programs. Often fees are charged on a sliding scale according to a person's ability to pay.

Fees are also important for psychological reasons. People who pay a fee are more likely to respect the service and take it seriously. If a person is paying a reasonable fee, he or she will not tend to miss sessions and will tend to be more engaged in treatment than if the service is free. If your members pay a fee, they will expect quality service from your organization and will hold the staff accountable.

Contracting   Governmental agencies such as departments of social services, mental health, and probation often contract with nonprofit agencies rather than administer their own programs. Departments of social services, for example, often contract with independent foster homes, small group homes, institutions, and counseling agencies. In California, regional centers for people with developmental disabilities contract with a wide variety of service providers called vendors. Regional centers contract with infant stimulation programs, speech therapists, day programs for adults, workshops, respite care programs, recreational programs, treatment centers, small family homes, group homes, and intermediate care facilities. A program that provides a service for a county or state agency must meet county or state licensing requirements, fulfill the specific requirements of the funding agency, and accept the fees that are part of the contract.

Private Foundation Grants   A private foundation is an organization set up as a charitable trust, and therefore is not taxable. Foundations are managed by their own trustees or directors, and have a principal fund to maintain or aid religious, charitable, scientific, literary, or educational activities. Many wealthy individuals use trusts as a way of reducing their taxable income as well as for worthwhile philanthropic purposes. College scholarships, for example, are educational grants, many of which are administered by a trust. Credit for the first modern foundation goes to Margaret Olivia Slocum Sage, who established the Russell Sage Foundation in 1907.[35] The Russell Sage

Foundation was of particular importance to the growth and development of the social work profession. In 1917, the Sage Foundation published the pioneering textbook on social casework, *Social Diagnosis,* by Mary Richmond, head of the Charity Organization Department of New York. They also published the first ten volumes of the Social Work Yearbook and many important books in social work.

In 1990, foundations awarded more than 12,000 grants to social welfare, representing more than 21% of the giving and constituting the second-largest group of recipients following education. While more than 24,000 grant-making foundations exist today, however, they generally do not fund minority-controlled social services in any significant way, although they do fund a number of programs that serve people of color. This is an area in which macro social workers could provide significant assistance.[36]

There are a number of kinds of foundations, each of which identifies specific purposes for which the grant money can be used. Among these are general purpose, family, community, corporate, special purpose, and operating foundations.

General Purpose Foundations   General purpose foundations have broad areas of interest, often national in scope. Often they are established by wealthy individuals and have their own staff who administer the foundation funds and a board that makes funding decisions. These foundations usually carry the name of the founder, for example, the Carnegie Foundation, Rockefeller Foundation, Kresge Foundation, Ford Foundation, R. W. Johnson Foundation, W. K. Kellogg Foundation, and Alfred P. Sloan Foundation.[37] While general purpose foundations are usually large and heavily funded, there is usually heavy competition for funds from these foundations

Family Foundations   While a general purpose foundation is one whose original founders have died, a family foundation is one still controlled by the family members. Because the family members make funding decisions, people who have a personal contact or relationship with a member of the family have the best entree to these funds.

Company Foundations   A corporate foundation usually gives its funds to organizations that provide some benefit to the company's interests, for example, community projects where the corporation does business, special interests of employees, or areas of corporate concern. The Crown Zellerbach Foundation in San Francisco provides funding for many local San Francisco social service organizations. Company foundations often offer support by donating equipment and supplies, loaning executives, providing conferences and meeting facilities, and extending in-kind services such as printing and management consulting.

Community Foundations   A community foundation, sometimes called a community trust, charitable trust, or community fund, is a vehicle for administering a number of separate charitable and combined funds in a given geographic area. Community foundations can be found in most major cities and are often named for the locality, such as the San Francisco Foundation. Community foundations are actually public charities supported by the contributions of a large number of individuals who pool their resources for the common good. These foundations may receive large gifts as well as small gifts from people who are charitably inclined but do not have large amounts of money. Donors can designate the organization they wish to fund, designate a type of service or geographic area, or leave an unrestricted gift. An unrestricted gift gives a community foundation much more leeway to respond to emerging community issues. A community foundation must by law and by spirit continually attract new donors to maintain its public charity status. Thus it is not unusual to see community foundations advertise for donors.

Macro social workers assist community members to approach wealthy and not so wealthy people to develop a community foundation that can enrich and enliven the community, equalize resources, improve neighborhoods, develop scholarship endowments for youth, assist minority businesses, and develop group services or community development corporations.

Special Purpose Foundations   Special purpose foundations assist programs within a single field or only a few fields of interest. Over the past decade the percentage of special-purpose grant dollars has increased steadily. Children and youth continue to be the single largest special beneficiary of foundation grant dollars.[38] A number of special purpose foundations, however, have evolved within the last decade to serve women, homeless, and people with AIDS.

Social Justice Foundations   A network of foundations that give to social justice and advocacy has significantly enhanced social reform. The overwhelming majority of these social justice foundations are family and special-interest foundations concerned with systems of change. The Arca Foundation supports a wide variety of organizations struggling for social and economic justice. The Compton Foundation has as one of its program priorities social justice, including the provision of adequate social services at the local level, with a particular interest in programs directed at youth.[39]

Operating Foundations   An operating foundation is dedicated to only one project, organization, or program. An organization may set up its own private foundation, which then solicits money for that organization or program. Many universities and hospitals use operating foundations. Fresno Pacific Foundation, for example, solicits funds and disburses them for scholarships, capital improvements, and other needs of Fresno Pacific University. The Bulldog Foundation supports the football team of California State University, Fresno.

Funding Collaborations   A trend in foundation giving is funding collaborations, partnerships between various foundations. For example, community-based organizations, businesses, universities, and public schools may establish a collaborative foundation to help low-income students gain access to college. The Pew Charitable Trusts, John D. and Catherine T. MacArthur Foundation, and Rockefeller Foundation joined to establish the Energy Foundation. The Ford Foundation established a national initiative in 1989 that allocates funds to community foundations to assess the demographic changes occurring in areas that the community foundations serve to determine how the change may affect their programs. Funders often work together to donate to a particular agency project, with each funder giving a specific amount that will help meet the budgetary need.[40]

Government Grants   Government organizations or agencies often have funds available for pilot projects, start-up grants, research grants, or ongoing funding grants. Sometimes government agencies want to experiment with new and innovative approaches and will ask for proposals for such projects. The National Institutes for Mental Health (NIMH), for example, often provides funding for pilot projects in the field of mental health. At other times, governmental agencies may be established to assist small, struggling organizations or programs. The National Endowment for the Arts, for example, was specifically established to fund artists and to underwrite theater productions, writing, and music projects that would otherwise not be produced.

Today government agencies fund many social organizations by contracting or by means of grants. The Area Agency on Aging, for example, receives federal money to distribute to local agencies for provision of services to the elderly. In this way, local communities have input on the specific needs and can better allocate and provide services.

How to Obtain a Grant

It is not easy to secure a foundation grant. There are always more applicants than grant awards. For instance, according to the *Annual Register of Grant Support* in 1993, the Ford Foundation received 30,000 proposals but funded only about 2,000. The Barbara Bush Foundation for Family Literacy typically receives 600–700 applications annually but funds only 10 to 20 projects each year.[41]

There are two different approaches to obtaining money from foundations or from government funding agencies. The first is a reactive approach; the second is a proactive approach. If you wait until grant announcements come to you and then apply, you are using a reactive approach. This approach is most common with government grants. Using the proactive approach means actively searching for potential funding sources. Many boards use both reactive and proactive approaches to seeking grants.

Find a foundation or governmental grant that supports the mission of your program. A number of sources of information can help you choose the right foundation. The Foundation Center, for example, is a national organization that has been established by foundations to provide a single authoritative source of information on foundation and corporate giving. It provides annually updated directories and guides and other publications covering grants and nonprofit funding. A bibliography of foundation resources is found in the Additional Readings section at the end of this chapter.

If you are interested in a particular kind of government funding, you can get on the agency mailing list or review the *Federal Register,* a daily publication that provides information on federal government legislation and guidelines for new and revised grants. Most large public libraries subscribe to the *Federal Register.* You can also obtain the *Catalog of Federal Domestic Assistance,* which provides basic information on federal resources, including a profile of each program, eligibility, deadlines, funding levels, and telephone numbers of places to contact.

Idea Statements   When you apply for funding to a private foundation, you must write an idea statement. An idea statement gets you in the door of the foundation. An idea statement is two to four pages long and tells the foundation what you want to do, how you intend to do it, and how much it will cost. An idea statement usually has the following components:

A summary or abstract of the entire proposal

An introduction to the idea statement

A need or problem statement

Goals of the project

Objectives (if they are different from goals)

The method by which you will accomplish the goals

The evaluation method you will use

A budget summary

Make sure that your idea statement is neatly typed and is in the best writing style you can muster. Send it with a cover letter to the foundation you have chosen. If interested, the foundation will request a meeting, ask for further information, or ask for a full grant proposal.

Requests for Proposals   Government agencies have a standardized grant process called a request for proposals (RFP). An RFP is an invitation for organizations to provide a proposal on a specific project, usually distributed through state or county agencies that have the responsibility to administer grants at the local level. Sometimes RFPs are announced in newspapers. Figure 10.3 shows an RFP distributed by the Shasta County Department of Public Health and received by e-mail from the Association of Community Organization and Social Administration (ACOSA), one of the major macro social work organizations.

If your organization is interested in applying for a government grant, it should respond to the RFP announcement and obtain application forms or documents. There may be a meeting for all applicants at which grant administrators provide specific information, distribute forms, and answer questions. Often, only applicants who attend the information session are permitted to apply for the grant.

Writing a Grant Proposal   When applying for a grant, most likely your organization will be asked to submit a formal proposal. Usually, foundations supply you with an outline of the kinds of information they require and which you use as a guide to write your proposal. One of the most important components of a proposal is the budget, which is an indication of the board's planning and management skills. The funds your program requires must be projected clearly so that the organization's needs can be understood and accepted by potential funders.[42] Government agencies often choose the proposal that offers the best program ideas at the least cost. Several sources on how to write grant proposals are listed in the Additional Reading section at the end of the chapter.

Carrying Out the Project   Once you receive a grant, you must keep records and statistics on services provided, clientele, staff service hours, and other items. As your organization monitors its effectiveness, you will be able to pinpoint what it needs to improve, where it needs to grow, and areas where it is functioning well. This information is invaluable in convincing funding agencies, foundations, constituents, members, and others who support your organization that their money has been well spent and that your program deserves continued funding. Agencies that are unable to show they are effective in carrying out their goals, that cannot account for meeting needs or making an impact in the arena of their service provision, cannot expect to receive ongoing support. Your board will need to evaluate the project at the end of the grant period. (The process of performing program evaluations is found in Chapter 11.)

FINDING CLIENTS

The best source of clientele for your social organization or its programs is referrals from other agencies in your area. Most social agencies welcome having additional resources and are interested in knowing more about your services. One way to get the word

Overview

The Health Improvement Partnership is a community collaborative engaged in long-term community health planning, using a primary prevention approach. The partnership uses a four-phase process: Assessment, Planning, Implementation, and Evaluation. As part of the implementation phase, four community groups are being funded to conduct a variety of activities in neighborhoods and small rural communities. Several of the groups have a neighborhood development/community organization component to their activities. We are seeking project proposals to provide basic training in Community Organizing/Community Development to all four groups.

Requirements

Each project proposal must contain the following:

1. A clear budget (and a brief but detailed budget justification narrative).
2. Two consecutive full-day trainings in Redding to be conducted before April 14, 2000.
3. A plan for ongoing consultation with funded community groups through December 2000.
4. At least two references from previously conducted trainings.
5. Proposals must be received by 5:00 p.m. on Tuesday March 7, 2000,
   and should be no more than four (4) single-spaced pages in length.

Priorities

Priority will be given to project plans that:

1. Have a clear training outline that is consistent with focus of the Community Grants Program and the Workplans of the funded community groups (see attached).
• Have clear outcome measures for participants
• Demonstrate experience in Community Development/Organizing training.
• Demonstrate experience in Community Development/Organizing in communities demographically/geographically similar to Shasta County.
• Use funds efficiently.

Attachments

1. A description of the "Project Focus" of the Community Grants Program, which formed the basis for the proposals submitted by the community groups.
2. A copy of the Workplan submitted by each community group, and accepted by the Health Improvement Partnership.

Please mail or deliver project proposals to:
Patrick Moriarty, Coordinator
c/o Shasta County Department of Public Health
2650 Breslauer Way
Redding, CA 96001
Shasta County Department of Public Health functions as the Fiscal Agent for the Health Improvement Partnership and will also function as Fiscal Agent for the purpose of this proposal.

FIGURE 10.3 A Request for Proposal

out about your new program is by networking. Join the local council of social agencies or other social services network in your area. Attend NASW meetings. Go to workshops and training programs where other professionals will be present. Visit agencies that will be the most likely referral sources. When you network or visit, carry a bunch of your flyers or brochures, and hand them out to people as you tell about your new program. Your brochures should be clear and specific about your services, the kinds of clients you accept, fees, and geographic boundaries or other limitations of your service. There is nothing like face-to-face contact to spread the word about your program.

Television and radio spots are also helpful and often can be obtained free in the form of a community service announcement. Have an open house to announce the opening of your program to community leaders, community agencies, and referral sources. This can be a gala affair with refreshments, a short presentation, and introductions of board members and those who have been instrumental in getting the program established. Make sure that you maintain positive relationships with all the members of the community and that everyone understands the services you are providing.

CONCLUSION

Program development is a natural outcome of macro social work change. A macro social work program developer helps the community form a program development group and perform a needs assessment. You work with your group to establish the corporation, assist the group to recruit and train the board, and work with the board to develop the organization. You assist the board to develop a statement of the organization's mission, vision, values, and goals. You also assist with deciding on an organizational structure, and with recruiting the staff of the organization.

You help set up the budget and accounting procedures, obtain funding, apply for grants, and find clients for the services of the organization. You and your program development group and the board of directors may feel proud that the lengthy process that began with a needs assessment has resulted in the development of a new social organization to help the members of your community.

KEY CONCEPTS

normative needs

demand needs

needs assessment

social indicators approach

rates under treatment

focused interviews

key informant

focus groups

community forum

surveys

board of directors

for-profit organization

not-for-profit organization

incorporation

articles of incorporation

constitution

by-laws

mission statement

independent solicitation

cooperative solicitation

membership dues

fundraising benefits

fees for service

foundation

operating foundation

community foundation

general purpose foundation

family foundation

corporate foundation

special-interest foundation

social justice foundation

government grant

idea statement

request for proposal

grant proposal

QUESTIONS FOR DISCUSSION

1. What changes in purpose, structure, and roles do you think may be required of a community planning group as it shifts to develop a community program?
2. You are thinking of setting up a small group home for persons who have mental illness problems. Discuss the benefits and disadvantages of being a profit-making organization and a not-for-profit organization and make a decision about which way is best for your program.
3. Social agencies, businesses, as well as your college or university more than likely have articles of incorporation, constitutions, by-laws, and mission statements. Collect as many of these as you can. Compare the mission statements. What are their common characteristics? What do they tell you about an organization? Do they leave out anything you think is important? How could you improve them?

4. Compare the articles of incorporation, by-laws, and constitutions that you have collected. What are the similarities and differences?

5. Obtain an organizational chart from your college or university. Examine the staffing patterns. Is the organization hierarchically structured? How many organizational layers are there? Does it have a flat structure in which decision-making is dispersed, or is it a thin vertical structure in which decision-making is concentrated at the top? Would you characterize the organization as simple or complex? Would you recommend any of these structures for a social organization?

EXERCISE 10.1

Developing a Mission Statement

You are a macro social worker with an inner-city task force on community development. The task force is particularly concerned about a number of problems that center on inner-city youth. These problems include dropouts, gangs, drug abuse, and crime. The lives of many inner-city youth are being wasted; they have few resources and opportunities. Recently, a young boy named Roy, one of the youth in your neighborhood, was killed in a gang fight. The task force has named a community project after Roy, calling it Reclaiming Our Youth (ROY). This innovative pilot program will include drug rehabilitation, counseling, group work, and job training.

Form subgroups of six to seven persons. Decide on a chairperson and a recorder. Develop a mission statement for the ROY program. After your task group has finished, share your statement with the other groups.

1. How did the mission statements differ?

2. How were they the same?

3. How could they be improved?

EXERCISE 10.2

Developing an Idea Statement

Your program development task force has decided that the ROY program will apply for a funding grant. In your community, there are about 300 school dropouts, at least 50 of whom are runaway youth. In addition to its initial ideas, the task force is also considering providing medical services, job finding, shel-ter, and reunification services. Reunification helps families become reunited after children have been removed and placed in foster homes.

You are also interested in working with law enforcement to prevent sexual exploitation of youth. Your program would provide youth with financial assistance, alternative education to prevent dropping out of high school, and legal services by which youth can become emancipated from their families of origin and live independently or in group settings.

Form groups of six or seven persons. These should be different groups than those in Exercise 10.1. Choose one of the program ideas mentioned above and develop an idea statement that could be used for a grant proposal. The idea statement should be no longer than four pages and follow the outline presented in this chapter.

Form into several groups, each one having an equal representation of members from the groups that wrote idea statements.

Each group plays the role of a Community Foundation Allocation Committee. Your task is to review the idea statements and rank them. First decide on the criteria that your allocation committee will use. Criteria may include soundness of the idea, cost effectiveness, potential community impact, capability of implementation, long-range benefits, or others. Review each of the idea statements and rank them in order according to your funding criteria.

After your allocation committee has ranked the idea statements, share your ranking with the class. Discuss the rankings and the criteria committees used.

1. Why did you decide on one idea statement rather than another?

2. Spend time discussing what you learned about the process. What constitutes a successful idea statement?

3. What did you discover about writing a good idea statement?

EXERCISE 10.3

Constituting the Board of the ROY Program

The Community Foundation Allocation Committee has accepted the idea statement submitted by the program development task force and has asked for a full proposal. If the proposal is accepted for funding, the task force must become incorporated as a non-profit organization and form a board of directors that can accept funds and operate the program. The new board would consist of 11 people. Five new members need to be selected. Existing task force members have approached several people. Each has exhibited initial interest. You will form yourselves into the Nominating Committee of the ROY board. The Nominating Committee plus the program development consultant consists of the following:

1. Joe Smith is a 43-year-old community resident who is unemployed because of a work-related injury. He has been a resident of the neighborhood for over 20 years and considers working in the community one of his most important priorities.

2. Sarah Rosenberg, 24, a social work graduate student in macro social work, has been assigned to do her second-year field internship with the ROY program.

3. Versie Fillmore, 55, is a minister of the local AME church. Rev. Fillmore, a charismatic leader, is very outspoken about the need for more programs for youth. She has attempted on her own to develop youth programs at the church and sees the ROY program as an important component to help young people lift themselves from poverty and get a new start in life.

4. Harry Whitmore, 67, the owner and operator of the Western Appliance Shop, is more conservative than some of the other board members and his interests come from his concern that the youth need to be kept busy and off the streets. He reflects the interests of the business community.

5. John Dokes, 35, is an insurance salesperson. As part of the United Way drive, he has been assigned by his boss, Leonard Moss, to assist on the board of the ROY program. John lives in a middle-class suburb about 5 miles from the ROY neighborhood. He is relatively new to the area and unfamiliar with social programs or with the youth culture and the neighborhood. He sees his role as bringing some business expertise to the program.

6. Ruth Dumore, 45, is the president of the St. James Neighborhood Association and represents the homeowners in the community. She is concerned about property values and the general deterioration of the neighborhood. But she also seems to have genuine concern for developing a program for youth.

7. Bill Hosokawa, 35, is the macro social work program developer who has worked with the task force. He acts in the role of consultant only and does not participate in the actual decision-making. He offers advice, observes the process, and helps the members arrive at a decision, but he does not influence the actual outcome. This will be his last role in helping the task force, since he is being assigned to another project.

1. Harriet Garcia is a 33-year-old math teacher at the local middle school.

2. Cheryl Lau is a 45-year-old social worker from the local mental health clinic.

3. Joe Sullivan, 40, is co-owner with his wife Jane of a neighborhood "mom and pop" convenience store, a favorite hangout of local youth. The Sullivans live in a residential neighborhood about 3 miles from the community.

4. Jane Sullivan, 38, is co-owner with her husband Joe of the convenience store. In addition to her work at the store, Jane is the primary caregiver for their 5-year-old daughter.

5. Hector Mendez is a 22-year-old youth leader in the local Catholic church and a former gang member.

6. Saul Adelman is a 47-year-old college professor at the State University School of Social Work.

7. Isaiah Washington, 67, is a retired maintenance worker from the local high school. A member of the board of a local AME church, he is a neighborhood resident of 30 years. He has three grown children, one of whom continues to live in the neighborhood.

8. June Southerland, 45, is a neighborhood resident and member of the St. James Neighborhood Association.

9. Ruben Kinsley, a 35-year-old bus driver, grew up in Watts and understands problems of teenagers. He has expressed interest in working with a group of youths.

10. George Allison, 38, is a city planner with ties to the mayor's office.

11. Harold Bennett, 47, owns an apartment complex in the neighborhood. He is president of the local business association and a neighborhood resident.

The instructor divides the class into groups of six or seven members each. Each group will simulate the

ROY Nomination Committee. The instructor will assign each member a role and will give specific individual instructions to each member about the role he or she is to play.

Task force members will decide how to organize themselves, develop criteria for selecting the members to be invited, and make their selection. The student assigned the role of Bill Hosokawa is to assist the task force in reaching a consensus.

The instructor may ask the task force to continue to meet outside of class if there is not enough time to process the exercise during class. However, each task force should at least begin in class, and the instructor should circulate among the groups to ensure that they are on track and carrying out the assignment.

After the task force groups have made their selections, the class reassembles. Each task force lists its selections on newsprint or a board so that all can observe. The instructor leads a discussion of the exercise by asking the following questions.

1. How did the group organize itself?
2. What criteria did the task forces use to decide?
3. How did each task force arrive at a decision: consensus, majority vote, or other decision rules?
4. What conflicts emerged?
5. How were the conflicts resolved?
6. Was each group satisfied with the outcome?
7. How successful do you think that the board configuration will be in helping the ROY program succeed?

ADVANCED EXERCISE 10.4

Board Committee Practice

The class will constitute itself as the board of the ROY program. The instructor is the board chair. The board divides itself into committees of roughly five students each. One committee will develop a fiscal plan for the ROY program. The second will compose job descriptions. The third will develop a plan for staff recruitment, and the fourth will compose an application form. Additional committees can duplicate these assignments. Each committee reports its findings to the board at its next regularly scheduled meeting.

Developing a Fiscal Plan

The board of the ROY program obtained a start-up grant of $85,000 for the first year of operation. This will cover the salaries of an executive director at $35,000, a social worker at $25,900, and a secretary/receptionist at $18,000, plus $7,000 for part-time maintenance services. The board has been able to obtain an old house owned by a church as the matching share donated by the board. However, repairs need to be made to the roof and plumbing, totaling $8,000, and office furnishings need to be obtained. In addition, utilities and supplies will need to be paid for, as well as additional staff positions to operate the halfway house. The estimated total expenses to get through the first year of operation will exceed $45,000.

You have been selected as a member of the fiscal committee of the board. The board chairperson has charged your committee to come up with a plan for raising the additional $45,000 needed for the first year of operation and to devise a plan for the second-year budget, which is estimated to be $150,000.

You know that there are a number of sources of funding available to you. For example, you may charge a fee for service, develop a campaign for direct solicitation, charge membership dues, put on benefits, or become a vendor for the Department of Social Services or Probation—that is, you could contract with these departments to provide services for them. You may also consider other avenues, such as getting donations. You have thought of applying for government grants, but that is not possible this year.

The board chairperson has asked the fiscal committee to contact at least one or more government agencies that might contract with your social organization for your group to be one of its service providers. The goal to find out what is involved in becoming a vendor or a contract agency, the amount of money contracts generate, and the process for qualifying to be a contract agency or vendor.

The chair has also asked you to contact at least two agencies who use fees, solicitation, membership dues, benefits, or donations in order to obtain information about the feasibility and practicality of these methods. You are to explore what is involved in these fundraising ventures and the amount of money these sources can develop.

Once information is obtained, develop a list of the most feasible funding sources, prioritize the list based on interviews with the various social agencies, and recommend a plan for fundraising. The board is expecting the report of the fiscal committee at its next full meeting.

Writing a Job Description

The board of the ROY program wants to develop a generic job application form that can be used for all staff positions. The board is aware that there are legally permissible questions that can be asked and questions that are not legally permissible. One of the board members has mentioned, for example, that it is not legally permissible to ask a person's race or to ask for a photo. The board as a whole, therefore, wants to develop a form that gives the personnel committee enough information so that job applicants can be screened appropriately, but that also falls within legal boundaries.

The board has asked you to be a member of the job application committee. The board chair has asked your committee to:

1 brainstorm about the various tasks and duties required to develop the job application and organize yourselves for your task.

2. obtain legal information from your State Fair Employment and Housing Agency or the public library about what is or is not permissible to ask on job applications:

Obtain job applications from at least six social agencies for ideas. Develop a job application that is legally acceptable and that provides enough information to help the board in making employee selections. Report the committee's findings to the board at its next meeting, and submit the proposed job application for approval, along with the six sample job applications that your committee has collected.

Writing a Position Description

The first staff person the ROY board of directors needs to hire is an executive director. The board knows that the executive must have experience in operating a small social service agency. They would also like someone who has experience in youth work, drug rehabilitation, and operating a halfway house. They would prefer a social worker, but are not sure whether other occupational categories should be considered. In addition, budgeting, program development, and program evaluation will be key operations if the ROY program will continue past its first year.

You have been selected as a member of the personnel selection committee. The task of the committee is to write a job description for the position of executive director, including the duties and tasks that the executive director would perform in operating the ROY program, and the education, experience, specific job skills, and personal qualities the executive director must have in order to perform those duties and tasks.

The committee's first task is to decide how to organize yourselves and how to go about writing a job description. The chair suggests that you:

1. Brainstorm about the various tasks and duties required to develop the job description.

2. Collect six job descriptions of executive director positions from other small social agencies to explore what kinds of education, experience, and job skills they normally look for, and the amount of money they pay. You might also find it helpful to interview an administrator about the kinds of tasks the position entails and the education, skills, and experience that are necessary.

3. Using the example in the textbook, write the job description for the position of executive director.

Present your job description at the next board meeting, along with examples from the agencies you contacted.

Recruiting Staff

The board will be faced with hiring several staff members in the next month. A plan for recruiting staff and a process for staff selection must be developed. You are a member of the recruitment and selection committee. You know that there are a number of ways of recruiting staff. Among these are job postings, obtaining referrals, college recruiting programs, holding job fairs, holding open houses, advertising in newspapers and professional journals, listing the job opening with the County Employment Office, or using private employment agencies.

Because the board does not want to waste time, the chair has asked your committee to visit at least three social agencies. Find out the methods they have used to recruit staff, discuss the cost of recruitment, and ask their recommendations as to the most effective way to recruit BA-level social workers, MSW-level social workers, supervisors, an executive director, and office personnel. In addition, the board has asked that you contact the County Employment Office and private employment agencies for information about their services and costs.

After gathering this information, you are to write up your findings and provide a prioritized listing of recruiting methods, evaluating the pros and cons of each method. Report your findings to the board at its next meeting.

ADVANCED EXERCISE 10.5

Assessing a Program Development Process

This exercise will help you assess a program development process. Read the following newspaper article and then answer the questions that follow.

Project Aims to Turn Homeless Into Producers

In 1998, John Williams, Executive Director of the Plains County Economic Opportunity Commission, decided to help break the cycle of criminal recidivism so prevalent in his community. Aware that about 80% of prison parolees are Hispanics or African Americans needing job training, education, and a residence to give them a start in a tight job market, Williams applied to the U.S. Department of Health and Human Services for an 18-month pilot project to set up a Center for Homeless Parolees. According to Williams, "Parolees aren't able to cope with the outside. Sometimes they fly off the handle and lose their jobs if an employer says something negative. The next thing you know, they are back in the joint. Or they receive a few checks and get dirty and go back on drugs."

EOC came up with $40,000 in their own funds and about $510,485 in bank financing to buy and rehabilitate a 25-bed residence on N. Wayne Street. Based on this funding, the U.S. Department of Health and Human Services awarded the EOC $290,000, the first time it has funded this kind of program. The State Department of Corrections also approved $292,000 in funds for the residential program that will be operated by the Sobriety House, a substance abuse treatment center.

The residence center will offer crisis intervention, shelter, food, health care, counseling, career development, legal aid, recreation, and transportation and referral services. Williams said the EOC expects to find permanent jobs each year for 100 people, surpassing the 65 people required by the contract.

Form into groups of five or six members. Using only the information in this article, apply the principles of program development you have learned in this chapter. Critique the process by which this program was developed.

1. What are its strengths? What are its weaknesses?
2. How closely did Williams follow the process recommended in this chapter? What components were followed? What components were left out?
3. Assess the sequence of the development process. What was done first, second, third? What sequence would you recommend?
4. Assuming the funding period is three years, would you expect this program to be successful during the initial funding period?
5. What do you think will happen once the program funding ends?
6. On what basis do you think Williams will decide whether the program has been successful? How would you assess the program's effectiveness?

Report back to the whole class and, with the help of your instructor, draw some conclusions about the program development process.

ADDITIONAL READING

History

Jane Addams. *Twenty Years at Hull House.* New York: Macmillan, 1910.
———. *The Second Twenty Years at Hull House.* New York: Macmillan, 1930.
F. A. Davis. *Spearheads for Reform: The Social Settlements and the Progressive Movement: 1890–1914.* New York: Oxford University Press, 1967.

Getting Started

Joan Flanagan. *The Successful Volunteer Organization: Getting Started, and Getting Results in Nonprofit, Charities, Grassroots, and Community Groups.* Chicago: Contemporary Books, 1984.
James L. Heskett, W. Earl Sasser, Jr., and Christopher W. L. Hart. *Service Breakthroughs: Changing the Rules of the Game.* New York: Freedom Press, 1990.
Jonathan D Crane, ed. *Social Programs That Work.* New York: Russell Sage Foundation, 1998.

Working With Boards and Staff

Bradford Leland Powers. *Making Meetings Work: A Guide for Leaders and Group Members.* San Diego, CA: Pfeiffer, 1976.
J. Carver. *Boards That Make a Difference.* San Francisco: Jossey-Bass, 1990.

W. R. Conrad and W. E. Glen. *The Effective Voluntary Board of Directors.* Athens, OH: Swallow Press, 1983.

Diane J. Duca. *Nonprofit Boards: A Practical Guide to Roles, Responsibilities, and Performance.* Phoenix, AZ: Oryx Press, 1986.

Darcy Campion Devney. *Organizing Special Events and Conferences: A Practical Guide for Busy Volunteers and Staff.* Sarasota, FL: Pineapple Press, 1990.

David Emenhiser. *Power Funding: Gaining Access to Power, Influence, and Money in Your Community.* Rockford, MD: Fundraising Institute, 1992.

Robert Greenleaf. *Trustees as Servants.* Peterborough, NC: Windy Row Press, 1973.

John D. Lawson. *When You Preside.* 5th ed. Danville, IL: Interstate Printers and Publishers, 1980.

Mary Bray Whetten, ed. *The Basic Meeting Manual: For Officers and Members of Any Organization.* Nashville, TN: Thomas Nelson, 1986.

Foundation Fundraising Resources

F. E Andrews. *Philanthropic Foundations*: New York: Russell Sage Foundation, 1998.

Foundation and Grant Information

The Foundation Center publishes grants directories, grants indexes, guidebooks, monographs, and bibliographies and offers a wide variety of services and information to grant seekers. The center has regional centers in New York, Washington, D.C., Atlanta, Cleveland, and San Francisco and cooperates with public libraries nationally to house its materials. The following are publications of the Foundation Center, 79 Fifth Avenue, New York, NY, 10003. Each of these sources is updated and published annually.

The Foundation Directory provides information on finances, governance, and giving information. It contains profiles of the largest U.S. foundations— those that have at least $2 million in assets and disperse $200,000. Includes information on 28,000 selected grants.

The Foundation Directory, Part 2: A Guide to Grant Programs $50,000 to $200,000. Data on over 4,200 mid-sized foundations, including more than 28,000 recently awarded foundation grants.

Foundation Grants Index Annual. An index of grant subject areas. Within each subject area, grant descriptions are listed geographically by state and alphabetically by foundation.

The Foundation 1000. Information on the thousand largest U.S. foundations responsible for 60% of all foundation grant dollars. Foundation 1000 grantmakers hold over $100 billion in assets and award $6 billion in more than 190,000 grants to nonprofit organizations annually.

National Directory of Corporate Giving. Information on corporate foundations.

National Guide to Funding for Children, Youth and Families. Information on foundations and corporate direct-giving programs.

National Guide to Funding for the Economically Disadvantaged. Information on foundations for employment programs, homeless shelters, welfare initiatives, and others.

Foundation Fundamentals: A Guide for Grant Seekers, also published by the Foundation Center, is an exceptionally useful book for people who are new to grant seeking.

The National Network of Grantmakers is an association of individual grantmakers committed to social and economic justice with a strong focus on advice. Members often describe their foundations as promoters of social change and as supporters of new approaches. The National Network publishes *The Grant Seekers Guide: Founding Sourcebook,* which identifies foundations with assets of $1 million or more that address social and economic justice issues. The guide is designed for smaller grassroots community-based organizations.

The Council on Foundations, a national organization to which foundations belong, publishes *Foundation News,* which can be helpful to grant seekers who might have interest in the latest concerns in the foundation world.

The Independent Sector is the primary support organization of nonprofit social organizations. Composed of more than 800 organizations, its mission is to create a national forum capable of encouraging giving and volunteering. Because its membership has a significant number of foundations, social welfare organizations that belong have an opportunity to interact with other foundations and can help keep foundations current on issues and concerns. The Independent Sector publishes the *Non-Profit Almanac* and *Dimensions of the Independent Sector,* which can serve as an important reference tool.

Government Funding Sources

Superintendent of Documents. *Catalog of Federal Domestic Assistance.* U.S. Government Printing Office, Mailstop SSOP, Washington, DC 20402-9328.

Federal Register and *Federal Register Index.* Superintendent of Documents, P.O. Box 371954, Pittsburgh, PA, 15250-7954.

Contracting

F. M. Alson et al. *Contracting With the Federal Government.* New York: Wiley, 1984.

Writing Grants and Proposals

D. G. Bauer. *The "How-to" Grants Manual.* New York: Macmillan, 1984.

Foundation Center. *The Foundation Center's Guide to Proposal Writing.* New York: Foundation Center, 1994.

Mary Hall. *Getting Funded: A Complete Guide to Proposal Writing.* 3d ed. Portland, OR: Continuing Education Publications, Portland State University, 1988.

Patricia Read. *Foundation Fundamentals: A Guide for Grantseekers.* 5th ed. New York: Foundation Center, 1994.

Virginia White. *Grant Proposals That Succeeded.* New York: Plenum Press, 1984.

J. R. Shellow and N. C. Stella, eds. *The Grant Seekers Guide.* 3d ed. Mt. Kisko, NY: Moyer Bell Limited, n. d.

Grassroots Fundraising Resources

Joan Flanagan. *The Grassroots Fundraising Book.* Chicago, IL: Contemporary Books, 1992.

———. *Successful Fundraising: A Complete Handbook for Volunteers and Professionals.* Chicago: Contemporary Books, 1991.

Kim Klein. *Fundraising for Social Change.* Berkeley, CA: Chardon Press, 1985.

Journals

Chronicle of Philanthropy, a national newspaper published twice a month.

Grassroots Fundraising Journal, P.O. Box 11607, Berekely, CA 94701.

11
Becoming a Social Work Administrator

We have grown up with the belief that control, consistency, and predictability are essential. We have separated managing the work from doing the work. We have created a class system inside our institutions. There is a management class and an employee or worker class. The management class enjoys privileges and prerogatives and is taught management skills. The worker class has fewer privileges and prerogatives and is taught operational or basic skills. The fundamental beliefs we have about how to run organizations and organize work aren't working.[1]

Peter Block

Now these are the last words of David.
He that ruleth over men must be just,
    ruling in the fear of God.
And he shall be as the light in the morning,
    when the sun riseth.
Even a morning without clouds,
    as the tender grass,
        springing out of the earth,
            by clear shining after rain.

II Samuel 23:1, 3–5

Ideas in This Chapter

HARRY HOPKINS, SOCIAL WORK ADMINISTRATOR

He wrote no books and gave few speeches. He never earned a large salary, and when he died he was nearly penniless. Rarely in good health, he was in pain much of his life. He was never elected to public office, and he did not earn advanced degrees. Throughout much of his career he was vilified in the press and by many politicians. Yet during the 13 years that Harry Lloyd Hopkins remained in public service, he was recognized as the second most powerful man in America and had a profound impact on every major crisis from the international economic collapse to the dawn of the atomic age.

Within five years of coming to Washington, Hopkins spent more money and employed more people than any other person in history. He directed programs that helped mobilize the nation for one of the greatest confrontations of the century and with that productivity paved the way for the defeat of the Axis powers during World War II. Emissary to two presidents, he forged the great alliance between the United States, Russia, and Great Britain that helped win the war and set the course for the postwar era.

Harry Hopkins, public social work administrator, was born in 1890. In all his endeavors, his mother impressed upon Harry, "You were put on earth to serve others. Don't be afraid to take risks. What counts is not words but actions." Hopkins attended Grinnell College, where he majored in the new field of political science, and was president of the senior class of 1912. An extrovert with acute powers of calculation, he had the ability to learn with speed and accuracy, his most remarkable attribute in later years. Hopkins had not made up his mind about a future career when he graduated, but he was offered a summer job at a camp for poor children in New Jersey, an experience that was to change his life forever. After two months at the camp, he was a zealous champion of the underprivileged.

Hopkins became a social worker at the Christadora House on New York's Lower East Side for room and board and $5 a month pocket money. The wrenching poverty and squalor of the city slums were to Hopkins alien and shocking. It was something he never forgot. During his first winter in New York, he asked for a job with the Association for Improving the Condition of the Poor (AICP) and was put on the payroll at $40 a month on a training basis. During the day he worked for Christadora House and at night went out on assignments for the AICP. Within two years this zealous social worker became the executive secretary of the New York City Board of Child Welfare.

He joined the Red Cross during World War I as director of the Gulf Division in New Orleans, and eventually he was overseeing all Red Cross activities in the Southeastern United States. After the war, Hopkins accepted a position as director of the Health Division of the AICP. He was charged with providing research into the health conditions of New York City. From there he became administrator of the New York Tuberculosis Association.

In 1928 Franklin Roosevelt was elected Governor of New York. After the crash of 1929, Roosevelt established the Temporary Emergency Relief Administration (TERA) and offered the position of deputy to Hopkins. TERA was the largest and most daring program for the relief of unemployment that had ever been undertaken by any state.[2] Within a year he was appointed chair, and by 1932 had given out 30 million dollars in aid and helped over a million destitute people.

Shortly after Roosevelt was elected President of the United States, he invited Hopkins to head the Federal Emergency Relief Administration (FERA), which meant a reduction in pay for Hopkins from $15,000 to $8,000. Roosevelt wrote of Hopkins, "Action had to be immediate." It was immediate. In his first two hours in office, Hopkins disbursed more than $5 million in aid to the states. But more than simply providing relief, Hopkins and Roosevelt were engineering a revolutionary change in the relationship between the American government and its citizens. Three-and-a-half weeks after he had entered federal service, Hopkins spoke at the National Conference of Social Work and announced the principle that relief was an obligation of government, breaking with the tradition of nongovernmental intervention that had been in place for the preceding 70 years.

At the end of his first year, Hopkins had helped in solving the vital problems of some 17 million people and spent a $1.5 billion in aid with an organization consisting of only 121 people and a payroll of only $22,000 per month. Hopkins believed in jobs, not welfare. He put together a program for putting people to work on governmental subsidized projects for the Civil Works Administration (CWA), one of the broadest programs ever instituted by the U.S.

government, and none too soon. By 1933, 42,000 businesses had failed and 25% of the entire workforce was unemployed. The country was near revolution. Nazism and Communism were barking at the door.

"Get the money out fast, and get it out honestly," was Roosevelt's charge, and Hopkins did it with incredible zeal and at a terrific pace, putting 4 million people to work in the first 30 days of CWA's existence. In three and a half months the CWA inaugurated 180,000 work projects. It built or improved 40,000 schools, laid 120,000 feet of sewer pipe, built 469 airports and improved 529 more, built 255,000 miles of road, employed 50,000 teachers, and built 3,700 playgrounds. Among the 4.26 million people for whom work was found, 3,000 were writers and artists, the inception of the Federal Arts Program. While compassion drove Hopkins onward, his genius for problem-solving drove him upward. Administration, for Harry Hopkins, was not simply putting a policy into motion. It was deciding to do something, seeing it work, seeking new opportunities, and being willing to live in a stream of events that couldn't be predicted.

With the passage of the Work Relief Bill in 1934, Hopkins was put in charge of the Works Progress Administration (WPA). Told by Roosevelt, "Do something and do it quickly, and don't come back with problems," Hopkins was eventually to spend over $10 billion on creating jobs, mobilizing more people than the army and navy combined during World War I. By 1935 he had found jobs for over 18 million workers and reported to Roosevelt, "Well, they're all at work, just don't ask me what the hell they're doing." Hopkins organized medical care, housing, education, school hot lunch programs, adult literacy programs, day care centers, rehabilitation for families, employment programs, and direct relief. The federal government became involved in almost every sector of American life.

In 1939, at the end of his second term, Roosevelt began grooming Hopkins as a presidential candidate and appointed him secretary of commerce to give him a less controversial role with more status. Hopkins developed a mysterious ailment, however, that prevented his body from absorbing nutrition. Fed intravenously and subsisting on vitamins and blood transfusions, he survived but became a semi-invalid. Gaunt and worn after his years of 18-hour days and constant pressure, Hopkins resigned from the cabinet and left public service. Having no

position, title, or salary, he was invited by his old friend Roosevelt to live as a guest the White House. Yet events would draw Hopkins back to even more important service to his country.

When Winston Churchill became Prime Minister in May 1940, Britain was financially bankrupt and threatened with imminent destruction by Hitler's aerial attacks. Roosevelt sent Hopkins as his personal envoy to Churchill, who found in Hopkins a staunch ally. Against the cries of those who advocated U.S. neutrality, Harry urged that America support Britain, arguing for a "Lend-Lease" program to arm the allies. Hopkins was put in charge. Working from a card table in his bedroom at the White House, he began the most massive undertaking this nation has ever known. With $7 billion to spend, Hopkins developed a program that exceeded the war production of Germany, Italy, and Japan combined.[3] Because of Hopkins, when Japan attacked Pearl Harbor, bringing America into the war, American war production was near full capacity, arming and supplying not only American soldiers but the Allied forces as well.

Harry Hopkins, public social work administrator, the personal envoy of two presidents, empowered by the time he died to spend $9 billion for the relief of others and billions more in Lend Lease, who guided America out of the Great Depression, and whose foresight forged the Great Alliance, was one of the most dedicated heroes of the war. Public service was his creed, his life, his legacy. He had conviction without limit and was without a doubt one of the great humanitarians of our time.

WHAT YOU WILL LEARN IN THIS CHAPTER

The word *administer* comes from the Latin *ad ministrare* meaning "minister to" or "to serve." Social administrators are social workers who provide service to both staff and clients in a community social agency. The role of a social administrator is to build a collaborative social organization that focuses on delivering social services and developing programs in service to its community.

In this chapter you will learn about supervision, departmental decision-making, budgeting, and personnel administration. You will learn about the role of the chief social work administrator in planning, working with the board, and program evaluation. Just as social workers and others are inventing social organizations as a new form of human association, you will discover that social work administration is breaking free of top-down, hierarchical, market-centered management, which has overwhelmed the field of public and social administration for well over 100 years. A new form of social administration is being constructed that is more congruent with social work values of partnership and service. Most social workers will have an opportunity to work in social organizations and experience the importance of administration in carrying out social work. Someday, you may decide to become a social administrator.

WHAT DO SOCIAL WORK ADMINISTRATORS DO?

Social work administrators help social workers and members of the community facilitate the work of social betterment by means of a social organization. In many hierarchically structured social agencies, depending on their size, there are three levels of administration. Line supervisors are at the first level. Social work supervisors usually are in charge of a unit of six or seven social workers. The supervisor helps social workers individually and the unit as a whole perform their jobs. Division or departmental administrators engage departments in joint decision-making, develop smooth working relationships between units, coordinate work of the units, and make sure that each unit is functioning properly. The chief social work administrator is responsible for much of the planning for the agency, manages the budget and personnel issues, sees to it that the agency is periodically evaluated, and relates to the social organization's board of directors, who make overall personnel, financial, and program policy decisions for the agency. Much of the success of any social work program depends on the quality of administrative leadership.

Supervision

A social work supervisor is at different times an information giver, instructor, problem-solver, coach, consul-

tant, mentor, and evaluator. The social model of administration expects social work supervisors in a joint venture to assist you to develop skill and collaborate in the provision of service to your clients. In a 1974 study by Al Kadushin, social workers asserted that "being able to share responsibility with supervisors and being able to obtain support for difficult cases was the greatest source of satisfaction." Both supervisors and workers believe that as you gain experience, the best relationship becomes one of consultant-consultee, a form of supervision preferred by many social workers.

Shulman reports that social workers often want supervisors to devote time to teach practice skills, discus research information, and provide feedback on performance. When a supervisor models rapport and caring as well as offering empathy, respect, mutuality, and trust, these qualities carry over in the way social workers assist your clients. Shulman found that "supervisees learn what a supervisor really feels about helping by observing the supervisor in action. More is often 'caught' by you than is 'taught' by the supervisor."[4]

Sometimes as a social worker you will need explicit, firm direction or direct answers to a policy or procedural question. Your supervisor should provide answers clearly and forthrightly. As you increasingly think about and make your own decisions, the trust and the support of your supervisor is important. Ongoing positive reinforcement, good communication, including active listening and giving feedback, and your supervisor's attempts to create a positive work environment are often essential in helping you become independent and self-directing.

In addition to working with you individually, your supervisor assists your entire work unit to set work priorities and goals and decide on work assignments. Your supervisor acts as a buffer between your unit and administration, providing you with information and training about the agency's plans and priorities. Your supervisor informs the department administrator about your unit's needs and performance. The ultimate objective of good supervision is to help your unit become a cohesive group of highly capable social workers who deliver the highest amount and quality of service to your clients.

Performance Appraisal   In most social agencies, social work supervisors monitor and evaluate your performance as an ongoing process. Performance appraisal often comes out of your discussions with your supervisor, may be based on your professional objectives as well as the agency's standards, and is performed collaboratively with you confirming what has been occurring during the year's period.

In larger, more hierarchically structured organizations, social workers are often evaluated by means of conventional performance evaluation processes developed by human resource specialists. Such evaluation is designed to measure the extent to which you achieve the requirements of your position by means of specific, realistic, and achievable criteria in relation to standards of agency performance. These organizations evaluate staff on at least an annual basis and use these evaluations to determine pay raises, promotions, future assignments, or the need for discipline.

Human resource specialists decide on performance standards. The kinds of measurement criteria they consider include output quality, output quantity, work habits and attitudes, learning ability, and judgment or problem-solving ability. They recommend that your supervisor objectively examine how you perform certain key skills such as devising a questionnaire or keeping records, your ability to perform essential practice functions such as community planning or performing casework, and concrete outputs such as the number of policies or programs developed, or children reunified with parents.

Human resource professionals also recommend your supervisor evaluate you subjectively by comparing your individual performance to others using group norms, assessing your performance on the basis of relatively fixed, independently determined standards, and judging performance by carefully observing what you do.[5]

This kind of conventional performance evaluation requires the imposition of externally applied measurable evaluation criteria, a form of consciously applied control that often bears little resemblance to actual social work practice. Management justifies such quantifiable evaluation as part of agency "quality control," as if you are a component of a machine. Implicit in such monitoring is basic distrust of social workers and an assumption that unless regularly scrutinized, you will fail to perform properly. Setting goals for you, defining your progress toward those goals, and then rewarding or punishing you in relation to them does not honor your capabilities. Not only does such con-

trol fail to respect you as a competent adult, a professional capable of self-direction, but it misuses supervisors as well. Some critics find such impersonal formal procedures "no more than a vehicle for the bureaucratic surveillance of social workers."[6]

An approach that is more consistent with social work values of self-determination and respect for the ability of social workers will reverse typical patriarchal management. Instead of measurement serving the interests of control, consistency, and predictability, social administrators will "let measurement and control serve core social workers," asserts Peter Block. "For example, measures should come out of conversation with clients, between workers themselves as well as supervisors," says Block. You and your social work team maintain control by your commitments to your jobs and to one another. These commitments become mutual agreements, not only between workers but also between workers and supervisors. Because contracts are between partners, expectations go both ways, with equal demands, between workers and supervisors, and between supervisors and department heads. The intent is to eliminate coercion as the basis for getting results. Performance contracts would not be tied to pay or punishment but to mutual accountability, teamwork, and accomplishing the goals of serving the community and clients, and increasing your skills and capacities for growth. "No one," asserts Block, "should be able to make a living simply planning, watching, and controlling or evaluating the actions of others." Social work administrators should "exist primarily to contribute to social workers who do the core work. Core social workers should have strong voices in determining what administrators can do to help them accomplish the common purposes of the social organization."[7]

Social work supervisors are valuable people. They have special knowledge and experience, and we choose them because we believe they are the best social workers we have. We need these talented individuals who are skilled in providing caring, concerned relationships and capable of passing their experience to others. We need to reorient our thinking about supervision. Instead of monitoring and controlling, we should allow our experienced social workers to coach, teach, support, and provide modeling and consultation in service of those who do social work with clients. The role that we call "supervision" should not be one of authority, but rather should assist and support you in becoming the best social worker you can be.

Brainstorming is useful when the solution to a problem requires the group's cumulative wisdom. (© Jane Scherr/Jeroboam, Inc.)

Administrative Decision-Making

All administrators engage in decision-making. Often, administrators make decisions alone, after gathering information and reviewing the strengths and limits of each alternative. The administrator often chooses the alternative that is cheapest, most efficient, or most effective in accomplishing a specific goal. At other times administrators play a facilitative role, collaboratively engaging a department's supervisors to solve a problem by arriving at several alternative decisions and selecting the best alternative solution.

Administrators are often preoccupied with instrumental questions such as: How can we improve service delivery to our clients? How can we increase our efficiency? How can we save money and eliminate waste? What can we do to expand our services? Instrumental questions, however, ask only about means. They rarely examine premises on which those questions are based. Social work administrators who see beyond instrumental questions and encourage social workers to ask more fundamental questions of value assist social workers to engage in broader questions that can improve the direction of the social organization. For example, the most efficient or cost-effective solution, if not in the interests

of members of the community or if imposed from the top, may only alienate people. Instead of asking about efficiency, it may be more important to ask "Is the department or unit going in the right direction?"

Arriving at Alternatives Once the real problem and the values implicit in the problem are clear, it is time to look at alternative solutions or decisions. Administrators may use a variety of techniques to make decisions in organizations: decision-analysis, linear programming, queuing, decision trees, benefit/cost analysis, and force-field analysis. These are common tools that administrators as well as staff can use and with which they should be familiar. These techniques were described in Chapter 6.

Administrators often use decision techniques with groups of staff members to develop solutions to social and administrative problems. Three kinds of decision techniques are common in meetings: (1) brainstorming, (2) reverse brainstorming, and (3) nominal group technique (NGT).

Brainstorming and Reverse Brainstorming *Brainstorming* allows a group to obtain the maximum amount of input in an orderly manner. Brainstorming reduces dominance by cliques and disruption by overly assertive, excessively garrulous, or domineering individuals. It also eliminates group dependency on a single authority figure and allows those who are generally silent to contribute. Brainstorming is useful when the solution to a problem requires the group's cumulative wisdom. It provides a means by which a number of ideas about a topic can be generated in a short amount of time.

When using brainstorming, explain the purpose and rules to insure an orderly process, especially in the early stages of a group, when members are still getting to know one another. The rules for brainstorming are:

1. *Expressiveness*—express any idea that comes to mind.
2. *Nonevaluation*—no criticism allowed.
3. *Quantity*—the more ideas the better.
4. *Building*—try to build on one another's ideas.

Write the issue on a blackboard or sheet of newsprint. Explain that the purpose of brainstorming is to generate as many ideas as possible, without thinking about the quality of the ideas. Any idea, no matter how far-fetched, is appropriate. In fact, the wilder and more audacious the idea the better, since one goal of brainstorming is to break through old ways of thinking and come up with new, innovative courses of action.

Stress that brainstorming should be fun, exciting, and interesting. Ideas will be stimulated and members will build on one another's ideas, or come up with new and different combinations. During the course of idea generation, no comments, criticism, evaluation, or discussion is allowed. As ideas are generated, write them down as quickly as members can think of them. Shy or reluctant members should be especially encouraged to participate.

In order to make sure that everyone has a chance and that all of the ideas are elicited, you may limit members to one idea at a time. Once members have exhausted themselves, the group reviews all of the suggestions, prioritizing them, and voting on those that seem worthwhile.

Brainstorming is a very popular technique; however, empirical evidence indicates that individuals working alone who are asked specifically to be creative tend to generate more solutions than brainstorming groups. When individual scores are added together to yield group scores, individuals working alone tend to outperform brainstorming groups. Finally, training, practice, and allowing subjects to record ideas *after* the brainstorming session tend to improve the group's proficiency.[8]

Reverse brainstorming is a technique for considering negative consequences of ideas that are generated through brainstorming. After lists of various ideas have been generated and your group is narrowing the list to the best ideas, ask group members, "What might go wrong with this idea?" Looking at the negative consequences of ideas can help to eliminate unworkable ones. Reverse brainstorming looks at the costs of decisions rather than benefits.

Nominal Group Technique   Andre Delbecq and Andrew Van de Ven developed an approach that combines the benefits gained when members of a group work alone to generate ideas (the members form a group in name only or a *nominal group*). They called their technique the *Nominal Group Technique* or *NGT*. NGT differs from brainstorming in that the process is not freewheeling but controlled and structured. While members may feel uncomfortable in using a highly structured process, discomfort usually diminishes after using the technique a time or two. The steps of the NGT process are as follows.

1. *Silent generation of ideas in writing.* The leader introduces the problem or issue in writing on a blackboard or newsprint pad, explains the theory of NGT and the procedure, and answers questions. Once everyone understands the process and the issue to be decided, each individual silently generates ideas about the issue in writing. Usually this takes about 10–15 minutes.
2. *Round Robin sharing.* Once everyone has finished generating ideas, each person in turn reads one idea from his or her list and the leader writes it on the board. If a member has an idea that is the same as one on the board, he or she moves to the next new one on his or her list. Members continue until all of the ideas are on the board.
3. *Discussion and clarification.* The leader asks members to look over the entire list to insure that it is comprehensive, clear, accurate, and nonrepetitive. The list is refined, but the merits

of differing ideas are not commented upon, discussed, or debated.

4. *Voting.* Because a large number of items may be on the board, it is often best to decide by multiple voting. A first choice will receive 3 points, a second choice 2 points, and a third choice 1 point. Each person writes his or her top three preferences on a card and passes it to the leader. The total points are added up and divided by the number of group members to obtain an average. The results are compared.

5. *Discussion (optional).* Because several rankings may receive close scores, discussion may help the group understand why they voted the way they did.

6. *Revoting.* The voting process can be repeated among the top scoring items until a clear winner emerges.

NGT protects individuals from group pressure, because anonymity is assured and discussion is not allowed. In the idea generation phase, each person is given the assurance that he or she will have opportunity to generate as many ideas as possible. This stimulates creativity, but in a quiet atmosphere in which everyone can give the problem the full concentration and attention.

The Round Robin phase provides for face-to-face contact and interaction at an appropriate time and in a controlled atmosphere. Each person knows that his or her ideas will receive equal and legitimate attention. The voting process provides for an explicit mathematical solution that fairly weighs all members' inputs.

Finally, in the discussion phase, member's subjective feelings, perceptions, and input can be factored into the final vote, while individuals understand that there will be joint group commitment to the final decision.

Administering Finances

Administering an organization's finances includes developing the budget, presenting the budget to the board of directors, overseeing how money is generated and spent, and insuring that there is good fiscal accountability. In a small agency, the chief social work administrator often takes the lead in overseeing the financial health of the agency, preparing the budget, raising funds, and assisting staff in managing the agency's finances. In a middle-size agency that has two or three social work departments, a finance manager is often responsible for managing agency funds. In a larger agency, administering the finances is usually delegated to a finance or accounting department.

The budget is your agency's most basic and important organizational plan. The budget sets out the financial outcomes that you intend to accomplish during a specific period, usually a year. According to Malvern Gross, a budget is a "plan of action that represents the organization's blueprint expressed in monetary terms, a tool to monitor the financial activities [of an agency] throughout the year."[9] Budgeting is intended to be a rational process. According to Wildavsky, "Making budgetary decisions depends on calculating which alternatives to consider and to chose. Calculation involves determining how problems are identified, get broken down into manageable decisions, how choices are made, and who shall be taken into account."[10]

However, arriving at a budget is far from perfectly rational. For one thing, according to Wildavsky, people are limited in their ability to calculate, time is severely limited, and "the number of matters that can be encompassed in one mind at the same time is quite small." As a result, people tend to make budgeting decisions *incrementally.* We "simplify in order to get by. We tend to make small moves, let experience accumulate, and use feedback from our decisions to gauge consequences." Social work agencies, in addition, often lack a well-understood financial base. "Spending agencies do not know how much they will need; reviewing bodies do not know how much they should allocate. Requests for spending and actual appropriations fluctuate wildly."[11] As a result budgeting, especially in small agencies, may often involve making educated guesses about a future state of affairs and what the needs of the agency will be.

Some budgets are "wish lists" in which administrators ask for what they want, but they must work within whatever amount is allocated to them. If the agency or program is new, the problem is compounded. Often a negotiated struggle takes place. Central funding sources, such as United Way, government agencies, or county or state budget departments will exert control, knowing that agencies will push for increases as hard as they can. The result is a game in which each attempts to maximize its position without regard for the other. Added to this mix is the self-interested pursuit of power by executives who see success in the budgeting arena as their "road to fortune." Budgeting in pubic social work agencies and to a certain extent in private ones is a mixture of rationality and politics.[12]

Three budgeting models used by social agencies are line item budgeting, functional budgeting, and program budgeting.

Line Item Budgeting   The line item budget, the most common form of budgeting in social agencies, is a description of revenue and expenditures on functional items such as salaries, rent, utilities, postage, office supplies, training, consultation, and others. A line item budget for an entire agency may include the following:

> *Personnel costs:* salaries, health and life insurance, staff development
>
> *Space*: rent, utilities, telephone, insurance
>
> *Equipment*: purchased equipment, leased equipment, equipment maintenance
>
> *Consumable items:* supplies, postage, books, subscriptions, printing, advertising
>
> *Petty Cash*
>
> *Other:* Conferences, travel, services purchased

The line item budgeting process is relatively easy to calculate and understand. Since line items may cut across departments or divisions, each department calculates how much it spent on these various items in a given year. Budget planners add up these line items, compare actual expenditures with last year's budget, and project costs on those items into the next year.

An advantage of line-item budgeting is "simplicity and expenditure control. The categories are limited and fixed over time, and increases and decreases projected in any given line are usually determined as a small increment"[13] over the previous year. Assume, for example, that last year your agency spent $100 on paper products. Allowing for inflation, this year the board approves a budget allocation of $105 for paper expenditure. Because of increased demand for paperwork, the agency actually spends $115 dollars. Based on those figures, it would probably make sense for the board to budget $130 next year, given increased usage and increased costs.

Sometimes line item budgets are developed by financial or accounting staff who often guess how costs might increase or decrease in the coming year.

They ask social work professionals what increases they expect to make. Based on those figures, the budget is submitted to the board, who, without further information or understanding, is asked to approve it.[14]

Line item budgeting may suffer because it is based on previous expenditures that may or may not be accurate predictors of future needs. It tells us nothing about the relative importance of budget items, or whether various departments or units needed them. Line item budgeting "does not depict efficiency, effectiveness, priorities, or programs of the agency,"[15] neither does it help you plan for new programs or for agency innovation.

Functional Budgeting   A functional budget places various organizational functions into categories that can be examined and monitored. As an administrator of a smaller social organization, you may divide finances into social work services and supporting or administrative services.[16] If you administer a larger organization, you may want to know if expenditures for social service programs, system maintenance (personnel, accounting), and support (clerical, facilities maintenance) are growing more quickly than others and whether the amounts allocated to these various functions are appropriate.

Program Budgeting   Administrators who use program budgeting "make budgetary decisions by focusing on end products of output." You may ask yourself, for example, "What do we do (program)?" "Why do we do it (objective)?" and "How are we doing (output in relation to objectives or results)?" You define program objectives in terms that are capable of being analyzed, have specific time horizons for accomplishing objectives, measure program effectiveness, and develop and compare alternative ways of attaining objectives.[17] For example, if the goal of a program is to rehabilitate 100 persons addicted to alcohol in the coming year, the administrator and staff calculate the resources needed to accomplish this goal. The meaning of "rehabilitation" may become an issue. Is an alcoholic considered rehabilitated when he or she has been sober for three months, six months, or one year? Is a person addicted to alcohol considered rehabilitated if he or she is capable of holding a job and attends Alcoholics Anonymous (AA) meetings regularly? Once a definition is decided upon, social workers can arrive at some goals. It is best to make goals specific, measurable, and time limited. You assess particular treatment methods. For example, if your definition of rehabilitation includes holding a job or enrolling in AA, you will probably add a job training program to your services, as well as referrals to and monitoring AA attendance. You and your staff calculate how much it will cost to rehabilitate 100 persons addicted to alcohol.

At various points during and at the end of the year, you can review the budget to assess the degree to which the program was successful in accomplishing its goals and if it is staying within its cost projections. You and the other social workers can also assess the effectiveness of various treatment modalities, arrive at more realistic operational definitions, and attempt to improve treatment effectiveness. Then you adjust your treatment goals and budgets.

Program budgeting has an advantage over line item budgeting and functional budgeting because it allows you to examine how effective services have been in the past year, and it provides a mechanism to plan a better program for the future. In addition, program budgeting involves everyone in the budgeting process who is responsible for program outcomes, particularly line social work staff. This makes budgeting an integral part of the treatment process, gives social workers increased control over their own work, and provides incentives in goal accomplishment. Program budgeting can also help evaluate treatment and program effectiveness.

Human Resources Management

Because social organizations are composed of people, and their purpose is to enhance people's lives, the human side of organizational life ought to be one of the most, if not *the* most important aspects of social work administration. The human side of organizational life, especially in larger hierarchically structured social work organizations, is often delegated to human resource managers whose role is to influence "the effectiveness of employees in the organization."[18] Human resources (HR) management is "the use, development, assessment, reward, and management of individual organizational members or worker groups." Human resources management includes the design and implementation of systems for staffing an organization and "developing employees, managing careers, evaluating per-

formance, compensating workers, and smoothing labor relations."[19]

MARY PARKER FOLLETT: ADMINISTRATION THEORIST

Born in Quincy, Massachusetts, an 1898 graduate of Radcliffe College, Mary Parker Follett was active in vocational guidance, industrial relations, civic education, settlement work, and social administration theory and practice. As a vocational counselor for Boston's Roxbury Neighborhood House, Follett became aware of poor working families in need of social, recreational, and educational facilities. In 1909 her lobbying efforts resulted in legislation that made her the initiator of the first public school community centers,[20] the Boston School Centers for after-school recreation and education programs.

A member of the Vocational Guidance Board of the Boston School Board and the Minimum Wage Board of the Women's Municipal League, Follett was active in the business community and addressed groups of business people. In 1924, Follett moved to England, where she was vice president of the National Community Center Association and a member of the Taylor Society, an organization concerned with scientific management, administration, and efficiency in industry.

Her theory of "Psychological Interpenetrating" pioneered the concept that was later described by Alfred Schutz as "intersubjectivity" and we-relations. In her 1924 book *Creative Experience*,[21] Follett advocated administration practice in which people of different socio-economic and occupational backgrounds understand one another's viewpoints. Her various writings on administration are contained in *Dynamic Administration: The Collected Papers of Mary Parker Follett*[22] and describe her perspectives on social administration.

In an era when management was the exclusive bastion of wealthy male business leaders, Mary Parker Follett brought a new perspective to social administration, concentrating on social work values. Of all the important organizational theorists and writers, she was the only social worker, and the only theorist, to challenge the scientific management model of business. Over 100 years ahead of her time, her voice is now beginning to be recognized for its uniqueness, creativity, and advocacy of authentic social work administration.

Recruitment and Selection   According to Sturgeon, since everything the organization does depends on the quality of its employees, recruiting and selecting people is the organization's most important function.[23] Recruitment provides the agency with an adequate number of applicants. When you perform recruitment and selection, use the following steps:

1. Develop a job description that outlines information regarding the minimum qualifications for the position in terms of education, experience, and skills.
2. Recruit employees by designing position announcements, advertising, and outreach.
3. Screen applicants using application forms, resume reviews, references, and tests if appropriate.
4. Conduct screening interviews.
5. Select the person and notify other applicants.

The details of how to carry out these functions are described in Chapter 10.

Administering Diversity   Sturgeon says that equal employment opportunity is common sense. In the 21st century, Caucasians will become a minority in the United States. America's ethnic diversity should be significantly represented in the workforce of every organization if only to avoid being out of sync with the organization's external environment. More important, every social organization has a responsibility to support the community that sustains it. One of the striking features of the United States is the strength of the belief held by people at all levels of society that achieving the "American dream" is really possible for many citizens. When Americans come to believe that they cannot better their lot through their own merit and efforts, society stands at risk. Equal employment opportunity is a responsibility that every social organization owes not only to its community but to society as a whole.[24]

Affirmative action involves taking steps to ensure proportional recruitment, selection, and promotion of qualified members of groups formerly excluded, such as ethnic groups and women. Many types of employer's unions and employment agencies are required to plan and document the steps they are taking to reduce underrepresentation of various groups through written Affirmative Action Programs (AAPs). Equal Employment Opportunity Commission (EEOC) guidelines cover such areas as the type of questions that can be asked on an employment application or in an interview (for instance criminal record, marital status, number of children, ethnicity) and the use of screening or interviewing committees composed of a mix of males, females, and ethnic group members.[25]

There are a number of differences between affirmative action and equal employment opportunity. Affirmative action is voluntary, allows for increased value for those with protected characteristics, and gives preference to members of protected groups in hiring and promotion. Equal employment opportunity, on the other hand, is legally mandated, neutral with respect to protected characteristics, and prohibits discrimination in promotions and hiring. Pecora says in addition to banning certain types of application or interview questions, EEOC guidelines require that the selection process of candidates not have an adverse impact on any social, ethnic, or gender group unless the procedure is validated through job analysis or employee selection research. *Adverse impact* is indicated with an employee selection rate for any race, sex, or ethnic group that is less than 80% of the rate of the groups with the highest rate of selection. Proscriptions against discrimination in employment mandate that any requirement (education or experience) used as a standard for employment decisions must have a manifest relationship to the employment in question.[26]

Americans With Disabilities Act   Enacted July 26, 1990, the Americans With Disabilities Act (ADA) extends broad civil rights protection to many Americans with disabilities and contains four major sections relating to: employment, state and local government service, public accommodations provided by private entities, and communications.[27] The law:

1. Provides a clear and comprehensive national mandate for the elimination of discrimination against individuals with disabilities.
2. Provides clear, strong, consistent, enforceable standards addressing discrimination against individuals with disabilities.
3. Insures that the federal government plays a central role in enforcing standards.
4. Allows government to apply the power of the 14th Amendment, to regulation of commerce, and to address discrimination faced by persons with disabilities.[28]

Nondiscrimination laws forbid all employers from making hiring decisions based on criteria that are either irrelevant to the job or inappropriately subjective, such as preferring an underqualified person over a qualified person who has a disability. The ADA requires employers to make allowances for disabled applicants so that they can compete on more equal terms.[29]

Orienting Staff When you hire someone, it is important to take time to introduce the employee to other staff members, explain his or her particular role, and review the important policies and procedures, including regulations pertaining to state and federal regulations or agency by-laws. Have copies of the organizational charts available. Relate the new social worker to the organization as a whole. In hierarchically oriented organizations, it is also important for you to orient the worker to the responsibility and authority structure.

Most often you will accomplish the basic components of such an orientation over several working days and follow it up by additional on-the-job orientations. In a case-management agency, for example, you provide policy on recording and documentation of files, and how to perform social case histories or other work-related procedures. If you are orienting social work students for internships, go through the same process as with any other professional social worker to replicate what they will experience when they get their first job.

Sexual Harassment Sexual harassment is increasingly recognized as one of the most sensitive employee issues you may be called on to handle. Agency supervisors, administrators, as well as entire organizations have been held liable by local and federal courts. Sexual harassment involves unwelcome sexual advances, requests of sexual favors, or other conduct of a sexual nature. Harassment can be verbal, visual, or physical. Visual harassment involves leering, suggestive ogling, offensive signs and gestures, or open display of pornographic or other offensive materials. Verbal harassment includes sexually explicit jokes, sexual suggestions, highly personal innuendoes, and explicit propositions. Physical harassment includes brushing up against the body, patting, squeezing, pinching, kissing, fondling, forced sexual assault, and rape.

Pecora reports that in a study of 23,000 randomly selected male and female civilian employees conducted by the Federal Merit system between May 1978 and May 1980, approximately 42% of the women and 15% of the men reported being harassed, and 1% reported the most severe form of harassment (actual or attempted rape). Sexual harassment is often widespread and occurs regardless of a person's age, marital status, appearance, ethnicity, occupation, or salary.

Because of the seriousness and extent of this kind of behavior, make sure that your social organization has clear standards of behavior in place. Help your staff understand what constitutes appropriate behavior and insure that everyone knows his or her rights and obligations. Train your social work supervisors how to handle complaints promptly and fairly.[30]

Handling Employee Performance Problems It is important for you to distinguish between social worker and agency performance problems. Employee performance problems are often assumed to be due to lack of a social worker knowledge or skills, poor attitudes, need for more supervision, or poor work habits such as carelessness, lack of attention to detail, lack of personal organization, or poor use of time.[31] Be sensitive, however, to the possibility that personal factors such as a social worker's health problems, family pressures, emotional difficulties or external stress may be contributing to poor performance.

A social worker's performance difficulties may also be a result of a host of nonworker factors, including stress due to unclear or inconsistent agency policies, resource limitations, and vague or shifting work priorities or performance standards. Performance problems can result from unsupportive or punitive supervision, excessive workload demands, and assignment of inappropriate cases. Before you decide on a course of action, make sure that you understand fully the source of a social worker's difficulties and can distinguish among those due to the worker's lack of ability, to personal problems, or to agency factors. (You will find more ideas about work- and nonwork-related personal problems and possible solutions in Chapter 12.)

Termination Discharging someone can be one of the most difficult and unpleasant tasks in working with employees. You should develop explicit policies that describe the conditions under which an employee can be terminated. A host of legal issues surround termination, and nearly all groups of employees have protections under the law enforced by local courts, state human rights agencies, the EEOC, and in the case of unions, the National Labor Relations Board (NLRB). Make sure that your social work staff and supervisors know the conditions under which termination may be considered and the process by which it may occur. Just as with any other sensitive issue, help your supervisors understand how to handle termination fairly, sensitively, and honestly.[32]

Human Resource Management and Social Work

In most rational-legal social work bureaucracies, the human relations management function is often considered necessary to ensure that employees are treated with procedural correctness, attention to the law, impartiality, and equity. Human relations managers enforce standardization and routinization that also protect the organization from accusations of discrimination and unfairness. While offering certain protections, however, the human resources management function tends to treat social workers as objects. We are seen as one of several organizational resources that are incapable of rational self-direction, whose behavior needs to be managed and controlled by others. The more highly bureaucratized and rationalized our society becomes, the greater will be the demand for converting social workers and others into objects to be controlled for efficiency, effectiveness, and legal compliance. This is an issue that social work administrators must work to resolve.

THE ROLE OF CHIEF SOCIAL WORK ADMINISTRATOR

A chief social work administrator helps to create conditions by which people's welfare can be improved by means of a social organization. A social work administrator will have an attitude of service rather than power and control. You help facilitate planning and help devise policies to assist social workers carry out their jobs effectively. You report to the community board of directors, providing information and taking direction from them. You insure that the organization's effectiveness is evaluated.

Service

Your administrative style, the way in which you disseminate decision-making, your approach to the community in which your organization is located, and the manner in which you relate to social work staff and the board will be reflected in many ways throughout the social agency. You work to maximize choice for social workers who are doing the day-to-day work with clients, not hoard decision-making as the exclusive prerogative of the top administrative team. You provide service to social workers, who provide service to their clients.[33] You encourage a climate of personal responsibility, individual choice, humanization, and independent action on the part of social workers and clients.

You maintain an attitude of service toward the social workers doing the work, rather than a presumption that social workers are servants of the administration in carrying out its plans, programs, goals, or directions. As much as possible you assist social workers to become involved in the design of the governance systems by which the social organization operates.

Planning

Strategic planning and policy formulation set parameters or limits within which day-to-day decisions are made.[34] Social organizations are always in a state of change. There are new services to consider, new problems to solve, new issues in the agency's environment, and new political and economic factors with which to contend. As a result, a good deal of social administrative effort goes into planning. In fact, planning is probably one of the major tasks that you accomplish. As a responsible social work administrator, you continually sift through the many issues confronting you and develop plans to deal with those issues. Rarely will you be caught off guard or unaware of problems in the agency's internal processes or in its external social environment.

Weinbach says that planning includes "those structures and activities that are used to shape future events in organizations."[35] Usually plans are written in some form that help social workers and clients orient themselves toward the organization's goals. For example, the mission statement of a social agency tells people the purpose for which the agency is established. Planning involves setting *goals* and *objectives* for the social organization and developing "work maps" such as programs and budgets that show how these goals and objectives can be accomplished.[36] In partnership with social workers and clients, you scan the organization's environment for "major discontinuities…that might provide opportunities or constraints" and monitor "gradual changes in environmental indicators"[37] to plan for client needs, and for ways that the social agency can meet those needs. While the community board of direc-

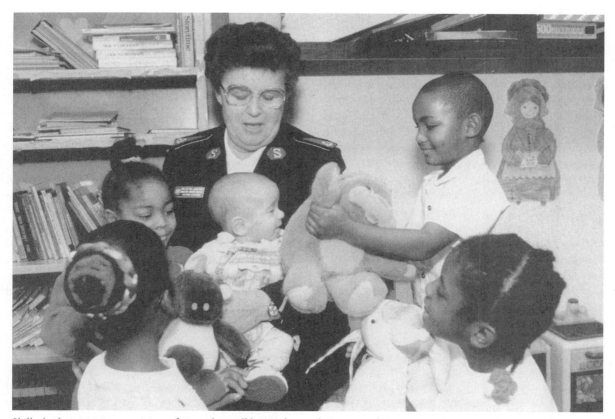

Skilled administrators envision a future that will bring about a better social environment and a stronger sense of community. (Courtesy of Salvation Army)

tors sets overall agency policy and direction, as chief social administrator you are responsible for developing internal organization policies and procedures. Koontz, O'Donnell, and Weinrich define policies as "general statements…which guide or channel thinking and action in decision-making."[38] Policies, according to Herbert Simon, are the premises of decisions.[39] They include not only ways of thinking but more importantly values implicit in decisions.[40]Work procedures flow from internal policies. Procedures are work plans that help people work in a coordinated fashion and facilitate communication. It is important for you to give a good deal of thought to internal agency policies, because they shape the culture of the agency.

Relating to the Board of Directors

The board of directors of a nonprofit social organization is responsible for evaluating the social work administrator and the agency's operations at regular intervals. Although as chief social work administrator you are delegated authority for the agency's day-to-day operations and for handling most personnel matters, the agency's by-laws invest your community board with the power and authority to make overall agency policy. The ultimate responsibility for the agency functioning and for the your performance and that of the agency staff resides with the board.[41] Most relationships between you and your community board members, therefore, involve elements of power and dependency that develop a creative tension that can work to the advantage of your organization as long as respect exists and the give-and-take is roughly equal.[42] Although board members can draw on your expertise and knowledge, they cannot allow their legal responsibility to be diluted or co-opted by over dependence on you. While you need to develop a collegial working relationship with the board members, you always remain an employee of the community board, no matter how seasoned you become.[43]

As chief social work administrator, you play a critical role in determining the nature and extent of the relationship between yourself and your board. You not only serve as an advocate with the board members but stimulate them to advocate for their social organization in the broader society. You provide your community board with statistics, interpret client, consumer, or patient needs, discuss program options, and provide information on funding possibilities. Because your board members are dependent on you for information, you are an integral part of the policy-making process. Although this works because you establish a balance in your role, the relationship between policy formation and administration is never settled for all time but involves a continuous process of negotiation.[44]

Evaluating the Program

Program evaluation today "has become ubiquitous in the planning and administration of social welfare policies and programs."[45] Government agencies and foundations want to know how much impact your program has had on the problems that it was to remediate. If you can show that your program did what you intended, you may be able to make a case to continue or even expand it. If the program your social work organization operates is successful, others may want to know about it so that it can be replicated elsewhere. Your clients want to be assured that they are receiving the best services that can be provided.[46] "Politicians demand that programs demonstrate their cost effectiveness and be accountable to the public."[47] More and more program evaluation is automatically built into the process of obtaining funding from either government or private foundations.

Carol Weiss says that program evaluation measures the effects of a program against its goals to help make decisions about your organization's future direction.[48] According to Rossi and Freeman, the purpose of program evaluation is to assess and improve the "conceptualization, design, planning, administration, implementation, effectiveness, efficiency, and utility of social interventions, and human service programs."[49] You will often find program evaluation to be most useful if it is conducted by an objective outsider whose skills you and your community board can trust.

Process Analysis Process analysis is one way for you as a program evaluator to assess the internal processes by which services are carried out in the social organization.[50] You can conceptualize the internal system state of a social organization by means of "systems fit." The organization's members, processes, structures and technologies, goals, strategies, and culture must fit together properly in order for the organization to function well.

You monitor organizational members' skills, attitudes, and values by asking: Do employee skills and training fit the job requirements? Does the organization attract and retain the best people? Are professionals and others who seek autonomy and challenge assigned to less structured and less closely controlled jobs? Do work-related organizational problems create undue stress or employee health problems? Your assessment may lead you to recommend improved recruitment and selection, counseling, stress management, and health maintenance programs.

Look at processes of organizational decision-making, leadership, and communication. Does the decision-making process use all available resources and arrive at decisions that further organizational goals? Does organizational leadership create a sense of mission and identity among members? Is communication effective and efficient, or does it result in mixed messages, misunderstanding, or delay? You may recommend sensitivity training, team building, process consultation, third-party interventions, or survey feedback techniques described in Chapter 12.

Assess organizational structures and technologies. Are people who work together closely grouped in units or otherwise linked structurally? Are procedures for coordinating work and information flow appropriate to the tasks and technology? Do members regard the rules and procedures as fair and sensible? As a result of your assessment you might recommend techniques such as job redesign, revised administrative procedures, reward mechanisms, redesigned divisions of labor, or new work procedures to improve effectiveness.

Evaluate organizational goals, strategies, and cultures by asking whether procedures are supported by the organization's culture and norms. Do power struggles or inter-unit rivalries prohibit achieving organizational objectives? Your recommendations may include promoting goal clarification, coping with change through workshops, or improving the organizational culture.

Ask practical questions to help a program improve its usefulness. Which fundraising strategy yields the most funds? What proportion of the target population is being served? What types of individuals are not being reached by the program? Do targeted individuals refuse services? Do clients drop out of the program prematurely? You may recommend different funding possibilities, ways of recruiting clients, or ways to help clients stay with services.

Outcome or Impact Analysis   In order to evaluate the extent to which the program is achieving its goals or outcomes in terms of quantity and quality, you must understand the program's goals.[51] Often, however, program goals are vague and nonspecific. For example, an organization may state that its goals are to reduce crime, assist the homeless, or support victims of domestic violence. While worthy endeavors, these are not goals that you can easily assess. Your first task, therefore, is to assist the organization's key stakeholders, including clients and the community in general, social workers, and other staff, as well as the board and administration to state their goals in clear, specific, and measurable terms,[52] and to decide which are the most practical and important. Other stakeholders are funding agencies and other social organizations and governmental agencies that partner with the social organization. Involve these stakeholders not only in the selection of goals and the evaluation design but also at every step by "sharing mutual incremental feedback throughout all phases of the evaluation."[53]

Effectiveness Criteria   Put goals in operational or measurable terms. To assess *quantity*, determine the volume, speed, or rate of services. For example, the goal of a probation department may be to maintain a certain rate of recidivism (the number of repeat offenses) made by offenders. The effectiveness criteria is the specific number of offenses per offender in a period of time. Other effectiveness criteria may be number or hours of services provided, percentage of target group reached, number of people served, and number of people rehabilitated.

You may also assess the effectiveness of a program by the *quality* of the services it provides. How good were the services? For example, the goal of an in-home support service to the elderly may be to provide food preparation, visitation, and transportation services. Evaluating the quality of the in-home support program would include determining how well food was prepared, the friendliness of the visitors, and the efficiency of transportation. Quality may be measured by assessing client satisfaction with services, the length of time treatment was effective, and the impact of services on the problem.

Measurements   Measurements are indicators of success or effectiveness. A number of scales, indices, tests, instruments, and measures exist that you can use for measuring organizations and groups. Among these are the Michigan Organizational Assessment Questionnaire, the Organizational Assessment Inventory, Group Effectiveness Survey, Organizational Diagnosis Questionnaire, and Job Diagnostic Survey.[54] Try to use multiple measures to develop a more rounded and truer picture of program outcomes[55] as well as multiple means of collecting data. The number and mix of sources of data are limited only by your ingenuity and imagination. Possible sources are:

1. Interviews
2. Questionnaires
3. Observation
4. Ratings (by peers, staff, experts)
5. Psychometric tests of attitudes, values, personality, preferences, norms, and beliefs
6. Institutional records
7. Government statistics
8. Tests of information, interpretation, and skills
9. Physical evidence
10. Clinical examinations
11. Financial records
12. Documents (minutes of meetings, newspaper accounts, transcripts of trials)

Designing the Evaluation   Three kinds of designs most useful in program evaluation research are pure experimental research, quasi-experimental research, and benefit-cost analysis.

Pure Experimental Research   Pure experimental research typically uses randomly selected subjects in controlled settings. If you are evaluating a new treatment program in an outpatient facility for juveniles addicted to drugs, for example, randomly select a group of typical drug users from all the facility's clients. Divide this number into two subgroups. One is the control group and the other is the experimental group. Next, assess the levels of drug abuse of each group to get a baseline before treatment begins. The control group receives conventional treatment. The experimental group receives the new treatment. After the treatment is completed, retest each group and compare the results. If the rate of drug use in the experimental group is considerably less than that of the control group, you might conclude that the new treatment approach was effective.

While experimental research is fairly straightforward, you may already see why this "pure" experiment might not work in actual practice. Because the offenders know who is receiving a treatment program, they may collude to interfere with its results. Any number of external factors that have nothing to do with treatment, such as the home, school, and peer relationships may affect the outcomes. Clients enter programs and leave them without notice. Staff come and go. Clients change and grow independently of treatment in ways that may affect results.

Quasi-Experimental Research   Quasi-experimental research allows you to assess program effectiveness in settings where you cannot control many of the variables. While there are many kinds of quasi-experimental research designs,[56] two that are useful in program evaluation are the time series and the nonequivalent control group designs. *Time series designs* account for events that give false indicators of success over time, such as changes in the program's environment, the life cycle of a program, or shifts in personnel. For example, heaviest drug users may drop out of the program, giving a false impression that the treatment program was successful. Staff may gradually gain skill in providing treatment, or less capable staff may have been replaced with more competent people, giving a misleading picture of effectiveness of the program itself.

Collect data at regular intervals over a period of time before the program is implemented to obtain a picture of normal changes in the program's service pattern. When you institute the new treatment program, measure it over time to allow for maturation of staff, adjusting to the new program routine, and changes in clients or staff. After enough evaluations are conducted to give a comprehensive picture of the new treatment's success rate, compare the pattern of program changes before and during the treatment to assess whether the new service is effective.

Nonequivalent control group designs are useful if it is impossible to divide a population into two random groups for an experiment. Instead of dividing a population find another group with similar characteristics against which you can compare the experimental group. For example, if you want to evaluate a new treatment program for youth in a residential facility, use a randomly selected control group of similar residents of another facility who are receiving no treatment or a conventional treatment. Use a time series design to obtain a baseline on both the experimental group and the control group. Then, implement the treatment program with the experimental group while continuing to take measurements on both groups. After the treatment is over, test both groups and compare the results. If the experimental group improved in comparison to the control group, you may have some confidence that the outcome was the result of the treatment and not due to extraneous factors.

Benefit-Cost Analysis   Benefit-cost analysis is an extension of rational problem-solving. It is a way of looking at various program alternatives and estimating the benefit in dollars that each alternative will provide in comparison to its potential dollar costs.[57] Once you establish a benefit/cost ratio for each program alternative, compare each one. Select the one with the highest ratio, the one that gives the best return. For example, if program A provides benefits of $200 and costs only $100, the benefit/cost ratio is 2/1 or 2. You get twice as much benefit as the program costs. On the other hand, if program B provides the same benefits of $200 but costs $300, its benefit/cost ratio is 2/3 or 0.667. You only get 2/3 return for the money you put into the project. Assuming that services are of equal quality and meet program objectives, you would normally give the highest rating to the one that gives the most benefits at the least cost.

Benefit-cost analysis tends to be most useful when you can easily obtain information about the degree of the program's impact, when its benefits can be reduced to dollar terms without extraordinary guesswork, and when you can easily identify the program's indirect costs.

The major difficulty in benefit-cost analysis is accounting for all of the costs and benefits of a program and converting often highly intangible results into dollar figures. For example, what are the costs to a community if a child is abused or the benefits in dollars when the cycle of abuse is broken? How much dollar benefit accrues when community members make decisions for themselves? Community empowerment may not be considered by some to be a benefit, because powerful groups may have a vested interest in keeping community members dependent on them. Some argue that trying to place dollar amounts on social costs is inappropriate, because activities like educating a child with an intellectual disability ought to be done for humanitarian reasons even though the costs far outweigh any monetary benefits that will result.

In spite of these difficulties, there are ways to develop measurable criteria for the purposes of benefit-cost analysis. Hornick and Burrows recommend that you:

1. Compare only agencies with similar objectives and similar clients.

2. Conduct a time budget study during a stable period if the organization's records are inadequate.

3. Use the same parameters or cost criteria for all agencies being compared.

4. Calculate the agency costs in as many ways as possible, such as cost per case, cost per client, and cost per hour of direct service to the client, and compare them to those of other agencies.[58]

CONCLUSION

A social organization ought to provide social workers with a socially healthy and congenial working environment. Ideally a social organization is staffed with compassionate and caring social work professionals trained in communication skills whose goals and ideals are service to others. You are invested in and skilled in relationships and social systems dynamics, and most of you want to make social systems better. Social work organizations are rich in resources for providing assistance and for empowerment of your clients as well as yourselves.

Social administration ought to be able to utilize this wealth of human capacity to create social organizations that are models of leadership, innovation, and compassion rather than rely on management models that use workers as a means of production. Social work administration is one of the most important arenas of macro social work practice, and because many large social work agencies continue to be based on business management, administration presents social work with some of its greatest challenges. You can be one of the social workers who can assist in reducing our dependency on management and instead find ways to implement authentic social administration back into social work organizations.

KEY CONCEPTS

administration

line supervisors

staff functions

brainstorming

reverse brainstorming

nominal group technique

budgeting

incrementalism

line item budget

functional budget

program budget

personnel administration

human resources management

recruitment

selection

orienting

performance appraisal

equal employment opportunity (EEO)

affirmative action

Americans With Disabilities Act

sexual harassment

planning

policy

program evaluation

process analysis

impact or outcome analysis

pure experimental research

quasi-experimental research

time series design

nonequivalent control group design

benefit-cost analysis

QUESTIONS FOR DISCUSSION

1. Charles A. Rapp and John Poertner, in their book *Social Administration: A Client-Centered Approach*, assert clients are "resources to be acquired," but administrators are to "promote the idea that clients are heroes."[59] Comment on the idea of a client-centered approach to social administration. In what sense can clients be considered "resources?" In what sense can they be considered heroes? In what sense can clients be considered both resources and heroes?

2. This chapter has referred to both administration and management. What are the differences between administration and management?

3. Should social organizations and social workers be managed or provided with administrative services? Is it possible to use both management as well as administration? Why or why not?

4. Human resources management assumes that social workers are resources who need to be managed. In what sense can social workers be considered organizational resources? In what sense do social workers need to be managed?

5. Comment on the need for the human resources management function in social organizations. What are the advantages and disadvantages? If you were a chief social work administrator how would you administer this function?

6. The text explains that affirmative action is voluntary, allows for increased value for those with protected characteristics, and gives preference to members of protected groups in hiring and promotion. Equal employment opportunity, on the other hand, is a legal obligation, neutral with respect to protected characteristics, and prohibits discrimination in promotions and hiring. What are the strengths of affirmative action? What are its limitations? What are the strengths of equal employment opportunity? What are its limitations?

7. Affirmative action assumes that there are times when discrimination in employment is warranted. Equal employment opportunity assumes that discrimination in employment is rarely warranted. Which is correct? Can both be correct? Which is congruent with social work values and principles?

8. Since 1883, the U.S. Civil Service Commission has required all nonpolitical appointees to be hired strictly on the basis of "job relatedness," preventing officials from hiring friends or relatives. This is called the "merit principle." Aside from ethnicity, should government ever provide or encourage public employment regardless of merit? If no, why not? If yes, why and under what circumstances? In the past 100 years has government ever done so?

9. Aside from ethnicity, should government ever offer preference to certain groups in public employment? If no, why not? If yes, why and under what circumstances? Has government ever done so?

EXERCISE 11.1

The Ideal Administrator

Think of the various jobs that you have had or organizations such as a social agency, school, church, or business with which you have been involved. Think of the very best administrator that you knew. What qualities elicited your admiration and respect? Individually make a list of the qualities you admire about that administrator.

Now think of an administrator that was the worst one that you have encountered. What kinds of qualities did that person exemplify? Make a list of these qualities. Compare both lists. Are there commonalities? Are there differences? What does this comparison say about the kinds of qualities that you think would make an ideal administrator?

Break into triads. Each person spends a few minutes sharing qualities that he or she admires in administrators. Share stories that you remember that illustrate those qualities and come to some conclusions about what makes for a good administrator. Review lists of those qualities that you saw as negative ones. Share stories that illustrate those qualities and come to a conclusion about them. Make up a composite listing.

Return to the class as a whole. Each triad writes positive and negative qualities on the blackboard or newsprint. As you discuss your various perceptions and experiences, try to come to some consensus about what makes an ideal administrator. What have you learned about qualities that are positive in an administrator and those that are negative?

Compare your class list with the model of social work administration presented in this chapter. Have you listed qualities that are similar to those described in this chapter? Have you discovered others that are not listed? As a class, draw conclusions about what makes for a good social administrator.

EXERCISE 11.2

Deciding on a Human Resources Model

Imagine yourself in the role of a newly hired human resources manager of a large social agency. Human resources management is responsible for personnel selection, training, evaluation, and termination of employees. The CEO has told you that one of the first things you need to do is establish a perspective on hiring personnel that will become the model reflected throughout the department and the agency as a whole. Your CEO has made things easy for you by having her assistant research three current personnel models in management literature. While she has not herself reviewed these models, she has told you to select the one that will assist the organization to efficiently and effectively meet the organization's personnel needs according to the NASW code of ethics— "The social worker should work to improve the employing agency's policies and procedures and the *efficiency and effectiveness* of its services."[60] You are to report back to her with your recommendation. She has defined the criteria as follows:

1. Effective: Will using this model accomplish the agency's goals?

2. Efficient: To what extent does the model take costs into consideration?

Because the CEO believes that the expert advice of personnel theorists should be followed as well as the principles of the NASW code of ethics, she asserts that you are to be *completely and strictly objective*

and not insert your own opinion or personal values into this assessment.

In order to be objective, you decide to weight the models according to a scale of

5=very effective	5=very efficient
4=moderately effective	4=moderately efficient
3=adequately effective	3=adequately efficient
2=somewhat effective	2=somewhat efficient
1=little effective	1=little efficient
0=not effective	0=not efficient

Model 1

People are functionaries—individuals who do what they are supposed to do in pursuit of the organization's goal. The human version of the cog is the *functionary*—a person who performs his function effectively regardless of its purposes. The functionary does his duty, applies his skills, and performs his routines regardless of what goal or whose goal is involved. A screwdriver does not choose among goals or owners. It does what it is told.[61]

Score:
Effective
Efficient
Total

Model 2

Human resources are equivalent to financial, material, or other resources, all of which contribute to the production of goods and services in an organization.[62] An effective organization exploits its environment to acquire scarce and valued resources. The function of the personnel department is to acquire human resources for the organization, much as a grocery store stocks goods for consumers.[63]

While organizations extract resources externally from their environment and maintain stocks of human material, they also utilize an internal extraction process. Personnel administrators create conditions within the organization to maximize the extraction of resources from the staff.[64]

Score:
Effective
Efficient
Total

Model 3

Accounting for human resources investment costs will make it possible to put rationality into the process of managing internal manpower movement (i.e., position turnover). Fully depreciated human resources can be given priority consideration for redevelopment investment. The moral choice between buying new (and usually young) talent and overhauling old (long service) people can be made explicit so that it can be regulated. Where employees with low development and acquisition account balances have valuable skills which are not being used in their present jobs, reassignment becomes "profitable."…The costs of developing and redeveloping human resources would become an explicit, rational process constrained principally by economic considerations….Depreciating human resources makes human resources accounting a meaningful and practical activity.[65]

Score:
Effective
Efficient
Total

Deciding on a Model

Individually calculate scores for each model. The model with the highest total becomes your individual recommendation.

After you have computed individual scores, arrange yourselves in groups of five. Do not change your individual scoring or engage in discussion. Based only on the results of your individual scores, determine which model your group calculates as most effective and efficient by assigning a 3 to your first choice, a 2 to your second choice, and a 1 to your last choice. Add up the scores each model receives from group members. The model with the highest score becomes your group recommendation. Keep your individual and group scores. Engage in group discussion for five minutes to decide if you or your group wants to change the recommendation to the CEO.

Your instructor will give you a questionnaire with discussion questions. After you have engaged in discussion for five minutes, fill out the questionnaire. Then return to the class as a whole and reflect on the class discussion questions.

EXERCISE 11.3

Creating a Shared Vision

Read the following excerpt from Peter Block. Then read the excerpt from Burt Nanus. Compare the two versions and answer the questions that follow.

Peter Block

There is something deep in each of us that wants a common vision articulated by those in power. To suggest otherwise is almost heresy. This longing for a common vision is the wish for someone else to create the unity we seek, someone above to create community, rallying cries, and common purpose.

We have bought the notion that vision must come from the top. What this means in practical terms is that a consultant or staff person has spent a lot of time interviewing executives and writing vision paragraphs. Ownership of the vision resides with those who craft a vision and with them alone. A statement created for a team to endorse is not owned by the team. Even more problematical is that, in most cases, the vision is created for the rest of the organization to live out. An appropriate task for management is to define business mission and set business goals, but a vision created for others is patriarchy in action.

Top management surely needs a vision statement, but for themselves alone to live out and be accountable for. As soon as top management creates a vision statement for the rest of the organization to embrace, the parenting relationship has begun cloaked in the robe of partnership.[66]

Burt Nanus

You must be able to relate skillfully to workers inside your organization who look to you for guidance, encouragement and motivation….You must be able to shape and influence all aspects of your organization. You must be able to set a course toward a destination that others will recognize as representing real progress…a vision so compelling that everyone in the organization will want to make it happen.

The leader is responsible for catalyzing changes in the internal environment….[Leaders]make the vision achievable in the future. They adopt challenging new visions of what is both possible and desirable, communicate their vision, and persuade others to become so committed to these new directions that they are eager to lend their resources and energies to make them happen.

These forces unleashed by the right vision can be summarized in one word that has become the theme for leadership in the 1990s: empowerment. Once people buy into the vision…they are empowered, to take actions that advance the vision.[67]

1. What values are implicit in Block's view of vision? In Nanus's view of vision?

2. Which version do you think is more effective?

3. Which version do you think is the right one? Are there circumstances in which both can be right?

4. Which version do you intuitively feel most akin to? What values are implicit in your choice?

5. Nanus asserts that once people buy into the vision, they are empowered to take action to advance the vision. How do you assess Nanus's definition of empowerment? Are you empowered when you advance another person's vision? Why or why not? If not, under what circumstances do you become empowered?

EXERCISE 11.4

Equal Treatment Dilemma

Review the following excerpt from Victor A. Thompson. Think about how this statement relates to the provision of social welfare services, and answer the questions that follow. In class, discuss your opinion with your classmates and come to some conclusion.

The modern administrative norm, which made efficient administration possible, was the rule that everyone in the same problem category should be treated equally.

The result of the norm was to strip away the uniqueness of individuals and to turn administration into an efficient mass processing of cases within each problem category. This resulted in an enormous lowering of unit costs plus other valuable consequences, such as predictability. Thus the norm was a necessary prerequisite of modern, mass-democratic government....

Nearly all administrative organizations...apply the norm of equality. Even in nondemocratic governments of industrial nations, the norm is applied to everyone, but the political elite. The "rule of law" in this sense is an administrative necessity in an industrial country.[68]

1. Do social workers follow the "modern administrative norm," that everyone in the same problem category should be treated equally? How does social work administration expect us to treat clients?

2. Do social workers "strip away the uniqueness of individuals and turn administration into an efficient mass processing of cases?"

3. Do you agree that the "rule of law" is an administrative necessity? What would happen if we abandoned the rule of law in our organizational arrangements and instituted personalized, individualized, unequal administration instead?

4. Is there any way to reconcile providing individual personal treatment for people as well as treating everyone equally?

5. Thompson asserts that the rule of equality is a "necessary prerequisite of modern, mass-democratic government." What does this statement mean? Do you believe that modern mass democratic government operates by a rule of equality? Why or why not? How do you think poor people in this country would answer that question?

ADVANCED EXERCISE 11.5

Reassembling an Organization for the Elderly

In this exercise you will have an opportunity to explore how to "reassemble" an agency that was in serious disrepair, applying your skills in organizational diagnosis and problem-solving. This is a real-life example, submitted by Dr. Charles Trent, Wurzweiler School of Social Work, Yeshiva University. After you have read the following vignette, answer the questions that follow. Once you have completed your assessment, read the description of how Dr. Trent reassembled the agency your instructor will give you. Compare your assessment with his approach.

One day, without notice, my predecessor walked out of the community-based nonprofit agency and never returned. All attempts to contact him were futile. With him went all undocumented administrative memory accrued during his tenure. He took all of his administrative records and other key files. The major question asked by the board in my hiring interviews was, "How will you help our little agency recover?" This little agency's challenges presented many significant organizational problems. Although it had historical successes advocating against injustices directed toward the elderly, the agency now needed an advocate. Its most serious problems were:

1. The executive director had arbitrarily abandoned the agency, taking key administrative memory and documents with him.

2. External accountability organizations were closing in and demanding appropriate action from the agency.

3. The entire staff was demoralized and had not been paid for two months.

4. Services were not being provided to the agency's constituents and they were angry.

5. Local agencies, sensing the agency's weaknesses, began to signal competitiveness for the agency's assets.

6. Local and federal politicians (the city councilman, state assemblyman, state senator, and congressman) wanted the agency to explain how it was going to recover.

7. Some board members were suggesting that the organization close its doors.

8. No administrative structure was in place to enable the agency to cope.

Although I was unsure I would draw a salary for awhile, I jumped at the chance to design an intervention. I figured that such intervention would help the enrolled clientele, the agency, and the larger community, and that it would help me develop my skill at managing, administering, and organizing. Of course my primary interest in line with the code of ethics was helping the constituents, members, clients, and consumers of the agency's services.

One major administrative objective was to disassemble the entire organization and renew it in one year so that current contracts would remain in place and new ones could be negotiated. Breaking down an automobile to know how it is put together is a frequent analogy in disassembly theory, which I had learned in management classes. Although one person can break down a car, disassembling a nonprofit organization is a group interactive process of collecting, classifying, and analyzing written documents (reports, minutes, letters, memos, by-laws, case files, and others) to know the earlier decisions and commitments that were made, by whom and to whom. When many key documents are missing, then interviewing available key informants is necessary. These data then form the foundation of restructuring and rebuilding a totally new organization that has a different mission statement, revised by-laws, a new organization chart, and new marketing tools.

Because there was an irrational change of executive leadership with no logical communication between either the board or the new executive with the old director, the entire agency had to be reassembled. I had to develop a theory on which to disassemble and reassemble the organization. Moreover, the probable decisions and commitments made by my predecessor had to be constructed, understood, and factored into current and future decision-making and control.

Case Analysis

You are a young, ambitious administrator of this small nonprofit organization for the elderly. Individually design a plan for helping the organization for the elderly to solve the problems Dr. Trent identified, keeping in mind there are no absolutely right or wrong answers.

1. How would you prioritize these problems?

2. How would you go about solving them?

In class, break into groups of five. Compare your action plan with those of your classmates. Then, compare your solutions to those that the administrator of this agency actually used.

1. Do you think your plan would be successful?

2. Do you think that the administrator's plans were successful?

3. What is your assessment of how the administrator applied theory to practice?

ADVANCED EXERCISE 11.6
Designing a Program Evaluation

This exercise refers to Exercises 10.2 and 10.3 in Chapter 10. One of the components of the ROY program in which foundations and government agencies are particularly interested is the drug rehabilitation program. The program includes both a halfway house in-patient treatment program and an out-patient program.

Each program offers counseling, medical care, and a twelve-step program. The counseling and medical care components use innovative treatment methods, and foundations and governmental agencies are interested in assessing the effectiveness of these methods. The halfway house has space for six youths and includes recreation and life skills training. The board of the ROY program has decided that it wants to assess the effectiveness of the counseling, medical care, and drug treatment services compared with those of other drug treatment programs. Second, it wants to measure the effectiveness of the in-patient drug treatment services in comparison with out-patient services to help in deciding which program should be refunded after the first year. Third, it wants an internal systems process analysis of the overall ROY program.

Form into teams of six persons. Develop a program evaluation design for each of the three components to be measured.

1. How would your team compare the effectiveness of the ROY program with other programs?

2. How would your team measure the in-patient and the out-patient program and compare them?

3. What internal systems issues in the overall ROY program would you choose to monitor, and how would you monitor them?

In your research design, describe:

1. How you would decide on the goals of your research.

2. How you would operationalize your goals, i.e., what effectiveness criteria you would use.

3. What tests, scales, indices, or other measures you would use.

4. What methods of data collection you would use.

5. What kinds of research designs you would choose, for example, a pure experimental research design, a quasi-experimental design, or a benefit-cost analysis?

After your group has developed its design, share it with other groups. What were the best features of the different designs? How could your design have been improved?

ADDITIONAL READING

Federal Regulations Dealing With Administration

Executive Order No. 11246.

Title VII of the Civil Rights Act of 1964 as amended in 1991.

Age Discrimination in Employment Act, 1967, as amended in 1978 and 1986.

Americans With Disabilities Act, 1990.

Equal Opportunity Act, 1972.

Equal Pay Act, 1963.

Fair Labor Standards Act.

Immigration Reform and Control Act, 1985.

Rehabilitation Act, 1973, especially handicap sections (sections 503 and 504).

Vietnam Veteran Era Veterans Readjustment Assistance Act of 1974 (veteran status).

Veterans Reemployment Rights Act.

1972 amendments to the 1964 Civil Rights Act.

General Administration

Carl J. Bellone. *Organization Theory and the New Public Administration.* Boston: Allyn and Bacon, 1980.

Joseph and Susan Berk. *Managing Effectively: A Handbook for First Time Managers.* New York: Sterling, 1991.

R. Carter. *The Accountable Agency.* Beverly Hills, CA: Sage, 1983.

Elliot M. Fox and Luther Urwick. *Dynamic Administration: The Collected Papers of Mary Parker Follett.* New York: Hippocrene Books, 1977.

Michael M. Harmon. *Action Theory for Public Administration.* New York: Longman, 1981.

David Schuman. *Bureaucracies, Organizations, and Administration: A Political Primer.* New York: Macmillan, 1976.

Social Administration

Peter Block. *Stewardship: Choosing Service Over Self-Interest.* San Francisco: Berrett-Koehler Publishers, 1993.

R. L. Edwards and David M. Austin. "Managing Effectively in an Environment of Competing Values," in *Skills for Effective Human Services Management.* Ed. R. L. Edwards and J. A. Yankey. Washington, DC: NASW Press, 1991, pp. 5–22.

Leslie H. Garner Jr. *Leadership in Human Services: How to Articulate and Implement a Vision to Achieve Results.* San Francisco: Jossey-Bass in collaboration with the National Child Welfare Leadership Center, School of Social Work, University of North Carolina, Chapel Hill, 1989.

C. A. Glisson. "A Contingency Model of Social Welfare Administration," *Administration in Social Work,* 5 (1981): pp. 15–30.

Burton Gummer. *The Politics of Social Administration: Managing Organizational Politics in Social Agencies.* Englewood Cliffs, NJ: Prentice-Hall, 1990.

P. R. Keys and L. Ginsberg, eds. *New Management in Human Services.* Silver Spring, MD: NASW, 1988.

Sharon M. Oster. *Strategic Management for Nonprofit Organizations: Theory and Cases.* New York: Oxford University Press, 1995.

R. E. Quinn. *Beyond Rational Management: Mastering the Paradoxes and Competing Demands of High Performance.* San Francisco: Jossey-Bass, 1988.

Charles A. Rapp and John Poertner. *Social Administration: A Client Centered Approach.* New York: Longman, 1992.

Earl Shorris. *Scenes for Corporate Life: The Politics of Middle Management.* New York: Penguin, 1981.

Rex Skidmore. *Social Work Administration: Dynamic Management and Human Relationships.* 2d ed. Englewood Cliffs, NJ: Prentice-Hall, 1990.

Simon Slavin, ed. *Social Administration: The Management of the Social Services.* New York: Haworth Press, 1978.

Sue Spencer. *The Administration Method in Social Work Education.* New York: Council on Social Work Education, 1959.

Robert Weinbach. *The Social Worker as Manager: Theory and Practice.* New York: Longman, 1990.

M. E. Weiner. *Human Services Management: Analysis and Applications.* 2d ed. Belmont, CA: Wadsworth, 1990.

Marvin R. Weisbord. *Productive Workplaces: Organizing, and Managing for Dignity, Meaning, and Community.* San Francisco: Jossey-Bass, 1987.

David M. Austin. "Management Overview," in *Encyclopedia of Social Work.* 19th ed. Washington, DC: NASW Press, 1995, pp. 1642–1659.

Supervision

M. J. Austin. *Supervisory Management for the Human Services.* Englewood Cliffs, NJ: Prentice-Hall, 1981.

R. Bolton. *People Skills.* New York: Simon and Schuster, 1986.

R. M. Bramson. *Coping With Difficult People.* New York: Ballantine Books, 1981.

S. Holloway and George Braeger. *Supervision in the Human Services: The Politics of Practice.* New York: Free Press, 1989.

Al Kadushin. *Supervision in Social Work.* 4th ed. New York: Columbia University Press, 1992.

Ruth Middleman and G. Rhodes. *Competent Supervision: Making Imaginative Judgements.* Englewood Cliffs, NJ: Prentice Hall, 1985.

Decision Making

Irving Janis. *Victims of Groupthink.* Boston: Houghton Mifflin, 1972.

———. *Decision-Making: A Psychological Analysis of Conflict, Choice, and Commitment.* New York: Free Press, 1977.

J. Rosehead, ed. *Rational Analysis for a Problematic World.* New York: Wiley, 1989.

John E. Tropman. *Effective Decisions in Meetings.* Beverly Hills: Sage, 1995.

———. *Effective Meetings: Improving Group Decision Making.* 2d ed. Beverly Hills, CA: Sage, 1996.

Budgeting

Aaron Wildavsky. *Budgeting: A Comparative Theory of Budgetary Processes.* Boston: Little, Brown, 1975.

———. *Politics of the Budgetary Process.* 3d ed. Boston: Little, Brown, 1979.

Finance

Arnold J. Olenick and Philip R. Olenick. *Making the Nonprofit Organization Work: A Financial, Legal, and Tax Guide for Administrators.* Englewood Cliffs, NJ: Prentice-Hall, 1983.

Administering to People

Brown University. *The American University and the Pluralist Ideal: A Report of the Visiting Committee on Minority Life and Education at Brown University.* Newport, RI: Brown University Press, 1986.

R. Coulson. *The Termination Handbook.* New York: Free Press, 1981.

P. Crul. *The Implications of Sexual Harassment on the Job: A Profile of the Experience of 92 Women.* Research Series Report No. 3. New York: Working Women's Institute, 1979.

Equity Institute. *Renewing Commitment to Diversity in the 90s.* Paper presented at the 16th Annual Nonprofit Management Conference, Cleveland, June 1990.

Girl Scouts of the United States of America. *Valuing Differences: Pluralism.* New York: Author, 1990.

W. B. Johnston and Alfred E. Packer. *Workforce 2000: Work and Workers for the Twenty-first Century.* Indianapolis: Hudson Institute, 1987.

D. E. Klinger and J. Nalbandian. *Public Personnel Management: Contexts and Strategies.* Englewood Cliffs, NJ: Prentice-Hall, 1985.

National Association of Social Workers. *NASW Standards for Social Work Personnel Practice.* Washington, DC: NASW Press, 1990.

Merit Systems Protection Board. *Sexual Harassment in the Federal Workplace: Is It a Prob-*

lem? Washington, DC: U.S. Government Printing Office, 1981.

Peter J. Pecora. "Personnel Management," NASW *Encyclopedia of Social Work.* 19th ed. Washington, DC: NASW Press, pp. 1828–1837.

Chief Administration

R. L. Clifton and A. Dahms. *Grassroots Administration: A Handbook for Staff and Directors of Small Community Based Social Service Agencies.* Prospect Heights, IL: Wavelin Press, 1983.

P. C. Nutt and R. W. Backoff. *Strategic Management for Public and Third Sector Organizations: A Handbook for Leaders.* San Francisco: Jossey-Bass, 1992.

C. N. Waldo. *A Working Guide for Directors of Not for Profit Organizations.* New York: Quorum Chapters, 1986.

Program Evaluation

Carl A. Bennett and Arthur A. Lumsdaine, eds. *Evaluation and Experiment.* New York: Academic Press, 1975.

Emil J. Posavac and Raymond G. Carey. *Program Evaluation: Methods and Case Studies.* Englewood Cliffs, NJ: Prentice-Hall, 1985.

Peter H. Rossi and Howard E. Freeman. *Evaluation: A Systematic Approach.* Beverly Hills, CA: Sage, 1982.

T. Tripodi. *Evaluative Research for Social Workers.* Englewood Cliffs, NJ: Prentice-Hall, 1983.

Carol Weiss. *Evaluation Research.* Englewood Cliffs, NJ: Prentice-Hall, 1972.

Benefit-Cost Analysis

M. S. Thompson. *Benefit-Cost Analysis for Program Evaluation.* Beverly Hills, CA: Sage, 1983.

Journals

Administration in Social Work, published by the National Network for Social Work Managers.

Administrative Science Quarterly

Social Work Administrator. Published by the Society for Social Work Administration in Health Care.

Public Administration Review, American Society for Public Administration (ASPA).

Public Welfare

Becoming an Organization Developer

While we are members of a society that protects freedom of speech, choice, and the rights of the individual, we work in places that…view the values underlying democracy with deep skepticism, if not contempt….We are still convinced that for large groups of people to get work done and succeed in the marketplace control, consistency and predictability, engineered from the top are absolute requirements.

You cannot solve [organizational] problems by using the same management strategies that created the problem, however. The very system that has patriarchy as the root problem uses patriarchal means to try to eliminate its symptoms.[1]

Peter Block

Ideas in This Chapter

JEAN CARLYLE TAKES A STAND

For the past ten years, Wells County has experienced a high level of growth. While welcome, growth has also produced traffic congestion, increased gangs, drug use, and crime, and as a result, a rise in the caseloads of the Wells County Probation Department. Several years ago, probation officers were generalists, each officer handling all the persons in a geographical area. As some areas grew more rapidly than others, however, continual shifting of boundaries became necessary. East Side, which contained many immigrant and low-income populations, experienced a large amount of growth and a greater degree of crime as well. Not only were caseloads in the East Side unit growing more rapidly, but also the crimes were of a different nature, necessitating more work. A vicious cycle developed. The more work, the less time to monitor cases and the more likely the charges would repeat offenses. Not only was their work more difficult and caseloads higher, but their success rates were far lower than other units whose workloads were lighter and whose charges were far less difficult.

The East Side Unit had younger, more inexperienced workers and some who were older and more burned out. It also had acquired some of the less competent workers. Many more assertive and capable workers having obtained valuable experience transferred to other units or were promoted to specialist positions. As a result, the unit began to think of themselves as the Siberia of the probation department, as less competent workers and victims of an unjust system.

In an effort to balance caseloads, Jean Carlyle, supervisor of the East Side Unit, had to change assignments often. With each change, workloads became even more backed up. While Jean did everything possible to develop equity, many members of the unit did not feel they could adequately supervise their wards. The six supervisors in other geographical areas where there was less growth, however, resisted shifting boundaries because they did not want to absorb more work for themselves and their workers, cause confusion in their units, or risk their success rates. Supervisory meetings often ended in heated arguments in which supervisors of units with smaller caseloads defended their territory against Jean, who staged what she considered a one-person battle and often felt discriminated against. Jean, however, did not give up because she wanted to make the East Side Unit into one of the best units in the agency and because of her commitment to serving Spanish Speaking and African American populations on the East Side.

Located physically away from the central office, the East Side staff had some status and privilege, resulting in greater cohesion. In addition, officers had private offices, unlike workers at Central, who were all located in one large pool with workers separated only by five-foot-high partitions. However, being isolated from Central, the East Side Unit was out of the loop of information and power. Because of agency growth, the entire agency moved into new headquarters, and the East Side Unit was merged into the new building. The members of the East Side office lost what little special status they had, and what is worse, in the new arrangement, they were deprived of their individual offices. Arthur Thompson, a new probation chief, began putting pressure on all units to meet demands from the state for accountability. His style was simply to apply pressure and weed out workers who were incompetent.

Farthest behind and with poorer success rates, Jean was under the gun to crank more work from staff who were already overwhelmed with more difficult loads and more change, and now had to travel farther to visit clients. The members of the unit blamed Jean for what they believed was her inability to adequately represent the needs of the unit in agency meetings, and for the increased workload. They were angry about losing their private offices. Now they were stressed because of the increased pressure from which Jean had sheltered her workers in the past.

Stress levels in the unit rose even higher. Conversations previously held in private were now heard by everyone. Members had little opportunity to blow off steam with one another. As a result, East Side Unit members began to take longer lunches, sometimes leaving on prolonged visits to clients' homes and not returning until the next day. Meeting behind closed doors, members of Jean's unit became openly hostile to her. "Wimp" could be heard whispered in corridors when she came by. Morale in the unit plummeted. Distrust, miscommunication, and conflicts were developing. One day, in the middle of a conversation, one of her workers started shouting at her. Jean was stunned, as were the rest of the probation officers, as the worker's screaming voice echoed through the agency. Jean went to Arthur Thompson, who only berated her for being ineffective. In spite of what she considered to be heroic measures to advocate for her workers, even they had turned on her. Jean felt helpless, alone, and stressed.

The county had recently hired Kathy Herbert, a social work organization developer, who had visited the probation department and explained her services. With no one else to turn to, Jean called Kathy. Meeting over coffee, Jean for the first time poured out her frustrations built up over years of being a buffer between her unit and the rest of the agency. Her feelings were deep and painful, and it was embarrassing for her to express her grief. She felt that her battles to help her unit, her concern for their good, and her compassion were being thrown back at her in the form of resentment and anger. She felt blamed for the very situations she had fought against.

Kathy provided a listening ear and over the course of several weeks helped Jean work through her anger, loss, and hurt. Together they began to problem-solve and worked on different approaches to the unit. Kathy met with Jean and her unit together, engaging in mutual problem-solving. Gradually, the unit began to see that they were in a self-defeating cycle, and while they were under stress and blaming Jean, their own attitudes and work habits were contributing to their low morale and lack of self-esteem. Jean also realized that she needed to be much more directive and began to make some changes in how she related to her unit. Her self-confidence began to return and she began to feel in control once again, developing a proposal for redistributing workloads on a more equitable basis.

As the East Side members began to take responsibility for themselves, not blaming the supervisor for issues beyond her control, Jean and her unit began to work together as a team once again. Jointly, they began to strategize for solutions. While the external pressures of work did not ease up, Jean and her unit were communicating on a regular basis and reworking their relationships.

WHAT YOU WILL LEARN IN THIS CHAPTER

It is probably safe to say that no organizational system is without defects. Everyone who works in organizational systems will, at times, find themselves under stress, experience burnout, or have their lives thrown into turmoil. They may become demoralized, in conflict with those with whom they work, or experience job dissatisfaction. In addition, if the organization experiences financial problems, people may find themselves out of work and their lives in disarray.

These problems can affect the provision of quality services to clients. Clients of social agencies may experience inefficient or ineffective services, rigid or inflexible responses to their needs, or an organizational system fraught with red tape. Because organizations affect people's lives in so many ways, therefore, macro social workers are increasingly turning their attention to these important social systems, finding that the methods, skills, and processes we use in healing families, groups, or communities also work with helping dysfunctional organizations.

In this chapter you will become acquainted with the emerging field of organization development. You will learn who organization developers are. You will also discover that there are two different kinds of organization development. You will learn about the most popular and well-known method of organizational intervention: conventional organization development. You will explore how to do conventional organization development step by step, including diagnosing and applying a variety of treatment tools and techniques at the individual, group, intergroup, and organizational level.

You will also learn about a much less well-known and rarely utilized method of assisting members of social organizations called the partnership model. You will discover that this model is more congruent with social organizations in social work. You will explore how a social organization developer uses the partnership model to help social organizations improve their effectiveness.

WHO ARE ORGANIZATION DEVELOPERS?

Organization developers help organizational members plan for and carry out change. There are two kinds of organization developers. An internal organization developer is an employee of a direct service social agency such as a county social services department, regional center for developmentally disabled, hospital, or mental health facility, who works exclusively with the employees, supervisors, and administrators inside that agency. Internal consultants may tend to be cautious and more thoughtful in their recommendations because they must live with the changes that they recommend.[2]

An external organization developer works either as a private management consultant or as a member of an organization development firm and provides management consultation, training, and problem-solving to many different organizations and agencies. Robbins says that while conventional external consultants can offer objective perspectives because they are from the outside, they often do not have an intimate understanding of the history, culture, goals, and procedures of the organization. As a result, external consultants may have a tendency to institute drastic changes because they do not have to live with the results.[3]

Organization development can be a very rewarding endeavor. Many social work organization developers have an MSW specializing in clinical social work. They often have acquired additional education at the master's or doctoral level in administration, applied organization behavior, or organization development, as well as experience working in complex organizations.

WHAT IS ORGANIZATION DEVELOPMENT?

Organization development is an "emerging behavioral science discipline that provides a set of methodologies for systematically bringing about organizational change, improving the effectiveness of the organization and its members."[4] Richard Beckhard says that organization development is a process of engaging in change that is "(1) planned, (2) organization wide, (3) managed from the top, (4) to increase organization effectiveness and health, (5) through planned interventions in the organization's processes (6) using behavioral science knowledge."[5]

Most organizations that require organization development services are more or less hierarchically oriented business or public organizations that have taken a reactive approach to solving problems. If you consult with them, it is probably most appropriate to use conventional organization development because it fits best with the managerial style and culture of these systems. The conventional approach is supported by major organization development professional organizations, universities, and writers.

The partnership model of social organization development is relatively new and fits most congruently with social organizations. The partnership model tends to be proactive and membership oriented, encouraging organizational members and the community to engage in a process of ongoing, mutual problem-solving rather than the conventional model of imposing change from the top down. A capable organization developer will be able to use both models as long as he or she is clear about his or her own value stance toward organizational change.

The environment of the organization developer is change. There are a number of factors that impel organizations toward change and factors that cause organizations to resist change. You must understand both of these forces in order to assist organizational members respond positively to the need for change. Robbins tells us that there are at least six forces that are "increasingly creating the need for change—the changing nature of the work force, technology, economic shocks, changing social trends, the 'new' world politics and the changing nature of competition."[6] According to Harvey and Brown, because of this "increasingly complex environment, it becomes even more critical for management to identify and respond to forces of social and technical change." Those organizations that adapt to changing circumstances will survive; those that fail to adapt will not.[7]

In spite of the need for change, however, there are a number of factors that create complications for administrators in trying to effect change in their own organizations. "Organizations," as Robbins says, "by their very nature are conservative. They actively resist change."[8] It is a paradox that while change and innovation is the heart of organizational survival, "organizations are not necessarily intended to change."[9] For example, the system's state, size, structure, chain of command, subordinate position of workers, organizational culture, and administrator may all contribute to an organization's resistance to change. According to systems theory, there is a tendency for an organization to exhibit inertia. An organizational system will tend to maintain a stable state that works against change. All organizations have inherent mechanisms to maintain homeostasis or stability.[10]

Smaller systems are more malleable and adaptable to change. The larger the system, the more difficult it is to shift direction. More people are involved in change, any one of whom can cause resistance. More subsystems must be integrated, coordinated, and linked together.

More important than size, however, are the organization's structural aspects. Modern complex organization, almost without exception, is based on hierarchical structure, unitary command, and one-way communication in which subordinates do what they are told. Each of these organizational components becomes entrenched in a self-reinforcing organization culture that resists change at every level. Top-down hierarchy, for example,

> promotes delays and sluggishness; everything must be kicked upstairs for a decision either because the boss insists or because the subordinate does not want to take the risk of making a poor decision. All this indecision exists at the same time that superiors are being authoritarian, dictatorial, rigid, making snap judgments which they refuse to reconsider, implementing on-the-spot decisions without consulting with their subordinates, and generally stifling any independence or creativity at the subordinate levels.… Hierarchy promotes rigidity and timidity.[11]

In modern hierarchical governance systems, change must proceed up and down the chain of command. In general, it will be resisted at each level, particularly when organizations are composed of highly trained professionals.[12] "Subordinates are under constant surveillance from superiors; thus they often give up trying to exercise initiative or imagination and instead suppress or distort information. Finally, since everything must go through channels, and these are vertical, two people at the same level in two different departments cannot work things ourselves, but must involve long lines of superiors."[13]

When managers see their roles as making decisions from the top, a model of obedience and dependency is established. Organizational problems that may be obvious to line workers go unrecognized by administration for long periods of time. Because workers are functionaries who do what they are told,

they may think it inappropriate to suggest changes and even self-defeating for them to do so. Individuals at lower levels of organizations may be reluctant to complain to their supervisors out of fear of causing trouble. They may not want to appear disgruntled, because this could reflect badly on their performance evaluations. Those who call attention to problems may even be subject to reprisal. "Subordinates are afraid of passing up bad news, or of making suggestions to change. (Such an action would imply that their superiors should have thought of the changes and did not.) They are also more afraid of new situations than of familiar ones, since with the new situations, those above them might introduce new evils, while the old ones are sufficient."[14]

People are very malleable. If the organization culture is patriarchal, people will adapt to those organization patterns. Patriarchy and resistance to change becomes self-reinforcing. According to Herbert Simon, "organizational environment provides much of the force that molds and develops personal qualities and habits."[15] Organization culture naturally shapes human character to conform to the premises of organization decisions. These premises, says Simon, "inject into the very nervous systems of organization members the criteria of decisions that the organization wishes to employ." Organization members are therefore able to make decisions by themselves as the organization would like them to decide.[16]

Organizational change becomes very difficult because "in changing these old patterns, people must alter not only their behavior, but also their values and their view of themselves [while at the same time] the organization structure, procedures and relationships continues to reinforce prior patterns of behavior and to resist the new ones."[17] As a result, "almost any change will be psychologically painful,"[18] bringing with it "upheaval and dissatisfaction."[19]

Organization leaders are, therefore, faced with a dilemma. "In a monocratic administrative system—a bureaucracy—the external owner has all the rights. He alone can innovate," asserts Victor Thompson. While "innovation will depend upon the psychology of the owner—his mood, confidence, faith and so forth,"[20] administrators may not want to hear about problems or may themselves have contributed to them. Even though the administrator may realize that change is needed, he or she may be reluctant or even be unable to change the hierarchical, patriarchal organization culture that he or she has created.

APPROACHES TO CONVENTIONAL ORGANIZATION DEVELOPMENT

Most conventional organization development "seeks to improve the ability of the organization to adapt to changes in its environment. It seeks to change employee behavior."[21] There are several conventional approaches that organization developers can take in planning for change. In the systems approach, the organization developer sees the system as a process of inputs, system maintenance, outputs, and feedback. A change strategy could occur at any point on this continuum. A change in one part of the system process could create changes in other parts of the system.

In the social ecology approach, the organization developer views an organization as an open system that is continually interacting with and adapting to its environment. A dysfunctional organization system is one that has failed to adapt. A system design that may at one time have been appropriate or workable has become outmoded or incongruent with new conditions. The organization becomes rigid, unable to scan its environment or cope with tensions or stresses that its environment presents. You try to help the administration and staff anticipate changes and initiate strategies to adapt to them.

In the levels of analysis approach, the organization developer might focus on the level of individual effectiveness, examining morale, absenteeism, or productivity. You focus at the level of the group or unit, helping units work more effectively together. You help resolve conflicts, communication problems, or coordination difficulties at the intergroup level. You could concentrate on the effectiveness of the organization as a whole, making sure its overall goals are being met and that the organization's culture is healthy.[22]

In the subsystems approach, the organization developer focuses on one or more subsystems in the organization. For example, you could begin by improving the reward system in hopes that improving compensation or benefits will increase organization effectiveness. You might examine the communication system, improving information flow between units. You might work with the decision-making system to improve the decision quality and quantity. You could focus on the fiscal budgeting system, improving efficiency and cost-effectiveness, and reducing waste.[23]

In the contingency approach, the organization developer may view the organization as a system composed of a variety of components, each of which must fit together harmoniously in order for the system to function effectively. You look at the relationship of all of the parts of the organization and attempt to discover which of the parts do not fit well with the others. Once the dysfunctional components are located, you adjust them so that the parts of the organization work smoothly together.

In the therapeutic approach, you assume a role of a therapist whose client is a dysfunctional organization. Just as a social work clinician uses personality theory to diagnose psychopathology, you use organization theory and a variety of theories of human behavior, group dynamics, and organization behavior to diagnose organizational problems. You look at different components of the system to determine where pain is located, and which level of analysis dysfunctions are occurring. You develop a treatment plan and provide an intervention to restore the system to better functioning, and you evaluate the treatment to insure its success.

The conventional approach taken here is one that combines all these various aspects of organization development.

HOW TO DO CONVENTIONAL ORGANIZATION DEVELOPMENT

Individuals in organizations may lack motivation, display decreased morale, or be prone to stress and burnout. Dysfunctions may show up in interunit rivalry, miscommunication, or conflict. The symptoms may manifest themselves in lessened organizational effectiveness, inefficiency, or poor adaptability to the organization's environment. If these problems persist or if an administrator becomes unable to

Conventional organization developers negotiate with the organization's board about their expectations and formalize a contract. (© Spencer Grant/Photo Edit)

resolve them, he or she may call upon an organizational developer to help.

As an organization developer, you begin by meeting with the administrator for a preliminary interview. After listening to the administrator's perception of the problem, talk to the organization's board of directors. Assess whether the problems they have identified are ones that you have the skills and capabilities of addressing. Explain your philosophy. Be clear about your own professional and personal commitment to bring about a better social environment. This may include empowering staff, or insuring that the agency is fully a part of the community in which it resides, for example.

Give the administrators and board members an idea of the time, resources, and cost to bring about the changes that they want to achieve so they can decide whether they are able and willing to undertake the process. Ultimately you must decide whether or not you can be of help to the organization and the extent to which the administration is serious about wanting to change.

Be clear about the methods you plan to use, and the extent to which you may need access to employees, agency records, and files. Stress the need for con-

fidentiality and your expectation that the agency will protect employees, clients, and the administration from reprisal or breaches of trust, which would irreparably damage the change process. Should you decide to proceed, negotiate with the administration and board about their expectations for the project and formalize a contract specifying the timing and nature of your activities.

Problem Identification

Your first task is to clearly identify the problem. One way to assess an organization's health is the effectiveness by which its components work together. You look at the organization's output, its internal system state, its adaptation to its social environment,[24] and its culture.

Outputs   You examine the quantity and quality of the organization's outputs. An effective casework agency will process a sufficient number of clients per month. One that is less effective will have a waiting list or backlog of clients. A recent study of child care programs in the United States found that only one in seven were "of good quality where children enjoyed close relationships with adults and teachers focused on the individual needs of the children." The study concluded that most child care centers, and especially in infant/toddler rooms, did not meet children's needs for health, safety, warm relationships, and learning.[25] In this case, the quality of output goals of many child care centers would be considered poor.

Internal System State   The internal system state is the capacity of the people in the organization to carry out their tasks effectively, interact well together, and engage in productive problem-solving, planning, and service provision. Questions you may explore might be: What is the ratio of service units to their cost? How much waste or downtime occurs in service provision? How effectively are problems resolved, plans carried out, or services provided?

Organizations need people who have effective interpersonal relationships, agree on goals and procedures, and express a level of work satisfaction. Examine how satisfied the employees are. You will be on the lookout for the extent to which members of an organization experience emotional pain and discomfort related to work stress. Employees may be absent or late more often than seems warranted, morale may be low, and work-related injuries may be high. The organization may experience a great deal of employee turnover.

Examine internal relationship processes by asking: What is the extent to which the members of the agency are engaged in destructive conflicts? How cohesive and cooperative are workers? Is there a smooth flow of information among people? How high is employee participation in decision making?[26]

Adaptation   Adaptation of the organization in relation to its wider environment is an important indicator of organizational health. Is there adequate financial support for the agency? Does it have enough human resources at its disposal? How proactively does it scan its environment and anticipate problems? How positive are its relationships with private, public, and not-for-profit agencies in its environment? What is its reputation in its wider community? What is its ability to use resources?

Organization Culture   The organization's culture is composed of the meanings that people attach to the organization and the underlying premises that an orga-

nization represents.[27] The culture is "shared values, beliefs, assumptions, perceptions, norms, artifacts, and patterns of behavior. It is the unseen and unobservable force that is always behind organizational activities. Culture is to the organization what personality is to the individual—a hidden, yet unifying theme that provides meaning, direction and mobilization."[28]

People in an agency with a strong culture will have a clear sense of its mission, believe that its mission is important, and believe that the agency provides necessary and needed services. They will be committed to the mission because there is congruence between what the agency does and what staff want to accomplish. The agency will be a place that helps employees do their best for their clients.

On the other hand, an agency with a weak culture has a vague sense of its purpose, and often there is a discrepancy between what it says about itself and what it actually does. People lack idealism, energy, and a sense of enthusiasm about the agency and what it does. People simply "put in their time" because they know that their efforts will not pay off, will not be recognized, or may be discouraged. There may be an underlying sense that what people do or think doesn't matter.

A weak culture occurs when staff members have little idea about the history or philosophy of the agency. They lose sight of who the heroes of the agency are and the values those heroes represent. Agencies with weak cultures give vague or conflicting messages about what is important or how to succeed in the agency. For example, an agency where the implicit message is "it's not what you know, but who you know" is one that encourages people to spend time appeasing others rather than getting the job done. An agency with a weak culture spends little time recognizing employee achievements and organizational successes.

The culture of an organization is weak or fragmented when employees in some units or work sites are given preferential treatment or when different classes of employees are treated differentially. When a culture is weak or in trouble, people get frightened. This shows up in emotional outbursts such as denouncement of an agency policy in the workplace and visible displays of anger or through personal problems such as a wave of divorces or drinking problems.

Gathering Information

There are a number of ways that you may gather information about the output, internal system state, adaptation, or culture of an organization. You talk to people using semistructured interviews. You may observe the organization's milieu as a participant observer, gather information by means of questionnaires, or examine agency records.

Talking to People   Begin with the administrator and his or her key staff because they are the ones who will implement changes and to whom you will report your findings. For example, ask about the administrator's perception of the problem. Where in the organizational system does it seem to be located? How is the problem manifesting itself? What kinds of effects does the problem cause? How effective is the organization's output, its internal system state, its ability to adapt, and its culture?

After you get key administrators' perceptions, you need to gather information from organization members. Just as a social work therapist offers an opener to a client, you can say, "Tell me your story." Establish rapport and communicate a caring attitude. Make sure that you cover as many people in the organization as you can. Even if you are concerned only with one unit or part of an organization, reach out beyond that unit's boundaries, because what affects one unit will often affect other units in the organization.

Participant Observation   In addition to interviewing people directly, use yourself as a research instrument by means of participant observation. Engage the day-to-day life of the organizational system, observing its culture and interactions. Listen to the gossip, participate in staff meetings, talk with employees as they gather around the coffeepot, and chat with the receptionist and secretaries. Immediately after you make an observation, take time to record the details as objectively as possible. A good participant observer will watch for signs of stress, tension, conflict, avoidance, poor performance, and communication problems.

Questionnaires   Talking individually to people and using yourself as a participant observer will help you pinpoint specific questions. You can devise a questionnaire and distribute it to all employees or, if the organization is large, to a random sample of them. Questionnaires can be helpful because of their anonymity, the speed by which information can be collected, their ability to reduce bias, and the ease by which data can be tabulated.

Existing Data   Existing data from the organization's files, records, budgets, and personnel information can help you obtain a clearer picture of the problem. Personnel information, for example, can give you a picture of employee turnover, an indication of how much sick time employees take, grievances, and other factors.

Diagnosing Organization Problems

After you have gathered information, examine it for patterns, themes, and common indicators that will tell you where in the system the problem is located and what the sources of the problem are. This becomes a tentative diagnosis. Listed below are several diagnostic indicators of problems in organizations.

The Sound of "If Only"   People are expressing hopelessness, alienation, and powerlessness in an organization when you hear things like: "If only I could work with that so and so." "If only this could be changed." "If only people would listen to me."[29]

Dualism   When a company operates on the basis of either/or dichotomies, organizational managers will demand that employees commit themselves by asking "Are you for it or against it?" The implied message is acquiescence to the manager's ideas or policies. Employees understand that they need to "toe the line." Questioning decisions or offering alternative ideas is seen as disloyalty or disagreement.

Unchallenged Ambiguity   If we leave things vague enough, we can't be challenged or held accountable. "We'll do that as soon as possible," "We're working on it," or "I'll get around to it" are typical responses to problems that never get resolution.

Inconsistencies   Supervisors or workers are given double messages, which leaves them in a position of trying to second guess administrators. When this happens, workers or supervisors either take literally what administrators say and risk making a mistake, or they ignore administration, using their own better judgment, but risk going against the administrators' demands. For example, an administrator tells supervisors to tighten services because of budget problems but gives no guidelines. Attempting to comply, a supervisor applies rules more strictly, but fairly, angering a client who complains to the director. The supervisor is threatened with termination if clients complain again.

Let George Do It   People in the organization see things going wrong and do nothing about it. Nobody volunteers. Mistakes and problems are habitually hidden or shelved.[30]

No Problem Here   One level of organization dysfunction occurs when ambiguities or inconsistencies cannot be discussed. A sign of greater dysfunction is when the fact that they can't be discussed cannot be discussed. "Don't talk, don't feel, don't think" becomes unspoken policy. People begin to say, "This is a place that's not prepared to address the issues" or "We can't challenge statements, decisions, or assumptions." Instead of confronting discrepancies directly, people begin to express their feelings indirectly by complaining, griping, and sniping in the break room.[31]

Too Hot to Handle   Workers will tend to stay away from conflicts when the source is their own supervisor or interaction between supervisors. If those in authority demand that workers take sides in these disputes, and workers are caught in the middle, they are in an untenable position.

Unresolved Conflicts   Conflicts remain unresolved when they are covert or are managed by office politics and other games. Arguments may be interminable and irreconcilable. In a crisis, staff members withdraw or blame each other.[32]

Triangulation   Triangulation occurs when people refuse to take responsibility for their feelings or avoid direct communication with others about issues. Instead they complain to a supervisor, who gets stuck with the problem. If the supervisor can solve the problem, he or she becomes a hero. If not, he or she becomes the stuckee. Stuckees tend to be rescuers who cannot say no. They perpetuate triangulation by encouraging people to air grievances with them rather than talk directly to one another.

The Sorry Circle   Sometimes triangulation expands to include several people. One person, for example, is offended or blocked by another worker. Instead of talking to the offender, the staff member goes to his or her supervisor. Rather than bring together the two who are in conflict, the supervisor continues the process, complaining to the supervisor of the offender. Instead of bringing everyone together, the second supervisor assumes the offender is guilty and reprimands him or her. If enough time is allowed to lapse until the offender is made aware of the problem, he or she may have completely forgotten the incident and be totally confused. A perpetrator of the sorry circle may operate even more subtly by sending a formal memo of complaint to supervisors and the administrator without copying the victim. Left out of the communication loop, the victim is presumed guilty, without knowing he or she has been accused.

Overcontrol   As Weinbach asserts, "People at the top try to control as many decisions as possible." Supervisors or administrators therefore can become bottlenecks. They may make decisions without adequate information or advice. They may tightly control small expenditures and demand excessive justification. They may allow little freedom for staff to make mistakes.[33]

Nero Fiddled While Rome Burned   During times of great organizational stress, administrators may tend to work hard at solving insignificant issues while the agency is crumbling about them. For example, in one social agency, the director was being accused of incompetent, its board was under siege, and the state was threatening to take over the agency's operation. Workers were demoralized, services had nearly ground to a halt, clients were up in arms, and the budget was in shambles. A crucial strategy meeting of the administration was held with all top management staff. It dealt with a procedure on how to answer phone calls from clients.

Scapegoating   Agency anger, frustration, and anxiety may get pinned onto one individual or subunit of the organization as a convenient target. The unit or individual ends up with the most difficult assignments, usually with fewer resources, and then is blamed when things go wrong. Ultimately, these scapegoats bear the pain and become vehicles for system dysfunction. "One more mistake and you're out."

I Get No Respect   When administrators are under stress, they may sometimes demand blind allegiance based on their position in the organization rather than on their leadership style or quality of decisions. Staff is expected to support and offer deference to shore up the administrator's sagging self-esteem, compromising their own integrity in the process.

Do As I Say, Not As I Do   In this dysfunctional game, mangers assume that they are a species apart, not liable for the same behaviors or procedures for which they hold others accountable. Dispensing favors or punishment with impunity, they set in motion a culture of favoritism. Double standards become the norm. People are treated progressively as objects the farther they are positioned down the hierarchy.

I'm All Alone Here   The ultimate result of "I get no respect" and "Do as I say and not as I do" is that mangers try to get things done by themselves without relying on others. Orders, policies, and procedures don't get carried out as intended. The manager becomes increasingly isolated, frustrated, and without support.

The Party Line   Overly stressed administrators stop listening to internal and external organizational reality, failing to adequately scan the organization. Instead, they fall back on rules, roles, and procedure manuals rather than what is required to meet changing conditions. When in doubt, they pull out the procedures manual as an authority to buttress their decisions.

Lack of Trust   Lack of trust flows into the culture of the entire organization. "The judgment of people lower down in the organization is not respected outside the narrow limits of their jobs. People compete when they need to collaborate. They are very jealous of their area of responsibility. Seeking or accepting help is felt to be a sign of weakness. Offering help is unthought of. They distrust each other's

motives and speak poorly of one another," asserts Weinbach.[34]

Playing Politics   If organization politics becomes the normal way of operating, the organizational culture operates not on "what you know, but who you know." Those who are "in" are listened to rather than those who raise disquieting questions; supervisors do what will best protect themselves, and the agency may be seen as a place by which maneuvering to get ahead is the norm.

We Have Always Done It This Way   People may be reluctant to admit that things are not going well because it may reflect on them and on their own performance. Because they are immobilized and cannot change, they resist seeing that current practices no longer fit changing circumstances and display blindness to problem situations. Instead of adaptability, they fall back on the adage, "We have always done it this way."

Helplessness   "People swallow their frustrations: 'I can do nothing. It's their responsibility to save the ship,'" says Weinbach.[35]

Burnout and Get Out   "People feel locked into their jobs. They feel stale and bored but constrained by the need for security. Their behavior in staff meetings is listless and docile," Weinbach asserts.[36] Ultimately people become so burned out, they end up getting out of the organization.

Developing a Treatment Plan

Organizational treatment is often complex and involves intensive work. Depending on your diagnosis of what the problem is and where it is located, you can treat systems at the individual level, the group level, the inter-group level, or the organization level.

Organization developers have devised numerous kinds of treatments, and the range of solutions is still in the process of development. You need to be aware that these solutions may or may not work in the particular setting for which you are seeking answers. A solution developed for one organization may not fit another. You always need to adjust any prescriptive solution to the particular situation with which you are faced. This may mean developing an entirely new and innovative solution.

At the Individual Level

People bring into organizations not only skills, but feelings, values, and personal problems. In addition, social workers are affected by the general dysfunctions, stresses, and culture that organizations create. Problems at the individual level usually begin to be expressed in lowered job performance and effectiveness, erratic attendance, increasing tardiness, or excessive absenteeism. An employee may have a negative attitude or become physically ill or accident-prone.

Personal life stresses such as divorce, death, marriage, or giving birth often affect individual job performance. Personal behavior problems such as alcohol, drug abuse, compulsive eating disorders, or gambling can impact work effectiveness. Some people are victims of emotional disorders such as chronic depression, bipolar psychosis, obsessive compulsive disorders, or phobias that affect their jobs. Workaholism is one such disorder that is particularly common in organizations.

When work-related problems are of a purely personal nature, make an assessment, and either provide short-term counseling or make a referral to a clinical social worker, usually one practicing in an employee assistance program. Employee assistance programs provide diagnosis, counseling, and referral for individuals under personal or job related stress.

Sometimes organizational leaders and social workers bring into their positions dysfunction carried over from childhood. Workers and managers who come from abusive, alcoholic, or addictive homes may use the organization as a source of their own addictions. Overworking because of a compulsion rather than enjoyment is an addiction common in organizations. People who are workaholics or who work under a workaholic boss are ultimately less rather than more productive. Driven workaholics inevitably induce stress in the workplace, and because they don't take care of themselves, they frequently feel a lot of anger and resentment, eventually displaying physical symptoms such as irritable bowel syndrome, headaches, or ulcers. Exhibiting denial, they operate by "don't think, don't feel, don't talk" rules. According to Rebecca

Jones, while "work addiction can be just as unhealthy as substance abuse, the majority of U.S. corporations not only tolerate it, they actually reward it."[37]

System-Wide Individual Problems   Organization developers are concerned with how organization systems contribute to individual well being. When system-wide patterns of organizational dysfunction cause stress-related burnout, interpersonal conflicts, or emotional and health problems, you should become personally involved in the treatment process.

Stress   One of the most common work-related problems is stress. Everyone experiences stress. In fact, a certain amount of stress is necessary for life. Positive stress includes experiences that are perceived as challenging, exciting, and stimulating. For some people, speaking in front of a group is a personally affirming and enhancing opportunity. On the other hand, negative stress is physically and emotionally damaging. Speaking in front of a group can be so painful and threatening that the person may become physically ill, forget what she or he was to say, and afterward have a feeling of shame or embarrassment.

Organizations often contain negative stressors that affect people. Excessive changes in organizational rules and procedures over a long period of time can lead to stress and burnout as well as lack of control over one's job environment. A 1988 study by the American Medical Association for example, reveals that "jobs causing the most problems were not those with a great deal of pressure to work hard and fast such as high-powered executive jobs often associated with heart attacks. Instead, the types of jobs causing increases in blood pressure were lower-level jobs where there were high psychosocial demands coupled with little control over the workplace and little use of skills."[38]

Stress caused by the need to conform to organizational premises, lack of opportunity to use all of your abilities, and the pressure of trying to please often conflicting demands of managers and clients is a situation ready-made for major health problems. An employee who is experiencing a high level of stress, for example, may develop high blood pressure, irritability, difficulty in making routine decisions, and loss of appetite.[39] A study by the California Worker's Compensation Institute states that the "increase in work-related mental stress claims in the 1980s was phenomenal." Claims of mental stress resulting in lost work time increased from 1,178 incidents in 1979 to 9,368 in 1988, a total of 540%. Job pressures caused employees mental stress 69% of the time, followed by harassment 35%, firing 15%, discrimination 7%, demotion 2%, and other grievances 11%. The authors of the report recommend that "we should start thinking about job design, about moving toward enhancement of skills, about better job training, and increasing worker participation in decision-making.[40]

Burnout Burnout is an occupational hazard that leaves people "vulnerable to doubt, disillusionment, and an eventual exhaustion of energy."[41] People who are experiencing burnout may also have physical symptoms such as backaches, frequent colds, or sexual dysfunction. Edelwich says that while burnout can occur in any kind of involvement, "it does not occur with anything like the same regularity or carry with it the same social costs in business as it does in the human services where it takes on a special character and special intensity." Burnout may occur due either to individual or system deficiency. Edelwich has developed a four-stage system of diagnosing burnout in the helping professions.

Stage 1: Idealistic Enthusiasm. Many who enter social work do so with a sense of altruism and idealism. You may lose yourself in your helping role, leading to unrealistic expectations in your work. For example, you may expect that your presence will make all the difference in the world to your clients, that the job will work a miracle in your own life, and that success and its rewards will be immediate, automatic, and universal. You may expect that every client will be highly motivated and respond with appreciation to your omniscience and omnipotence.

Stage 2: Stagnation. When the expectations of Stage 1 go unrealized, social workers may lose momentum. The job does not meet all of your personal needs, such as the need to earn a decent living, to be respected, to have satisfying family and social relationships, or the leisure to enjoy them. If you give all of your energy to clients during the day and have little left over, you may retreat from family, or from the sources of rejuvenation that are available. While you may expect the small world of the agency to provide identity and meet your social needs, in reality the agency sucks you dry.

Stage 3: Frustration. Being bogged down and losing your energy and enthusiasm leads to frustration, dis-

appointment with yourself and others, and disillusionment about your role and about the social work profession. You may display symptoms of frustration such as emotional outbursts, exhaustion, or depression.

Stage 4: Apathy. If unrecognized and untreated, frustration leads to apathy, the final stage of burnout. Apathy exhibits itself in detachment, boredom, indifference, and retreat. The job is no longer exciting or fulfilling.

Treatment for Job-Related Stress A number of techniques such as stress reduction, biofeedback, meditation, stress management training, and physical exercise are available to treat individual stress. Companies often provide counseling services, memberships to fitness clubs, and even on-site exercise rooms to help employees cope with job-induced stress. Johnson and Johnson company, for example, has developed a Live for Life (LIL) program, a "total immersion" approach including fitness, smoking cessation, moderation of drinking, nutrition, weight control, blood pressure control, and stress management. By the third year of the program involving 8,000 employees, LIL showed enough profit in the time and money saved by reducing absences and illnesses to pay back expenses incurred the first year.[42]

Agencies can treat burnout by reducing the amount of time that a social worker spends working directly with clients each day, each year, or over the course of a career. After a number of years in direct service, the worker could shift to administrative or educational roles, or provide support groups or peer counseling groups. The best way to deal with burnout, however, is prevention. Help workers at the beginning of their careers establish realistic expectations. Provide education in stages of burnout. If burnout does occur, assist the social worker to assess his or her goals and expectations and make personal or job-related changes.

Quality of Working Life Programs Overspecialization, rigid rules and roles, and formalized procedures can make jobs routine, boring, and lacking in challenge. Quality of Working Life (QWL) programs such as job rotation, job modules, job enlargement, job enrichment, and training can make work more meaningful and increase worker motivation.

Rotating jobs is a way you can provide increased skill variety for employees who are no longer challenged with their assignments. By diversifying employee activities, workers learn new skills, and administrators obtain more flexibility in scheduling work, adapting to change, and filling vacancies. On the other hand, rotating jobs can mean increased training costs, job disruption, and increased inefficiency because of lag time in job changeover.[43]

Work modules spread undesirable jobs among everyone in a unit rather than assigning them permanently to only a few people. At the beginning of a workday, employees request a set of job modules that constitute a day's work, rotating jobs as often as three or four times per day. Work modules allow individuals greater autonomy over work, take into account their own particular job preferences, and build skill variety into the workday.[44]

Job enlargement increases the number of different operations required in a job, thereby increasing its diversity. When you expand assignments by adding a variety of interesting, meaningful tasks, you help employees identify with and make projects their own. If, however, you merely add more boring or meaningless jobs to existing ones, your workers will lose the value of job enlargement.[45]

Job rotation, work modules, and job enlargement deal with increasing the number of operations of a job. Job enrichment involves the content of the work. You expand workers' job functions to include decision-making, planning, executing, and inspecting their work. Successfully enriched jobs add not only increased responsibility but also autonomy, independence, self-reliance, and self esteem. You trust the worker to perform an entire job. You provide feedback so the worker corrects his or her own performance.[46]

At the Group Level

While groups are powerful systems for accomplishing work, they can also create difficulties if they become dysfunctional. Communication problems, interpersonal relationship problems, poor leadership, undefined tasks or roles, and intra-unit rivalry or conflict are all issues you may confront. Organization developers and theorists have developed a number of techniques for improving group effectiveness. Among these are T-groups, integrated work teams, project management, quality circles, team development, and group conferences.

T-Groups   T-groups, or training groups, are also known as sensitivity, encounter, or growth groups. They were developed in 1946 by Kurt Lewin at the National Training Laboratory for Group Development in Bethel, Maine. Lewin and his associates discovered that feedback of data about group interaction was a rich learning experience, helping people develop self-awareness, communication skills, and interpersonal effectiveness.[47]

Begin a T-group with a structured activity such as a "trust walk," or "nonverbal communication" exercise aimed at generating interpersonal feelings. After the exercise, have members share their feelings. You are intentionally nondirective to promote member interaction and insure that the group develops its own leadership.

By the late 1970s, most organization developers moved away from using T-groups even though they can be sources of rejuvenation, particularly to managers who live "drab and muted lives."[48] Team-building, group discussions and conferences aimed at organizational problem-solving replaced the T-group movement.[49]

Integrated Work Teams   One way to increase job satisfaction among individuals is to transform functional work groups into integrated work teams. Instead of several groups performing a single role independently of one another, assign several tasks to each team. Team members decide on specific member assignments and are responsible for rotating jobs as tasks require. Many work crews operate as integrated teams. For example, in cleaning a large building, a supervisor will identify tasks but allow workers as a group to choose how the tasks will be allocated. Roadwork crews, outside maintenance crews, or construction crews often distribute work this way.[50]

Project Management   Project management is another way to structure teams for effective work accomplishment. You pull together social workers from several departments or units and assign them to work on a specific project. Because project teams are generally temporary, a leader needs to know how to build a team quickly, adapt his or her leadership style to the situation, and help the group become a functioning unit. The leader must help members understand and accept their new role assignments.

If not organized correctly, a project management team has potential for role or task conflict. You can assist the new project team leader to think through these issues before the project team is developed, and assist the leader to help the group through its life cycle.

Integrated work teams, such as this group of employees at East Wind Nutbutters, a cooperatively run company, decide on specific member assignments and the responsibility for rotating jobs. (Courtesy of East Wind Community, Tecumseh, MO)

Quality Circles   A quality circle is a voluntary group of workers, often a normal work unit, that has a shared area of responsibility. They meet together weekly on company time and on company premises to discuss their quality problems, investigate causes of problems, recommend solutions, and take corrective action. Members not only take responsibility for solving problems but generate and evaluate their own feedback. Part of a quality circle's success means developing trust, sharing, and good communication skills, much as occurs in a T-group.[51]

Team Development and Group Conferences   A team is a "group of individuals who depend upon one anther to accomplish a common objective."[52] You can use team building or team development to assist work group members who are either unfamiliar with one another or who are experiencing difficulty in working together. Your goal is to increase the communication, cooperation, and cohesiveness of units to increase their effectiveness.

This process is also appropriate for engaging two departments experiencing interunit rivalry. Bring them together to consider how to better attain organizational objectives. A meeting of two or more units is called a group conference.

There are six steps in the team development/group conference process:

Step 1: Establish the need for a team or a team development process.

Step 2: Diagnose the Problem. Hand out questionnaires and meet with the team to formulate a diagnosis of the level of team development and to establish an agenda of issues.

Step 3: Planning. Provide feedback to the team members on the issues, establish a set of objectives, and develop a group contract with the team asking for a commitment to work on specific issues over a span of time.

Step 4: Decide on Problems. Ideally have the team meet for several days away from the office. Restate the objectives and lay out the issues. Ask members to develop an agenda and rank the issues in order of priority. Ask them to write down five problems they consider detrimental to the group's functioning and task accomplishment. Rank the problems from 1 to 5, 1 being the most serious problem. Make five columns, ranking each column in order of importance or urgency, the first column being most urgent or important and the last column not urgent:

1. Most Urgent, needs immediate response
2. Very Urgent, needs response within the week
3. Urgent, needs response within the month
4. Less Urgent, can wait more than one month
5. Not Urgent, can be put off for the immediate future

Place the problem issues that members ranked 1 or most serious under the heading "most urgent," those ranked 2 under "very urgent," and so on. Once group members are satisfied with the completeness of the listing, ask them to determine the "ease" and "speed" of arriving at solutions. For each problem, weight ease of solution: E for easy, MD for moderately difficult, and H for hard. Indicate amount of time it will take to reach resolution. Speed can be indicated by Q for quick, M for moderate, and L for lengthy. Members can now see which issues are most important and most urgent, and how difficult and long it will take to resolve them. With this new information, group members can decide which problems to tackle first. Sometimes a very important problem may appear to have a fairly easy solution. On the other hand, the team may decide on dealing with shorter term, more immediate solutions that can easily be resolved even though they may not be most important.

Step 5: Resolution Process. Help members reach agreement to work in new ways, restructure roles, and develop time-lines to test out new processes. The means by which the group works on its own internal problems can be a beginning for restructuring the group's internal dynamics. For example, if the leadership is identified as a major problem, assign the unit supervisor or division chief to observe or record the process, and appoint someone else to lead the group. This will enable the administrator to be objective and involved, and insure that she or he hears what is said about administration without the need to be defensive.

If there are subgroup rivalries within the group, break the subgroups apart and place them in different groups to promote interaction with others. If communication problems or conflicts exist between particular members, form them into triads. Ask each triad to choose a problem to focus on. One member tells his or her perceptions of the problem while the listener reflects back. Message senders and receivers exchange roles so each practices communication and listening, while an observer gives feedback. During these exchanges, work closely with each subgroup, listening, facilitating, modeling, coaching, giving feedback, and structuring activities to help members work more closely together.

Once members have resolved an interpersonal issue, they may be ready to deal with task-related issues. The goal is to arrive at specific action plans to which all members can commit themselves. Before the meeting ends, the team should list action items to be dealt with, who will be responsible for each item, and a time schedule.[53]

Step 6: Evaluation. Develop criteria for evaluating whether the team has been effective, provide training in the new processes, and, if needed, make periodic reassessments and adjustments.

At the Intergroup Level

Organizational problems often exist at the boundaries between subunits in an organization where different groups, units, or departments interact, communicate, and relate.

Problem-Solving Task Forces A problem-solving task force is a short-term conference group made up of two departments that are having trouble coordinating their work. The following process is a modification of a technique called intergroup team building developed by Robert Blake, Herbert Shepard, and Jane Mouton.[54]

Bring both units together. Elicit as many symptoms as possible to get a clear picture of the performance problems and uncover their dynamics. Have each unit go to separate rooms. Using information developed in the discussion phase, ask them to develop a list of problems that interfere with performance between the units. After the lists are complete, the units meet together and record their lists on a board for all to see. Facilitate a process of narrowing the lists to specific underlying issues or causes. Divide the larger group into several subgroups, comprised of equal representation from each of the two units. Ask them to arrive at solutions to the problems they have identified.

Have the subgroups return to the larger group to report on solutions and reach a consensus. Develop a mutual contract in which both units commit themselves to the joint solution, agree to assess its effectiveness, and report back to evaluate on a specific date.

Problem-solving task forces are useful in solving problems that have reached a crisis point. For longer term solutions, however, you may need to develop ongoing coordination task forces composed of representatives from various units whose role is to monitor, assess, and propose solutions to continuing interunit coordination problems, to resolve disputes, and facilitate planning or production between units.

Boundary Spanning   Boundary spanners are staff troubleshooters who are on the lookout for problems and work to insure that the relationships between units are smooth. Boundary spanners coordinate efforts between units, teams, or task forces by bringing them together for problem-solving. They help resolve conflicts between supervisors or department heads, facilitate integration and work flow, listen to complaints, and in general make sure that communication and integration of the units occur.[55]

Conflict Resolution Strategies

The Chinese word for change contains two symbols, one meaning danger the other opportunity. While change can create opportunity, it is not without risk. One of the darker aspects of change is conflict in which some attain their goals but at the expense of others who perceive themselves as being blocked. Conflict is common in organizations, especially when there is a great deal of interdependency creating rivalry and communication and performance problems.[56] One of your roles as an organization developer is to help manage conflict constructively. Most conflicts follow predictable stages or steps (see Figure 12.1).[57]

Stage 1: Tension Development. A minor conflict occurs. The issue may seem insignificant, but it creates discomfort. While this is the best time to deal with the irritation, people tend to avoid recognizing or confronting the situation, hoping it will pass or not repeat itself.

Stage 2: Role Dilemma. As conflicts continue, a dilemma is created and tension builds. While parties

may feel that this situation should not have occurred, they experience increased powerlessness and helplessness. In order to resolve their confusion and reach equilibrium, parties may try to understand who is at fault, pinpoint the cause of the problem, and attach it to an incident, issue, event, or person. The injured parties try to get out of the dilemma by asking themselves, "What am I doing to cause this tension?" "What is the other person doing?" "What went wrong?" "What is happening here?" "Because individuals often struggle alone with the issue, their questions may remain unanswered, perceptions may become entrenched, and dilemmas continue. Issues become more urgent and it may become difficult for the parties to break the cycle on their own.

Stage 3: Injustice Collecting. If the cycle is not broken, people begin to attach blame. Hurts multiply, piling up with each new confrontation. They nurse their wounds, inventory injustices, dwelling internally on their own injuries. Each party feels justified in his or her anger, actively blaming the other party. The parties involved unconsciously prepare for battle. At this point, it is still possible to break the cycle by having the parties face each other and talk about the issues. But because individuals have withdrawn into their hurts, dialoguing with themselves, and cataloging their own injuries, communication will tend to be tense and difficult.

Stage 4: Confrontation. The original problem may have been forgotten or swallowed up in each person's accumulated hurts. The focus of the conflict is now on getting even, obtaining revenge, or restitution. Trading hurts, however, only exacerbates injuries, further damaging relationships, blocking communication, and separating the parties from understanding or resolving the issue. Conflict at this stage is often destructive. If people remain inflexible at this stage, conflict may escalate into a fight or the parties may refuse to interact at all. If the parties are able to stop trading verbal punches or open themselves to one another, however, you may be able to trace the conflict back to the original problem and work toward resolution.

Stage 5: Adjustments. If the parties have chosen to either fight or withdraw, they will have locked themselves in a standoff. In families this leads to separation and divorce; in international conflict it leads to a battle or a "cold war." In organizations, an employee may ask for a transfer or quit, rival units may refuse to work on common projects, and labor unions may go on strike. If, however, the parties have been able to engage one

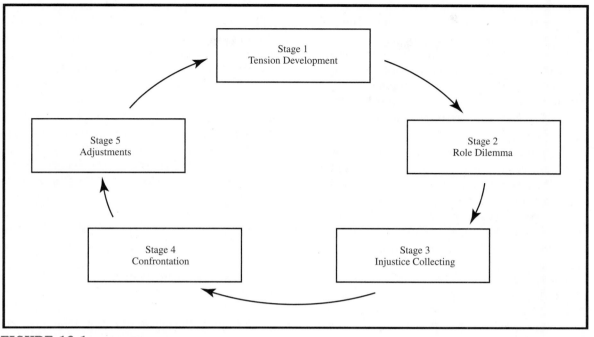

FIGURE 12.1 The Conflict Cycle

another, you may be able to assist them to make adjustments using intensive third-party peacemaking, mediation, or arbitration.

Unconditional Commitment If you become engaged in conflict resolution, remember that jumping into the content of a dispute without laying groundwork will often only escalate the conflict and produce negative results. The best resolutions come about when both parties have made an unconditional commitment to be constructive and to do only those things that will be good for the interunit groups' relationship.[58] The following list is an adaptation of ideas derived from the "Unconditionally Constructive Strategy" developed by Roger Fisher and Scott Brown of the Harvard Negotiating Project.[59]

1. I will commit myself to make things right, even if I may not be sure of how that may occur or how committed others may be at the moment. I will declare my intention to resolve the conflict and work toward reconciliation even if others' commitment seems to waver.

2. I will work at expressing and owning my negative as well as positive feelings so that what caused them can be worked through and resolved.

3. I will balance reason and emotion even if other parties are acting only emotionally or only logically.

4. I will work at understanding. Even if they misunderstand me, I will try to understand them.

5. I will work at good communication. Even if others are not listening, I will listen to them and consult with them on matters that affect them.

6. I will be reliable. Even if others are trying to deceive me, I will neither offer blind trust nor will I try to deceive them.

7. I will use persuasion rather than coercion. Even if they are trying to coerce me, I will be open to persuasion, and I will try to persuade them.

8. I will work at acceptance. Even if others reject me and my concerns as unworthy of their consideration, I will accept others as worthy of consideration.

9. I will be open to learning. Even if others seem to be unbending, I will be accessible and committed to my own growth and learn from this experience.

10. I will relate with respect. I will respect ideas, feelings, and perceptions even if they differ from my own. Likewise I will uphold respect for my own perceptions and expect that others will offer me the same respect.

There are three different processes that you can use in resolving conflicts. Use mediation if the problem involves healing an injury or injustice that has broken a personal relationship. Use negotiation when the issue is external to each party, or to reach agreement in a dispute or arrive at a settlement to which both parties must agree. Use mutual problem-solving to resolve a breach in a working relationship.

Mediation   Mediators are advocates for both parties in a disagreement. Mediators help those involved recognize injustice, restore equity, regain relationships, and commit to future resolution. Have both parties describe how they became involved in the conflict. Ask party A to describe the conflict, including both facts and feelings while party B listens and takes notes. When party A is finished, ask party B to summarize the main facts and feelings until party A can say, "Yes, that is what I said." The process is repeated with party B describing the conflict while A listens, takes notes, and summarizes what party B said.

Explain that this stage is to restore what was broken or bring balance back to the relationship. Ask each party to use the following "four R's," and suggest what would be needed to restore equity: (a) related to the hurt, (b) reasonable, (c) respectful, and (d) restorative.

Make suggestions and help parties formulate alternatives. After all of the suggestions are expressed, help see commonalities and areas of agreement. Work through each suggestion in turn until both parties agree that the solutions will restore the broken relationship. If there are still unspoken or unresolved hurts, these need to be expressed.

Both parties then contract with one another to implement the mutually arrived upon solutions. Ask both parties to what behaviors or actions they will commit to prevent future conflicts. What agreements need to be made to build trust? How will accountability be dealt with? Write a summary and have each party sign an agreement. Schedule a follow-up meeting to check what each party is doing to keep the contract, follow their agreements, or make adjustments.

Negotiation   Negotiation is a universal process in which an issue or dispute affecting two parties is settled so that a mutual agreement is reached. People negotiate every day over many issues.[60] The most successful negotiation is one that ends in a win/win situation, in which both parties get something they want, and each will be willing to negotiate again. However, there are also win/lose and lose/lose outcomes. Negotiators work hard to prevent one or both sides from losing.

Preparation: Examine the situation in which both parties find themselves, including the background, culture, and the reasons each side takes the position they do. Ask for or gather information from both parties about their positions, what each is willing to give up, and the demands that each party is making. You cannot negotiate what the other side is not capable of or authorized to give. Asking what is impossible for the other side will only result in a deadlock or a lose/lose situation.

Presentation of Demands: Meet with both parties. Choose a neutral setting in which both parties are comfortable and at a time when neither will be rushed. Ask each party to present his or her position and formally lay out demands. The demands should be specific, clear, and measurable. Plan an agenda.

Negotiating Rounds: Plan on holding several negotiating rounds. In Round 1, you meet with party A, the most inflexible party, and obtain as many concessions you can that will come close to what you know party B will accept. Explain what you think the chances of success are. Tell in which areas and to what extent they may need to give ground.

In Round 2, meet with party B and present the concessions of party A. Depending on your assessment of B's position, you may offer only part of party A's demands. Try to come to agreement on as many issues as possible. On those areas where party A's concessions are not acceptable, extract from party B a compromise that will come as close as possible to what you know A will accept.

In Round 3, as party B considers their position and strategy, meet again with party A and present the items on which you have obtained agreement, pressing A to make concessions on the remaining issues to obtain as much of B's demands as possible.

Negotiate in continuing rounds until a compromise is reached. If either party becomes inflexible, try to understand why and problem-solve, helping to arrive at creative solutions. Then, present those solutions to the other party, asking them to likewise consider alternative solutions until an acceptable compromise is reached.

Mutual Problem-Solving   Mutual problem-solving relies on "seeking fundamental points of difference rather than on determining who is right, who is wrong, who wins or who loses."[61] This technique requires you to bring the conflicting parties together and encourage them to face the underlying causes for their conflict. The purpose is to solve the problem through collaboration rather than merely accommodate different points of view as with negotiation.

Have each party define the problem and commit themselves to a resolution. Ask each party to privately make a list of its concerns and the reasons for taking a particular position.

Combine each party's listings, taking one item from one group and one from the other, rewording the concerns in a positive manner. For example, " I don't want to have to put up with your reneging on our agreements" becomes "Keeping our agreements is important." Write the reworded lists in full view on a board or sheet of newsprint.

Each party silently writes down possible solutions to the problems that have been listed. Place all of the suggested solutions in plain view. Participants assess the solutions in terms of their particular interests and goals. Modify, shape, combine, adapt, or change the solutions until both groups adopt one or possibly a series of solutions.

Develop a mutual contract in which each conflicting party is held mutually accountable for the solution. If a solution does not work because one or the other violates the contract, bring the parties together again to air grievances and renegotiate the contract. If each side tries the solution in good faith, but it does not work, have the parties join together to review why the approach did not work and adjust the solution to accommodate the issues that continue to get in the way.

Management by Objectives

One method of increasing organizational effectiveness is Management by Objectives (MBO). MBO is a process whereby each unit of an organization develops long-range goals and short-term objectives.[62]

The administrator establishes long-range goals and strategic plans for the organization and breaks them down into specific overall organization objectives for each department. Objectives are statements of measurable results the organization is to achieve within a specific time period. Each department head breaks down the departmental objectives for each subunit. Then, within each work unit, line supervisors develop specific job objectives for each worker.

Action plans are developed that contain the sequence of tasks, key activities, and budgets required to accomplish the objectives. Managers develop methods for ensuring the accomplishment of the objectives for which they have responsibility. The action plans are implemented, and individuals are assigned responsibility for specific tasks. Usually managers develop a series of behavior reinforcements and motivational incentives to strengthen performance through training, compensation, or other techniques. Feedback by means of periodic progress reviews adjusting objectives, action plans, and control methods is built into the process.[63]

SOCIAL ORGANIZATION DEVELOPMENT: THE PARTNERSHIP MODEL

Social organizations are different from modern, complex organizations and are based on different premises.[64] Social organization development is not about efficiency, effectiveness, or improving the management of people. Neither is it about "humanizing" modern complex organizations. Instead it presents a challenge to social administrators who genuinely value service, individual dignity, personal self-determination, and freedom of choice. The partnership model of social organization development is for social workers and administrators who have a vision of transforming social organizations into authentic tools of social service, not control of social change, not conformity, and making them congruent with the principles of social work.

The partnership model of social organization development shifts the emphasis from top-down planning and puts responsibility and choice in the hands of ordinary employees of the organization. They are the ones who do the organization's work, who experience its failures and dysfunctions, and who must endure being deprived of full humanity in complex organizations. It is they who must survive the impersonality that organization imposes on daily existence, that robs them of creativity and keeps them dependent. Partnership, more than leadership, offers hope that freedom, opportunity, and service can be rediscovered in the renunciation of organizational dependency. According to Block, social organization development asserts that "I discover my freedom through the belief that my security lies within and is assured by acts of congruence and integrity. I can be of real service only when I take responsibility for all my actions, and when the choices I make are mine which is the only safety I have. Service out of obligation is co-dependency and a disguised form of control. Service that fully satisfies is done with no expectation of return, and is freely chosen."[65]

Social organization development asks: What will it take for me to claim my own freedom and create an organization of my own choosing? What is it I uniquely have to offer and what do I wish to leave behind here? When will I finally choose adventure and accept the fact that there is no safe path, that my underlying security comes from counting on my own actions or from some higher power?

Saying yes to questions of freedom, service, and adventure opens up the possibility of beginning your own experiment in partnership and service. It only takes one instant to decide for freedom and autonomy, one moment of decision to affirm your life and move in another direction. You only have to choose it and have the courage to live with the consequences.

The partnership model of social organization development presents these challenges to administrators and to members of the organization as a means of transforming social organizations from control and threat systems into an authentic means of service and social liberation. When social administrators as well as social workers accept this challenge for themselves and their social organizations, they can begin to assist clients to do the same.

When you begin to carry out the partnership model of organization development, you generally use the steps described below. Keep in mind that you follow the lead of the people you are assisting. The important thing is not rigidly following a process, but being familiar enough with the various steps so that you can apply them when they are called for.

Entry

Helping people choose autonomy, partnership, and service is difficult. When staff and administration choose to create their own experiment, it is like walking into an unlit room, says Block. For this reason, a partnership model of social organization development often begins as an act of faith and gets built when responsibility and commitment are widely shared. The faith of the partnership model asserts that "creating our own practice is the basis of ownership and responsibility," and claims that change can start from wherever

a person happens to be. Partnership and service are exercises of faith, responsibility, and commitment.

You must be clear at the outset that the partnership approach is unlike conventional organization development, but you need to be equally clear that it will improve organizational functioning, effectiveness, and service in ways that will insure genuine congruence with social work principles and values.

Develop a Contract

Try to determine how ready and able the board, administration, and members of the organization are in following through on a project of self-determination and mutual responsibility in taking charge of their futures together. Your goal is to assist in helping social organizations become a community that can be used for transformative purposes. You want to empower board members, social workers, and clients so that they control the organization, instead of the organization controlling people.

You engage the board, administration, and members jointly about your expectations for the project and formalize them in a written contract specifying the timing and nature of their mutual activities. This includes the difficult issues, such as a commitment to improved quality and service. It concludes with the principles for the redesign effort.

Renegotiate Control and Responsibility

You renegotiate control and responsibility with members, administrators, and staff. With each group you ask for exemptions from business as usual to provide space for engaging in change.

Core Social Workers   Your discussion with core social workers is about purpose and responsibility. They join in designing the kind of unit in which they will operate. They exercise more choice and control. In return they claim ownership and real responsibility for the work process and outcomes. Self-management is one way to talk about this.

Everyone has doubts and fears. Even though history may be on the side of the doubtful and their wounds are real, people can choose to have faith in the face of that experience. You affirm their version of history and support them in their doubts by acknowledging the part of you that agrees with their position. You acknowledge their perceptions of reality, while you affirm your faith and commitment in the face of your own reservations and invite the same choice from the other person. You replace unobtrusive control, persuasion, or coercion with an invitation to choice and opportunity.

What is critical in this whole process is that people make choices in spite of the doubts they have. You affirm the choice that you have made. For the cynics, you too can name other programs that have started and resulted in nothing of value. But you can also own the risks of the path you are choosing. For the victims, you acknowledge their feelings of helplessness and their wish that people in power will not disappoint them. You have the same desire and the same doubt. For the bystanders, support their desire for more data, more proof that this story has been written elsewhere and will have a happy ending. You too may have searched for reassurance and wanted more. But you continue in spite of the unknown.

Administrators   The stakes are raised when bosses or people in key staff positions are cynical about what you want to do. They often want to maintain tight control and consistency even after your best arguments have been made. Despite the risk, the process is similar to the one dealing with core workers.

Make the case for reform. State the results you are seeking, the harsh realities the core workers face. Be clear about the principles you want to reach toward and the constraints you have established. Affirm the choice you have made for responsibility, organizational service, quality, and empowerment and ask administrators to support what you are trying to do.

When administrators lack faith or commitment, don't argue or negotiate. All you can do is communicate understanding to them. In a sense, take their side, acknowledge the risks, and ask to be treated as an exception, a human pilot project. You have to be willing to absorb all the risk. You will deliver results to administration, and if you do not, you expect to pay a price. All you want from the boss is tolerance or indifference. You do not require sponsorship, commitment, or even deep interest. If you get enthusiasm, take it but don't set it up as a requirement.

Acknowledge that you want an exemption to normal requirements for control and consistency. Let administration know that you understand the problem your request creates for them. The discussion with administrators is about their giving up control in

exchange for a promise. You ask them to yield on their wish for consistency and let you and the core workers conduct your experiment.

In return for the exemption, you are committing to deliver specific results. Along with core workers you are promising certain operational outcomes in return for the freedom to purse a unique path. You are promising that clients will be better served and the organization will function better. Merely promising higher morale or better teamwork is not enough. You promise that core workers will honor the requirements of the organization, you will keep the administrators fully informed, and you will live with the consequences.

Staff Functions   Staff groups hold specialized positions in management functions. Their jobs were created to insure consistency and control in personnel administration, financial operations, and information systems technology. Discuss with staff groups the need for an exception. In return you agree to give them what they require in terms of accountability, paperwork, time limits, and formal processes so that their work is not hampered, but explain that core social workers and units operate internally as they choose. Let staff functions know that you understand the risks of deviating from the standard ways of operating. The boss as broker may be helpful in getting this exception.

Offer an Invitation to Change

Invite members to make a choice. There is no promise in this invitation, nor is there an immediate demand for acceptance. You only ask to keep doubts and excuses in the background where they belong. For example, say to the cynics, "I understand what you say. The doubts and perhaps bitterness you express, I in some way share. I, though, have decided to have faith that this time we can do something here that will matter, and I hope you will make the same choice and join in this effort." This may not be persuasive and it may not change their position, but it neutralizes the power they have over the organization. While they have a right to their own stance, they do not have a right to hold back others.

Workers have a right to say no to your invitation. They may want a boss who will take care of them in return for hard work and loyalty. Their choice needs to be acknowledged, but it also has consequences. In the longer run, they will have a hard time getting what they want from the organization, and the organization may not have a place where they can contribute. Despite this, there usually is no need to force the issue at this moment. People need to be given time and support to make fundamental choices about faith and responsibility. Block asserts that "we do not need everyone to chose partnership and service. All you need is about 25% to commit and the way the organization operates will start to shift. Over time this 25% will pull the others along and another 20% will usually move on out of their own discomfort."

Create a Desired Future

Partnership is created as each of us defines a vision for the areas of our responsibility. The focus is on the future your group wants to create for the organization. Ask the group to participate in expressing a joint vision of the organization, its purpose, governance, and structure for the future. What is the best way of including the organization as part of the community? How do you create partnership? How does the organization engage in mutual empowerment of members and clients? How is accountability to be provided? How can clients be part of organization and community building?

Form Improvement Teams

Encourage each unit to begin a dialogue about what values are important to each person at this stage of life and how these can be lived out more deeply in this workplace. Dialogue is key. The hallmark of partnership in action, says Block, is to ask people to talk about what matters to them, not to ask people to support what matters to you or the leaders.

Have groups meet regularly to discuss improvement ideas. General Electric has a process called a workout, in which departments meet to discuss and decide on how to streamline the business. It is their vehicle for creating a more entrepreneurial mindset. Quality circles were an early version of a improvement teams. Many improvement teams cross functions and levels. Their focus is usually on cost cutting, quality enhancement, reducing cycle time, and satisfying customers.

Change Work Practices

Core social work, clerical work, and custodial teams meet together to rethink questions of service provision, meeting client expectations and needs, ways of approaching social problems, arranging for services, delivering services, or new ways of making social change. Procedures in budgeting, funding, structuring the work, hiring, and evaluations all come under the umbrella of changing management and work practices.

Many groups set up steering committees and task forces to shape this activity. Steering committees guide the whole effort, setting priorities, establishing study groups or task forces, making final decisions on changes, and monitoring the effort. Task forces get set up to address specific changes and make recommendations.

The section from conventional organization development on "Developing a Treatment Plan" covers this process. You can share your experience about how to implement techniques of work redesign, ecology of work, implementing high-performance work teams, total quality management (TQM), reinventing the workplace, and others. This step is where the idea of service and partnership begins to get institutionalized.

Redesign the Organization

As a social organization developer, you help administrators and members redesign the structure or architecture of the organization. Even when chief administrators initiate reforms, all they can do is initiate. Changes in management practices may not touch the basic structure of how work gets done. Partnership, on the other hand, acknowledges that social workers are capable of defining for ourselves the rules and yardsticks by which we live and work. If you want the middle and core social workers to treat the organization as their own, they have to steer the reform efforts with their own hands. Give people at the bottom more control over how the change happens.

The substantive work of redesign has to be done by self-managing teams of social work and staff groups. Each team of core social workers designs what is right for its unit. Members must struggle with how much of the traditional supervisor's tasks to take on. How does the team do discipline, schedule work, hire and train new members, monitor outcomes, manage suppliers, reassign roles? There is no one answer.

Offer Learning Opportunities

If you want social workers in each unit to design their own experiments, they also should define their learning requirements. The partnership model of social organization development puts choice in the hand of the learner. If training is needed, those who require it define it, choose it, and manage it. Let different units choose their own ways and place for learning. Let the agenda and environment for learning emerge, rather than be a cornerstone of the change strategy. For example, offer management training to core workers in areas like team skills, conflict management, communication skills, quality tools, and work process improvement. Most social organizations create a menu that teams can choose from. Each team chooses its own agenda, and team members attend sessions together.

Trust the Social Workers

With your assistance, core social workers, office workers, and other staff implement the plans they have devised. If you want social work staff to take ownership and responsibility, they will have to define and create the means for successfully living out those responsibilities on their own. You, the administration, and the board must trust that mature social workers have the skills, training, and capabilities to take control of their work, their workplaces, and their futures.

A CODE OF ETHICS FOR SOCIAL ORGANIZATION DEVELOPMENT

In addition to the values and ethical norms of the social work profession, the following is a proposed oath of conduct for social work organization developers:

1. I will begin my involvement by developing a grasp of the organization members' unique subjective appreciation of the organization, despite whatever critical stance I may take later toward the organization.

2. I will determine for myself the degree to which the overall purposes of the agency are compatible with my personal values and the norms of the social work profession.

3. I will be frank in revealing my values and assumptions, explaining my goals, and describing the techniques and processes I will use to achieve them.

4. I will not impose my viewpoint on the agency. I will work to create a climate in which moral-

ethical issues may be critically evaluated, and I may even play an active part in that criticism.

5. I will work to bring about shared responsibility, accountability, worker involvement, and mutual engagement in task accomplishment and problem-solving.

6. I will work to bring about an institutional culture compatible with human dignity and self-determination.

7. I will work to bring about changes in either the organization's ends or means to achieve a healthier setting for the agency's employees and its clientele.

CONCLUSION

Probably no organization in existence does not have problems at some level: employees with stress-related personal problems, units or teams that do not function effectively, departments experiencing interunit rivalries, or entire organizations whose workers are dissatisfied and in conflict with management. Conventional organization developers find a great deal of challenge and satisfaction in helping organization members develop healthier, more satisfying and productive work environments. Organization development can be a very exciting and rewarding arena of social work practice.

Social organization developers use techniques developed to help change organizational systems, but always in the service of means and ends that are ethically good. Social organization development is a new wave of organization development designed to help social workers create social organizations that practice empowerment and self-determination, and that treat organization members as mature adults who can and should chart their own future.

KEY CONCEPTS

organization development
internal organization development
external organization development
systems process approach
social ecology approach
levels of analysis approach
subsystems approach

contingency theory approach

therapeutic approach

problem recognition

problem identification

gathering information

systems effectiveness

output goals

internal system state

adaptation to social environment

stress

burnout

work-related personal problems

system-wide personal problems

Quality of Work Life (QLW)

T-groups

team building

group conferences

integrated work teams

project management

quality circles

problem-solving task forces

boundary spanning

conflict cycle

conflict resolution

mediation

negotiation

mutual problem solving

management by objectives (MBO)

social organization development

partnership model of organization development

QUESTIONS FOR DISCUSSION

1. How are the role, skills, and process of an organization developer similar or different from those of a psychotherapist?
2. How is the role of an organization developer similar or different from that of a community developer?

3. Organization developers are charged with improving the effectiveness of the organization with which they have contracted. Are there situations in which an organization developer may find his or her social work values in conflict with helping the organization become more effective? What are some ethical conflicts organization developers might encounter?
4. Social organization development prescribes a role of moral actor. Is this role appropriate or inappropriate? What limitations or dangers are implicit in this role for action therapists? Is being a moral actor a role with which you would feel comfortable in carrying out organization development? Why or why not?
5. Organizations are tools for implementing the predetermined ends of the owners. Does an organization developer have a right to question those ends? Why or why not? Would you ever find work if you questioned the ends to which client organizations were directed?

EXERCISE 12.1

How to Reduce Resistance to Change

You may be placed in a situation where the demands of the organization and social work values are in conflict. For example, because management uses the force of command, there may be an implied or overt message that employees must participate in a change process whether they want to or not. Change can be imposed on people even if it is against their own wishes. In this case, greater autonomy and worker participation is sacrificed for organizational control.

This exercise will help you explore employee self-determination, mutual participation, and people's right to choose in organizational change. Read the following description of social work values by Lowenberg and Dolgoff and the extract on how to reduce resistance to change, particularly those parts in italics. Answer the questions that follow.

Primary Social Work Values
Frank Lowenberg and Ralph Dolgoff describe some of the primary values of social work as:

1. Regard for individual worth and human dignity furthered by mutual participation, acceptance, confidentiality, honesty, and responsible handling of conflict.

2. Respect for people's right to choose, to contract for services, and to participate in the helping process.

3. Contributing to making social institutions more humane and responsive to human needs.

4. Demonstrating respect for and acceptance of the unique characteristics of diverse populations.[66]

Reducing Resistance to Change

As most organizational change can be expected to generate resistance, it can also be postulated that *the greater the participation of staff in the change process, the more likely that they will have an opportunity to coalesce and organize against the change.* This is especially true when major system change is at stake. In such cases, *use of power and authority may be required to effectively initiate the change.*[67]

1. Compare the advice in this excerpt with the ethical principles cited by Lowenberg and Dolgoff. With which principles is the excerpt congruent? With which principles does the excerpt conflict?

2. The excerpt postulates that the greater the staff participation, the more likely staff will organize against change in organizations. What assumptions about employees are implicit in such a postulate? Is the reverse of this postulate true, that is, that the less participation of staff in the change process, the less likely they will have opportunity to organize against change? What does your knowledge about unions and labor relations tell you about this assumption?

3. The except asserts that when major system change is at stake, power and authority may be required to bring about change. What assumptions about the use of power and authority are implicit in these statements? Do you think that escalating power and authority facilitates change or hinders it?

4. As an organization developer, if you were asked by management to force change onto workers and given power and authority to do so, would you comply? Why or why not? Are there any circumstances under which you should force organizational change onto employees against their wishes? What circumstances might these be?

5. The advice in the excerpt places organizational goal achievement over employee self-determination. As an organization developer, what would you do if you were asked by management to facilitate a change process that might weaken mutual participation, interfere with the right of employees to choose or participate in the helping process?

EXERCISE 12.2
Conflict Resolution

The purpose of this exercise is to discover alternative ways of resolving conflicts in an agency setting.

Scenario

You are a manager of the program development section of a relatively young, innovative, private vocational rehabilitation agency engaged in the competitive world of providing case management, training, education, counseling, advocacy, and legal services for a variety of clients who are SSI (supplemental security income) recipients. Services are up and the company is expanding.

You report to the chief of research and development. Your section is a key one because of need for envisioning services to meet needs in new and innovative ways.

The chief of research and development has decided to establish teams which would oversee each new program service. A team consists of a member each from research, planning, program development, case management, and personnel and is responsible for seeing a new program idea through its original conception, research, planning, funding, and implementation stages. The representative from case management has been appointed as chair of your team.

Recently a promising new program idea has been devised that will create a whole new market niche. At a team meeting you present a plan for the new program idea, including demographics, needs, existing services, cost, and a proposed time schedule. Of special interest, you think, is the introduction of a new computerized system of record keeping which would provide better quality client services, efficiency, and accountability. It would provide better communication among staff, since staff members could immediately access client files, do recording in the field, and send e-mail messages to other staff members, among many other uses. While there would be considerable cost savings in the long run, the short-term costs of purchasing portable computers and software and training people in the use of the new equipment would be considerably greater than using the current method—handwritten notes.

During the meeting the planning manager voices serious objections. He is interested in getting the new program implemented soon, but the delay in time caused by setting up and training people in the use of computerized equipment, he says, would lose the company's competitive edge and overcome any long-term cost savings. He wants to proceed immediately but eliminate the computerized recordkeeping system. As manager of program development, you disagree and note that without computerized recordkeeping, the efficiency of the new program would be diminished considerably, plus the record-keeping system could be useful in all of the agency's programs and services. Its long-term uses would outweigh short-term costs.

Arguments on both sides become heated. The manager of case management sides with you, but the personnel manager sides with planning. The result is a stalemate. After the meeting you reflect on what you consider to be a personal loss. You also realize, however, that your own department agrees with your position and that the planning department is behind the shorter term consideration. Because this is an important issue, you try to figure out what your alternatives are. As you think about it, you see them in the following ways:

1. You can have a meeting with the planning representative and stress the positive aspects of your idea, indicating that the equipment will make the company the most innovative and foremost vocational rehabilitation provider in the state.

2. You can rework your plan to go along with the objections of the planning representative, doing the best you can with the long-term cost considerations of the plan.

3. You can send a letter to the president of the organization, resigning your position on the team.

4. You can tell the planning representative that if he goes along with your position now, you will give full support to his new agency reorganization plan that is to be presented to the team in the near future.

5. You can go to the chief of research and development and request that he intercede for your position.

6. You can ask the planning representative to meet with you for a full day next week in order to work out your differences and come up with an alternative solution.

7. You can ask a member of the chief of research and development's staff to sit in on all team meetings and act as the new chairperson and arbitrator of all problems.

8. You can send the planning representative a letter (with copies to all team members, the chief of research and development, and the president) indicating that his or her opposition to your plan is holding up a potentially profitable project.

9. You can ask the chief of research and development to attend the next team meeting in order to stress the importance of this project to the continued growth of the company.

10. You can immediately walk into the planning representative's office and ask him to justify his position to you.

11. You can ask for the intervention of a third-party negotiator.

12. You can complain to your unit and urge them to campaign for your position to the rest of the agency, hoping to sway opinion your way.

Rank the preceding twelve alternatives. After you finish, break into random groups of five to seven people each. Discuss your individual rankings and come to a group consensus. Record the group ranking. Then, return to the class as a whole. Compare group rankings. What were the most preferred solutions? What were the least preferred? Why were these solutions chosen? How did your individual rankings compare to the group rankings?

EXERCISE 12.3

Process Consultation

This exercise will give you an opportunity to conduct a process consultation. Each student will practice taking consultant, client, and observer roles and practice active listening, giving feedback, and formulating a diagnosis. Form yourselves into triads and choose a role as client, consultant, or observer. Read the following role descriptions:

Client: Think of an organizational problem with which you are involved, at work or in school, that needs resolution. The problem can be at the individual, group, intergroup, or organization level. Write the problem down. You will present this problem to the consultant.

Consultant: You are an organization development specialist. Your role is to help the client tell his or her story by listening actively to the client. For example, you will use empathy, practice perception checking, clarify the problem, use reflection, and give feedback. Review attending, active listening, and feedback techniques. You will try to avoid giving advice or trying to solve the problem for the client by offering solutions. Avoid being judgmental, blaming, or moralizing. Finally, avoid small talk or getting side-tracked.

Observer: You are to carefully watch the interaction between the client and the consultant. Using the "Process Consultation Observer Form," record your observations as accurately as you can.

Each triad will have a total of seven minutes to complete one role-play round. The instructor will keep track of the time.

After consultant and consultee interact, the observer shares his or her observations. Once the observer has shared, the consultant should solicit feedback from the client. The best feedback is nonevaluative. Feedback should not be judgmental. Feedback should describe in objective terms behaviors that were observed.

Role-Play Guidelines

The following questions can be used as a guide.

As observer, what patterns did you observe?

1. Did the process proceed smoothly or did the interaction get stuck?

2. Was there mutual engagement or did client/consultant talk past one another?

3. Was there good communication or did one or the other not listen accurately to what the other said?

4. Did the consultant try to help the client formulate his or her problem or did the consultant try to solve the problem for the client or offer advice instead of active listening?

5. Did you observe moralizing or judgmental behavior?

6. Did the consultant and client stay on track or did they get involved in side issues or engage in small talk?

As client, how do you assess the consultant's integration with you?

1. Did the consultant listen actively? Did the consultant give feedback?

2. Did the consultant seem to exhibit empathy?

3. Did the consultant help you clarify the problem?

4. Were you helped to moved ahead in reaching a diagnosis?

5. What would your next steps be?

As consultant, how do you assess your engagement of the client?

1. Do you feel you were able to follow the issue?

2. Do you feel you were able to grasp the problem concretely and help the client verbalize it?

3. Did the client seem resistant?

4. What do you think your next steps with the client would be?

After a few minutes of sharing, roles are exchanged and a second round is initiated.

Process Consultation Observer Form

Observer:

Consultant:

1. Showed empathy:
   low   **1**   **2**   **3**   **4**   **5**   **6**   *high*
   Observations:

2. Used active listening:
   low   **1**   **2**   **3**   **4**   **5**   **6**   *high*
   Observations:

3. Practiced perception checking:
   low   **1**   **2**   **3**   **4**   **5**   **6**   *high*
   Observations:

4. Clarified the problem:
   low   **1**   **2**   **3**   **4**   **5**   **6**   *high*
   Observations:

5. Used reflection:

   low   1   2   3   4   5   6   *high*

   Observations:

6. Gave feedback:

   low   1   2   3   4   5   6   *high*

   Observations:

7. Reached a diagnosis:

   low   1   2   3   4   5   6   *high*

   Observations:

8. Gave advice:

   low   1   2   3   4   5   6   *high*

   Observations:

9. Solved problem for client:

   low   1   2   3   4   5   6   *high*

   Observations:

10. Was judgmental or blaming:

    low   1   2   3   4   5   6   *high*

    Observations:

11. Engaged in side issues:

    low   1   2   3   4   5   6   *high*

    Observations:

ADDITIONAL READING

At Work: Stories of Tomorrow's Workplace (bimonthly). Berrett-Koehler Publishers, 155 Montgomery St., San Francisco, CA 94104-4109.

Peter Block. *Stewardship: Choosing Service Over Self-Interest.* San Francisco: Berrett-Koehler, 1993.

George Brager and Stephen Holloway. *Changing Human Service Organizations: Politics and Practice.* New York: Free Press, 1978.

Ray Redburn et al. *Confessions of Empowering Organizations.* Cincinnnati: Association for Quality and Participation, 1991.

Marvin R. Weisbord. *Discovering Common Ground: How Future Search Conferences Bring People Together.* San Francisco: Berrett-Koehler, 1992.

Conflict Resolution and Negotiation

Roger Fisher and Scott Brown. *Getting Together: Building a Relationship That Gets to Yes.* Boston: Houghton Mifflin, 1988.

Roger Fisher and William Ury with Bruce Patton, ed. *Getting to Yes: Negotiating Agreement Without Giving In.* 2d ed. New York: Penguin Books, 1991.

Organization Development

Richard Beckhard. *Organization Development: Strategies and Models.* Reading, MA: Addison-Wesley, 1969.

Warren Bennis et al. *The Planning of Change.* 4th ed.. New York: Holt, 1985.

Wendell French and Cecil H. Bell Jr. *Organization Development: Behavioral Science Interventions for Organization Improvement.* 2d ed. Englewood Cliffs, NJ: Prentice-Hall, 1978.

Gary M. Gould and Michael L. Smith, eds. *Social Work in the Workplace: Practice and Principles.* New York: Springer, 1988.

Rosabeth Moss Kanter. *The Change Masters.* New York: Simon and Schuster, 1983.

Tom Peters and R. Waterman. *In Search of Excellence: Lessons From America's Best Run Companies.* Harper and Row, 1982.

Management Consultation

Peter Block. *Flawless Consulting: A Guide to Getting Your Expertise Used.* San Diego: Pfeiffer, 1981.

L. Goodstein. *Consultation With Human Service Systems.* Reading, MA: Addison-Wesley, 1978.

G. L. Lippitt. "A Study of the Consultation Process" *Journal of Social Issues,* 15 (1959): pp. 43–50.

G. Lippitt and R. Lippitt. *The Consulting Process in Action.* La Jolla, CA: University Associates, 1978.

Edgar A. Schein. *Process Consultation: Its Roles in Organization Development.* Reading MA: Addison-Wesley, 1969

*M*acro Social Work at the Societal and Global Levels

Four

By almost any standards, democratic participation has dramatically declined in the past 15 years. Voter turnout has dwindled. Political party identification is rare. Those with money almost completely dominate electoral politics and the policy making process.... Citizens distrust politicians. Most are deeply cynical about and alienated from public life. Civic culture has devolved into a brutish individualism. Only the private—personal and family issues—seem to matter.[1]

Robert Fisher

It must be considered that there is nothing more difficult to carry out, or doubtful of success, or more dangerous to handle than to initiate a new order of things. For the reformer has enemies in all those who profit by the old order, and only lukewarm defenders in those who would profit by the new.[2]

Niccolo Machiavelli

*D*emocracy in America, as well as other nations, is a top-down process in which policies formulated at the national level are intended to solve social problems at the local level. Local communities and their members are generally left out of the democratic decision-making process. We are often ignored while we wait passively for legislators, corporate leaders, and governmental officials to solve problems for us. The result is generalized apathy and our uninvolvement in the political process.

Gradually, however, many of us discovered that politics of big government and the welfare state has not worked, and that government and large business corporations were, in large measure, a good part of the problem. We realized that social change cannot be left up to professional politicians and we began to challenge top-down decision-making, hierarchical democracy. We have come to realize what macro social workers have known all along: that social change is the role of the citizen.

Everyone has a right and an obligation to make our society a better place. It is a process that is nowhere near completion. It may not even be an occurrence that is completely recognized, accepted, or even understood, but it is a process that has begun. Social change is being accomplished by local citizens and macro social workers—community planners, community organizers, community developers, program developers, social administrators, and organization developers—working together at the grassroots level.

In Part 4 you will learn the role of macro social work in making societal level and global social change. In Chapter 13 you will learn about politics and social policy. You will explore various ideas about how social policy is supposed to originate and exercise your own imagination to discover a better way to devise social policy in America.

While social policy is intended to grasp the major issues about which we are concerned and give direction to government about those issues, there are times when vitally important concerns are ignored or even resisted by policy makers. When this happens, we exert our freedom of expression and right of assembly to petition the government for a redress of grievances. Macro social workers help ordinary people actively demonstrate for social change. In Chapter14 you will see how social activists have organized mass modern social movements to obtain women's suffrage, labor reform, civil rights reform, and disabilities reform. You will learn how to become involved in such movements and that an entirely new kind of movement is developing at the birth of the new millennium. You will discover that these new social movements may be among the most powerful means to bring about a better society.

Macro social workers work not only to develop a better society, but to develop a better world. Macro social workers are especially drawn to the developing world nations where poverty, violence, disease, famine, and oppression continue to steal the lives of men, women, and children. In Chapter 15 you will learn about global social problems, and you will find out how macro social workers help communities engage in planning, community development and community organization at the international level. You will see how new social organizations called non-governmental organizations (NGOs), are revolutionizing our global society. You will find that societal and global social work not only can be among the most personally rewarding kinds of social work, but it can help bring about a better world.

13

Becoming a Social Policy Advocate

If anyone else still has illusions about this country, it's not the poor. They know that this country will spend $20 billion to put a man on the moon, but will not spend $20 to put a man on his feet. They know it will spend more to keep weevils from eating the cotton than to keep rats from eating the fingers of a baby in Harlem. They know it will pay a U.S. Senator over $100,000 a year not to plant cotton, but will not pay $1 to the families on his plantation not to raise hookworms in the stomachs of their own children.

Si Kahn[1]

Every gun made, every warship launched, every rocket fired signifies, in the final sense, a theft from those who hunger and are not fed, those who are cold and not clothed. This world in arms is not spending money alone. It is spending the sweat of its laborers, the genius of its scientists, the hopes of its children.

Dwight D. Eisenhower

Ideas in This Chapter

347

JOAN CLAYBROOK: SOCIAL POLICY ADVOCATE

The tall, bespectacled woman at a makeshift lectern in a Capitol Hill hearing room doesn't look particularly fierce. Her face is scrubbed, her shoes sturdy, her smile ready. In a brightly colored suit and pearls, she looks like an aging version of the Junior Leaguer she once was. But make no mistake; consumer policy advocate Joan Claybrook is no pussycat.[2]

As president of Public Citizen, the consumer-advocacy group founded by Ralph Nader in 1971, Claybrook has a point of view on just about every issue affecting the public good, from health care to insurance, from legal rights to banking. But there are two things that really get to her: automobile safety and campaign finance. In 1992 she hammered away at how much public money President Bush took in during his presidential and vice presidential campaigns ("over $420 million by the end of 1992," she says), while he said he would veto any campaign-finance reform bill that provided for public funding of congressional elections or restricts spending on them. In early May 1992, a bill doing just that landed on his desk, and Joan Claybrook was one of the people who pushed it there. As she sees it, she represents the interests of the people, and the people deserve to win.

"It's important to approach people in the best way that you can," says Claybrook. "We think very hard about that. What is the best way to communicate the message?" She goes about it by studying the issues, learning their history, including previous congressional votes. She also works the media by staging press conferences, writing opinion pieces, and sending letters to the editor.

Claybrook was reared to be a social policy analyst. At her parents' house, dinner conversations were about politics. Her father, a bond attorney and Baltimore City Council member, stalwart of the local civil rights movement in the 1950s, was a founder of the Maryland Americans for Democratic Action. Her mother, a homemaker, was a natural organizer who believed that their three children ought to be encouraged to do anything they wanted, even if they failed. After her parents died, Joan's attitude changed. "I never thought about having to achieve either before or after their deaths, but I realized that I was the older generation now, and that I had a lot to give."

One of the original Nader's Raiders, Claybrook became a consumer advocate even earlier. She came to Washington in 1965 as a fellow of the American Political Science Association, the first time the program included women. Required to work for a member of Congress, Claybrook signed on with James MacKay, a Southern Liberal Democrat who asked her to work on auto safety. She had just read an amazing book, *Unsafe at Any Speed*, by Ralph Nader. When MacKay decided to introduce an auto-safety bill, the first regulatory bill for the auto industry, he asked Claybrook to draft it. As Claybrook followed the bill through Congress, she was introduced to lobbying Nader-style. "I saw Ralph in operation, how he manipulated, maneuvered, pushed and pulled, how he used disclosures to shock people," she recalls. "It was an incredibly fast education."

The following September, the bill, which established safety standards for motor vehicles, was enacted into law. At the end of her fellowship, Claybrook moved to the National Traffic Safety Bureau (NTSB), where she became assistant to the director. She stayed there until 1970, when she joined Nader. In 1973 she founded and directed Congress Watch, Public Citizen's congressional lobbying group, and when Jimmy Carter was elected president, she was asked to head the NTSB. She pushed to require automobile makers to provide air bags or at least passive seat belts. In 1980 she was back in the trenches of the consumer movement as president of Public Citizen. "I have a love of battle," she says. "I work on issues I care deeply about and get paid enough to live on. Who could ask for anything more?"

WHAT YOU WILL LEARN IN THIS CHAPTER

Macro social workers practice in the arena of social policy and politics. You need to know how to develop policy, understand how social policies can be made better, and be able to decide among competing policy preferences. In this chapter you will learn what social policies are and explore who decides on social policies in America. You will critique conventional policy-making and learn about community-centered policy. You will find out how to apply community-centered policy-making step by step, conduct policy research, apply value thinking to policy questions, decide among various policy alternatives, and implement social policy.

WHAT ARE SOCIAL POLICIES?

Public policies are operating principles by which governmental systems carry out their goals in domestic and foreign affairs. Domestic policies have to do with such areas as farm policy, economic policy, and environmental policy, among many others. Foreign policy articulates our country's position to friendly and unfriendly nations.

Social policies provide direction to government in the resolution of social problems. Social policy issues raise some of the most important and fundamental questions of people's rights and social justice. They include such questions as: Should U.S. citizens have inalienable rights to possess handguns? Should women have a right to abortion and should the federal government subsidize abortions for poor women who cannot afford them? Should people who are gay be afforded the same legal rights and protections as other citizens? Should government be permitted the right to execute certain criminals? Should people in poverty be provided with entitlement to financial assistance? Answering policy questions such as these provides positions that guide us in problem resolution.

SOCIAL WORK POLITICIANS

Jeanette Ranking was the first woman and first social worker elected to the U.S. Congress, an extraordinary accomplishment considering the status of women in public life at the beginning of this century. Ranking completed professional studies at the New York School of Philanthropy (studying under Frances Perkins and Louis Brandies) in the summer of 1909. She won a seat in the U.S. House of Representative as a Republican from Montana in 1916. After her service in the House of Representatives, Jeanette Ranking continued to be an activist and spokesperson for women's rights, civil rights, election reform, and social and economic justice.[3]

In 1991 a NASW Pace survey revealed 113 social workers in elected office. In 1993, 165 elected office holders were identified, a 50% increase in two years. In 1992 an unprecedented number of social workers ran for Congress, ten in all. At that time there were five social workers in Congress, nine serving in state legislatures, 26 in county or borough governments, 47 in city or municipal offices, and 11 in other elected capacities. Among the social workers in elected office, 132 were women and 72 were men, 154 were white, 28 African American, 17 Hispanic, and 5 Asian American.[4]

WHO DECIDES: MODELS OF POLICY-MAKING

Before you can have an impact on social policy, you need to have a grasp of who makes social policy. Several models are described in the sections that follow.

Elite Model

In the elite model of policy-making, policy is in the hands of a few individuals who pull the strings of government and business, deciding on the rules according to their preferences and values. They use government as a resource to exact policy preferences in their favor and have influence on and access to policy arenas far beyond others who lack such resources. Galbraith asserts, for example, "the president of General Motors has a prescriptive right, on visiting Washington, to see the President of the United States. The president of General Electric has a right to see the Secretary of Defense and the president of General Dynamics to see any general." Many of these corporate elites are appointed to high-level policy-making or cabinet-level posts in government. Elites often shift from running large business corporations to running federal bureaucracies, and vice versa. They exert enormous influence, imposing their own policy preferences on the agencies they direct.[5]

Elitists believe "the masses are largely passive, apathetic and ill-informed," Dye asserts. Public policy, therefore, does "not reflect demands of 'the people' so much as it does the interests and values of elites."[6]

Institutional Model

In the institutional model, policy is the purview of the formal institutions of government, particularly legislatures. Legislatures of provincial, state, and federal governments make the policy, which then becomes the responsibility of the executive branch to carry out. The U.S. Congress and Canadian Parliament, for example, develop laws governing services to the elderly, child welfare, people with disabilities, and criminal offenders, among many others. Likewise, state legislatures mandate policies for state departments of education, transportation, health, and others. County boards of supervisors set policies regulating departments of social services, mental health, probation, and public health. At the local level, policy is developed by city councils over city agencies.

BARBARA MIKULSKI

Born on July 30, 1936, Barbara A. Mikulski is the great-granddaughter of Polish immigrants and the oldest of three daughters. Her parents, William and Christine Mikulski, operated a neighborhood grocery store in East Baltimore, where she worked during her high school years. Mikulski was educated at local parochial schools in Baltimore. She graduated in 1958 from Mount St. Agnes College and received her MSW from the University of Maryland School of Social Work in 1965. As a community organizer, she helped improve a working-class district of Baltimore.

Because of her engagement in community organization and her leadership ability, she ran for a public office, serving in the U.S. House of Representatives from 1977 to 1987 and then in the U.S. Senate. With her election and reelection to the Senate, Mikulski achieved a number of firsts. She is the first Democratic woman to hold a Senate seat not previously held by a husband, the first Democratic woman to have served in both houses of Congress, and the first woman to win a statewide office in Maryland. She is deputy minority whip and serves on the Appropriations and Labor and Human Resources Committees.

Interest Group Model

While the legislative process may be the means by which policy becomes legitimized, William Morrow asserts that "government institutions have accepted interest-group liberalism as the official public philosophy"[7] by which policy is actually conceived and created. Government institutions operate within a milieu of intersecting interest groups and a political culture of pluralism, both of which determine the direction of public policy in America.

According to Morrow, pluralism is "a mutual balance of power among religious, ethnic, economic and geographical groups, with overlapping membership, all of which participate in policy-making through mutual adjustment of conflicting goals within policy arenas."[8]

James Madison, one of the framers of the Constitution, wrote that a democratic state contains a multiplicity of interests, among which are "landed interests, a manufacturing interest, a mercantile interest, a moneyed interest." Because the natural propensity of these interests "is to vex and oppress each other rather than co-operate for the common good,"[9] government offices should be divided and arranged "in such a manner so that each may be a check on the other that the private interest of every individual may be a sentinel over public rights."[10] Government carries out its conflict management function by establishing rules of the game, enacting and enforcing compromises in the form of public policy,[11] the outcome of which is equilibrium in which "ambition must be made to counteract ambition."[12]

Social problems, Morrow asserts, are supposed to "work their way to decision-making arenas for action. Involvement in interest-group politics helps generate loyalty to the system with the result that society remains relatively stable. Policies that ultimately emanate from group interaction represent a consensus of diverse opinion."[13]

Because of the fundamentally pluralistic nature of the American political environment, policy-making occurs as various interest groups press for policy outcomes on both the institutional as well as agency structures of government. Businesses, for example, continually lobby government for favorable legislation. Corporations bargain for preferential policy treatment in the form of subsidies, price supports, tax breaks, tariff protection, interest-free loans, contracts, or the free or below-cost use of public land, water, and other benefits. Policy-making is a reflection of the success or failure of these groups in having their particular preference schedules enacted in legislation.

Interest groups exert their influence by means of political action committees (PACs). PACs sponsor particular viewpoints and perspectives on legislation and exert their influence by funneling campaign contributions to candidates they hope will favor legislation benefiting them. Wealthy PACs such as the National Rifle Association (NRA) have been able to influence legislation allowing nearly anyone to own handguns and various kinds of military style weapons. While the corporate sector establishes many PACs, the social sector including social action, environmental, and social welfare advocacy groups establishes other PACs, although these are not nearly as prolific or as wealthy. For example, the National Association of Social Workers established Political Action for Candidate Election (PACE), which makes contributions to candidates who profess positions similar to those of the association.

Social policy analysts may work for or against various interest groups, all of which compete with one another for scarce resources. Social policy advocates, for example, perform research and policy analysis and develop policy proposals in favor of children, the poor, homeless, and mentally ill, pressuring government for policy outcomes in their favor. Child welfare organizations, welfare rights groups, community organizations, and others lobby the government to enact policies that will advance their causes.

A problem with the pluralist paradigm of policymaking is that interest-group politics does not result in equally contending actors, each of whom operate on a level playing field, but rather in unequal struggles of powerful elites using organized groups to press for policy prizes. E. E. Schattschneider, for example, once remarked that "the flaw in the pluralist heaven is that the heavenly chorus sings with a strong upper-class accent."[14] Powerful, organized interests headed by well-educated, experienced leaders in control of special interests that have access to policy-makers win out in the struggle over resources.[15]

Public life in America becomes a subsidiary component of private affairs, and government an arena of imperialistic enterprise or "marketplace politics" in which private interests seek preferential treatment in the form of policy concessions. Morrow calls this a "bazaar" model of politics in which organized interest groups bargain in the public arena for goods, services, and policy concessions. Government pro-vides arenas of opportunity for those who exploit its resources to increase their power and influence at public expense. Absent in marketplace politics is the notion of the "common good" or "public interests." The interest group model reduces American politics to conflict resolution between contending actors, which in the opinion of Frank Coleman, "is corrupt, sterile and deprived of purpose."[16]

WHO GETS WELFARE IN AMERICA?

House Republicans took a hard look at corporate welfare in 1995—and liked what they saw.[17] Rather than slashing special-interest tax loopholes, corporate subsidies, and promotional programs, House Republicans chose instead to preserve many of those programs and in some cases increased their funding. "One of the lessons we've learned," said Stephen Moore, director of fiscal policy studies at the Cato Institute, "is that the corporate lobby is extraordinarily powerful in this town." Corporate welfare, in general, includes tax breaks, subsidies, direct purchases, and interest-free loans that provide benefits to a particular company or industry. In 1994 the federal government spent an estimated $51 billion on direct subsidies to industries and provided $53 billion more in tax breaks.[18] In contrast, the total amount of money spent on social welfare in 1994 by federal and state governments combined was a little more than $22.5 billion, less than one-fourth the amount spent by the federal government subsidizing business corporations. Although Congress cut billions in social programs in 1995, it provided corporate subsidies to 129 private industries totaling $87 billion. In that same year a Washington watchdog group found that the federal government provided $167.2 billion in welfare for wealthy corporations.[19]

The situation may even be worse at the state level. In 1995, for example, of concern was what one newspaper termed "the festering pile of special interest tax bills moving through the California State Legislature. What smells worse than hundreds of millions of dollars in tax breaks to multinational corporations at a time when the state's treasury is so empty that lawmakers must cut grants to the blind and disabled?"[20]

One bill sponsored by Pepsico would redefine restaurants and coffee shops as "manufacturers," entitling them to California's 6% investment credit on equipment. A bill sponsored by the Air Transport Association would restore a loophole that exempted airlines from sales tax on fuel and petroleum products. The worst case is Sony, which has not paid corporate taxes in California for years and still wants to take advantage of the new manufacturing investment tax credit. A bill was written to make the credit refundable to Sony alone, entitling them to a huge government gift. As the *Fresno Bee* noted, "Writing tax legislation company by company, to put it mildly, doesn't pass the smell test."

Rational Actor Model

Those who claim that policy-making is a primarily rational process assume that interest groups as well as local, state, and national governments operate as unitary actors who attempt to maximize their self-interest by means of a set of value preferences. This "concept of rationality is important mainly because, if a government, like a person acts rationally, its behavior can be *fully* explained in terms of the goals it is trying to achieve."[21]

Governments compete for scarce resources or attempt to reach prescribed goals in an environment of other like-minded, competitive, maximizing, self-interested rational actors. The question why nations engage in seemingly "irrational" activities such as war can, therefore, be understood in terms of rational action. Each governmental actor is in competition with every other actor to maximize its national interest. These interests have to do with appropriating resources, maintaining the integrity of boundaries, developing "spheres of influence," and obtaining markets for goods, as well as such intangibles as maintaining national pride and honor.

Sometimes social planners or social policy analysts become confused when their arguments to convince political actors about the necessity of policies based on needs, facts, human concern or compassion fall on deaf ears. As a social policy analyst, you need to understand that political actors often operate primarily out of their own rational self-interests. You need to appeal to those interests if you are to be successful.

Administrative Actor Model

While legislatures or parliaments may set broad policies, it is the organizational actors and agencies that interpret, implement, and decide on policy at the local level where it really counts.[22] Public organizations come into being as a result of problem arenas and policy agitation on the part of claimants for a voice in policy-making, a response by government to regulate and mediate conflicting interest groups, provide access to government processes, and act as spokespersons for interpreting government policy. Often there are overlapping jurisdictions, and mandates reflecting a multiplicity of interests and policy arenas. Power is not only fragmented among the branches and levels of government, therefore, but also among this "fourth branch" of government.

Administrative organizations move ahead in small, incremental steps, scanning the horizon of the political environment, responding marginally to pressures. They build on past decisions on a short-term, yearly basis from a budget that has past program commitments. The staffs of these organizations have watched politicians come and go while they continue to exert influence and carry out their routines at the grassroots level. They collect an immense amount of experience, wisdom, and information over the years with which to address problems, much of which is extremely useful in policy debates on one or another solution to problems. As a result, these organizations are often impervious to the demands of politicians, who may attempt to divert or utilize the agency's resources on behalf of their constituents, their own interests, or ideology. Allison asserts that "government behavior relevant to any important problem reflects the independent output of these agencies. Government leaders can substantially disturb, but not substantially control, the behavior of these organizations."[23]

Morrow asserts that "when administrative agencies are established, the expectation is that the structure and jurisdiction of these agencies will facilitate the legitimization of some values at the expense of others."[24]They constitute "intrabureaucratic lobbies for certain biases" or particular value preferences.[25] Public agencies relate to their constituents, provide services, address needs, bargain with claimants for the organization's resources, develop expertise on the policy arena they are mandated to address, arrange interorganizational alliances, scan their environment for resources, and predict the consequences of current conditions. They give policy concessions, impose rules, and propose laws in the favor of claimants and their constituents.

Public organizations become targets of vested interest groups who seek to maximize their value preferences by capturing agencies or by influencing the policy outcome expressed by those agencies.

Public agency staffs often become accomplices to special interests and those who control resources in the private marketplace by helping extend the private marketplace into public arenas.[26]

Interest groups that achieve the establishment of an administrative agency mandated to allocate resources and carry out policies on their behalf, therefore, have a powerful tool in their hands to extract additional policy concessions. The Department of Agriculture, for example, reflects and responds to the particular needs and preferences of the farming industry, particularly the American Farm Bureau Federation. So successful has the federation been that in 1995 it won $10 billion per year in federal crop subsides for farmers.[27] In the same way, the Department of the Interior reflects voices of conservationists. The Defense Department "is subjected to claimant pressure from the various branches of the armed forces, as well as powerful corporations of the defense industry, each of which seeks to amplify its own role within the defense establishment."[28]

EDOLPHUS TOWNS

Edolphus Towns was born on July 21, 1934, in Chadbourn, North Carolina, and served in the U.S. Army from 1956 to 1958. Towns received his MSW degree from Adelphi University in New York, taught in the New York City public school system, and was assistant administrator at Beth Israel Medical Center and a professor at Medger Evers College and Fordham University. Towns became the first African American deputy borough president in Brooklyn's history and in 1982 was elected to the U.S. House of Representatives. He is a member of the Commerce and Government Reform and Oversight Committees and gained stature as chair of the Congressional Black Caucus. He chaired the Human Resources and Intergovernmental Relations Subcommittee of the Government Operations Committee and served as a member of numerous subcommittees in the areas of health, the environment, and consumer protection.

Towns has been a primary player in promoting universal health care. He advocated Medicaid coverage for drug and alcohol treatment for pregnant women and higher reimbursement rates for nonphysicians to improve access to health care in poor communities. He fought to improve training opportunities for prospective physicians of color, equalize the quality of medical

service in urban-rural communities, reform the welfare system, and for the Family and Medical Leave Act.

Bargaining and Negotiation

The Environmental Protection Agency (EPA) was established as a result of intense lobbying by environmentalists who wanted to protect public and private land from exploitation by private interest groups. The Bureau of Land Management was established on behalf of miners, loggers, and ranchers to protect their private access to mineral, forest, and grazing rights on public lands. Often these groups conflict. The outcome is determined by bargaining among these groups and their supporters in legislatures and administrative agencies. This bargaining "nearly always results in compromise among the numerous interests, with each making concessions in the interests of securing at least a portion of its goals." According to its advocates, Morrow asserts, bargaining or negotiation represents the most practical view of the common good or public interest.[29]

Systems Model

The systems model is possibly the most comprehensive model available because it includes many of the other models already described. The policy process is seen as a total system in which the variety of political actors including wealthy corporate executives and governmental elites, legislatures, administrative agencies, political parties, and interest groups operate in various ways to determine policy.

This model suggests that the policy-making process is a closed system in which claimants to policy preferences provide inputs to the policy process. These inputs are processed in the political decision-making arena, resulting in outputs that then impact the political, social, and economic environment. A feedback loop is then created in which the subsystems in the political environment react to policy outputs and generate new inputs. The outputs of one policy decision create material for the inputs to a new decision.

The systems model of policy-making, therefore, assumes a self-contained, self-regulatory, automatically self-adjusting process. Several policy processes work together to form a complex intermixture of activities, each of which plays a role in the ultimate formulation of a policy. Politics becomes much like a mechanism that moves of its own volition. Social policy analysts who are familiar with systems thinking and the systems model, however, can intervene at salient points in the systems process and use the system to achieve policy ends.

CIRO RODRIGUEZ

Born December 9, 1946, Ciro D. Rodriguez attended San Antonio College and received his BA in political science from St. Mary's University in San Antonio. He received his MSW from Our Lady of the Lake University. From 1975 to 1987, Rodriguez served as a board member of the Harlandale Independent School District and worked as an educational consultant for the Intercultural Development Research Association and as a caseworker with the Texas Department of Mental Health and Mental Retardation. From 1987 to 1996 he taught at our Lady of the Lake University's Worden School of Social Work. He was elected to the Texas House of Representatives in 1987 and chaired the important Local and Consent Calendar Committee. He served on the Public Health and Higher Education Committees and as vice chairman of the Legislative Study Group, a coalition of progressive Texas House members.

Rodriguez joined the U.S. House of Representatives after a special election in April 1997 to fill the unexpired term of the late Frank Tejedo. He serves on the National Security and Veterans Affairs Committees and is interested in increasing educational opportunities, protecting vital social programs such as Medicare and Social Security, expanding access to health care, and promoting economic development and small business throughout south Texas.[30] Most recently Rodriguez introduced the House version of a bill to create a Center for Social Work Research, most likely within the National Institute of Health.

EXERCISE 13.1

Critiquing Policy-Making Models

Models are representations. Even though several models have been presented in the preceding discussion, they may not completely describe the operative realities of modern politics. Moreover, models are not normative. They do not explain how politics ought to work. Before reading on, exercise your critical sensibilities and decide if areas of political

engagement have been left out of these policy-making models. Think of a normative model of the political process. What should an ideal model of politics and policy-making include? After you have developed your own critique, read the one below.

CRITIQUE OF POLICY-MAKING MODELS

The various policy-making models comprise groups, organizations, and systems that political scientists generally concur are the actors in policy-making. The only difference between them is the choice as to which of the top echelon of actors is the most important. However, one institution is ignored in virtually every compendium of policy-making. Policy-making is almost never seen by theorists or practitioners as a process located at the level of ordinary citizens in their *neighborhoods,* the community where people live and have opportunity to express their most vital interests. This oversight is revealing because it demonstrates the extent to which policy-making is seen as a top-down process pursued exclusively by those few who are in positions of power.

People in community have been so far removed from modern politics and policy that hardly anyone considers their absence remarkable or even important. It is somewhat ironic that the original meaning of *politics* and *policy* is derived from the Greek *polis,* a small unit of governance like a community or small town where people engage in mutual decision-making and construction of the rules and processes that guide their lives. It is even more ironic that although America is generally conceived to be a government "of the people," the people are nowhere considered as direct actors in the policy-making process. The political and policy-making systems that politicians have constructed obliterate the involvement of the vast majority of ordinary citizens in the political process, and there is little recognition that this has even happened.

Most of us have little or no say in the policies that affect our lives. We seem to be willing to live with the pretense that we hold the keys to the gates of government when in fact those doors firmly lock us out. We tend to be generally content with our social noninvolvement in public affairs as long as political systems allocate resources and provide decision-making arrangements that do not diverge significantly from our interests. Those in power who do exercise their political voices and assert their policy preferences, however, are content with such public apathy and uninvolvement because it provides them with a free field in which to operate.

There are, however, groups of other people, who know what the powerful have forgotten, and what most North American citizens rarely reflect upon: that in order to be fully human, and for democracy to survive, they can no longer afford to leave the machinery of politics to the wealthy, the professionals, the influential. These groups, more often than not, are the large number of citizens who do not share equally in the benefits that society offers. They comprise many ordinary citizens in working-class and poor neighborhoods, the marginalized, the handicapped, people who have routinely been kicked out, left out, and kept out of the policy-making system. African Americans, Native Americans and women were legally excluded from decision-making prior to emancipation and suffrage, and even after emancipation, African Americans and Native Americans were prevented from voting by regulations designed to keep them out.

Social policy carried out by those involved in the policy system may reflect the "assumptions about the human condition that may be reasonable to the upper socioeconomic groups who make them, but bare little resemblance to the reality of the lower socioeconomic groups that are supposed to be beneficiaries." The policy-making process is often, therefore, not only "irregular and irrational, it is also unrepresentative."[31] Politics and policy do not engage people at the local level of community or neighborhood where they can make decisions themselves often about things that matter most—quality of community life, education, social and neighborhood services. They ignore most ordinary people in general, and explicitly avoid those at the bottom who have the least power and the most to gain by being involved in making their own decisions.

NORMATIVE COMMUNITY-CENTERED SOCIAL POLICY

A theory of policy and politics that resists taking the assumptions of conventional policy-making for granted is called a *normative* theory of policy-making. Norma-

tive policy theory is less concerned about describing how policy takes place than exploring how it ought to occur.[32] Self-perpetuating political systems may be difficult to change, but many macro social workers believe that it is nevertheless possible and above all necessary to change them. By conceiving of a normative process of politics and social policy, macro social workers may be able to work toward substantive political change.

The Self as a Political Actor

To the extent that social policy becomes divorced from us, and politics becomes the purview of mass political processes in control of the influential, we are disallowed from making crucial choices that determine the shape of our society. The power that ordinary people are alleged to possess becomes deprived of content, and we lack control over the premises and social contexts by which we live. Even more important, while the machinery of politics and policy-making grinds along, it crushes people's vital spirit of independence, self-reliance, and self-determination, the very social goods on which democracy depends, and leaves in its path the ruins of apathy, alienation, and disengagement. "The domain of political action," says Abe Kaplan, "is itself one of the loci of increasing depersonalization and dehumanization. The political leader is not a person, but an image, and to him you are not even that, only a vote, or at best, a constituent."[33]

People ought to be active in shaping policy that affects their lives. Social policy ought to be primarily the purview of citizens, not social elites, governmental institutions, administrative decision-makers, or the outcome of bargaining and negotiation of political actors far removed from people. Policy is best made when people exercise decision-making that combines justice, fairness, equity, and a sense of the public good rather than an aggregation of public interests.[34]

In order for people to become authentic political actors, individual citizens need direct access to political processes by face-to-face deliberation first in their own neighborhoods on policy matters that affect their lives and then at progressively higher levels of involvement.

Communal Politics

One of the most debilitating results of modernization is a "feeling of powerlessness in the face of institutions controlled by those whom we do not know, whose values we often do not share," and whose motives we may question.[35] Berger and Neuhaus assert that human beings in their own communities understand their needs better than anyone else. Neighborhood and ethnic associations, community, social, and religious organizations exist where people are, and that is where sound public policy should originate. Neighborhood politics aims at empowering poor people to do the things that the more affluent can already do. Politics at the neighborhood level spreads the power around a bit more—and they do so where it matters, in people's control over their own lives. It is at the level of community neighborhoods that people can "generate principled expression of the real values and the real needs of people in our society."

Community structures, therefore, are essential for a vital democratic society. Public policy should recognize, respect, and where possible empower community and neighborhood institutions. Government needs to support community political involvement by designating policy-making structures at the community level. We should learn to ask about the effects of public policies on community structures and at the very minimum put in place policies that prevent government and corporate power from damaging neighborhood communities any further. For example, we should work against the flight of people from inner cities, which has created wastelands of abandoned buildings and businesses, or decimating neighborhoods in the name of "redevelopment." Instead of exploiting the community for human resources, tax breaks, and other incentives, private organizations and government should operate in a truly interactive fashion with the community as a whole.

DEBBIE STABENOW

Born on April 29, 1950, in Gladwin, Michigan, Debbie Stabenow was raised in Clare. She received her BA in 1972 and MSW in 1975 from Michigan State University. Her career has been dedicated to public service and leadership. She served as the Ingham County Commissioner and spent 12 years in the Michigan House of Representatives and four years in the Michigan State Senate. She was the Democratic nominee for lieutenant governor in 1994. She is cofounder of the Michigan Leadership Institute, which specializes in leadership development and team-building training for organizations and individuals.

Now in the U.S. Congress, Stabenow serves on the Agriculture and Science Committees as well as the House Democratic Steering Committee, the Northeast Midwest Congressional Coalition, the Congressional Caucus for Women's Issues, and the Public Pension Reform Caucus. Stabenow has authored more than 50 public acts. She has been recognized nationally for her leadership on issues such as domestic violence, child support and visitation enforcement, drunk driving, Alzheimer's disease, mental health, child abuse prevention, and foster care reform. She has been a leading advocate for small businesses, a leader on property tax and school finance reform, and instrumental in several important environmental reforms

Value Education

Values are the substance of politics and policy. Public education systems, however, do not generally emphasize skills in value-oriented decision-making, depriving students of an important tool for graduation into adult citizenship. Having reduced politics to possessive pursuit of self-interest and decision-making to the pragmatic compromise between contending actors, ethical political discourse tends to be gradually eliminated as a serious arena of thought and action in American public affairs.

Local communities, however, are value-generating, value-bearing, and value-transmitting agencies of society. In neighborhood social structures, the process of social valuation occurs continually as we communicate, engage, and relate face to face. The values which infuse each community's history and culture reproduce those same social values in the lives of community members.[36] Neighborhood social organizations that involve us in community-building projects, social service, and direct grassroots political engagement are important components of civic and social consciousness. By actively engaging one another in making informed value decisions in areas that affect their lives and incorporating those values in the life of the community, we become political actors.

Closely allied with value education is character education. Early in its history, social work understood the role of character education as a vital component of democracy. *Character Education in a Democracy* by social worker S. R. Slavson, who later became the father of American group psychotherapy, laid the foundation for the character-building role in social group work. Professional social group work was identified as a method of character building and citizenship[37] and pioneered helping character-building programs of the YM and YWCA, Boy and Girl Scouts, and Boys and Girls Clubs.

However, the two arenas of social work practice most intimately connected to neighborhoods—social group work and community social work—have become devalued arenas of social work practice. A revitalized social group work could once again provide value and character education to prepare citizens for value-centered decision-making, to activate their own sense of what is good and right, and to engage in difficult value questions. The efforts of social group workers could come to maturity as community social workers work with citizens in building strong community organizations, community development corporations, and community associations. Exercising one's values in community life, as an outgrowth of value and character education provided by social group workers and community social workers, is fundamental to democracy, value decision-making, and the development of sound social policy.[38] A renewed commitment to social policy in social work practice cannot occur only at the top levels of government but must begin as social workers assist individuals to practice citizenship, leadership, and public service and become engaged in the political life of their communities

---

FLORENCE KELLY

Born in Philadelphia on September 12, 1859, Florence Kelly was the daughter of Caroline and William "Pig Iron" Kelly, a member of Congress. Since no American Law School would accept women, she studied law at the University of Zurich, where she published a translation of Friedrich Engles's *The Conditions of the Working Class in England in 1844* for which Engles himself wrote a preface. In 1891 Kelly joined Jane Addams at Hull House and, because of her intense interest in women's and child labor, she was commissioned by Illinois Governor Altgeld to survey the Chicago slums and report on the employment of children in sweat shops. Kelly's analysis resulted in a new state child-labor law, including the development of a Department of Factory Inspection, to which she was appointed as its first chief.

When the district attorney refused to cooperate with her, she decided to conduct her own court battles on behalf of children. She obtained an LLB in 1894 and, as a lawyer, worked though the legal system to improve policies and conditions of the poor. So vivid and compelling were her demands for better protection of children at work that she succeeded in obtaining another child-labor law in 1897.

In 1899 Kelly moved to Henry Street Settlement in New York City to become General Secretary of the National Consumers. For the next 25 years, Kelly built a distinguished pattern of social reforms, including minimum wage laws, women's suffrage, federal aid to mothers and babies, and radical reforms in the employment and education of children, working conditions for women, and factory hygiene. In 1903 when a challenge to the state's ten-hour workday law was coming before the Supreme Court, Kelly and her associates compiled the brief for Justice Brandeis that provided the basis for the historic Supreme Court decision ratifying the ten-hour law.

Kelly was a courageous social work advocate of women and children, workers and consumers, and as a legal scholar and policy analyst, she authored many reforms and laws. She was ahead of her time in her belief that the cause of destitution was modern industrialism and that industry must be controlled by the state. Florence Kelly, macro social work advocate, was a Quaker by religion, a socialist by politics, and a humanitarian in character. She died in Germantown, Pennsylvania on February 17, 1932, at the age of 73.[39]

Grassroots Democracy

Representative democracy was practical and efficient in early America when distance and lack of instantaneous communication meant that direct democracy was impossible. Because of the small size and homogeneity of most towns, politicians were often truly "representative" of the culture and values of the communities that elected them. Thomas Bender says that in 1790 there were only 24 places in the United States with a population over 2,500 people. Most people lived in a town or village of this size or smaller, and politics was embedded in social relations, which promoted political consensus and "allowed the town to speak to the larger society with one political voice." Bender notes that after votes on the Constitutions of 1778 and 1780, the returns from Massachusetts towns "included detailed criticisms and suggestions, and each of these was phrased as the sense of the town, which indeed it was."[40]

Today there is such a mixture of groups in many locales that no one representative can adequately speak for all. The massive size of many cities and the pluralistic and complex nature of our society make representative democracy increasingly ineffective and dysfunctional. Modern technology, however, has made politics accessible to each person in ways never before conceived as possible. Computers, television, and the "information highway" make distance or time no barrier to communication and decision-making.

If social work policy advocates utilize creative thinking, a "populist" or people's orientation to democracy, often termed "grassroots" democracy, may still be possible. The citizen's role in the political process could consist of more than choosing officials, providing the means by which groups pursue their own private interests, or engaging in arrangements by which the system can function. Politics and policy-making may begin to occur as a daily and normal role of all citizens who exert their sense of what is good and right in mutual interaction at the level of the community, not in back rooms of legislative chambers, in the corridors of power, or in the board rooms of multinational corporations. Government would become truly "of the people, by the people, and for the people" rather than "of the elites, by the Congress, and for special interests."

The State as a Good Society

A normative perspective on social policy would view the state as a good society comprised of a variety of pluralistic communities, each of which develops its own cultural milieu by means of value education and interaction with other communities. The ethnic, historical, and cultural diversity of these communities would be recognized and honored as building blocks of the social order.

Society would not be seen merely as an aggregation of conflicting individual interests, tastes, or opinions, each of which competes in the policy arena on an equal level. Instead, certain overarching ideals would be recognized toward which the society ought to move. Within the policy arena, some values will be subordinated to those ideals. Where the two conflict, the public interest ought to generally supersede purely private self-interest, for example. Privilege and position will give way to equalizing opportunity of the less privileged and less powerful. Rewarding accumulation of wealth, for example, would receive less policy recognition than assisting those who lack means of survival.

HOW TO DO COMMUNITY-CENTERED POLICY ANALYSIS

Most modern policy analysis occurs today at high levels of governmental policy decision-making and results in lengthy reports on specific social problems. Professional experts skilled in policy research provide policy-makers with pragmatic, action-oriented recommendations for alleviating social problems.[41] Sometimes a policy analysis is commissioned by the President or by a congressional committee. Sometimes it is performed by an interest group concerned about the policy question that tries to influence public policy. For example, *The State of America's Children,* a report by the Children's Defense Fund, provides information, analysis, and recommendations on many issues concerning children. These policy assessments are often very valuable, and many times the policy recommendations they contain are implemented.

At times, however, worthwhile but politically unpopular policy recommendations are never implemented. A policy analysis commissioned by one national administration may be ignored by a succeeding administration whose policy preferences are different. Policy analysis generated by experts may offer recommendations for, rather than with, people and miss the mark of what is most important or helpful. At other times, policy decisions may be manipulated to serve the interests of those in power rather than assist victims of social problems.

In contrast to top-down policy assessment, community-centered policy analysis is performed at the local level by people who are directly affected by the social policy, not by a professional analyst who acts alone or as part of an independent policy research group. These local policy recommendations are combined at the regional or national levels into a unified proposal, often by coalitions or federations of community organizations concerned about the policy issue.

Community-centered policy analysis provides a tool, derived from a variation of rational problem-solving and action research, that you can use to help people in their own communities develop and design social policy. It includes preparation for analysis, defining the policy problem, getting the facts, finding the real problem, relabeling, developing potential solutions, assessing the feasibility of alternative solutions, ranking alternative solutions, choosing the most feasible solution, and communicating recommendations to policy makers.

Developing a Policy-Making Group

Developing a community social policy may come as an offshoot of community organizing, community development, or community planning. Members of these community-centered organizations may propose changes in city ordinances or zoning laws, propose new laws governing the allocation of city services, or ask for watchdog commissions that have authority to investigate police brutality, discrimination, or human rights violations. Community groups may ask for neighborhood authority to participate in the city budgeting process or for new police procedures regarding use of tactical squads or firearms that may endanger innocent citizens. They may work for local neighborhood-based government, laws governing the use of drugs, or any of a host of other issues that will lead to a better community and a more responsive local government.

The first step in developing community policy recommendations is the formation of a community policy-making group. The group should be representative of the community as a whole and chosen by its members in a democratic election process. The macro social worker assists the policy-making group as consultant, trainer, information gatherer, liaison to local government, group facilitator, or technical advisor.

Defining the Problem

In order to develop policy alternatives, the community policy-making group needs to define the policy issues in ways that they can be solved.[42] Your group members ask themselves: What part of the policy problem do we want to resolve? Are we interested in certain aspects of the issue, or should we try to tackle the problem as a whole? How do we define a policy problem in such a way that it is solvable, given the limitations on our resources—time, manpower, funding, and expertise?

Solutions may often seem very obvious. It is tempting for members to pull solutions out of the air.

However, your group needs to be able to work through the policy definition process systematically. As you assist members to define the problem, you help them navigate through a number of initial pitfalls.

Premature Labeling   Labeling helps you see the policy in a clear way, restricts the range of choices, and identifies what is, as well as what is not, to be considered. Labeling a problem too early in the process, however, may prevent the group from considering the problem completely. Premature labeling may lead group members to be concerned with symptoms rather than causes, with causes when symptoms are all that realistically can be treated, or with the wrong problem. At the beginning of policy analysis, therefore, leave options open until the real problem emerges clearly.

The Solution in Search of a Problem   Sometimes people come to the policy table armed with a full repertoire of solutions gleaned from articles, journals, meetings, research, and their own experience and values. As soon as people encounter a condition which one of these ready-made solutions might fix, they may phrase the problem to fit their preconceived solution, so that their answers are the best and most logical remedies. If they are lucky, their solution will fit the problem, but more than likely the situation is more complicated and, having already made up their minds, they may have foreclosed other possibilities.

Each of the solutions may appear logical and, to the individuals proposing them, necessary. In the battle of solutions that ensues, each group member attempts to persuade the group that his or her idea is best. This process is almost always destructive. It rarely leads to effective solutions because the problem has not been clearly defined based on its characteristics. Moreover, the group may accept a statement with which most, if not all, are uncomfortable. While those whose ideas prevailed may "win," it is at the expense of those who may feel they were forced to capitulate or compromise. They may go along but not be really committed to the issue.

If your policy-making group seems to focus on solutions before clearly examining the problem, you need to recognize that they are playing the "solutions in search of a problem" game and help members disengage themselves from this process.

Accepting the Leader's Definition   If you are a social work policy analyst who has a highly developed intuitive sense, you may have a knack for putting your finger on the crux of the problem. Allowing your own intuitive sense to dominate the problem identification process, however, may work for you some of the time, but it won't work all of the time.

The community policy-making group may accept your version of the problem because of your expertise, track record, or power position. None of these is a valid reason for deciding on a problem definition. If you happen to be wrong, you will have wasted valuable time and tarnished your own reputation. If you have hunch about what the real problem is, it is best to wait, watch, and use the group process to confirm your intuition rather than make a pronouncement. Keep in mind that you need to help the whole group work through a process in which all can learn. You are not helping if you move too far ahead of your policy group.

Personal Influence   Be careful about those who tend to be most persuasive, influential, or assertive. Often their version may be accepted by the group, or parts of different problem perceptions may be pieced together or a compromise may be reached among dominant members. None of these may reflect the ideas of the group as a whole. The result is a problem statement based on personalities and personal influence of the members and not the real problem itself.

One way to help your group avoid these pitfalls is to explore the origins and history of the problem arena. Knowing these antecedents will help your group understand the variety of factors that have led to the present situation, the length of time the problem has been in existence, its scope and severity. Knowing what has been tried in the past will help avoid dead-end solutions or blind alleys, and understanding what has worked will help prevent your group from reinventing the wheel.

Help the group ask themselves the "when, who, what, where, why, and how" questions in relation to the problem. This will get your group started on being objective.

When did the problem first appear? Through what historical events or circumstances has the social problem evolved to the present state of affairs? Did it come about suddenly or does it have a long history?

Who are the major actors? These may be decision-makers, agency or organizational administrators, various interest groups, community leaders, or legislators. Who has contributed to the problem? Are there groups of perpetrators or potential targets that may have caused or potentially may have added to the policy issue? Who are the prime victims of the policy problem? Who has the most to gain and who has the most to lose by solving the problem?

Why did the policy problem come about? What events or conditions have led up to the current state of affairs? Are there particular cycles or trends that tell you which factors may be causally related to the problem?

What are some of the major consequences of the policy problem? This question deals with symptoms of the problem. What are the economic, social, and political affects of the problem? What social situations or social conditions have contributed to the problem's continuance or added to its complexity? A second question deals with solutions. What kinds of policy solutions have been tried in the past? How effective were these policy solutions? Have the social policies themselves changed or been modified?

Where is the problem located? Is the problem generalized throughout the community or are particular areas affected more than others? Obtaining an idea of where the problem is located will give your group an idea of where to start.

How important is the problem? How widespread is it? How many people are affected by it?

Focus Groups   Bring together those representatives who have a stake in the problem to help define the problem from their perspective, and ask them questions your community policy-making group has prepared. Focus group participants may be politicians, planners, community leaders, agency administrators, victims, and service providers. As members of the policy-making group meet with focus groups, be alert for persons who may want to work with you on the solution after the problem has been identified sufficiently.

Defining the "Real" Problem   After the community policy-making group has gathered, asked themselves questions, and engaged focus groups of key actors, your members' perceptions of the problem may bear little resemblance to the issue they initially formulated.[43] This is to be welcomed because your group members' perceptions of the problem will have been refined, clarified, and shaped by the new information they have developed.

Even though there may be many perspectives on the problem, your policy-making group has control over the way they define the problem. There is no one best problem statement, nor is there only one real problem. "Each problem situation contains within its boundaries—however vague and fuzzy those boundaries might be—numerous potential 'real' problems."[44]

Most problems are laden with subjective perceptions and values. For example, if your group explores its concern about violence in your neighborhood, any number of issues may occur to you. Does the problem concern the availability of handguns, assault rifles, or hunting weapons? Is the problem the number of shop owners or dealers who sell guns? Does the problem lie in the laws that permit easy access to weapons? Is your group interested in violence on television or about specific kinds of violence such as domestic violence, rape, or violence used in the commission of robberies? Are they concerned about youth-oriented violence such as gang violence?

Choose a problem definition that is meaningful and valid for the community. Certain problems will intuitively speak to the policy-making group members. Look at the scope of the problem, for example. Some problems may seem so large or unwieldy that they appear unsolvable. The group may have to break them down into smaller, more manageable pieces. On the other hand, members may see patterns of smaller problems that they want to group together into a larger one.

One criteria of choice may be whether the problem is one that the community members can actually do something about. It doesn't make sense to try to fight violence in general, for example. But you can help your group choose the family aspect (domestic violence is on the rise), the youth aspect (gang violence is killing innocent people), or the legal aspect (allowing people to carry concealed weapons should be outlawed). The group could narrow its focus to a particular neighborhood (Northside) or location (Lincoln High School).

Relabeling　　Help your group relabel the problem and come up with a working problem statement from which they will continue the problem-solving process.

For example, using the hypothetical problem of violence, your group may redefine the problem to focus on controlling handguns in Northside.

Gathering Information

Two general ways to approach policy research are focused synthesis and epical research. A *focused synthesis* is a think piece that pulls together information from a variety of sources in support of a policy position, including published articles, discussions with experts and stakeholders, focus interviews, reports from congressional hearings, anecdotal stories, experience of researchers, unpublished documents, staff memoranda, existing research data, and published materials. One Agency for International Development (AID) study of rural water supply problems, for example, used available literature, the researchers own field experiences in the past five years, and discussions with individuals at several agencies and organizations. *Epical research* involves formulating policy questions, operationalizing variables, collecting and analyzing data. The most useful kinds of data for policy analysis include secondary research, social surveys, and case studies.[45]

Combine a number of different research methods, such as a survey with focused synthesis, or case studies with secondary analysis. An ideal combination is to use qualitative methods such as participant observation and quantitative methods such as a social survey. Using several different combinations increases the perceived validity of the study; both methods corroborate one another and can give your group additional insight that one method alone could not provide.[46]

Formulate Specific Research Questions　　The process of formulating specific research questions should include malleable variables that will most likely impact the social problem. Malleable variables are those aspects of the problem that can be changed. People's attitudes, for example, cannot generally be changed easily, but social conditions that affect those attitudes can be changed. Look for those aspects of the problem that the community can do something about. Then formulate research questions around those malleable variables.

Select questions that address an *important* aspect of the problem given the financial and manpower limits of the policy group. Questions should provide information that will be useful for current and future decision-making and address issues in a manner that will help policymakers act on the social problem.[47]

Operationalize Variables
To operationalize means to define the variables in terms of specific measurable indicators. Some problem variables, however, may not be directly measurable. For example, there may be no single, universally accepted measure of racial tolerance. On the other hand, a number of indicators to measure such variables as crime, unemployment, or poverty may be available from which your group may choose.

You can help the policy-making group find proxy or substitute indicators for those variables that are not directly measurable. Proxy indicators are measures that reasonably substitute for the issue about which your group wants information. You may look at such indicators as unemployment rates of different ethnic groups, a racial attitude survey of randomly selected citizens, or affirmative action policies of corporations. While none of these separately or together measure racial tolerance, they can provide a partial substitute.[48]

Secondary Research
Using secondary research, or data produced by universities, governmental agencies, and policy research institutes, is the most cost-efficient method for answering policy research questions and provides answers more quickly than information you collect yourself, which is called primary research.[49] Secondary data come in many forms, such as large statistical studies provided by the federal government and other government bodies, government reports, industry studies, and information from syndicated information services, traditional books, and journals found in libraries, as well as the unpublished observations of a knowledgeable observer. If your policy-making group wants to use existing research information, they will need to ask their own questions about the data and subject it to their own statistical analysis.

Social Surveys
Surveys are ways of following up on issues that have been raised from focus interviews, or from the examination of secondary data. A survey is a systematic inquiry of perceptions or attitudes about problems affecting an entire population or a sample of that population. Surveys, described in Chapter 6, are best used when you want to narrow down issues, ask respondents to rank the importance

of particular concerns, or give you an indicator of a range of preferences among items.

Case Studies
Case studies tend to be frequently used in policy research because they are often quick, cost efficient, allow room for impressionistic analysis of a situation,[50] and provide a relatively complete understanding of a situation's complexity. Case studies also promote examination of the process by which intervention or policy actions have been implemented. For example, Graham Allison's assessment of the Cuban Missile Crisis is a case study that examines the decision-making process.[51] Case studies are particularly useful for developing recommendations about the future implementation of a policy question.

Developing Alternative Solutions

After your group has identified the problem and gathered enough information about it, you can devise possible solutions or interventions. Examine which issues can be changed and which cannot. Eliminate those issues about which you can do nothing. For example, in considering the problem of controlling access to handguns, your policy-making group may decide that the manufacture of guns and the importation of guns into the community are issues they cannot change. Try to be conservative when deciding what the group cannot change. Things that at first appear unchangeable may turn out to be amenable to change after all.

Your group is left with those elements of the problem over which it has some control. For example, your group may be able to impact the legality of handguns in the community or affect gun safety and training in the use of guns. Your group may examine interdicting weapons or provide gun-free areas where weapons are excluded. You may limit availability of weapons to those that are nonlethal. You may persuade police to limit the use of "tactical" squads in which police raid suspected crack houses, sometimes injuring innocent people in the process. These are windows of opportunity where changes can bring about different consequences for people. List your group's "change points" on a board to make them explicit.

Help your members manipulate the change points to eliminate or ameliorate the problem by asking the following questions.

1. Who will be affected?
2. Who will pay and by what means?
3. Who will have jurisdiction?

4. Who will implement the policy?

5. How will the policy be regulated?

Consider the problem of guns in Northside. For each category, list as many items as you can think of. For example, those affected would be citizens, police, gun shop owners, hunters, criminals. Who will pay includes citizens, businesses, and others. Financial measures include taxes, grants, contracts, loans, rewards, incentives, subsidies, and compensation for loss. Regulation may be by means of standards, licenses, codes, warning, fines, probation, and incarceration. Place each of these lists in columns and go through each column, putting together different combinations of items. Some will make no sense, but using this technique will open your group to think of alternatives they may not have visualized.

Using these criteria, your group should develop as many alternatives as possible. The group then examines the list and eliminates those that are obviously not workable. Then the group ranks the viable alternatives in order. Leaving things just as they are is an option that should always be considered.

Public Forum   Call a public forum or arrange for focus groups to get input from the community on the issues and on the various alternatives that your group is now considering. The community forum or focus groups are intended to present the alternatives and to solicit input. Out of these community gatherings you may be able to sharpen your perspectives, discover issues not previously considered, and obtain a clear sense of the community's interests and directions, as well as the power of its concern about the issues.

Choosing Among Alternatives

Decide on a final ranking of the alternatives using input from the community forum. In the best of all worlds the policy-making group would chose the policy alternative that members consider the best one. However, it is very possible that a good policy alternative may not be politically, economically, or socially feasible. It is useless to press for a policy that has little hope of being enacted. Your group, therefore, needs to assess which of their most highly ranked alternatives have the best chance of being implemented.

Assessing Political Feasibility   Many political actors will have a stake in the outcome of any policy.[52] Each of these individuals or groups have pre-ferred solutions that will compete with your solution in the political arena. Politicians may be interested in your group's policy solution only to the extent that it enhances or detracts from their chances for reelection or affects their constituencies. If your community policy-making group intends to implement a policy proposal, political actors—those who hold power—and their influence are important for you to consider.

One way to assess the amount of support various alternatives can expect from key political decision-makers is by means of the PRINCE political accounting system developed by O'Leary and Coplin. PRINCE requires scoring each political decision-maker in areas of issue position, power, and salience. By comparing the total support score of each alternative solution, members can see which alternatives are most politically feasible. Assume, for example, that one solution that your group favors is to establish a special agency paid for by taxpayers and fines that would restrict the number of handguns in Northside. Determine the political actors who would be involved in the decision. The political actors in this case are the mayor, the city council, a local chapter of the NRA, the local taxpayers association, a local chapter of Handgun Control Inc., and the chief of police. Figure 13.1 illustrates how the PRINCE model works.

The first variable to be considered is issue position. Issue position indicates the strength of support an actor expresses for this particular alternative solution. Score issue position with a range from +3 to -3. A plus indicates support and a minus indicates opposition. A "3" indicates the political actor is unequivocally in favor of or opposed to the alternative. A "1" or a "2" indicates the actor is less clearly in favor of or opposed to the alternative. A "0" indicates the actor is neutral.

The power variable estimates the amount of power possessed by the actor to decide on the alternative. If the actor has maximum influence to decide, a "3" is assigned. A "1" or "2" is assigned for moderate influence and a "0" for no capability of influencing at all.

The third variable is salience, the degree to which the actor cares about and pays attention to the issue. Salience measures how high the issue stands on the actor's list of concerns in contrast to issue position, which indicates how strong is her or his preference for this particular alternative solution. For example, the problem of violence may be very salient for an

Actors	Issue Position	x	Power	x	Salience	=	Total Support by Actors
Mayor	-1	x	2	x	2	=	-4
City Council	+1	x	3	x	3	=	9
NRA	-3	x	2	x	3	=	-18
Taxpayers Association	+1	x	1	x	1	=	1
Handgun Control, Inc.	+3	x	1	x	3	=	9
Police Chief	+1	x	1	x	3	=	3
						Net Score	0

FIGURE 13.1   PRINCE Political Accounting System. Alternative: Establish a special agency to restrict handguns.

actor, but his or her preference for your group's particular alternative (issue position) may be low. A "3" for salience indicates that a problem is high on the political actor's agenda, a "1" or "2" indicates that a problem is of low to moderate salience, and a "0" indicates it is of no importance at all.

After your policy-making group estimates the three variables, multiply across the rows to determine each actor's support for this alternative. Then add up the final product of the scores to obtain a net score. The larger the positive number, the more likely that support for this alternative will be strong. The closer the net score to zero, the more likely the alternative will be politically contentious. The larger a negative score, the more likely this particular alternative will be infeasible. Calculate the political feasibility for each of your top alternatives.

Assessing Economic Feasibility   After you calculate which alternative solution is most politically feasible, your group should determine which is most economically feasible. There are three ways to assess economic feasibility: Benefit-cost analysis, cost-effectiveness analysis, and decision analysis.

Benefit-Cost Analysis   Benefit-cost analysis is a method by which your group compares costs and benefits to society of alternative policy options. Given two proposals each of which will meet your goals, the one that has the highest benefit/cost ratio will often be more appealing to decision-makers. Generally speaking a benefit/cost ratio that equals or exceeds 1 will tend to attract attention because the benefits of that alternative will equal or exceed costs.

Add all of the benefits in dollars that will be incurred by implementing that alternative. These benefits are then divided by a sum of all of the costs to obtain a benefit/cost ratio. For example, suppose your group decided on the three most politically feasible alternatives to control access to guns in Northside. Assume that each has equal benefits, that is, the life of one child saved. The hypothetical benefit/cost ratios are:

1. Require all guns to have a special child-proof safety device at $10 additional cost, to be born by the buyer. Assuming there are 1,000 guns, the estimated total cost is $10,000. The benefit/cost ratio is 1/10,000 or 0.0001.

2. Require anyone owning a gun to have special training in safety, paid by the owner. Training costs $100 per owner for 1,000 owners, totaling $100,000. The benefit/cost ratio is 1/100,000 or 0.00001.

3. Institute an amnesty program in which guns would be accepted by the local government for destruction in return for a $200 rebate per gun, paid for by taxpayers. The benefit/cost ratio for 1,000 guns recaptured is 1/200,000, or 0.000005.

Given these three proposals, the most favorable benefit/cost ratio is to provide guns with safety devices, especially because the cost is born by the buyer. The amnesty program is least cost/beneficial, not only because it is most expensive, but also because the cost is born by all taxpayers.

A limitation of benefit-cost analysis is the difficulty in assigning monetary costs to such intangibles as a human life and the difficulty of calculating future unknowns with any accuracy. (Benefit-cost analysis was described in Chapter 10.)

Cost-Effectiveness Analysis Sometimes costs and benefits of different policy options cannot be clearly identified to allow for analysis. When this occurs, benefit/cost analysis is often replaced by cost-effectiveness analysis. Cost-effectiveness analysis expresses the actual monetary cost per unit of benefit or expected outcome. Examples of costs effectiveness include:

The number of dollars needed to reduce the number of handguns by a certain amount.

The number of dollars needed for an alcohol abuser to achieve abstinence.

The number of dollars needed for a former convict to not recidivate.

The number of dollars needed to achieve a certain percentage increase in the literacy rate of the population.

The number of dollars needed to reduce infant mortality by a certain percentage.

By themselves, cost-effectiveness dollar amounts say little about whether a policy should or should not be implemented. Therefore, policy-makers often compare the cost-effectiveness of several different options. For example, the cost of rehabilitating an alcoholic convicted of drunk driving may be compared to the costs of incarcerating drunk drivers, withholding the driver's license and imposing a fine, mandating community service and driver training courses, or doing nothing. The costs of doing nothing may be determined by the average cost of property damage, injuries, and deaths incurred per alcoholic. Policy-makers can then judge which of these alternatives is the best use of taxpayers' money.

An advantage of cost-effectiveness is the ease by which expenses of one alternative can be calculated in comparison to other alternatives. Policy-makers can judge whether a policy option is sufficiently effective to warrant its cost.

Decision-Analysis Decision analysis requires a panel of experts to assign a numeric score on an agreed upon common denominator to all benefits and costs. For example, the cost of the abuse of a child or the benefits of preventing or rehabilitating abuse would be calculated. With such numeric scores, statistically expected values of each alternative policy solution can be computed. Comparing these values for each policy alternative will then yield the optimal policy.[53]

Assessing Social Feasibility Social feasibility estimates the impact on people, groups, organizations, and communities that will result from one or more policy options. Social feasibility is measured by means of a Social Impact Assessment (SIA), based on similar principles that ecologists use in making Environmental Impact Assessments. For example, in developing a SIA for the Chicago Crosstown Expressway, policy analysis first studied a variety of costs including aesthetics, traffic, and directness of route in addition to construction and maintenance costs. Then they assessed potential beneficial impacts of the expressway on employment, urban renewal, and property values. Each variable was assigned a subjective score of acceptability.

While SIA acceptability scores cannot be used to calculate social benefits in monetary terms, by considering a range of costs and benefits, SIAs do consider less tangible but important aspects of social concern.[54] Because SIAs help policy-makers assess the extent to which an alternative will have an adverse impact on the public, they give some indication of public acceptability of an alternative.

Deciding on the Best Solution

Your policy-making group now has four different measures they can use to gauge the alternatives: (1) rankings that express your community group's preferences, and (2) the political, (3) economic, and (4) social feasibility of those alternatives. Your group can arrive at a numeric score for each alternative by multiplying each constraint: group ranking × political feasibility × economic feasibility × social feasibility. When ranking your group's five most preferred solutions, assign a 5 to the most preferred, a 4 to the second most preferred, and so on, ending with a 1 for the least preferred. Use the numerical indicator already assigned to the three feasibility measures.

Your group may consider one or more of these measures to be more important than others. For example, your group may decide that social feasibility carries more weight than political feasibility. The process of giving weight to one or another of the feasibility measures is very simple. If your group thinks that economic feasibility is twice as important as social feasibility, multiply the figures for economic feasibility by 2. After you have weighted the measures, multiply the weighted scores of your group's preferred solution by economic, political, and social feasibility scores for each alternative. Compare the final scores of each alternative. The alternative with the highest score should have the best chance of being implemented successfully.

Developing a Policy Proposal

In a written report, set forth the policy-making group's recommendations for resolving the social problem. Describe the policy issue under consideration and the three or four top policy alternatives that the group recommends, including the feasibility measures for each solution. Explain why each received its ranking. Offer short-term and long-term recommendations, as well as strategies for implementation. When issuing a statement or report, help your group present the results as simply as possible so the report is easily understood. Present the conclusion and major caveats first. Be concise. Use examples and anecdotes. Avoid jargon. Discuss the effectiveness of several of the group's alternatives and reduce your proposal to its essential elements.

Implementing Policy

Implementing policy is the "real world" of politics. Present the policy proposal to your community organization, community development corporation, or community planning council. Once your organization accepts the policy proposal, they will be the group that pursues implementation. Your role is to help devise ways of getting the policy proposal accepted by governmental leaders by means of case conferences, fact gathering, position taking, committee work, petitions, media campaigns, or working directly through politicians by means of lobbying or political pressure tactics.

The Case Conference Hold a conference with agencies that have responsibility in your policy initiative's area. Your goal is to help agency administrators realize that policies or procedures that are dysfunctional for your group may also be problematical for others. Raising the issue in a case conference may assist in getting the policy changed.

Fact Gathering Having the right information in a form that can be used properly gives you leverage and influence for change.

Position-Taking Issue a public statement or report that puts your policy-making group or community organization on public record as a participant in a change process. Taking a position informs people about where you stand, clarifies your objectives, and provides a point of identification. You put agencies and politicians on notice that your organization is fighting for change and you make clear what you want to accomplish.[55]

Committee Work Government policy committees serve several purposes in the decision-making process. They provide a public forum for the discussion of ideas. They also publicize potential alternative solutions. Social workers help the community by serving as committee members or as consultants to committees.[56]

Petitions Petitioning can indicate public support for a particular solution to a problem. "It informs decision-makers that there are people 'out there' who have a stake in the decision."[57]

Media Campaigns The use of radio, television, and newspapers can be an important part of the policy change process. Publicity, stories, and pictures bring issues to public attention and create a climate in which change is possible.

Lobbying Lobbying is a fundamental part of the American system of government.[58] While large business corporations work for their self-interest, you and your members lobby governmental officials in the public interest, equalizing the power balance and insuring that "individuals, groups and communities who cannot lobby for themselves" are represented in the political bargaining process. You and your community policy group can lobby face to face, by telephone, letter, or by giving testimony. Keep in mind that a legislator needs your information and assistance. Be honest and factual. Know your issue thoroughly. Anticipate the opposition's claims and formulate persuasive counter arguments. Acknowledge the merits of competing proposals. If you are unwilling to acknowledge strengths of alternative proposals or weaknesses of your own, you may be seen as a propagandist and damage your credibility.

Straightforward presentations with data are generally the most persuasive. Be able to answer two critical concerns of legislators: what the proposed legislation will cost, and what will be the bill's social impact. Pro-

Petitioning serves to proclaim public support for a policy alternative. (© Laima Druskis/Jeroboam, Inc.)

vide succinct supportive documents. Thank the legislator for the appointment and for being open-minded. Follow up with a thank-you letter that includes a synopsis of the position taken by that legislator during the meeting and with anything that you have agreed to do.

Letter Writing   Letters to legislators are an effective way to get your point across. Make them short, to the point, and credible, one or two pages at most. Describe your position exactly and provide documentation. State the action you want the legislator to take, such as voting yes or no on legislation or co-sponsoring legislation.

Avoid form letters. The more personal the letter, the more effective. Clearly written handwritten letters on your own stationery are the most effective. End your letter with a short thank you for considering your proposal or request.

Telephoning   Phone calls, usually 48 hours before a legislative vote, will signal a legislator which way the wind is blowing on a piece of legislation and may swing those who are undecided. When calling, state who you are and the message you wish to convey. For example, "I would like to urge Representative Smith to vote yes

on Bill 33 because…" Leave your name, address, and phone number to confirm that you are a constituent.

Testifying   Legislative committees gather as much information as possible from a wide variety of viewpoints. You or your members may be asked to testify. The key to offering successful testimony is preparation. Briefly introduce yourself. Tell who you are, what program you are representing, how many people you represent, and your qualifications. State your goal and outline your main points. Talk about the problem. Discuss the significance of the issue and try to relate it to the district represented by the legislators before you. Talk about current efforts to resolve the problem—what solutions have been tried; which ones have worked; which have failed. Explain why current efforts are insufficient and how they can be improved. Offer specific recommendations. What can the legislators do to help solve the problem at hand? Summarize your main points, thank the panel or committee, and tell them you would be happy to answer questions. Keep your presentation to ten minutes or less. Never read a statement, but make your testimony interesting and conversational.[59]

The key to offering successful testimony is preparation. Richard Codd, president of the American Planning Association, testifies before Congress, February 1995, against H.R. 925, the Private Property Protection Act. (Courtesy of the American Planning Association)

Blending Approaches   Blend political pressure, legal tactics, and confrontation approaches. If the goal of the organization is to increase the city's commitment to open housing, representatives of the organization might lobby to get strong open-housing ordinance on the books (a political pressure tactic), simultaneously seeking a court injunction to halt the city's receipt of state development funds until its housing profile improves (a legal tactic), while conducting demonstrations in the plaza in front of city hall to publicize the difficulties facing the poor in finding housing (a confrontation tactic). Confrontation and legal action tactics are described more fully in Chapter 14.

CONCLUSION

Social policy occurs as institutional political actors, competing interest groups, government agencies, and business corporations bargain for policy concessions in an interlocking system of decision-making. Macro social workers work with community groups and community organizations to propose policies that can improve communities and society as a whole. To abdicate this role inevitably means leaving the field of policy and politics to those who wield power at the highest levels of influence.

We need to understand theories of policy-making and how to decide on, propose, and get policy implemented. We need to have a vision of a normative process of politics and social policy that helps move America toward what it could become in today's highly technological, fast-paced world. One such model provides a an understanding of the necessity for locating policy at the community level. It includes a vision of the self as a political actor, a belief in the value of mediating structures, grassroots democracy, community politics, value-based education, and a vision of the state as a good society.

KEY CONCEPTS

public policy

social policy

policy-making models

elite model

institutional model

interest group model

pluralism

rational actor model

administrative actor model

bargaining and negotiation

systems model

normative policy-making

self as political actor

communal politics

value education

grassroots Democracy

state as good society

policy analysis process

change points

political feasibility

PRINCE

economic feasibility

benefit/cost analysis

cost-effectiveness

decision analysis

social impact analysis

case conference

fact gathering

position-taking

committee work

media campaigns

petitions

lobbying

letter writing

telephoning

testifying

QUESTIONS FOR DISCUSSION

1. In this chapter the point was made that "modern technology has made politics accessible to each person in ways never before conceived possible. Computers, television, and the 'information highway' make distance no barrier to communication and decision-making." How will technology make politics and social policy processes more accessible to people, increasing the quality and representativeness of policy solutions?

2. A proposal was made in this chapter for direct citizen access to policy and politics, rather than leaving politics to professions such as elected and appointed officials and lobbyists. What are the advantages of this proposal? What are its disadvantages?

3. Given the fact that often less than 50% of those eligible to vote actually exercise this right, is it realistic to expect that citizens will want to become more directly involved in politics even if they have the opportunity?

4. DiNitto and Dye assert that social policy is a *continuing political struggle* over "conflicting goals and objectives, competing definitions of problems, alternative approaches and strategies, multiple programs and policies, competing proposals for reform, and even different ideas about how decisions should be made."[60] If this is an accurate statement about social policy, can decisions that are good in themselves ever be made about social issues?

5. Can policies be made on any other basis than conflict resolution or on a set of majoritarian decision rules? Explain your answer.

6. If resolving policy disputes by bargaining or voting are the only options available, what assurance is there that policies will be developed that rise above dominance by those groups that have the most power or the most votes?

7. Can you think of a different model of politics that would be more appropriate for our highly mobile, technological society than those discussed in this chapter?

8. John McNutt of the Boston College School of Social Work asserts that the information divide—access to computers and computer information—between haves and have nots is the policy problem of the new century.[61] What do you think of McNutt's assertion? (For more information, you can obtain a PBS series on the *Information Divide* which discusses this policy issue.)

9. Simon and Aigner state that "Social work is neither pro capitalism nor pro socialism. As they presently exist, both capitalist and socialist political economies fail to provide the conditions

necessary for all members to meet their basic needs, accomplish their life tasks, and realize their values and aspirations. There are oppressed, victimized, and neglected groups in all societies."[62] Do you agree or disagree that both capitalism and socialism fail to provide for people's needs?

10. Does social work have a responsibility to help correct market failures and help people meet needs, accomplish life tasks, and realize their aspirations? What solutions can you recommend?

11. The National Rifle Association has successfully carried the battle of upholding the right of people to bear arms. The result has been little gun control legislation in this country. Some people assert that the Second Amendment provides a moral, if not legal, right to own handguns. Are there ethical values that override this moral and legal right? If so, what does that higher good consist of?

EXERCISE 13.2

Solving a Housing Problem

Read the following excerpt from John Perkins's book, *With Justice for All*. Then respond to the questions that follow.

Once I was talking with some of the staff members of the housing authority in Atlanta. They asked me, "What can we do to help change the dehumanizing conditions of these apartment buildings?"

My answer was simple. "Give the apartments to the people."

They thought I was crazy. But that's exactly what we need to do. These apartments can be turned into cooperatives or condominiums. Rent subsidies need to be replaced with mortgage-payment subsidies. We don't need a new program or any more money to do this at all. We just need to redirect the subsidies to the poor family and subsidize home ownership among the poor, rather than to subsidize landlords and local and county governmental housing authorities.

Ownership creates responsibility. If I go into one of these housing authority apartments and see a broken screen and ask, "Why isn't your screen fixed?" The mother may answer, "The landlord hasn't gotten around to fixing it yet."

Then if I ask, "Who broke it?" She'll say, "My kids broke it." Her lack of ownership has removed her sense of responsibility. If she owned that apartment, she would feel responsible enough to fix it herself. She would also feel responsible to teach her children to take care of the apartment.

The key to redistribution and empowerment of the poor is helping people accept responsibility for their own development.[63]

1. What is your opinion of John Perkins's solution to the housing problem? Do you think it would work?

2. Would helping people become home owners develop empowerment and commitment?

3. Why do you suppose a solution like Perkins's meets with surprise? Who would be for it? Who would be against it?

4. How does Perkins's solution relate to the assertion by Simon and Aigner about capitalism and socialism in discussion question 9? What would capitalists think of his solution? What would socialists think of his solution?

5. Can you think of similar solutions to social problems such as drugs, crime, gang violence, or others that affect our communities which would empower people and assist people to gain affiliation, mastery, and community ownership?

EXERCISE 13.3

Community Control or National Control?

Writing about community development, S. K. Khinduka asserts that "Local institutions can no longer remain unaffected by the extra-community system. Local destinies cannot be decided locally. Nor can the major problems of a locality—poverty, unemployment, housing, and discrimination—be solved merely or mainly by mobilizing local efforts." Khinduka is discussing broad national, centralized policy-making that can impose an overall ethic of justice. He asserts that communities are often parochial and unjust, perpetuating racism and oppression. He asserts, "There are champions of local rights who oppose federal intervention so that they can perpetuate the injustice of local political and economic arrangements. The principle of local rights is thus invoked mainly to defeat, delay, or dilute national policies designed to correct the inequities of the local system." Khinduka calls this "local self-determination." In contrast, he says, when African Americans ask for control over local institutions "they are, in effect, saying that they no longer want white domination of their lives and institutions. This is a demand for self-determination, *not local* self-determination." According to Khinduka, self-determination "seeks to restore respect for a group often subjected to conscious and unconscious indignities," while local self-determination "is calculated to deny precisely this egalitarian end."[64]

1. Do you believe Khinduka's assertion that the major problems of a locality—poverty, unemployment, housing, and discrimination—cannot be solved merely or mainly by mobilizing local efforts?

2. Khinduka asserts that "there are champions of local rights who oppose federal intervention so that they can perpetuate the injustice of local political and economic arrangements. The principle of local rights is thus invoked mainly to defeat, delay, or dilute national policies designed to correct the inequities of the local system." What is your assessment of this assertion?

3. What is your perspective on the distinction that Khinduka makes between self determination and local self determination? Is this a valid distinction?

4. Will local self-determination in community generally result in a denial of egalitarianism and a lack of respect for groups, as Khinduka asserts?

5. If local self-determination results in injustice, how would you as a policy developer help restore justice in such a community?

EXERCISE 13.4

Thomas Bender on Politics

Read Thomas Bender's assessment and discuss the questions that follow.

"A sense of commonwealth, rather than community, provides the essential foundation for a vigorous and effective political life. A commonwealth is based upon shared public ideals, rather than upon acquaintance or affection. Personal knowledge of fellow citizens…is not necessary. What is necessary is full political communication that examines the consequences of proposed and enacted public policies. Such public communication undergirds civic respon-

sibility and enables us to determine whether we share a common interest in certain public policies affecting the whole. . . . Power and political problems in modern society are more extensive than a neighborhood or a community. . . . Any effort to concentrate one's efforts on neighborhood or community political activity may mask a denial of access to sources of power affecting local life through the general polity."[65]

1. Do you agree that community is not the level at which politics should be conducted?

2. Is Bender correct when he states that community political activity may mask a denial of access to sources of power affecting local life though the general polity? How would community organizers Cesar Chavez, Gale Cincotta, or Ernesto Cortes respond to this assertion?

3. Does Bender's argument preclude community level politics?

4. What arguments for or against Bender's assertion can you present?

EXERCISE 13.5

Allocating Water: The Elixir of Life

This exercise will provide experience in grappling with a difficult policy question and help you come to some consensus. Divide yourselves into five interest groups. One group is to represent ecological interests, another agribusiness. The third represents urban interests of Los Angeles and other urban areas. The fourth represents the power industry. The fifth represents the public interest in the use of lakes, rivers, and bays. Choose one observer for each group and select two class members as mediators.

Outside of class, each group reads "Allocating Water: The Elixir of Life," prepares a policy statement reflecting the group's interests, and answers the questions at the end of the excerpt. Additional research may be needed. In class, each group presents its written proposal to the other interest groups. Outside of class, each group reads their competitors' proposals and prepares a response that will bring them closer together on the issues. Then the class as a whole meets to develop a joint policy statement to which each group can agree. Groups should choose two members each as representatives who will speak for the group as a whole. Groups can lobby, join one another, request mediators to negotiate differences, or form power blocks. Mediators refer to Chapter 12 on the techniques of doing negotiating and bargaining. Observers take notes during the process and give feedback to policy advocates. The instructor will monitor the process, keep order, help facilitate communication, and direct groups to help them come to some agreement. The instructor may set a specific time limit on the entire consensus-building process. At the end of the exercise, the instructor will lead a discussion on the following questions.

1. What did you learn about compromising differences?

2. If your class was able to come to an agreement, was everybody happy with the decision?

3. What values did your group use in advocating for your position?

4. What kind of power politics emerged?

5. Do you think that the decision that your class arrived at would be accepted or later contested by rival groups?

Allocating Water: The Elixir of Life

In California the allocation of water is a major policy controversy. Water is regulated by the State Water Resources Control Board, and nearly everyone in California is affected by its policy decisions. The problem is, as Boyd Gibbons, director of the state Department of Fish and Game said, "there is not enough water to supply all beneficial uses in all years."

On the one hand are farmers whose 40-year contracts for federally subsidized water are now expiring. Many of these farmers insist that when the public paid to build the Central Valley Water Project, a huge system of reservoirs and canals, the public gave up all claim to the water that flows into it. Agribusiness insists now that the government has to renew the contracts without reducing their supplies by one drop—no matter how desperately the water may be needed elsewhere in the state.

On the other hand, urban areas such as Los Angeles claim proprietary rights to water that has systematically drained Mono Lake, lowering its level and nearly destroying it. Power companies, insisting on building more dams even on small and insignificant creeks in order to produce more energy, have systematically destroyed many of California's wild rivers and the ecosystems on which those rivers depend. Environmentalists point to the need for water to prevent the destruction of endangered species of fish and the winter run of Chinook salmon. The public in general depends on California's rivers and lakes for fishing and recreation.

The battle even takes on regional overtones. Most of the water exists in the northern part of the state, while many of the thirsty urban dwellers in Los Angeles and farmers in the Central Valley and the Imperial Valley are located in middle and southern portions of the state. Into this battle step the contending groups, lawyers, lobbyists, and government agencies, all of whom want a piece of the action in hammering out allocation policy.

Who has rights to the water? Who really needs it? How much should be allocated? Who will pay and how much? Is preserving California's ecosystems, particularly its wildlife, rivers, streams, deltas, and bays more or less important than subsidizing agriculture and power industries? Should agriculture receive huge breaks on the water it buys from federally supported irrigation projects while urban dwellers pay full cost? Will jobs and thereby one of California's largest industries be jeopardized if they are not given all the water they want?

EXERCISE *13.6*

Developing Social Policy

Listed below are a series of social policy questions. Break into groups of six or seven. Choose one of these questions or another social issue of concern.

1. Should drugs be legalized?

2. Should a system of national health insurance be developed?

3. Should the welfare system be revised?

4. Should the death penalty be abolished?

5. Should the Equal Rights Amendment be ratified?

6. Should the remaining old-growth forests in the United States be protected?

7. Should affirmative action programs be eliminated?

Gather facts by asking the who, why, what, where, and how questions in relation to the issue. Gather information and decide on the "real" problem to be worked on by role-playing and using the fishbowl technique. Decide on several solutions to the real problem by locating change points. Rank your solutions according to those you think are the best ones to solve the social problem.

Present your policy statement to the rest of the class, including how you decided on the problem, the problem definition your group decided on, and at least three solutions. Compare the process that each group used. Was the process effective or ineffective? How could your policy-making process be improved?

EXERCISE 13.7

Using PRINCE to Test Political Feasibility

Choose at least four actors who have control over the policy issue you worked on in exercise 13.6. For each of the three alternative solutions you have chosen, use the PRICE political feasibility model to decide on the issue position, power, salience, and total support of the actors. Calculate the scores, rate each alternative solution, and rank the alternative solutions. Did the PRINCE ranking turn out as you expected?

ADDITIONAL READING

Donald L. Bartlett and James B. Steele. *America: What Went Wrong?* Kansas City, MO: Andrews and McMeel, 1992.

Marvin Cetron and Owen Davies. *American Renaissance: Our Life at the Turn of the 21st Century.* New York: St. Martin's,1989.

C. Chambers. *Seedtime of Reform: American Social Services and Social Action, 1918–1933.* Minneapolis: University of Minnesota Press, 1963.

William Greider. *Who Will Tell the People: The Betrayal of American Democracy.* New York: Simon and Schuster, 1992.

B. Jansson. *Becoming an Effective Policy Advocate: From Policy Practice to Social Justice.* 3d ed. Pacific Grove, CA: Brooks/Cole, 1999.

Ralph Nader and William Taylor. *The Big Boys: Power and Position in American Business.* New York: Pantheon, 1986.

John McKnight. "Do No Harm: Policy Options That Meet Human Needs," *Social Policy* (Summer 1989): pp. 5–15.

David Osborne and Ted Gaebler. *Reinventing Government: How the Entrepreneurial Spirit Is Transforming the Public Sector.* New York: Addison-Wesley, 1992.

Kevin Phillips. *The Politics of Rich and Poor.* New York: Random House, 1990.

Center for Urban Affairs and Policy Research. *Politics of the Helping Professions.* Evanston, IL: Northwestern University, n. d.

Aaron Wildavsky. *Speaking Truth to Power: The Art and Craft of Policy Analysis.* Boston: Little, Brown, 1979.

Elite Model

William G. Domhoff. *The Power Elite and the State: How Policy Is Made in America.* Hawthorne, NJ: Aldine De Gruyter, 1990.

———. *The Powers That Be: Processes of Ruling-Class Domination in America.* New York: Random House, 1979.

———. *The Higher Circles: The Governing Class in America.* New York: Random House, 1970.

———. *Who Rules America?* Englewood Cliffs, NJ: Prentice-Hall, 1967.

Michael Parenti. *Power and the Powerless.* 2d ed. New York: St. Martin's, 1978.

———. *Democracy for the Few.* 5th ed. New York: St. Martin's, 1988.

John Kenneth Galbraith. *Economics and the Public Purpose.* Boston: Houghton Mifflin, 1973.

C. Wright Mills. *The Power Elite.* New York: Oxford University Press, 1956.

Institutional Model

David B. Truman. The *Governmental Process.* New York: Knopf, 1971.

Rational Actor Model

Graham T. Allison. *The Essence of Decision: Explaining the Cuban Missile Crisis.* Boston: Little, Brown, 1971.

George C. Edwards III and Ira Sharkansky. *The Policy Predicament: Making and Implementing Public Policy.* San Francisco: W. H. Freeman, 1978.

Edith Stokey and Richard Zeckhauser. *A Primer for Policy Analysis.* New York: W. W. Norton, 1978.

Interest Group Model

Theodore Lowi. *The End of Liberalism.* New York: W. W. Norton, 1969.

V. Smith. "How Interest Groups Influence Legislators," *Social Work,* 24(3) (1979): pp. 234–239.

J. Walker Jr. *Mobilizing Interest Groups in America: Patrons, Professions, and Social Movements.* Ann Arbor: University of Michigan Press, 1991.

Administrative Actor Model

C. Kerwin. *Rulemaking: How Government Agencies Write Law and Make Policy*. Washington, DC: Congressional Quarterly Press, 1994.

William L. Morrow. *Public Administration: Politics and the Political Process*. New York: Random House, 1975.

Systems Model

David Easton. *A Framework for Political Analysis*. Englewood Cliffs, NJ: Prentice-Hall, 1965.

———. "An Approach to the Analysis of Political Systems," *World Politics,* 9 (1957): 383–400.

Social Policy and Social Work

Thomas R. Dye. *Understanding Public Policy*. 2d ed. Englewood Cliffs, NJ: Prentice-Hall, 1975.

Neil Gilbert and Harry Specht. *Dimensions of Social Welfare Policy*. 2d ed. Englewood Cliffs, NJ: Prentice-Hall, 1986.

Nathan Glazer. *The Limits of Social Policy*. Cambridge, MA: Harvard University Press, 1988.

Michael Harrington. *The Other America: Poverty in the Unites States*. New York: Macmillan, 1962.

Thomas M. Meenaghan and Robert O. Washington. *Social Policy and Social Welfare*. New York: Free Press, 1980.

M. Miringoff and S. Opdycke. *American Social Welfare Policy Reassessment and Reform*. Englewood Cliffs, NJ: Prentice-Hall, 1986.

Dean Pierce. *Policy for the Social Work Practitioner*. New York: Longman, 1984.

Charles S. Prigmore and Charles R. Atherton. *Social Welfare Policy Analysis and Formulation*. 2d ed. Lexington, MA: D. C. Heath, 1986.

W. Rican. *Beyond Altruism: Social Welfare Policy in American Society*. New York: Haworth Press, 1988.

John E. Tropman et al. *Strategic Perspectives on Social Policy*. New York: Pergamon Press, 1976.

Politics and Social Work

Jane Addams. "Pragmatism in Politics," *The Survey,* 29(12) (1912).

R. Albert. "Social Work Advocacy in the Regulatory Process," *Social Casework* (1983): pp.473–481.

A. Davis. "Settlement Workers in Politics, 1890–1914," *Review of Politics,* 26(4) (1964): pp. 505–517.

R. Dear and R. Patti. "Legislative Advocacy: Seven Effective Tactics," *Social Work,* 26(4) (1981): pp. 289–296.

R. Fisher. "Political Social Work," *Journal of Social Work Education* 31(2), (1995): pp. 194–203.

Jeffrey H. Galper. *Politics of Social Services*. Englewood Cliffs, NJ: Prentice-Hall, 1975.

K. Giles. *Flight of the Dove: The Story of Jeanette Rankin*. Beaverton, OR: Touchstone Press, 1980.

K. Haynes and J. Mickelson. *Affecting Change: Social Workers in the Political Arena*. 3d ed. New York: Longman, 1997.

M. Mahaffey and J. Hanks, eds. *Practical Politics: Social Work and Political Responsibility*. Silver Spring, MD: NASW Press, 1982.

M. Mahaffey. "Lobbying and Social Work," *Social Work,* 17(1) (1972): pp. 3–11.

Betty Reid Mandell and Ann Withorn. *Keep on Keeping on: Local Politics in the Era of the Global City*. Urban Affairs Annual Review 41. Newbury Park: Sage, 1993.

R. Patti and R. Dear. "Legislative Advocacy: A Path to Social Change," *Social Work,* 20(2) (1975): pp. 108–114.

S. Rees. *Achieving Power: Practice and Policy in Social Welfare*. North Sydney, Australia: Allen and Unwin, 1991.

A. Ribicoff. "Politics and Social Workers," *Social Work,* 7(2) (1962): pp. 3–6.

W. Richan. *Lobbying for Social Change*, 2d ed. New York: Haworth, 1996.

R. Salcido and E. Seck. "Political Participation Among Social Work Chapters," *Social Work,* 37(6), (1992): pp. 563–564.

J. Wolk. "Are Social Workers Politically Active?" *Social Work,* 25(5) (1981): pp. 283–288.

14

Becoming Active in Social Movements

Those who profess to favor freedom, and yet deprecate agitation are men who want crops without plowing up the ground. They want rain without thunder and lightning. They want the ocean without the mighty roar of its many waters.

This struggle may be a moral one; it may be a physical one; or it may be both moral and physical; but it must be a struggle.

Power concedes nothing without a demand. It never did and it never will. Find out just what people will submit to and you have found the exact amount of injustice and wrong that will be imposed upon them; and these will continue until they are resisted with either words or blows, or with both.

The limits of tyrants are prescribed by the endurance of those whom they oppress.

Frederick Douglass

Ideas in This Chapter

MARTIN LUTHER KING JR. AND THE WAR IN VIETNAM

On January 14, 1967, Martin Luther King Jr. bought a copy of *Ramparts* magazine and read the illustrated story "The Children of Vietnam." This event was to be a turning point in the history of social movements.[1] Many photos showed the burn wounds suffered by youngsters who had been struck by American napalm. As he looked at the pictures from Vietnam, King's attention froze. He saw a picture of a Vietnamese mother holding her dead baby, a baby killed by American military. He pushed the plate of food away from him. His friend Bernard Lee looked up and said, "Doesn't it taste any good?" King answered, "Nothing will ever taste any good for me until I do everything I can to end that war."

The anti-war protests and other postmodern social movements of the 1960s were watershed events in the history of social protest, but more importantly they marked, for perceptive observers of American society, a turning point in our modern era as well. There is no clearer indicator of this change than the little understood shift by Martin Luther King Jr. from protest against segregation to protest against the war in Vietnam. Many people considered this shift a dilution of the civil rights movement. Others considered it subversion of national policy. Even more thought it an effort to exploit the protest against the war to boost the waning influence of King's Southern Christian Leadership Conference (SCLC).

King's inclusion of the protest against the war in Vietnam in the civil rights struggle was a matter of conscience that deepened the meaning of nonviolence and called America to face its commitment to freedom and justice. Even more important, in choosing that path, King confronted the ideals and values of modernity and began to lead America into the postmodern era. He saw that the struggle for equal opportunity was not only about jobs, but about human dignity; that nonviolence on the streets of Selma, Birmingham, or Chicago was meaningless when children were slaughtered in My Lai, and that racism and colonialism at home could not be defeated unless America repudiated racism and colonialism abroad.

In the earlier days of the civil rights movement, like most civil rights activists before him, King pursued political and economic freedom for African Americans. King articulated the essence of modern social movements. "Gentlemen," he said to those who were trying to prevent a protest march, "you know we don't have much. We don't have much money. We don't really have much education and we don't have political power….We are not trying to overthrow you. We're trying to get in. We are trying to make justice a reality."

For civil rights leaders, and for most African Americans, the goal of civil disobedience was to "get in" to make justice real for all Americans. Getting in has been the goal of all modern social movements. The goal of the suffrage movement was for women to get in; of the labor movement, for workers to get in; now for African Americans, the goal was also to get in.

King realized that unless he took a stand against the war, however, his years of struggle for African Americans to "get in" meant participating in the very things he had fought against: racism, violence, injustice, and oppression. Unless he worked to change the foundations of American culture that promoted paternalism and racism, getting in might be worse than staying out. He saw that racism was only a part of the modern system built on domination, exploitation, privilege, and power; that racism was violent no matter how distant; that colonialism was violent, no matter how benevolent; that exploitation was violent, no matter how profitable. The struggle to "get in" to the benefits of the American dream also meant to get into this world of violence, not as a victim but as a perpetrator, as a prosperous American who benefited by the suffering, oppression, and even death of others. It was something he could not accept.

"I spent a lot of time in prayerful meditation," King said. "I came to the conclusion that I could no longer remain silent about an issue that was destroying the soul of our nation." Later King said to a *New York Times* correspondent, "We are merely marking time in the civil rights movement if we do not take a stand against the war." King clearly announced his intention not merely to reform but to change society. "It is out of this moral commitment to dignity and the worth of human personality," King said, "that I feel it is necessary to stand up against the war in Vietnam. If we are to get on the right side of the world revolution, we as a nation must undergo a radical revolution of values. We must rapidly begin the shift from a thing-oriented society to a person-oriented society." King began to lead America out of the wilderness of modernity and into the promised land of the new postmodern era.

WHAT YOU WILL LEARN IN THIS CHAPTER

Social work is called to transform society and to create a more just social order. In fact, says Gustavo Gutierrez, "to do nothing in favor of those who are oppressed is to act against them." Macro social workers ought to be "building a world where every man, regardless of race, religion, or nationality can live a fully human life, free of the servitude that comes from other men and from the incompletely mastered world about him."[2]

Social action is for those social workers who "are deeply troubled by our present world, seek a vision of a society which supports life,"[3] and are committed to a process of social change and an end to violence and human misery. Social action has nothing less as its goal than making fundamental changes in social structures which foster oppression and injustice.

In this chapter you will learn what social action is. You will learn about modern social movements. You will explore the heritage of modern social action, how social workers were among the foremost champions of freedom and equality for all Americans. You will learn how to conduct a modern campaign of social action, unfreeze inequitable systems, move to action, and establish ways that are more just. You will explore the process, tactics, and techniques by which social activists brought the nation's attention to their just causes and how social activists have, for the most part, brought to completion the social promise of modernity.

You will discover how social activists laid a foundation for the emergence of the new postmodern social era in which we now live and about new social movements that are occurring in the United States and around the globe today. You will explore how postmodern social activists generate these new social movements and how you too can become involved in constructing the new society of the future.

MODERN SOCIAL ACTION

America was founded in the fires of protest and revolution by those seeking to end tyranny and construct a modern nation of liberty and justice. It was peopled, by and large, by those who were disaffected, outcasts, protestors, idealists, visionaries, dreamers, seekers, true believers, and religious dissidents who often fled their homeland because of persecution and who wanted to make the modern dream of opportunity and freedom from oppression a reality. When those ideals failed to materialize, however, Americans continued to press government for redress by means of social action.

Modern social action has been practiced under many names. It has been variously called social reform, social revolution, counter-revolution, social protest, and resistance. Social action tries to slow down or stop practices that citizens perceive as unethical or immoral. Social movements have occurred under the labels of war resistance, cultural resistance, civil disobedience, and civil insurrection.

Social action occurs when an oppressed, disadvantaged, or injured people engage in mutual action against an oppressor, aim at redistribution of power at the political or economic levels, reorder organizational alliances at top levels of the bureaucratic apparatus, and ultimately change public policies. It is a process by which people attempt "to realize the democratic dream of equality, justice, peace, cooperation, equal and full opportunities for education, full and useful employment, health and the creation of those circumstances in which man can have the chance to live by values that give meaning to life."[4]

Social action is most often expressed as a single-issue "movement," often national in scope, that engages people from all walks of life to bring about changes in social policy and structures. Social action deals with the most pressing and important issues of our time. Some of the most impressive and long-standing social victories in the human struggle for justice and equality have come from social action. Many of these, such as regulating nuclear arms, protecting the environment, and ending racism, affect all of us.

MODERN SOCIAL MOVEMENTS

While the history of modern social protest has occurred over the entire course of American experience, it has been most visible in four major social movements: the labor movement, the abolitionist movement, the progressive movement, and the movements of the 1960s.

Labor Movement

The struggle of American laborers for decent working conditions, fair wages, and decent hours began as early as 1636 when a group of fishermen in Maine mutinied when their wages were withheld.[5] In 1806 the Journeymen Cordwainers of Philadelphia struck for higher wages and were indicted for criminal conspiracy. One of the worst strikes of all, the Great Pullman Strike of 1886, occurred when the company laid off more than 3,000 of its 5,800 Chicago employees and cut the wages of the others from between 25 to 40% without reducing the rents workers paid for living in company houses. The consequences were economically disastrous as thousands of people were left completely destitute. "In one instance, an employee found that after payment for rent was taken out, his paycheck came to two cents."[6]

The fight for decent working conditions and fair pay, and against exploitation of workers, continued through the early 1900s, prompting confrontations with paid henchmen of wealthy business owners and their cohorts in law enforcement. In company after company, activists and organizers fought for worker rights. At times the struggle was brutal and bloody. Workers at the Carnegie-owned Homestead steel plant in Pennsylvania, for example, refused to accept wage cuts, instigating the Great Homestead Strike of 1892. General manager Henry Clay Frick shut the plant down and hired special deputy sheriffs to guard the buildings. The striking workers ran them out of town, whereupon Frick called in 300 Pinkerton detectives armed with rifles to subdue the workers. A battle ensued as the workers opened fire on Frick's private army and attempted to sink their barges with a small brass cannon. Eventually the detectives ran up a white flag of surrender. Infuriated that seven of their number had been killed, however, the workers again attacked the detectives, who escaped but had to run the gauntlet of an angry mob of men and women. Six days later the governor of Pennsylvania mobilized a militia

of 8,000 men who took over Homestead and placed it under martial law. Frick then brought in scabs—non-union workers hired to take the jobs of the striking workers—reopening the plant with militia protection.

During this period, metal miners in Coeur d'Alene, Idaho, switchmen in Buffalo, and coal miners in Tennessee walked off their jobs in defiance of their employers. Workers in the minefields of the western states had established the Western Federation of miners in 1897 and engaged in a series of strikes in the gold, silver, lead, and copper mines of the West. In each instance, the strikes were forcibly broken through the intervention of the state militia. In 1903–1904, miners in the Cripple Creek area of Colorado attempted to go on strike and were attacked by strikebreakers. The miners fought back. Mine owners escalated violence, hiring vigilantes and calling in the state militia against the striking miners. Miners sabotaged trains and exploded mines. In retaliation, miners were murdered or arrested and imprisoned. Miners' meetings were machine-gunned. The strike was finally crushed by vigilantes, deputized sheriffs, police, and militia.

It was not until millions of laborers in the United States had suffered through years of bitter unemployment in the midst of the Great Depression that in March 1932, Congress passed the Norris-LaGuardia Act. By this legislation, the welfare of industrial workers was made a direct concern of government, and the principle was established that only organized labor could deal on equal terms with organized capital.

In July 1935, the National Labor Relations Act (NLRA) was passed, legalizing labor unions, prohibiting employers from interfering with unions or refusing to bargain collectively, and upholding the rights of workers to negotiate for their rights on an equal basis with management. The NLRA also established a regulatory agency, the National Labor Relations Board (NLRB), which had sole authority to determine bargaining units and the power to supervise elections, hear complaints of unfair labor practices, issue cease and desist orders, and petition the court for enforcement of its orders.

BERTHA CAPEN REYNOLDS

Bertha Capen Reynolds, social worker, educator, and activist, advocated for working-class and oppressed groups and stressed the importance of working together for a more humane world. Born in 1885 and raised in Stoughton, Massachusetts, she graduated from the Boston School of Social Work in 1914. She participated in the first course in psychiatry ever offered to social workers at Smith College in 1918, and in 1925 she was appointed associate director of Smith College School of Social Work.

In 1938, Reynolds was asked to resign from the college because she encouraged social workers to unionize to improve their working conditions and the lives of their clients. After her dismissal, she continued to write extensively in *Social Work Today,* the journal of the Rank and File Movement, on the need for social workers to become more politically active and concerned about the civil rights of their clients. In 1942, she published *Learning and Teaching in the Practice of Social Work.* However, in spite of her background and scholarship, she found it difficult to obtain employment either in schools of social work or social agencies, coming to the conclusion that she had been blacklisted for her union activities. In 1943, however, the National Maritime Union hired her.

After her retirement in 1948, Reynolds wrote three more books, *Social Work and Social Living* (1951), *McCarthyism versus Social Work* (1954), and her autobiography, *An Uncharted Journey* (1963). Although she did not stand alone in her perspectives, Reynolds has come to symbolize the historical tradition of progressive social work. What distinguished her was her serious and lifelong commitment to understanding the forces behind oppression, war, and human degradation. Reynolds died in 1978 at the age of 92. In 1985, progressive social workers, compelled to resist the conservative drift of the social work profession and their increasing marginalization, rallied around the centennial celebration of her life and legacy and formed a national organization, the Bertha Capen Reynolds Society (BCRS).

Abolitionist Movement

In the early 19th century, modern social activists observed with rising concern the horrors that slavery and racism brought upon the American nation.[7] They worked in many ways and in increasing numbers to establish the beginnings of the abolition movement. By 1831, agitation against slavery began to grow. William Lloyd Garrison of Newburyport, Massachusetts, published the first issue of the *Liberator*, a rabid antislavery newspaper. The very next year the New England Anti-Slavery Society was founded, and by 1833 delegates from several states founded the American Anti-Slavery Society, which was dedicated to

immediate emancipation. In 1837 the abolitionists began to agitate for social legislation by circulating petitions directed at Congress. Speakers spread the message of abolition and inspired the "formation of town, country, and state antislavery groups. By 1838 the Anti-Slavery Society claimed a membership of 250,000 with over 1,300 auxiliaries."

The success of the movement, however, inspired active and vengeful retaliation. In 1835 a mob in Charleston, South Carolina, broke into the post office and stole and burned antislavery publications. President Andrew Jackson applauded the riot along with southern and a few northern public officials. In that same year, rioters in Boston led Garrison through the streets on a rope, and two years later Elijah Lovejoy, an antislavery editor, was murdered while defending his press in Alton, Illinois.

From 1850 onward, events began to escalate. The Fugitive Slave Act required northerners to assist in capturing and returning escaped slaves. African Americans resisted and protested slavery by escaping from bondage, by day-to-day resistance, and by staging occasional insurrections. Engaging in civil disobedience, African Americans and abolitionists alike fought slave-catchers. They rescued fugitives from courtrooms and jails, inspiring the single most effective piece of antislavery propaganda, *Uncle Tom's Cabin* by Harriet Beecher Stowe, published in 1852.

In 1857, in spite of the moral and human rights issues involved, the U.S. Supreme Court rendered the Dred Scott decision, ruling that ownership of people was constitutional and that Congress had no authority to ban it from the territories. In October 1859, abolitionist John Brown and a small band of followers attacked the federal arsenal at Harper's Ferry, Virginia. A little over a year later, on December 20, 1860, South Carolina seceded from the Union over the issue of slavery, and the Civil War began, the bloodiest conflict this nation has ever experienced. By its end in 1865, almost 500,000 had died in the struggle, more than any other war before or since, and hundreds of thousands more Americans were maimed for life. The war, however, led to the end of slavery in the United States.

HARRIET TUBMAN

In about 1821, Araminta Ross was born into slavery in Dorchester County, Maryland. When she was thirteen, a plantation overseer struck her on the head so severely that Araminta's skull was fractured, leaving her physically handicapped for the rest of her life. In 1844, however, she married Samuel Tubman, a free black man, and changed her name to Harriet, renouncing her former life of slavery. In that same year she fled to Philadelphia with her husband but clandestinely returned to Baltimore a year later and helped several members of her family to escape from bondage.

Encouraged by her success, Tubman devoted all of her energy to guiding runaway slaves to freedom from the plantations of Maryland through the Underground Railway. When the fugitive slave law was rigidly enforced in Maryland, she moved her fugitive refugees at first to New York and afterward to Canada, aiding in the escape of more than 300 slaves. Her activity became so obnoxious to the southern states that a reward of $40,000 was offered for apprehending the 'Negro Moses.' During the Civil War, Tubman served as a spy for the Union army and as a nurse in Union army hospitals.

Progressive Movement

Progressivism began convulsively in the 1880s and waxed and waned afterward to insure the survival of democracy in the United States by the enlargement of government to control and offset the power of private corporations over the nation's institutions and life. One of the foremost groups of progressives was the emerging profession of social workers. Progressive social workers became involved in nearly every issue of the times, in an era that was rife with social movements including charities and corrections, temperance, women's suffrage, health insurance, social settlements, and more.

Charities and Corrections Movement   The charities and corrections movement was a response of idealistic reformers to the misery and despair that accompanied industrialization in the United States in the years following the Civil War. The movement was based on a powerful belief in the perfectibility of society. While the major arm of the charities and corrections movement was the establishment of Charity Organization Societies (COS), its aims were much broader. Charities and corrections people were concerned about every corner of darkness, despair, and deprivation on earth. They sought to aid criminals, drunks, the poor, children, and people suffering from

mental or physical illness. They worked to improve food and drug safety, sanitation, playgrounds, and slums. Many of the reforms they sought—the 40-hour work week, social security, child labor laws, disaster relief—have become institutionalized and we now take them for granted, but in the nineteenth century, these ideas were considered radical.

Temperance Movement   Encouraged by the inexpensive production of corn in the Midwest after the Revolutionary War, whiskey drinking became something of a national pastime for men, women, and children.[8] Between 1800 and 1830, whiskey consumption increased to more than 5 gallons per person per year. Many people were concerned about the relationship of alcoholism to unemployment, poverty, and family breakdown. Alcoholism caused of loss of time from work and physical abuse within families. Ultimately its eradication was seen as a matter of women's and family rights.

In 1826 the American Society for the Promotion of Temperance was founded, motivated by a spirit of religious and humanitarian reform. So successful was this movement that the annual consumption of whiskey after 1830 dropped from 5 to less than 2 gallons per person per year. In the 1830s and 1840s, thousands of local temperance societies were formed to prohibit the sale of liquor altogether. By 1860 the temperance movement boasted a membership of more than a million individuals. The members of the movement became more and more politically active. Even though women lacked the right to vote, they entered the political arena. In 1869, women formed the Prohibition Party, along with the Women's Christian Temperance Union (WCTU), and the Anti-Saloon League. Frances Willard, the militant leader of the prohibition forces, carried the battle into the enemy territory of the saloons, where women sang hymns, prayed, and at times engaged in acts of symbolic protest, destroying bottles of whisky and kegs of beer.

By the beginning of the twentieth century, seven states had voted to prohibit alcohol. By World War I, two-thirds of the U.S. population lived in areas where drinking was outlawed. In 1919 the Eighteenth Amendment to the Constitution was passed, completely outlawing manufacture, sale, import, or export of alcoholic beverages in the United States. Social protest by women against drinking was overwhelmingly effective, but implementation proved to be another matter. Enforcement of prohibition by interdiction ultimately proved to be impossible. Bootlegging, speak-easies, smuggling, and the manufacture of "bathtub gin," and "white lightning" in homemade stills (distilleries) proved that the human predisposition to alcohol was more potent than government enforcement. In 1933, the Eighteenth Amendment was repealed.

Women's Suffrage Movement   Women have been involved at the center of every major social movement in the United States, "moving from concern for rooting out individual imperfections that would lead to unhappy family living to a demand for explicit political recognition and power, and then to larger social issues."[9] In 1848 the first Women's Rights Convention was held in Seneca Falls, New York. Women's suffrage was demanded, and a Declaration of Independence was adopted. In 1900 the National American Woman's Suffrage Association was founded, along with a number of other women's groups, among them, the National Consumer's League, the National Women's Trade Union League, and the Young Women's Christian Association. All of these organizations "were at once concerned with matters affecting women as women and the potential of the vote for righting wrongs."

Social activists such as Carrie Chapman Catt and social workers Jane Addams, Florence Kelly, and others led the fight for women's rights—writing pamphlets and tracts, lobbying state legislatures and Congress, demonstrating, marching, and picketing. The Nineteenth Amendment to the Constitution, giving women the right to vote, was approved by Congress on June 4, 1919, and ratified by the states on August 26, 1920. The National American Women's Suffrage Association dissolved but later revived as the League of Women Voters.

Settlement House Movement   Settlement workers were at the forefront of every major social movement in an era that was filled with reform efforts. They were tireless fighters for social justice, helping to mobilize people who were desperate for social change. When New York City politicians in collusion with construction companies proposed an elevated loop connecting the Brooklyn and Williamsburg Bridges as a way to skim money from the public treasury, for example, settlement workers of the Henry

Street and University Settlements in New York City organized mass meetings, sent out letters to influential people, persuaded newspapers to present their point of view, and bombarded the city council with letters and petitions.

Settlement workers at the Chicago Commons, including Allen T. Burns and Raymond Robins, "made surveys, filed reports, checked for voting frauds, organized political rallies and torch parades, and distributed posters and handbills." They also served as campaign managers, advisers on policy, statistics gatherers, and 'brain trusters'" for reform political administrations.[10]

Settlement staff were active in the labor movement, especially the women's and child labor movements. Florence Kelly was instrumental in obtaining the constitutionality of the 10-hour work day. Settlement workers fought for laws to protect employed women, helping organize the National Women's Trade Union, and picketed with women workers in strikes against sweatshop owners. Jane Addams was instrumental in the creation of the State Boards of Conciliation and Arbitration in Illinois. In 1902 Lillian Wald and Florence Kelly mobilized 32 settlement houses in New York City to abolish the horrors of child labor, stimulating the 1903 Conference of Charities and Corrections that built opposition to child labor on national lines. In 1904 the National Child Labor Committee was organized, including founding members Jane Addams, Florence Kelly, and Lillian Wald.[11]

Settlement workers were prime advocates in the child welfare movement, pushing for child welfare legislation. Lillian Wald and Florence Kelly organized the first White House Conference on Child Dependency in 1909, bringing the issue of dependent children before the entire nation. The White House Conference was instrumental in developing the Children's Bureau, established in 1912, the first Child Welfare agency of the Federal Government. Settlement workers helped organize the juvenile criminal justice movement, agitating for a separate juvenile court system, and they provided leadership in establishing the first probation service in Chicago and the Juvenile Protective Association.[12]

Hull House workers organized the Immigrant Protective League, easing immigrants' adjustment to their new country and helping to prevent political exploitation of immigrants by corrupt political machines.

Settlement workers formed the Municipal Voters League, provided national leadership to the General Federation of Women's Clubs, and were on the forefront of passage of the Women's Suffrage Amendment to the Constitution in 1919.[13]

Settlement house staff were active in the progressive political movement. Jane Addams, for example, contributed to the platform and the organizational work of the Progressive Party in 1912. She was a delegate to the first national convention of the Progressive Party and seconded the nomination of Theodore Roosevelt as presidential candidate.

A number of settlement workers became active in the pacifist movement during World War I, among them Jane Addams. In 1915 Jane Addams founded the Woman's International League for Peace and Freedom and continued to press for peace during the war. Social workers who were members of religious groups including Quakers, Mennonites, and Seventh Day Adventists held pacifist and nonviolent beliefs and were jailed for their resistance to the war. Out of those efforts, however, conscientious objection to war became recognized as a legitimate right.

Progressive social work activists did not oppose the premises of modern American society. They worked to reform society, not revolutionize it. They wanted a society that carried out in practice the social principles of justice and opportunity that the Constitution guaranteed in theory to all our citizens. They struggled to create a level playing field, to make society more just and equitable, to seek out those who had been excluded and seat them in the banquet hall of the American dream. Progressive social workers and other modern activists promoted "economic growth and prosperity, social security and social control, individual freedom and self-interest, private consumption and material progress"[14] for all people, and they worked against the powerful who distorted these components of opportunity.

Social Action of the 1960s

Even though social movements had already accomplished a great deal, a reaction set in through much of the 1920s to the 1960s. Social movements tended to be conceptualized as potentially dangerous to the stability of established ways of life. Between World War I and II, social movements became identified with fascism, communism, anarchism, and subversion of the social order. For most people, communism, fascism, and anarchism posed enormous threats to enlightened reason, liberty, democracy, and capitalistic free enterprise, which were central to Western civilization. Protests were seen as resulting in disruptive strikes, demonstrations, and riots. As a result, mass social movements of any kind were often tinged with a fear of tyranny, accusations of un-Americanism, distaste for irrational behavior, and concern about mob violence.[15]

The period between 1920 and 1960 perpetuated silencing minorities, women, and the least skilled. But while social protest went underground during this period, a process was covertly being generated out of sight of the mainstream that would bring about a convulsive outburst to end discrimination and bring about the beginning of an era of new social movements. The 1960s are generally recognized as the decade of protest. The many movements of this period included those for human potential, free speech, the counter culture, the environment, women's liberation, civil rights, welfare rights, and ending the war in Vietnam. The thrust of the Kennedy-Johnson administrations was, in many respects, the last great attempt to bring the modern Enlightenment project to a culmination, including not only the triumph of modern reason and science, but individual freedom and liberty, economic self-determination, and democracy. The ideals they championed included the virtues of the welfare state and to bring the poor and racially excluded groups, especially African Americans, into full political, economic, and social equality. The great contradictions of discrimination and segregation could no longer stand the combined pressure that the welfare and civil rights movements exerted in an age that celebrated progress, justice, and the democratic way of life as a model for the world.

Welfare Rights Movement.　During the late 1960s and early 1970s, the National Welfare Rights Organization (NWRO), founded by Syracuse CORE chairman George Wiley, provided the structure for a powerful welfare rights movement.[16] All around the country, but especially in the North, poor women organized to stop what they saw as ill treatment from welfare workers. Then they organized to change rules that made it impossible for them to survive and began demanding more benefits at the local and state levels. By the early 1970s the role of the NWRO became more pronounced, and local organizing efforts began to follow a national strategy. Their efforts were instrumental in leading Congress to consider a guaranteed national income and to reject President Nixon's Family Assistance Plan. Nevertheless, organizing became more difficult as state and county welfare departments learned better how to routinize benefits and limit worker discretion, so that one critical focus of early organizing—its attacks on the arbitrary allotment of benefits—was reduced.

With the death in 1973 of NWRO founder George Wiley, and the defeat of the Family Assistance Plan, however, the national focus of the welfare rights movement quickly collapsed. The movement splintered into remnants, with some areas losing any organizational form, while others maintained small organizations that struggled to retain at least a watchdog role in regard to state programs to organize around particularly offensive polices.

Civil Rights Movement   The civil rights movement began as far back as the Progressive Movement with the formation of two major civil rights organizations. The National Association for the Advancement of Colored People (NAACP) came into being in 1910 as an embodiment of the political and legal activism advocated by W.E.B. Dubois. A year later the National Urban League was established to help southern migrants adjust to urban living conditions in the North, expressing Booker T. Washington's view that African Americans should concentrate on economic progress.[17]

The inception of the modern civil rights movement can be traced to 1941, when A. Philip Randolph, president of the International Brotherhood of Pullman Workers, and the NAACP used the threat of a march on Washington to force President Roosevelt into signing Executive Order 8802, creating a temporary Committee on Fair Employment Practice to give African Americans fair and equal treatment in jobs. Although southern conservatives in Congress killed the committee in 1946, this political victory demonstrated the power African Americans could wield by using collective action. It inspired the vision that social justice could be attained when African Americans refused to endure injustice any longer.

Shortly after Randolph's victory, A. J. Muste, James Farmer, and others founded the Congress for Racial Equality (CORE), an offshoot of the Quaker-sponsored Fellowship of Reconciliation, and began to use techniques of nonviolent direct action to fight racial discrimination at the University of Chicago. In 1943 members of CORE used sit-in demonstrations to successfully desegregate a Chicago restaurant, and in April 1947, CORE and its allies sent black and white Freedom Riders into the South to test compliance with federal court decisions on interstate bus routes, tactics that would later be used all over the South. A year later, President Truman ordered the desegregation of the U.S. Armed forces. Momentum was beginning to build among champions of civil rights that segregation could be stopped.

While CORE was waging action at the grassroots level, Thurgood Marshall, one of the NAACP's chief litigants and later a Supreme Court justice, used legal action to build precedent after precedent in court victories against segregation in higher education, including *Sweatt v. Painter, McLaurin v. Oklahoma State Regents,* and *Henderson v. United States.* Direct grassroots action by CORE and precedents established by the NAACP began to pay off when in 1953 the Supreme Court banned segregation in restaurants in Washington, D.C. A year later, the landmark rulings in *Brown v. Board of Education of Topeka* and *Bolling v. Sharpe* found that segregated schools were a violation of the 14th Amendment. The Supreme Court made clear its determination to prohibit government-sanctioned forms of racial discrimination. The Supreme Court decision was dramatically tested in September 1957 when Governor Orval Faubus used the Arkansas National Guard to prevent nine African American children from attending school in Little Rock. Defying Governor Faubus, President Eisenhower enforced the Supreme Court decision by sending federal troops into the South for the first time since the end of Reconstruction.

While the tide was clearly beginning to turn against segregation in the United States, the battle against discrimination could not be won by the courts or by governmental intervention alone. The real struggle to end racism would have to be won on the streets and playgrounds, in classrooms and churches, in stores and restaurants, in factories and offices, and it would have to be won by African Americans themselves.

Throughout the 1960s, the principle civil rights organizations—the NAACP, National Urban League, Congress of Racial Equality (CORE), Southern

Christian Leadership Conference (SCLC), and Student Nonviolent Coordinating Committee (SNCC)—promoted mass, nonviolent resistance to segregation by means of sit-ins, boycotts, picketing, marches, and legal action all over the South. After the Montgomery, Alabama, bus boycott of 1955–1956, for example, the SCLC was organized by Martin Luther King Jr. and Ralph Abernathy, becoming the largest and most active civil rights group. The SCLC-affiliated Student Nonviolent Coordinating Committee organized by Stokely Carmichael in 1960 was the most vocally militant of the major civil rights organizations and was instrumental in developing the organizational infrastructure for SCLC in a number of southern states, including Alabama and Mississippi.

Although fading in the 1950s, CORE revived when James Farmer returned as national director in 1961. While CORE fought southern segregation with Freedom Rides and other tactics, in the North it increasingly relied on the boycott as a weapon to force racial quotas on targeted corporations. Between 1960 and 1962, CORE inspired boycotts, coordinated by almost 400 religious leaders, that brought 24 corporations including Pepsi-Cola, Esso, Gulf Oil, and Sun Oil to an agreement to hire African Americans in specific numbers. Completely committed to racial quotas by 1962, CORE disseminated the strategy of boycotts for quotas in New York, Boston, and Detroit and continued to be involved in issues affecting blacks in northern urban centers, particularly housing and job discrimination. In 1961 the new executive director of the National Urban League, macro social worker Whitney M. Young Jr., proselytized for a "decade of discrimination" in favor of African Americans by means of racial preferences in employment.

Throughout these years of turbulence, members of activist civil rights organizations, blacks and whites, Rabbis and ministers, Christians and Jews, social workers and social activists were vilified, spat on, yelled at, threatened, beaten, tear-gassed, jailed, and some even murdered in the cause of civil rights. The vision of these events on television and in newspapers and magazines captured the nation's attention. But opposition was also mounting, and the forces of racism used every tactic at their disposal to intimidate civil rights activists.

While each victory added to the groundswell of momentum, A. Phillip Randolph, who had used the threat of a march on Washington in 1941 to gain the first major civil rights victory, believed that if civil rights organizations acted together, they could give a final push to obtain passage of the civil rights bill that was pending in Congress. Using his influence with organized labor, Randolph persuaded the unions to jointly sponsor a mammoth March on Washington with the civil rights organizations in 1963. The "I Have a Dream" speech of Martin Luther King captured the nation's moral consciousness, and at that moment the tide turned. Less than a year later, the Civil Rights Act of 1964 was passed, prohibiting racial, sexual, or ethnic discrimination in employment or public accommodations in the United States. It established an enforcement mechanism, the Equal Employment Opportunity Commission, to implement the law. In short order, Congress passed the Voting Rights Act of 1965, and in 1968 the Fair Housing Act. Later, the Supreme Court struck down miscegenation laws, the most offensive apartheid measures of all (as late as World War II, 30 of 48 states outlawed black-white marriage).

Modern social movements in the United States have, to a large degree, eradicated injustice and oppression and broadened the benefits of political liberty and economic opportunity for all Americans. They ended the scourge of child labor, sweatshops, and 12-hour workdays, and have given laborers the legal right to bargain collectively with management. They expanded suffrage to every citizen and opened voting booths to citizens who were prevented from voting on the basis of race. Modern social movements have broken the back of slavery and segregation and destroyed numerous barriers to opportunity.

WHITNEY YOUNG, MACRO SOCIAL WORKER AND CIVIL RIGHTS ACTIVIST

Born in 1921, Whitney Moore Young Jr. served in the segregated U.S. Army in Europe during World War II, where he acted as a liaison between white officers and African American enlisted men. He later referred to his experience as the inspiration for his subsequent career as an expert in race relations. With a MSW degree from the University of Minnesota School of Social Work, Young worked for the Urban League of St. Paul and later become executive secretary at the branch office in Omaha, Nebraska. At age 33 he was named dean of the Atlanta University School of Social

Work, acquiring a formidable reputation as an administrator and fundraiser. In 1961 Young returned to the National Urban League, where he served for ten years as executive director. During his tenure he successfully secured jobs and training for African Americans in areas traditionally closed to them. Selective placement was the name he gave to this pioneering employment program responsible for moving African American professionals into well-paid white-collar jobs in major business and industry.

Young's innovative plan was considered a major inspiration for the War on Poverty of the Johnson administration. He was an advisor on race relations to Presidents Kennedy, Johnson, and Nixon. From 1969 until his death in 1971, macro social worker Whitney M. Young Jr. served as president of NASW. He is considered one of the principal pioneers in community organization, demonstrating its use in advocacy for oppressed people, and he pioneered the development of social work in industrial settings with both union and management.

HOW TO ENGAGE IN SOCIAL ACTION

Modern social activists often rely heavily on mechanistic power tactics and moral persuasion to unfreeze dysfunctional systems that are frozen in oppressive structures, move to action, and then refreeze these systems into patterns that are more equitable.[18]

Unfreezing the System

The process of social action may be seen as an attempt to move or change a social system into a direction that is better, more just, and equitable. In any social action movement there will be continual forces of resistance to change. Resistance can be seen as the enemy against which you are working. Among these enemies are inertia and homeostasis, fear of the unknown, disruption of routine, threats to security, and threats to power.

Inertia and Homeostasis   At the simplest and most mechanistic level, any social system manifests strong forces that tend to keep it moving in one direction. This is called inertia. It is very difficult to derail a system once it is moving along a prescribed path.

Another tendency that keeps the system from changing is homeostasis. Systems have built-in mechanisms for self-correction that keep them stable; they resist external forces that would disturb their equilibrium.

Fear of the Unknown   On a more personal level, change creates anxiety. It is often less threatening to keep something old and familiar, even if it is dysfunctional, than trade it in for something that is new, unknown, and filled with potential risk, uncertainty, and lack of information.

Disruption of Routine   People are creatures of habit and routine. Change in the social system tends to upset this routine, disturbing lifestyles, often requiring us to change behaviors, ways of thinking, and attitudes, that have served us over the years. It is sometimes difficult for us to adjust to new ways of being.

Threats to Security   Our livelihood or job security frequently depends on and is a result of fitting into a system, learning the rules and procedures, and becoming socialized to that organizational setting. We establish security by building a family, putting down roots, and investing time and energy in that effort. Social change may disrupt or threaten our jobs, families, social situations, or place in a community.

Threats to Power   Entrenched powers want to keep things the way they are, often because they have developed a system that benefits them at the expense of others. They have a vested interest in maintaining the systems over which they have control. Control means that they have freedom to mobilize values, influence policy, pursue their own interests, and develop social tools such as organizations to create wealth and more power. Social action develops new countervailing power bases that threaten to usurp this power. Perhaps more than anything else, it is the struggle for social, political, and economic power that motivates people in influential positions to resist social change.

Life Cycle of Resistance to Change   If you understand the life cycle of resistance, the process of change becomes easier; you can work in small increments, measure your progress, and predict eventual victory.[19] If you attempt to unfreeze social systems, you may be encouraged by the realization that movements are cyclical, "having their own life cycles and their own internal dynamics."[20] While most change efforts move through all the phases of resistance to change, every change effort is unique. Some phases may be shortened, omitted, or there may be regression to previous phases. Inevitably the process is a slow one.

One factor that influences the cycle of resistance is the magnitude of the social problem. The greater the extent and pervasiveness of the social problem, the more resistance and the greater the forces that will oppose any change effort. The greater the degree of change that needs to be made, the more difficult it will be to make successful changes.

Another important factor is the time frame. The longer the history of the problem, the more likely that change will need to proceed slowly and take longer before victory is reached. Often the more gradual the change process, the more successful it will be. Sometimes, however, rapid changes are indicated. The massive social changes that were instituted during the Great Depression and the urgency to end the war in Vietnam are examples of the necessity for speedy change.

Phase 1 At the beginning of the change effort, the existing state of affairs—the status quo—is solidly entrenched. The status quo benefits those in power, has evolved over time, or has become part of the system's culture and way of operating. Keeping the system going is accepted as the way things are or even should be. Sometimes the oppressed have been socialized to accept their situation, or have developed a mentality in which they perpetuate the very systems that oppress them.

In the beginning stage of change, therefore, social work activists take a prophetic stance. Like a "voice in the wilderness," you are in the minority, alone, and isolated. You can expect to be openly criticized, ridiculed, scapegoated, or persecuted by whatever means the entrenched interests have at their disposal. Personal attacks on your character or on members of your organization in the form of harassment, intimidation, threats, and even physical attacks may be used to force you to conform to the norm and not disturb the system's equilibrium. Resistance to the change effort appears to be massive. Unless you and your members understand, prepare for, and are willing to encounter this phase of resistance, the change effort may be overwhelmed.

Harvey and Brown describe, for example, how the environmental movement began with a small group of concerned conservationists, scientists, and young people in the 1960s. Rachel Carson's book *Silent Spring* raised the nation's consciousness about the dangers of pesticides, and the first Earth Day was held in 1970. However, because of opposing political forces that emerged during the late 1970s and throughout the 1980s, commitment to environmental concerns waned. Environmentalists were portrayed as alarmists and radicals who were concerned about saving insignificant species at the expense of jobs and progress.

Because resistance will be massive at the beginning of a change effort, Rubin and Rubin suggest that before commencing, you and your members consider the following issues.

1. How can you obtain the power you need to either overcome opponents or to reduce the forces that resist change?

2. How can your organization achieve legitimacy?

3. What kinds of symbols can you design that will allow the organization to get its issues high on the agendas of those who can influence change?

4. What strategies can the organization develop to increase chances of victory?

5. What can the organization do to maintain people's morale until victories occur?[21]

Phase 2 As the movement for change grows, it encounters the second stage of resistance. Forces for and against change become more clearly defined. Your members gather facts and patterns begin to emerge. As your members and others become more aware of the issues and the consequences, what at first may have been perceived as being an insignificant issue begins to be recognized as a legitimate social problem that concerns everyone. The more you engage and sensitize people to the problem, the initial threat that exposure posed begins to lessen, and your forces for change gain understanding and recognition.

During the 1980s, for example, growing bodies of evidence on a number of fronts supported the position of the environmentalists, who persisted through court actions and pressure on elected officials. Research confirmed that pollution was destroying the ozone layer in the atmosphere and the greenhouse effect was a reality. Data on the harmful effects of pesticides, not only on wildlife but also on humans, was documented. Information showed that shrinking habitats and decimation of wilderness areas resulted in the extinction of numerous species of plants and animals. Massive oil spills brought home to people the dangers of technology. The inability to process raw sewage and dispose of nuclear waste became national concerns. The dangers to the environment could no longer be ignored. In fact, they were becoming an international problem.

Phase 3   In the third phase of resistance to change, lines have been drawn and there is direct confrontation between forces battling for change and those that are struggling to maintain the status quo. Those fighting against change marshal all of their forces, realizing that they need to take the activists seriously. The stakes are raised and an all-out attempt is made to destroy the change effort once and for all. When this occurs, you refine your strategies, sometimes using direct confrontation tactics such as sit-ins, marches, leaflets, demonstrations, and rallies. You make use of the media, attacking specific perpetrators and gaining publicity.

In the early 1980s, for example, the environmental movement became increasingly well-organized, vocal, and active on a number of fronts. Numerous environmental groups began agitating for change locally as well as nationally. Specific companies that engaged in pollution were targeted. James Watt, secretary of the interior, one of the most vocal and visible opponents of environmental concerns, became a lightning rod for pro-environmental forces such as the Sierra Club and the Wilderness Society. Demonstrations occurred. People boycotted environmentally insensitive companies or specific products that harmed the environment. Media attention increased.

Phase 4   If you and your organization are successful at persuasion and have won decisive battles, those who continue to resist are seen as stubborn, ignorant, and obstructionist. However, resistance forces can still mobilize enough power to regain their momentum. This is a time for you to shift gears, use tact, patience, and wisdom, keep your balance, and persuade those who are not openly opposed to change, but may not yet be completely convinced about the need for change. Your change strategies move from direct confrontation to legal action, negotiation, and policy development. You shift from a confrontive to a visionary stance.

In the environmental movement, for example, the struggle moved from confronting lumber, mining, and oil corporations to the development of policy culmi-

nating in the Endangered Species Act, Clean Air Act, creation of the Environmental Protection Agency, and development of the Environmental Super Fund. Each piece of legislation meant compromise and bargaining with agribusiness, miners, and oil interests who continued to press for concessions favoring their interests. With each successive victory, however, the environmental movement gained strength and power.

Phase 5   In the final phase, those who resist change are as few and as alienated as you and your organization were in Phase 1. Even those who were opposed to change jump on the bandwagon and try to show how they too are part of forces for change. Corporations that were major opponents of the environmental movement, for example, have begun to take out advertisements showing how they contribute to cleaning the environment. Being environmentally sensitive is now "politically correct."

Battles for social change are never finished once and for all, but must be refought over and over. The forces against change may still be mobilized to undermine changes that have been so hard won. The congressional elections of 1994 saw the Republican Party win a majority of House and Senate seats. Conservative forces lost no time in establishing strategies to dismantle as much environmental, social welfare, and other progressive social legislation as possible.

Moving to Action

Often unfreezing a system occurs incrementally. Parts of the structure are broken down one piece at a time and gradually reduced to a condition in which they are malleable enough to be resolidified into new and more wholesome patterns. There are three different approaches that you can take when moving to social action. You can lessen resistance so that the forces for change can prevail by using media, moral demonstrations, and nonviolent resistance. Your movement organization can overpower resistance by direct action, including rallies, marches, sit-ins, vigils, slowdowns of services, and traffic blockages. Your organization can move in both directions at once, reducing resistance and strengthening the driving forces that promote change. Informational campaigns, for example, can mobilize people while pressuring the opposition. Community education programs that inform citizens can be followed by community forums on the issue. "A frequent side effect is that when confronted by knowledgeable opponents, the opposition shows itself to be ignorant of technical details, which makes them look foolish and denies them legitimacy."

Public disruptions can place a social issue on the public agenda by gaining media coverage and implying the potential for violence. The change forces may gain support if opponents react belligerently.

Action Strategies and Tactics

Strategies are broad plans to achieve goals. *Tactics* are shorter term actions designed to carry out a strategy. Each campaign for social justice may require a variation in tactics, depending on the unique situations you are confronting. "A campaign may begin with a confrontation to attract media attention," say Rubin and Rubin, "then proceed to political pressure tactics to make long-term changes. Or, it may begin with mild pressure tactics, and if success is not forthcoming, gradually apply more power, using first legal, and finally, confrontation tactics. Or, the campaign may run several tactics simultaneously. Social work activists need to know how to combine tactics in an overall strategy to achieve a desired effect."[22]

Saul Alinksy recommends that you "keep the pressure on, with different tactics and actions, and utilize all events of the period for your purpose."[23] Some of the strategies by which social action organizations mobilize change are:

1. Active noncooperation with oppression; resistance and refusal to participate in the cycle of victimization.

2. Active exposure of perpetrators and acts of oppression to public scrutiny.

3. Using information to actively challenge misinformation and distortions of truth where they occur.

4. Public relations including media coverage, to gain public recognition.

5. Legal action, including legislation and lobbying.

6. *Satyagraha* or nonviolent resistance, soul force, or truth force.

7. Direct confrontation and challenging perpetrators of oppression.

Active Noncooperation With Oppression   One of the key strategies in breaking cycles of victimization is to refuse to participate in self-defeating oppression, not cooperating with required behaviors, and refusing to accept laws, policies, and procedures that are demeaning. For African Americans in the South, this meant sitting in white-only sections of public transportation, using white-only restrooms in defiance of existing practices, and using sit-ins at restaurants that would not serve them.

Noncooperation with oppression may also include not acting in the role of a victim. A victim may act in stereotyped ways that reinforce the perception of oppressors that the victim is inferior. Retraining oppressed individuals to develop skills, habits, dress, appearance, and language helps overcome demeaning, stigmatizing behavior. During the civil rights movement, African Americans mounted campaigns emphasizing "black pride" and education in African American Studies. Many African Americans adopted African names, African dress, and "natural" hairstyles.

Education, however, not only means acquiring cognitive skills and changes in outward appearance, but also the inner social presence and self-presentation skills that stimulate others to treat the oppressed with respect and dignity. To the extent that oppressed and stigmatized persons no longer act the role of victim, oppressors will have difficulty in relating to them as victims.

Exposure of Perpetrators   Make every effort to expose perpetrators to the victims of their oppression. This puts often impersonal, distant, and sanitized oppression where it belongs—at the personal level. Victims gain power as they see their oppressors as real people, not shadowy processes, procedures, rules, or policies. They learn that behind the seemingly impenetrable maze of rules and norms are individuals. This places the victims, often for the first time, on an equal footing with those who have taken advantage of them.

You publicly disclose the plight of the disadvantaged, showing who is responsible for their situation. Your campaign members target specific individuals rather than institutions. "Who can attack the telephone company or the government? It is far easier to attack the callousness of the president of the company, Mr. Smith, who won't let shut-in elderly people have affordable phones, while he has a telephone in his limousine."[24] You challenge oppressors by making demands, giving ultimatums, and delivering messages to them personally. They may be shielded by layers of bureaucracy, networks of inter-locking relationships with others in power, the right of protection from self-incrimination, and skillful use of evasion, but you demand to have your members meet those in charge face-to face. Saul Alinsky puts the point this way: "Pick the target, freeze it, per-sonalize it and polarize it."[25]

Information Campaigns Don't be so naive as to believe that oppressors will play fairly. You can expect that forces of oppression will "make a mockery of the democratic…process by misrepresenting cases, improperly invoking authority, making false promises, or distracting attention from key issues."[26] Some oppressors will very selectively inform and misinform citizens. They may call attention to partic-ular needs and obscure others…. They may appear to welcome legitimate, open discussion and public edu-cation while simultaneously ignoring the need for affected populations to join in those discussions. They may omit a careful analysis of legitimate alternatives and thus misrepresent actual options.[27] Sometimes officials of a government agency or corporate man-agers will give in during a demonstration but then renege on agreements after everyone has gone home.

Information campaigns dig up facts and data that oppressors would rather hide or obfuscate in their attempts at keeping power and domination. For decades the tobacco industry consistently denied, distorted, and suppressed research that indicated smoking caused cancer. Once evidence was shown to be irrefutable, they resisted facts that secondhand smoke was likewise cancer causing. The exposure of tobacco company disinformation and evidence of the dangers of tobacco smoke have led to laws banning smoking in public places and requiring warning labels on cigarette packages, as well as lawsuits by state and federal governments on behalf of people addicted to nicotine.

Forester recommends that your activist organi-zation "anticipate the attempts of established interests to shape the perceived needs of citizens…and work against such needs-shaping rhetoric." Activists counter those who shape information to keep people in subservient positions.

> Confront misrepresentations, distortions, and stereotyping of the poor by gathering facts and presenting them in newspapers, magazines, and on television.

> Demand that reports and information about vic-tims of oppression be intelligible to the public and actively explored at public hearings, not simply noted and passed over.

> Challenge misrepresentations of costs, risks, and available alternatives to social problems by those in power.

> Temper exaggerated claims.

> Demystify organizations and bureaucratic or cor-porate processes.

> Encourage mobilization and action of affected citizens.[28]

Public Relations As your movement organization strategizes and maneuvers, you gain media attention. Newspaper and TV investigative reporters can help you expose injustice. Exposure may mean finding a vulnerable spot and exploiting it. One of the most powerful tactics of the civil rights demonstrators, for example, was the television exposure of the brutality, anger, and hate aimed at nonviolent resisters as they sought equal rights and access guaranteed in the Con-stitution. The media captured national attention by showing that civil rights was a compelling moral cause that could not be denied. A group of journalists and novelists called "muckrakers" exposed oppres-sors in the early twentieth century, aiding social activists in their cause. Carey McWilliams exposed discrimination with such books as *Brothers Under the Skin*, and John Steinbeck publicized the story of migrant workers in California in his novel *Grapes of Wrath*. Like the muckrakers, your members can use public relations by giving speeches, making personal appearances, and writing articles, pamphlets, books, newsletters, and flyers.[29]

Legal Action Legal tactics are a way of forcing a solution by using the court system and existing laws to force those in power to live up to their own rules and agreements.[30] By using the legal process, social movement organizations can ask judges to clarify the responsibility of governmental agencies in cases where vaguely written legislation makes implemen-tation difficult. You can force governmental officials to faithfully and responsibly carry out laws in situa-tions where they have been pressured by particular interest groups to dilute or not comply with existing laws. For example, courts can order slum landlords to stop evicting people from their homes, order school districts to provide equal educational opportunities, or mandate compensation for damages caused by toxic waste. Using the legal process enhances your organization's legitimacy. It places your movement organization on an equal level with business or governmental organizations, forcing them, for example, to recognize the rights of migrant workers for redress, the legitimate grievances of the homeless poor, the just cause of victims of discrimination.

Getting an injunction can assist your organization stop practices that are damaging. Injunctions are court orders to stop possibly harmful action until additional facts are gathered. The instant papers have been served, the recipient must cease actions or risk being in contempt of court. Such tactics place the full weight of the government behind your movement organization, giving your members time to rally their forces, gather information, and plan their next tactic.

Another legal tactic is discovery, which allows lawyers to examine an opponent's documents. Through discovery, for example, movement organizations found internal reports of the Department of Interior showing that public water was being sold far below market costs to large-scale commercial farmers.

A lawsuit is another major legal action that movement organizers can take against perpetrators of oppression. A lawsuit can be filed to "right a wrong, claim compensation for harm done, or make a party perform as agreed." A performance suit is a lawsuit that forces individuals or corporations to live up to a contract. Sometimes even the government will deny people rights or benefits to which they are legally entitled. During the Reagan administration, for example, many people were wrongly denied social security benefits because policies were interpreted too narrowly. Many of these people sued to obtain aid.

Sometimes advocacy groups or regulatory agencies whose legal role is to protect the public will file a class action suit. Class action suits are helpful when the overall societal damage is large but the damages suffered by any single person is relatively small, making individual suits prohibitively expensive. Consumer activists have filed class action suits on behalf of citizens who have been overcharged by utility companies or insurance companies, or who have purchased defective products.

If regulatory agencies do not follow their own procedures, your organization can file a procedural suit. You greatly improve your bargaining power if you can show that governmental agencies do not follow rules or adjudicate claims fairly. Consumer movement activists, for example, file procedural suits against the Food and Drug Administration for ignoring scientific evidence and force them to regulate food additives.

Sometimes city councils illegally hold closed hearings, planning commissions give preferential treatment to developers, or general services agencies do not use sealed bids but give favored treatment to certain contractors. These agencies may begin to follow correct procedures if challenged with a lawsuit.

Because legal tactics can be so expensive, the mere threat of a lawsuit may often lead oppressors to the bargaining table. Builders, for example, can only make a profit when houses are sold and loans paid off. If your movement organization gets an injunction against the builder, construction is delayed, costing the builder money on the loans incurred. To avoid these expenses, as well as those of a potential court battle that could drag on for months or years, a developer might be willing to negotiate, giving your organization its demands.

Legal action has disadvantages, however. Court processes are slow and expensive. Suits filed in one state are not valid in other states. Lawsuits may stimulate opponents to file counter suits against your organization. Even when the courts give a social movement the victory, this may only be temporary. Laws may be repealed, or past legal actions revoked.

Satyagraha   Mahatma Gandhi remains one of the foremost movement activists of our time. A diminutive man, he challenged the weight of the entire British Empire and nearly single-handedly mobilized colonial India into a massive effort to gain independence. In doing so, he pioneered one of the most compelling principles of social action. This is the principle of *satyagraha*. It has been described as "soul force" or "truth force."

Ferguson says that satyagraha has been misunderstood in the West as "passive resistance" or "nonviolent resistance."[31] Gandhi disavowed these terms because they suggest weakness, nonaction, or simply passivity in the face of violence and oppression. Timothy Flinders asserts, "to call satyagraha passive resistance is like calling light non-darkness: it does not describe the positive energy of the principle."[32]

Satyagraha is a combination of two opposite forces: fierce autonomy and total compassion. It asserts:

> I will not coerce you. But, neither will I be coerced by you. While I will not allow you to behave unjustly toward me, I will not oppose you by violence (physical force), but by the force of the truth and the right—by the integrity of my beliefs and by my commitment to what is just and good.
>
> My integrity shines forth because I will not compromise my commitment by acting unjustly or falsely or try to overturn violence with violence, humiliation, injury, or subjugation. Instead I will show my integrity by my willingness to suffer, to pour myself out for my community, to place myself in danger, go to prison, and die if necessary. But I will not condone, cooperate, or allow by inaction injustice, oppression, or violence to continue.
>
> Ultimately the moral force of my restraint, seeing my intention, sensing my compassion and openness, and by treating myself with intense respect and dignity, you must also treat me with respect and dignity. By my unrelenting commitment to justice, you too must also begin to respect justice.

Satyagraha opens the heart of the adversary and stirs the conscience of the indifferent. Satyagraha removes social action from the arena of confrontation or threat, bargaining or negotiation, deal making, game playing, or pleading. Satyagraha requires heroic restraint and courage to forgive. Martin Luther King Jr. used oppression of African Americans as a moral force with which to confront oppressors. He resisted being oppressed, and he even submitted to imprisonment and death. To his Atlanta congregation he said, "I choose to give my life for those who have been left out of the sunlight of opportunity. I choose to live for and with those who find themselves seeing life as a long and desolate corridor with no exit sign. This is the way I'm going. If it means suffering a little bit, I'm going that way. If it means sacrificing, I'm going that way. If it means dying for them, I'm going that way. Because I heard a voice saying, 'Do something for others.' "[33]

King demonstrated that while oppressors could imprison his body, they could not imprison his self or break his spirit. He challenged injustice with just demands, demonstrating justice in every action, and he did not let himself be treated unjustly. He demonstrated to the oppressor that injustice would not be accepted, and he challenged America to live up to the values it espoused, to become a just nation in its actions as well as its words.

Conflict and Confrontation   Gaining power for people who are oppressed cannot be resolved without negative consequences for those who must give up power.[34] Whenever your movement organization stimulates social action, you will inevitably generate conflict. When your organization conducts demonstrations, rallies, marches, strikes, sit-ins, boycotts, leafleting, or picketing, therefore, be prepared for retaliation. The targets of your action will almost always strike back.

In its mildest form, the response of targets may only be an attempt to deny the legitimacy of protests. They may charge that the protest is un-American or they will mount their own campaigns against social change. Phyllis Schlafly established a national movement called STOP ERA to prevent adding the Equal Rights Amendment to the Constitution, and Jerry Falwell of the religious right established the Moral Majority to counteract abortion rights and gay rights activists.

Sometimes the opposition "will turn one group against another, exploiting tensions between groups." They may use slander and personal defamation. "Opponents may accuse the group's leader of being a communist, homosexual or lesbian, an embezzler, or a philanderer." Retaliation efforts against African American and Native American militants included eavesdropping, propaganda, disinformation, harassment, infiltration, and manufacturing evidence that some activists were police informers.[35]

Sometimes, however, counterstrikes are brutal and may decimate the membership. Your members can be threatened with intimidation, insults, arrests, physical attacks, or even death. The Ku Klux Klan attempted to intimidate civil rights activists by their own demonstrations. During the civil rights movement of the 1960s, police officials raided homes of African American militants and killed them, allegedly in self-defense. Union organizers have been fired, threatened, beaten, and murdered. Twenty-three students were shot in the "Kent State massacre" in Ohio during a demonstration for peace.

"Direct action campaigns, therefore, must not be undertaken lightly," assert Rubin and Rubin; "they require people's time and moral commitment to the issues, and sometimes they involve risk. Only try direct action after a conventional approach has failed,

Prayer vigils, in which demonstrators silently light candles, display moral and spiritual nonviolence. (© Jim West/Impact Visuals)

and then do so cautiously by engaging in testing actions."[36] Consider the issues involved and plan the confrontation carefully, taking into consideration the abilities of the participants, their commitment to the issues, and the effectiveness of the tactic you are using. Prepare and train participants well. Anticipate retaliation and strategize for it in advance.

Planning the Confrontation In planning picketing, you must consider many details. Some cities have laws about the materials with which pickets signs can be made to prevent them from being used as weapons. Picketers should be located where they get attention, but if they obstruct traffic or violate private property, they may anger the public and risk arrest. Your members need to work out a plan to get picketers out of jail.

Likewise, an enormous amount of planning is required for a successful march. For example, when Martin Luther King Jr. led marches in Chicago in 1966, "months of negotiation were required to determine which groups would participate and to ensure that King's overall philosophy of nonviolence would be observed. The choice of which streets to march down were argued over for weeks because some streets showed the deterioration of housing but other streets better illustrated the effects of discrimination."[37]

Training Confrontation tactics must be "planned with an awareness of how far members of the action organization are willing to go in a campaign."[38] They must be rehearsed and participants trained in their use, especially for non violent tactics. "Few people can be beaten and arrested without wanting to defend themselves. People who by temperament are not nonviolent must be kept out of the actions. During the Montgomery bus Boycotts, there were training schools in nonviolence, and only people trained and experienced in nonviolence were allowed to become Freedom Riders."[39]

Training is also crucial for picketing and marching. Picketers, for example, "must be trained not to respond to taunts or unpleasant distractions. Giving in to taunts, the picketers look disorderly and thereby lose legitimacy."[40]

Anticipating Retaliation Always expect and try to anticipate counterattacks. Rubin and Rubin alert organizations to expect that "opponents will try to seize the organization's books, records, and mailing lists. They will search for financial irregularities…and try to taint the organization with scandal." Make sure that your organization's books are squeaky clean, be aware of skeletons in the closet of organizational leaders, keep books and mailing lists in secure places, and watch what is put in writing that might give the appearance of slander. Your movement organization must be "very cautious to avoid the appearance of impropriety" because it is trying to take the high moral ground.

Plan what to do in the face of massive assaults such as imprisonment of your movement's leaders, attempts to demoralize your membership, and threats or bribes. The more aware and prepared your organization is, the better it will resist counterattacks. Try not to play in a game you don't think you can win, and never take on more than your organization can handle.

There are, however, some tactical advantages to being retaliated against. "Overt repression," for example, "denies the enemy legitimacy and often grants it to protesters…. Evoking a response (even a high negative response as with the use of excessive force) from the opposition is a sure indication that a direct action organization has reached and scared its target."

TOYOHIKO KAGAWA, RENEWER OF SOCIETY

Toyohiko Kagawa was born in 1888 in Kobe, Japan. Orphaned early, he lived first with his widowed stepmother and then with an uncle. He enrolled in a Bible class in order to learn English, and in his teens he became a Christian and was disowned by his family. In his late teens, he attended Presbyterian College in Tokyo for three years.

Kagawa decided that he had a vocation to help the poor, and that in order to do so effectively he must live as one of them. Accordingly, from 1910 to 1924 he lived for all but two years in a shed six feet square in the slums of Kobe. In 1912 he unionized the shipyard workers. He spent two years (1914–1916) at Princeton studying techniques for the relief of poverty. In 1918 and 1921 he organized unions among factory workers and among farmers. He worked for universal male suffrage (granted in 1925) and for laws more favorable to trade unions.

In 1923 he was asked to supervise social work in Tokyo. His writings began to attract favorable notice from the Japanese government and abroad. He estab-lished credit unions, schools, hospitals, and churches, and wrote and spoke extensively on the application of Christian principles to the ordering of society. He founded the Anti-War League, and in 1940 was arrested after publicly apologizing to China for the Japanese invasion of that country. In the summer of 1941 he visited the United States in an attempt to avert war between Japan and the United States. After the war, despite failing health, he devoted himself to the reconciliation of democratic ideals and procedures with traditional Japanese culture. He died in Tokyo April 23, 1960. A day of remembrance has been set aside for this hero of social work and Christianity in the Christian Church Year.

Kinds of Direct Confrontation Direct confrontations include rallies, moral demonstrations, picketing, marches, sit-ins, boycotts, and symbolic demonstrations, among other actions.[41] *Rallies* mobilize numbers of people for a cause and provide supporters and potential supporters with information and a sense of unity. They also attract media attention and make a statement about the issues you are raising. One of the most impressive rallies in the history of protest was the 1963 March on Washington for Civil Rights. The rally was seen on national television with a crowd of between 200,000 and 500,000 participants. The Louis Farrakhan's "Million Man March" is another example.

Moral demonstrations include voluntary jailing, fasts, and prayer vigils. In these kinds of demonstrations individuals may often become the focus of attention. For example, Gandhi placed himself at the center of attention by going on hunger strikes in his efforts to free India from British rule. Cesar Chavez's fast during the grape boycott in California gained national attention. This demonstration solidified the strikers and brought Senator Robert Kennedy on the side of the farm workers. Prayer vigils, in which demonstrators silently light candles, demonstrate both moral and spiritual nonviolence. Some anti-abortion protesters use peaceful prayer walks rather than militant tactics.

Picketing focuses attention on the targeted oppressor and is intended to achieve immediate political solutions. Protesters have picketed corporations, nuclear reactors, government offices, governors, and Presidents, among other real or symbolic targets. *Marches* demonstrate the power of the activist organization, provide an arena of media attention, and bring together other organizations in a show of solidarity.

Sit-ins inconvenience the opponent, obtain media attention, and avoid violence by taking over offices, highways, lunch counters, stairways, lobbies, or other public places. A sit-in puts protesters on the opponent's turf and often leads to arrest, because those involved are trespassing. Sometimes sit-ins seek immediate gains, such as when welfare rights activists demand services to which they are legally entitled. Others aim at broader issues, such as the Native American "capture" of Alcatraz that publicized the abnegation of Indian Treaty Rights.

A *boycott* is an economic pressure campaign designed to force an immediate solution to a problem by advocating that people refuse to purchase a particular product, or all products from a particular company. For example, Cesar Chavez initiated a national boycott of table grapes to force commercial farmers to yield to union demands. Environmentalists organized a boycott of tuna fish caught with nets that endanger dolphins. Another kind of boycott is renter strikes in which people refuse to pay rent until landlords take responsibility for repairs or provide services such as adequate heat. Sometimes, however, such boycotts are illegal. In some states it is illegal to withhold rent no matter what the landlord does. In other states, tenants can place funds in an escrow account until the problem is settled.

Symbolic demonstrations are powerful ways of demonstrating goals and values of protest. For example, students protesting apartheid in South Africa constructed shanty-towns on the lawns of universities to show the living conditions of black South Africans. When Greenpeace protesters surround nuclear naval vessels with small dinghies, or place themselves between a whaling ship and whales to protest their destruction, they engage in a symbolic action of David taking on Goliath. Demonstrators advocating awareness for AIDS research have developed a huge quilt, each section of which has the name of a person who died from AIDS sewn into it by a friend or relative. The quilt is unrolled at demonstrations and rallies, symbolizing in graphic detail the numbers of people who have died as their names are read into a microphone.

What If the Strategy Fails   You will not win every battle. If your social action strategy fails, spend time debriefing to figure out what happened and why.

What tactics could have been changed? Was the timing of the campaign poor? Did the opponents capture the symbols that garner public support? Was there too much fragmentation in the movement organization to bring about a coherent effort? What could be done differently the next time?

Burnout and Demoralization   Because of the stress of confrontation, the long-term nature of the issues, and the strength of the opposition, your members may burn out and demoralization may occur. How do you cope with burnout? First of all, keep in mind that capacity building, rectification of social injustice, strengthening community, and empowerment are long-term issues. There will always be ups and downs, victories and defeats. Prepare for the long haul. Be careful not to take on too much too soon. Pace yourselves so that you or your organization does not become overwhelmed. Take on issues that will motivate and energize your organization. When you or your organization begin to become weary of the struggle, it may be time to take a break. Saul Alinsky says, "A tactic that drags on too long becomes a drag. A good tactic is one your people enjoy."[42]

Give yourself time to step away from the conflict and assess how far you have come. Then, celebrate your successes together. Let yourselves enjoy what you have accomplished, and allow yourselves to feel renewed in one another's presence. Share your feelings of accomplishment and affirm one another's importance. Give recognition and reflect on your victories. Have fun and find rejuvenation in the relationships you have developed.

Solidifying Change

If your movement organization is successful in your social action efforts, the unjust, harmful, dehumanizing systems or processes that have been exposed and broken up now need to be replaced with ones that are just, helpful, and humanizing. This is the refreezing or solidifying stage of the change process. While confrontation tactics force opponents to pay attention and make short-term changes, political pressure tactics are intended to change laws and enforce regulations that preserve the short-term victories. Tenants can't demonstrate each time a landlord turns off the heat in a building. Instead, a tenants organization needs to have a city code adopted and enforced that guarantees warm apartments. This means using political pressure tactics and asking for policy concessions in which people are protected against unequal treatment and unfair advantage, with the government acting as a referee of a new set of procedures, rules, or laws. Solidifying change may also take the form of establishing new agencies to oversee and enforce the laws.

Politics   Political tactics require detailed knowledge of laws and regulations, the power structure, interest groups, and the political process. Social activists must become involved in the political arena, obtaining the political support of elected officials such as local, county, and state legislators, judges, lawyers, lobbyists, and administrators of public agencies.

Policy   The ultimate goal of modern social action is to institute new social policies that widen the scope of justice, equality, and freedom, that bring more and more people under the umbrella of opportunity and prosperity and keep the power and influence of the wealthy from usurping the rights of others. One way to obtain policy concessions is to negotiate and bargain with public officials. If the issues are large enough, you may have to move the political process in your favor by petitioning or developing referendums and initiatives. You can form an interest group that can lobby for changes in the law, or propose new laws. For example, the civil rights movement resulted in the passage of the Civil Rights Act, the environmental movement in the Clean Air Act, and the labor movement in the National Labor Relations Act.

Establish an Agency   If your organization has been successful in obtaining policy concessions, try to obtain a public agency that will operate programs and propose legislation on your behalf. The Civil Rights Act established affirmative action agencies, and the National Labor Relations Act established the National Labor Relations Board. Educators have a Department of Education to represent their interests, farmers the Department of Agriculture, veterans, the Veterans Administration, and small business owners the Small Business Administration.

Monitoring and Enforcement   Even with laws, policies, and agencies in place, however, the social action process is still not complete. There is no guar-antee that the same social or cultural forces will not continue to work to undermine the new structures you have created. For example, even though the Emancipation Proclamation freed the slaves and the 14th Amendment guaranteed equality and gave African Americans the right to vote, racism continued to be practiced even more virulently by means of the Black Codes, racist organizations such as the Ku Klux Klan, and the *Plessy v. Ferguson* Supreme Court decision which institutionalized "separate but equal" facilities in the United States.

A mechanism of monitoring, enforcement, and consequences needs to be instituted to insure that social systems abide by the new behavioral constraints. Clear sanctions or punishments for those who refuse to live by the new, nonoppressive standards must be established. An agency, usually a regulatory commission, must be authorized as a watchdog to ensure compliance with standards. The Equal Employment Opportunity Commission and Affirmative Action Agencies, for example, have been established to insure compliance with nondiscrimination in employment.

The governor or President must establish those regulatory agencies and then follow through in a way that meets the spirit and intent of the law, and there needs to be a commitment on the part of the executive branch of government to enforce the laws. Appropriations of funds must follow the establishment of advocacy agencies and regulatory commissions so that the executive branch of government has resources to enforce the law.

An unsympathetic executive can easily undermine all of your efforts to change social policy by not enforcing the regulations. In a more subtle fashion, the composition of the regulatory commission can be so arranged that the very perpetrators of injustice and oppression become the regulators, and the agencies are transformed into systems that reinforce oppression. Finally, enforcement of the laws can be twisted, loopholes found, exceptions made, delays granted, and a host of obfuscating processes developed that destroy the gains you and other social activists have worked hard to achieve. While the main outlines of these issues may already have been won for most people, the battle is really never over. Macro social work activists need to be continually vigilant when the megastructures of society attempt to extend their domain at the expense of others.

LIMITATIONS OF MODERN SOCIAL ACTION

Modern issue-oriented social movements may be one of the few means of resisting the defects of an increasingly centralized, organized, technological society. Critics of the activist perspective, however, argue that social action is essentially reactive rather than proactive. They assert that modern social activists tend to become engaged where oppression and injustice are fully entrenched, using confrontation tactics to fix a system that is broken rather than prevent injustice in the first place.

While broad social justice issues such as peace or ethnic intolerance capture the attention of many citizens, much modern social action tends to stop excesses here and there. It works for limited short-term objectives, such as forcing a slumlord to be responsive to tenants rights, confronting a company that is polluting the water supply, or protesting a nuclear power site. Activists may force one organization to be more socially responsible but patriarchal, value-free, instrumental reason continues to perpetuate a modern culture of unobtrusive dehumanization. Direct action tactics are often only mitigating forces. By attacking injustices one by one, activists may win battles but lose the war.

While necessary as a countervailing effort against large complex organization, social action often plays the same game that organizations play for limited stakes. Modern social action tends to ask for reform rather than revolution, for concession instead of asserting the power to change the premises by which the system operates.[43] Modern social action slows down injustice and may bring society closer to the values inherent in the Constitution, but is less effective in developing measures to change the entrenched system. If social activists want to make long-term, fundamental changes in the premises and structures of society, reforming one corporation, one governmental agency, or one social policy at a time by means of modern social movements will not work. The vision of the social activist must be on far deeper and longer range issues.

The challenge for macro social work activists of the new millennium is to engage in new social movements to enhance the human condition, develop personal identity, create meaning, and add to the pursuit of a good life for all and in the process reconstruct the profession of social work itself. New social activists will think in new ways, grasp a new understanding of the social, and of the self, and engage with others in building a completely new social order. This is the goal of new postmodern social movements.

POSTMODERN SOCIAL MOVEMENTS

"Some time between 1965 and 1973," says Peter Drucker, "we passed over a divide and entered the 'next century.' We are in political *terra incognita* with few landmarks to guide us."[44] We are in a transition period between the modern world of the Enlightenment, which is passing away but is still much with us, and the new postmodern era, the outlines of which remain to be fashioned.

It is the contention of many thinkers today that the postmodern era cannot be constructed from the ideology of capitalism, representative democracy, individualism, modern instrumental reason, complex organization, or science and technology. Instead, this new era will be shaped by socially conscious actors who create new social movements unlike anything that has been seen before. Eyerman and Jamison assert that society is "continuously being recreated through complex processes of interaction and innovation in particular contexts"[45] by means of a variety of new social movements. By 1983, for example, the major media were reporting a new kind of social action around the country, or what John Herbers of the *New York Times* called a "new wave of citizen initiatives." The environmental movement and the movement to end the nuclear arms race, new consumer movements, women's liberation, gay rights, and animal rights represented a new kind of citizen involvement in which ordinary people became knowledgeable about the most complex issues.[46] They often reached beyond issues of economics to include issues of collective identity and new modes of consciousness.

The shared logic of the new movements was the demand that society should be structured so that people themselves working together can shape the conditions of their lives. Feminism, for example, is not just about gender equality; it aims at the fundamental restructuring of power relations between the sexes. The peace and environmental movements are fundamentally efforts to make public decision-making fully accountable to those affected and to give people in their communities the chance to control their own futures.[47]

Women's Movement

In the late 1960s, the women's movement took on renewed vigor with the National Organization for Women (NOW), the Equal Rights Amendment (ERA) to the Constitution, and the issues of promoting equal pay for equal work and the right of women to obtain an abortion. While the ERA did not obtain the approval of two-thirds of the states needed for ratification, it heightened the consciousness of America to women's issues. Women were elected to public office in increasing numbers. Even more importantly, the women's movement worked at redefining the role of women in society, searching for a way for self-expression and a new identity that did not depend on modern stereotypes. The new identity was encapsulated in the term "feminism." Feminism was not merely an attempt to reach parity with males. Feminism was not merely a rejection of male dominance, but of dominance itself as a framework on which human relationships ought to be based. It was a rejection of the mentality of paternalism. Women were reaching for a new way of being. They rejected the premise that some people have an innate claim to superiority based on membership in a racial, gender, or sexual-orientation category. Such claims always deny others the right to their own self-determination, to control their lives, and to decide who they want to become.

Peace Movement

The civil rights movement created an atmosphere of ferment that became translated into the protest movement against the war in Vietnam in the mid 1960s and a general sense of disenchantment with government, large complex organizations, and the values of the "establishment." The movement to end the war in Vietnam decisively rejected the American colonialist mentality and imperialist national policy of modern politics that used war as a way of defending America's hegemony of power. It revealed the misunderstanding of authentic democracy by those who believed that democracy could be imposed on a small, underdeveloped nation "for their own good," and the utter futility of thinking that modern rationality and weaponry could make any difference against a communally based culture of defiance. The peace movement was not merely "anti-war," it was a challenge to the presumption that a powerful nation, under the pretense of democracy, had a right to interfere with the self-determination of a

Social protest is an important form of social action. (© Ellis Herwig/Photo Edit)

weaker nation. Ultimately the peace movement was a challenge to modern colonial mentality.

Environmental Movement

While the miracles and benefits of science and technology have been the hallmarks of modernity since the Enlightenment, since the 1960s the relationship between the general public and those who create, manage, and profit from technology soured. The litany of ecological disasters and technical failures from Love Canal and the space shuttle Challenger explosion, massive oil spills, the destruction of wildlife, industrial and agricultural pollution, and the Chernobyl nuclear meltdown turned many Americans away from technological optimism. The environmental movement that resulted involved people of every age and station in life around the issue of preserving a sustainable environment. People realized that while they could do little to influence major environmental problems caused by ineptitude, corruption, and greed at the highest levels of business and government, they could often limit the dangerous side effects of technological miscalculations in their own neighborhoods. The result was a reaction against the most cherished ideals of the modern era and rejection of technological progress for its own sake, not only by the poor whose neighborhoods were used to dump hazardous wastes, but by intellectuals, professionals, and middle class alike.

CHARACTERISTICS OF POSTMODERN SOCIAL MOVEMENTS

Post-modern social movements are concerned with self-determination rather than dominance, the right to choose and decide rather than have others decide for us, and the necessity to shape our own futures with friends and neighbors in our own communities. Postmodern social movements arise around communities of interest or geography, not necessarily against companies, factories, or wealthy executives, as did many modern social movements.[48] They tend to be made up of heterogeneous groups of people across the spectrum of social life. A post-modern movement on behalf of a woman's right to choose, for example, may include people of different economic and social status and different cultural identities, such as whites, African-Americans, and other ethnic groups, working women and professionals, the poor and wealthy, the young and old.[49]

Although modern social movements were large, single-issue, highly organized, mass movements, postmodern social movements are often small, loose, and open, tap local knowledge and resources, and respond to problems rapidly and creatively. They have deeper and more complex channels, often remaining underground for long periods of time as new identities are forged. These hidden networks are composed of small, separate groups, in a circuit of exchanges. Information circulates though the networks, and specific agencies insure a certain amount of unity and allow multiple membership.[50] They function as social laboratories, experimenting with new ways of understanding, new kinds of communally based social rela-

tionships, new organizational forms, and new ways of conceiving politics and of devising policy.

The new forms of consciousness discovered in new social movements provide something crucial in the constitution of postmodern society. They focus on community self-help and empowerment. For example, emerging postmodern social movements of the 1960s brought about a new awareness of the power of community as the locus where social problems need to be solved. Community building thus becomes the natural focus of the new social movement efforts— not necessarily community as mere locality, but as a center of political and social action. New social movements redefined community as a form of social relationship not restricted to time or place, generating a flexible group that transforms society internally.

Community is increasingly seen as assuming responsibility for itself and is envisaged as the center of a new conception of grassroots politics and problem-solving. The ideology of community participation is sustained by the belief that the power of the state has extended too far, diminishing the freedoms of ordinary people and their rights to control their own affairs. Top-down solutions and centralized welfare state solutions to social problems are seen as a dead end.

The rejection of the welfare state and the substitution of community suggest a radically redefined role of government in society. Richard Flacks says that postmodern social movements fundamentally reconceptualize the nature of the state. The state would not be seen as the source of social welfare but as a vehicle for community empowerment and local control. The state would be the source of capital and law that would enable people to solve their problems at the level of the community.[51] Government is to validate new community-generated solutions, provide institutional legitimization of community, and act as financial sponsor of community projects either directly or by means of third-party social organizations.

Postmodern social movements challenge the "closed and settled" questions of modern liberal politics and the "frozen decisions" that constitute complex organizational megastructures. Postmodern social movements are "transforming agents of political life," allowing for new understanding. Postmodern social movements "are distinct from modern protest organizations or mobilization campaigns. They are characterized by self-conscious awareness that the very foundations of society are at stake or in contest."[52]

New postmodern social movements struggle against interlocking megastructures that override the public interest. Megastructures tend to assert that their solutions are the only ones possible, while they often hide their specific interests and their core of arbitrary power and oppression. New social movements reveal "what the system does not say of itself." They unmask the deception, paternalism, and violence that is often covert in modern society.

Postmodern social movements support the rights of people to frame and develop their own cultures and the need for people everywhere to construct their own social reality. New social movements reject authoritarianism in social organization, paternalism in government, unitary leadership in social relationships, and individualism in the creation of human meaning. Some see postmodern social movements as nonideological because they dismiss the old ideologies of capitalism and socialism, nationalism and imperialism, paternalism and colonialism. Participants engage in the process of defining new historical projects by reflecting on their own identities[53] and by articulating values such as respect for the environment as an end in itself. They encourage people to resist becoming trapped in commodifying, dehumanizing social systems, and reject technological progress as an unqualified social good.[54]

Postmodern social movements reject passive, atomistic individualism in which people are treated as components, objects, or functions of social systems. Michel Foucault argues that postmodern social movements "assert the right to be different and underline everything which makes individuals truly individual."[55] They encourage us to resist forfeiting our individuality for individualism. Instead of being forced back on ourselves, we fall back into community. Postmodern movements attack everything that separates us from one another, alienates us, or splits up community life.

Of most importance, however, postmodern social movements develop new conceptualizations and associational forms that can serve as social laboratories for trying out new ways of thinking and being.[56] Just as modern reason was born out of the Enlightenment and shaped our institutions and mentality, social thinking is being born out of postmodern social movements, and is reciprocally shaping the frameworks and structures that are emerging from them. New social movements attempt to broaden unidimensional and unitary modern reason that limits thinking to instrumental means, accepts prepro-grammed ends as valid, and reduces thinking to mere calculation. When complex organization restricts people's actions, values, or ideas to narrow operational arenas, postmodern social movements encourage consideration of multiple ways of thinking, the exploration of rival ends or goods, the value of creativity, and new ways of meaning creation arrived at by means of social interaction. The result is the creation of arenas of social space for the consideration of new ideas that differ from the programmed ideas and functional thinking of systems processes.

It is precisely in the creation, articulation, and formulation of new thoughts and ideas that a postmodern social movement defines itself in society. New social movements create new types of knowledge as well as recombine or connect previously separate types of knowledge. They are "cognitive movements" that seek entirely new approaches to understanding. Social knowledge is not the "discovery" by an individual genius, nor is it the determined outcome of systemic interactions within an established research and development system. Knowledge is primarily a social creation, and the postmodern social movement is the source and model of this way of understanding and thinking socially. Knowledge is the product of a series of social encounters, within movements, between movements and their established opponents. Knowledge creation is seen as the collective creation of social groups. The collective articulation of movement identity can be likened to a process of social learning in which movement organizations act as structuring forces, opening a space in which creative interaction between individuals can take place.

THE POSTMODERN SOCIAL MOVEMENT PROCESS

Postmodern social movements attempt to forge a new construction of social reality.[57] They are cognitive processes that develop new ways of social thinking and new understandings about the world. The process includes cognitive dissonance, shared perceptions and meanings, envisioning a new future, collective identity and submerged networks, and moving to action.

Cognitive Dissonance

Social learning begins with experience. While we all seek positive, harmonious experiences, our negative experiences tend to be the most important and valuable. Negative experiences are those in which some injury occurs, an injustice is felt, a trust is betrayed, a loss is sustained. We are shaken out of our everyday routines. Our normal way of thinking becomes disturbed. Something altogether new enters the picture that requires our understanding and integration. It is out of socially negative experiences that personal growth, social learning, and value choices often occur.

More important, however, when we encounter betrayal, loss, and deceit in our engagement with the megastructures of the modern project, we experience discontinuities out of which postmodern social movements form. These discontinuities are called cognitive dissonance. Cognitive dissonance is the perception that current ways of thinking, belief systems, and structures are not congruent with the way things ought to be, the feeling that "there is something wrong here." For example, if we expect to be treated personally in our encounters with modern organizations and experience dehumanization and impersonality instead, our experience of social reality becomes problematic and begs for resolution. When such experiences are compounded daily, they add up to a generalized disenchantment with the premises on which modernity rests and eventually promote a need to change our social environment. Over time we may generate a feeling that modernity has outlived its usefulness, that it overextended itself and is becoming destructive to the human condition.

Shared Perceptions and Meanings

In a social movement, the "personal grievances that we experience in our everyday lives become translated into a collective sense of injustice." This commonality forms an arena of opportunity to restructure the social world and align it more closely with a new perception of the human condition. As we collectively dialogue about our common experiences of alienation and apathy, for example, the dissonance caused by passive individualism becomes the cause of its own correction.

We link the structured practices of social life with the collective action of a social movement through the intermediate step of face-to-face interaction and meaning construction. We define the social discontinuities that we experience. We attach them to concepts. We give them names and labels. As we articulate

our feelings, we often ask one another, "What do these experiences mean?" While we may not have all of the facts, we intuitively reach for deeper meaning and come to some consensus. When we explore our understanding of social policies in relation to our new understanding of truth and congruence with meaning we intuitively recognize that certain policies are basically wrong and in need of correction. We assert our common refusal to accept such policies or the premises on which they are based.

Envisioning a New Future

New visions, hopes, dreams, and the values they embody begin to become real. Envisioning future possibilities begins a process of understanding and conceptualizing a different worldview and the construction of a new social reality. Imagination produces alternative possibilities which may not currently exist, but if we stretch our perceptions, we can see beyond present reality. We imagine a future that is different, more congruent, and more aligned with the truth of the human condition.

Collective Identity and Submerged Networks

From the initial experience of injustice to the perception of cognitive dissonance, reflection, agreed upon shared meanings in close face-to-face interaction, we develop a strong emotional investment that encourages us to share in a collective identity. These new collective identities are formed during an incubation period by means of submerged networks out of the view of the public eye. The submerged network is a system of small groups of people who experiment with new definitions of their situation, alternative perceptions of the world, different societal truths and cultural norms, and new ways of thinking. These postmodern movement groups are not special-interest groups like modern social movements that compete in the political arena for policy consideration. They are like a cognitive territory or a new conceptual space filled with dynamic interaction. As groups and organizations interact in those conceptual spaces, they form the collective identity of a postmodern social movement organization.[58]

Leaders and members work to give permanence to this collective identity. At a certain point, however, movement organizations take on a further dimension as different forms of association carve out an actual societal space together. They transform what began as interpersonal interests into interorganizational concerns and then define themselves in wider social terms.

Action

Social engagement in new social movement organizations is ultimately action oriented. It includes a goal and tactics and a strategy for collective action to resolve shared grievances. It is action that cements social thinking into new social forms. When postmodern groups come out into the open, they confront political authority and proclaim opposition against the decision-making logic and values that result in specific policies.[59] Postmodern movements act as a medium that reveals to the rest of society the connection between a specific problem and the logic that dominates the system. Members proclaim that alternative cultural models are possible, specifically those that they already display and practice by means of their collective action.

CONCLUSION

Social activism has a long, rich, and successful history in America. It continues to be a strong and viable means of social change when social problems become entrenched in economic and political institutions of our society. Modern social movements, often assisted and sometimes led by macro social workers, have helped bring many collective groups of people to share in the benefits of modernity: immigrants, women, laborers, children, and others. However, just as macro social workers at the turn of the twentieth century engaged in major social reform, macro social workers at the turn of the twenty-first century face another challenge. We are in the early stages of an entirely new and unprecedented era, the outlines of which are still not entirely clear. But what is becoming increasingly understood is that the new postmodern era will not merely reform modernity, but will supercede it. It will usher in new ways of social thinking, new forms of communality, new social identities, and new forms of social consciousness. New postmodern social movements will be one of the major means by which this new era will be born, and macro

social workers such as yourselves who are perceptive social actors will have opportunity to be at the center of these changes.

KEY CONCEPTS

Freedom Riders
sit-in demonstrations
rallies
marches
satyagraha
picketing
prayer vigils
boycotts
NAACP
CORE
SNCC
SCLC
modernity
postmodernity
modern social movements
postmodern social movements
cognitive dissonance

QUESTIONS FOR DISCUSSION

1. What is the modern era and what are some of its leading ideologies, prominent values, and most important structures?
2. What is the postmodern era? What are some of its leading ideologies, values, and most prominent structures?
3. What is the difference between modern social movements and postmodern social movements?
4. Describe two of the most notable modern social movements. Why do you consider them "modern"?
5. Describe two postmodern social movements. Why do you consider them "postmodern?"
6. The opening narrative asserts that the turning point in the history of social movements was the shift in thinking by Martin Luther King Jr. as he broadened his vision from wanting African

Americans to "get in" on the benefits of modernity to protesting against modernity's fundamental defects. Comment on this assertion and its implications for the future of social work.

EXERCISE 14.1

Developing a Social Action Problem

Think about a social problem in your own community that may be appropriate for social action strategies and tactics. Write a short paragraph describing the problem.

How would you organize people to get involved? What strategies and tactics would you use? What if your efforts failed? How would you deal with resistance to change and the life cycle of resistance?

EXERCISE 14.2

Rules for Radicals

Listed below are Saul Alinsky's 13 tactical rules for overpowering the opposition.

1. Power is not only what you have but what the enemy thinks you have.
2. Never go outside the experience of your people.
3. Wherever possible, go outside the experience of the enemy.
4. Make the enemy live up to their own book of rules.
5. Ridicule is man's most potent weapon.
6. A good tactic is one that your people enjoy.
7. A tactic that drags on too long becomes a drag.
8. Keep the pressure on with different tactics and actions.
9. The threat is usually more terrifying than the thing itself.
10. The major premise for tactics is the development of operations that will maintain a constant pressure on the opposition.
11. If you push a negative hard and deep enough, it will break into its counterside.
12. The price of a successful attack is a constructive alternative.
13. Pick the target, freeze it, personalize it, and polarize it.

After reviewing Alinsky's rules for radicals, answer the following questions.

1. Can you apply these rules to social change?
2. Can you apply them to other situations where you are encountering resistance to change?
3. Do you agree with rule 5? Would you be able to use this rule? What repercussions are there?
4. What does rule 11 mean?
5. Describe what you think Alinsky means by rule 13. How would you put it into practice?

EXERCISE 14.3

Fighting Ministers

For 100 years, Duchesne, Pennsylvania, was a thriving steel town. Then the dream of the good life turned into a nightmare. On Thanksgiving Day 1983, 14 steel mills in Pennsylvania closed, and 250,000 people in the valley lost their jobs. In Pittsburgh, nine out of ten blast furnaces shut down. The steel industry had gone from boom to bust. Suicide and divorce rates skyrocketed.

A group of Lutheran pastors whose congregations were hard hit by the plant closings organized themselves into a group called the Denominational Ministry Strategy, or DMS, to help the unemployed steelworkers. DMS discovered that Pittsburgh's unemployment was not simply the result of fate or a natural downturn in the business cycle but rather the deliberate decision of Pittsburgh's corporations to eliminate heavy industry in the area. Mellon Bank, Pittsburgh's most powerful institution, with $28 billion in assets, much of it in steelworker pension funds, was foreclosing steel mills in Pittsburgh while at the same time loaning money to build mills in another country where labor was cheaper and profits higher. Politicians, the steel industry, and banks colluded in a conscious plan to rid themselves of their own steelworkers. Hundreds of thousands of people who depended for their livelihood on the steel industry were jettisoned like so much excess baggage.

The pastors believed that if they set up a dialogue with the power brokers, help for the unemployed would come. Instead of help, they found deaf ears. When the milltown of Clairton was shut down, the pastors thought that if they petitioned the governor to declare the town an economic disaster area, he would listen, but he turned away from them. They thought that if they went to corporate leaders and showed how people were being destroyed while corporations were making the highest profits in years, the CEOs would listen. But the leaders of industry refused to help.

The Lutheran pastors decided to go to the people. But Pittsburgh's unemployed failed to join the ministers in massive numbers. It had been 30 years since anyone had seen a strike, and the workers had become complacent. The pastors preached on the steps of Mellon Bank, urging customers to take their savings out of Mellon and invest in another bank. They laid the blame for Pittsburgh's unemployment on Pittsburgh's doorstep.

Corporate leaders began to retaliate. While this was to be expected, what was not expected was the reaction from the pastors' own synod. Castigated in a synod meeting, the DMS pastors were declared outcasts. The synod withdrew its support and the DMS pastors were alone. Then a group of labor leaders who called themselves the Network to Save the Monohio Valley joined the DMS pastors. The pastors and labor leaders banded together and became more militant. They began to stage demonstrations to spotlight Pittsburgh's abandonment of its workers. They dumped dead fish and skunks in lobbies of corporate offices, scattered coins on the floor of Mellon Bank, milled about, and disrupted business.

These tactics, however, brought only ridicule and resentment. Trinity Lutheran Church voted to oust the Reverend Douglas Roth because of his activism. Having many members of the congregation on his side, he refused to leave. When the synod appointed a substitute minister to take over, the board president refused to allow him to preach. Finally, Roth barricaded himself in the church.

Hiring the same law firm that represented Mellon Bank, the synod filed an injunction against Roth and directed the county sheriff to arrest him. Roth was sentenced to 90 days in jail and fined $1,200. One person commented, "Look at Nazi Germany. Who do they lock up first? The ministers and union leaders. It's a dangerous thing to put a minister in jail for standing up for what he believes in."

The wives of the DMS ministers had struggled for over a year on the sidelines. Now they decided to act as a group by visiting St. John's Lutheran Church, the church attended by the synod bishop and many church administrators. When confronted outside the church by the sheriff and a contingent of armed police officers, the women refused to leave, insisting on their right to worship with their fellow Lutherans. The bishop gave silent assent as the wives of his pastors were arrested and taken away to jail for trying to attend church on Sunday.

When the Lutheran Church in America (LCA) took title to Trinity Church, sealing the church building, a number of church members, union leaders, DMS pastors, and their wives barricaded themselves inside. Breaking down a rear door, the sheriff arrested the entire group. They were all sentenced to between 30 and 60 days in jail and fined.

Meanwhile, Douglas Roth, who had been given an extra 60 days in jail for taping sermons and sending them to his parishioners, was finally released after a total of 122 days in jail. He was immediately removed from the clergy roster, the first minister ever to be defrocked by the Lutheran Church in America.

Since the synod had locked them out of the church, members of Trinity Lutheran church-in-exile continued worship in a bus and in warmer weather held services on the sidewalk. Like Martin Luther, who began the Protestant Reformation 500 years earlier, these Lutheran pastors had taken action against an oppressive system and even against their own church.

The description of the fighting ministers tells of a social action effort that seemed to end in failure for the change agents.

1. Do you agree that the effort failed? Why or why not?

2. Did the fighting ministers follow the methods described in this chapter? Which did they use? Which did they not use?

3. Were their tactics successful or not successful? Why or why not?

4. What tactics or strategies would you have used?

5. The change effort shifted from the unemployed steelworkers to the church itself as a focus of social action. Why did this happen?

6. What would you do if the social agency or social organization for which you work opposes your organizing effort?

ADDITIONAL READING

Theory of Social Movements

B. Moyer. *The Movement Action Plan: A Strategic Framework Describing the Eight Stages of a Successful Social Movement.* San Francisco: Social Movement Empowerment Project, 1987.

Stuart Lowe. *Urban Social Movements: The City After Castells.* London: Macmillan, 1986.

Enrique Larana, Hank Johnston, and Joseph R. Gusfield, eds. *New Social Movements: From Ideology to Identity.* Philadelphia: Temple University Press, 1994.

Aldon D. Morris and Carol McClurg Mueller, eds. *Frontiers in Social Movement Theory.* New Haven, CT: Yale University Press, 1992.

Ron Eyerman and Andrew Jamison. *Social Movements: A Cognitive Approach.* Cambridge: Polity Press, 1991.

Doug McAdam, John D. McCarthy, and Mayer N. Zald. *Comparative Perspectives on Social Movements: Political Opportunities, Mobilizing Structures, and Cultural Framing.* New York: Cambridge University Press, 1996.

Anthony Oberschall. *Social Movements: Ideologies, Interests, and Identities.* New Brunswick, NJ: Transaction Publishers, 1993.

Stanford M. Lyman, ed. *Social Movements: Critiques, Concepts, Case-Studies.* Washington Square, NY: New York University Press, 1995.

Cyrus Ernesto Zirakzadeh. *Social Movements in Politics: A Comparative Study.* New York: Longman, 1997.

Practice of Social Activism

L. Reeser, *Professionalism and Activism in Social Work.* New York: Columbia University Press, 1990.

Kim Bobo, Jackie Kendall, and Steve Max. *Organizing for Social Change: A Manual for Activists in the 1990s.* 2d ed. Santa Ana, CA: Seven Locks Press, 1996.

Harry Boyte, Heather Booth, and Steve Max. *Citizen Action and the New American Populism.* Philadelphia: Temple University Press, 1986.

Huenefeld, John. *The Community Activist's Handbook: A Guide to Organizing, Financing, and Publicizing Community Campaigns.* Boston: Beacon, 1970.

Civil Rights Movement

Martin Luther King Jr. *Stride Toward Freedom: The Montgomery Story.* New York: Ballantine, 1958.

Stokely Carmichael and Charles V. Hamilton. *Black Power: The Politics of Liberation in America.* New York: Random House, 1967.

David J. Garrow. *Bearing the Cross: Martin Luther King Jr. and the Southern Christian Leadership Conference.* New York: William Morrow, 1986.

Malcolm X. *Autobiography of Malcolm X.* New York: Ballantine Books, 1981.

A. Morris. *Origins of the Civil Rights Movement.* New York: Free Press/Macmillan, 1984.

Alden Whitman. *American Reformers.* New York: H. W. Wilson, 1985.

Environmental Movement

Rachel Carson. *The Silent Spring.* Boston:Houghton Mifflin, 1962.

Charles Piller. *The Failsafe Society: Community Defiance and the End of American Technological Optimism.* New York: Basic Books, 1991.

Labor Movement

David M. Gordon, Richard Edwards, and Michael Reich. *Segmented Work, Divided Workers: The Historical Transformation of Labor in the United States.* New York: Cambridge University Press, 1982.

Student Protest Movement

James Miller. *Democracy Is in the Streets: From Port Huron to the Seige of Chicago.* Cambridge, MA: Harvard University Press, 1994.

Tenant Movement

R. Lawson and M. Naison, eds. *The Tenant Movement in New York City, 1904–1984*. New Brunswick, NJ: Rutgers University Press, 1986.

Welfare Rights Movement

Gary Delgado. *Organizing the Movement: The Roots and Growth of ACORN*. Philadelphia: Temple University Press, 1986.

J. Diamond. *For Crying Out Loud: Women and Poverty in the U.S.* New York: Pilgrim, 1986.

S. H. Hertz. *The Welfare Mothers Movement: A Decade of Change for Poor Women*. Nadham, MD: University Press, 1981.

Paul A. Kurzman. *The Mississippi Experience: Strategies for Welfare Rights Action*. New York: Association Press, 1971.

Frances Fox Piven and Richard A. Cloward. *Poor People's Movements*. New York: Pantheon, 1977.

J. Pope. *Biting the Hand That Feeds Them: Organizing Women on Welfare at the Grass Roots Level*. New York: Praeger, 1989.

Women's Movement

Temma Kaplan. *Crazy for Democracy: Women in Grassroots Movements*. New York: Routledge, 1997.

Sara Evans. *Personal Politics: The Roots of Women's Liberation in the Civil Rights Movements and the New Left*. New York: Random House, 1980.

History of Social Movements and Social Protest

Robert Allen. *Reluctant Reformers: Racism and Social Reform Movements in the United States*. Washington, DC: Howard University Press, 1983.

Terry H. Anderson. *The Movement and the Sixties: Protest in America from Greensboro to Wounded Knee*. New York: Oxford University Press, 1995.

Walter Anderson. *The Age of Protest*. Pacific Palisades, CA: Goodyear, 1989.

Robert A. Goldberg. *Grassroots Resistance: Social Movements in Twentieth Century America*. Belmont, CA: Wadsworth, 1991.

G. Parris and L. Brooks. *Blacks in the City: A History of the National Urban League*. Boston: Little, Brown, 1971.

Upton Sinclair. *The Cry for Justice: An Anthology of the Literature of Social Protest*. New York: Lyle Stuart, 1964.

Ronald G. Walters. *American Reformers: 1815–1860*. New York: Hill and Wang, 1978.

Progressive Social Work

B. Simon. "Rethinking Empowerment" *Journal of Progressive Human Services*, 1(1) (1990), pp. 27–39.

———. *The Empowerment Tradition in American Social Work*. New York: Columbia University Press, 1994.

Related Works

Paulo Freire. *Pedagogy of the Oppressed*. New York: Continuum, 1992.

Catherine Ingram. *In the Footsteps of Gandhi: Conversations With Spiritual Social Activists*. Berkeley, CA: Parallax Press, 1990.

Donna Schaper. *A Book of Common Power: Narratives Against the Current*. San Diego, CA: Lura Media, 1989.

Timmon Milne Wallis. *Satyagraha: The Gandhian Approach to Nonviolent Social Change*. Northampton, MA: Pittenbrauch Press, 1995.

15

Social Work at the Global Level

If anything human is foreign to me, I am myself, by just so much, less human. . . . It is a fact of man's makeup…that I am indeed my brother's keeper; the voice of my brother's blood cries out to me from the ground, because, in the most significant sense, his blood is my very own.

As the range of our fellow-feeling contracts, the boundaries of the self close in, and become at last the walls of a prison. As we withdraw from the problems of the aged, the young, the poor, from suffering humanity in any part of the world, it is our own individualities that shrink.

Abraham Kaplan[1]

Just because you own the land doesn't mean you own the people.

Philippine Land Reform saying[2]

Ideas in This Chapter

HOW TO ELIMINATE A SOCIAL PROBLEM

"Everyone is afraid," he said as he fiddled with a piece of plastic tape, keeping his eyes on the table. Sister Beatriz Semiano and a social worker, Wolmer Nascimento, a coordinator for the National Movement for Street Boys and Girls, listened as A. G., a thin, dark boy, one of the ragged legion of street kids who live by their wits in Sao Paulo, Rio, and Reclife, told how death squads hired by local merchants roam the streets exterminating homeless children. "He was sleeping," A. G. said, "and they filled his face with bullets." Cleiton, 12, used to steal from stores in a shopping gallery near the center of Duque de Caxias, Brazil, one of the grimy, violent suburbs only a few miles from the swaying palms, elegant hotels, and white sand beaches of Rio de Janeiro. Cleiton's death was not an isolated incident.

Hundreds of children are murdered each year by bands of private security guards, many of them off-duty or former police officers, the very people who should safeguard the children. A. G. said that he had known "a heap" of youngsters killed in Duque de Caxias. One was Luciano, 16, picked up by his killers and shot in the head. "He robbed stores," A. G. said of Luciano. Two weeks after Luciano's death, gunmen killed his friend Ademir, 16. "He also robbed," A. G. said. There is no doubt, A G. insisted, about who the killers work for. "The store owners pay them to kill us." A. G. has slept on the streets for 11 of his 16 years. He said the killers almost got him when he was 13. The merchants treat the children like rats. Kill them and the problem goes away. Sometimes in a shrewd if twisted scheme, they pay members of some street gangs to exterminate children in rival gangs.

Sr. Beatriz confirmed the dangers A.G. described. "He lives in the street, he sleeps in the street, and he is threatened with death," she said. "It is a terrible problem in Brazil." The problem, she and others say, has its roots in urban poverty, antiquated laws, police corruption, and ineffective systems for providing child welfare and criminal justice.

WHAT YOU WILL LEARN IN THIS CHAPTER

On every continent and in virtually every nation of the globe, international macro social workers engage in some of the most difficult social problems that people face. In this chapter you will explore what macro social workers do in the poorest nations of the world. You will learn about global social problems. You will discover that modern development which has produced affluence, political liberty, and technological advances in North America, Japan, and Europe has often failed to replicate those achievements in many of the world's more impoverished nations.

You will learn how indigenous people, however, are using grassroots social movement organizations to shape their own identities, construct their cultures, and take ownership of their lives. The result is a global movement on a scale unlike anything that has ever been known in history. Few people even know of its existence, and yet in hidden networks, in the most out of the way places, and among the least likely people, the postmodern social movement is revolutionizing the way economics is being practiced and politics is being carried out. You will discover that this world-wide movement is comprised of tens of thousands of new social organizations spread throughout almost every nation of the world, and on an immensely wider scale than is occurring in North America. You will explore how you, as an international macro social worker, can assist members of the world's poor and destitute nations to strengthen their communities, overcome poverty, and engage in social change on a global scale.

BRAVE NEW MILLENNIUM: SOCIAL PROBLEMS IN OUR GLOBAL SOCIETY

Beginning in the sixteenth century, the Enlightenment on the subcontinent of Europe brought about the scientific revolution, free enterprise capitalism, and representative democracy. This movement created a new society and formed the basis of what is commonly referred to as the modern era of Western culture. Over the past five centuries, modernity has become international and now global in character.[3]

Although free enterprise has brought economic prosperity for most nations of Europe and North America, it has created disparities of wealth and economic ruin for the rest of the world's population. Representative democracy has provided freedom from autocratic state governments of the West, but has taken away decision-making from people of Asia, Africa, and South America, placed control in the hands of a few, and brought oppression to many. The efforts of Western nations to export development to poverty-stricken nations has invariably resulted in dependency. People in these communities "confront a seemingly endless list of issues stemming from underlying issues of poverty, environmental degradation and the population explosion. Among these are ethnic violence, political instability, corruption, lack of education and health care, and now AIDS."[4]

Failure of the Modern Market Economy

For hundreds of years, indigenous peoples throughout the world have experienced colonization. While overt colonization has generally ended, economic exploitation continues unabated as the fabric of their societies continues to erode. The developmental paths of modern industrialized societies, in either their socialist or capitalist variants, have destroyed the economies of less "developed" nations, bringing massive and pervasive poverty to four-fifths of the world's population. Today 1.2 billion people of the world live beneath the threshold of basic needs, while 20% of the world's population use 80% of the world's resources.[5] In most third world cities, between 35% and 75% of the population are poor. The gap dividing the rich from the poor has never been wider: the top fifth of the population on the global economic ladder enjoy 60 times the goods and services of the lowest fifth.[6]

Julian Bond asserts that if we could shrink the world's population to a village of only 100 people, 6 of the 100 people would own 59% of all the wealth in the world, and all of those people would be from the United States; 80 would live in substandard housing; 70 would be unable to read and write; 50 would suffer from malnutrition. One would have a college education.[7] In Bombay, India, a million people live in a slum built on a giant garbage heap. On the other side of the Indian sub-continent, between 500,000 and 750,000 Bengali live their entire lives on the streets of Calcutta—never once to experience a roof over their heads. In Lagos, Nigeria, 75% of families live in one-room shacks. More than a million people—half the population of Nairobi, Kenya—live in the giant slums of Mather, Korogocho, and Kibura. In Guayaquil,

Ecuador, 60% of the people live in shantytowns amid garbage-strewn mud flats and polluted water.[8]

In the summer of 1999, according to the World Food Program, 1.2 million people were in danger of starving in the southern part of the African nation of Sudan in a famine caused by civil war, drought, and displacement, four times the estimate just two months before. In Bahr el Ghazal province, death has become so common that people say they have forgotten how to weep.[9]

The burden of poverty falls most heavily on the shoulders of the world's children. Fifteen thousand of Manila's street children survive through prostitution. Forty thousand children are prostitutes in Bangkok, Thailand. In Sao Paulo, Brazil, 700,000 street children have been abandoned by their parents[10] and face a daily struggle to outrun death by starvation, disease, or police extermination squads.

The desperation of the majority of the world's population is not the result of indifference by the United Nations or its global economic affiliates the International Monetary Fund, World Bank, or the World Trade Organization. Global impoverishment is not due to the unwillingness of powerful nations to pump aid, money, or technical resources into countries that are poor. Neither is it caused by a lack of effort by the major economic powers of the world to hasten a global market mentality or to rationalize and commodify the thinking of the impoverished people of the earth.

Since the end of World War II, the three major global economic networks affiliated with the United Nations—the International Monetary Fund (IMF), the World Trade Organization, the World Bank—have struggled to maintain economic stability in world markets. The IMF consults with and applies economic pressure on nations to change economic policies that are failing. The World Trade Organization, by means of the General Agreement on Trade and Tariffs (GATT), works to eliminate protective barriers between nations, stimulating open trade, reducing debt, and increasing the flow of capital. The World Bank provides long-term, low-interest loans exceeding $15 billion annually to build dams for power and irrigation, develop industry, and engage agriculture projects in less developed nations.[11]

While these global organizations attempt to develop the world's economy, their efforts have not always met with success. Instead of improving the economic capacity of underdeveloped nations, they have stabilized world economies for the benefit of large multinational corporations, preserved the balance of payments structure, or protected the investments that wealthy nations have made in nations that do not have strong market economies. At other times, large global financial institutions have been used by world superpowers to obtain political, economic, and strategic advantage over one another in the struggle for world dominance. Margaret Thatcher of Britain and Ronald Reagan of the United States, for example, "carried their conservative zeal into the international arena using such powerful agencies as the International Monetary Fund (IMF) to restructure other societies to their liking." As a condition for giving loans to poor nations to finance their huge debts, the IMF required them to accept Structural Adjustment Programs (SAPs) that cut off subsidies to the poor, reduced welfare state bureaucracy, and raised prices for goods and services while reducing wages for labor. Instead of investing in their own domestic production and consumption, impoverished nations were expected to import Western products to increase their foreign currency reserves and pay off their debts. Reagan and Thatcher made non-market-centered countries into instruments for boosting Western capitalism and guinea pigs on which to test neo-liberal policies before putting them in place in the United States and Britain.[12]

Even the well-intentioned efforts of institutions such as the World Bank often create conditions the opposite of those intended. Rather than assist the efforts of nongovernment organizations (NGOs) in poor nations, Mansour Fakih asserts the World Bank is their biggest obstacle.[13] As a result of long-term, low-interest loans for large agricultural, energy, transportation, and other development projects, the environment on which local people depend is destroyed and poor farmers are forced off their land. A few people become dependent on the low-level jobs at subsistence wages that these projects offer, while the rest take their families to cities in a desperate search for employment. The raw materials, food, or other resources these projects develop are sold at prices the poor cannot afford and are often exported to economically developed nations, profiting rich entrepreneurs and government officials.

What is even worse, however, is that sometimes funds are diverted from authentic economic develop-

ment and spent instead on military weapons manufactured by wealthy market-centered nations, including the United States. The defense industry, using government-subsidized technology, profits by selling arms to governments of impoverished nations, which often use the weapons to repress their own people or make war on one another, eroding their economies and weakening their own infrastructure.

Even if long-term development funds are used to directly benefit local poor people's projects in their own communities, people have sometimes become dependent on foreign capital. Infusion of money has reduced local initiative and created dependency. Although poor people in villages cannot prevent governments from accepting development money that benefits the rich, they can decide whether dependence on outside funds is in their own interests. Residents of Kujupukur village in India, for example, considered the question of accepting government aid in developing their agriculture, health, and literacy: "We have realized that ours is a country of villages and if villages want money from the government, either the government has to take from us and give back, or beg for us from other countries. So we decided not to ask anything from anybody."[14]

Global economic organizations such as the World Trade Organization, IMF, or World Bank may be able to offer resources, but the answer to poverty will never come from top-down solutions, capital investment, or gigantic corporate or governmental development projects. The cure to poverty will not come by converting local economies into high-powered market systems, or by inducing people to accept the premises on which modern market economies are based. We cannot create wealth in poor nations when we appropriate people's land for our benefit, or exploit people as cheap sources of labor.

Poverty will only be eradicated as people in their own local communities take charge of their lives. It will begin when people reject an image of themselves, often imposed by the "developmental" mentality, that impoverishment is due to their inability, laziness, and lack of intelligence or desire to be dependent on others. The economic capacity of people will continue to grow as they work together on common projects for the benefit of all. It will come to fruition as they develop self-sufficiency, using primarily their own resources, guided by their own ideas, engaging in their own common effort to better the lives of their children and their communities.

Failure of Modern Politics

There is little doubt that modern political institutions have generally failed people in impoverished nations. Even in countries where free elections are held, there is no guarantee that those elected will serve the interests of the people. Democratically elected governments have often been rife with corruption, using public office as a means of enriching themselves and their friends. At other times, they use their power to block the freedom of people to decide. Because governmental leaders often come from rich elites, they have rarely been willing to break the chain of exploitation on which their own wealth has been built. Land reform and wage and labor reforms, for example, are rarely forthcoming from such governments. Not only have many governments failed to help their citizens obtain liberty, but they have often been the worst perpetrators of tyranny. At times, governments in poor nations have permitted wealthy corporations to exploit their resources and their people. Military or civilian dictatorships have engaged in acts of appalling atrocities against their own citizens to keep them intimidated, helpless, and compliant, often supported by the most developed nations, including the United States.

These circumstances have at times provoked people to challenge the systems that steal their freedom, culture, and rights to be human. Land possessed by Guatemalan peasants, who experience the lowest ratings in health, literacy, housing, school attendance, and nutrition of any group in the nation, was systematically plundered by the wealthy with the consent and support of government. The army conscripted the men and forced the rest to move. Their culture, language, and religion were taken and their labor exploited. Under normal conditions, the poor were so locked into a culture of oppression that they could not break free, but in February 1976 an earthquake disrupted the army's communications, opening a window of opportunity for the poor people to organize. They found trustworthy leaders and established contact among the 22 ethnic groups as well as with priests and students. By April 1978 they formed the Committee of United Peasants (CUC) that united all Guatemalan ethnic groups for the first time.

The response by the Guatemalan army was predictable and violent. On May 29, 1978, the army occupied the village of Panzos, killing men, women, and children and raping women. In a calculated move they allowed a few to escape so that their terrified reports would spread all over the country as a warning. Rather than submit to intimidation, however, the CUC organized massive demonstrations and strikes that were joined by almost all ethnic groups and peasant organizations. In brutal reprisal, the army burned alive 27 activists who had taken over the Spanish embassy. In a genocidal action known as "land cleaning," the Guatemalan army destroyed villages, murdered pregnant women and children, burned houses, harvests, and grain reserves, slaughtered domestic animals, and stole belongings. They captured the fleeing population along with those hiding in the mountains and resettled them in concentration camps.[15]

Experiences like this have been repeated in Uganda, Haiti, Colombia, Argentina, Chile, the Philippines, Nicaragua, Peru, and many other developing nations, the most recent of which has been the appalling genocide of the people of East Timor by the Indonesian dictatorship, exceeding even the "killing fields" of Pol Pot in Cambodia.

While larger and larger numbers of people are no longer willing to accept repressive political regimes, however, many have come to realize that armed conflict aimed at the capture of state power is not the answer. But neither is acceptance of modern top-down, mass representative democracy of the kind practiced in North America.[16] Mass representative democracy atomizes subjects as citizens and limits decision-making to a token gesture of voting annually for officials who may or may not serve the interests of the people. Decisions are made by a few, and authentic participation by ordinary people is denied. These limitations weaken the legitimacy of nation states and their capacity to protect or advocate for people who are most vulnerable. As a result, the modern political system is becoming increasingly irrelevant to people at the local level in many poverty-stricken nations.

In contrast, the poor people of the earth are constructing authentic democratic structures in which they directly participate in decisions that affect their lives, not where power is delegated to a few distant politicians. They are using frequent, deliberative, face-to-face decision-making that arises out of shared values and discussion. Consensual political engagement enables citizens of non-market-centered nations to proclaim that "we too are human beings."[17]

If people are to be authentically free and liberated, says Ponna Wignaraja, "they must be the final arbiters of their lives. They need to form their own organizations and through their own organizations to counter the socio-economic reality that keeps them in poverty."[18]

Failure of Modern Development

During the 1950s and 1960s, many political leaders believed that the living standards of the poor in "stagnant" and "backward" regions could be "modernized" by development aid and massive transfers of capital, technology, and labor in the form of volunteers.[19] Popular interpreters of this idea such as Walt Whitman Rostow and others conceived of history as progressing from uncivilized to civilized, from undeveloped to developed, from east to west, culminating in the most modern nations of North America.[20] Modernization theory, as this approach to comparative history came to be called, emerged as the dominant explanation of societal change in the 1960s. The progressive development of history was seen to move in a straight line from past to the present, involving the replacement of premodern economies, ways of thinking, and modes of communal human association with market economies, rational thinking, and modern complex organizations. Social evolution was seen as an inevitable sequential process in which all urban and modern societies converge as a single societal type, exemplified by liberal democratic capitalist nations of the West.[21]

Modernization theorists assumed that problems of poverty, health, and lack of education among "underdeveloped" people lie in their primitive cultures and not in the social conditions they have been forced to accept. The solution was to change these people's thinking and their premodern economic and political systems, bringing them into the modern world as rapidly as possible. Led by the United States, economically developed nations engaged in technology transfer, doled out aid, and supported political regimes that claimed to encourage free enterprise capitalism, industrialization, modernization, and urbanization. The cumulative effect of these improvements was expected to automatically "trickle down" to those at the bottom, or else be handed down in an administrative fashion. Public and private material accumu-

lation along with formal democratic elections were expected to solve other social problems of the world's impoverished people.[22]

Inspired by the modernization model and the success of the Marshall Plan, which helped rebuild European economies after World War II, John F. Kennedy launched the Alliance for Progress in 1961, which pumped billions of dollars into Latin America and was expected to create markets for U.S. products. Community development programs were masterminded by national planners and operated under a centralized system of rational management and resource allocation. Top-down development adopted in much of South America and other regions was an unequivocal failure.[23] "Despite a number of development efforts," asserts Mansour Fakih, "both the absolute number and percentage of the world's people who lived in utter poverty continued to increase."[24] Economic and political experts created poverty instead of eradicating it, and they increased the dependence of these countries within an inequitable global order.[25]

Modernization deprived the people of their identities, disallowed from making decisions on their own behalf, and ignored their traditional ways of thinking. People were invariably worse off than before, stripped of their culture, their communities, their land, or even themselves. The forest dwellers of India report that

> We lived with the forest as one organic whole—there was no separation between us and the trees physically, culturally, or emotionally in daily living and growing together. Then you came, with your notion of "development," and separated us. To you the forest was just a "resource," but you could not even develop this resource because now the forest is disappearing. Even we did not count to you.
>
> The path of your "development" did not lead us to mansions but to the slums. Because of "development" we had to give up our lifestyle, and our culture. You deprived us of our habitat and deprived our country of its environment.
>
> We feel cheated and our country has been cheated too. It is strange that what is good for us has been decided by those who have cheated our country and us. To us real development is not a negation of nature and its forces, but being a part of it. Our consensus is that we have to preserve what we have and develop a new perspective based on the flowering of our own eco-regions.[26]

The failure of modern global change occurs because it is based on deceitful premises. According to Mansour Fakih, "the ideas of modernization and developmentalism create a hegemony of thinking that distorts human consciousness." Modernization hegemony is an organizing principle or worldview diffused by modern complex organizations, including universities, corporations, and governments, that supports the rationalization of world processes and inserts premises of ideological control, domination, and patriarchy into every area of human life. The modernization/developmentalist worldview has created a climate in which people incorporate into their consciousness the pretense that competition, self-interest, economic growth, wealth accumulation, interest-group liberalism, and a host of other modern premises are the epitome of civilization.[27]

Many people today, however, reject the modern developmentalist hegemony as a "false consciousness." New social movements in poor nations struggle against the dominant modernization worldview. Their main concern is to develop a collective "critical consciousness" that will bring about human liberation and create diverse grassroots structures in which people construct their own social reality.

NEW GLOBAL SOCIAL MOVEMENTS

Many people in wealthy nations of the West are unaware that for the past 40 years the majority of the world's population has been spontaneously developing a global social movement constructed by people in community and based on their own social consciousness and values. We have entered an age that the French social theorist Alain Touraine describes as the "self-production of society."[28]

These new social movements are qualitatively different from earlier movements against colonialism and for liberation, land reform, or labor unions.[29] While new global social movements do not aim at overthrowing governments or seizing the assets of the world's global corporations, they represent a rupture with authoritarian political cultures[30] in South America, Africa, and Asia, a rejection of market-centered thinking, and repudiation of the developmentalist worldview of the West.

Their goals are modest and simple. They seek to reclaim their lives and the cultures that modernity has taken from them. The forest people of India speak for many: "The major interest [of first world leaders] is the development of the forest as a resource rather than as a habitat of people. This basic difference distinguishes 'us' [the forest dwellers of India] from 'you.' You believe that we should reap the dubious benefits of 'development,' and become like you or your serfs. We reject your notion of development and we want back our lives."[31]

The 80% of the world's population that comprises the poor people of the earth is disarming the modern developmental worldview by disassociating themselves from its methods, abandoning belief in its promises, not participating with its goals, and ignoring its premises. Instead, they are developing their own alternative cultures, values, identities, decision-making infrastructures, and local economies. They are utilizing social thinking, asserting their self-determination and self-reliance, and engaging in their own social construction of reality. They are creating a completely new global culture from the ground up.

New Global Social Organizations

Global postmodern social movements are occurring by means of multitudes of new social organizations springing up in every impoverished nation. These new social forms began developing spontaneously and autonomously during the 1960s and first came to prominence in the jungles and barrios of Brazil, and from there quickly spread to other regions of Latin America.[32]

In the 1960s, Catholic priests in Central America and Brazil were impressed with the way the poor survived by helping each other. They generated their own perspective on biblical interpretation known as liberation theology and began organizing grassroots communities called *Communidades Ecclesiales de Base,* or base ecclesial communities. These *communidades* define themselves as base or basic because they are composed of the simplest and poorest of people, but also because they are the most basic and foundational structures of the Church. Being from the base, these new social organizations take care of the whole of human life, its spiritual as well as its worldly aspects. They are called "Church of the Poor" or "Popular Church" because they are "of the people." *Communidades* also grew under the auspices of Popular Education Centers, Social Promotion Centers, and Advice and Support Centers in Brazil. It was in those centers that the work of Paulo Freire germinated.[33]

Just like new social movement organizations of North America, *communidades* are small, unobtrusive, low-profile, nonhierarchical groups within submerged networks in villages, barrios, and neighborhoods that raise people's consciousness about social problems. *Communidades* remained underground because of the authoritarian regime that imposed itself on Brazil with a right-wing military coup of 1964 and also because they needed time to develop creativity and flexibility, which allowed them to survive and grow.[34] Because of their small size and community orientation, the *communidades* were able to maintain their space in a civil society dominated by oppression. Evans and Boyte assert that their roots in community define these free spaces, the dense, rich networks of daily life "that nurture values associated with citizenship and a vision of the common good."[35]

During this period of submergence, *communidades* developed their collective identity, communal culture, and a vision of what might constitute a new society. Their unity and values became an integral part of the self-understanding of each of their members.[36] Poor people realized that oppression and poverty are not "givens" in the nature of things. They worked to understand their situation, not to accommodate to it but to change it.

The so-called "work of the ants" was consolidated by a wide range of submerged groups in cities and in the country.[37] The communal culture that emerged rejected the premises of modernity that had brought indigenous people nearly 400 years of oppression, poverty, and genocide. They refused self-interested market economies, top-down decision-making, impersonal liberal democratic politics, and self-serving "development." This new awareness energized them for social, ecclesial, and political action that would have been unthinkable in the past. Vatican Council II, for example, empowered the faithful of the estimated 80,000 *communidades* in Brazil to perform the sacraments in remote areas lacking priests, and entrusted to the faithful the conduct of priestly functions within *communidades* in Panama, Guatemala, Argentina, and Peru. This is why Gustavo Gutierrez has characterized these new expressions of community as "an irruption of the poor" into the mainstream of church and society. The "absent ones" are making their presence felt.[38]

Gradually, many *communidades* secularized. They consolidated themselves to engage in decision-making without being a political party. They concentrated in participatory education, active social learning, and participant action research without being a university. They created small economic projects, experimented with self-help, and formed an economic base with the community's own resources without becoming market-centered corporations.

At the same time *communidades de base* were emerging in Latin American, similar social organizations began developing autonomously and spontaneously in Africa, India, and Asia. People came together in villages, neighborhoods, and shantytowns around the world in response to modern forces that endanger their communities and the planet.[39] They not only emerged independently of one another but have diffused transnationally more rapidly than has any other social movement.[40] In Indonesia, for example, in the late 1960s and 1970s only a handful of these organizations existed. Less than two decades later more than 3,000 had formed.[41]

What is remarkable about the new social movement organizations is "the speed with which the masses in each country converged on particular strategies, coordinated their operations, and successfully executed their plans."[42] In the Bhoomi Sena (land army) movement in Maharastra, India, for example, poverty-stricken villagers spontaneously formed people's social organizations called Tarun Mandals, whose membership includes all the people in the village. In three years the Bhoomi Sena movement spread to 120 villages, with Tarun Mandals in about 40 of them. Functioning systematically and holding weekly meetings, they have managed to free villagers who were virtually enslaved as bonded laborers. A minimum wage is now in effect in Bhoomi Sena villages and in many others. Tarun Mandals are spontaneously creating people's institutions to settle disputes, provide education, sponsor elections, and develop a labor union.

According to Mansour Fakih, by 1985 the lives of more than 100 million peasants in Latin America, Africa, and Asia had become directly affected by the activities of the new global social organizations, and no doubt their influence has increased since then.[43]

The picture shows an expanding latticework covering the globe. At the local level, particularly among the close to 4 billion humans in developing lands, it appears that the world's people are better organized today than they have been since European colonialism disrupted traditional societies centuries ago. Fisher asserts, "the proliferation of grassroots efforts is in fact a hallmark of our era."[44]

At the local grassroots level, these new social movement organizations are often located in rural villages or the slums of larger cities and are characterized by their lack of official corporate status. They are informally structured, and range in size from three-member groups to communities of 20 to 30 members. The members carry out all the functions of the social organization, including common education, self-help projects, and political action. Just as decision-making, tasks, learning, and participation are shared, leadership is also shared, as Julie Fisher makes clear: "After an entire *communidade* in a small town was arrested and brought before the local police chief on charges of subversion, he demanded to be told who was behind them, guiding and manipulating them. They at first replied, 'Nobody. It is all of us that you see here.' The police, unconvinced, insisted, 'Take me to your leader.' They answered, 'The one who encourages us and guides us is our Chief. It is our Lord Jesus Christ.'"[45]

Many of these small grassroots social organizations are broad-based, responding to the circumstances, issues, and concerns of their members. Some devote themselves to charitable work. Others engage in *conscientization* (consciousness raising) and discussion of social and political problems while others become actively involved in social outreach, social action, and social services. Members of base ecclesial communities gather for Sunday Liturgy of the Word, engage in Bible reading and reflection, and discuss the social conditions that affect their lives. They help organize community social events such as festivals and celebrations. *Communidades* in larger cities organize literacy classes and neighborhood crime watches, build and maintain community centers, provide aid for those most in need of economic assistance, and petition the local government for better municipal services.[46] Often they join with others to obtain training and develop joint strategies for community improvement. By the end of 1984, for example, 2,000 base social organizations in the diocese of Machakos in

Kenya, with over 60,000 participants, were actively involved in tree planting, cooperatives, savings groups, water projects, enterprise development, and consumer shops.

In addition to broad based community enrichment, some *local grassroots social organizations* form single-issue organizations around women's issues, ecology, or social action. Each single-issue organization has its own separate clan of activists with its guiding truths and ideology. They are composed entirely of volunteer members who carry out all the functions of the organization, and they have devoted themselves to such diverse and specific areas as defense of flora and fauna, organic agriculture, alternative medicine, alternative journalism, agricultural communities, esoteric knowledge, meditation, defense of indigenous communities, antinuclear struggles, alternative physical therapies, and others.[47]

When larger social movement organizations become formally structured and incorporated by the state, they are generically labeled *nongovernmental organizations* or *NGOs*, just as their counterparts in the United States are called nonprofit organizations. Formal social movement organizations, however, cannot be usefully defined by what they are not. In the Philippines the name NGO was rejected and the term Self-reliance Promoting Organization (SPO) was adopted instead.[48] In Indonesia they are called Community Self-reliance Organizations. In India formal social movement organizations are called voluntary agencies or nonparty political formations.

Smaller NGOs rarely have paid staff and almost never have any structure resembling hierarchy except at the most formally organized levels. NGOs nearly always comprise members who organize themselves with full participation and engagement of all. They represent a "bewildering mix of ideologies, objectives, working styles, social composition, funding and support sources."[49]

Some NGOs operate as free-standing social movement organizations with a single-issue focus in ecology, health, economic development, or social policy. Others are the multimember organizational coalitions composed of hundreds of *communidades,* such as the broad-based Six-S Movement in Burkina Faso, which covers nearly two-thirds of the country's villages and has become a regional movement spreading to a number of other countries, including Senegal, Chad, Niger, and Mali. These broad-based NGOs operate in ways that reflect the different needs, cultures, and situations of the great variety of their members. In the 1970s, larger and more urban-oriented NGOs in Brazil, for example, engaged in reorganizing and restructuring the unions, organized neighborhood associations, cooperatives, consumer groups, small trades, and peasant associations of all kinds. They took on projects in economic action, communication, human rights, participant research, health, and education,[50] as well as relief, training, social service, and political action.[51]

Many broad-based NGOs concentrate in rural areas. In 1980, for example, a group of concerned persons in Matabeleland, one of the most depressed areas in Zimbabwe with acute poverty and the highest rate of illiteracy in the country, decided to help people understand their poverty, question its causes, regain their dignity, and take collective initiative for their self-development. They structured themselves into a formal organization, the Organization of Rural Associations for Progress (ORAP), and formally registered as an NGO in 1981. Six years later, ORAP included 500 grassroots village groups with an average membership of about 75, as well as 30–40 umbrella organizations and 10 associations.

ORAP uses the local cultural tradition of people working together to help themselves (*amalima*) and rural mutual help groups (*ilima*). People's groups in the villages grew out of the village committees formed during liberation and some out of existing women's clubs. Out of a great deal of discussion about their problems and needs, they took action, mobilizing their labor and skills with the help of external donors. Assisted by professional and semi-professional staff, village groups federated into "umbrellas" and the umbrellas federated into "associations." Each association elects representatives to the ORAP advisory board. Ordinary villagers form themselves into mass community associations called development centers to consolidate and plan their mutual efforts.[52]

Community economic development is one of the more important areas in which NGOs become active. Many NGOs work to develop alternatives to capitalistic industrial models, state-controlled social programs, or centralized hierarchical, top-down institutionalized structures of decision making. In some ways they resemble North American asset-based community development projects, helping communities become economically sustainable, using the communities' resources and building on their strengths in ways that are compatible with the ecology and with their own culture. Community economic development NGOs promote solidarity and foster self-management, while working to improve the life chances and well-being of their residents.[53]

In Latin America a majority of the estimated 20,000 squatter settlements have created their own community economic development organizations. In the Lima squatter settlement Villa El Salvado, nearly 350,000 people, for example, have constructed hundreds of thousands of neatly designed homes. The nearly 200 nursery, primary, and secondary schools were built mostly by community volunteers. Virtually everyone knows how or is learning to read and write. Residents piped in water, and desert areas that were once barren now yield tons of oranges, vegetables, sweet potatoes, papayas, and corn. What most impresses visitors is organization. Every block and every activity is intensely organized through crisscrossing neighborhood associations, women's groups, youth groups, artisan associations, and production cooperatives. An estimated 2,000 organizations are nestled within federations of larger federations and these confederations largely control the democratically elected local government.[54]

Just as in North America, many community economic development NGOs emphasize housing. In Colombia there are over 700 public nonprofit community housing organizations. A grassroots community organization in Costa Rica built 1,300 houses in two years at final construction costs that were 40–50% lower than houses of comparable quality built by either government or the private sectors. Ordinary people learned to erect prefabricated walls and use computers for accounting, planning, and compiling data.[55]

Many community economic development NGOs engage in a wide variety of other self-help projects, including carpentry, sewing, building, basketry, wood carving, livestock grazing, school uniform making, vegetable gardening, poultry keeping, cement sheet making, knitting, mat making, ox-yoke making, baking, grinding mills, food storage, water, and sanitation.[56]

Some economic development NGOs help provide needed programs of assistance. In Peru, urban social movement organizations developed popular kitchens. In 1986, 625 kitchens existed in Lima and by 1990 the number had grown to 1,500 community kitchens averaging fifty members. One hundred thousand people, mostly mothers, are organized into barrio, zonal, and district organizations that raise funds for 7,500 Vaso de Leche (glass of milk) committees that work through community kitchens to distribute powdered milk as well as participate in developing popular libraries and health projects.[57]

The common goals of all these projects are to foster individual and communal self-reliance, control their own futures, and provide a forum by which members can express and discuss ideas and projects. They work to construct their communal reality out of their values, history, culture, and traditions, and by their own action regardless of and often in spite of those in authority. Many times community economic development NGOs resist accepting government assistance. Imported capital and technology can be helpful. But assistance must be based on people's ability to use credit productively, on accurate perceptions of need, and on their own initiative. External assistance can be supplementary if it is not dependency creating, and it must be under the control and planning of community members themselves.

One of the areas of largest impact of both informal grassroots and formally recognized social movement organizations is at the *political level*. NGOs as well as grassroots *communidades* work at institutional change in many communities. "Transformational" social movement organizations engage in a battle against the modernization/developmentalist worldviews that try to dominate the thinking of poor people. Like community organizations in North America, transformative social movement organizations in poor nations of the world work to promote people's "critical consciousness" to help them transform the "false consciousness" of modernity into a socially conscious society that names and denounces the philosophies of dominance.[58]

They engage in popular resistance and social change worldwide. Multiple and varied activist projects range from the struggle of members of a Caracas barrio to prevent the removal of a tree to the armed defense of their culture by ethnic groups in Guatemala. They include the efforts of small, politically oriented *communidades ecclesiales de base* that engage in social action in local villages to global

social movements that help bring about social justice, equality, and equal rights to people who have been oppressed and exploited.[59] In 1973, in the midst of Brazil's military dictatorship, mother's clubs in south Rio de Janeiro initiated a neighborhood movement against the high cost of living and denounced the high levels of pollution in the water supply, mobilizing 20,000 in a street demonstration that remained a landmark in the struggle for democracy.[60] Tens of thousands of students in Mexico City led mass demonstrations to eliminate obstacles to university entry, and in Buenos Aires grandmothers and mothers continue their daily march around the Plaza de Mayo, protesting the disappearance of their children and grandchildren.

New social movement organizations have begun to involve thousands of people in political advocacy. In 1976, Mexican grassroots social movement organizations joined to agitate for the defense of nature,[61] while ecological movements in India and people's movements against the commercial destruction of rain forests in Brazil and other kinds of predatory development projects built countervailing political power. A Brazilian congressman, for example, asserted that legislation against deforestation of the Amazon had been passed not because of international pressure or because congress understood the Greenhouse Effect, but because it was facing intense, organized pressure from Brazil's environmental movements and networks of Indian tribes.[62]

Such advocacy-based social movement organizations raise special questions of human development for women in developing nations where women often have a doubly subhuman status. Social movement organizations help them think and act independently of the men to whom they are often held to be subordinate.[63] Landless women's groups assert, for example, "We know that there is no easy or quick solution to our problem of food and clothing. But we as women did not even have the right to speak. In our organization we can now meet and speak, and share and discuss our problems. We feel that we are now human beings. We look forward to our weekly meetings where we stand up and speak—we can release ourselves as we have never been able to do before, and we now have the courage to speak the truth."[64]

Not only do advocacy-based movement organizations work on behalf of their own particular concerns, but they form alliances with one another. In Mexico, neighborhood organizations systematically join with independent workers, peasants, and teachers in their struggle for housing, clean air, education, a decent environment, solidarity, and democracy. Economic development Glass of Milk committees in Peru became integrated with broad-based community organizations, with the workers movement, and with women's movement organizations.[65] In addition, many direct-service NGOs are forming permanent networks at regional and national levels to debate common problems and perspectives and develop policy initiatives, much like national federations of community organizations in the United States and Canada.

The cumulative effect of direct political action by these social movement organizations has begun to change the political climate in many impoverished nations. Voluntary associations in urban areas in Africa have promoted social change by spearheading struggles for independence.[66] New democracy movements and people's struggles in the Philippines, Pakistan, Bangladesh, and some Latin American countries have been dramatic responses to repressive regimes and military dictatorships. By 1991, political reform in 25 countries in Asia, Africa, and Latin America now allows for a wide voter participation in free elections with multiple candidates.[67] Some social movement organizations align themselves with environmental, human rights, and women's movements nationally and internationally, mobilizing around a vision of people-centered development and policy and political reforms.[68]

Social movement organizations engage in more than economic development and political action projects. Special NGOs called *nongovernmental support organizations (NGSOs)* provide resources, training, staff, and technical assistance for NGOs and help support the NGO social movement. Some of these NGSOs maintain linkages with international social work organizations in North America and Europe or with the United Nations.

Transnational social movement organizations (TSMOs) are NGOs that have members in two or more states and an international office that coordinates or facilitates transnational activities. Amnesty International, for example, is a TSMO that mobilizes an international base of human rights advocates who question individual states about their human rights practices and provide material resources and legal services for victims of human rights abuse.[69] Many TSMOs operate at the people-to-people level, providing educational campaigns, citizen exchanges, information sharing, or services that increase pubic awareness. They maintain international solidarity networks,[70] educate the public about development issues, provide training for new social movement organizations, or act as advocates for specific groups. TSMOs work to bring policies of individual states in line with international standards by lobbying delegates at international meetings and monitoring compliance with international agreements.

International Social Work Organizations

Secular and faith-based international social work organizations are important adjuncts to social movement organizations in the poorer nations of the world. Oxfam, Africares, World Vision, Lutheran World Relief, the Mennonite Central Committee, the International Red Cross, the Christian Children's Fund, CARE, and many others are active in helping local indigenous communities. They provide assistance in community development and community organization, relief, immigration, human rights, advocacy, education and training, funding, and technical assistance, and they operate as nongovernmental support organizations (NGSOs), or transnational social movement organizations (TSMOs).

The Save the Children Federation, for example, organized a network of women's clubs in Colombia to promote small enterprise development and health education. Technoserve has provided assistance in agrarian reform cooperatives in Peru and El Salvador.[71] The Inter-American Foundation and the African Development Foundation fund international grassroots support organizations. All of these international social welfare organizations are important sources of assistance, support, direct involvement, coordination, and information that would not otherwise be available. They are a means by which social workers from North America and Europe can find a way of direct involvement in international social work.

The United Nations, founded in 1945, is the world's largest, oldest, and most important international support and advocacy organization.[72] Operating

International community development targets traditional communities in Africa, Asia, and South America. (Courtesy of Freedom From Hunger, [info@freefromhunger.org])

under the auspices of its Economic and Social Council, the United Nations provides community development programs and services to developing nations worldwide in the arenas of information, technical assistance, and a variety of specialized programs. Information is an important resource in community development efforts.

The United Nations is a central collection repository for social data and statistics from all member nations and publishes its own *World Economic Survey*, a *Report on the World Social Situation*, and the *State of the World's Children* compiled by UNICEF. This data is complemented by periodical statistical collections such as the *UN Statistical Yearbook* and the monthly *Statistical Bulletin*.[73]

The UN Development Program (UNDP) is a major UN vehicle for community development. The Development Program, for example, provides expert assistance to developing countries, regional training centers, scholarships, and planning projects for investment. The UN Fund for Population Activities (UNFPA) assists communities in applying knowledge of population dynamics to family planning services and training, and the UN Capital Development Fund

(UNCDF) provides grants and low-interest loans for community development in the least developed countries. The UN also recruits a corps of volunteers who do community development work.

The UN provides a variety of specialized programs that complement its community development efforts. One of the most well-known UN community development programs is UNICEF, the United Nations International Children's Emergency Fund. Initially established to provide aid to children who had suffered during World War II, it now develops long-term programs for health, social welfare, and teaching. The UN continues to provide assistance and protection to refugees who are displaced because of political reasons, war, famine, floods, and other disasters, through the UN Disaster Relief Organization (UNDRO). This agency "is on the scene first to protect the human rights of people outside their own countries and to offer material assistance where forced migrations occur."[74]

The World Food Program is designed to take agricultural surplus or gifts in kind to send food to developing countries. The UN is also involved in health issues, mainly by means of its affiliated World

Health Organization (WHO). WHO coordinates research, provides a system for notification of infectious diseases, and assists developing countries to organize their own public health services and control health-related problems such as poor sanitation.[75]

Becoming Involved in International Social Work

The easiest and most accessible way to become involved in international social work is to become a social work intern or volunteer, or obtain a paid position in an international social welfare organization such as Oxfam, CARE, World Vision, or UNICEF that provides relief or promotes community development.[76]

When you perform international social work, you will need to learn the language and understand the culture, customs, and history of the people with whom you are working. Only with a mind freed from the presumption that Western ideas are superior can you prevent yourself from unintentionally reinforcing the conditions you intend to change. You may, for example, come with a sincere intention to help develop people in an impoverished nation. Social workers who come from Canada or the United States, however, cannot develop the poor or anyone else. The only person you can develop is yourself, and the only people who can develop the poor are poor people themselves. Modern developmental models represent top-down, rational, market-orientation ideas of "progress." You cannot be a representative of these ideas. Instead, you honor the ideals of human potential, self-determination, self-development, and the necessity for people to construct their own social reality and community culture. You disassociate yourself from enlightenment reason. You assert that self-reliant action by the people will not be determined by others' knowledge but by the people's own knowledge and action.

You cannot assist in the process of liberation, if you are not first liberated yourself. Tarun Mandals (poor people's village organizations) give you this advice.

> We need outside help for analysis and understanding our situation and experience, but not for telling us what we should do. Initially we had genuinely thought that outsiders had our good at heart and knew better. We did not think much of ourselves and did not have ideas of our own.

> An outsider who comes with ready-made solutions and advice is worse than useless. He must first understand *from us* what our questions are, help articulate the questions better, and then help *us* to find solutions.

> An outsider also has to change. He alone is a friend who helps us to think about our problems *on our own*. The principle should be minimum intervention.

Once you have become clear about the difference between the values, methods, and processes of modernization and the principles of helping people generate their own ideas and decisions, you may be ready to begin. Your primary task is to assist local people to attain a liberated mind in which they not only affirm that their ideas are of value, but they trust their beliefs and culture and respect their own judgment. Only with a liberated mind can poor people release their creative potential to conceive the new world that lies ahead of them and then act on that vision.

While you may raise questions and sharpen thinking, your goal is to assist members of communities to make their own decisions, not judge whether the direction is the right one. The strength of your method is your conviction that ordinary working people are capable of social inquiry and analysis, and this capability can be enhanced by practice. Liberating education is more than the transfer of information; it is the practice of freedom. You affirm that poor villagers have the capacity to direct their own development and discover a "truth" of their community that becomes as valid for them as scientific truth is to technologically minded members of the West.

You engage community members on their own territory and on their own terms. You must be willing to give up your own lifestyle and economic attainments to gain the trust, respect, and confidence of the community members. By living in impoverished communities, you demonstrate that you are willing to live the same life that they live, breath its air, eat the same food, and as much as possible become attuned to its culture.

One of the hallmarks of an international social worker is your ability to engage people. In the early stages of community work, your main job is simply to get to know the community and make friends with the people there. Talk to them about their lives, about the life of this community, and their feelings about living in this community. Share with them who you are and be as real and genuine as you can. Express real interest in people, their surroundings, hopes, fears, and personal situations. Try to relate their lives with something in your own life. When you develop common ground or rapport, real understanding and communication can begin. The more you talk with people and get to know them, the more closer to them you will become, and the more you become one of them.

Relationships and communication develop trust. Trust is essential in all community social work. Your influence in a community will depend to the extent to which its members trust you. The fastest way to develop trust is visibility. Go to places where people congregate. Any place people in the community gather is a good place for you to spend time. Go to religious celebrations and traditional festivals. Try to become close to several key people. If you can gain acceptance by one or more members of a particular subgroup, you have established a toehold in that community. Once you have done this, you will more than likely be able to expand to other subgroups, because most communities have overlapping networks of relationships.

When you meet with a group of community members, listen to the issues, gather information, take time to talk to key community leaders, or simply act as a participant-observer in the community itself. Stimulate an attitude of self-reliance in the people from the very beginning. Help them ask questions such as, What can we do ourselves to solve this problem? Do we need the NGO worker to solve this problem? If we absolutely need outside help, how fast can we make ourselves independent? What can we do to facilitate this purpose?

GETTING STARTED IN A PUERTO RICAN COMMUNITY

In early January, 1985, we arrived at our farm in Cubuy. Living in the hills and on a farm was entirely foreign to both of us. We quickly learned that two women living alone would need some help with the heavy work. John Luis, a young man in the area, was a member of a crew of handymen that helped us out. As custom requires, he became like a family member rather than simply a "stateside" handyman. He was unemployed and his prospects for a job were dismal. We began to informally involve him in sessions on entrepreneurship skills. Eventually, he asked whether his friends and family members could join him in these sessions. Before we could proceed to accept his suggestion, John Luis explained that we had to talk with his family and the parents of other youths who would be coming. We visited homes to introduce ourselves and explain the purpose of the youth sessions. Before long, the sessions expanded to formal Saturday morning meetings with eight of his relatives and friends.

Word spread around the small village that two "American" teachers from California had come to live in the area and that they were teaching the children. Within a week, John Luis brought a verbal invitation for us to present ourselves at a meeting of the local association. Not knowing what to expect, we arrived at the meeting fully equipped, carrying documentation as to who we were. We were seated in a small room opposite eight older gentlemen and one woman who never spoke throughout the meeting. The men were dressed in the true "jibara" style. They wore sparkling clear and ironed "guayaberas." We introduced ourselves and they asked why we had come to their village. We spoke for several hours.

At the end, fully satisfied, the association asked us to work with the entire community in solving its serious unemployment problem. We told the association that we needed a planning and action committee. They named a committee, immediately including some of those present and others whom they could notify. Our work began that night. Every Thursday evening we met to plan and create a model of action. As a result of our work, Producir Inc., an economic and community development corporation, was legally incorporated in June 1986.[77]

One of your first tasks is to help members break the bonds of oppression that hold them in chains. Overt oppression itself, however, is not the main problem confronting the people of poor nations. The oppressed people's perception of their situation and their internalization of that oppression is their most persistent and insidious enemy. After centuries of conditioned helplessness, many people are trapped in "self-colonization." Freire calls this "playing host to the oppressor." Poor people participate in their own self-oppression. They accept their role as an oppressed people and often act in helpless and dependent ways rather than reject those roles. They internalize the opinions that the oppressor holds of them as if they are true. They believe

Community Development NGOs help communities become economically sustainable by using their own resources and building on their strengths. (© Billy E. Barnes/Jeroboam, Inc.)

themselves to be nothing more than "things" owned by oppressors. Poor people often blame themselves for the conditions that oppressors have placed on them. You help raise the consciousness of these people.

You can do this by using Paulo Freire's model of education of critical awareness and critical evaluation. *Conscientization* is a deepened consciousness of one's situation that leads you to understand your situation as a historical reality susceptible to transformation.[78] You help members by means of dialogue, simulation exercises, consciousness raising, and critical assessment exercises in which members examine their situation and self-perceptions. You may ask your members: "Who are we? For what reason do we exist? Why are we poor?" You help them understand that they are no different from the rich and the powerful, and you assist them to understand that poverty is not inherent in them but lies in situations that they can change.[79]

Stimulate people's reflection and analysis, assisted but not dominated by the knowledge and considerations that you may have. Provide consultation and raise questions. Assist each person to speak his or her mind

with a spirit of acceptance, and listen carefully to his or her ideas, concerns, questions, and issues. As you listen, try to help develop commonality and look for patterns that you can use in helping them organize in a common direction. Clarify objectives and develop a sharper direction of their work. Ask people to deliberate what they want to do long range, and how the social movement organization can help them.

At the end of the meeting or meetings, assist the group to come to some sort of decision. The key value in decision-making within a community is not efficiency, but participation. The time required to reach a decision should not be the shortest time required, nor should a small, select group make the decisions. Only those directly involved have the right to decide whether to implement or refuse an idea. You may provide information and support, but the ultimate strategy must remain the possession of those affected by the consequences. Involve them in understanding principles of good decision-making.[80]

Help members organize around their decision and come up with a plan. When they are ready, assist them to move toward implementation. Implementation of change in modern communities includes initiating a community project of volunteer effort, coordinating efforts with other communities, and developing a project that the community members agree will benefit them.

One of your most important goals is to help move members toward becoming leaders. You liberate members from the need for a trainer so that they become self-educators in their own learning. You help train members as facilitators who assist one another or consult with other *communidades de base* in cultural, political, and economic self-reliance and decision-making.

Those who dominate and exploit people control most of the material and financial resources in less developed nations. Your members may decide to work toward justice and equity in the use of public resources. Depending on the kinds of projects or issues with which your community group is confronted, you may need to arrange for training in legal rights, government policy, or process. You help people obtain their rightful share of normal public resources, learn how to use them, and engage in this process on their own. For example, it does not make sense to help poor people be dependent on voluntary agencies or special donors to obtain financial help for their projects when public resources are available. You may help your members use an NGO to obtain a loan to establish credit for a brief period, and help them gain confidence and skill in using credit wisely. At the same time, however, you help the poor understand that they have a right to receive credit from the banking system just as others. You assist them in learning how the banking system works, how to negotiate for credit, and how to utilize their combined strength.

When a system unjustly discriminates against your community, you help them affirm their rights. You assist your members to organize themselves to exercise their collective power. You assess the strengths of your members and train them in direct-action tactics and strategies. You engage them in decision-making and challenge oppressors over issues that they have a reasonable possibility of winning.

Community members periodically evaluate their own experience and review their progress collectively and draw lessons from successes and failures. Help develop a consciousness among the poor so they see short-run failures as a learning process upon which

subsequent strategy is to be built. A struggle is never lost if constructive lessons are drawn from its failure. After your members have reviewed their own work, ask NGO workers to do a more systematic and formal assessment based on the members' own objectives.

Encourage your members to engage in remembrance so that their history is not forgotten, their shared stories are passed down, and their collective memories remain in the unconscious of the community. Members themselves are the main researchers who collect or document this history in simple language, assisted if necessary by locally educated youth or teachers. Encourage them to record their traditions, songs, stories, truths, and experiences and share them with other groups and villages. Help them explore the meaning behind their experiences and stories. It is out of the meaning of these stories and myths that a culture is born, traditions are generated, and symbols developed that sustain them through the difficulties ahead.

AN AGENDA FOR THE NEW GLOBAL SOCIETY

An agenda for a new global society for the 21st century may consist of:

1. Communities expressing a variety of cooperative, responsible, self-reliant indigenous peoples as the social basis for the new society, including creation of the self, social learning, and decision-making.

2. Participatory, face-to-face democracy at the grassroots community level.

3. Bottom-up and interactive decision-making enhanced by advanced information technology that will make political decision-making at the grassroots level a reality.

4. Encouragement of rich ethnic and cultural diversity, and respect for the social, including social justice, social ethics, and social action, rather than a market-centered economic society in which thinking, systems, and people become categories of the market.

5. Restriction of modern hierarchical organization systems to their proper enclaves and recognition that they are tools of community and not command instruments.

6. Dissolving the state governance apparatus from a source of power and control to a system of community support.

7. Promotion of partnerships with government, institutions, and professional groups by developing social relationships among diverse communal forms.

CONCLUSION

In the 500 years since European explorers first encountered indigenous people, the Enlightenment has increased the wealth of European and North American nations, but it has created poverty for much of the remainder of the world's population. Modernity continues to destroy communal identity and negates freedom, self-determination, and humanity, which are fundamental to indigenous cultures of non-market-centered nations.[81] The modern project generates violence, creates hopelessness, breeds dependency, and undermines the human spirit. It endangers the land and decimates wildlife, forests, rivers, lakes, and oceans.

With the help of international macro social workers, members of the least developed nations are exercising their rights of refusal to accept the market-centered, rational, goal-maximizing Enlightenment tradition and reject colonial mentality and patriarchal rule. They are autonomously and spontaneously reasserting their prerogative as humans to choose new social forms worldwide that provide room for the social, renewed communal relations, and recognition of the value of their indigenous cultures. Where windows of opportunity emerged, they began to create small base communities. As they acquired experience and strength, they began joining forces in an amazing variety of processes and organizational forms expressing the ingenuity, diversity, and creativity that people generate when they solve problems together. They have become a global social movement of momentous proportions.

International social work is the "conquest of a small piece of humanity for the common heritage of human kind."[82] When you engage in international social work, you participate in an emancipatory project with people who construct their own communal reality. International macro social workers who work for global social justice and human rights engage in

one of the most important and vital arenas of social work. Those of you who become involved in international social work will no doubt play an increasingly important role in shaping the future world. Helping people build a new social world, create their own communities, and in the process construct themselves is what social work is all about. The new global social revolution and world of international social work waits for you to accept its challenge.

KEY CONCEPTS

global social movements

modernization

development

developing nation

least developed nation

developed nation

World Bank

IMF

World Trade Organization

GATT

UN

social movement organization

communidades ecclesiales de base

communidades de base

conscientization

NGO

TSMO

NGSO

UNICEF

United Nations Development Program (UNDP)

United Nations Fund for Population Activities (UNFPA)

United Nations Capital Development Fund (UNCDF)

United Nations Disaster Relief Organization (UNDRO)

World Food Program (WFP)

World Health Organization (WHO)

hegemony

QUESTIONS FOR DISCUSSION

1. What are some of the premises, ideas, and characteristics of the modern developed nations? How do they affect people in developing and least developed nations?

2. What is meant by development? What positive benefits has development provided? What negative consequences has it had? Can development be used to help poor people in developing nations enter modernity? What would happen if the entire world were to become completely modern? Would this be an event that you would welcome? Why or why not?

3. The point was made that because of modernity, the developed nations of Europe and North America have prospered economically and politically. Critique this assertion. In your critique, consider the comment of Alberto Ramos, a Brazilian scholar/politician, who asserts that modernity has won a Phyrric victory. In what sense has modernity benefited Europe and North America? In what sense is the triumph of modernity a Phyrric victory?

4. What is the new postmodern global revolution? What are some social movements that make up this revolution? Why is it called a revolution rather than a reform movement? Is this a revolution that you welcome? Why or why not? Do you believe macro social workers should work to help bring this revolution about or resist it?

EXERCISE 15.1

Money or Ideas

For three years you have been working with a social movement organization in a developing nation. You have become fluent in the language and are familiar with the culture and history of the people. Along with a native-born social worker, you are beginning to work directly with a village in a poor area of the nation. You are meeting with 40 of the villagers. As you talk with them, they say to you, "Don't give us money, give us ideas, because ideas would permit us to forge our own means of fighting hunger."

What is your response? Meet with a triad of your classmates and come to a group decision. Return to class, and your instructor will lead a discussion.

EXERCISE 15.2

Paulo Freire and Social Ecology

Review the ideas and premises on which social ecology is based, particularly social adaptation, empowerment, and social transformation. Think about the way that social ecology theory assumes that humans either adapt to or transform the social environment which they inhabit. Consider Paulo Friere's assertion that "If for animals, orientation in the world means adaptation to the world, for man it means humanizing the world by transforming it."

1. What is the social ecology idea of social adaptation?

2. What is the social ecology theory of social transformation?

3. Is the role of social work to help people adapt to their social environment or transform it? Do we do both?

4. Do people gain empowerment by adaptation or transformation?

5. Can the social ecology model assist you in your work to help empower people?

EXERCISE 15.3

Social Critique

Review the following statement.

The modern global economy has made a few people wealthy at the expense of the rest of the world's population. It has provided a fraction of the world's people with an adequate income. It is no longer possible that a small minority can appropriate the material and human resources of the globe for their own benefit. This state of affairs is untenable. It cannot be a way that the growing world's population may be sustained.

1. Critique this statement. Is it completely true, partially true, or false?

2. If you were asked to change this statement to reflect your own understanding of the facts, what changes would you make?

3. If you were to change this statement to reflect your own beliefs about the correct diagnosis of the world economy, what changes would you make?

4. If you were to asked to change the last two sentences to reflect your position about the modern global economy, what would you say?

Bring your written statements to class. Form into triads and compare your statements. Develop a composite response to the various questions and return to class. Your instructor will lead a discussion reflecting your responses.

ADDITIONAL READING

Base Ecclesial Communities

Alvaro Barreiro. *Basic Ecclesial Communities: The Evangelization of the Poor,* trans. Barbara Campbell. Maryknoll, NY: Orbis, 1982.

Leonardo Boff. *Ecclesiogenesis: The Base Communities Reinvent the Church*, trans. Robert R. Barr. Maryknoll, NY: Orbis, 1986.

Guillermo Cook. *The Expectation of the Poor: Latin American Basic Ecclesial Communities in Protestant Perspective.* Maryknoll, NY: Orbis, 1985.

W. E. Hewitt. *Base Christian Communities and Social Change in Brazil.* Lincoln: University of Nebraska Press, 1991.

Thomas A. Kleissler, Margo A. LeBert, and Mary C. McGuinness. *Small Christian Communities: A Vision of Hope.* Mahwah, NJ: Paulist Press, 1991.

Sergio Torres and John Eagleson, eds. *The Challenge of Basic Christian Communities,* trans. John Drury. Maryknoll, NY: Orbis, 1981.

John Paul Vandenakker. *Small Christian Communities and the Parish: An Ecclesiological Analysis of the North American Experience.* Kansas City, MO: Sheed and Ward, 1994.

International Social Work

M.C. Hokenstad, S. K. Khinduka, and J. Midgley, eds. *Profiles in International Social Work.* Washington, DC: NASW Press, 1992.

Development Planning

Anis Chowdhury and Colin Kirkpatrick. *Development Policy and Planning: An Introduction to Models and Techniques.* London: Routledge, 1994.

Abhimany Singh. *Planning for Developing a Backward Economy.* New Delhi: Vikas Publishing, 1991.

Development Policy

Yamond Apthorpe and Des Gasper, eds. *Arguing Development Policy: Frames and Discourses.* London: Frank Cass, 1966.

John Friedman. *Empowerment: The Politics of Alternative Development.* Cambridge, MA: Blackwell, 1992.

Hope Kempe. *Development in the Third World: From Policy Failure to Policy Reform.* Armonk, NY: M. E. Sharpe, 1996.

Oskar Kurer. *The Political Foundations of Development Policies.* Lanham, MD: University Press of America, 1997.

Development Practice

Hubert Campfens. *Community Development Around the World.* Toronto: University of Toronto Press, 1997.

Julie Fisher. *The Road From Rio: Sustainable Development and the Nongovernmental Movement in the Third World.* Westport, CT: Praeger, 1993.

Allen Jedlicka. *Volunteerism and World Development: Pathway to a New World.* New York: Praeger, 1990.

Frances Moore Lappe and Joseph Collins. *World Hunger: Twelve Myths.* New York: Grove Press, 1986.

Dominque La Pierre. *The City of Joy.* Garden City, NY: Doubleday, 1995.

Philip McMichael. *Development and Social Change: A Global Perspective.* Thousand Oaks, CA: Pine Forge Press, 1996.

John Rapley. *Understanding Development: Theory and Practice in the Third World.* Boulder, CO: Lynne Rienner, 1996.

K. Subbarao et al. *Safety Net Programs and Poverty Reduction: Lessons From Cross-Country Experience*. Washington, DC: World Bank, 1997.

World Bank. *Liveable Cities for the 21st Century*. Washington, DC: World Bank, 1996.

Development Theory

Arturo Escobar. *Encountering Development. The Making and Unmaking of the Third World*. Princeton, NJ: Princeton University Press, 1995.

Bjorn Hettne. *Development Theory and the Three Worlds*. 2d ed. Edinburgh Gate, England: Addison Wesley Longman, 1995.

David McClelland. *The Achieving Society*. New York: VanNostrand, 1961.

W. W. Rostow. *The Stages of Economic Growth*. Cambridge: Cambridge University Press, 1960.

Jeremy Seabrook. *Victims of Development: Resistance and Alternatives*. London: Verso, 1993.

Liberation Theology

Jon Bonino. *Doing Theology in a Revolutionary Situation*. Philadelphia: Fortress, 1975.

Gustavo Gutierrez. *Theology of Liberation*. Maryknoll, NY: Orbis, 1973.

———. *The Power of the Poor in History*. Maryknoll, NY: Orbis, 1983.

Modernization

Cyril E. Black. *The Dynamics of Modernization*. New York: Harper, 1967.

Richard D. Brown. *Modernization: The Transformation of American Life, 1600–1865*. New York: Hill and Wang, 1976.

S. C. Dube. *Modernization and Development: The Search for Alternative Paradigms*. Tokyo: United Nations University, 1988.

Charles Inkeles and David Smith. *Becoming Modern*. Cambridge, MA: Harvard University Press, 1974.

Social Critique

Samir Amin. *Unequal Development*. New York: Monthly Review Press, 1976.

Paulo Freire. *Pedagogy of the Oppressed*. New York: Herder and Herder 1970.

———. *Education for Critical Consciousness*. New York: Seabury Press, 1973.

Antonio Gramsci. *Selections From the Prison Notebooks*. New York: International Publishers, 1971.

Jurgen Habermas. *Knowledge and Human Interest*, trans. Jeremy Shapirs. Boston: Beacon, 1983.

Timothy Luke. *Social Theory and Modernity: Critique, Dissent, and Revolution*. Newbury Park, CA: Sage, 1990.

Rigoberta Menchu. *I, Rigoberta Menchu: An Indian Woman in Guatemala*, trans. Ann Wright. London: Verso, 1984.

PART FIVE

Macro Social Work Resources

*I*n the Epilogue, you will discover more about the heritage of macro social work, and you will find exercises that bring this book and your course to closure.

The appendices at the end of this book provide directories to help you increase your own understanding of macro social work. Appendix A provides you with a listing of volunteer opportunities in domestic as well as international social work. Appendix B offers you a listing of some social organizations that you can contact for more information about each of the arenas of macro social work and possible internships. Appendix C offers a description of how to access usergroups, newsgroups, and the Internet and listings of newsgroups and websites useful in obtaining more information about macro social work, for doing research, writing reports, or even finding internships or jobs in macro social work.

Epilogue

Macro Social Work:
A Profession of Heroes

> We ought always and in every way treat mankind and every other rational being as an end and never merely as a means only.
>
> *Immanuel Kant*, Groundwork of the Metaphysic of Morals

The woman who took care of my daughter when she was little was a Greek Jew. She was very young, nine, ten, eleven when the war broke out, and was lying on the crematorium door when the American troops came through. So she has a number tattooed on her arm. And it was always like being hit in the stomach with a brick when she would take my baby and sit and circle her with her arm, and there was the number. So encircled by love and suffering shared, we are no longer in the "giving-getting" mode. We know ourselves as social selves, parents and children, members of a people, inheritors of a history and a culture that we must nurture through memory and hope.[1]

Ideas in the Epilogue

As a macro social worker, you can help overcome oppression, exploitation, and suffering, and make the world a better place for the generations to come. (© Susanne Arms Wimberley/Jeroboam, Inc.)

IRENA SENDLER: SOCIAL WORK RESCUER

In 1940, Nazis confined 500,000 Polish Jews in the Warsaw Ghetto to await their deaths.[2] Most people in Warsaw turned their backs, but not Irena Sendler. A Warsaw social worker, Sendler decided to invest herself in this community and wangled a permit to check for signs of typhus, a disease that the Nazis feared.

Sendler decided to do something about what she saw. Joining Zegota, a tiny underground cell dedicated to rescuing the Jews, she took on the code name "Jolanta." Because the deportations of Jews had already begun, it was impossible to save the adults, so Sendler began smuggling children out in an ambulance. Over the next three years Sendler successfully transported more than 2,000 Jewish children to safety, giving them temporary new identities. In order to keep track of the children's real names, she placed information about their identities in bottles, which she buried in her garden.

It was difficult for Sendler to find people willing to help these children. However, after much effort, she did find families and developed a network of churches and convents that were willing to help. "I have clothing for the convent," she would write, and the nuns would come and pick up the children.

In 1943, the Gestapo arrested and tortured Sendler, and sentenced her to die. Her colleagues in the Polish underground, however, bribed a prison guard to free her at the last minute, listing her as "executed" on the official form. In hiding, Sendler continued her work of rescuing children. After the war, she dug up her bottles and began searching for the parents of the children she had rescued. She could find only a few of the parents because most had died in Nazi concentration camps. Years later, when Irena Sendler was honored for her rescue work and her picture appeared in a newspaper, "a man, a painter, telephoned me," Sendler said. "I remember your face," he said. "It was you who took me out of the Ghetto." Sendler had many calls like that.

MACRO SOCIAL WORKERS AND HEROES OF SOCIAL JUSTICE

Macro social work is a profession that aims at community betterment, making a good society and a better world. We need social workers of vision, commitment, and courage who see a future in which social relationships among people are as important as technological improvement; in which community solidarity and engagement are prized as much as organizational efficiency and effectiveness; in which heroes of social justice are revered as much as flamboyant entertainment celebrities or sports figures.

This text opened with the observation that the trend in social work for the last several decades has been away from macro social concerns and toward micro social work practice. Counseling and psychotherapy are needed, and there are many rewards in treating individuals, couples, and families and helping people change their lives and overcome personal troubles. Much good is being done helping people break cycles of abuse, codependency, and addictions as well as treating depression, anxieties, and other emotional and behavioral disorders. As important as micro social work is, however, the extent to which we focus our professional energies on individual problems rather than the social conditions that may have brought them about, the more we tend to ignore our wider and more fundamental social problems.

"It would be tragic," asserts Noam Chomsky, "if those who are fortunate enough to live in the advanced societies of the West were to forget or abandon the hope that our world can be transformed to a world in which the creative spirit is alive, in which life is an adventure full of hope and joy, based rather upon the impulse to construct than upon the desire to retain what we possess or seize what is possessed by others."[3] But even today, the focus on social problems is shifting to a more proactive vision of the future. The reactive social problem approach is giving way to social change. Instead of weaknesses, macro social workers are looking at people's strengths, from problems to possibilities.

You have learned that the modern world is giving way to a new postmodern social era. These changes are being brought about by the poor and not by the powerful. You have explored how the poor people of the earth who have been exploited by unjust economic and political systems of the modern age are reinventing society. They are creating new planning councils, faith-based community organizations, community development corporations, social organizations, new social movements, and *base comunidades* that are transforming the way we think about social problems, leadership, social relationships, and the nature of the human condition. It is my hope that you have learned how you too can be a part of bringing this new postmodern era into existence, and I hope that you will want to be a participant with the poor in that effort. If so, you will become a member of a group of outstanding macro social workers. You will join people of the stature of Saint Elizabeth Ann Seton, Charles Booth, Dorothea Dix, Reverend Samuel Barnett, Reverend Charles Loring Brace, Homer Folks, Graham Taylor, Clara Barton, Sojourner Truth, Mary Parker Follett, Mary Simkhovitch, Grace and Edith Abbott, Clifford Beers, Harriet Tubman, Lord Robert Baden-Powell, Sophonisba Breckinridge, Sir George Williams, Lillian Wald, Dorothy Day, Reverend William Booth, Jane Addams, Harry Hopkins, Mary McLeod Bethune, Saint Frances Cabrini, W.E.B. Du Bois, Michael Harrington, Whitney Young Jr., Florence Kelly, Josephine Shaw Lowell, Bertha Capen Reynolds, and Si Kahn.

You will become partners with heroes of social justice in the United States as well as around the world who want to bring an end to oppression, inhumanity, and injustice: Frederick Douglass, Thadeus Stevens, Rev. Walter Rauschenbusch, Rev. Dr. Martin Luther King Jr., George Wiley, Roy Wilkins, Rev. John Perkins, Cesar Chavez, Saul Alinsky, Toyohiko Kagawa, and many others. The contributions of these macro social workers and workers for social justice have changed the direction of our nation and improved the quality of our lives.

We need to remember these heroes and their accomplishments. They form a "cloud of witnesses" whose vision and dedication support our efforts today and on whose shoulders we ride. From these heroes we can learn about compassion in a world that is often uncaring, altruism in a world of selfish consumption, sacrifice in a world of self-interest, and humanity in a world rife with dehumanization. Not only are the accomplishments of these macro social workers impressive, but the writing by and about them is prodigious. Read about some of these macro social workers and the books they have written. You will be inspired and come to a better understanding of what macro social workers have accomplished. You will learn about the challenges that await you and discover how you too can become a hero for others.

Edith Abbott (1876–1957)

Edith Abbott. *Democracy and Social Progress in England*. Chicago: The University of Chicago Press, 1918.

———. *Historical Aspects of the Immigration Problem*. New York: Arno, 1969.

———. *Immigration. Selected Documents and Case Records*. New York: Arno, 1969.

———. *The One hundred and One County Jails of Illinois and Why they ought to be Abolished*. Chicago: 1916.

———. *Some American Pioneers in Social Welfare*. Chicago, IL: University of Chicago Press, 1937.

———. *The Tenements of Chicago, 1908–1935*. 1936. Reprint. New Salem, NH: Ayer, 1970.

———. *Women in Industry: A Study in American Economic History*. New York: Appleton, 1910. Reprint. New Salem, NH: Ayer, 1969.

Grace Abbott (1878–1939)

Grace Abbott. *The Child and the State, Select Documents*. New York: Greenwood, 1968.

———. *From Relief to Social Security: The Development of The New Public Welfare Services and their Administration*. New York: Russell and Russell, 1966.

———. *The Immigrant and the Community*. 1917. Reprint. New York: J. S. Ozer, 1971.

———. *The Juvenile Court and a Community Program for Treating and Preventing Delinquency*. Chicago: 1936.

———. *The Social Security Act and Relief*. Chicago: 1936.

Lela B. Costin. *Two Sisters for Social Justice: A Biography of Grace and Edith Abbott*. Urbana: University of Illinois Press, 1983.

Jane Addams (1860–1935)

Jane Addams. *Democracy and Social Ethics*. Cambridge: Belknap Press of Harvard University, 1964.

———. *Jane Addams on Peace, War, and International Understanding. 1899-1932*. Allen F. Davis, ed. New York: Garland, 1976.

———. *A New Conscience and an Ancient Evil*. New York: Arno, 1972.

———. *Newer Ideas of Peace*. New York: J. S. Ozer, 1972.

———. *Peace and Bread in Time of War*. New York: J. S. Ozer, 1972.

———. *Philanthropy and Social Progress*. Montclair, NJ: Patterson Smith, 1970.

———. *The Social Thought of Jane Addams*. Christopher Lasch, ed. New York: Irvington, 1982.

———. *The Spirit of Youth and the City Streets*. New York: Macmillan, 1909. Reprint. Urbana: University of Illinois Press, 1989.

———. *Twenty Years at Hull House*. New York: Penguin Books, 1998.

———. *The Second Twenty Years at Hull House*. New York: Macmillan, 1930.

Frank E. Aloise. *Jane Addams*. New York: Crowell, 1971.

Allen F. Davis. *American Heroine: The Life and Legend of Jane Addams*. Chicago: Ivan Dee, 2000.

Mary Jo Deegan. *Jane Addams and the Men of the Chicago School, 1892–1918*. New Brunswick, NJ: Transaction Books, 1988.

John C. Farrell. *Beloved Lady: A History of Jane Addams' Ideas on Reform and Peace*. Baltimore, MD: John Hopkins Press, 1967.

Mary Kittredge. *Jane Addams: Helper of the Poor*. New York: Chelsea House, 1988.

Daniel Levine. *Jane Addams and the Liberal Tradition*. Westport, CT: Greenwood, 1980.

James Linn. *Jane Addams: A Biography*. Urbana: University of Illinois Press, 2000.

Eleanor J. Stebner. *The Women of Hull House: A Study in Spirituality, Vocation, and Friendship*. Albany: State University of New York Press, 1997.

Margaret Tims. *Jane Addams of Hull House, 1860–1935*. New York: Macmillan, 1981.

Lord Robert Baden-Powell (1857–1941)

Robert Baden-Powell. *Scouting for Boys*. London: C. A. Pearson, 1910.

Howard Fast. *Lord Baden-Powell of the Boy Scouts.* New York: J. Messner, 1941.

Tim Jeal. *The Boy-Man: The Life of Lord Baden-Powell.* New York: Morrow, 1990.

Duncan W. Grinnell-Milne. *Baden-Powell at Mafekin.* London: Bodley Head, 1957.

William Hillcourt. *Baden-Powell: The Two Lives of a Hero.* New York: G. P. Putnam's Sons, 1964.

Ernest Edwin Reynolds. *Baden-Powell: A Biography of Lord Baden-Powell of Gilwell.* London: Oxford University Press, 1943.

Canon Samuel Barnett (1844–1913)

Samuel Barnett. *Religion and Progress.* New York: Macmillan, 1907.

———— and Henrietta Barnett. *Towards Social Reform.* New York: Macmillan, 1909.

Henrietta Barnett. *Canon Barnett: His Life, Work, and Friends,* 2 vols. Boston: Houghton Mifflin, 1919.

Clara Barton (1821–1912)

Clara Barton. *The Story of the Red Cross: Glimpses of Field Work.* 1904. Reprint. New York: Airmont, 1968.

————. *The Red Cross in Peace and War.* Meriden, CT: Journal Publishing, 1912.

————. *The Story of My Childhood.* New York: Arno, 1980.

William E. Barton. *The Life of Clara Barton: Founder of the American Red Cross.* New York: AMS Press, 1969.

David Burton. *Clara Barton: In the Service of Humanity.* Westport, CT: Greenwood, 1995.

Jeannette Covert. *The Story of Clara Barton of the Red Cross.* New York: J. Messner, 1941.

Leni Hamilton. *Clara Barton.* New York: Chelsea House, 1988.

Stephen B. Oates. *A Woman of Valor: Clara Barton and the Civil War.* New York: Free Press, 1994.

Elizabeth Pryor. *Clara Barton: Professional Angel.* Philadelphia: University of Pennsylvania Press, 1987.

Susan Sloate. *Clara Barton: Founder of the American Red Cross.* New York: Fawcett, 1990.

Clifford Beers (1876–1943)

Clifford Beers. *A Mind That Found Itself: An Autobiography.* Pittsburgh, PA: University of Pittsburgh Press, 1981.

————. *The Aftercare of the Insane.* New Haven, CT: Bradley and Scoville, 1909.

————. *A Society for Mental Hygiene as an Agency for Social Service and Education.* New Haven, CT: 1910.

Norman Dain. *Clifford W. Beers: Advocate for the Insane.* Pittsburgh, PA: University of Pittsburgh Press, 1980.

Mary McLeod Bethune (1875–1955)

Mary McLeod Bethune. *Building a Better World: Essays and Selected Documents.* Audrey McCluskey, ed. Bloomington: Indiana University Press, 1999.

Rackham Holt. *Mary McLeod Bethune: A Biography.* Garden City, NY: Doubleday, 1964.

Catherine O. Peare. *Mary McLeod Bethune.* New York: Vanguard, 1951.

Beth P. Wilson. *Giants for Justice: Bethune, Randolph, and King.* New York: Harcourt, Brace, Jovanovich, 1978.

Rinna Wolfe. *Mary McLeod Bethune.* New York: F. Watts, 1992.

Charles Booth (1840–1916)

Charles Booth. *Life and Labour of the People of London,* 9 vols. New York: Macmillan, 1892–1897.

————. *Pauperism: A Picture.* London: Macmillan, 1892.

————. *Old Age Pensions and the Aged Poor: A Proposal.* London: Macmillan, 1899.

T. S. Simey and M. B. Simey. *Charles Booth: Social Scientist.* Westport, CT: Greenwood Press, 1980.

William Booth (1829–1912)

William Booth. *In Darkest England and the Way Out.* London: International Headquarters of the Salvation Army, 1890.

————. *Training of Children.* London: Salvation Army, 1888.

———.*The Vagrant and Unemployable.* London: Salvation Army, 1909

Richard Collier. *The General Next to God: The Story of William Booth and the Salvation Army.* New York: Dutton, 1965.

Ervine St. John. *God's Soldier: General William Booth.* New York: Macmillan, 1935.

Norman E. Nygaard. *Trumpet of Salvation: The Story of William and Catherine Booth.* Grand Rapids, MI: Zondervan, 1961.

Harold C. Steele. *I Was a Stranger: The Faith of William Booth: Founder of the Salvation Army.* New York: Exposition, 1954.

Charles Loring Brace (1826–1890)

Charles Loring Brace. *The Best Method of Disposing of Our Pauper and Vagrant Children.* New York: Wynkoop, Hallenbeck and Thomas, 1859.

———. *The Dangerous Classes of New York and Twenty Years Among Them.* 1880. Reprint. Silver Spring, MD: National Association of Social Workers, 1978.

———. *The Life of Charles Loring Brace.* Emma Brace, ed. New York: Arno, 1976.

Sophonisba Preston Breckenridge (1866–1948)

Sophonisba Breckenridge. *Women in the 20th Century.* 1933.

——— and Edith Abbott. *The Delinquent Child and the Home.* New York: Survey Associates, 1912.

——— and Edith Abbott. *The Housing Problem in Chicago.* Chicago: University of Chicago Press, 1910–1915.

St. Frances Cabrini (1850–1917)

Lucille Papin Borden. *Francesca Cabrini.* New York: Macmillan, 1945.

Pietro Di Donato. *Immigrant Saint: The Life of Mother Cabrini.* New York: St. Martin's, 1991.

Dorothy Day (1897–1980)

Dorothy Day. *From Union Square to Rome.* New York: Arno Press, 1978.

———. *Little by Little: Selected Writings of Dorothy Day.* Maryknoll, NY: Orbis Books, 1992.

———. *Loaves and Fishes.* Maryknoll, NY: Orbis Books, 1997.

———. *The Long Loneliness: Autobiography of Dorothy Day.* San Francisco: Harper, 1981.

———. *On Pilgrimage.* Grand Rapids, MI: W. B. Eerdmans, 1999.

———. *On Pilgrimage: The Sixties.* New York: Curtis Books, 1972.

———. *Selections From her Writings.* Michael Garvey, ed. Springfield, MD: Templegate, 1996.

Michele Teresa Aronica. *Beyond Charismatic Leadership: The New York Catholic Worker Movement.* New Brunswick, NJ: Transaction Books, 1987.

Robert Coles. *Dorothy Day: A Radical Devotion.* Reading, MA: Addison-Wesley, 1989.

David R. Collins. *Got a Penny? The Story of Dorothy Day.* Boston: Pauline Books and Media, 1996.

Marie Dennis. *A Retreat With Oscar Romero and Dorothy Day: Walking With the Poor.* Cincinnati, OH: St. Anthony Messenger Press, 1997.

James S. Forest. *Love Is the Measure: A Biography of Dorothy Day.* Maryknoll, NY: Orbis Books, 1994.

Deborah Kent. *Dorothy Day: Friend to the Forgotten.* Grand Rapids, MI: W. B. Eerdmans, 1996.

William D. Miller. *Dorothy Day: A Biography.* San Francisco: Harper and Row, 1982.

June O'Connor. *The Moral Vision of Dorothy Day: A Feminist Perspective.* New York: Crossroad, 1991.

Nancy Roberts. *Dorothy Day and the Catholic Worker.* Albany: State University of New York Press, 1984.

Dorothea Lynde Dix (1802–1887)

Dorothea Lynde Dix. *Asylum, Prison, and Poorhouse: The Writings and Reform Work of Dorothea Dix in Illinois.* David L. Lightner, ed. Carbondale: Southern Illinois University Press, 1999.

———. *The Lady and the President: The Letters of Dorothea Dix and Millard Fillmore.* Charles M. Snyder, ed. Lexington: University Press of Kentucky, 1975.

————. *On Behalf of the Insane Poor: Selected Reports.* New York: Arno Press, 1971.

————. *Remarks on Prisons and Prison Discipline in the U.S.* Montclair, NJ: Patterson Smith, 1984.

Thomas J. Brown. *Dorothea Dix: New England Reformer.* Cambridge, MA: Harvard University Press, 1998.

Penny Colman. *Breaking the Chains: The Crusade of Dorothea Lynde Dix.* White Hall, VA: Shoe Tree Press, 1992.

David Gollaher. *Voice for the Mad: the Life of Dorothea Dix.* New York: Free Press, 1995.

Frederick Herrmann. *Dorothea L. Dix and the Politics of Institutional Reform.* Trenton NJ: New Jersey Historical Commission, 1981.

Helen E. Marshall. *Dorothea Dix: Forgotten Samaritan.* New York: Russell and Russell, 1967.

Charles Schaifer and Lucy Freeman. *Heart's Work: Civil War Heroine and Champion of the Mentally Ill, Dorothea Lynde Dix.* New York: Paragon House, 1991.

Francis Tiffany. *Life of Dorothea Dix.* Ann Arbor, MI: Plutarch Press, 1971.

Dorothy Clarke Wilson. *Stranger and Traveler: The Story of Dorothea Dix, American Reformer.* Boston: Little, Brown, 1975.

W.E.B. Du Bois (1868–1963)

W.E.B (William Edward Burghart) Du Bois. *The Autobiography of W.E.B. Du Bois.* Reprint. New York: International Publishers, 1968.

————. *Against Racism: Unpublished Essays, Papers Addresses 1887–1961.* Herbert Aptheker, ed. Amherst: University of Massachusetts Press, 1985.

————. *In Battle for Peace.* Millwood, NY: Kraus-Thomson, 1976.

————. *Black Reconstruction in America 1860–1880.* New York: Atheneum, 1992.

————. *The Correspondence of W.E.B. Du Bois.* Herbert Apthecker, ed. Amherst: University of Massachusetts Press, 1973.

————. *Darkwater: Voices From Within the Veil.* Mineola, NY: Dover, 1999.

————. *Dusk of Dawn: An Essay Toward an Autobiography of a Race Concept.* New Brunswick: Transaction Books, 1984.

————. *The Emerging Thought of W.E.B. Du Bois: Essays and Editorials From the Crisis.* New York: Simon and Schuster, 1972.

————. *The Gift of Black Folk.* Millwood, NY: Kraus-Thomson, 1975.

————. *The Negro.* Mineola, NY: Dover, 2000.

————. *The Negro American Family.* Cambridge: MIT Press, 1970.

————. *The Oxford W.E.B. Du Bois Reader.* New York: Oxford University Press, 1996.

————. *W.E.B. Du Bois: A Reader.* David Lewis, ed. New York: Holt, 1995.

————. *Souls of Black Folk.* Las Vegas, NV: Classic Americana, 1997.

————. *The Writings of W.E.B. Du Bois.* New York: Crowell, 1975.

Herbert Aptheker. *The Literary Legacy of W.E.B. Du Bois.* White Plains, NY: Kraus International, 1989.

Francis L. Broderick. *W.E.B. Du Bois: Negro Leader in a Time of Crisis.* Stanford, CA: Stanford University Press, 1959.

Seamus Cavan. *W.E.B. Du Bois and Racial Relations.* Brookfield, CT: Millbrook Press, 1993.

Joseph DeMarco. *The Social Thought of W.E.B. Du Bois.* Lanham, MD: University Press of America, 1983.

Virginia Hamilton. *W.E.B. Du Bois: A Biography.* New York: Harper-Row, 1972.

Gerald Horne and Mary Young, eds. *W.E.B. Du Bois: An Encyclopedia.* Westport CT: Greenwood, 2000.

Melissa McDaniel. *W.E.B. Du Bois: Scholar and Civil Rights Activist.* New York: Franklin Watts, 1999.

Kwadwo O. Pobi-Asamani. *W.E.B. Du Bois: His Contribution to Pan Africanism.* San Bernardino, CA: Borgo Press, 1994.

Mary Parker Follett (1868–1933)

Mary Parker Follett. *Creative Experience*, New York: Longmans, Green, 1924.

————. *Dynamic Administration: The Collected Papers of Mary Parker Follett.* Henry Metcalf and Luther Uwick, eds. London: Hippocrene Books, 1973.

———. *Freedom and Coordination: Lectures in Business Organization.* New York: Garland, 1987.

———. *The New State: Group Organization: The Solution of Popular Government.* University Park: Pennsylvania State University Press, 1998.

Pauline Graham, ed. *Mary Parker Follett—Prophet of Management: A Celebration of Writings From the 1920s.* Boston: Harvard Business School Press, 1995.

Homer Folks (1867–1963)

Homer Folks. *The Care of Destitute, Neglected and Delinquent Children.* New York: Arno, 1971.

———. *The Human Costs of War.* New York: Harper and Brothers, 1920.

Walter I. Trattner. *Homer Folks: Pioneer in Social Welfare.* New York: Columbia University Press, 1968.

Michael Harrington (1928–1989)

Michael Harrington. *The Other America: Poverty in the United States.* New York: Collier Books, 1994.

———. *The Accidental Century.* New York: Macmillan, 1965.

———. *Decade of Decision: The Crisis of the American System.* New York: Simon and Schuster, 1980.

———. *Fragments of the Century.* New York: Simon and Schuster, 1977.

———. *The Long Distance Runner: An Autobiography.* New York: Holt, 1988.

———. *The New American Poverty.* New York: Holt, 1984.

———. *The Next America: The Decline and Rise of the United States.* New York: Holt, 1981.

———. *The Vast Majority: A Journey to the World's Poor.* New York: Simon and Schuster, 1976.

Loren Okroi. *Galbraith, Harrington, Heilbroner: Economics and Dissent in an Age of Optimism.* Princeton, NJ: Princeton University Press, 1988.

Harry L. Hopkins (1890–1946)

Harry L. Hopkins. *Spending to Save: The Complete Story of Relief.* Seattle: University of Washington Press, 1972.

Henry Hitch Adams. *Harry Hopkins: A Biography.* New York: Putnam, 1977.

Searle F. Charles. *Minister of Relief: Harry Hopkins and the Depression.* Westport, CT: Greenwood, 1974.

June Hopkins. *Harry Hopkins: Sudden Hero, Brash Reformer.* New York: St. Martin's Press, 1999.

Paul Kurzman. *Harry Hopkins and the New Deal.* Fairlawn, NJ: Burdick, 1974.

George McJimsey. *Harry Hopkins: Ally of the Poor and Defender of Democracy.* Cambridge, MA: Harvard University Press, 1987.

Robert Sherwood. *Roosevelt and Hopkins: An Intimate History.* New York: Harper, 1950.

Dwight Matthew B. Wills. *Wartime Missions of Harry L. Hopkins.* Raleigh, NC: Pentland, 1996.

Toyohiko Kagawa (1888–1960)

Toyohiko Kagawa. *Behold the Man.* New York: Harper and Brothers 1941.

———. *Brotherhood Economics.* New York: Harper and Brothers, 1936.

———. *The Challenge of Redemptive Love.* New York: Abingdon Press, 1940.

———. *Living Out Christ's Love: Selected Writings of Toyohiko Kagawa.* Nashville, TN: Upper Room Books, 1998.

———. *Meditations on the Cross.* Chicago: Willett, Clark, 1935.

———. *Songs From the Slums: Poems by Toyohiko Kagawa.* Nashville, TN: Cokesbury Press, 1935.

William Axling. *Kagawa.* New York: Harper and Brothers, 1946.

Emerson Bradshaw. *Unconquerable Kagawa.* St. Paul, MN: Macalester Park Publishing, 1952.

Cyril J. Davey. *Kagawa of Japan.* New York: Abingdon Press, 1961.

Masao Takenaka. "The Impact of Kagawa and his Movement," *The Study of Christianity and Social Problems,* vol. 6, July 1993, pp. 55–99.

Robert Schildgen. *Toyohiko Kagawa: Apostle of Love and Social Justice.* Berkeley, CA: Centenary Books, 1988.

Jessie M. Trout, ed. *Kagawa: Japanese Prophet: His Witness in Life and Word.* New York: Association Press, 1960.

Florence Kelley (1859–1932)

Florence Kelley. *On the Inside.* New York: Sanford, 1890.

———. *Minimum Wage Laws*. New York: National Consumers League, 1912.

———. *Modern Industry in Relation to the Family, Health, Education, Morality*. Westport, CT: Hyperion, 1975.

———. *Some Ethical Gains Through Legislation*. New York: Arno, 1969.

———. *A Privileged Industry*. New York: National Consumers League, 1912.

———. *Wage-earning Women in War Time: The Textile Industry*. New York: National Consumers League, 1919.

———. *The Working Child*. Chicago: Hollister, 1986.

Dorothy Rose Blumberg. *Florence Kelley: The Making of a Social Pioneer*. New York: Augustus M. Kelley, 1966.

Josephine Goldmark. *Impatient Crusader: Florence Kelley's Life Story*. Westport, CT: Greenwood, 1976.

Katherine Kish Sklar. *Florence Kelley and the Nation's Work*. New Haven: Yale University Press, 1995.

Martin Luther King Jr. (1929–1968)

Martin Luther King Jr. *Strength to Love*. New York: Harper and Row, 1968.

———. *Stride Toward Freedom: The Montgomery Story*. New York: Harper and Brothers, 1958.

———. *The Trumpet of Conscience*. New York: Harper and Row, 1968.

———. *Where Do We Go From Here: Chaos or Community?* New York: Harper and Row, 1967.

———. *Why We Can't Wait*. New York: New American Library, 1964.

John J. Ansbro. *Martin Luther King Jr.: The Making of a Mind*. Maryknoll, NY: Orbis, 1982.

David J. Garrow. *Bearing the Cross: Martin Luther King Jr. and the Southern Christian Leadership Conference*. New York: William Morrow, 1986.

Lerone Bennett Jr. *What Manner of Man: A Biography of Martin Luther King Jr.* Chicago: Johnson Publishing, 1968.

Thomas C. Clemens. *Martin Luther King: Man of Peace*. Washington, DC: USIA, 1965.

Bennie E. Goodwin. *Dr. Martin Luther King Jr.: God's Messenger of Love, Justice and Hope*. Jersey City, NJ: Goodpatrick, 1976.

James P. Hanigan. *Martin Luther King Jr. and the Foundations of Nonviolence*. Lanham, MD: University Press of America, 1984.

Walton Hanes Jr. *Political Philosophy of Martin Luther King Jr.* Westport, CT: Greenwood, 1971.

William D Watley. *Roots of Resistance: The Nonviolent Ethic of Martin Luther King Jr.* Valley Forge, PA: Judson Press, 1985.

Bertha Capen Reynolds (1885–1978)

Bertha Capen Reynolds. *Between Client and Community: A Study in Responsibility in Social Case Work*. New York: Oriole, 1973.

———. *Learning and Teaching in the Practice of Social Work*. Silver Spring, MD: NASW Press, 1985.

———. *Social Work and Social Living: Explorations in Philosophy and Practice*. New York: Citadel Press, 1951.

———. *An Uncharted Journey: Fifty Years of Growth in Social Work*. Silver Spring, MD: NASW Press, 1991.

St. Elizabeth Ann Seton (1774–1821)

Elizabeth Ann Seton. *Collected Writings*. Regina Bechtle, Judith Metz, eds. Hyde Park, NY: New City Press, 2000.

Joseph I. Dirvin. *Mrs. Seton: Foundress of the American Sisters of Charity*. New York: Farrar, Straus and Giroux, 1975.

Leonard Feeny. *Mother Seton: Saint Elizabeth of New York*. Cambridge, MA: Ravengate Press, 1991.

Sr. Mary Celeste. *The Intimate Friendships of Elizabeth Ann Bayley Seton, First Native-Born American Saint*. Lanham, MD: University Press of America, 2000.

Alma Power-Waters. *Mother Seton: First American-Born Saint*. New York: Pocket Books, 1976.

Lord Shaftesbury (Anthony Ashley Cooper) (1801–1885)

Georgina Battiscombe. *Shaftesbury: The Great Reformer: 1801–1885*. Boston: Houghton Mifflin, 1975.

Barbara Blackburn. *Noble Lord: The Life of the Seventh Earl of Shaftesbury.* London: Home and Van Thal, 1949.

Mary Simkhovitch (1867–1951)

Mary K. Simkhovitch. *The City Worker's World in America.* New Salem, NH: Ayer, 1971.

———. *The Church and Public Housing.* New York: Department of Christian Social Service, National Council, 1934.

———. *Group Life.* New York: Association Press, 1940.

———. *Neighborhood: My Story of Greenwich House.* New York: Norton, 1938. Reprint. New Salem, NH: Ayer, n. d.

———. *Quicksand: The Way of Life in the Slums.* Evanston, IL: Row, Peterson, 1942.

———. *The Red Festival.* Milwaukee, WI: Morehouse, 1934.

Graham Taylor (1851–1938)

Graham R Taylor. *Chicago Commons Through Forty Years.* Chicago, IL: University of Chicago Press, 1936.

———. *Pioneering on Social Frontiers.* New York: Arno Press, 1976.

———. *Religion in Social Action.* New York: Dodd, Mead, 1913.

Louise C. Wade. *Graham Taylor: Pioneer for Social Justice.* Chicago: University of Chicago Press, 1964.

Sojourner Truth (1797–1883)

Catherine Bernard. *Sojourner Truth: Abolitionist and Women's Rights Activist.* Berkeley Heights, NJ: Enslow, 2001.

Jacqueline Bernard. *Journey Toward Freedom: The Story of Sojourner Truth.* New York: Norton, 1967. Reprint. New York: Feminist Press, 1990.

Arthur H. Fauset. *Sojourner Truth: God's Faithful Pilgrim.* New York: Russell and Russell, 1971.

Suzanne P. Fitch. *Sojourner Truth as Orator: Wit, Story and Song.* Westport, CT: 1997.

Carleton Mabee. *Sojourner Truth: Slave, Prophet, Legend.* New York: New York University Press, 1993.

Olive Gilbert. *Narrative of Sojourner Truth: A Bondswoman of Olden Time with a History of her Labors and Correspondence.* New York: Penguin, 1998.

Nell Irvin Painter. *Sojourner Truth: A Life, a Symbol.* New York: W. W. Norton, 1996.

Erlene Stetson. *Glorying in Tribulation: The Lifework of Sojourner Truth.* East Lansing: Michigan State University Press, 1994.

Margaret Washington. *The Narrative of Sojourner Truth.* New York: Vintage Books, 1993.

Harriett Tubman (1820-1913)

Sarah H. Bradford. *Harriet Tubman: The Moses of Her People.* Magnolia, MA: Peter Smith, n. d.

Dan Elish. *Harriet Tubman and the Underground Railroad.* Brookfield, CT: Millbrook Press, 1993.

Ann Petry. *Harriet Tubman: Conductor on the Underground Railroad.* New York: Crowell, 1955.

Lillian Wald (1867–1940)

Lillian Wald. *The House on Henry Street.* New York: Holt, 1915. Reprint. New Brunswick, NJ: Transaction, 1991.

———. *Windows on Henry Street.* Boston: Little, Brown, 1934.

Clare Coss. *Lillian D. Wald: Progressive Activist.* New York: Feminist Press at the City University of New York, 1989.

Doris Daniels. *Always a Sister: The Feminism of Lillian D. Wald.* New York: Feminist Press at the City University of New York, 1989.

Robert Duffus. *Lillian Wald: Neighbor and Crusader.* New York: Macmillan, 1938.

Alberta Eiseman. *Rebels and Reformers: Biographies of Four Jewish Americans.* Garden City, NY: Zenith Books, 1976.

Beatrice Siegel. *Lillian Wald of Henry Street.* New York: Macmillan, 1983.

Sir George Williams (1821–1905)

J. E. Hodder-Williams. *The Life of Sir George Williams: Founder of The Young Men's Christian Association.* New York: Association Press, 1915.

E. G. Lentz. *George Williams: A Tribute to the Founder of the Red Triangle.* Carbondale: Illinois Area YMCA, 1959.

Cecil B. A. Northcoat. *Sir George Williams: Founder of the YMCA.* London: Religious Tract Society, n. d.

GETTING A JOB, BECOMING A VOLUNTEER, DOING AN INTERNSHIP

Macro social work presents a compelling opportunity to become involved at the grassroots level where it really matters and to assist people with issues about which they are vitally concerned. It offers an array of possibilities to use your skills, expand your horizons, and deepen your life experiences as your journey leads you onward. There is an arena in macro social work waiting for you to seek new challenges, and find new ways to help people and to create a better world.

If this book has inspired an interest in macro social work, the best way for you to discover whether you are meant for this field is to get involved in it personally. In Appendix A, you will find a listing of volunteer agencies. Appendix B contains a list of the names, addresses, and phone numbers of many social organizations that could offer an internship or job possibility. Contact one or more today. Find out if there is a future for you as a macro social worker. Another resource is the Guidestar website (http//www.guidestar.org) which contains information on 700,000 nonprofit and social organizations, and has continuously updated listings of paid and volunteer positions available.

CONCLUSION

While devotion to the individual has grown in professional social work, its active participation in solving social problems has tended to shrink, diverting "social work from its original mission and vision of the perfectibility of society."[4] In spite of these trends away from macro oriented practice, the field of macro social work has a unique opportunity to reclaim its heritage as the profession committed to community enrichment and conceiving a society that is ethically good as well as economically prosperous.

You too can add your name to the list of those social workers who saw a better future and gave their lives to bring hope and possibility, and to defeat oppression and injustice.

EXERCISE 16.1

A Renewed Ethical Code

One of the hallmarks of a renewed social work is its substantive ethical base. This exercise will help you exercise your ethical thinking skills. Write down at least five of the most important ethical values that you think the profession of macro social work ought to espouse. In triads, share your lists and come up with a composite list. In class, compare your lists with the one that follows. Then, develop an ethical code that can guide the field of macro social work.

A Proposed Ethical Code

Macro social workers work to create a society that aims toward the truth, seeks justice, and becomes good. As we seek those values, there are a number of principles to which we attend.

1. Macro social workers challenge society to be everything that it can potentially become, while living with the reality of conditions as they are.

2. Macro social workers must have the courage and the will to challenge those forces that condone, perpetuate, or cause human suffering.

3. Macro social workers speak for those who cannot speak for themselves, advocate for those who have no voice, seek empowerment for the powerless and well-being for those whose lives are deprived.

4. Where required, macro social workers stand outside the social consensus, shatter norms, and challenge the status quo. We may refuse to participate in social processes or systems that are destructive to the human condition.

5. Macro social workers value and seek to rekindle in the life of society a sense of authentic community, a substantive conception of democracy, economic justice, and a way of ethical reason in which individuals realize their potential. We have a vision of and a desire to restore community among people.

6. Macro social workers are committed to society's future. We work to bring about the very best that

society can become, even when it actively resists becoming that best. We try to bring new creative energies to bear on society, forging a pathway to its future.

7. Macro social workers are against death makers, violence, and destruction. We fight against oppression of people and of the human spirit wherever they occur. We are against greed and avarice, compulsive exploitation, ruthless competition, and mindless individualism. We are against dehumanizing social systems and the divisiveness that undermines others.

8. Macro social workers are against deception that saps the human spirit. We fight against denial in any of its forms. We question the conventional wisdom of our age when it promotes injustice, poverty, inequality, powerlessness, and helplessness.

EXERCISE 16.2

Critiquing Social Work's Mission

Specht and Courtney make a claim about what they believe ought to be the mission of social work that places community at its center. They state

Social work's mission should be to build a meaning, a purpose and a sense of obligation for the community. It is only by creating a community that we establish a basis for commitment, obligation, and social support. We must build communities that are excited about their child care systems, that find it exhilarating to care for the mentally ill and the frail aged, and make demands upon people to behave, to contribute, and to care for one another. Psychotherapy will not enable us to do that, and the farther down the psychotherapeutic path social workers go, the less effective they will be in achieving their true mission.[5]

This statement implies that the profession of social work is on the wrong path, and that its current emphasis on clinical treatment is inappropriate. Break into triads and discuss this statement. In your triads, reflect on the following questions. After the class reassembles, come to some conclusions about social work's mission and the place of macro social work vs. micro social work.

1. What are the strengths of Specht and Courtney's argument?

2. What are its limitations?

3. Do you agree with their assessment of the mission of social work? If so, why? If not, what do you think the mission of the social work profession ought to be?

4. What role do you think communal social work ought to play in the social work profession?

5. What role do you think psychotherapy ought to play in social work?

EXERCISE 16.3

Life Journey

In Chapter 1, I described my life journey. In this exercise you will have an opportunity to explore your own life journey and project it ahead into the future. You may want to review my life journey to grasp some of the important events. On a blank piece of paper, draw your life journey so far. Start as far back as you can remember and stop at the present time. Draw your journey as a graph. The peaks are to represent the highs in your life—successes, achievements, accomplishments, and goals met. They can also be personal issues resolved, or relational, spiritual, career, or other high points. The level spots represent periods of evenness, transition, and steadiness. The valleys represent the lows, periods of hurt or crisis, struggle, or defeat.

Next to each peak, write a word or two identifying the peak experience. Do the same for the plains and the valleys.

Go back over each peak. For each peak, make a few notes on why this was a peak experience for you. Put your approximate age at the time of the peak and what the experience helped you learn or accomplish. Do the same for the plains and valleys.

Analyze your notes.

1. What themes and patterns are revealed by your life journey?

2. What important personal strengths are revealed?

3. What do these themes and patterns tell you about what you are likely to find personally compelling about the future?

As you review your journey, project your journey ahead.

1. What do you expect it will be?

2. Where are you going next on your journey?

3. What is your vision of your future?

4. What role do you see yourself playing in the field of social work?

5. What role, if any, does macro social work play in your future career?

Form into groups of four. In your group, compare your life journeys. Make a list of the common peaks, plains, and valleys. Hand these in to the instructor. While the instructor is charting these on the board, discuss the commonalities and differences of your life journeys. Come to some conclusion about the patterns and try to name any similarities that you can see. Out of your discussion, draw a group life journey that traces those common patterns.

Discussion Questions

The instructor reassembles the class and leads a discussion of the following questions.

1. What have you learned about your past and the future direction of your life?

2. What kinds of experiences have affected you and the direction of your life?

3. What role or roles in social work does your life journey indicate?

4. What kinds of values are the most important in your life journey?

5. What kind of life world are you creating for yourself?

EXERCISE 16.4

The Stance of a Macro Social Worker

In Chapter 1 you may have completed Checklist 1.2 The Stance of a Macro Social Worker. Without looking at your previous responses and without trying to remember your answers, quickly rate each of the following questions. Do not think deeply or meditate about what is the best answer. Rate the questions quickly so as to give your unconscious intuition a chance to operate. This will give you your best self-assessment. On a scale of 1–5 with 1 being the lowest and 5 the highest, mark the ones that are especially meaningful for you, placing them in the columns below. For example, if the statement describes you to a high degree, assign a 5. If it is generally descriptive,

assign it a 4. If it is sometimes descriptive of you, give it a 3. If it rarely is descriptive of you, give it a 2. If it is not descriptive of you, give it a 1.

It is important for me to:

1. Take part in a movement to bring an end to injustice.

2. Become involved with a community and help mold the destiny of a people.

3. Use my vision to look for possibilities in the future.

4. Shape a system in the here and now over the long term.

5. Gather information and facts to correct dishonesty or deceit.

6. Develop relationships strengthening communities or organizations.

7. Exert my creativity and ability to see the big picture to try out something new.

8. Fix a broken system by applying my technical skills.

9. Help the underdog obtain redress and empower the powerless.

10. Engage others in constructing a social world and forging social bonds.

11. Be a part of something positive that is larger than myself.

12. Make a tangible contribution by implementing concrete decisions today.

13. Get involved in social action and social justice.

14. Get involved in building community or neighborhood.

15. Get involved in developing new programs, plans, or projects.

16. Get involved in making things happen by implementing the details of decisions.

Place your scores for each sentence in the following columns and add up your answers at the bottom.

A	B	C	D
1 ____	2 ____	3 ____	4 ____
5 ____	6 ____	7 ____	8 ____
9 ____	10 ____	11 ____	12 ____
13 ____	14 ____	15 ____	16 ____
SA/SP	**CD/OD**	**PD/PL**	**AD/R**

If you scored highest in column A, you may have more interest in either social action or social policy analysis. If you scored highest in column B, you may have more aptitude in the areas of community or organization development. If you were higher in column C, you might have more interest in either program development or social planning. Those of you who were higher in column D could be better at either administration or social research.

Compare your scores with those in Chapter 1. Are they generally the same or are they different? If they are different, what do they say about your motivation and stance as a macro social worker now that you have finished the course? Compare your rankings with those of others in class. Have the ratings of others changed? If so, how?

EXERCISE 16.5
Unfinished Business

You will have an opportunity to express any questions, issues, or concerns that remain unresolved. Your instructor will ask you to reflect on the course as a whole and make a list of issues, questions, and concerns that remain unanswered or unresolved and bring them to class. Form into triads. Combine similar issues and rank the list in order. List the issues on the board. The instructor reassembles the class. Similar issues are combined. The instructor leads a general class discussion and responds to as many issues as time allows, bringing closure to issues of importance to class members. The instructor collects the lists and may respond individually as needed to those issues that were not addressed in class.

EXERCISE 16.6
Final Self-Assessment

You will assess the learning that you have achieved in the course. Your instructor will ask you to review your original and/or revised individual contracts. Reexamine your personal learning objectives. Evaluate the extent to which you were able to meet your objectives by listing:

Learning Activities
These can include reading the text, additional outside reading, completing checklists, debates, forums, dis-

cussions, writing papers, engaging in field experiences, experiential exercises, and others.

Major Achievements
For example, obtaining the grades you aimed at, finishing papers on time, obtaining a field placement, finding a job or volunteer position in macro social work, or finishing reading and reporting on a major book in macro social work.

Kinds of Learning Acquired

1. Learning about yourself: personality functions, leadership functions and abilities, membership skills, personal journey, and motivation as a macro social worker.

2. Learning about macro social work: problem-solving, social thinking methods, skills in leading groups, writing idea statements, doing research, history, decision techniques, macro social work heroes.

3. Learning about process: forming a group, leading, decision-making or problem-solving skills, how to work with communities, organizations, or society as a whole.

Assessment of Capacities

1. What are your strengths?
2. What areas do you want to develop more?
3. Where do you go from here?

Objectives
Using the information above, develop a set of education/career goals.

1. What is your career objective?
2. How will you reach this objective?
3. What additional education/training/graduate school will you need?
4. What kinds of jobs will you need to look for?

Bring your self-assessments to class, form into triads, and review your lists. Share activities, achievements, learning, capacities, and objectives. Give the self-assessments to your instructor, who may use them for giving personal feedback, making observations, and giving encouragement, support, or affirmation.

EXERCISE 16.7
Career Goals

One of the goals of this course is to stimulate your interest in the field of macro social work as a career. This exercise will assist you to clarify your career goals and the place of macro social work as part of those goals.

Career planning involves resolving the following issues: (1) determining where you are now, (2) deciding where you want to be, and (3) developing a plan for getting where you want to be.

Prepare a list of career and life goals including:

1. professional goals
2. personal goals, including educational, artistic, cultural, self-expression, awareness expansion, personal fulfillment
3. relational goals, including social, friendship, marital, community relationships

In class, form into dyads. One person will play the role of consultant and the other consultee. The consultant and consultee clarify the lists, examine them for consistency, and prioritize them. Partners reverse roles and the process is repeated.

Individually, both partners make another list: (1) things that bring the most satisfaction, (2) accomplishments that each person is proud of, and (3) experiences that are least satisfying or ones to be avoided.

Form into the same consultant/consultee dyads. The consultant and consultee review lists for consistency, conflicts, or discontinuities between the lists. Roles are reversed and the second consultation round is carried out.

Based on new information, reformulate or reorder your goals. Develop a plan of action indicating the steps you must take to get from where you are to where you would like to be.

EXERCISE 16.8
The Gift of Feedback

You will have an opportunity to share feelings and give closure to the course experience. This closure exercise is especially useful for classes in which there were a lot of experiential sharing and engagement. This exercise allows you and your instructor to offer positive feedback on the learning you have acquired from one another. Your instructor has an opportunity to share his or her feelings about you, give a final assessment, and say goodbye.

This exercise is best accomplished when the class size is no more than 20. If the class is larger or if task groups were used in the class, then subgroups can be used.

Your instructor will ask you to think about the things you have learned from *each* person in the group, including the instructor, and answer the question, "What will I take from this person when I leave the class?" These should be positive things. Outside of class, write your feelings in the form of a signed letter for each person in the class. Place each letter in an envelope with the person's name on the outside (or fold the letters and put each person's name on the outside), and bring the letters to class. Form into a circle, distribute your "mail" to one another, and silently read your mail.

Your instructor will ask you to choose one of the letters that was most memorable and read it to the class members or to reflect on the impact you have had on others in the class and to offer feedback to the class on your learning experience. Finally, the instructor offers to read one or two pieces of his or her mail and share reflections about the class members, the learning experience, and what he or she will take from this class as a whole, bringing closure to the class experience.

ADDITIONAL READING

History of Psychotherapy

Walter Bromberg. *Man Above Humanity: A History of Psychotherapy.* Philadelphia: J. B. Lippincott, 1954.

Jan Ehrenwald. *Psychotherapy: Myth and Method.* New York: Graune and Stratton, 1966.

Jerome Frank. *Persuasion and Healing: A Comparative Study of Psychotherapy.* Baltimore: Johns Hopkins University Press, 1973.

Thomas K. Freedheim, ed. *History of Psychotherapy: A Century of Change.* Washington, DC: American Psychological Association, 1991.

Thomas S. Szasz. *The Manufacture of Madness: A Comparative Study of the Inquisition and the Mental Health Movement.* New York: Harper and Row, 1970.

Critiques of Psychotherapy

Paul Halmos. *The Faith of Counselors.* New York: Schocken Books, 1966.

Perry London. *The Modes and Morals of Psychotherapy.* 2d ed. New York: Hemisphere Publishing, 1986.

O. Hobart Mowrer. *The Crisis of Psychiatry and Religion.* Princeton, NJ: Van Nostrand, 1961.

Philip Rieff. *The Triumph of the Therapeutic: Uses of Faith After Freud.* New York: Harper and Row, 1966.

William Schofield. *Psychotherapy: The Purchase of Friendship.* Englewood Cliffs, NJ: Prentice-Hall, 1964.

Heroes of Social Work

Clarke A. Chambers. *Paul U. Kellogg and the Survey: Voices for Social Welfare and Social Justice.* Minneapolis: University of Minnesota Press, 1971.

Robin McKown. *Pioneers in Mental Health.* New York: Dodd, Mead, 1961.

Herbert Stroup. *Social Welfare Pioneers.* Chicago: Nelson-Hall, 1986.

Heinz VonHoff. *People Who Care: An Illustrated History of Human Compassion.* Philadelphia: Fortress Press, 1971.

Mary Ormsbee Whitton. *These Were the Women: USA, 1776–1860.* New York: Hastings House, 1954.

Altruism and Caring

George Bach and Laura Torbet. *A Time for Caring.* New York: Delacourte, 1982.

Allen Luks and Peggy Payne. *The Healing Power of Doing Good.* New York: Fawcett, 1992.

Samuel P. Oliner and Pearl M. Oliner. *The Altruistic Personality: Rescuers of the Jews in Nazi Europe.* New York: Free Press, 1988.

Milton Meltzer. *Who Cares? Millions Do: A Book About Altruism.* New York: Walker, 1994.

Richard Zimmerman. *What Can I Do to Make a Difference? A Positive Action Source Book.* New York: Plume, 1991.

Roy Lubove. *The Professional Altruist: The Emergence of Social Work as a Career, 1880–1930.* New York: Atheneum, 1969.

APPENDIX A

Volunteer and Job Opportunities

I don't know what your destiny will be, but one thing I do know: the only ones among you who will be really happy are those who have sought and found how to serve.
Albert Schweitzer

Those who train many in the ways of justice will sparkle like stars for all eternity.
Daniel 12:3

Volunteer and Job Opportunities

The best way to understand about social work in general and macro social work in particular is to work in a social organization. Not only is volunteering a satisfying experience, but you will begin your career of giving service to others. The more you gain experience, the more skilled you become. Begin now. Find out about the fulfilling and exciting experiences that await you. You might discover a possibility for using one of these social organizations as an internship.

Volunteer Organizations

Fourth World Movement—USA, 7000 Willow Hill Dr., Landover, MD 20785, Tel. 301-336-9489, Fax: 301-336-0092, e-mail: 4thworld@his.com (see description, Appendix B, Chapter 2).

Revitalization Corps, PO Box 1625, Hartford, CT 06101, Tel. 203-249-7523. Founded in 1964, the Revitalization Corps assists suburban families, college students, and others to become personally involved in the problems of the inner city.

Points of Light Foundation, 1737 H St. NW, Washington, DC 20006, Tel. 202-223-9186, Fax: 202-223-9256. Founded in 1990, PIF maintains a network of 400 affiliated volunteer, technical assistance, and training centers. Publications include *News From the Points of Light Foundation, Volunteer Action Leadership* (a quarterly magazine), and *Volunteer Readership Catalog of Publications.*

Volunteers in Service to America (VISTA), 1100 Vermont Ave. NW, Suite 8100, Washington, DC 20525, Tel. 202-606-4845, Fax: 202-606-4921. Founded in 1964 as part of the War on Poverty, VISTA is a national volunteer organization administered by ACTION, an independent government agency. Volunteers serve in areas of drug abuse, literacy, runaway youth, neighborhood revitalization, and economic development in the United States, Puerto Rico, the Virgin Islands, and Guam. They are provided with health insurance, a basic subsistence allowance, and stipend upon completion of service.

International Volunteer Service, Overseas Development Network (ODN), 333 Valencia St., Suite 330, San Francisco, CA 94103, Tel. 415-431-4204, Fax: 415-431-5953, e-mail: odn@igc.org, http://www. igc.apc.org/odn. Founded in 1983, ODN is a national, student-based, nonprofit organization addressing global issues such as hunger, poverty, and social injustice through grassroots development projects in the United States and overseas. Publications include *Development Opportunities Catalog,* a guide of internships, volunteer work and employment opportunities with development organizations, *A Handbook for Creating Your Own Internship in Community Development, Global Links Newsletter, and Education for Action,* a guide to progressive graduate programs in community development.

International Opportunities Clearinghouse, Overseas Development Network (ODN), 333 Valencia St., Suite 330, San Francisco, CA 94103, Tel. 415-431-4204, Fax: 415-431-5953, e-mail: odn@igc.org, http://www.igc.apc.org/odn. The research and referral service will provide you with an application questionnaire. Return this questionnaire and a research fee and you will be provided with referrals to organizations, along with publications such as *A Handbook for Creating Your Own Internship in International Development, Guide to Fundraising for Grassroots Development,* and advice sheets with tips on fundraising, preparing for your trip, and planning your return.

International Voluntary Services, 1424 16th St. NW, Suite 603, Washington, DC 20036-2211, Tel. 202-387-5533, Fax: 202-387-4234. Founded in 1953, IVS provides skilled technicians in Bolivia, Cambodia, Ecuador, Bangladesh, Thailand, and Vietnam.

National Service League, 821 N. Broadway, Irvington, NY 10533-1232, Tel. 914-591-5168. Founded in 1990, the service places volunteers ages 18–24 in community service programs. After four months of training with U.S. corporate, elected, and community leaders in fields such as computers, journalism, business management, marketing, and the environment, volunteers are assigned to projects in Central Europe for eight months.

Brethren Volunteer Service, 1451 Dundee Ave., Elgin, IL 60120, Tel. 847-742-5100, Fax: 847-742-6103, e-mail: COB-BVSparti@Ecunet.com. Founded in 1948, BVS sends people 18 years of age and over for a year of service in the United States or two years overseas, working with children, senior citizens, community services, disabled, street people, prisoners, and in areas of hunger, peace, domestic violence, housing, health care, and community development. Volunteers receive room and board, medical expenses, and a monthly allowance. Publications include *Brethren Volunteer Service Projects Booklet.*

Council of Religious Volunteer Agencies, c/o Jack F. Reents, Lutheran World Mission Volunteers, 8765 W. Higgins Rd., Chicago, IL 60631, Tel. 312-380-2631, Fax: 312-380-2410. Founded in 1946, CRVA prepares a catalog of service opportunities, including work camps, community services, institutional service, and individual service in the United States and abroad sponsored by 200 private organizations. Publications include *Volunteer,* a semiannual publication about volunteer opportunities.

SCI-International Voluntary Service, Route CI 2, Box 506, Crozet, VA 22932, Tel. 804-823-1826, Fax: 804-823-5027. Founded in 1920, SCI operates in 24 countries in economic development, peace, work refugees, emergency service, work, and study camps. Volunteer programs in the United States are carried out from New York to California and last two to three weeks. Publications include *Service Civil International USA Workcamp Listing* and *Workcamp News.*

Winant and Clayton Volunteers, 109 E. 50th St., New York, NY 10022, Tel. 212-751-1616. Founded in 1948, WCV is named for John Winant, U.S. Ambassador to England, and Rev. Dr. P. B. (Tubby) Clayton, Chaplain to the Queen. WCV places U.S. volunteers in British social work agencies, youth clubs, correctional institutions, mental health centers, and programs assisting the homeless and persons with AIDS. British volunteers are placed in U.S. social work and social service agencies. Volunteers pay their own transportation to and from Great Britain but receive free room and board while they work.

Institute for Food and Development Policy (FoodFirst), 398 60th St., Oakland, CA 94618, Tel. 510-654-4400, Fax: 510-654-4551, e-mail: foodfirst@ igc.apc.org (see Appendix B, Chapter 14).

Peace Corps, P-301, Washington, DC 20526, Tel. 800-424-8580; United Nations, United Nations Headquarters, New York, NY 10017, Tel. 212-963-1234 (see Appendix B, Chapter 15).

Jobs

Guidestar: lists over 700,000 continuously updated organizations, including listings of paid and volunteer job opportunities and possible internships. http//: www.guidestar.org.

USA Jobs: best Internet source for information about federal jobs. Lists of federal job openings, updated daily. Search the listings by type of job, location, and pay level, then apply online. Also information about searching for a federal job, student employment, outplacement assistance, and more. http://www.usajobs. opm.gov; e-mail: usajobs_webmaster@opm.gov.

Additional Reading

Allen Jedlicka. *Volunteerism and World Development: Pathway to a New World.* New York: Praeger, 1990.

APPENDIX B

How to Get Involved

The "I" that does not want to get involved is something less than an individual.
If an individual has an identity and not just an identification, a personality and not
merely a complex of data to be fed into a computer, is not isolated from others
but open to them, not encapsulated, but sharing common concerns—you are in a word,
involved.... The more we are involved with others the more of an individual [each
of us] become[s].[1]

Abraham Kaplan

*H*ere is a listing of only a few social agencies, social organizations, and services utilized by or integral to the practice of macro social work.[2] This listing testifies to the vibrant, growing activity of macro social work practice and to the wealth of resources developed not only by macro social workers but by concerned and involved citizens. These social organizations continually rebuild the infrastructure of society, adding to the wealth of social capital without which our society would fail.

Contact as many of them as spark your interest. Write, phone, or e-mail to get more information or request their publications. Make financial contributions if you are able. Join one or more of them to become active and involved. Find out how you can volunteer. Visit them with your class or invite their staff or members to your class discussions. Find out about internship opportunities. Write a paper as a course project about one that interests you.

This list is not intended to be comprehensive, but only to give an indication of the huge number of social organizations with which macro social work engages. My apologies if any of the more important social organizations has inadvertently been omitted from this listing.

In addition to the hundreds of organizations listed in this appendix, please access Guidestar at http://www.guidestar. org. Guidestar is a nonprofit organization developed by Arthur "Buzz" Schmidt that lists 700,000 nonprofit social organizations. It is a great resource to find out more about specific organizations and displays the extraordinary number of resources, services, and programs that macro social workers use in planning, community development, community organization program development, social policy, and administration. It includes job listings and volunteer positions for students looking for jobs, internships, or volunteer opportunities. It provides opportunities for making charitable donations to nonprofit organizations, for teaching about nonprofit organizations, potential research, and conferences.

Chapter 1 Overview of the Practice of Macro Social Work

Association for Community Organization and Social Administration (ACOSA)

ACOSA was formed in 1987 to strengthen community organization and social administration in social work practice and education. ACOSA consists of organized activities and symposium sessions that have been a part of the annual program of the Council on Social Work Education (CSWE) since 1982.

The purposes of ACOSA are to facilitate and support an annual national symposium, provide a forum for sharing information on teaching, models, research and practice; facilitate networking among educators and practitioners; promote the development of community organization and social administration and to influence the direction of other +3professional associations in promoting community organization and social administration. ACOSA sponsors an annual symposium in conjunction with the Annual Program Meeting of the Council on Social Work Education (CSWE). Visit the ACOSA home page at http://www.acosa.org.

For information about membership in ACOSA, contact Terry Mizrahi, ACOSA, Hunter College, School of Social Work, 129 E. 79th St. New York, NY 10021. Fax: 212-452-7150 (e-mail: Tmizrahi@hunter. cuny.edu).

ACOSA publishes the *Journal of Community Practice,* a multidisciplinary journal designed to provide a forum for the development of research, theory, practice, and curriculum strategies for the full range of work with community groups, grassroots organizing, and interorganizational and interagency planning, collaboration, and coalition building. E-mail: jcomm@ email.unc.edu.

You can also join the ACSOA-L listserve to keep up to date with ACOSA and discussions of key issues. Send an e-mail request to listserv@wvnvm. wvnet.edu.

Bertha Capen Reynolds Society

Columbus Circle Station
PO Box 20563
New York, NY 10023

Founded in 1985, the Bertha Capen Reynolds Society is a national organization of progressive workers in social welfare dedicated to promoting collective and individual action and is formed around a set of 10 principles that are implemented at the national level and though the activity of local chapters in several cities throughout the country. Progressive social workers in BCRS chapters gather for discussions, study groups, and informal support. These processes typically lead to activism in local communities on wide-ranging social concerns. BCRS holds an annual national meeting where strategies for social change are proposed, skills for progressive practice are developed, and progressive views are affirmed and refined.[3]

Chapter 2 Social Problems and Social Change

Hundreds of thousands of social organizations and agencies in the United States and Canada exist, dealing with the vast array of social problems. For more information about local organizations, consult your local directory of social agencies or access Guidestar at http://www.guidestar.org. The small sampling in this list is only intended to give you an idea of the variety of issues with which macro social workers are involved, the kinds of programs they have developed, and the kind of work with which they are engaged.

Aging

National Council of Senior Citizens

1331 F St. NW
Washington, DC 20004-1171
202-347-8800
Fax: 202-624-9595
Founded in 1961. Assists with social and political action and sponsors the National Senior Citizens Education and Research Center.

The National Hispanic Council on Aging

2713 Ontario Rd., NW
Washington, DC 20009
202-265-1288
Fax: 202-745-2522

Founded in 1980. Develops educational resources, conducts policy analysis research, demonstration projects, and training, and offers a speakers bureau and many publications.

National Indian Council on Aging

City Centre, Suite 510 W
6400 Uptown Blvd., NW

Albuquerque, NM 87110
505-888-3302
Fax: 505-888-3276

Founded in 1976. Provides comprehensive services to Indian and Alaskan tribal organizations on elderly, information on Indian aging programs, technical assistance, and training.

Jewish Association for Services for the Aged

400 W. 68th Street
New York, NY 10023
212-724-3200
Fax: 212-769-1218

Founded in 1968. Provides case management, information and referral, counseling, financial assistance, legal services, protective services, immigrant services, hot lunch programs, homemaker, and many other services. Trains students from schools of social work at New York University, Hunter College, Yeshiva University, and Adelphi Universities.

National Caucus and Center on Black Aged

1424 K St. NW, Suite 500
Washington, DC 20005
202-637-8400
Fax: 202-347-0895

Founded in 1970 to improve living conditions for low-income elderly black Americans; community awareness, employment services, rental housing, training in nursing home administration, long-term care, housing management, and commercial property maintenance.

National Asian Pacific Center on Aging

Melbourne Tower, Suite 914
1511 3rd Ave.
Seattle, WA 98101
206-624-1221
Fax: 206-624-1023

Founded in 1979. Offers planning, technical assistance, program development, and training. Publishes Registry of Services for Pacific/Asian elderly.

National Council on the Aging

409 3rd St. SW, Suite 200
Washington, DC 20024
202-479-1200
Fax: 202-479-0735

Founded in 1950, administers National Association of Older Worker Employment Services, Health Promotion Institute, National Center on Rural Aging, National Institute on Community Based Long-term Care, National Institute of Senior Centers, National Center for Voluntary Leadership in Aging, among several others.

Child Abuse

American Professional Society on the Abuse of Children

407 S. Dearborn St., Suite 1300
Chicago, IL 60605

312-554B0166
Fax: 312-554-0919

Founded in 1987. Works to improve response to abused and neglected children.

International Society for Prevention of Child Abuse and Neglect

332 S. Michigan Ave., Suite 1600
Chicago, IL 60604
312-663-3520
Fax: 312-939-8962

Founded in 1977. Works to alleviate child abuse, neglect, and sexual abuse. Publications include *Child Abuse and Neglect: The International Journal* and a newsletter, *The Link.*

Child Welfare

Child Welfare Institute

1349 SW Peachtree NE, Suite 900
Atlanta, GA 30309
404-876-1934
Fax: 404-876-7949

Founded in 1984. Supports programs promoting foster parenting, minor emancipation, adoption, reunification, and combating child abuse and neglect. Publishes *Ideas in Action.*

Christian Children's Fund

2821 Emerywood Pky.
Richmond, VA
804-756-2700
Fax: 804-756-2718

Founded in 1938. Assists with physical, spiritual, and mental health needs of children of all ethnic backgrounds, and publishes *Childworld* quarterly and *Fieldnotes* monthly.

Childhelp USA

1345 N. El Centro Ave., Suite 630
Los Angeles, CA 90028-8216
800-423-4453

Founded in 1959. Operates residential treatment facilities and group homes, provides foster family placement, recovery programs for survivors of abuse, referrals, and research.

Civil Rights

Simon Wiesenthal Center

9760 W. Pico Blvd.
Los Angeles, CA 90035
213-553-5486

Congress of Racial Equality (CORE)

1457 Flatbush Ave
Brooklyn, NY 11210
718-434-3580

National Urban League

500 E. 62nd St.

New York, NY 10021
212-310-9000

Southern Christian Leadership Conference (SCLC)

334 Auburn Ave., NE
Atlanta, GA 30303
404-522-1420

Disability

Association for Children With Down Syndrome (ACDS)

2616 Martin Ave.
Bellmore, NY 1710
516-221-4700
Fax: 516-221-4311

Founded in 1966. Operates outreach programs, referral services; infant, toddler, and preschool programs, research, and conferences. Publishes *ACDS Newsletter* and videos.

Congress of Organizations of the Physically Handicapped

16630 Beverly
Tinley Park, IL 60477-1904
708-532-3566

Founded in 1958. Assists organizations with program development, technical assistance, and liaison to professional groups.

National Center for Disability Services

201 I.U. Willets Rd.
Albertson, NY 11507
516-747-5400
Fax: 516-747-5378

Founded in 1952. Operates Abilities Health and Rehabilitation Surveys, Career and Employment Institute, Henry Viscardi Schools, and a Research and Training Institute.

Crime and Crime Prevention

Friends Outside

3031 Tisch Way, Suite 507
San Jose, CA 95128
408-985-8807
Fax: 408-985-8839

Founded in 1955. Provides educational, recreation, social, and support groups for adult and juvenile offenders and families. Offers work-furlough and reentry programs for parolees, victim/juvenile offender mediation, and conflict resolution workshops.

Prison Fellowship Ministries

PO Box 17500
Washington, DC 20041
202-478-0100
Fax: 202-834-3658

Founded in 1976. Trains volunteers. Organizes seminars, and community service projects in prison ministry.

Administers correspondence and visitation programs for ex-offenders and families.

U.S. Office of Juvenile Justice and Delinquency Prevention
633 Indiana Ave. NW
Washington, DC 20531
202-307-0751

The primary federal agency monitoring and advancing juvenile justice. Develops and funds programs in illegal drug use and serious juvenile crime prevention. The National Youth Gang Clearinghouse centers on youth gangs. Publishes the *OJJDP Juvenile Justice Bulletin*.

Domestic Violence

National Coalition against Domestic Violence
PO Box 18749
Denver, CO 80218
303-839-1852
Fax: 303-831-9251

Founded in 1978. Coalition of battered women's service organizations and shelters. Provides technical assistance, trains, makes referrals, and maintains a speakers bureau.

Ethnic Services

International Black Women's Congress
1081 Bergen St.
Newark, NJ 07112
201-926-0570
Fax: 201-926-0818

Founded in 1983. Provides support groups, assistance in business startup, education, research, charitable programs, awards, and scholarships to women.

Puerto Rican Association for Community Affairs
853 Broadway, 5th Fl.
New York, NY 10003
212-673-7320
Fax: 212-529-8917

Founded in 1953. Provides foster care, adoptions, emergency housing, day care, casework, medical, dental, and an alternative high school for dropouts.

National Puerto Rican Forum
31 E. 32nd St., 4th Fl.
New York, NY 10016
212-685-2311
Fax: 212-689-5034

Founded in 1957. Implements programs in career services, job placement, English language training.

Housing

Enterprise Foundation
10227 Wincopin Cir., Suite 500
Columbia, MD 21044-3400
410-964-1230
Fax: 410-964-1918

Assists nonprofit neighborhood housing organizations to provide affordable housing and other basic human needs to low income families.

Cooperative Housing Foundation
8300 Colesville Rd., Suite 420
Silver Spring, MD 20910
301-587-4700
Fax: 301-587-2626

Founded in 1952, sponsors cooperative and self-help housing, economic development, and planning.

Habitat for Humanity International
121 Habitat St.
Americus, GA 31709-3498
912-924-6935
Fax: 912-924-6541
e-mail: Public-info@habitat.org

Founded in 1976. Ecumenical Christian housing organization, builds shelters sold to poor at no profit through no-interest loans. Chapters at more than 2,100 colleges and universities.

Hunger

Food for the Hungry
7729 E. Greenway Rd.
PO Box E
Scottsdale, AZ 85260
602-998-3100
Fax: 602-443-1420

Founded in 1971. Disaster relief, direct relief, developmental assistance in third-world countries, including a child sponsorship program. Hunger Corps conducts volunteer community development, including food distribution, water development, animal husbandry, gardening programs.

Food Research and Action Center
1875 Connecticut Ave. NW, Suite 540
Washington, DC 20009
202-986-2200
Fax: 202-986-2525

Founded in 1970. Technical assistance, training research, and community organizing assistance to low-income organizations.

Second Harvest
116 S. Michigan Ave., Suite 4
Chicago, IL 60603
312-263-2303
Fax: 312-236-5626

Founded in 1979. Distribute donated food and grocery products to food pantries, soup kitchens, and homeless shelters through a network of 185 food banks.

Female Offenders

Women's Prison Association
110 2nd Ave.

New York, NY 10003
212-674-1163
Fax: 212-677-1981

Founded in 1844. WPA advocates alternatives to incarceration, provides training programs, and assists homeless ex-offenders seeking to reunite with children.

Homelessness

National Alliance to End Homelessness

1618 K St. NW, Suite 206
Washington, DC 20005
202-638-1526
Fax: 202-638-4664

Founded in 1983. NAEH is a policy advocacy, research, and educational agency for successful program solutions.

National Coalition for the Homeless

1612 K St. NW, Suite 1004
Washington, DC 20006
202-775-1322
Fax: 202-775-1316
e-mail: nch@ari.net

The NCH is a clearinghouse of information on homelessness.

Juvenile Criminal Justice

National Association of Juvenile Correctional Agencies

55 Albin Rd.
Bow, NH 00304-3703
606-271-5945

NAJCA promotes legislation and research for the improvement of juvenile justice. Opposes the death penalty for juveniles, and publishes the *NAJCA News.*

National Council on Crime and Delinquency

685 Market St., No. 620
San Francisco, CA 94105
415-896-6223
Fax: 415-896-5109

Founded in 1907. NCCD develops community-based treatment instead of imprisonment for juvenile offenders, including programs and courses. Publishes *Crime and Delinquency* and *Journal of Research on Crime and Delinquency* quarterlies.

Mental Illness

National Alliance for the Mentally Ill

200 N. Glebe Rd., Suite 1015
Arlington, VA 22203
703-524-7600

Poverty

American Public Welfare Association

810 First St. NE, Suite 500

Washington, DC 20002

APWA was founded in 1930. Publishes the *APWA News.*

Fourth World Movement USA

7000 Willow Hill Dr.
Landover, MD 20785
301-336-9489
Fax: 301-336-0092
e-mail: 4thworld@his.com

Founded in 1957. FWM works for full inclusion of the poorest and most excluded families in society by street libraries, literacy programs, and internships. Publishes *Fourth World Journal.*

Refugee Services

American Refugee Committee

2344 Nicollet Ave. S., Suite 350
Minneapolis, MN 55404
612-872-7060
612-872-4309
e-mail: kraus024@maroon.tc.umn.edu

Founded in 1979. ARC helps insure survival and well-being of international refugees, displaced persons, and others resulting from social and political unrest, civil wars, and famine.

Immigration and Refugee Services of America

1717 Massachusetts Ave. NW, Suite 701
Washington, DC 20036
202-797-2105
Fax: 202-797-2363

Founded in 1958. IRSA assists refugees and immigrants adjust to American life in service centers in 34 cities, providing technical assistance in immigration, language training, and social casework.

Lutheran Immigration and Refugee Service

390 Park Ave. S.
New York, NY 10016-8803
212-532-6350

LIRS was founded in 1939 to provide advocacy, refugee sponsorship, and foster homes for refugees. Publications include *Face To Face: The Ministry of Refugee Resettlement,* the *LIRS Bulletin,* and *Seeking Safe Haven: A Congregational Guide to Helping Central American Refugees in the United States.*

United States Catholic Conference/ Migration and Refugee Services

3211 4th St. NE
Washington, DC 20017-1194
202-541-3352
Fax: 202-541-3399

Founded in 1920. Provides training, housing, and employment assistance, legal services, social security registration for arriving refugees. Publications include *MRS Annual Review, MRS Resettlement,* and *Immigration Directory.*

Relief

Cityteam Ministries
PO Box 143
San Jose, CA 95103
408-998-4770
Fax: 408-292-9406
　　Founded in 1957. Provides emergency services, meals, shelter, food boxes, and medical assistance to destitute inner-city residents, as well as job training, recovery programs for alcohol and drug addicts, youth club programs, and winter and summer camp programs for youth. Publishes *Cityteam Report,* and *Newsletter.*

National Voluntary Organizations Active in Disaster
American Red Cross Disaster Services
8111 Gatehouse Rd., 2nd Fl.
Falls Church, VA 22042
301-270-6782
Fax: 703-206-8635
　　Founded in 1971. NVOAD coordinates national and local voluntary organizations in disaster relief activities and encourages training programs. Publishes a *National Directory* and newsletter.

Research

Society for the Study of Social Problems
906 McClung Tower
University of Tennessee
Knoxville, TN 37996-0490
432-974-3620
Fax: 432-974-7013
　　Founded in 1951. Conducts research in a number of social problem areas. Publishes *Social Problems* quarterly.

Violence

National Institute Against Prejudice and Violence
31 S. Greene St.
Baltimore, MD 21201
301-3218-5170
　　NIAPV works to prevent violence motivated by racial, religious, ethnic, or sexual prejudice.

Mothers Against Gangs
110 W. Madison St.
Chicago, IL 60602
312-853-2336
　　MAG is an association of community members and parents. Lobbies for legislation, better law enforcement, and youth activity programs in neighborhoods. Provides education about gangs for neighborhood organizations and publishes quarterly newsletter, *Mothers Against Gangs.*

Youth Organizations

Camp Fire Boys and Girls
4601 Madison Ave.

Kansas City, MO 64112-1278
816-756-1950
Fax: 816-756-0258
　　Founded in 1910 for youth up to 21 years of age. Small-group character building, leadership, responsibility, self-direction, creativity, decision-making, and planning skills, and work with others. Publications include *Camp Fire Annual Report,* manuals, pamphlets, and *Teens in Action* newsletter.

Chapter 4 Leadership: The Hallmark of Macro Social Work

American Center for International Leadership
2200 S. Josephine St.
Denver, CO 80208
303-733-6143
Fax: 303-733-6122
　　ACIL was established in 1985. Promotes understanding between potential leaders ages 25–45 in the United States and globally in politics, arms control, industry, trade, health care, and other areas. Presents Dag Hammarskjold and George C. Marshal awards and issues several publications.

American Council of Young Political Leaders
1612 K St. NW, Suite 300
202-857-0999
Fax: 202-857-0027
　　Founded in 1966. ACYPL promotes understanding among political leaders ages 25–41 in all countries. Conducts meetings, conferences with government officials, business people, and academicians, and sponsors annual study exchanges.

Center for the New Leadership
2641 Mann Ct.
Falls Church, VA 22046
　　Identifies, trains, and promotes America's new leaders. Operates clearinghouse and resource center for leadership studies, citizen activism, and social innovation. Maintains Rapid Deployment Solutions Program, crisis resolution, and leadership development for communities.

National Association for Community Leadership
200 S. Meridian St., Suite 340
Indianapolis, IN 46225
317-637-7408
Fax: 317-637-7413
　　Supports and promotes community leadership, leadership organizations, leadership training, and consultation.

National Black Leadership Roundtable
1424 Longworth House Bldg.
Washington, DC 20515
　　Composed of 300 chief executives of national black organizations, NBLR provides a forum for exchange of ideas in political and economic issues important to the black community and offers an annual youth award.

National Indian Training and Research Center

2121 S. Mill St., Suite 216
Tempe, AZ 85282
602-967-9484
Fax: 602-921-1015

NITRC was founded in 1969 to improve American Indian leadership, training, and research for social and economic betterment.

Leadership Research

Center for Public Leadership Studies
Texas A&M University
College Station, TX 77843-4348
409-845-3038
Fax: 409-847-8924
e-mail: e339av@poliscsi.tamu.edu

Founded in 1993. Examines the impact of leadership on policy formation and implementation, including group conflict, volunteerism, and international affairs.

Reflective Leadership Center

University of Minnesota
Hubert M. Humphrey Institute, Rm. 55
Minneapolis, MN 55455
612-625-7377
Fax: 612-625-6351

Founded in 1981. Studies leadership theory and practice, including cooperative leadership, organizational leadership, leadership in public issues, global problems, and political, ethical, and visionary leadership.

Chapter 5 Communities

Community Associations Institute

1630 Duke St.
Alexandria, VA 22314
703-548-8600
Fax: 703-684-1581

Clearinghouse for encouragement of residential community housing and community associations. Publications include *Common Ground, Community Association Law Reporter.*

Community Service

PO Box 243
Yellow Springs, OH 45387
513-767-2161
Fax: 513-767-1461

Founded in 1940. CS promotes understanding of the nature of community and information on intentional communities and land trusts. Publications include *Annual Booklists, Community Service Newsletter.*

Fellowship for Intentional Community

PO Box 814
Langley, WA 98260
206-221-3064
Fax: 206-221-7828

Founded in 1948. Promotes the establishment of cooperative living, opportunities for personal and community development, and nurturing peaceful social transformation. Publications include *Communities: Journal of Cooperative Living* and *Directory of Intentional Communities.*

Foundation for Community Encouragement, Inc.

PO Box 449
Ridgefield, CT 06877
203-431-9434

Founded in 1984 by M. Scott Peck, author of *The Road Less Traveled.* Encourages development of community wherever it does not exist and assists existing communities. FCE provides leadership training, workshops, and referral of individuals to communities.

Michigan Futures, Inc.

30400 Telegraph Rd., Suite 370
Bingham Farms, MI 48025

Works to create community on a statewide scale based on a new kind of politics of partnership and service rather than power and self-interest.

Community Research

Comparative Study of Community
    Decision-Making
University of Chicago
112 E. 59th St.
Chicago, IL 60637
312-962-8686
Fax: 312-702-9673
e-mail: tnc@cicero.spc.uchicago.edu

Founded in 1967. Examines community decision-making in the United States and other countries.

Chapter 6 Becoming a Social Work Planner

American Planning Association

122 S. Michigan Ave., Suite 1600
Chicago, IL 60603
312-431-9100
Fax: 312-431-9985
e-mail: bklien@uhurv.uchicago.edu

APA analyzes urban, suburban, and rural change, including land use, transportation, housing, citizen participation, economic development, social equity, and community facilities. Publications include monthly journal Planning, Land Use Law and Zoning Digest, Zoning News, Environment and Development, JOBMART, Planners Press PASS Reports.

National Association of Area Agencies on Aging

1112 16th St. NW, Suite 100
Washington, DC 20036
202-296-8130
Fax: 202-296-8134

Established in 1975. Assists 665 member Agencies on Aging networking, advocacy, responses to federal legislation, disseminates information to federal government, and provides administrative, training, and technical assistance to area agencies.

National Planning Association
1424 16th St. NW, Suite 700
Washington, DC 20036
202-265-7685
Fax: 202-797-5516

Prepares studies on national goals and priorities, welfare and dependency problems, employment and workforce needs, and other social problems. Publications include *Looking Ahead* and *North American Outlook*.

Planners Network
379 DeKalb Ave.
Brooklyn, NY 11205
718-636-3496
Fax: 718-636-3709

Progressive analysis of planning issues. Promotes change in American politics and economics, support network to influence national and local policies eliminating inequalities of wealth and power, expanding human services over military. Publishes *Membership Roster*.

Planning Assistance
1832 Jefferson Pl. NW
Washington, DC 20036
202-466-3290
Fax: 202-466-3293

Founded in 1972, PA assists organizations in the United States and developing countries to improve planning and managing economic and social development programs. Provides management training programs.

Chapter 7 Becoming a Community Developer

ACCION International
120 Beacon St.
Somerville, MA 02143
617-492-45930
Fax: 617-876-9509

Founded in 1961. Creates and supports organizations which provide financial services to the poor.

Community Development Society
1123 N. Water St.
Milwaukee, WI 53202
414-276-7106
Fax: 414-276-7704

Established in 1969. A forum for exchange of ideas in community programs, scholarship, and research.

First Nations Development Institute
The Stores Bldg.
11917 Main St.
Fredericksburg, VA 22408
540-371-5615
Fax: 540-371-3505

Founded in 1980. Provides technical assistance, grants, and loans for economic development, development of nonprofit organizations, and commercial enterprise among Native American Tribes.

Native American Community Board
PO Box 572
Lanke Andses, SD 57356-0572
605-487-7072
Fax: 605-487-7964

Founded in 1984. Social and economic development, training American Indians, Native American Women's Health Education Resource Center. Publishes *Wicozanni-Wowapi*.

National Association for Community and Economic Development
1200 19th St. NW, Suite 300
Washington, DC 20036
202-429-5118
Fax: 202-223-4579

Founded in 1978. Stimulates and implements community, economic, and housing development programs. Liaison between counties and HUD.

National Association of Community Action Agencies
1875 Connecticut Ave. NW, Suite 416
Washington, DC 20009
202-265-7546
Fax: 202-265-8850

Founded in 1971. Promotes a unified approach and advocacy in problems of poverty, promotes community development, informs members of legislation and progress in community action and community development programs. Publishes *Directory of Community Action Agencies, NCAA Network, Training Manual*.

Economic Development

National Center for American Indian Enterprise Development
953 Juanita Ave.
Mesa, AZ 85204
602-831-7524
Fax: 602-491-1332

Founded in 1969. Business, economic development training to Native American tribes, operates Management Institute: Training for Indian Managers, and a development company, American Indian Fellowship in Business, and publishes the *Directory of American Indian Businesses,* and the *Indian Business and Management* quarterly.

National Center for Neighborhood Enterprise
1367 Connecticut Ave. NW
Washington, DC 20036
202-331-1103
Fax: 202-296-1541

Supports low-income communities, technical assistance, promotes alternative approaches to community development, identifies successful programs, needs, recommends policy, educates public, sponsors programs in youth entrepreneurship and seminars in public housing management.

National Congress for Community Economic Development

1875 Connecticut Ave. NW, Suite 524
Washington, DC 20009
202-234-5009
Fax: 202-234-4510

Monitors legislation and provides information to new community-based economic development organizations, community development corporations, community action agencies, and rural cooperatives.

National Council for Urban Economic Development

1730 K St. NW, Suite 915
Washington, DC 20006
202-223-4735
Fax: 202-223-4745

NCUED works for global economic development, job creation, and building local economies.

National Development Council

41 E. 42nd St., Suite 1500
New York, NY 10017
212-682-1106
Fax: 212-573-6118

Founded in 1972. Provides innovative economic development financing programs to communities, trains local staff, gives advice to Congress and federal government.

National Economic Development and Law Center

2201 Broadway, Suite 8215
Oakland, CA 94612
510-251-2600
Fax: 510-251-7217

Founded in 1969. Legal services counseling, representation, planning assistance to Community Development Corporations, co-ops, and other community organizations.

Community Development Research

Milton S. Eisenhower Foundation

1660 L St. NW, Suite 200
Washington, DC 20036

Founded in 1981. Provides research on community programs to improve the life of inner-city neighborhoods. Publishes *Youth Investment and Community Reconstruction* and the monthly newsletter, *Challenges From Within.*

Chapter 8 Becoming a Community Organizer

Association of Community Organizations for Reform Now (ACORN)

1024 Elysian Fields Ave.
New Orleans, LA 70117
504-943-0044
e-mail: acorn@acorn.org

Founded in 1970. ACORN has 80,000 members and is affiliated with 800 local organizations. Helps low- and moderate-income families fight utility rate increases, prescription drug prices. Promotes national health insurance, subsidized utility rates for the elderly.

Center for Community Change

1000 Wisconsin Ave. NW
Washington, DC 20007
202-342-0519
Fax: 202-342-1132

Founded in 1968. Provides technical assistance in beginning and developing community organizations. Publishes *Center for Community Change, Annual Report, Citizen Action Guides,* and *Community Change.*

Coalition for Economic Survival

1296 N. Fairfax Ave.
Los Angeles, CA 90046
213-656-4410
Fax: 213-656-4416

Founded in 1972. Conducts tenants rights clinics, helps organize tenants unions against rent increases and displacement. Publications include *Coalition for Economic Survival* bulletin, *Organizing Times* quarterly newsletter, and *Gone but Not Forgotten* video.

Grassroots Leadership

1300 Baxter St., Suite 200
PO Box 36006
Charlotte, NC 28236
704-332-3090
Fax: 704-332-0445

Founded by macro social worker Si Kahn in 1980. Provides organizing assistance in multiracial organizing, direct-action campaigns, strategies, tactics, coalitions, fundraising, leadership development, meeting skills, public relations, communication, and others. Provides skilled facilitation for meetings and retreats, folksong concerts, and a speakers bureau on civil rights, organizing, and social change in the new millennium.

Industrial Areas Foundation (IAF)

220 W. Kinzie St., 5th Fl.
Chicago, IL 60610-4412
312-245-9211
Fax:312-245-9744

Founded in 1940 by Saul Alinsky. IAF helps poor, working, and middle-class communities in larger municipalities to organize themselves to have power over matters that affect their own interest. Maintains a training institute.

Interreligious Foundation for Community Organization

402 W. 145th St., 3rd Fl.
New York, NY 10031
212-926B5757

Fax: 212-926-5842

Founded in 1967. Assists organizations in more than 40 cities in housing, education, job training, and legal aid.

Jewish Fund of Justice

260 Fifth Ave., Suite 901
New York, NY 10001
212-213-2113
Fax: 212-213-2233

Established in 1985 with assistance by Si Kahn, founding chair. JFJ provides technical and financial assistance to grassroots community organizations in Central Harlem, Oakland, Chicago, organizing for legal, educational, and human rights. Publications include *Justice, Justice Shalt Thou Pursue, American Jews Building Grassroots Partnerships for Social Change.*

National Association of Neighborhoods

1651 Fuller NW
Washington, DC 20009
202-332-7766
Fax: 202-332-2314

Founded by Milton Kotler, NAN is the primary nationwide community organization building network that assists community organizations and coalitions in 120 cities in local issues, welfare reform, crime, and safety programs.

National Center for Urban Ethnic Affairs

PO Box 20, Cardinal Station
Washington, DC 20064
202-319-5129
Fax: 202-319-6389

Founded in 1970. Helps urban communities, parishes, and congregations develop networks of neighborhoods, neighborhood organizations, and coalitions of neighborhood organizations, government agencies, and private sector for neighborhood revitalization, self-help in education, human services, economic opportunities, and housing. Provides summer internships.

National Neighborhood Coalition

1875 Connecticut Ave., No. 710
Washington, DC 20009
202-986-2096
Fax: 202-986-2539

Founded in 1979. National educational clearinghouse on national policies and federal programs on inner-city neighborhood groups.

National Peoples Action (NPA)

810 N. Milwaukee Ave.
Chicago IL 60622
312-243-3038

Founded in 1972 by Gale Cincotta. A coalition of neighborhood organizations, unions, senior citizens groups, and churches. Organizes low-income people in drugs, utility rates, health care. Instrumental in passage of Home Mortgage Disclosure Act and Community Reinvestment Act.

Pacific Institute for Community Organizations (PICO)

171 Santa Rosa Ave.
Oakland, CA 94610
510-655-4816

Founded in 1972 by Fr. John Bauman. PICO sponsors church-based community organizations and coalitions in 29 cities such as the San Francisco Organizing Project, Oakland Community Organizations, Orlando Interfaith Sponsoring Committee, Kansas City Church Community Organization, and others by means of using community-congregation model of community organization in drug prevention, education, housing, public safety, jobs.

Community Organization Training

Center for Third World Organizing

1218 E. 21st St.
Oakland, CA 94606-33132
510-533-7583
Fax: 510-533-0923

Founded in 1980. CTWO provides training and issue analysis to low-income minority organizations. The Minority Activist Apprenticeship Program develops minority community organizers and leaders of minority communities. Publications include *CTWO Time, Directory of Church Funding Sources, Issue Pacs.*

Direct Action Research and Training Center (DART)

314 NE 26th Terrace
PO Box 370791
Miami, FL 33137-0791
305-576-8020
Fax: 305-576-0789
Internet: www.fiu.edu/~dart

Founded in 1982. Builds new congregation-based organizations, consults and trains existing organizations in the DART network. Organizes workshops on community organizing skills for community groups and religious institutions, recruits training organizers.

Institute for Social Justice

1024 Elysian Fields Ave.
New Orleans, LA 70117
504-943-5954
Fax: 504-944-7078

Provides training and technical assistance, seminars, and workshops in community organizing. Especially for church social activists and lawyers involved with community groups and basic skills of community organizing to persons new to the field. Publishes community organization handbooks.

National Training and Information Center (NTIC)

810 N. Milwaukee Ave.
Chicago, IL 60622
312-243-3035

Fax: 312-243-7044

Founded in 1972, by Shel Trapp and Gale Cincotta. Provides training in community organizing and on-site consultation services and technical assistance. Courses dealing with organizing in areas of housing, block club organizing, issue development, community drug problems, and neighborhood reinvestment. NTIC has produced dozens of publications as well as the newspaper *Disclosure*.

Midwest Academy

225 W. Ohio, Suite 250
Chicago, IL 60610
312-645-6010
Fax: 312-645-6018

Founded in 1973 by Heather Booth for training in community organization. Offers five-day workshops in Organizing for Social Change, consulting services in planning, strategy, staff development, fundraising, and leadership development.

Organize Training Center

442 A Vicksburg
San Francisco, CA 94119
415-821-6180
Fax: 415-821-1631

Founded in 1973 by Mike Miller. Initiates community organizing projects and provides training in community organizing. Workshops on history, philosophy, strategy and tactics of mass-based organizing. Provides consulting services to community, church, and labor organizations.

Chapter 9 The Social Sector and the Rise of the Social Organization

This listing includes some of the premier nonprofit, voluntary, third-sector social organizations in the United States. These organizations have become institutions in their own right. The Congress of the United States has chartered two of these organizations, and two have been recipients of the Nobel Peace Prize. All have made historically significant contributions to American society. As a social worker, you can be proud to claim these historic agencies as part of your heritage, and as a macro social worker, I hope you will be inspired by the dedication, vision, and commitment of the people who have founded these organizations.

Also included are organizations that support and provide funding assistance and research about the nonprofit, voluntary social sector.

Premier Nonprofit Voluntary Organizations

Alcoholics Anonymous World Services

475 Riverside Dr.
New York, NY 10163
212-870-3400
Fax: 212-870-3003

Founded in 1935. AA is the prototype for all other 12-step self-help groups such as Narcotics Anonymous, Gam-blers Anonymous, Overeaters Anonymous, Codependents Anonymous, and Sexaholics Anonymous. Tens of thousands of AA and other 12-step groups exist throughout the United States and the world, providing renewed community relationships and assisting in rebuilding the lives and social networks of millions of people since its inception.

American Civil Liberties Union

132 W. 43rd St.
New York, NY 10036
212-944-9800
Fax: 212-869-9065
gopher://aclu.org:6601/

Founded in 1920. The ACLU is the premier human rights organization in America, keeping a close watch on how government and business maintain human rights guaranteed in the Declaration of Independence and the U.S. Constitution. The ACLU brings many lawsuits intended to protect individual civil rights as well as to promote national policy on behalf of women's rights, gay and lesbian rights, and children's rights. The ACLU publishes the monthly newsletter *First Principles* and the bimonthly newspaper *Civil Liberties*.

American Friends Service Committee

1501 Cherry St.
Philadelphia, PA 19102
215-241-7000
Fax: 215-864-0104
e-mail: afscinfor@afsc.org

Founded in 1917 by the Quakers to relieve human suffering and discover approaches to world peace and social justice through nonviolence. Currently AFSC operates in 22 countries, working in development, refugee relief, peace education, and community organizing. Supports resistance to militarism. AFSC was a corecipient of the Nobel Peace Prize in 1947.

American Red Cross

431 18th St. NW
Washington, DC 20006
202-737-8300

Founded in 1881 by Clara Barton. One of the few organizations charted by the United States Congress, and fulfills America's obligations under international treaties. For well over 100 years the Red Cross has served members of the armed forces, aided disaster victims, and assisted other Red Cross societies in times of emergencies. Maintains regional blood centers, trains volunteers, and provides community services and international refugee and relief activities.

Amnesty International of the U.S.A.

322 8th Ave.
New York, NY 10001
212-807-8400
Fax: 212-627-1451

Founded in 1961. Works for the release of men, women, and children detained anywhere for their beliefs, color, ethnic origin, sex, religion, or language provided they have not used or advocated violence. Amnesty International opposes torture, disappearance, and executions and advocates fair and prompt trials for all political prisoners. AIUSA monitors and prevents human rights abuses in 151 countries, and maintains a variety of networks for volunteer involvement. Publishes the Amnesty International Report. In 1977 Amnesty International was recipient of the Nobel Prize for Peace.

National Association for the Advancement of Colored People
4805 Mt. Hope Dr.
Baltimore, MD 21215
410-358-8900
Fax: 410-4816-9257
Founded in 1909. The NAACP works to achieve equal rights and elimination of racial prejudice discrimination in housing, employment, voting, schools, courts, transportation, recreation, prisons, and business enterprises. Sponsors NAACP National Housing Corporation to develop low- and moderate-income housing, referral, tutorials, and day care.

Association for Retarded Citizens
500 E. Border St., Suite 300
Arlington, TX 76010
817-261-6003
Fax: 817-277-3491
Founded in 1950. Provides programs, services, and research, and promotes public understanding and legislation for persons with intellectual disabilities. ARC publishes *Advocates Voice, ARC Government Report, ARC NOW, and ARC Today.*

Big Brothers/Big Sisters of America
230 N. 13th St.
Philadelphia, PA 19107
215-567-7000
Fax: 215-567-0394
Founded in 1904. Offers a one-to-one program matching a child from a single-parent home with an adult volunteer who serves as a mentor and role model. The match is made with the assistance of a trained social caseworker who also supervises and supports the relationship. Publications include *Annual Report, Agency Director,* and a newsletter.

Boys and Girls Clubs of America
1230 W. Peachtree St. NW
Atlanta, GA 30309
404-815-5700
Fax: 404-815-5757
Founded in 1906. Offers services to more than 2 million disadvantaged youth, primarily in inner cities. Focuses on drug and alcohol prevention, delinquency prevention, health and fitness, career exploration, educational enhancement, leadership development, character building, and healthy social growth and development. Publications include *Connections* and *Program Newsletter.*

Boy Scouts of America
1425 W. Walnut Hill Ln.
PO Box 152079
Irving, TX 75015
214-580-2000
Founded in 1910 by Lord Robert Baden-Powell. Chartered by the U.S. Congress as a youth-oriented educational and character-building program. Training in citizenship, mental and physical fitness for boys and young adults through locally sponsored scout groups offering camping, service projects, wilderness experiences, leadership training, and outdoor experiences. Publications include *Boy Scouts of America Annual Report to Congress, Boys Life Magazine, Exploring Magazine, Scouting Magazine: A Family Magazine,* as well as *The Boy Scout Handbook* and other books on scouting.

Catholic Charities USA
1731 King St., Suite 200
Alexandria, VA 22314
703-549-1390
Fax: 703-549-1656
Founded in 1910. Provides consultation, information, research in social problems including alcohol and drug abuse, teen pregnancy, child hunger, care for elderly, and disaster relief. Publications include *Charities USA* quarterly, *Directory of Diocesan Agencies of Catholic Charities in the US, Puerto Rico and Canada.*

Child Welfare League of America
440 First St. NW, Suite 310
Washington, DC 20001
202-638-2952
Fax: 202-638-4004
Organized in 1920 to improve the care and services of abused, dependent, or neglected children, youth, and their families. Provides consultation, research, and information, and develops standards for child welfare practice. Publications include *Child Welfare,* a bimonthly journal, *Child Welfare League of America Children's Monitor, Children's Voice* magazine, and the *CWLA Directory of Member Agencies.*

Family Service America
11700 W. Lake Park Dr.
Milwaukee, WI 53224
414-359-1040
Fax: 414-359-1074
Founded in 1911 as a direct descendant of the Charity Organization Societies. Provides family counseling, family life education, and advocacy services.

Girl Scouts of the USA
420 Fifth Ave.
New York, NY 10018-2702
212-852B8000
Fax: 212-852-6517
Founded in 1912. For girls age 5 to 17, and women 18 and over, provides programs in character building, leader-

ship development, self-sufficiency, resourcefulness, self-awareness, development of values, service, new skills, career possibilities, and international exchange programs. Publications include *Environmental Scanning Report, Girl Scout Leader: For Adults in Girl Scouting and the Girl Scouts of the USA.*

Goodwill Industries International

9200 Wisconsin Ave.
Bethesda, MD 20814
301-530-6500
Fax: 301-530-1516

Founded in 1902. Provides employment, training, evaluation, counseling, placement, job training, and vocational rehabilitation for people with disabilities, collects donated goods, repairs and sells them in retail stores.

Jewish Community Centers Association of North America

15 E. 26th St.
New York, NY 10010
212-523-4949
Fax: 212-481-4174

Founded in 1917. Aids Jewish community centers in planning, personnel, camping, health, administration, research, and public relations. Serves religious and welfare needs of Jewish military personnel and local Armed Services committees, Jewish chaplains in all branches of the Armed Forces.

John Howard Association

59 E. Van Buren St., Suite 1600
Chicago, IL
312-554-1901
Fax: 312-554-1905

Founded in 1901. Named after John Howard, an eighteenth-century English prison reformer. One of the oldest programs devoted to prison reform in the United States. Provides consultation and development of volunteer programs in criminal justice, and conducts research.

National Easter Seal Society

230 W. Monroe
Chicago, IL 60606
312-726-6200
Fax: 312-726-1494
e-mail: Nessinfo@seals.com

Founded in 1919. Serves one million persons with disabilities by means of advocacy, program development, fundraising, and resource development, offers physical, occupational, speech, and language therapy, vocational evaluation and training, and camping.

92nd Street Young Men's and Young Women's Hebrew Association

1395 Lexington Ave.
New York, NY 10128
212-427-6000

Fax: 212-410-1254
e-mail: gsllipman@92ndsty.org

Founded in 1874, a merger of the Young Women's and Young Men's Hebrew Associations. Serves the education and recreation needs of more than 300,000 members and nonmembers, maintaining program centers in Jewish arts, classes, workshops, lectures, senior programs, libraries, parenting center, preschool kindergarten, health center, professional music and theatrical performance.

Planned Parenthood Federation of America

810 Seventh Ave.
New York, NY 10019
212-541-7800
Fax: 212-245-1845

Founded in 1916. Provides medically supervised reproductive health services and education in reproductive health and voluntary fertility regulation.

National Council of U.S. Society of St. Vincent DePaul

58 Progress Pky.
St. Louis, MO 63043-3706
314-576-3993
Fax: 314-576-6755

Founded in 1833. Provides social service to the poor, summer camps, salvage operations, drop-in centers for the homeless, and personal visitation services. Publications include *Ozanam News, Society Diocesan Council Newsletter, Vincepaul* monthly newsletter.

National Council of Young Men's Christian Associations

101 N. Wacker Dr.
Chicago, IL 60606
312-977-0031
Fax: 312-977-9063

Founded in 1851. Powerful volunteer movement in meeting the community needs of people of all ages, races, religions, abilities, and incomes worldwide. YMCA-USA has nearly 14 million members nationwide. Works to nurture healthy social development of children, promote leadership, and strengthen families by providing an array of group activities for children and young adults, physical fitness facilities and training, camping programs, aquatics instruction, parent-child programs such as the Y-Indian Guides and Y-Indian Princess programs as well as programs in juvenile criminal justice, job retraining, relief work, and international exchange. Publications include *Discovery YMCA, Yearbook and Official Roster,* and the *YMCA Directory.*

Salvation Army

National Headquarters
615 Slaters Ln.
PO Box 269
Alexandria, VA 22313
703-684-5500
Fax: 703-684-34-78

Founded in 1865. All commissioned officers of the Salvation Army are ordained ministers devoted to full-time religious and social welfare activities. Provides adult alcoholic and drug rehabilitation centers, clinics, outpatient programs for unwed mothers, recreation centers, camping programs, senior and children's day care, senior housing and activity centers, emergency feeding and shelter. Publications include *Marching to Glory Program Aids, War Cry,* a biweekly magazine, *What Is the Salvation Army,* and the *Young Salvationist.*

UNICEF
3 United Nations Plaza
New York, NY 10017
212-326-7000
Fax: 212-702-7100
Organized in 1946 as an agency of the United Nations. Works for the survival, protection, and development of children throughout the world by low-cost community-based programs in social service, health, nutrition, education, water and sanitation, and status of women. Helps children in armed conflicts, provides relief and rehabilitation in emergencies. Publications include *First Call for Children, The Progress of Nation, State of the World's Children, the UNICEF Annual Report,* and *UNICEF At A Glance.*

Volunteers of America
3939 N. Causeway Blvd.
Metairie, LA 70002
504-837-2652
Fax: 504-837-4200
Founded in 1896. Christian human service organization offering programs for elderly, youth, families, alcoholics, drug abusers, and the disabled. Publications include *History of the Volunteers of America, Something Wonderful, Spirit* quarterly, and *The Volunteers Gazette* monthly.

Young Women's Christian Association
726 Broadway
New York, NY 10003
212-614-2700
Fax: 212-677-9716
Founded in 1858. Provides women and girls over 12 with opportunities for service in health education, recreation, clubs, classes in employment, education, human sexuality, self-improvement, volunteerism, citizenship, social esteem, empowerment and character building, and leadership skills abilities.

Nonprofit Organization Support Organizations

Association of Jewish Family and Children's Agencies
3086 Hwy. 27, Suite 11
PO Box 248
Kendall Park, NJ 08824-0248
908-8121-0909

Fax: 908-821-0493
e-mail: ajfca@aol.com
Founded in 1972. AJFCA serves Jewish family and children's agencies in the United States and Canada, providing opportunities for the exchange of experiences, consultation on programs, and administration, develops guidelines and statements.

Independent Sector
1828 L St. NW, Suite 1200
Washington, DC 20036
202-223-8100
Fax: 202-416-0580
Founded in 1980. Primary resource organization on nonprofit or voluntary social sector organizations in the United States. Supports, educates, conducts research, engages government regarding the nonprofit social sector and effective management of its philanthropic, voluntary organizations.

National Alliance of Black Organizations
3724 Airport Blvd.
Austin, TX 78722
512-478-9802
Fax: 512-478-9804
Founded in 1976. Serves as a forum for black organizations and associations for exchange of ideas, voter registration, and charitable assistance.

National Assembly of National Voluntary Health and Social Welfare Organizations
1319 F St. NW, Suite 601
Washington, DC 20004
202-347-2080
Fax: 202-393-45217
Founded in 1923 as the National Social Work Council. Facilitates cooperation among national voluntary health and social welfare organizations to increase impact of agencies and voluntarism. Publications include *Community Collaborations Manual,* and *Salary and Benefits Survey of National Voluntary Human Service Organizations.*

National Charities Information Bureau
19 Union Sq. W, 6th Fl.
New York, NY 10003-3395
212-929-6300
Fax: 212-463-7083
Founded in 1918. Provides standards in philanthropy and promotes informed giving by means of reports on origin, purpose, program, leadership and finances, and contributions of charitable organizations.

National Coalition of Hispanic Health and Human Services Organizations
1501 16th St. NW
Washington, DC 20036
202-387-5000
Founded in 1973. Assists Hispanic community-based health, mental health, and human services organizations

develop new models, strengthen infrastructure, conduct research, and increase funding.

National Collaboration for Youth

1319 F. St., Suite 601
Washington, DC 200014
202-347-2080
Fax: 202-393-4517

Founded in 1973. A coalition of youth development organizations to improve public awareness of the needs of youth, public policy, directing national resources to youth development, and youth decision-making. Collaborates in community service, youth employment, education, health, family life, and juvenile justice. Publications include *The Community Collaboration Manual, Directory of Internships for Youth Development, Salaries and Benefits in the Youth Development Field.*

Non-Governmental Organizations Committee on UNICEF

c/o UNICEF NGO Liaison Sect.
3 United Nations Plaza, H-6F
New York, NY 10017
212-326-7305
Fax: 212-326-7260

Research

Association for Research on Nonprofit Organizations and Voluntary Action

550 W. North St., Suite 301
Indianapolis, IN 46202
317-684-2120
Fax: 317-684-8900

Founded in 1971. Research in voluntary action, citizen participation in social movements, interest groups, political participation, community development, and disseminates information about voluntary action and nonprofit organizations.

International Society for Third-Sector Research

Johns Hopkins University
Institute for Policy Studies
Wymun Bldg., 5th Fl.
Baltimore, MD 21218
410-516-4678
Fax: 410-516-4870

Founded in 1992. Supports research and interdisciplinary study of national and international nonprofit, charitable, and voluntary organizations. Publishes *Inside ISTR.*

Chapter 10 Becoming a Program Developer

This listing provides you with information about various foundations and funding organizations that may be helpful in developing social programs.

Council on Foundations

1828 L St. NW, Suite 300
Washington, DC 20036
202-466-6512
Fax: 202-785-3926

Founded in 1949. Provides consultation and research and publishes *Council of Foundations Annual Report, First Steps in Starting a Foundation, Foundation Management Report* and *Handbook on Private Foundations.*

Council of Jewish Federations

730 Broadway, 2nd Fl.
New York, NY 10003-9596
212-475-5000
Fax: 212-529-5842

Founded in 1932. Coalition of local federations, welfare funds, and community councils that raises funds for local, national, and overseas Jewish needs.

Foundation Center

79 Fifth Ave.
New York, NY 10003
212-620-4230
Fax: 212-807-3677

Founded in 1956. Develops and disseminates information about foundations and grants, sponsors orientations on foundations and funding research, maintains research libraries collections. Publishes directories of all major foundations in the United States.

Funding Exchange

666 Broadway, 5th Fl.
New York, NY 10012
212-529-5300
Fax: 212-982-9272

Assists community-based alternative foundations, grants to grassroots organizations in their local areas. Offers services and seminars for foundation donors. Publishes *Grantmaker Docket, Funding Exchange,* and *We Gave Away a Fortune.*

National Black United Fund

40 Clinton St.
Newark, NJ 07102
201-643-5122
Fax: 201-648-8350
e-mail: nbuf@tnt.org

Founded in 1972. Solicits funds in education, human services, economic development, social justice; provides financing and technical support to projects serving black communities. Administers the National Black United Federation of Charities, supports self-help, volunteerism, and mutual aid programs.

National Center of Nonprofit Boards

2000 L St. NW, Suite 510
Washington, DC 20036
202-452-6262
Fax: 202-452-6299

Founded in 1988. Strengthens governing boards of nonprofit organizations in youth development, public policy, and social welfare; assists nonprofit organizations design board member training. Publishes *Board Member*, a bimonthly journal, booklets, books, and a catalog.

United Black Fund of America

1101 14th St. NW, Suite 601
Washington, DC 2005
202-783-0430
Fax: 202-347-2564

Founded in 1969. Funds member nonprofit agencies serving low-income or disabled blacks and other minorities in health and welfare, day care, education, senior services, drug and alcohol rehabilitation programs. Publishes the *United Black Fund Agency Directory*.

United Way of America

021 N. Fairfax St.
Alexandria, VA 22314
703-836-7100
Fax: 703-683-7840

Founded in 1918, an outgrowth of the Community Chests and Councils of America and Charity Organization Society movement. Providing national, regional, and local program support, consultation in fundraising, budgeting management, fund distribution, planning and communications, corporate giving, and volunteer development training though the National Academy for Volunteerism.

Chapter 11 Becoming a Social Work Administrator

Listed below are organizations that social work administrators have formed or with which they associate to better develop the field of social work administration. To learn more about what social work administrators are doing in your area, contact one of these organizations or join the National Network for Social Work Managers.

Association for Volunteer Administration

PO Box 4584
Boulder, CO 80306
303-541-0238
303-541-0277

Founded in 1960. AVA is a professional association of administrators of volunteer programs, educators, researchers, and students in training, and competency certification. Offers service awards. Publishes *Journal of Volunteer Administration*.

National Council of Local Public Welfare Administrators

810 S St., NE Suite 500
Washington, DC 20002
202-682-0100

Founded in 1940. Works to influence national policy and strengthen professional ability and leadership in local public welfare administration.

National Council of State Human Services Administrators

810 First St. NE, Suite 500
Washington, DC 20002
202-682-0100
Fax: 202-289-6555

Founded in 1939. Provides a forum for exchange of ideas on national policy affecting state welfare administration and service.

National Network for Social Work Managers

1316 New Hampshire Ave. NW, Suite 602
Washington, DC 20036
202-785-2814
Fax: 202-785-2904
e-mail: brotmandc@aol.com

Founded in 1985. Strengthens social work administration planning, budgeting, finance, and legislative practice, provides networking for social work administrators. Conducts National Management Institute and regional workshops. Administers Chauncey Alexander Lifetime Achievement Award in Social Work Management and the National Management Excellence Award for Social Work Executives and Managers. Publishes *Administration in Social Work* quarterly, *Social Work Executive* quarterly, monographs, and newsletter.

Society for Social Work Administrators in Health Care

c/o American Hospital Association
One North Franklin
Chicago, IL 60606
312-422-3000
Fax: 312-422-4580

Founded in 1965. Provides information and dialog to support and develop the profession of social work health care administration. Publishes *Continuum* bimonthly and *Social Work Administrator*.

National Association of State Mental Retardation Program Directors

113 Oronoco St.
Alexandria, VA 22314
703-683-4202

Founded in 1963. Monitors and reports on administrative, legislative, and other issues affecting the administration of programs for persons with intellectual disabilities. Publishes the monthly newsletter *Capitol Capsule* and *New Directions*.

Chapter 12 Becoming an Organization Developer

Organization development is a growing field in macro social work. Listed below are some organizations you can contact if you want more information about how to become an organization developer or what organization developers do in the field of social work.

Association for Quality and Participation

801-B West 8th St.
Cincinnati, Ohio 45203
513-381-1959

Provides support and information about the quality movement and managing organizational change. According to Peter Block, "their conferences are among the best places to hear about innovative practice in participation and new work places."

American Society for Training and Development

640 King St., Box 1443
Alexandria, VA 22313-2043
703-683-8100
Fax: 703-683-8103
Internet: www.astd.org/virtual.community/

Founded in 1944. Premier professional association for workplace learning and performance. Provides leadership to individuals and organizations in work-related competence, performance, and fulfillment. Has 70,000 members in 150 countries, 47 specialty groups, volunteer opportunities.

Black Affairs Center for Training and Organizational Development

109181 Jarboe Ct.
Silver Spring, MD 20901
301-681-9827
Fax: 301-681-3186

Founded in 1970. A multidisciplinary management consulting organization engaged in organizational renewal, systematic problem-solving, skills development, training, and consultation in employee motivation, women's issues, single parents, aging, sexual harassment, and stress management. Publications include *National Minority Business Association* quarterly journal.

Center for Human Services

7200 Wisconsin Ave., Suite 600
Bethesda, MD 20814
301-654-8338
Fax: 301-941-8427

Founded in 1968. Provides technical assistance to human services organizations in organization development diagnosis and intervention, leadership, human resource management, quality assurance, performance appraisal, job design, systems analysis, total quality management, strategic planning, team building, management coaching and counseling, as well as training in labor-management relations, sexual harassment protection, equal opportunity, affirmative action, and stress management.

Independent Community Consultants

Planning and Training Office
PO Box 41

Hampton, AR 71744
501-798-4510
Fax: 501-798-4513

Founded in 1972. A nonprofit management consulting and training organization providing planning, research, evaluation, conflict resolution, and information services to social organizations.

Management Assistance Group

1555 Connecticut Ave. NW, 3rd Fl
Washington, DC 20036
202-659-1963
Fax: 202-659-3105

Founded in 1972. MAG provides consultation to nonprofit social organizations in organizational and managerial problems, promotes discussions and workshops on organizational development.

National Staff Development and Training Association

810 First St. NE, Suite 500
Washington, DC 20002-4267
202-682-0100
Fax: 202-289-6555

Founded in 1984. NSDTA engages welfare workers in staff development and training, maintains network of contacts for individuals and technical assistance.

Organization Development Network

71 Valley St., Suite 301
South Orange, NJ 07079-2825
973-763-7337
Fax: 973-763-7488
Internet: http://www.odnet.org/

Primary organization for organization development professionals. Provides information on assessment tools, large group interventions, structural interventions, organization behavior, and trends. Sponsors an annual conference, a journal, and local chapters.

Chapter 13 Becoming a Social Policy Advocate

There is an amazing number of organizations in the United States that are concerned with issues of social justice, social action, and social policy, and in the arena of social policy there are a large number of social policy research organizations, many of which are connected with universities. I have listed here only the more well-known social action, social policy, and social justice organizations. There are hundreds of others. If there is a policy issue that interests you, contact one of these organizations. They will tell you how you can become active in working for social change, provide you with information, and tell you what efforts are being made in your local community. Your local NASW chapter can also help you discover areas where you can make a difference.

Civil Rights

Asian-American Legal Defense and Education Fund

99 Hudson St.
New York, NY 10013
212-9666-5932
Fax: 212-966-4303

Founded in 1974. Works on immigration, employment, voting rights, racially motivated violence against Asian-Americans, and Japanese American Redress. Litigates cases, monitors and reports incidence of racial discrimination, sponsors training sessions to inform community workers and residents of rights and benefits. Publishes *Outlook*.

Mexican American Legal Defense and Education Fund

634 S. Spring St., 11th Fl.
Los Angeles, CA 90014
213-629-2512
Fax: 213-629-1916

Founded in 1968. Protects civil rights of Hispanics, engages in class action civil rights litigation, and maintains litigation departments in education, employment, immigration, and voting rights.

National Urban League

500 E. 62nd St.
New York, NY 10021
212-310-9000
Fax: 212-593-8250

Founded in 1910. Works to eliminate institutional racism. Operates programs in justice administration, education, employment, health, social welfare, including Black Executive Exchange Program, Seniors in Community Service, and a Summer Internship Program. Publications include *Community Surveys and Reports, The Urban League News*.

Puerto Rican Legal Defense and Education Fund

99 Hudson St., 14th Fl.
New York, NY 10013
212-219-3360
Fax: 212-431-4276

Founded in 1972. Works to protect the civil rights of Puerto Ricans and other Latinos by conducting class-action litigation in education, employment, voting rights, and housing. Facilitates pursuit of legal careers for Puerto Ricans. Publications include *Pregonero*.

Southern Christian Leadership Conference

334 Auborn Ave., NE
Atlanta, GA
404-522-1420
Fax: 404-659-7390

Founded by Martin Luther King Jr. Works to end discrimination and segregation.

Southern Poverty Law Center

PO Box 2087
Montgomery, AL 36102
334-264-0286
Fax: 334-264-0629

Founded in 1971. Works to protect legal and civil rights of poor people through education and litigation, especially individuals injured or threatened by white supremacy groups. Publications include *Klanwatch Intelligence Report, SPLC Report*, and *Teaching Tolerance*.

Human Rights

Antidefamation League

823 United Nations Plaza
New York, NY 10017
212-490-2525
Fax: 212-867-0779

Founded in 1913. Works to end defamation of Jewish people, attain justice and fair treatment for all people. Promotes interfaith and intergroup relationships. Operates the Jewish Foundation for Christian Rescuers, Braun Center for Holocaust Studies, Hidden Child Committee, and A World of Differences educational project.

Gay and Lesbian Alliance Against Defamation

150 W. 26th St., Suite 503
New York, NY
212-807-1700
Fax: 212-807-1806

Founded in 1985. GLAAD opposes media and public defamation of gay and lesbian individuals and assists the gay community organize, counter homophobia, defend legal rights, and promote fair treatment nationwide. Publications include *GLAAD Bulletin, GLAAD Tidings, Images* quarterly, *Media Guide to the Lesbian and Gay Community*.

International League for Humans Rights

432 Park Ave. S., Rm. 1103
New York, NY 10016
212-684-1221
Fax: 212-684-1696
e-mail ILHR@undp.org

Founded in 1942, accredited by the UN, Council of Europe. Promotes human, political, civil, racial, and human rights. Investigates and intervenes in human rights violations.

Human Rights Watch

485 Fifth Ave., 3rd Fl.
New York, NY 10017
212-972-8400
Fax: 212-972-0905

Monitors human rights worldwide, evaluates human rights practices of governments, identifies, publicizes, and protests abuses, observes human rights practices, sponsors missions to countries violating human rights, meets with government officials, conducts interviews with victims, families, and witnesses, attends court proceedings, examines court records. Publications include *Human Rights Watch Publication Catalog, Human Rights Watch Quarterly Newsletter, Human Rights Watch: Questions and Answers, Human Rights Watch World Report.*

Clergy and Laity Concerned
340 Mead Rd.
Decatur, GA 30030
404-377-1983
Fax: 404-377-5367

Founded in 1965. Brings to bear moral, ethical, and religious values on issues of human rights, racial and gender justice, militarism, economic justice. Publications include *Martin Luther King on Hunger, Poverty, Unemployment and Peace, Beyond Vietnam, The Truth Is Out.*

Policy Research

Brookings Institution
1775 Massachusetts Ave. NW
Washington, DC 20036
202-797-6000
Fax: 202-797-6004

Founded in 1916. Conducts nonpartisan research, education, economics, government, and foreign policy. Conducts conferences, forums, and seminars. Publishes *Brookings Newsletter, Brookings Papers on Economic Activity, Brookings Review,* and a *Media Guide/Directory of Scholars.*

Center for Public Policy,
Union Institute
1731 Connecticut Ave. NW, Suite 300
Washington, DC 20009
202-667-1313
Fax: 202-265-0492

Works with nonprofit organizations on social problem issues to increase engagement with public policy-making process. Publications include *A Place at the Table: A Study of State-wide Nonprofit Association Movement, Building Our Might: Establishing a Statewide Nonprofit Association, Neighbors Building Community: A Report on the Neighborhood Assistance Act, Part of the Solution: Innovative Approaches to Nonprofit Funding.*

Center for the Study of Youth Policy
University of Michigan School of Social Work
1015 E. Huron St.
Ann Arbor, MI 48104-1689

Examines juvenile criminal justice and juvenile corrections. Publishes many booklets, including *Programs for the Serious and Juvenile Offenders,* and *Violent Juvenile Crime: What Do We Know About It and What Can We Do About It?*

Center for the Study of Social Policy
1250 Eye St. NW, Suite 503
Washington, DC 20005-3922
202-371-1565
Fax: 202-371-1472

Founded in 1979. Attempts to identify policy directions for better financing and human service delivery. Analyzes effects of social policy on states, communities, families.

Public Agenda
6 E. 39th St., 9th Fl.
New York, NY 10016
212-686-6610
Fax: 212-889-3461
www.publicagenda.org/contact.htm

Founded in 1975 and presided over by Daniel Yankelovich. Helps citizens understand policy issues, conducts public opinion and attitudes research, policies. Students will probably come across some of Yankelovich studies on social problems and policy. Publications include *America Agenda* quarterly and many reports, some of which are *Assignment Incomplete: the Unfinished Business of Education Reform, Mixed Messages: A Survey of the Foreign Policy Views of Americas Leaders, Values We Live By: What Americans Want From Welfare Reform.*

Social Justice Organizations

Advocacy Institute
1707 L St. NW, Suite 400
Washington, DC 20035
202-659-8475
Fax: 202-659-8484
e-mail: ai001@hgdinst.org

Founded in 1984. Provides training in advocacy skills, democratic participation in civil, children's, human rights, and other public policy issues, to environmental, consumer, health, and other nonprofit organizations. Studies the role of public interest advocacy. Publishes *Advocates Advocate, Action,* and information bulletins.

Social Policy Organizations

Policy and Policy Practice Group
Rick Hoefer, President
Box 19129
School of Social Work,
University of Texas at Arlington
Arlington, TX 76019

Advocates social policy as important component of social work education and research. Promotes socially and economically just policy at local, state, national, and international levels. Publications include *Social Policy Journal.*

Chapter 14 Becoming Active in Social Movements

Getting involved in social action means bringing about a more just society. Many organizations are dedicated to bringing about justice and an end to oppression. The following represents only a small number of the many social action and social justice organizations in the United States. Write or call one today to explore how you can get involved in making a better society.

Social Action Organizations

Children

Children's Defense Fund
25 E St. NW
Washington, DC 20001
202-628-8787
Fax: 202-662-3530
Founded in 1973 by Marian Wright Edelman. Provides advocacy on behalf of America's children and teenagers, engages in research, public education, monitoring of federal agencies, litigation, legislation, assistance to groups and community organizations in child welfare, child health, adolescent pregnancy prevention, child care and development, family services, prevention of violence against and by children, child neglect and maltreatment, and adequate funding for essential programs for children. Among its many publications are *CFD Reports, The Health of America's Children: Maternal and Child Health Data Book*, and *The State of America's Children.*

Death Penalty

Death Penalty Information Center
1606 20th St. 2nd F.
Washington, DC 20009
202-347-2531
Fax: 202-332-1915

**National Coalition to Abolish
the Death Penalty**
918 F St. NW, Suite 601
Washington, DC 20004
202-347-2411
Fax: 202-347-2510
e-mail: NCADPI@aol.com
Founded in 1976. Oldest national organization to end the death penalty. Provides national forum, compiles statistics, litigation, and many publications including monthly newsletter *Lifelines.*

Disabilities

Disability Rights Center
2500 Q St. NW, Suite 121
Washington, DC 20007
301-324-0112
Founded in 1976. DRC assists political activists, consumer activists, and advocates about the disability movement, exacts compliance with federal laws, and monitors federal employment and the disabled.

People First International
PO Box 12642
Salem, OR 97309
503-362-0336
Fax: 503-585-0287

Founded in 1974. Provides persons with intellectual and developmental disabilities training in leadership skills, advocacy, consultation, and assistance for new groups.

Voice of the Retarded
5005 Newport DSR, Suite 108
Rolling Meadows, IL 60008
847-253-6020
Fax: 847-253-6054
Founded in 1983. Advocates to improve services and public awareness, monitors legislation, promotes of freedom of choice and residential alternatives for persons with intellectual disabilities.

Elderly

Gray Panthers
PO Box 21477
Washington, DC 20009-9477
202-466-3132
Fax: 202-466-3133
Founded in 1970. Works to combat ageism in national health care, affordable housing, environment, peace, education, economic justice, social justice. Publications include *Gray Panther Network,* and *the Network Newsletter.*

Guns and Violence

Coalition to Stop Gun Violence
100 Maryland Ave. NE
Washington, DC 20002
202-544-7190
Fax: 202-4544-7213
Works to ban the private sale and possession of handguns, conducts research, compiles statistics on deaths involving handguns, handgun production and marketing. Maintains speakers bureau.

Handgun Control, Inc.
1225 Eye St. NW, Suite 1100
Washington, DC 20005
202-898-0792
Fax: 202-37;1-9615
Founded in 1974. Public citizens' lobby on manufacture, importation, sale, transfer, and civilian possession of guns. Compiles information, works for policy change, develops legislation and research. Publishes progress reports, films, and books.

Hispanic

National Council of La Raza
810 First St. NE, 3rd Fl.
Washington, DC 20002
202-2819-380
Fax: 202-2819-8173
Founded in 1968. Technical assistance to Hispanic community organizations in economic development, community organization, housing, employment, social service;

performs research, policy analysis, training in community resources development, and board of directors training.

Native Americans

Association on American Indian Affairs
PO Box 2268
Tekakwitha Complex Agency Rd. 7
Sisseton, SD 57262
605-698-3998
Fax: 605-698-3316

Indian Law Resource Center
602 N. Ewing St.
Helena, MT 59601
406-449-2006
Fax: 4-6-449-2031
Founded in 1978. Human rights advocacy and environmental protection, free legal services, consultant to the UN Economic and Social Council.

Native American Policy Network
Barry University
11300 2nd Ave. NE
Miami, FL 33161
305-899-3473
Fax: 305-899-3279
Hunger

Bread for the World
1100 Wayne Ave., Suite 1000
Silver Spring, MD 20910
301-608-2400
Fax: 301-608-2401
e-mail: Bread@igc.org
Founded in 1973. Multinational organization working against hunger and poverty. Maintains the Bread for the World Institute. Publishes *Christian Faith and Public Policy: No Grounds for Divorce* and *Harvesting the Peace: The Arms Race and Human Need.*

Institute for Food and Development Policy (FoodFirst)
398 60th St.
Oakland, CA 94618
510-654-4400
Fax: 510-654-4551
e-mail: foodfirst@igc.apc.org
Founded in 1975. Research documentation and public education organization focusing on the social and economic causes of world hunger. Publishes directory of volunteer opportunities in developing nations, a speakers bureau, books and catalogs.

Peace

Episcopal Peace Fellowship
PO Box 28156
Washington, DC 20038-8156

202-783-3380
Fax: 202-393-3695
Founded in 1939. Works against capital punishment, racism, militarism, nuclear weapons, and the draft. Provides prisoner support and services to conscientious objectors. Publications include *Cross Before Flag, Episcopal Peace Fellowship Newsletter,* and *The Voice of Conscience: A Loud and Unusual Noise?.*

Fellowship for Reconciliation
PO Box 271
Nyack, NY 10960
914-358-4601
Fax: 914-358-4924
e-mail: fornatl@igc.org
Founded in 1915. Interfaith organization for peace and justice by means of education, coalition-building, and non-violent action, affiliated with the individual Peace Fellowship organizations of the Baptist, Buddhist, Catholic, Disciples, Episcopal, Jewish, Lutheran, and Presbyterian Churches.

Women

Institute for Women's Policy Research
1400 20th St. NW, Suite 104
Washington, DC 20036
202-785-5100
Fax: 202-833-4362

National Conference of Puerto Rican Women
5 Thomas Cir. NW
Washington, DC 20005
202-387-4716
Fax: 305-885-6558
Founded in 1972. Promotes equal participation of Puerto Rican and Hispanic women in politics and social, and economic life.

National Council of Negro Women
1001 G St. NW, Suite 800
Washington, DC 20006
202-628-0015
Fax: 202-785-8733
Founded in 1935 by Mary Mcleod Bethune. Coalition of national organizations. Operates Women Center for Educating and Career Advancement, the Bethune Museum, Archives for Black Women's History. Offices in West and Southern Africa. International projects to improve status of rural women in third-world countries.

National Organization for Women
1000 16th St. NW, Suite 700
Washington, DC 20036
202-331-0066
Fax: 202-785 8576
Founded in 1966. Works to end discrimination against women, promotes passage of the Equal Rights Amendment, enforcement of legislation, engages in lobbying and litigation.

United Nations Commission on the Status of Women

2 United Nations Plaza, Rm. DC2-1220
New York, NY 10017
212-963-4668
Fax: 212-963-3463

Founded in 1946. Serves 45 member countries promoting women's political, economic, civil, and social rights, and education; advises the UN and member bodies.

Women's Legal Defense Fund

1875 Connecticut Ave. NW, Suite 710
Washington, DC 20009
202-986-2600
Fax: 202 986-2539

Founded in 1971. Attempts to secure equal rights for women by advocacy, monitoring, and public education in areas of family law, employment, women's health, and others.

Chapter 15 Social Work at the Global Level

Listed here are a small number of U.S.-based organizations whose arena is international social work. There is probably no more fulfilling or more exciting experience than to volunteer in one of these organizations and devote a year or two to helping people in developing nations. If you want to expand your horizons in the field of social work, contact one of these organizations and find out how you can become involved in international social work.

International Social Service, American Branch

390 Park Ave. S.
New York, NY 10016
212-532-6350
Fax: 2112-532-8558

Founded in 1924. ISS provides casework related to family separation or migration across national boundaries in custody, intercountry adoptions, immigration, family reunions, rights to benefits.

United Nations

United Nations Headquarters
New York, NY 10017
212-963-1234

Founded in 1945. Comprising 159 member nations. Member nations consider major international issues, develop standards, study global social problems, formulate policy, and administer programs in economic and community development, refugees, women's rights, children, disaster relief, population control, research and training, health. Sends volunteers in community development to member nations worldwide. Publications include *Bibliographic Information, Monthly Bulletin of Statistics, Population and Vital Statistics Report, UNDOC: Current Index, Yearbook of the United Nations.*

International Women's Social Work

Association for Women in Development

1511 K. St. NW, Suite 825
Washington, DC 20005
202-628-0440
Fax: 202-628-044

Center for Development and Population Activities

1717 Massachusetts Ave. NW, Suite 200
Washington, DC 20036
202-667-1142
Fax: 202-332-4496

Administers community-based development projects in Africa, Asia, Latin America, the Middle East, and Eastern Europe in partnership with local women-operated organizations. Conducts leadership training programs in developing countries on institution building, and strategic planning. Projects include ACCESS to Family Planning Through Women Managers, and Better Life Options for Girls and Young Women.

Coalition for Women in International Development

3035 Chain Bridge Rd.
Washington, DC 20016
202-363-6140
Fax: 202-775-0596

Founded in 1976. Promotes American women's participation in U.S. foreign policy and economic, social, and political development and policy affecting women in developing countries.

International Child Welfare

Children's Aid International

PO Box 83220
San Diego, CA 92138-3220
619-694-0095
Fax: 619-694-0188

Founded in 1977. Provides nutritional, medical, educational assistance to needy children. Operates primary health care clinics in Nairobi, Kenya, and Malaysia. Educates community members in preventive health care. Publishes *Focus on Children* and a newsletter.

Children's Watch

22 Towbridge St.
Cambridge, MA 02138
617-492-4890

Founded in 1994. A multinational organization to improve the quality of children's status and children's human rights, particularly victims of violence, child prostitution, and child labor in hazardous industry, and armed conflicts. Publications include *Children's Watch Annual Report.*

Compassion International
3955 Cragwood Dr.
PO Box 7000
Colorado Springs, CO 80933
719-594-9900
Fax: 719-594-6271

Founded in 1952. Ministry to children in underdeveloped and developing countries, providing financial support to schools, care centers, children's homes, hostels, meal sponsorship, scholarships, student centers, and medical supplies.

Save the Children Federation
54 Wilton Rd.
Newport, CT 06880
203-221-4000
Fax: 203-454-3913

Founded in 1932. Provides community development, family self-help, health education, disaster relief in 45 countries, American inner cities, Appalachia, and American Indian reservations.

International Community Development

Alliance for Communities in Action
PO Box 30154
Bethesda, MD 20824
301-229-7707
Fax: 301-229-0457

Provides funding, supplies, and technical assistance to Latin American community-based organizations and grassroots cooperatives, neighborhood organizations, church and women's groups. Sponsors development programs through TECHO institute (housing), Food For Families (food production), and Agua Pura (potable water) programs.

Grassroots International
4848 Grove St., No. 103
Somerville, MA 02144
617-628-1664
Fax: 617-628-4737

Founded in 1983. Funds community-based relief, development projects worldwide. Assists local social change in Eritrea, South Africa, the West Bank, and Gaza, Haiti, Mexico, and the Philippines.

Oxfam America
26 West St.
Boston, MA 02111-1206
617-482-1211
Fax: 617-728-2594

A worldwide network of development and disaster assistance organizations. Funds small-scale self-help projects in Asia, Africa, and the Americas and emergency needs of refugees by funding food, water, and medical aid programs.

Private Agencies Collaborating Together
1901 Pennsylvania Ave. NW, Suite 501
Washington, DC 20006

202-466-5666
Fax: 202-466-5669

PACT was founded in 1972. An international development organization in microenterprise, health care, AIDS treatment, child welfare, environmental protection, nonformal education, and women's issues and human rights.

United Nations Development Programme
1 United Nations Plaza
New York, NY 10017
212-906-5315
Fax: 212-906-5364

Formed in 1965. Funds 6,000 projects in more than 150 developing countries to enhance self-reliance, sustainable human development, grassroots development, management development, women in development. Publishes *UNDEP Annual Report, UNDP Human Development Report.*

World Vision
PO Box 5002
Monrovia, CA 91016-9918

International Development Training

Center for Organizational and Community Development
University of Massachusetts
School of Education
377 Hills St.
Amherst, MA 01003

Founded in 1985. Provides materials and training in international community development, organizing, and fundraising. Publishes manuals and books on international community development methods and processes.

International Refugee Services

International Organization for Migration
1750 K St. NW, Suite 1110
Washington, DC 20006
202-862-1826
Fax: 202-862-1879
e-mail: promigrant@washington.iom.ch

Provides assistance to refugees, displaced individuals, and migrants in transportation, language, vocational training in 65 countries. Participates in development activities in Latin America and African countries.

International Rescue Committee
386 Park Ave. S., 10th Fl.
New York, NY 10016
212-679-0010
Fax: 212-689-3459

Founded in 1933 by Albert Einstein. Assists refugee victims of religious, political, and racial persecution, civil strife, famine. Publications include *Children in Flight, International Rescue Committee Annual Report, and Flight.*

Jesuit Refugee Service/USA

1424 16th St. NW, Suite 300
Washington, DC 20036
202-462-5200
Fax: 202-462-7009

Founded in 1983. Sends people to provide direct services to refugees worldwide. Publications include *The Mustard Seed.*

International Relief Organizations

Adventist Development and Relief Agency International

12501 Old Columbia Pike
Silver Spring, MD 20904
301-680-6380
Fax: 301-680-6370

Founded in 1956. Nonsectarian community development, AIDS awareness and prevention, refugee programs, constructs housing, builds schools, roads, and water systems, provides aid to disaster-stricken areas, builds hospitals, retirement homes, and orphanages worldwide.

American Jewish World Service

15 W. 26th St., 9th Fl.
New York, NY 10010
212-683-1161
Fax: 212-683-5187

Founded in 1985. Provides nonsectarian assistance to impoverished populations, particularly women, children, and threatened minorities. AJWS Jewish Volunteer Corps sends professional to work with NGOs for one to six months.

Americares Foundation

161 Cherry St.
New Canaan, CT 06840
203-966-5195
Fax: 203-972-0116

Founded in 1979. Dedicated to saving lives and fulfilling emergency medical needs worldwide in disasters caused by earthquakes, famines, floods, political upheavals, and wars.

CARE

151 Ellis St.
Atlanta, GA 30303-2439
404-681-f2552
Fax: 404-597-5977

Founded in 1945. Provides international disaster aid, promoting self-help community development programs including small enterprise development, water, primary health care, nutrition, agricultural development, and education.

Catholic Relief Services

209 W. Lafayette St.
Baltimore, MD 21201
410-625-2220
Fax: 410-6815-1635

Founded in 1943. Conducts disaster response, refugee relief, social welfare, and economic development in 67 countries, supports indigenous development agencies. Publications include *Catholic Relief Services Annual Report, The Wooden Bell* quarterly.

Church World Service

PO Box 968
Elkhart, IN 46515
219-264-3102
Fax: 219-262-0966

Founded in 1947. Provides blankets, food, health care, seeds, tools, water resources development, and basic education and vocational training worldwide. Sponsors the Annual CROP walk program and publishes a variety of brochures, films, and videos.

Mennonite Disaster Service

21 S. 12th St.
PO Box 500
Akron, PA 17501
717-859-2210
717-859-3875
e-mail: meno_disaster_service@ecunet.org
http://www.mbnet.mb.ca/mcc/mds

Founded in 1950. Coordinates response to disasters, provides cleanup, repair, rebuilding, helping in home building in ghettos and rural poverty areas.

Presiding Bishop's Fund for World Relief

815 2nd Ave.
New York, NY 10017
212-992-5129
Fax: 212-983-6377

Founded in 1940. Provides relief of worldwide human suffering in natural disasters and other emergencies, and developmental grants to eliminate famine, disease, and drought.

Refugee Advocacy

Refugees International

21 Dupont Circle NW
Washington, DC 20036
202-828-0110
Fax: 202-828-0819

Founded in 1979. Advocacy, information, and community support to refugees and displaced persons worldwide, supports existing refugee relief and resettlement programs. Publications include *Bosnia Relief Watch, Refugee and Relief Alert,* and *RI Bulletin.*

International Advocacy Organizations

American Association for International Aging

1900 L St., Suite 510
Washington, DC, 20036-5002
202-833-8893
Fax: 202-833-8762

Founded in 1983. Advocates aged worldwide, through self-help, mutual support, and economic development activities, international development, education and small grants to economic development projects. Publishes reports, *International Directory of Organizations in Aging.*

Global Research Organizations

Center for the Study of Global Problems
University of Georgia
017 Franklin House
Athens, GA 30602-4240
705-542-6633
Fax: 706-542-6633
e-mail: globis@uga.cc.uga.edu
Founded in 1980. Studies global policy, cooperative solutions for global peace, human rights, and sustainable development.

Worldwatch Institute
1776 Massachusetts Ave. NW
Washington, DC 20036
202-452-1999; 800-555-2028
Fax: 202-296-7365
e-mail: wwpub@igc.apc.org
Founded in 1975. Global problem-solving efforts include agriculture, population growth, renewable energy, water, biodiversity, health and environmental justice. Publications include *Environmental Alert Series, State of the World,* annual *World Watch,* and *World Watch Papers.*

Epilogue

You can become involved with professional social workers and learn more about what social work is doing to promote a better society. Several social work organizations are listed below. Join one today.

Professional Social Work Organizations

Association for the Advancement of Social Work with Groups
John H. Ramey, General Secretary
School of Social Work
University of Akron
Akron, OH 44325-8050
800-807-0793
330-836-0793

Association of Jewish Center Professionals
15 E. 26th St.
New York, NY 10010
212-532-4949
Fax: 212-481-4174
Founded in 1918. Supports staff of Jewish community centers, camps, youth groups, and students in schools of social work. Offers Professional of the Year Awards, affiliated with the Jewish Communal Service Association of North America.

Canadian Association of Social Workers
383 Parkdale Ave., Suite 402
Ottawa, ON, Canada K1Y 4R4
613-729-6668
e-mail: casw@casw-acts.ca

International Federation of Social Workers
PO Box 4649
N-0506 Oslo, Norway
47-22-0311-52
Fax: 47-22-0311 14

Jewish Social Services Professional Association
3086 State Hwy. 27, Suite 11
PO Box 248
Kendall Park, NM 08824-0248
908-821-0909
Fax: 908-634-7346
Founded in 1965. Professional association of social work employees united to provide a forum for discussion of topics concerning Jewish family and Children's services.

National Association of Black Social Workers, Inc.
8436 W. McNichols
Detroit, MI 48221
313-862-6813
Founded in 1968. Promotes accountability of the social welfare system in the black community, decision-making and policy setting, alternative service delivery, advocacy, human services and research, transracial adoption, health, aged, recruitment and retention of black social work students and faculty. Publishes *National Black Caucus Journal, National Newspaper,* and *Conference Proceedings.*

National Association of Puerto Rican Hispanic Social Workers
PO Box 651
Great Neck, NY 11717
516-864-1536
Fax: 516-864-1536
e-mail: sonia1536@aol.com
Founded in 1955. Promotes professional development of Hispanic social workers, creates standards and a code of ethics, and lobbies for the issues concerning Hispanic social work and for people of Hispanic or Puerto Rican heritage.

National Association of Social Workers
750 First St. NE, Suite 700
Washington, DC 20002-4241
202-408-8600
Fax: 202-336-8312
Founded in 1955. Develops professional standards for social work practice, operates National Center for Social Policy and Practice, conducts research. Publishes *Encyclopedia of Social Work, Health and Social Work* quarterly, *NASW News, Social Work Almanac, The Social Work Dictionary, Social Work in Education: A Journal for Social Workers in Schools,* and *Social Work* bimonthly, books and information.

National Institute for Social Work Information Service
ATTN: Mark Watson, 5 Tavistock Pl.
London, WCIH 9SN
071-387-9681

North American Association of Christians in Social Work
Box 7090
St. Davids, PA 19087-7090
610-687-5777
Fax: 610-687-5777

Founded in 1954. Organization of professional social workers who share a Christian worldview in social work, encourages awareness within the Christian community of human need and social work as a means of ministering to this need. Publications include *A Christian Response to Domestic Violence, Giving and Taking Help, Integrating Faith and Practice: A History of the North American Association of Christians in Social Work, The Poor You Have With You Always, Social Work and Christianity Journal,* books, and monographs.

1. Abraham Kaplan, "Perspectives on the Theme," in *Individuality and the New Society,* ed.

Abraham Kaplan (Seattle: University of Washington Press, 1970), pp. 19–20.

2. Information for compiling this list has been edited and adapted from *The Encyclopedia of Associations, 32d* ed., ed. Christine Maurer and Tara E. Sheets (Detroit, MI: GALE Research, 1998); Linda May Grobman, ed., *Days in the Lives of Social Workers* (Harrisburg, PA: White Hat Communications, 1996); *Research Centers Directory,* 21st ed., 1996-1997; David L. Bender, *Youth Violence* (Current Controversies Publishers, 1992); David Walls, *The Activists Almanac: The Concerned Citizens Guide to the Leading Advocacy Organizations in America;* Alan Edward Schorr, *Refugee and Immigrant Resource Directory,* 3rd ed. (Deanali Press, 1994).

3. Mari Bombyk, *Social Work Encyclopedia,* 19th ed. (Washington, DC: NASW Press), p. 1939.

APPENDIX C
Internet Ancillaries

*T*his appendix provides discussion lists, use groups, and newsgroups of interest to macro social workers, as well as information about how to access these materials. It includes a listing of federal government websites and e-mail addresses of many government agencies. Many of these sites may be helpful in obtaining help in researching papers or general information about topics of interest to macro social workers.

Usenet

Usenet is the world's largest bulletin board in the broadest sense of the word, a vast collection of people who communicate with each other in thousands of newsgroups or groups that share a special interest. It is so big that you cannot possibly sample it all. Instead you will want to look for the parts of usenet that you might find useful. Once you learn how to read and post on it, you will find a wealth of information available to you. Much of that information, however, is raw and unedited. Take the time necessary to find newsgroups of interest to you, and then read them for a period before posting.

You get your usenet news from a news server. That news server will most likely be located on your campus or somewhere else nearby. Ask your local system administrator or fellow users in your area for information about your local news server. If you do not have a local news server, you may have to resort to using the services of a commercial Internet provider. Even if you cannot access usenet, you can still get usenet news postings via e-mail or the World Wide Web. Stanford University sponsors a free NetNews Filtering Service in which you can specify the subjects you would like to read. Those are then sent to you via e-mail or via a Web home page created for you by the service. To get the e-mail version instructions, send an e-mail message to netnews@hotpage.stanford.edu.

Newsgroups

Because over 10,000 newsgroups exist, you will not be able to read them all. Your local server can only carry a small portion of them, and each individual post has a short lifetime, chiefly determined by the system administrator of the server from which you get your Usenet news. However, many newsgroups archive or collect their postings, making them available to you for much longer periods. Usenet newsgroups have been divided into subject categories. The "Big 8" categories are:

comp	computers in general
humanities	arts and literature
misc	topics not covered by the other categories
news	news
rec	recreation
sci	science
socs	social behaviors and culture
talk	problems and issues
alt	subjects of all kinds

The names become more specific as you read to the right. For example the group alt.activism covers more general material than alt.activism.death-penalty. The only way to really know what a particular newsgroup is interested in is to read what that group posts. The following is a short list of newsgroups filtered by Stanford NetNews that may be of interest to macro social work. The news.announce.newusers site gives information on how to use newsgroups for new users. Most news-reader software packages have a feature that will allow you to search the server you use for particular topics. If you cannot find a newsgroup that you know exists on your news server, contact your systems administrator.

alt.abortion.inequity

alt.abuse.recovery

alt.activism

alt.activism.death-penalty

alt.adoption

alt.culture.usenet

alt.individualism

alt.missing-kids

alt.politics.economics

alt.politics.equality

alt.politicalreform

alt.prisons

alt.recovery

alt.recovery.aa

alt.recovery.na

alt.recovery.codependency

alt.war

ba.jobs.offered

comp.edu

dc.jobs

dc.admin.news.groups

misc.jobs.mis

misc.jobs.offered

misc.jobs.offered.entry

misc.jobs.resumes

abuse.announce

news.groups

news.groups.questions

news.announce.newusers

Social Work Internet Sites

The Internet is ideal for networking and for linking up with resources that you can use for research as well as for finding resources. Most of the Internet sites useful to social work are interactive, which promotes networking. The Internet can help you access the latest data and can be a link between social work researchers and social work practitioners assisting social workers. The sites below link data, research, professional discussion, and information about specific social problems and may help you more easily find information you need.

Advocacy Groups

Oasis Research Center
http://www.matisse.net/politics/activist/
activist.html

American Civil Liberties Union (ACLU)
gopher://aclu.org:6601/

Anti-racist Training and Materials Project
www.mun.ca/cassw-ar

Bread for the World
http://www.bread.org/

Center of Budget and Policy Priorities
http://www.cbpp.org/

Child Trends
http://www.childtrends.org/

Child Welfare League of America
http://www.cwla.org/

Children Now
http://www.childrennow.org/

Children's Defense Fund
http://www.childrens defense.org/

Families USA
http://www.familiesusa.org/

Food Research and Action Center (FRAC)
http://www.frac.org/

Kids Count
http://www.aecf.org/aeckids.htm

Social Work Advocacy Network (SWAN)
http://falcon.cc.ukans.edu/~pthomas/
national.html

Stand For Children
http://www.stand.org/

Community

Alliance for National Renewal
http://www.ncl.org/anr/index.htm

Community Organization
http://comm-org.utoledo.edu/

Community Tool Box
http://ctb.ukans.edu

Cyber-Rural Network
http://www.cyber-rural.org/html/
english_version.html

National Association for Community Leadership
http://www.community leadership.org/

National Community Building Network
http://www.ncbn.org/welcome.html

Midwest Academy
http://www.mindspring.com/~midwestacademy/

Fundraising

National Network of Grantmakers
http://www.nng.org/

Andrew W. Mellon Foundation
http://www.mellon.org/

Ben & Jerry's Foundation
http://benjerry.com/scoop/partnershops.html

Foundation Center
http://www.fdncenter.org

Global Fund for Women
http://www.igc.apc.org/gfw/

MacArthur Foundation
http://www.macfdn.org/

Rotary Foundation
http://rotary.org/foundation/

Russel Sage Foundation
http://tap.epn.org/sage/

Student Services, Inc. (database of scholarships, grants, fellowships, loans)
http://www.student services.com

Twentieth Century Fund
www.tcf.org

Wested (grant information)
http://www.wested.org/tie/grant.html

Winston Foundation for World Peace
http://www.crosslink.net/~wfwp/

Federal Information Exchange
http://web.fie.com

Social Action and Social Administration

Political Activism Resources
http://www.kimsoft.com/kimpol.htm

Social Activist Movements in California
Audio Archive
http://www.lib.berkeley.edu/MRC/pacifica.html

Social Administration and Planning Links
http://www.geocities.com/john_g_mcnutt/
administ.htm

Social Organizations

Guidestar
http://www.Guidestar.org

Impact Online
http://www.impactonline.org/

Independent Sector
http://www.indepsec.org/

Internet Nonprofit Center
www.nonprofits.org

Institute for Global Communications Guide to
Progressive Organizations and Resources
www.igc.org/index.html

Latino Web Nonprofit Organizations
www.latinoweb.com/index.html

Nonprofit Information Center
http://www.silcom.com/~paladin/
nonprofits.html

Nonprofit Resources Catalog
http://www.clark.net/pub/pwalker/

Putnam Barber's Resources for Nonprofits
www.nonprofit-info.org/

Social Work Resources

National Association of Social Workers (NASW)
www.naswdc.org

World Wide Web Resources for Social Workers
http://www.nyu.edu/socialwork/wwwrsw/

Volunteer Information Organizations

America's Promise
www.americspromise.org/

Neighborhoods Online
http://www.lilbertynet.org/nol/natl.html

Points of Light Foundation
www.pointsoflight.org/default.html

Servnet
www.servenet.org

Volunteer Centers and Listings Online
http://dnai.com/~chldren/volunteer.html

Descriptions of Selected Social Work Sites

Anti-racist Training and Materials Project,
www.mun.ca/cassw-ar
Hosted by School of Social Work, Memorial University of Newfoundland, St. John's, NF Canada A1C 5S7. Extensive national inventory of resources and materials on anti-racism, anti-oppression, and diversity. Includes print and audio-visual resources, websites, virtual libraries, journals, publishers, organizations, teaching tools, course outlines, a bulletin board, discussion forum, research information, regional reports, the CASSW Accreditation Standards, and transcripts of conference proceedings and an anti-racism workshop.

Community Tool Box,
http://ctb.ukans.edu
Over 5,000 pages of resources for all types of community work, real-life applications, interactive format, how-to sections on many topics covered in this textbook such as community assessment, advocacy, leadership evaluation, writing grant applications, by-laws; welcoming, training, and maintaining a board of directors, choosing a group, and much more.

Cyber-Rural Network,
http://www.cyber-rural.org/html/
english_version.html.

A virtual dialogue/discussion forum hosted by the social development organization Matawinie Community Futures. Explore benefits and challenges that new information and communication technologies (NICT) offer rural communities. Community developers and organizers establish new contacts and share experiences, current projects, and ideas for innovative ventures.

Social Activist Movements in California,
http://www.lib.berkeley.edu/MRC/pacifica.html

A web-based collection of historical audio recordings related to California social activist movements of the 1960s. First phase has 30–40 hours of programming on the Free Speech Movement, including speeches of Mario Savio and others; deliberations of the UC Berekely Academic Senate on the FSM; songs of the FSM; a variety of on-site recordings of FSM events. Requires a sound card and speakers and either RealAudio or StreamWork audio players (available from www.real.com and www.xingtech.com, respectively).

Social Administration and Planning Links,
http://www.geocities.com/john_g_mcnutt/
administ.htm

These links are provided courtesy of John G. McNutt, Graduate School of Social Work, Boston College, Chestnut Hill, MA 02467. Please express your appreciation and let him know of other useful links that you are aware of. You can reach him at http://www.geocities.com/john_g_mcnutt/ or fax to 617-552-1080.

World Wide Web Resources for Social Workers,
http://www.nyu.edu/socialwork/wwwrsw/

More than 30, links to full-text articles from professional journals, including *Academic Psychiatry; Australasian Journal of Disaster and Trauma Studies; Canadian Journal of Psychiatry; Current Research in Social Psychology; Early Childhood Research & Practice; Journal of Rural Community Psychology; Future of Children; Journal of Ethics.*

Federal Government Internet Sites

Government Agencies

GPO Access (Federal Register)
    http://www.access.gpo.gov/

IFAS (e-mail members of Congress)
    http://www.ifas.org/activist/index.html

Links to State Governments
    http://www.nasire.org/ss/Ststates.html

Links to County Governments
    http://www.naco.org/members/counties/
    stlist.htm

U.S. Department of Agriculture
    http://www.usda.gov/

U.S. Department of Education
    http://www.ed.gov/

U.S. Department of Health and Human Services
    http://www. dhhs.gov/

U.S. Department of Justice
    http://www. usdoj.gov/

U.S. Department of Labor
    http://www.dol.gov/

White House
    http://www.whitehouse.gov

Statistical Agencies

Bureau of Labor Statistics
    http://www.stats.bls.gov/

Centers for Disease Control and Prevention
    http://www.cdc.gov/

Health Care Financing
    http://www.hcfa.gov/

National Center for Education Statistics
    http://nces.ed.gov/

National Center for Health Statistics
    http://www.cdc.gov/nchswww/index.htm

Social Security Administration
    http://www.ssa.gov/

U.S. Census Bureau
    http://www.census.gov/

Federal Government Links

Administration on Aging

Information about health-related matters, links to sites operated by state agencies on aging, directories of area agencies on aging, Older Americans Act, and others.
http://www.aoa.dhhs.gov
e-mail: esec@ban-gate.aoa.dhhs.gov

Administration for Children and Families

Includes programs operated by Administration for Children and Families, as well as information on grants, welfare reform, and more.

http://www.acf.dhhs.gov
e-mail: Webmaster@acf.dhhs.gov

American Memory

Thousands of prints, photographs, and documents of American history, including writings by African Americans, Civil War photographs, books, pamphlets from women's suffrage movement, and more.
http://lcweb2.loc.gov

CDC National AIDS Clearinghouse Servers

Database on private and government funding opportunities for community-based and HIV/AIDS service organizations, articles and summaries of newspapers, magazines, and journals.
http://www.cdcnac.org
e-mail: aidsinfo@cdcnac.aspensys.com

Current Population Survey

Monthly survey of 50,000 households regarding the U.S. labor force.
http://www.bls.census.gov/cps/cpsmain.htm
e-mail: cpshelp@info.census.gov

Federal Bureau of Investigation Homepage

Crime reports, current investigations, hate crimes and others.
http://www.fbi.gov
e-mail: webmaster@www.fbi.gov

FedWorld

A gateway to 100 federal bulletin boards and 14,000 files and databases including federal job openings, U.S. Supreme Court decisions, White House documents, and many others.
http://www.fedworld.gov
e-mail: webmaster@fedworld.gov

Historical, Social Economic, and Demographic Data From the U.S. Census

U.S. Census data from 1790–1860 for every county in most states, including slave ownership, churches, population, manufacturing, real estate, and more.
http://icg.fas.harvard.edu/census
e-mail: icg@fas.harvard.edu

Human Rights Home Page

Discusses development of the human rights movement, hyperlinks to copies of many of the famous documents that have shaped the human rights movement.
http://traveller.com/-hrwebhistory.htm

Justice Department Agencies.

http://www.ojp.usdoj.gov
e-mail: webmaster@ojp.usdoj.gov

Justice Information Center

Hundreds of reports about criminal and juvenile justice and links to other sites. Publications including *Boot Camps for*

Juvenile Offenders, Asssessing Exposure of Urban Youth to Violence, and more.

Library of Congress Home Page

Links to Internet sites operated by local, state, federal, and foreign governments and much more.
http://lcweb.loc.gov
e-mail: lcweb@loc.gov

National Archive of Criminal Justice Data

More than 500 technical datasets related to criminal justice, community studies, corrections, delinquency, victimization, and others.
http://www.icpsr.umich.edu/NACJD
e-mail: web-support@icpsr.umich.edu

National Clearinghouse on Child Abuse and Neglect Information

http://.calib.com/nccanch
email: nccanch@calib.com

National Institute on Alcohol Abuse and Alcoholism

Pamplets on alcoholism, aging and alcohol abuse, drinking and pregnancy, free research monographs.
http://www.njaaa.nih.gov
e-mail: webmaster@www.niaaa.nih.gov

National Institute on Drug Abuse

Fact sheets, articles about research, extensive grant information, catalog of publications, and more.
http://www.nida.nih.gov
e-mail: Webmaster@lists.nida.nih.gov

National Rehabilitation Information Center

Extensive information about disabilities and rehabilitation, Americans With Disabilities Act (ADA), hundreds of Internet sites about disability, and summaries of 14,000 disabilities-related books, articles, videos, and reports.
http://www.naric.com/naric

New Deal Network

Thousands of images related to culture, construction projects, social programs, people, and events of the New Deal Era.
http://newdeal.marist.edu

Oyez Oyez Oyez: A Supreme Court WWW Resource

Oral arguments from more than 75 historic Supreme Court cases. Must have RealAudio software installed. *Roe v. Wade, Hustler Magazine v. Falwell, Regents of University of California v. Bakke,* and others.
http://oyez.at.nwu.edu
e-mail: j-golman@nwu.edu

Queer Resources Directory

Hundreds of files about gays in military, bills, court decisions, government policies, and actions affecting gays. List of openly gay elected and appointed public officials and more.
http://www.qrd.org/qrd
e-mail: staff@qrd.org

Social Science Data Center

Many databases from Census Bureau, FBI, and others.
http://www.lib.virginia.edu/socsci/interactives.html
e-mail: ssdc@viva.lib.virgina.edu

United States Government Information

Hundreds of annotated links to federal Internet sites, divided by dozens of subjects including affirmative action, civil rights, crime statistics, international aid, welfare and welfare reform, and others.
http://www-libraries.colorado.edu/ps/gov/
    us/federal.htm
e-mail: govpubs@colorado.edu

United States Institute of Peace

Reports about international conflict, bimonthly magazine, grants, fellowships, books, links to sites devoted to international relations.
http://www.usip.org
e-mail: usip_requests@usip.org

U.S. Agency for International Development

Information about aid programs in developing nations, USAID telephone directory, and more.
http://www.info.usaid.gov
e-mail: inquiries@usaid.gov

USA Jobs

Best source on Internet for information about federal jobs. Federal job openings updated daily. Search listings by type of job, location, and pay level, then apply online. Also information about searching for a federal job, student employment, outplacement assistance, and more.
http://www.usajobs.opm.gov
e-mail: usajobs_webmaster@opm.gov

U.S. Census Bureau

Data on poverty, crime, housing, up to the second projections of current U.S. and world populations. You can extract data and display them in maps by state or county, showing violent crime rates, population growth by age groups, and much more.
http://www.census.gov
e-mail: webmaster@census.govU.S. Government Printing Office
    Home Page
Offers full text of bills introduced in Congress, the Congressional Record, the Federal Register, and many other databases, as well as federal depository libraries around the country that provide dial-in and Internet gateways into the GPO.
http:/www.access.gpo.gov
e-mail: wwwadmin@www.access.gpo.gov

Voices of the Civil Rights Era

Download audio recordings of some of the important speeches made during the civil rights movement.
http://webcorp.com/civilrights/index.htm

YouthInfo

Links to sites about adolescents, youth topics. Operated by Department of Heath and Human Services.
http://youth.dhhs.gov
e-mail: youth@osaspe.dhhs.gov

NOTES

Chapter 1: Overview of the Practice of Macro Social Work

1. Adapted from Alex Pulaski, "A Difficult Death in a Strange Land," *Fresno Bee,* February 16, 1993, pp. A1, A18. Used with permission.
2. Peter Berger and Richard John Neuhaus, *To Empower People: From State to Civil Society,* 2d ed., Michael Novak (New York: AEI Press,1996).
3. Robert Presthus, *The Organizational Society,* rev. ed. (New York: St. Martin's Press, 1988), and Hendrik M. Ruitenbeek, ed., *The Dilemma of Organizational Society* (New York: E. P. Dutton, 1963).
4. Ibid.

Part 1: Solving Social Problems and Making Social Change

1. F. A. Hayek. *The Counter-Revolution of Science: Studies on the Abuse of Reason* (New York: Free Press of Glencoe, 1964), pp. 32–33.
2. Paulo Freire, *Pedagogy for the Oppressed* (New York: Continuum, 1992), pp. 28, 42.
3. Gibson Winter, *Elements for a Social Ethic: The Role of Social Science in Public Policy* (New York: Macmillan, 1966), pp. 7–9.
4. Michael M. Harmon, *Action Theory for Public Administration* (New York: Longman, 1981), p. 59.
5. Winter, *Elements for a Social Ethic,* p. 8–10.
6. Antonia Pantoja and Wilhelmina Perry, "Community development and restoration: A perspective," in Felix G. Rivera and John L. Erlich, eds., *Community Organizing in a Diverse Society* (Boston: Allyn and Bacon, 1992), p. 227.
7. Hans Falck, *Social Work: The Membership Perspective* (New York: Springer, 1982), p. 16.
8. Harmon, *Action Theory for Public Adminsitration,* pp. 4, 5.
9. Freire, *Pedagogy for the Oppressed,* p. 42.

Chapter 2: Social Problems and Social Change

1. Si Kahn. *How People Get Power: Organizing Oppressed Communities for Action,* rev. ed. (Washington, DC: NASW Press, 1994), p. 132.
2. Pope John Paul II, San Antonio, Texas, September 13, 1987.
3. *Children's Defense Fund. The State of America's Children: A Report From the Children's Defense Fund, Yearbook 1998* (Boston: Beacon Press, 1998), p. xii.
4. Stefan Fatsis, "Recession Aside, Majority of Rich Are Getting Richer," *Fresno Bee,* October 21, 1991, pp. A1, A12.
5. *Pulling Apart: A State-by-State Analysis of Income Trends* [.pdf] http://www.cbpp.org/1-18-00sfp.htm.
6. Donald L. Bartlett and James B. Steele, "Middle Class Is Squeezed As Rich Get Richer and Poor Poorer," *Fresno Bee,* Sunday, October 27, 1991, p. A8.
7. Ibid.
8. Children's Defense Fund. *The State of America's Children,* pp. xi, xii.
9. D. Stanley Eitzen and Maxine Baca-Zinn, *Social Problems,* 6th ed. (Boston: Allyn and Bacon, 1994), p. 55.
10. Ruth Leger Sivard, *World Military and Social Expenditures,* 1991 (Washington, DC: World Priorities, 1991), pp. 33, 9.
11. Eitzen and Baca-Zinn, *Social Problems,* p. 10.
12. Robert C. Linthicum, *Empowering the Poor: Community Organization Among the City's "Rag, Tag and Bobtail"* (Monrovia, CA: MARC, 1991), p. 6.
13. Ronald C. Frederico, *Social Welfare in Today's World* (New York: McGraw Hill, 1990), p. 294.
14. Richard L. Means, *The Ethical Imperative: The Crisis in American Values* (Garden City, NY: Anchor Books, 1970), p. 1.
15. Frank M. Coleman, *Hobbes and America: Exploring the Constitutional Foundations* (Toronto: University of Toronto Press, 1977), pp. 30, 4.
16. Harry Specht and Mark Courtney, *Unfaithful Angels: How Social Work Has Abandoned Its Mission* (New York: Free Press, 1994), p. x.
17. H. Wayne Johnson, *The Social Services: An Introduction,* 3d ed. (Itasca, IL: F. E. Peacock Publishers, 1990), p. 24.
18. C. Wright Mills, *The Sociological Imagination* (London: Oxford University Press, 1959). p. 8.
19. Thomas J. Sullivan and Kenrick S. Thompson, *Introduction to Social Problems* (New York: Macmillan, 1988), p. 3; and Charles Zastrow, *Social Problems: Issues and Solutions* (Chicago: 1988), p. 6.
20. Robert K. Merton and Robert Nisbet, *Contemporary Social Problems,* 2d ed. (New York: Harcourt, Brace, and World, 1966), p. 799.
21. Soroka and Bryjak assert, "Social problems…are perceived as unacceptable by an influential segment of a society's population," in Michael P. Soroka and George J. Bryjak, *Social Problems: A World at Risk* (Boston: Allyn and Bacon, 1995), p. 22.
22. Robert Bellah, Richard Madsen, William M. Sullivan, Ann Swidler, and Steven M. Tipton, *Habits of the Heart: Individualism and Commitment in American Life* (New York: Harper and Row, 1985). See also Coleman, Hobbes and America.
23. Milton Friedman, *Capitalism and Freedom.* See also F. A Von Hayek, *The Road to Serfdom.*
24. Means, *Ethical Imperative,* p. 8.
25. Linthicum, *Empowering the Poor,* p. 9.
26. Michael Lind, *The Next American Nation: The New Nationalism and the Fourth American Revolution* (New York: Simon and Schuster), 1996.
27. Judith Rich Harris, *The Nurture Assumption: Why Children Turn Out the Way They Do* (New York: Simon and Schuster, 1999), p. 299.
28. Soroka and Bryjak, *Social Problems,* p. 9.
29. Timothy M. Cook, "A Little History Worth Knowing," *Dialogue on Disabilities,* Mennonite Central Committee, vol. 14, no. 3, Summer 1993, p. 1.
30. William Ryan, *Blaming the Victim* (New York: Pantheon Books, 1971).
31. Peter Breggin, in Eilen Gambril, *Social Work Practice: A Critical Thinkers Guide* (New York: Oxford University Press, 1997), p. 11.

32. Robert L. Woodson Sr. asserts that "Evidence abounds of the failure of an approach that relies merely on behavior modification or therapeutic intervention," in "Success Stories," Peter L. Berger and Richard John Neuhaus, *To Empower People: From State to Civil Society*, 2d ed. (Washington, DC: American Enterprise Institute Press, 1996), p. 107.

33. Thomas Szasz, *Insanity and Its Consequences* (New York: Wiley, 1987), p. 11.

34. M. Blenker , M. Baloom, and M. Neilsen, "A Research and Demonstration Project of Protective Service," *Social Casework*, 52 (1971), 483–499.

35. R. M. Dawes, *House of Cards: Psychology and Psychotherapy Built on Myth* (New York: Free Press, 1994), in Gambril Social Work Practice, p. 11.

36. Specht and Courtney, *Unfaithful Angels*, pp. 131, 155.

37. Woodson, "Success Stories," asserts that "A recidivism rate as high as 60% has been reported from boot camps for delinquent youth," p. 107.

38. Eitzen and Baca-Zinn, *Social Problems*, p. 14.

39. Stewart E. Perry, *Communities on the Way: Rebuilding Local Economies in the United States and Canada* (Albany: State University of New York Press, 1987), p. 34.

40. Linthicum, *Empowering the Poor*, p.10.

41. Harris, *Nurture Assumption*, p. 327.

42. Steven Pinker, Foreword, in Harris, *Nurture Assumption*, p. xii.

43. Harris, *Nurture Assumption*, p. 355.

44. Ibid., p. 155.

45. The principle of taking on roles was observed as early as 1890 by the first modern psychologist, William James, in his book *The Principles of Psychology* (New York: Henry Holt). James asserted, "A man has as many social selves as there are individuals who recognize him and carry an image of him in their mind. But we may practically say that he has as many different social selves as there are distinct groups of persons about whose opinion he cares. He generally shows a different side of himself to each of these different groups. Many a youth who is demure enough before his parents and teachers, swears and swaggers like a pirate among his 'tough' young friends."

46. Robert H. Lauer and Linda Boardman, "Role-Taking: Theory, Typology and Proposition," *Sociology and Social Research* 55 (January 1971), pp. 137, 105.

47. Harris, *Nurture Assumption*, p. 60.

48. Lauer and Boardman, "Role-Taking," pp. 104, 126–127.

49. Harris, *Nurture Assumption*, pp. 220, 199.

50. Ibid., p. 391.

51. Ibid., p. 28.

52. James M. Henslin, *Social Problems*, 4th ed. (Upper Saddle River, NJ: Prentice Hall, 1996), p. 146.

53. Ibid., p. 147.

54. Harris, *Nurture Assumption*, p. 298.

55. Ibid., p. 359.

56. H. Hortshorne and M. A. May "Studies in the Organization of Character," in H. Munsinger, ed., *Readings in Child Development* (New York: Holt, Rinehart and Winston, 1971), pp. 190–197.

57. Harris, *Nurture Assumption,* pp. 357–358.

58. Samuel R. Slavson, *Character Education in a Democracy.* (New York: Association Press, 1937).

59. Harris, *Nurture Assumption*, pp. 357–362.

60. Ibid., pp. 212–213.

61. Robert Linthicum, "Memorandum to William Brueggemann," Partners in Urban Transformation, Los Angeles, CA, July 22, 1998, p. 1.

62. James Madison, Alexander Hamilton, and John Jay, *The Federalist Papers*, no. 10.

63. Soroka and Bryjak, *Social Problems*, p. 15.

64. Henslin, *Social Problems*, pp. 42, 46.

65. Linthicum, "Memorandum," pp. 3, 4.

66. Charles Zastrow, *The Practice of Social Work*, 3d ed. (Homewood, IL: Dorsey Press, 1989), p. 217.

67. Augustus Y. Napier with Carl A. Whitaker, *The Family Crucible: One Family's Therapy—An Experience That Illuminates All Our Lives* (Toronto: Bantam Books, 1978), p. 47.

68. Eitzen and Baca-Zinn, *Social Problems*, p. 4.

69. Ritchie P. Lowry, *Social Problems* (Lexington, MA: D. C. Heath, 1974), p. 205.

70. Perrow, Charles, *Complex Organizations*, 2d ed. (Glenview, IL: Scott Foresman, 1979), p. 190.

71. Victor A. Thompson, *Without Sympathy or Enthusiasm: The Problem of Administrative Compassion* (University, AL: University of Alabama Press, 1975), pp. 90–94.

72. Perry, *Communities*, pp. 33–34.

73. Eitzen and Baca-Zinn, *Social Problems*, p. 9.

74. Ibid., pp. 5–6.

75. Peter M. Berger and John Neuhaus, *To Empower People: From State to Civil Society*, 2d ed. (Washington, DC: American Enterprise Institute Press, 1996), p. 159.

76. Gibson Winter, *Elements for a Social Ethic: The Role of Social Science in Public Policy* (New York: Macmillan, 1966), p. 15.

77. Michael M. Harmon, *Action Theory for Public Administration* (New York: Longman, 1981), p. 37.

78. Jerome G. Manus, *Analyzing Social Problems* (New York: Praeger, 1976), p 16.

79. Thomas P. Holland, "Organizations: Contest for Social Services Delivery" in *Encyclopedia of Social Work*, 19th ed. (Washington, DC: NASW Press, 1995), p. 1789.

80. Coleman, *Hobbes and America*, pp. 6, 16.

81. Richard Hofstadter, "Woodrow Wilson: Democrat in Cupidity" in *The Progressive Era: Liberal Renaissance or Liberal Failure*, Arthur Mann, ed. (New York: Holt, Rinehart and Winston, 1963), p. 71.

82. Coleman, *Hobbes and America*, pp. 55, 59.

83. Milton Friedman, *Capitalism and Freedom* (Chicago: University of Chicago Press, 1962), p.5.

84. Thomas M. Meenaghan and Robert O. Washington, *Social Policy and Social Welfare: Structure and Applications* (New York: Free Press, 1980), pp. 89, 81.

85. Bellah et al., *Habits of the Heart*, pp. 142–144, 38.

86. Herbert Simon, *Administrative Behavior: A Study of Decision Making Processes in Organization*, 3d ed. (New York: Free Press, 1976), pp. 85, 86.

87. Bellah et al., *Habits of the Heart*, p. 153.

88. Henry S. Kariel, *Beyond Liberalism: Where Relations Grow* (New York: Harper and Row, 1977), p. 5.

89. Coleman, *Hobbes and America*, p. 125.

90. MacIntyre, *After Virtue*, 2d ed. (Notre Dame, IN: University of Notre Dame Press, 1984), p. 227.

91. Elbert V. Bowden, *Economic Evolution* (Cincinnati: South-Western Publishing 1981), p. 193.

92 Charles L. Schultze, *The Public Use of Private Interest* (Washington, D.C.: Brookings Institution), p. 18.

93. Coleman, *Hobbes and America*, p. 10.

94. Bellah et al., *Habits of the Heart*, p. 33.

95. Coleman, *Hobbes and America,* p. 77.

96. Reinhold Niebuhr, "The Children of Light and the Children of Darkness," in *Gibson Winter, Social Ethics: Issues in Ethics and Society* (New York: Harper and Row, 1968), p. 148.

97. Coleman, *Hobbes and America*, pp. 116, 99.

98. Means, *Ethical Imperative*, p. 31.

99. Walter A. Weiskopf, *Alienation and Economics* (New York: Dell, 1971), p. 16.

100. Eizen and Baca-Zinn, *Social Problems*, p. 8.

101. Coleman, *Hobbes and America*, p. 21.

102. Ralph Brody, *Problem Solving: Concepts and Methods for Community Organizations* (New York: Human Sciences Press, 1982), p. 18.

103. Mills, *Sociological Imagination*, p. 187.

104. Joseph M. Kling and Prudence S. Posner, eds., *Dilemmas of Activism: Class, Community, and the Politics of Local Mobilization* (Philadelphia: Temple University Press, 1990), p. 40.

105. Eitzen and Baca-Zinn, *Social Problems*, pp. 14, 15.

106. Specht and Courtney, *Unfaithful Angels*, pp 152–175.

107. Ann Weick and Dennis Saleeby "Postmodern Perspectives for Social Work," in Roland G. Meinert, John T. Pardeck, and John W. Murphy, eds, *Postmodernism, Religion and the Future of Social Work* (New York: Haworth Pastoral Press, 1998), p. 29.

108. Editor, "Babies—The Future at Risk," *Fresno Bee*, April 26, 1990, p. B4.

109. Ibid.

110. Paulo Freire, *Pedagogy of the Oppressed* (New York: Continuum, 1992), p. 61.

111. Donald C. Reitzes and Dietrich C. Reitzes, *The Alinsky Legacy: Alive and Kicking* (Greenwich, CT: JAI Press, 1987), pp. 30–31.

112. Ibid., p. 31. Saul D. Alinsky, *Reveille for Radicals* (New York: Vintage Books, 1969), p. 115.

113. Mills, *Sociological Imagination*, p. 187.

Chapter 3: The Method of Solving Social Problems

1. Thomas Hobbes, *Leviathan: Or the Matter, Forme, and Power of a Commonwealth Ecclesiastical and Civil,* ed. Frederick J. E. Woodbridge (New York: Scribner, 1930), ch. 5, pp. 174–175.

2. Karl R. Popper, *In Search of a Better World: Lectures and Essays From Thirty Years* (London: Routledge and Kegan Paul, 1992), p. 149.

3. Hobbes, *Leviathan*, ch. 13, p. 253.

4. Hobbes, *Leviathan*, p. 136. Hobbes begins his great work by describing his new model of such an artificial social system, initiating the idea of systems theory. "For what is the *heart* but a spring; and the *nerves* but so many *strings;* and the *joints,* but so many *wheels,* giving motion to the whole body....Therefore, if God can create nature which is *nothing but a system* composed of a 'motion of limbs,' is it not also possible for humans by following the same creative process or art, to make an artificial animal? Thus [is created] the great Leviathan called a Commonwealth, or State, which is but an artificial man....in which the *sovereign* is an artificial *soul*;...the *magistrates* [are] artificial *joints*; *reward* and *punishment*...are the *nerves*."

5. Michael Oakeshott, introduction to Thomas Hobbes, *Leviathan: Or the Matter, Forme, and Power of a Commonwealth Ecclesiastical and Civil,* ed. Michael Oakeshott (New York: Collier Books, 1962), p. 19.

6. See John Locke, *Two Treatises of Government,* 1698.

7. Adam Smith, *An Inquiry Into the Nature and Causes of the Wealth of Nations,* ed. Edwin Cannan (New York: Modern Library, 1994, originally published in 1776).

8. Alexander Hamilton, James Madison, and John Jay, *The Federalist Papers,* ed. Clinton Rossiter (New York: Mentor, 1999).

9. Hobbes, Leviathan, ch. 5, pp. 41–42.

10. Herbert Simon, *Administrative Behavior,* 4th ed. (New York: Free Press, 1997). Simon states that the "major value premise of the administrator's decision is thereby given him, leaving to him only the implementation of these objectives," p. 11.

11. Mary Zey, *Rational Choice Theory and Organizational Theory: A Critique* (Thousand Oaks, CA: Sage, 1998), p. 2.

12. Simon, *Administrative Behavior*, p. 11.

13. Graham T. Allison, *The Essence of Decision: Explaining the Cuban Missile Crisis* (Boston: Little, Brown, 1971), p. 29.

14. Zey, *Rational Choice,* p. 1. Zey says that there are other labels for this theory. It is called "public choice theory" by political scientists and public administrators; "neoclassism" and "rational choice theory" by economists; "expected utility theory" by psychologists; and "rational choice theory" by sociologists.

15. Zey, *Rational Choice*, p. 2.

16. The closer a benefit/cost ratio is to or exceeds 1 (B/C=1), the more attractive it becomes. Furthermore, this is the same definition of efficiency. E=I/O, the more efficient (E) decision is one where inputs (I) are equal to or less than the outputs. If we receive more output than we put into a project or work, we have achieved efficiency. If a decision gives us more benefits than it costs, we have profit.

17. Gary Becker, *A Treatise on the Family* (Cambridge, MA: Harvard University Press, 1981), p. ix.

18. Mary Zey, "Criticisms of Rational Choice Models" in *Decision Making: Alternatives to Rational Choice Models,* ed. Mary Zey (Thousand Oaks, CA: Sage, 1992), pp. 9–10.

19. John Dewey, *How We Think,* rev. ed. (Lexington, MA: D. C. Heath, 1933).

20. Allison, *Essence*, pp. 10–36.

21. Herbert Simon, *Administrative Behavior,* 4th ed. (New York: Free Press, 1997), pp. 92–95.

22. C. West Churchman, *The Systems Approach* (New York: Dell, 1968), pp. 146–176.

23. Edith Stokey and Richard Zeckhauser, *A Primer for Policy Analysis* (New York: W. W. Norton, 1978), pp. 3–44.

24. See Ronald Lippitt, Jeanne Watson, and Bruce Westley, *The Dynamics of Planned Change* (New York: Harcourt, Brace and World, 1958), pp. 131–43. They examined the work of a variety of social workers, psychiatrists, and organization consultants and confirmed that most professionals used a process consisting of the following seven phases: (1) Development of a need for change; (2) Establishment of a change relationship; (3) Clarification or diagnosis of the client's system problem; (4) Examination of alternative routes and goals, establishing goals and intention of action; (5) Transformation of intentions into actual change efforts; (6) Generalization and stabilization of change; (7) Achievement of a terminal relationship.

25. See, for example, Irving L. Janis and Leon Mann, *Decision Making: A Psychological Analysis of Conflict, Choice, and Commitment* (New York: Free Press, 1977); A. L. George, *Presidential Decision-Making in Foreign Policy: The Effective Use of Information and Advice* (Boulder, CO: Westview); and Zey, *Decision Making: Alternatives to Rational Choice Models* (Thousand Oaks, CA: Sage, 1992).

26. Allison, *Essence,* pp. 29–30.

27. Helen Harris Perlman, *Social Casework: A Problem-Solving Process* (Chicago: University of Chicago Press, 1957.)

28. *Curriculum Policy Statement for Baccalaureate Degree Programs in Social Work Education* (Alexandria, VA: Council on Social Work Education, 1992); *Curriculum Policy Statement for Master's Degree Programs in Social Work Education* (Alexandria, VA: Council on Social Work Education, 1992).

29. Ronald L. Simons and Stephen M. Aigner, *Practice Principles: A Problem-Solving Approach to Social Work* (New York: Macmillan, 1985) pp. 25–29.

30. Richard M. Grinnell Jr., *Social Work Research and Evaluation*, 3d ed. (Itasca, IL: F. E. Peacock Publishers, 1988), p. 15.

31. Simon, *Administrative Behavior*, p. 75.

32. Kurt Lewin, "Frontiers in Group Dynamics: Concept, Method and Reality in Social Science, Social Equilibria, and Social Change," *Human Relations*, 1(1) (June 1947): pp. 5–41.

33. Ralph Brody, *Problem-Solving: Concepts and Methods for Community Organization* (New York: Human Sciences Press, 1992), p. 107.

34. Simon, *Administrative Behavior*, p. 57.

35. Alberto Guerreiro Ramos, *The New Science of Organizations: A Reconception of the Wealth of Nations* (Toronto: University of Toronto Press, 1981), p. 106.

36. Gibson Winter, *Elements for a Social Ethic: The Role of Social Science in Public Policy* (New York: Macmillan, 1966), p. 186.

37. Zey, *Rational Choice Theory*, p. 2.

38. Ramos, *New Science*, p. 106.

39. Harry Blamiers, *The Christian Mind* (New York: Seabury Press, 1963), p. 22.

40. Solomon Schimmel, *The Seven Deadly Sins: Jewish, Christian, and Classical Reflections on Human Nature* (New York: Free Press, 1992), p. 5.

41. See Max Weber, "Bureaucracy" in *Economy and Society: An Outline of Interpretive Sociology*, 3 vols., trans. Guenther Roth and Claus Wittich (New York: Bedminster Press, 1968), p. 975, and Victor A. Thompson, *Without Sympathy or Enthusiasm: The Problem of Administrative Compassion* (University: University of Alabama Press, 1975).

42. Weber, "Bureaucracy," p. 975.

43. Zey, *Decision Making*, p. 20. "Rational choice values self-serving individualized choice over collective choice and public goals."

44. Mancur Olson, *The Logic of Collective Action* (Boston: Harvard University Press), pp. 2–3.

45. Michael Heus and Allen Pincus, *The Creative Generalist: A Guide to Social Work Practice* (Barneveld, WI: Micamar Publishing, 1986), pp. 47–65, 108–126, 271.

46. Chris Valley, "One Community Organizer's Career Path in Program Development" (Atlanta, GA: Families First), unpublished manuscript, n.d. p. 6.

47. Julio Morales and Migdalia Reyes, "Cultural and Political Realities for Community Social Work Practice With Puerto Ricans in the United States," in Felix G. Rivera and John L. Erlich, eds., *Community Organizing in a Diverse Society*, 3d ed. (Needham, MA: Allyn and Bacon, 1992), p. 77.

48. Walter A. Weiskopf, *Alienation and Economics* (New York: Dell, 1971), p. 6.

49. Ramos, *New Science*, pp. 4, 17, 82.

50. Robert H. Lauer and Warren T. Handel, *Social Psychology: The Theory and Application of Symbolic Interactionism* (Englewood Cliffs, NJ: Prentice-Hall, 1983), pp. 30, 89, 90.

51. Otto Pollak, *Human Behavior and the Helping Professions* (New York: Spectrum, 1976), p. 10.

52. Lauer and Handel, *Social Psychology*, p. 23.

53. Ibid.

54. Walter Kaufman, ed., *Existentialism from Dostoevsky to Sartre* (New York: Meridian, 1956), p.136.

55. David L Miller, *Individualism: Personal Achievement and the Open Society* (Austin: University of Texas Press, 1967), pp. 19–20.

56. Harry Blumer, *Symbolic Interactionism: Perspective and Method* (Englewood Cliffs, NJ: Prentice-Hall, 1969), p.14.

57. George Herbert Mead, in Lauer and Handel, *Social Psychology*, p. 25.

58. Ibid., p. 15.

59. Blumer, *Symbolic Interactionism*, p. 15.

60. Lauer and Handel, *Social Psychology*, p. 25.

61. Ann Weick and Dennis Saleebey, "Postmodern Perspectives of Social Work" in Roland G. Meinert, John T. Pardeck, and John W. Murphy, eds., *Postmodernism, Religion, and the Future of Social Work* (New York: Haworth Pastoral Press, 1998), p. 29.

62. Zey, *Rational Choice*, p. 2.

63. Kenneth J. Arrow, "Rationality of Self and Others in an Economic System," in Zey, *Decision Making: Alternatives to Rational Chioice Models*, pp. 63–64.

64. Barry Checkoway, "Core Concepts for Community Change," in Marie Weil, ed., *Community Practice: Models in Action* (New York: Haworth Press, 1997), p. 13.

65. Harmon, *Action Theory*, p. 126.

66. Blumer, *Symbolic Interactionism*, p. 12.

67. Victor A. Thompson, *Without Sympathy or Enthusiasm: The Problem of Administrative Compassion* (University of Alabama Press, 1975), p. 10.

68. Simon, *Administrative Behavior*, pp. 80–83.

69. Aaron Wildavsky, *The Politics of the Budgetary Process*, 2d ed. (Boston: Little, Brown, 1974); William L. Morrow, *Public Administration: Politics and the Political System* (New York: Random House, 1975).

70. Robert Formaini, *The Myth of Scientific Public Policy* (New Brunswick, NJ: Transaction, 1990), pp. 1, 5, 91, 95.

71. *Curriculum Policy Statement for Baccalaureate Degree Programs in Social Work Education* (Alexandria, VA: Council on Social Work Education, 1992); *Curriculum Policy Statement for Master's Degree Programs in Social Work Education* (Alexandria, VA: Council on Social Work Education, 1992).

72. Charles Zastrow, *Introduction to Social Work and Social Welfare*, 7th ed. (Belmont, CA: Brooks/Cole Wadsworth, 2000), p. 71.

73. Zey, "Criticisms of Rational Choice Models," p. 27.

Chapter 4: Leadership: The Hallmark of Macro Social Work

1. Daniel Levine, *Jane Addams and the Liberal Tradition* (Westport, CT: Greenwood Press, 1971), p. ix.

2. Ibid., p. xi.

3. Ibid., p. 42.

4. Ibid., p. 129.

5. Ibid., p. 179.

6. Ibid., p. xi.

7. Ibid., p. 181.

8. Ibid., p. x.

9. Hans Falck, *Social Work: The Membership Perspective* (New York: Springer, 1982), p. 161.

10. Elenore L. Brilliant, "Social Work Leadership: A Missing Ingredient?" *Social Work*, 31(5) (Sept.–Oct., 1986): p. 326.

11. Burton Gummer, *The Politics of Social Administration: Managing Organizational Politics in Social Agencies* (Englewood Cliffs, NJ: Prentice-Hall, 1990), p. 122.

12. Chauncey Alexander, "Professional Social Workers and Political Responsibility," in Maryann Mahaffey and John W. Hanks, eds., *Practical Politics: Social Work and Political Responsibility* (Silverspring, MD: National Association of Social Workers, 1982), p. 15.

13. Gummer, *Politics of Social Administration*, p. 123.

14. Peter Block, *Stewardship: Choosing Service Over Self-Interest* (San Francisco: Berrett-Koehler, 1993), p. 21.

15. Charles Perrow, *Complex Organizations,* 2d ed. (Glenview, IL: Scott, Foresman, 1979), p. 4.
16. Herbert A. Simon, *Administrative Behavior,* 4th ed. (New York: Free Press, 1997), p. 196. Simon asserts that "authority refers to the *acceptance* by the subordinate of the decisions of the superior and not the power of the superior to apply sanctions in case of noncompliance." (p. 13).
17. Ibid., pp. 9, 179.
18. Ibid., p. 180.
19. Ibid.
20. Ibid., p.112. Simon asserts, for example, "training prepares the organization member to reach satisfactory decisions himself without the need for the constant exercise of authority or advice. . . . Training procedures are alternatives to the exercise of authority or advice as a means of control over the subordinate's decisions" (p. 13).
21. James M. Kouzas and Barry Posner, *The Leadership Challenge: How to Get Extraordinary Things Done in Organizations* (San Francisco: Jossey-Bass, 1987). Herbert Simon, *Administrative Behavior,* p. 186, looks at this issue differently. He says, "The leader…is merely a bus driver whose passengers will leave him unless he takes them in a direction they want to go. They leave him only minor discretion as to the road to be followed."
22. Block, *Stewardship: ChoosingService Over Self-Interest,* pp. 19, 21.
23. Simon, *Administrative Behavior,* p. 185.
24. Block, *Stewardship,* pp. 147–48.
25. Frederick Winslow Taylor, *Scientific Management* (Westport, CT: Greenwood, 1972). Originally published 1910.
26. David C. McClelland, *Power: The Inner Experience* (New York: Irvington, 1975), p. 260.
27. Block, *Stewardship,* pp. 36–37.
28. Arturo S. Rodrigues in Felix G. Rivera and John L. Erlich, *Community Organizing in a Diverse Society,* 3d ed. (Boston: Allyn and Bacon, 1998), p. vi.
29. Burton Gummer, *Politics of Social Administration,* p. 132.
30. Ibid., p. 187.
31. Edgar Schein in Kouzas and Posner, *The Leadership Challenge,* p. 83.
32. Kouzas and Posner, *The Leadership Challenge,* p. 7.
33. Theodore Hesburgh in Rapp and Poertner, *Social Administration: A Client Centered Approach* (New York: Longman, 1992), p. 281.
34. Kouzas and Posner, *The Leadership Challenge,* p. 83.
35. Ibid., p. 19.
36. Ibid., p. 83.
37. Ibid., p. 115.
38. Ibid., p. 113.
39. Warren Bennis and Burt Nanus, *Leaders: The Strategies for Taking Charge* (New York: Harper and Row, 1985), p. 3.
40. Kouzas and Posner, *The Leadership Challenge,* p. 222.
41. Paul Hersey and Kenneth H. Blanchard, *Management of Organizational Behavior: Utilizing Human Resources,* 5th ed. (Englewood Cliffs, NJ: Prentice-Hall, 1988), pp. 116–122.
42. Ibid., pp. 177–181.
43. William G. Brueggemann, "Group Centered Leadership," unpublished paper, Leadership Conference, Fresno Pacific University, Fresno, CA, January, 1986.
44. Adapted from B. Tuckman, "Developmental Sequence in Small Groups," *Psychological Bulletin,* 63 (1963): pp. 384–399.
45. Ronald W. Toseland and Robert F. Rivas. *An Introduction to Group Work Practice,* 2d ed. (Boston: Allyn and Bacon, 1995), p. 301.

46. Ibid., p. 300.
47. Ibid., p. 307.
48. Kouzas and Posner, *The Leadership Challenge,* p. 162.
49. Ibid.
50. Ibid., p. 184.
51. Burt Nanus, *Visionary Leadership* (San Francisco: Jossey-Bass, 1992), p. 12.
52. Ibid., pp. 18–19.
53. Henry Kissinger in Charles A. Rapp and John Poertner, *Social Administration: A Client Centered Approach* (New York: Longman, 1992), p. 281.
54. Adapted from John E. Jones, "Adjectives Feedback," Exercise 168 in William Pfeiffer, *Structured Exercises* (La Jolla, CA: University Associates, 1976).
55. Stephen P. Robbins, *Essentials of Organizational Behavior,* 3d ed. (Englewood Cliffs, NJ: Prentice-Hall, 1992), pp. 156–157.
56. Warren Bennis, *Why Leaders Can't Lead* (San Francisco: Jossey-Bass, 1989), p. 18.

Part II: Social Work with Communities

1. Harry Specht and Mark E. Courtney, *Unfaithful Angels: How Social Work Has Abandoned Its Mission* (New York: Free Press, 1994), p. 27.
2. Hans Falck, *Social Work: The Membership Perspective* (New York: Springer, 1988), p. 6.
3. Albert Borgmann, *Crossing the Post Modern Divide* (Chicago: University of Chicago Press, 1992), p. 57.

Chapter 5: Communities

1. Jeremiah 29:7.
2. First governor of Massachusetts Bay Colony in his sermon "A Model of Christian Charity," delivered aboard ship in Salem harbor just before landing in the new land. From Robert N. Bellah, Richard Madsen, William M. Sullivan, Ann Swidler, and Steven M. Tipton, *Habits of the Heart: Individualism and Commitment in American Life* (New York: Harper and Row, 1985), p. 28.
3. Excerpted and adapted from the *Weapons of the Spirit,* a film by Pierre Sauvage Productions and Friends of Le Chambon, Inc., 1988. See also Philip Hallie, *Lest Innocent Blood Be Shed: The Story of the Village of Le Chambon and How Goodness Happened There* (New York: Harper and Row, 1979).
4. Acts 2:44–46, 4:32–35, 5:12b.
5. Nobel Prize–winner Herbert Simon asserts that "It is impossible for the behavior of a single, isolated individual to reach any high degree of rationality. . . .the organization permits the individual to approach reasonably near to objective rationality." *Administrative Behavior,* 4th ed. (New York: Free Press, 1997), pp. 92–93.
6. Herbert Blumer, *Symbolic Interactionism: Perspective and Method* (Englewood Cliffs, NJ: Prentice-Hall, 1969), p.145.
7. George Herbert Mead, *Mind, Self and Society From the Standpoint of a Social Behaviorist* (Chicago: University of Chicago Press, 1962), p. 6n.
8. Gibson Winter, *Elements for a Social Ethic: The Role of Social Science in Public Policy* (New York: Macmillan, 1966), p. 8.
9. P. Ramsey, "The Transformation of Ethics," in *Faith and Ethics: The Theology of H. Richard Niebuhr,* ed. P. Ramsey (New York: Harper and Row, 1965), p. 141.
10. Ibid.
11. Michael M. Harmon, "Toward an Active Social Theory of Administrative Action," in *Organization Theory and the New*

Public Administration, ed. Carl J. Bellone (Boston: Allyn and Bacon, 1980), p.186.

12. Winter, *Elements for a Social Ethic*, p. 97.

13. Ibid., pp. 40–41.

14. David L. Miller, *Individualism: Personal Achievement and the Open Society* (Austin: University of Texas Press, 1967), p. 40.

15. Ibid., p. 36.

16. Ibid., pp. 40–42.

17. Robert H. Lauer and Warren T. Handel, *Social Psychology: The Theory and Application of Symbolic Interactionism* (Englewood Cliffs, NJ: Prentice-Hall, 1983), pp. 115–116.

18. Douglas Browning, *Act and Agent* (Coral Gables, FL: University of Miami Press, 1964), pp. 14, 19–20.

19. Miller, *Individualism*, p. 15.

20. John P. Hewitt, *Self and Society: A Symbolic Interactionist Social Psychology,* 7th ed. (Boston: Allyn and Bacon, 1997), p. 50.

21. Mead, *Mind, Self and Society,* p. 6n.

22. Lauer and Handel, *Social Psychology*, pp. 115–116.

23. Bellah et al., *Habits of the Heart*, p. 69.

24. Mead, *Mind, Self and Society*, p. 105.

25. Ibid., pp. 16–17.

26. Winter, *Elements for a Social Ethic,* p. 21.

27. Antonia Pantoja and Wilhelmina Perry, "Community Development and Restoration: A Perspective," in *Community Organizing in a Diverse Society,* ed. Felix G. Rivera and John L. Erlich (Boston: Allyn and Bacon, 1992), p. 237.

28. Winter, *Elements for a Social Ethic,* p. 21.

29. Pantoja and Perry, "Community Development and Restoration," p. 237.

30. Peter L. Berger and Richard John Neuhaus, *To Empower People: From State to Civil Society,* 2d ed. (Washington, DC: American Enterprise Institute Press, 1997), p. 158.

31. Ibid. See also Ralph Hummel, *The Bureaucratic Experience* (New York: St. Martin's Press, 1977).

32. Ibid.

33. Frank Coleman, *Hobbes and America: Exploring the Constitutional Foundations* (Toronto: University of Toronto Press, 1977).

34. Victor A. Thompson, *Without Sympathy or Enthusiasm: The Problem of Administrative Compassion* (University: University of Alabama Press, 1977).

35. Victor Thompson, *Bureaucracy and the Modern World* (University: University of Alabama Press, 1976).

36. Alberto Ramos, *The New Science of Organization* (Toronto: University of Toronto Press, 1981).

37. C. Wright Mills, *The Sociological Imagination* (London: Oxford University Press, 1959), pp. 307–308.

38. Lawrence Haworth, "The Good Life: Growth and Duty," in *Social Ethics: Issues in Ethics and Society,* ed. Gibson Winter (New York: Harper and Row, 1968), p.173.

39. Berger and Neuhaus, *To Empower People*, p. 159.

40. Samuel Bowles and Herbert Gintis, *Democracy and Capitalism* (New York: Basic Books, 1987), p. 179.

41. Blumer, *Symbolic Interactionism*, p. 15.

42. Dewey, *The Public and Its Problems* (Denver: Swallow Press, 1927), p. 131.

43. Francis Schussler Fiorenza, "The Church as a Community of Interpretation: Political Theology Between Discourse Ethics and Hermeneutical Reconstruction," in *Habermas, Modernity and Public Theology,* ed. Don S. Browning and Francis Schussler Fiorenza (New York: Crossroads, 1992), p. 79.

44. Pantoja and Perry, "Community Development and Restoration," p. 237.

45. Robert Fisher, *Let the People Decide: Neighborhood Organizing in America* (New York: Twayne, 1994), pp. xix, xxii.

46. Wynetta Devore, "The African American Community in 1990: The Search for a Practice Method," in *Community Organizing in a Diverse Society,* ed. Felix G. Rivera and John L. Erlich (Boston: Allyn and Bacon, 1992), p.83.

47. Judith Rich Harris, *The Nurture Assumption: Why Children Turn out the Way They Do* (New York: Simon and Schuster, 1998), pp. 298–299.

48. Myron Orfield, *Metropolitics: A Regional Agenda for Community and Stabiliity* (Cambridge, MA: Brookings Institution Press; Washington, DC: Lincoln Institute of Land Policy, 1997).

49. Ibid.

50. Ann Schaef, *When Society Becomes an Addict* (San Francisco: Harper and Row, 1987).

51. Thomas Bender, *Community and Social Change in America* (New Brunswick, NJ: Rutgers University Press, 1978), p. 146.

52. Si Kahn, *How People Get Power: Organizing Oppressed Communities for Action* (New York: McGraw-Hill, 1972), p. 124.

53. Gustavo Gutierrez, *We Drink From Our Own Wells* (Maryknoll, NY: Orbis, 1985), pp. 36–37.

54. Wynetta Devore, "The African American Community in 1990," p. 84.

55. John M. Perkins, *With Justice for All* (Ventura, CA: Regal Books, 1982), p. 35.

56. Berger and Neuhaus, *To Empower People,* pp. 185–186.

57. Ibid., p. 187.

58. Ibid., p. 185.

59. Ibid., p. 189.

60. Fiorenza, "The Church as a Community of Interpretation," pp. 79–80.

61. Jews, for example, experience a continuous historical existence of being aliens who "sing the Lord's song in a strange land" (Psalm 137:4). Christians see themselves as being "in the world but not *of* the world" (John 17:16–18).

62. Ernest Kurtz and Katherine Ketcham, *The Spirituality of Imperfection: Storytelling and the Journey to Wholeness* (New York: Bantam, 1992), p. 87.

63. Karen Lebacqz, *Justice in an Unjust World: Foundations for a Christian Approach to Justice* (Minneapolis: Augsburg Publishing House, 1987), p. 59.

64. Deuteronomy 14:29b; James 1:27.

65. Kurtz and Ketcham, *Spirituality of Imperfection,* pp. 82, 85.

66. Isaiah C. Lee, "The Chinese Americans—Community Organizing Strategies and Tactics," in *Community Organizing in a Diverse Society,* ed. Felix G. Rivera and John L. Erlich (Boston: Allyn and Bacon, 1992), pp. 153–155; reprinted with permission of the publisher.

67. Interview with Carter Camp originally in *Akwesasne Notes*, published by the Mohawk Nation; in Shirley Jenkins, *The Ethnic Dilemma in Social Services* (New York: Free Press, 1981), p. 16.

68. Thompson, *Without Sympathy or Enthusiasm,* p. 40.

69. Vu-Duc Vuong and John Duong Huynh, "Southeast Asians in the United States: A Strategy for Accelerated and Balanced Integration," in *Community Organizing in a Diverse Society,* ed. Felix G. Rivera and John L. Erlich (Boston: Allyn and Bacon, 1992), p. 217.

70. Ibid., p. 219.

71. Harry Specht and Mark Courtney, *Unfaithful Angels: How Social Work Has Abandoned Its Mission* (New York: Free Press, 1994).

72. Julio Morales, "Community Social Work Practice With Puerto Ricans in the United States," in *Community Organizing in a Diverse Society,* ed. Felix G. Rivera and John L. Erlich (Boston: Allyn and Bacon, 1992), p. 98.

73. Pantoja and Perry, "Community Development and Restoration," p. 227.

74. Sam Roberts, "America On the Move: How Mobile a Nation Is It?" *Fresno Bee,* Dec. 12, 1994, p. A1.

75. S. K. Khinduka, "Community Development: Potentials and Limitations," in *Strategies of Community Organization: Macro Practice,* 4th ed., ed. Fred M. Cox, John L. Erlich, Jack Rothman, and John E. Troppman (Itasca, IL: Peacock, 1987), p. 353.

76. Ibid.

Chapter 6: Becoming a Social Work Planner

1. John Forester, *Planning in the Face of Power* (Berkeley: University of California Press, 1989), p. 28.

2. The material in this opening section of the chapter is drawn from William M. Rohe and Lauren B. Gates, *Planning With Neighborhoods* (Chapel Hill: University of North Carolina Press, 1985), and is used by permission of the publisher.

3. Robert R. Mayer, *Policy and Program Planning* (Englewood Cliffs, NJ: Prentice-Hall, 1985), p. 4.

4. Armand Lauffer, "The Practice of Social Planning," in *Handbook for Social Services,* ed. Neil Gilbert and Harry Specht (Englewood Cliffs, NJ: Prentice-Hall, 1981), p. 583.

5. Rohe and Gates, *Planning With Neighborhoods,* pp. 80, 107, 108, 82.

6. Ibid., pp. 80, 82, 108.

7. Ibid., p. 82.

8. Ibid., pp. 82, 108.

9. Paul A. Kurzman, "Program Development and Service Coordination as Components of Community Practice," in *Theory and Practice of Community Social Work,* ed. Samuel H. Taylor and Robert W. Roberts (New York: Columbia University Press, 1985), p. 97.

10. Walter I. Trattner, *From Poor Law to Welfare State: A History of Social Welfare in America,* 4th ed. (New York: Free Press, 1989), p. 88.

11. Margaret E. Rich, *A Belief in People: A History of Family Social Work* (New York: Family Service Association of America, 1956), p. 13.

12. Kurzman, "Program Development," p. 97.

13. Ibid.

14. Beulah H. Compton, *Introduction to Social Welfare and Social Work: Structure, Function, and Process* (Homewood, IL: Dorsey, 1980), p. 162.

15. Arthur Dunham, *The New Community Organization* (New York: Crowell, 1970), p. 73.

16. Kurzman, "Program Development," p. 97.

17. Howard W. Hallman, *Neighborhoods: Their Place in Urban Life* (Beverly Hills, CA: Sage, 1984), p. 108.

18. Diana M. DiNitto and C. Aaron McNeece, *Social Work: Issues and Opportunities in a Challenging Profession* (Englewood Cliffs, NJ: Prentice-Hall, 1990), p. 72.

19. Kurzman, "Program Development," p. 98.

20. Jack Rothman and Mayer N. Zald, "Planning Theory and Social Work Community Practice" in *Theory and Practice of Community Social Work,* ed. Samuel H. Taylor and Robert W. Roberts (New York: Columbia University Press, 1985), p. 130.

21. Kurzman, "Program Development," p. 99.

22. Rothman and Zald, "Planning Theory," p. 142.

23. Ibid., p. 131.

24. Ronald L. Simons and Stephen M. Aigner, *Practice Principles: A Problem Solving Approach to Social Work* (New York: Macmillan, 1985), p. 208; and Neil Gilbert and Harry Specht, "Who Plans?" in *Strategies of Community Organization,* 3d ed., ed. Fred. M. Cox, John L. Erlich, Jack Rothman, and John E. Tropman (Itasca, IL: Peacock, 1979), p. 347.

25. Hallman, *Neighborhoods,* pp. 116–118.

26. Gilbert and Specht, "Who Plans?" p. 347.

27. Hallman, *Neighborhoods,* p. 118.

28. Simons and Aigner, *Practice Principles,* pp. 208–209.

29. Gilbert and Specht, "Who Plans?" p. 347.

30. Hallman, *Neighborhoods,* p. 118.

31. Ibid., pp. 118–119.

32. Ibid., p. 125.

33. Ibid., p. 126.

34. The ensuing discussion of social work planning for mental health draws on the work of Madelene R. Stoner, "The Practice of Community Social Work in Mental Health Settings," in *Theory and Practice of Community Social Work,* ed. Samuel H. Taylor and Robert W. Roberts (New York: Columbia University Press, 1985), pp. 285–308. The material is included here with the permission of the publisher.

35. Rothman and Zald, "Planning Theory," p. 131.

36. Gilbert and Specht, "Who Plans?" p. 348.

37. Linda Ruth Pine, "Economic Opportunity Act (EOA) 1964" in *American Community Organizations,* ed. Patricia Mooney Melvin (New York: Greenwood Press, 1986), p. 54.

38. Kurzman, "Program Development," p. 100.

39. Trattner, *From Poor Law,* p. 293.

40. Pine, "Economic Opportunity Act," pp. 54–56.

41. Neil Gilbert, "The Design of Community Planning Structures," *Social Service Review,* 53 (1979): p. 647.

42. Linda Ruth Pine, "Demonstration Cities and Metropolitan Development Act, 1966" in *American Community Organizations* ed. Patricia Mooney Melvin (New York: Greenwood Press, 1986), pp. 45–46.

43. The discussion of social work planning for aging in this section draws on the work of Abraham Monk, "The Practice of Community Social Work With the Aged," in *Theory and Practice of Community Social Work,* ed. Samuel H. Taylor and Robert W. Roberts (New York: Columbia University Press, 1985), pp. 268–272. The material is included here with the permission of the publisher.

44. *Cyclopedia of American Biography*, vol. 31, pp. 79–80, and *Social Work Encyclopedia*, 19th ed. (Washington, DC: NASW Press, 1995), p. 2576.

45. Hallman, *Neighborhoods,* pp. 132–133.

46. Ibid.

47. Hallman, *Neighborhoods,* p. 133.

48. Guy Benveniste, *Mastering the Politics of Planning: Crafting Credible Plans and Policies That Make a Difference* (San Francisco: Jossey-Bass, 1989) pp. 264, 263.

49. Jamshid Gharajedaghi in collaboration with Russell L. Ackoff, *A Prologue to National Development Planning* (New York: Greenwood Press, 1986), p. 27.

50. John Forester, *Planning in the Face of Power* (Berkeley: University of California Press, 1989), p. 28.

51. Ibid., p. 35.

52. Benveniste, *Mastering the Politics,* p. 264.

53. Alan Walker, *Social Planning: A Strategy for Socialist Welfare* (Oxford: B. Blackwell, 1984), p. 137.

54. Armand Lauffer, *Social Planning at the Community Level* (Englewood Cliffs, NJ: Prentice-Hall, 1978), p. 9.

55. George J. Wahrheit, Robert A. Bell, and John J. Schwab, "Selecting the Needs Assessment Approach," in *Tactics and*

Techniques of Community Practice, 2d ed., ed. Fred M. Cox, John L. Erlich, Jack Rothman, and John E. Tropman (Itasca, IL: Peacock, 1984), p. 49.

56. Allen Rubin and Earl Babbie, *Research Methods of Social Work* (Belmont, CA: Wadsworth, 1979), p. 503.

57. Wahrheit, Bell, and Schwab, "Selecting the Needs Assessment Approach," p. 41.

58. Harvey L. Gochros, "Research Interviewing," in *Social Work Research and Evaluation,* 3d ed., ed. Richard M. Grinnell Jr. (Itasca, IL: Peacock, 1988), p. 275.

59. Rebecca F. Guy, Charles E. Edgley, Ibtihaj Arafat, and Donald E. Allen, *Social Research Methods: Puzzles and Solutions* (Boston: Allyn and Bacon, 1987), p. 220.

60. Herbert Rubin and Irene S. Rubin, *Community Organizing and Development,* 2d ed. (New York: Macmillan, 1992), p. 160.

61. Guy et al., *Social Research Methods,* pp. 191–197.

62. Rubin and Babbie, *Research Methods,* p. 322.

63. Ibid., p. 320; Guy et al., *Social Research Methods*, p. 243.

64. Martin Gannon, *Management: An Integrated Framework,* 2d ed. (Boston: Little, Brown, 1982), p. 144.

65. Ibid., p. 145.

66. Ibid., p. 146.

67. Ibid., p. 142.

68. Edith Stokey and Richard Zeckhauser, *A Primer for Policy Analysis* (New York: Norton, 1978), p. 177.

69. Gannon, *Management,* pp. 151–153.

70. Forester, *Planning,* p. 5.

71. Ibid., pp. 5, 41.

72. Ibid., pp. 28, 40.

73. Ibid., p. 213.

74. Hallman, *Neighborhoods,* p. 132.

75. Rohe and Gates, *Planning With Neighborhoods,* p. 49.

76. Ibid., p. 50.

77. Friedrich A. Hayek, *The Road to Serfdom* (Chicago: University of Chicago Press, 1944), p. 35.

78. Summarized and adapted from Garrett Hardin, "The Tragedy of the Commons," *Science,* 162 (Dec. 1968): pp. 1243–1248.

79. Summarized and adapted from Henrik Ibsen, *Enemy of the People,* in *Four Great Plays by Ibsen* (New York: Bantam Books, 1959), pp. 130–215.

Chapter 7: Becoming a Community Developer

1. Marilyn Ferguson, *The Aquarian Conspiracy* (Los Angeles: J. P. Tarcher, 1980) p. 207.

2. This section draws on the work of Stewart E. Perry, *Communities on the Way: Rebuilding Local Economies in the United States and Canada* (Albany: State University of New York Press, 1987), pp. 6–8.

3. Howard W. Hallman, *Neighborhoods: Their Place in Urban Life,* vol. 154, Sage Library of Social Research (Beverly Hills, CA: Sage, 1984), pp. 130–131.

4. Bryan M. Phifer with E. Frederick List and Boyd Faulkner, "History of Community Development in America," in *Community Development in America*, ed. James A. Christenson and Jerry W. Robinson Jr. (Ames: Iowa State University Press, 1980), p. 12.

5. Antonia Pantoja and Wilhelmina Perry, "Community Development and Restoration: A Perspective," in *Community Organizing in a Diverse Society,* ed. Felix G. Rivera and John L. Erlich (Boston: Allyn and Bacon, 1992), p. 240.

6. Jack Rothman with John E. Tropman, "Models of Community Organization and Macro Practice Perspectives: Their Mixing and Phasing," in *Strategies of Community Organization,* 4th ed., ed. Fred M. Cox, John L. Erlich, Jack Rothman, and John E. Tropman (Itasca, IL: F. E. Peacock, 1987), p. 5.

7. Ibid.

8. S. K. Khinduka, "Community Development: Potentials and Limitations," in *Strategies of Community Organization,* ed. Cox et al., p. 353.

9. Phifer et al., "History of Community Development,"p. 18.

10. Ibid., p. 13.

11. Ibid., pp. 19–20, and Robert Fisher *Let the People Decide: Neighborhood Organizing in America* (New York: Twayne, 1994), p. 21.

12. Fisher, *Let the People Decide,* p. 23, and Hubert Campfens, ed., *Community Development Around the World: Practice, Theory, Research, Training* (Toronto: University of Toronto Press, 1997), pp. 18–19.

13. Beulah R. Compton, *Introduction to Social Welfare and Social Work: Structure, Function and Process* (Homewood,IL: Dorsey, 1980), p. 418.

14. Phifer et al., "History of Community Development," p. 35.

15. Ibid., p. 26.

16. Linda Ruth Pine, "Demonstration Cities and Metropolitan Development Act 1966," in *American Community Organizations: A Historical Dictionary,* ed. Patricia Mooney Melvin (New York: Greenwood Press, 1986), pp. 45–46.

17. Linda Ruth Pine, "Economic Opportunity Act (EOA) 1964," in *American Community Organizations: A Historical Dictionary,* ed. Patricia Mooney Melvin (New York: Greenwood Press, 1986), pp. 53–56.

18. Compton, *Introduction to Social Welfare,* p. 460.

19. Linda Ruth Pine, "Housing and Urban Development Act, 1968," in *American Community Organizations: A Historical Dictionary,* ed. Patricia Mooney Melvin (New York: Greenwood Press, 1986), p. 83.

20. Fisher, *Let the People Decide,* p. 181.

21. Neil R. Peirce and Carol F. Steinbach, *Enterprising Communities: Community-Based Development in America* (Washington, DC: Council for Community Based Development, 1990), pp. 15–16.

22. Fisher, *Let the People Decide,* pp. 157, 181.

23. Susan Redman-Rengstorf, "Neighborhoods U.S.A. (NUSA) 1975," in *American Community Organizations: A Historical Dictionary,* ed. Patricia Mooney Melvin (New York: Greenwood Press, 1986), pp. 131–132.

24. Susan Redman-Rengstorf, "Neighborhood Reinvestment Corporation (NERC) 1978," in *American Community Organizations: A Historical Dictionary,* ed. Patricia Mooney Melvin (New York: Greenwood Press, 1986), p. 129.

25. Robert R. Fairbanks, "Housing and Community Development Act (HCDA) 1974," in *American Community Organizations: A Historical Dictionary,* ed. Patricia Mooney Melvin (New York: Greenwood Press, 1986), pp. 81–83.

26. Lynne Navin, "Neighborhood Self-Help Development Act, 1978," in *American Community Organizations: A Historical Dictionary,* ed. Patricia Mooney Melvin (New York: Greenwood Press, 1986), p. 130.

27. Fisher, *Let the People Decide,* p. 181.

28. Patricia Mooney Melvin, ed., "National Neighborhood Policy Act 1977," in *American Community Organizations: A Historical Dictionary* (New York: Greenwood Press, 1986), pp. 127–129.

29. Pierce and Steinbach, *Enterprising Communities,* p. 26.

30. Renee Berger, *Against All Odds: The Achievement of Community-Based Development Organizations* (Washington, DC: National Congress for Community Economic Development, 1989), p. 4.

31. Alan C. Twelvetrees, *Organizing for Neighbourhood Development: A Comparative Study of Community Based Development Organizations,* 2d ed. (Aldershot, Eng: Avebury, 1996), pp. 147–148.

32. Hallman, *Neighborhoods,* p. 137.
33. Ibid., p. 138.
34. Fisher, *Let the People Decide,* p. 180.
35. Perry, *Communities on the Way,* p. 8.
36. Twelvetrees, *Organizing for Neighbourhood,* p. 148.
37. Thand Williamson, "Church-Based Community Economic Development: Perspectives and Prognosis," *Religious Socialism,* Fall 1997, p. 8.
38. Ibid.
39. Ibid.
40. Fisher, *Let the People Decide,* p. 182.
41. Williamson, "Church-Based Community Economic Development," pp. 8–9.
42. Twelvetrees, *Organizing for Neighbourhood,* pp.148–149.
43. Ibid., p. 151.
44. Perry, *Communities on the Way,* p. 37.
45. Ibid.
46. Si Kahn, *How People Get Power: Organizing Oppressed Communities for Action* (New York: McGraw Hill, 1970), p. 5.
47. The section on the three-tiered model is drawn from F. G. Rivera and John L. Erlich, *Community Organizing in a Diverse Society,* copyright (c) 1992 by Allyn and Bacon, pp. 10–12. Reprinted/adapted by permission.
48. Pantoja and Perry, "Community Development and Restoration," p. 237.
49. This section on how to diagnose community culture is summarized and adapted from Terrance E. Deal, *Corporate Culture* (New York: Addison-Wesley, 1982), pp. 130–139.
50. Adapted from Armand Lauffer, *Assessment Tools for Practitioners, Managers and Trainers* (Beverly Hills, CA: Sage, 1982), p. 9.
51. Ibid., p. 12.
52. Perry, *Communities on the Way,* p. 35.
53. G. Thomas Kingsley, Joseph B. McNeely, and James O. Gibson, *Community Building: Coming of Age* (Development Training Institute and Urban Institute, n. d.), p. 7.
54. Perry, *Communities on the Way,* p. 35.
55. Twelvetrees, *Organizing for Neighbourhood,* p. 115.
56. Ibid., p. 174.
57. Ibid., p. 149.
58. Williamson, "Church-Based Community Economic Development," p. 3.
59. Ibid.
60. Ibid., pp. 3–4.
61. Joan Walsh, *Stories of Renewal: Community Building and the Future of Urban America* (New York: Rockefeller Foundation, M.d.), p. 2.
62. Ibid., p. 35.
63. Si Kahn, *How People Get Power,* p. 116.
64. Ibid., p. 120.
65. Ibid., p. 121.
66. Fisher, *Let the People Decide,* pp. 182, 184.
67. Ibid., pp. 186–188.
68. Marilyn Gittell with Bruce Hoffacker, Eleanor Rollins, Samuel Foster, and Mark Hoffacker, *Limits of Citizen Participation: The Decline of Community Organizations* (Beverly Hills, CA: Sage, 1980) pp. 48–49.
69. Emily Mitchell, "Getting Better at Doing Good," *Time,* Feb. 21, 2000, pp. B9–B12.
70. Harry Specht and Mark E. Courtney, *Unfaithful Angels: How Social Work Has Abandoned Its Mission* (New York: Free Press, 1994), p. 27.
71. From Julio Morales, "Community Social Work With Puerto Rican Communities in the United States: One Organizer's Perspective," in *Community Organizing in a Diverse Society,* ed. Rivera and Erlich, pp. 102–104. Copyright (c) 1992 by Allyn and Bacon. Reprinted/ adapted by permission.

Chapter 8: Becoming a Community Organizer

1. Paulo Freire, *Pedagogy of the Oppressed* (New York: Continuum, 1992), p. 28.
2. Joan E. Lancourt. *Confront or Concede: The Alinsky Citizen-Action Organizations* (Lexington, MA: D. C. Heath, 1979), pp. 156–157.
3. Summarized and adapted from Harry Boyte, *Community Is Possible: Repairing America's Roots* (New York: Harper and Row, 1984), pp. 127–128, 133–135, 140–148, 151–152.
4. David Moberg, *All Together Now,* 27(3), Oct. 7, 1997, n. p.
5. Boyte, *Community Is Possible,* pp. 25–26.
6. Ibid.
7. The key ideas that formed this definition are those of Rev. Robert Linthicum, Partners in Urban Transformation, Los Angeles, CA. Memorandum to the author, July 22, 1998, p. 1.
8. Alan C. Twelvetrees, *Organizing for Neighbourhood Development: A Comparative Study of Community Based Development Organizations,* 2d ed. (Aldershot, Eng: Avebury Press, 1996), p. 139.
9. David Finks, *The Radical Vision of Saul Alinsky* (New York: Paulist Press, 1984), p. xi.
10. Janice Perlman, "Grassrooting the System," *Social Policy,* 9 (Sept./Oct. 1976): p. 8.
11. Stuart Langton, "Citizen Participation in America: Reflections on the State of the Art," in *Citizen Participation in America: Essays on the State of the Art,* ed. Stuart Langton (Lexington, MA: D. C. Heath, 1978), p. 3.
12. Finks, *Radical Vision,* p. xi.
13. Michael R. Williams, *Neighborhood Organization: Seeds of a New Urban Life* (Westport, CT: Greenwood Press, 1985), p. 76.
14. Karen Paget, "Citizen Organizing: Many Movements, No Majority," *American Prospect,* 7 (Summer 1990): pp. 115–116.
15. Williams, *Neighborhood Organization,* p. 76.
16. Ibid., p. 224.
17. Lancourt, *Confront or Concede,* pp. 156–157.
18. Herbert Simon. *Administrative Behavior,* 4th ed. (New York: Free Press, 1997), p. 93.
19. Lancourt, *Confront or Concede,* pp. 156–157.
20. Ibid., p. 156.
21. Williams, *Neighborhood Organization,* p. 227.
22. Ibid., p. 225.
23. Finks, *Radical Vision,* p. 266.
24. Alinsky, *Reveille for Radicals,* p. 219.
25. Ibid., p. 103.
26. Finks, *Radical Vision,* p. 28.
27. For example, Charles L. Harper, *Exploring Social Change: America and the World,* 3d ed. (Upper Saddle River, NJ: Prentice-Hall, 1998), p. 57. Harper says: "The political system [in America] is becoming less effective in representing the truly general interests and is more likely to reflect the narrower interests of the wealthy and special interests with lots of cash."
28. Harry Boyte, *The Backyard Revolution: Understanding the New Citizen Movement* (Philadelphia: Temple University Press, 1980), 49–50.
29. Robert Fisher, *Let the People Decide: Neighborhood Organizing in America.* (New York: Twayne, 1994), p. 4.
30. Hallman, *Neighborhoods,* p. 108.
31. Williams, *Neighborhood Organization,* p. 227.
32. This section has been adapted and summarized from Sidney Dillick, *Community Organization for Neighborhood Development, Past and Present* (New York: William Morrow, 1953), pp. 34–35.
33. Arthur Dunham, *The New Community Organization* (New York: Crowell, 1970), p. 74.
34. Fisher, *Let the People Decide,* p.14.

35. Ibid., p. 16.
36. Hallman, *Neighborhoods,* p. 109.
37. Dillick, *Community Organization,* 58–66.
38. Fisher, *Let the People Decide,* p. 16.
39. Dillick, *Community Organization*, pp. 61, 63.
40. Fisher, *Let the People Decide,* p. 19.
41. Dillick, *Community Organization,* p. 61.
42. Fisher, *Let the People Decide,* p. 20.
43. Hallman, *Neighborhoods,* p. 110.
44. The material on Saul Alinky's life has been adapted and summarized from Donald C. Reitzes and Dietrich C. Reitzes, *The Alinsky Legacy Alive and Kicking* (Greenwich, CT: JAI Press, 1987), pp. 3–9.
45. Saul Alinsky, *Reveille for Radicals,* p.72.
46. Finks, *Radical Vision,* pp. 21, 23.
47. Saul Alinsky, *Rules for Radicals: A Pragmatic Primer for Realistic Radicals* (New York: Vintage Books, 1974), p. xx.
48. Alinsky, *Revellie for Radicals*, p. 7.
49. Ibid., p. 116.
50. Ibid.
51. Williams, *Neighborhood Organizations,* pp. 31, 11, 12.
52. Finks, *Radical Vision,* pp. 274, 267.
53. Marilyn Gittell with Bruce Hoffacker, Eleanor Rollins, Samuel Foster, and Mark Hoffacker, *Limits of Citizen Participation: The Decline of Community Organizations* (Beverly Hills, CA: Sage, 1980), pp. 29–31.
54. Hallman, *Neighborhoods,* p. 121.
55. Gittell, *Limits,* p. 30.
56. Hallman, *Neighborhoods*, pp. 122–123.
57. Ibid., pp. 123–124.
58. Ibid.
59. Ibid., pp.134–135.
60. Ibid., p. 135.
61. National Training and Information Center, *Disclosure: The National Newspaper of Neighborhoods* (Chicago: National Training and Information Center, 1998), p. 7.
62. Hallman, *Neighborhoods,* pp. 135–136.
63. Williams, *Neighborhood Organizations,* p.77.
64. Ibid.
65. Twelvetrees, *Organizing for Neighbourhood Development,* pp. 151–152.
66. Si Kahn, biographical information from *How People Get Power: Organizing Oppressed Communities for Action* (Washington, DC: NASW Press, 1994), pp. 143–144.
67. Freire, *Pedagogy of the Oppressed,* p. 47.
68. Alinsky, *Reveille for Radicals.* p. 90.
69. From Julio Morales, "Community Social Work With Puerto Rican Communities," in *Community Organizing in a Diverse Society,* ed. Felix G. Rivera and John L. Erlich (Boston: Allyn and Bacon, 1992), pp. 96–97. Reprinted and adapted by permission of publisher.
70. Ibid., p. 101.
71. Warren C. Haggstrom, "The Tactics of Organization Building," in *Strategies of Community Organization,* 4th ed., ed. Fred M. Cox, John L. Erlich, Jack Rothman, and John E. Tropman (Itasca, IL: Peacock, 1987), p. 406.
72. Si Kahn, *How People Get Power: Organizing Oppressed Communities for Action* (New York: McGraw-Hill, 1978), p. 2.
73. Haggstrom, "Tactics of Organization Building," p. 408.
74. Ibid., pp. 407–411.
75. Reitzes and Reitzes, *The Alinsky Legacy,* p. 36.
76. Ibid., pp. 36–37.
77. Haggstrom, "Tactics of Organization Building," p. 411.
78. Ibid., 409–410.

79. Robert Fisher, *Let the People Decide,* p. 53.
80. This section adapted and summarized from Gary Delgado, *Organizing the Movement: The Roots and Growth of ACORN* (Philadelphia: Temple University Press, 1986), p. 22.
81. *Western Organizing Review,* Feb. 1998, n. p.
82. Information on the house meeting model has been adapted and summarized from *Western Organizing Review,* and Fisher, *Let the People Decide,* pp. 149–150.
83. Saul D. Alinsky, *Rules for Radicals,* p. 3.
84. Fisher, *Let the People Decide,* p. 53.
85. Delgado, *Organizing the Movement,* p. 22.
86. Reitzes and Reitzes, *The Alinsky Legacy,* p. 35.
87. Williams, *Neighborhood Organizations,* p. 226.
88. Si Kahn, *How People Get Power,* pp. 48–49.
89. Jack Rothman with John E. Tropman, "Models of Community Organization and Macro Practice Perspectives: Their Mixing and Phasing," in *Strategies of Community Organizing,* 4th ed., ed. Fred M. Cox, John L. Erlich, Jack Rothman, and John E. Tropman (New York: Free Press, 1989), p. 34.
90. Williams, *Neighborhood Organizations,* p. 226.
91. Reitzes and Reitzes, *The Alinsky Legacy,* p. 36.
92. Alinksy, *Rules for Radicals,* pp. 114, 159.
93. Finks, *Radical Vision,* p. 273.
94. Delgado, *Organizing the Movement,* p. 28.
95. Twelvetrees, *Organizing for Neighbourhood Development,* pp. 151–152.
96. Delgado, *Organizing the Movement,* p. 28.
97. Fisher, *Let the People Decide,* pp. 194–195.
98. Williams, *Neighborhood Organizations,* p. 76.
99. Oakland Community Organizations Profile, *PICO: 25 Years Reweaving the Fabric of America's Communities* (Oakland, CA: PICO, 1997), p. 25.
100. Thai Walker, "Living Wage Effort May Sprout Wings: Organizers Flush With Oakland Success," *San Francisco Chronicle,* Mar. 26, 1998, p. E.
101. Walter Wright, "Church Coalition Leads Way for Renovation of Kalihi Housing Project," *Honolulu Advertiser,* Feb. 2, 1998, n. p.
102. Richard Chacon, "1000 Work on Community at Interfaith Meeting," *Boston Sunday Globe,* Mar. 15, 1998, n. p.
103. Fink, *Radical Vision,* p. x.
104. This section summarized and adapted from Williams, *Neighborhood Organizations,* pp. 236–238.
105. Alinsky, *Rules for Radicals,* p. 3.
106. Hallman, *Neighborhoods,* p. 119.
107. Alinsky, *Rules for Radicals,* pp. 72–76.
108. Williams, *Neighborhood Organizations*, p. 48.
109. Shel Trapp. *Blessed Be the Fighters: Reflections on Organizing. Collected Essays of Shel Trapp* (Chicago: National Training and Information Center, 1986), pp. 15–16.
110. Sandra M. O'Donnell and Sokoni T. Karanja, "Transformative Community Practice: Building a Model for Developing Extremely Low-Income African American Communities," *Journal of Community Practice,* 7(3) (2000): p. 68.

Part 3: Social Work Practice with Organizations

1. Max Weber, "Bureaucracy," in *Economy and Society: An Outline of Interpretive Sociology,* 3 vols., ed. Guenther Roth and Claus Wittich, trans. Elphraim Fischoff et al. (New York: Bedminster, 1968), p. 987.
2. Robert Presthus, *The Organizational Society,* rev. ed. (New York: St. Martin's, 1978).

Chapter 9: The Social Sector and the Rise of the Social Organization

1. In Peter Block, *Stewardship: Choosing Service Over Self-Interest* (San Francisco: Berrett-Koehler, 1993), p. 186.
2. Max Weber, "Bureaucracy," in *From Max Weber: Essays in Sociology,* ed. H. H. Gerth and C. Wright Mills (New York: Oxford University Press, 1946), pp. 215–216.
3. This section is summarized and adapted from Peter F. Drucker, *New Realities in Government and Politics, in Economics and Business, in Society and World View* (New York: Harper and Row, 1989), pp. 200–204. Reprinted with permission.
4. Corporation data: "Fortune's Global 500: The World's Largest Corporations," *Fortune Magazine,* Aug. 7, 1995, n. p. Country data: "World Development Report," The World Bank, 1996, n. p., n. d.
5. Victor A. Thompson, *Bureaucracy and the Modern World* (Morristown, NJ: General Learning Press, 1976), p. 101.
6. Alberto Guerreiro Ramos, "A Substantive Approach to Organizations," in *Organization Theory and the New Public Administration,* ed. Carl J. Bellone (Boston: Allyn and Bacon, 1980), p. 146.
7. Marcel Mauss, in *Primitive, Archaic, and Modern Economies; Essays of Karl Polanyi,* ed. G. Dalton (Boston: Beacon Press, 1971), p. ix.
8. Karl Polanyi, *The Great Transformation* (Boston: Beacon Press, 1971), p. 71.
9. Ibid., p. 149.
10. Thompson, *Bureaucracy,* p. 115.
11. Ibid., p. 113.
12. Max Weber, "Politics as a Vocation," in *From Max Weber: Essays in Sociology,* ed. H. H. Gerth and C. Wright Mills (New York: Oxford University Press, 1946), p. 95.
13. Thompson, *Without Sympathy,* p. 67.
14. Ralph P. Hummel, *Bureaucratic Experience* (New York: St. Martin's, 1977), pp. 42–43.
15. Soren Kierkegaard, *Fear and Trembling and the Sickness Unto Death,* trans. Walter Lowrie (Garden City, NY: Doubleday, 1958), p. 145.
16. Paul Tillich, "The Person in a Technical Society," in *Social Ethics: Issues in Ethics and Society,* ed. Gibson Winter (New York: Harper and Row, 1968), pp. 125–126, 134.
17. Alberto Guerreiro Ramos, *The New Science of Organizations: A Reconceptualization of the Wealth of Nations* (Toronto: University of Toronto Press, 1981), p. 147.
18. Hummel, *Bureaucratic Experience,* p. 42.
19. Thompson, *Without Sympathy or Enthusiasm,* p. 28.
20. Tillich, "The Person in a Technical Society," pp. 150–151.
21. Ramos, *New Science,* p. 158.
22. Hummel, *Bureaucratic Experience,* pp. 133–137.
23. Max Weber, "Bureaucracy," pp. 215–216.
24. Thompson, *Without Sympathy,* pp. 1–7.
25. Alasdair MacIntyre, *After Virtue,* 2d ed. (Notre Dame, IN: University of Notre Dame Press, 1984), pp. 23–24. Thompson, *Without Sympathy,* pp. 110–114.
26. Hummel, *Bureaucratic Experience,* p. 13.
27. Thompson, *Without Sympathy,* p.117.
28. Hummel, *Bureaucratic Experience,* p.16.
29. Thompson, *Bureaucracy,* p. 10.
30. Herbert Simon, *Administrative Behavior: A Study of Decision-Making Processes in Administrative Organizations,* 4th ed. (New York: Free Press, 1997), pp. 92, 112.
31. Block, *Stewardship,* pp. 7, 51.
32. Ramos, *New Science,* p. 158.
33. The main ideas for this section have been obtained from George Brager and Stephen Holloway, *Changing Human Service Organizations: Politics and Practice* (New York: Free Press, 1978), p. 15.
34. Ibid.
35. Lester M. Salamon. *Partners in Public Service: Government-Nonprofit Relations in the Modern Welfare State* (Baltimore: Johns Hopkins University Press, 1995), p. 15.
36. Drucker, *New Realities,* p. 198.
37. Ibid.
38. Peter Hall. "A Historical Perspective on Nonprofit Organizations," in *The Jossey-Bass Handbook of Nonprofit Leadership and Management,* ed. Robert D. Herman and Associates (San Francisco: Jossey-Bass, 1994), pp. 3–4.
39. Drucker, *New Realities,* pp. 196–199.
40. Hall, "An Historical Perspective," pp. 3, 30, 19.
41. Alan B. Durning, "Poverty and the Environment: Reversing the Downward Spiral," Worldwatch paper no. 89, Worldwatch Institute, 1989, n. p.
42. Hall, "An Historical Perspective," p. 19.
43. Drucker, *New Realities,* p. 199, and Salamon, *Partners,* p. 52.
44. Hall, "An Historical Perspective," p. 30.
45. Ibid., pp. 3–4.
46. Salamon, *Partners,* pp. 65, 54, 89.
47. Drucker, *New Realities,* pp. 195–196.
48. Salamon, *Partners,* p. 117.
49. Ibid.
50. Darlyne Bailey, "Management: Diverse Workplaces," in *Encyclopedia of Social Work,* 19th ed. (Washington, DC: NASW Press, 1995) pp. 1659–1660.
51. Hall, *Historical Perspective,* pp. 3–4.
52. Drucker, *New Realities,* pp. 196–197.
53. Ibid.
54. Block, *Stewardship,* pp. 104, 200.
55. Ramos, *New Science of Organization,* p. 128.
56. Salamon, *Partners,* p. 54.
57. Drucker, *New Realities,* p. 205.
58. Ibid., pp. 197–198.
59. This section is adapted and sumarized from Salamon, *Partners,* pp. 5, 15–19, 33–34, 60–69, 91, 94.
60. John Forester, *Planning in the Face of Power* (Berkeley: University of California Press, 1989), p. 79.
61. Charles Perrow, *Complex Organizations: A Critical Essay,* 2d ed. (Glenview, IL: Scott Foresman, 1979), pp. 55–56.
62. Ramos, *New Science,* p. 160.
63. Donald Shon, *Beyond the Stable State* (New York: Random House, 1971), pp. 33–38.
64. Thompson, *Without Sympathy,* pp. 90–94.

Chapter 10: Becoming a Program Developer

1. Si Kahn, *How People Get Power: Organizing Oppressed Communities for Action* (New York: McGraw-Hill, 1978), p. 124.
2. The material on Barton is drawn from *Cyclopedia of American Biography,* vol. 15, pp. 314–315, and Jean K. Quam, *Encyclopedia of Social Work,* 19th ed. (Washington, DC: NASW Press, 1995), p. 2573.
3. This section adapted and summarized from Robert C. Linthicum, *Empowering the Poor: Community Organizing the City's "Rag, Tag and Bobtail"* (Monrovia, CA: MARC, 1991), pp. 22–23, 45–46.

4. Joseph P. Hornick and Barbara Burrows, "Program Evaluation," in *Social Work Research and Evaluation,* 3d ed., ed. Richard M. Grinnell Jr. (Itasca, IL: Peacock, 1987), p. 142.

5. Allen Rubin and Earl Babbie, *Research Methods for Social Work* (Belmont, CA: Wadsworth, 1989), p. 500.

6. Hornick and Burrows, "Program Evaluation," p. 403.

7. Rubin and Babbie, *Research Methods,* p. 500.

8. Ibid., p. 502.

9. *PICO: 25 Years Reweaving the Fabric of America's Communities* (Oakland Community Organizations Profile, 1997), p. 6.

10. "African American Pioneeers in Social Work," *Encyclopedia of Social Work*, 19th ed. (Washington, DC: NASW Press, 1995), p. 117.

11. This section is summarized and adapted from Joan M. Hummel, *Starting and Running a Nonprofit Organization,* 2d ed., revised by the Center for Nonprofit Management, Graduate School of Business, University of St. Thomas (Minneapolis: University of Minnesota Press, 1996), pp. 21–26, 12–15. Used with permission.

12. This section is summarized and adapted from Hummel, *Starting and Running,* pp. 16–18. Used with permission.

13. *Encyclopedia of Social Work*, 19th ed. (Washington, DC: NASW Press, 1995), p. 2573, and *National Cyclopedia of Biography*, pp. 166–167.

14. Hummel *Starting and Running*, p. 13.

15. Ibid., p. 15.

16. Ibid., p. 41.

17. *PICO: 25 Years Reweaving the Fabric*, p. 2.

18. Gordon Mayer, *National Training and Information Center— 25 Years: Neighborhood Dreams, Neighborhood Issues, Neighborhood Organizing* (Chicago: NTIC, 1997). Used with permission.

19. Hummel, *Starting and Running*, p. 41.

20. *PICO: 25 Years Reweaving the Fabric,* p 2.

21. Ibid., p. 5.

22. Hummel, *Starting and Running,* pp. 43–44.

23. Ibid., p. 103.

24. Ibid., p. 104.

25. Except where noted, this section is summarized and adapted from Hummel, *Starting and Running*, pp. 11–12, 101–105.

26. Sheldon R. Gelman, "Boards of Directors," in *Encyclopedia of Social Work*, 19th ed. (Washington, DC: NASW Press, 1995), p. 309.

27. Hummel, *Starting and Running*, p. 110.

28. Ibid., and Sturgeon, "Finding and Keeping," p. 540.

29. Hummel, *Starting and Running*, p. 111.

30. Ibid.

31. The following is summarized and adapted from M. Sue Sturgeon, "Finding and Keeping the Right Employees," in *Jossey-Bass Handbook of Nonprofit Leadership and Management* (San Francisco: Jossey-Bass, 1994), pp. 542–555. Used with permission.

32. Ibid., p. 544.

33. This section is summarized and adapted from Hummel, *Starting and Running*, pp. 51–59, 73–74.

34. Joan Flanagan, "How to Ask for Money," in *Tactics and Techniques of Community Practice,* 2d ed., ed. Fred M. Cox, John L. Erllich, Jack Rothman, and John E. Tropman (Itasca, IL: Peacock, 1984), p. 310.

35. Peter Dobkin Hall, "Historical Perspectives on Nonprofit Organizations," in *Jossey-Bass Handbook of Nonprofit Leadership and Management* (San Francisco, Jossey-Bass, 1994), p. 16.

36. Ione D. Vargus, "Charitable Foundations and Social Welfare," in *Encyclopedia of Social Work*, 19th ed. (Washington, DC: NASW Press, 1995), pp. 342–343.

37. Ibid., p. 342.

38. Foundation Center, 1994, p. xxi, in Vargus, "Charitable Foundations," p. 343.

39. Vargus, "Charitable Foundations,"p. 343.

40. Ibid.

41. Ibid., p. 342.

42. Hummel, *Starting and Running*, p. 52.

Chapter 11: Becoming a Social Work Administrator

1. Peter Block, *Stewardship: Choosing Service Over Self-Interest* (San Francisco: Berrett-Koehler Publishers, 1993), pp. 50–51.

2. Robert E. Sherwood, *Roosevelt and Hopkins: An Intimate History,* rev. ed. (New York: Harper and Brothers, 1950), p. 32.

3. Ibid., p. 281.

4. Lawrence Shulman, "Supervision and Consultation," in *Encyclopedia of Social Work*, 19th ed. (Washington, DC: NASW Press, 1995), pp. 2373–2374.

5. Peter J. Pecora, "Personnel Management," in *Encyclopedia of Social Work*, 19th ed. (Washington, DC: NASW Press, 1995), p. 1833.

6. Hugh England, *Social Work as Art: Making Sense for Good Practice* (London: Allen and Unwin, 1986), p. 41.

7. Block, *Stewardship*, pp. 65-66.

8. Donelson R. Forsyth, *An Introduction to Group Dynamics* (Monterey, CA: Brooks/Cole, 1983), pp. 166–167.

9. Malvern J. Gross, "The Importance of Budgeting," in *Social Administration: The Management of the Social Services,* ed. Simon Slavin (New York: Haworth Press, 1978), p. 233.

10. Aaron Wildavsky, *Budgeting: A Comparative Theory of Budgetary Processes* (Boston: Little, Brown, 1975), p. 5.

11. Ibid., pp. 5–6. See also Herbert Simon, *Administrative Behavior,* 4th ed. (New York: Free Press, 1997), pp. xxviii, xxx.

12. Wildavsky, *Budgeting*, p. 7.

13. Charles A. Rapp and John Poertner, *Social Administration: A Client-Centered Approach* (New York: Longman, 1992), p. 219.

14. Roderick K. Macleod, "Program Budgeting in Nonprofit Institutions," in *Social Administration: Management of the Social Services,* ed. Simon Slavin (New York: Haworth Press and Council on Social Work Education, 1968), p. 251.

15. Rex Skidmore, *Social Work Administration: Dynamic Management and Human Relationships,* 2d ed. (Englewood Cliffs, NJ: Prentice-Hall, 1990), p. 69.

16. Rapp and Poertner, *Social Administration*, p. 219.

17. Wildavsky, *Budgeting*, p. 297.

18. Herbert G. Heneman III, Donald P. Schwab, John A. Fossum, and Lee D. Dyer, *Managing Personnel and Human Resources* (Homewood, IL: Dow Jones-Irwin, 1981), p. 2.

19. Judith R. Gordon, *Human Resource Management: A Practical Approach* (Newton, MA: Allyn and Bacon, 1986), p. 5.

20. David M. Austin, "Management Overview," in *Encyclopedia of Social Work*, 19th ed. (Washington, DC: NASW Press, 1995), p. 1653.

21. Maryann Slyers, *Encyclopedia of Social Work*, 19th ed., (Washington, DC: NASW Press, 1995), p. 2585.

22. Elliot M. Fox and L. Urwick, *Dynamic Administration: The Collected Papers of Mary Parker Follett* (New York: Hippocrene Books, 1977).

23. M. Sue Sturgeon, "Finding and Keeping the Right Employees," in *Jossey-Bass Handbook of Nonprofit Leadership and Management* (San Francisco: Jossey-Bass, 1994), p. 535.

24. Sturgeon, " Finding and Keeping," pp. 541–542.

25. Pecora, "Personnel Management," p. 1830.

26. Ibid., pp. 1830–1831.

27. Ibid.
28. Wright Davis and Tremaine Law Firm, "Special Summary of the ADA Prepared for the Casey Family Program," in Pecora, "Personnel Management," p. 1831.
29. Sturgeon, " Finding and Keeping," p. 543.
30. Pecora, "Personnel Management," p. 1834.
31. Ibid., p. 1833.
32. Ibid., pp. 1833–1834.
33. Rapp and Poertner advocate for a "new metaphor" in which the traditional organizational chart is inverted so that "the pinnacle of the chart is the client and all organizational personnel are subservient. In fact, supervisors are subservient to frontline workers, and the executive is subservient to supervisors and frontline workers," *Social Administration*, p. 277.
34. Ibid., p. 138.
35. Robert Weinbach, *The Social Worker as Manager: Theory and Practice* (New York: Longman, 1990), p.75.
36. Paul Hersey and Kenneth H. Blanchard, *Management of Organizational Behavior: Utilizing Human Resources*, 5th ed. (Englewood Cliffs, NJ: Prentice-Hall, 1988), p. 6.
37. Robert H. Miles, *Macro Organizational Behavior* (Santa Monica, CA: Goodyear Publishing, 1980), pp. 322–323.
38. Harold Koontz, Cyril O'Donnell, and Heinz Weinrich, *Essentials of Management* (New York: McGraw-Hill, 1986), p. 79.
39. Herbert Simon, *Administrative Behavior: A Study of Decision-Making Processes in Administrative Organization*, 3d ed. (New York: Free Press, 1976), pp. xvii, xxxvii.
40. Ibid, pp. 48–52; see also John P. Flynn, *Social Agency Policy Analysis and Presentation for Community Practice* (Chicago: Nelson-Hall, 1987), pp. 133–172.
41. Sheldon R. Gelman, "Boards of Directors" in *Encyclopedia of Social Work*, 19th ed. (Washington, DC: NASW Press, 1995), p. 309.
42. Ibid., pp. 309–310.
43. Ibid., p. 310.
44. A. Gurin "Conceptual and Technical Issues in the Management of Human Services," in *The Management of Human Services*, ed. R. C. Sarri and Y. Hasenfeld (New York: Columbia University Press, 1978), pp. 289–308.
45. Ibid., 482.
46. Joseph P. Hornick and Barbara Burrows, "Program Evaluation," in *Social Work Research and Evaluation,* 3d ed., ed. Richard M. Grinnell Jr. (Itasca, IL: Peacock, 1988), p. 402.
47. Allen Rubin and Earl Babbie, *Research Methods for Social Work* (Belmont, CA: Wadsworth, 1989), p. 482.
48. Carol H. Weiss, *Evaluation Research: Methods of Assessing Program Effectiveness* (Englewood Cliffs, NJ: Prentice-Hall, 1972), p. 4.
49. Peter H. Rossi and Howard E. Freeman, *Evaluation: A Systematic Approach* (Beverly Hills, CA: Sage, 1982).
50. This section adapted and summarized from Michael I. Harrison, *Diagnosing Organizations: Methods, Model, and Processes* (Newbury Park, CA: Sage, 1987), pp.77–78. Used with permission.
51. Harrison, *Diagnosing*, p. 34.
52. Weiss, *Evaluation*, p. 26; Rubin and Babbie, *Research Methods*, p. 496.
53. Ibid., p. 30.
54. Harrison, *Diagnosing,* pp. 139–140.
55. Weiss, *Evaluation*, p. 36.
56. See, for example, Donald T. Campbell and Julian C. Stanley, *Experimental and Quasi-Experimental Designs for Research* (Chicago: Rand-McNally, 1963), for a description of three pre-experimental designs, three true experimental designs, and ten quasi-experimental designs.
57. I use the term "benefit-cost" analysis because ratios of benefits to costs are normally expressed benefit/cost rather than the reverse. Information in this section is summarized from E. J. Mishan, *Economics for Social Decisions: Elements of Cost-Benefit Analysis* (New York: Praeger, 1972), p. 88.
58. Hornick and Burrows, *Program Evaluation,* p. 416.
59. Rapp and Poertner, *Social Administration,* pp. 17, 6.
60. NASW Code of Ethics, 1979. This mandate was taken from section IV, The Social Worker's Ethical Responsibility to Employers and Employing Organizations: "(L) Commitments to Employing Organization. The social worker should adhere to commitments made to the employing organization. (1) The social worker should work to improve the employing agency's policies and procedures, and the efficiency and effectiveness of its services."
61. Drawn from Victor A. Thompson, *Bureaucracy and the Modern World*, (Morristown, NJ: General Learning Press, 1976) pp. 34, 17; and Victor A. Thompson, *Without Sympathy or Enthusiasm: The Problem of Administrative Compassion* (University: University of Alabama Press, 1977), p. 10.
62. Judith R. Gordon, *Human Resource Management*, p. 5.
63. Stanley E. Seashore and Ephraim Yuchtman, "A System Resource Approach to Organizational Effectiveness," *American Sociological Review*, 32(6) (Dec. 1967): 891–903, in *The New Public Personnel Administration,* ed. Felix A. Nigro and Lloyd G. Nigro (Itasca, IL: Peacock, 1976), pp. 31, 37.
64. Ibid., p. 59.
65. Glen A. Bassett, "Employee Turnover Measurement and Human Resources Accounting, "*Human Resources Management* (Fall 1972): pp. 29–30.
66. Block, *Stewardship*, p. 190.
67. Burt Nanus, *Visionary Leadership* (San Francisco: Jossey-Bass, 1992), pp. 11–14, 18.
68. Thompson, *Without Sympathy or Enthusiasm*, p. 41.

Chapter 12: Becoming an Organization Developer

1. Peter Block, *Stewardship: Choosing Service Over Self-Interest* (San Francisco: Berrett-Koehler, 1993), pp. 239–240, 251.
2. Stephen Robbins, *Essentials of Organization Behavior*, 3d ed. (Englewood Cliffs, NJ: Prentice-Hall, 1992), p. 276.
3. Ibid.
4. Donald F. Harvey and Donald F. Brown, *An Experiential Approach to Organization Development*, 4th ed. (Englewood Cliffs, NJ: Prentice-Hall, 1992), p. ix.
5. Richard Beckhard, *Organization Development: Strategies and Models* (Reading, MA: Addison-Wesley, 1969), p. 9.
6. Robbins, *Essentials*, p. 270.
7. Harvey and Brown, *Experiential Approach*, pp. 13, 39.
8. Stephen P. Robbins, *Organization Theory: The Structure and Design of Organizations* (Englewood Cliffs, NJ: Prentice-Hall, 1983), p. 266.
9. Harvey and Brown, *Experiential Approach*, p. 10.
10. Robbins, *Organization Theory*, pp. 13–14.
11. Charles Perrow, *Complex Organizations: A Critical Essay*, 2d ed., (Glenview, IL: Scott, Foresman, 1979), p. 34.
12. Victor A. Thompson, *Bureaucracy and the Modern World* (Morristown, NJ: General Learning Press, 1976), p. 96.
13. Perrow, *Complex Organizations*, p. 34.
14. Ibid.
15. Herbert A. Simon, *Administrative Behavior: A Study of the Decision-Making Processes in Administrative Organizations*, 3d ed. (New York: Free Press, 1976), p. xvi.
16. Simon, 4th ed., p. 112.

17. Ibid., p. 9.
18. Thompson, *Bureaucracy,* p. 96.
19. Harvey and Brown, *Experiential Approach*, p. 41.
20. Thompson, *Bureaucracy,* p. 84.
21. Robbins, *Essentials,* p. 276.
22. Harvey and Brown, *Experiential Approach*, pp. 57–59.
23. Robbins, *Essentials,* pp. 288–295.
24. Ibid., pp. 33–35.
25. Barbara Vobejda, "Most Child-Care Centers Inadequate, Study Says," *Fresno Bee,* February 6, 1995, p. A1.
26. Michael I. Harrison, *Diagnosing Organizations: Methods, Models, and Processes* (Newbury Park, CA: Sage, 1987), p. 35.
27. This section adapted and summarized from Terrence E. Deal, *Corporate Culture* (Reading, MA: Addison-Wesley, 1982), pp. 130–139.
28. J. Steven Ott, *The Organizational Culture Perspective* (Homewood, IL: Irwin, 1989), p. ix.
29. Tom Jones, Organization Developer, Worx, Inc., personal interview, Dec. 22, 1993, Fresno, California.
30. Robert W. Weinbach, *The Social Worker as Manager: Theory and Practice* (White Plains, NY: Longman, 1990), p. 316.
31. Tom Jones, personal interview.
32. Weinbach, *Social Worker as Manager*, p. 318.
33. Ibid., pp. 317–318.
34. Ibid.
35. Ibid., p. 319.
36. Ibid., p. 318.
37. Rebecca Jones, "Workaholic Women Suffer When They Put Boss First," *Fresno Bee,* May 14, 1991, p. A10.
38. Harvey and Brown, *Experiential Approach*, p. 306.
39. Robbins, *Essentials,* p. 286.
40. Harvey and Brown, *Experiential Approach*, p. 307.
41. Except where noted, this section is adapted and summarized from Jerry Edelwich with Archie Brodsky, *Burn-out: Stages of Disillusionment in the Helping Professions* (New York: Human Sciences Press, 1980), pp. 5, 114, 143–182.
42. Harvey and Brown, *Experiential Approach*, pp. 308–312.
43. Robbins, *Essentials,* p. 64, and Robbins, *Organization*, p. 252.
44. Robbins, *Essentials,* p. 65.
45. Robbins, *Organization*, p. 254.
46. Ibid., p. 255.
47. Edgar H. Schein, *Organizational Psychology*, 3d ed. (Englewood Cliffs, NJ: Prentice-Hall, 1980), pp. 162–163.
48. Charles Perrow, *Complex Organizations*, p. 109.
49. Harvey and Brown, *Experiential Approach*, pp. 293–296; see also Paul Hersey and Kenneth H. Blanchard, *Management of Organizational Behavior: Utilizing Human Resources*, 5th ed. (Englewood Cliffs, NJ: Prentice-Hall, 1988), pp. 149–151.
50. Robbins, Essentials, p. 67.
51. Harvey and Brown, *Experiential Approach*, pp. 452–458, and Robbins, Essentials, pp. 68–69.
52. Harvey and Brown, *Experiential Approach*, p. 336.
53. Ibid., p. 351.
54. Robert R. Blake, Herbert Shepard, and Jane S. Mouton, *Managing Intergroup Conflict in Industry* (Houston: Gulf Publishing, 1964). See also Robert R. Blake and Jane S. Mouton, *Solving Costly Organizational Conflicts: Achieving Intergroup Trust, Cooperation, and Teamwork* (San Francisco: Jossey-Bass, 1984).
55. Robert H. Miles, *Macro Organizational Behavior* (Santa Monica, CA: Goodyear Publishing, 1980), pp. 339–348.
56. Ibid., pp. 131.
57. Louis Kriesberg, *The Sociology of Social Conflicts* (Englewood Cliffs, NJ: Prentice-Hall, 1973). A form of the conflict cycle appeared in Jerry Robinson and Roy Clifford, *Managing Conflict in Community Groups* (Champaign-Urbana: University of Illinois, 1974), and in Norman Shawchuck, *How to Manage Conflict in the Church: Understanding and Managing Conflict* (Indianapolis: Spiritual Growth Resources, 1983).
58. Roger Fisher and Scott Brown, *Getting Together—Building a Relationship That Gets to Yes* (Boston: Houghton Mifflin, 1988), p. 37.
59. Ibid., p. 40.
60. This section was summarized and adapted from Freda Gomes, "How to Be a Winning Negotiator," *Toastmaster,* June 1984, pp. 15–19.
61. Robbins, *Organizational Theory*, p. 303.
62. Ibid., p. 24.
63. Harvey and Brown, *Experiential Approach*, pp. 417–423.
64. This section is drawn from Block, *Stewardship,* pp. 182–237.
65. Ibid., p. 237.
66. Frank Lowenberg and Ralph Dolgoff, *Ethical Decisions for Social Work Practice,* 2d ed. (Itasca, IL: F. E. Peacock, 1985), p. 14.
67. Bernard Neugeboren, *Organization, Policy, and Practice in the Human Services* (New York: Longman, 1985), p. 182.

Part 4: Macro Social Work at the Societal and Global Levels

1. Robert Fisher, *Let the People Decide: Neighborhood Organizing in America* (New York: Twayne, 1994), p. xii.
2. Niccolo Machiavelli, *The Prince,* trans. George Bull (London: Penguin, 1961), p. 51.

Chapter 13: Becoming a Social Policy Advocate

1. Si Kahn, *How People Get Power: Organizing Oppressed Communities for Action* (New York: McGraw-Hill, 1978), p. 124.
2. This section is summarized and adapted from Judith Weinraub, "Consumer Advocate Doesn't Back Down From a Good Fight," *Fresno Bee,* June 21, 1992, p. F5.
3. Weismiller and Rome, *Encyclopedia of Social Work,* 19th ed. (Washington, DC: NASW Press, 1995), p. 2309.
4. NASW, *Social Workers Serving in Elective Office* (Washington, DC: NASW, PACE, 1997).
5. John Kenneth Galbraith, *Economics and the Public Purpose* (Boston: Houghton Mifflin, 1973), pp. 46, 66.
6. Thomas R. Dye, *Understanding Public Policy,* 2d ed. (Englewood Cliffs, NJ: Prentice-Hall, 1975), p. 25.
7. William L. Morrow, *Public Administration: Politics, Policy, and the Political System,* 2d ed. (New York: Random House, 1980), p. 83.
8. Ibid., p. 50.
9. James Madison, Federalist No. 10, in Alexander Hamilton, James Madison, and John Jay, *The Federalist Papers* (New York: New American Library, 1961), p. 79.
10. Ibid., Federalist No. 51, p. 322.
11. Dye, *Understanding Public Policy,* p. 21.
12. Madison, Federalist No. 51, p. 322.
13. Morrow, *Public Administration,* pp. 50–51.
14. E. E. Schattschneider, *The Semi-Sovereign People* (New York: Holt, Reinhart, and Winston, 1960), p. 40.
15. Morrow, *Public Administration,* p. 51.
16. Coleman, *Hobbes and America,* p. 38.
17. Summarized and adapted from "The Stench of the Tax Giveaways," *Fresno Bee,* Sept. 2, 1995, p. B10.
18. Eric Planin, *Fresno Bee,* Aug. 21, 1995, p. A6. Used with permission.
19. Phillis J. Day, *A New History of Social Welfare,* 2d ed. (Boston: Allyn and Bacon, 1997), pp. 429–430.
20. "The Stench," p. B10.

21. John Harsanyi, "Some Social Science Implications of a New Approach to Game Theory," in Graham Allison, *The Essence of Decision: Explaining the Cuban Missile Crisis* (Boston: Little, Brown, 1971), p. 31.

22. Morrow, *Public Administration,* pp. 63–66.

23. Allison, *Essence of Decision,* p. 67.

24. Ibid., p. 79.

25. Ibid., p. 63.

26. Ibid., p. 83.

27. Michael Doyle and Jim Boren, "Dooley Harvested Subsidies," *Fresno Bee,* March 29, 1995, p. A1.

28. Ibid., p. 64.

29. Morrow, *Public Administration,* p. 90.

30. NASW, *Social Workers in Elective Office,* p. 5.

31. Howard J. Karger and David Stoesz, *American Social Welfare Policy: A Structural Approach* (New York: Longman, 1990), pp. 63–64.

32. For some critics of modern political and policy theory, see Eric Voegelin, *The New Science of Politics* (Chicago: University of Chicago Press, 1952), and Sheldon Wolin, *Politics and Vision* (Boston: Little, Brown, 1960).

33. Abraham Kaplan, "Perspectives on the Theme," in *Individuality and the New Society,* ed. Abraham Kaplan (Seattle: University of Washington Press, 1970), p. 15.

34. Michael M. Harmon, "Toward an Active Social Theory of Administrative Action: Some Empirical and Normative Implications," in *Organization Theory and the New Public Administration,* ed. Carl Bellone (Boston: Allyn and Bacon, 1980), p. 197.

35. This section is adapted and summarized from Peter L. Berger and Richard John Neuhaus, *To Empower People: From State to Civil Society,* 2d ed. (Washington, DC: American Enterprise Institute Press, 1996), pp. 163–164.

36. For an alternative educational model congruent with the action approach, see Paulo Freire, *Pedagogy of the Oppressed* (New York: Continuum, 1991).

37. Kenneth E. Reid, *Social Work Practice With Groups: A Clinical Perspective* (Pacific Grove, CA: Brooks/Cole, 1991), pp. 26–27, and *From Character Building to Social Treatment: The History of the Use of Groups in Social Work* (Westport, CT: Greenwood Press, 1981).

38. For a perspective on a value-centered theory of politics, see Stephen Salkever, "Virtue, Obligation, and Politics," *Political Science Review,* 68 (1976): pp. 78–91.

39. *Cyclopedia of American Biography,* vol. 23 (1925), pp. 111–112.

40. Thomas Bender, *Community and Social Change in America* (New Brunswick, NJ: Rutgers University Press, 1978), pp. 74–75.

41. Ann Majchrzak, *Methods for Policy Research,* Applied Social Research Methods Series, vol. 3 (Newbury Park, CA: Sage, 1984), p. 12.

42. This section is adapted and summarized from Christopher Bellavita and Henrik L. Blum, "An Analytical Tool for Policy Analysts and Planners," unpublished manuscript, 1981, pp. 5, 6, 12, 13.

43. Ibid., p. 12.

44. Ibid., p. 13.

45. Majchrzak, *Methods,* pp. 58–63.

46. Majchrzak, *Methods,* p. 66.

47. Ibid., pp. 47, 52.

48. Ibid., p. 57.

49. This section is summarized and adapted from David W. Stewart, *Secondary Research: Information, Sources, and Methods,* Applied Social Research Methods Series, vol. 4 (Newbury Park, CA: Sage, 1984), pp. 59–63, 11–12.

50. Ibid., p. 63.

51. Allison, *Essence of Decision.*

52. This section is adapted and summarized from William D. Coplin and Michael K. O'Leary, *Everyman's PRINCE: A Guide to Understanding Your Political Problems,* 2d ed. (North Scituate, MA: Duxbury Press, 1976), pp. 64–65, 72.

53. Ibid., p. 65.

54. Ibid.

55. Charles S. Prigmore and Charles R. Atherton, *Social Welfare Policy: Analysis and Formulation,* 2d ed. (Lexington, MA: D. C. Heath, 1986), p. 195.

56. Ibid., p. 196.

57. Ibid.

58. This section is summarized and adapted from Karen S. Haynes and James S. Mickelson, *Affecting Change: Social Workers in the Political Arena,* 2d ed. (New York: Longman, 1991), pp. 64, 72–76.

59. Child Welfare League of America, *Washington Workbook for Child Advocates,* in Haynes and Mikelson, *Affecting Change,* pp. 76–77.

60. DiNitto and Dye, *Social Welfare,* p. xiv.

61. John McNutt [online], Available e-mail 1/17/00.

62. Ronald L. Simons and Stephen M. Aigner, *Practice Principles: A Problem-Solving Approach to Social Work* (New York: Macmillan, 1985), p. 21.

63. John Perkins, *With Justice For All* (Ventura, CA: Regal Books, 1982), pp. 161–162.

64. Quotes are from S. K. Khinduka, "Community Development: Potentials and Limitations," in *Strategies of Community Organization: Macro Practice,* 4th ed., ed. Fred M. Cox, John L. Erlich, Jack Rothman, and John E. Tropman (Itasca, IL: Peacock, 1987), p. 358.

65. Bender, *Community and Social Change in America,* p. 148.

Chapter 14: Becoming Active In Social Movements

1. Summarized and adapted from J. Garrow, *Bearing the Cross,* (New York: William Morrow, 986) pp. 513, 536–553.

2. Gustavo Gutierrez, "Notes for a Theology of Liberation," *Theological Studies* (Baltimore: Waverly Press, 1970), pp. 254, 247.

3. George Lakey, *Strategy for a Living Revolution* (San Francisco: W. H. Freeman, 1973), p. xiii.

4. Saul D. Alinsky, *Rules for Radicals: A Pragmatic Primer for Realistic Radicals* (New York: Vintage Books, 1974), p. 3.

5. June Axinn and Herman Levin, *Social Welfare: A History of American Response to Need,* 2d ed. (New York: Longman, 1982), p. 248.

6. Except where noted, this section is adapted and summarized from Foster Rhea Dulles, *Labor in America: A History,* 3d ed. (New York: Crowell, 1966), pp. 22, 30, 166–172, 209–210, 263–275.

7. Adapted from Ronald G. Walters, *American Reformers 1815–1860* (New York: Hill and Wang, 1978), pp. 78, 80, 85.

8. This section is summarized and adapted from Axinn and Levin, *Social Welfare,* pp. 46–48.

9. This section is summarized and adapted from Axinn and Levin, *Social Welfare,* pp. 141–143.

10. Allen F. Davis, "Settlement Workers in Politics, 1890–1914," in *Practical Politics: Social Work and Political Responsibility,* ed. Maryann Mahaffey and John W. Hands (Silver Spring, MD: NASW), pp. 36–38.

11. Axinn and Levin, *Social Welfare,* p. 147.

12. Jane Addams, *Twenty Years at Hull House* (New York: New American Library, 1938), pp. 227–229.

13. Ibid., pp. 126–127.
14. Claus Offe, "Challenging the Boundaries of Institutional Politics: Social Movements Since the 1960s," in *Changing Boundaries of the Political,* ed. Charles Maier (New York: Cambridge University Press, 1987), p. 73.
15. Ron Eyerman and Andrew Jamison, *Social Movements: A Cognitive Approach* (Cambridge: Polity Press, 1991), pp. 10, 49.
16. This section is summarized and adapted from Robert Fisher and Joseph Kling, *Mobilizing the Community: Local Politics in the Era of the Global City.* Urban Affairs Annual Review, 41 (Newbury Park: Sage, 1993), pp. 127–129.
17. Ibid., p. 127.
18. Kurt Lewin, "Frontiers in Group Dynamics: Concept, Method and Reality in Social Science, Social Equilibria and Social Change," *Human Relations,* 1(1) (June 1947), pp. 5–41.
19. Except where noted, this section has been summarized and adapted from Donald F. Harvey and Donald R. Brown, *An Experiential Approach to Organization Development* (Englewood Cliffs, NJ: Prentice-Hall, 1991), pp. 199–200.
20. Eyerman and Jamison, *Social Movements,* p. 79.
21. Herbert J. Rubin and Irene S. Rubin, *Community Organizing and Development,* 2d ed. (New York: Macmillan, 1992), p. 245.
22. Ibid., p. 266.
23. Alinsky, *Rules for Radicals,* p. 128.
24. Ibid., p. 304.
25. Ibid., p. 130.
26. John Forester, *Planning in the Face of Power* (Berkeley: University of California Press, 1989), pp. 46–47.
27. Ibid., p. 45.
28. Ibid., pp. 46–47.
29. Rubin and Rubin, *Community Organizing,* p. 313.
30. This section is summarized and adapted from Rubin and Rubin, *Community Organizing,* pp. 296–298.
31. Marilyn Ferguson, *The Aquarian Conspiracy* (Los Angeles: Tarcher, 1980), p. 199.
32. Ibid.
33. Garrow, *Bearing the Cross,* p. 524.
34. This section is summarized and adapted from Rubin and Rubin, *Community Organizing,* pp. 264–265, 318.
35. Ibid., 89, 90.
36. Rubin and Rubin, *Community Organizing,* pp. 320, 302.
37. Ibid., pp. 313–314.
38. Ibid., p. 303.
39. T. Branch, *Parting the Waters: America in the King Years, 1954–1963* (New York: Simon and Schuster, 1988), p. 438.
40. Rubin and Rubin, *Community Organizing,* p. 313.
41. This section adapted and summarized from Rubin and Rubin, *Community Organizing,* pp. 309, 312–317.
42. Alinsky, *Rules for Radicals,* p. 127.
43. Ibid.
44. Peter F. Drucker, *New Realities in Government and Politics, In Economics and Business, In Society and World View* (New York: Harper and Row, 1989), pp. 3–4.
45. Eyerman and Jamison, *Social Movements,* p. 162.
46. Harry C. Boyte, *Community Is Possible: Repairing America's Roots* (New York: Harper and Row, 1984), pp. 26, 28.
47. Richard Flacks, "The Party's Over," in *New Social Movements: From Ideology to Identity,* ed. Enrique Larana, Hank Johnston, and Joseph R. Gusfield (Philadelphia: Temple University Press, 1994), p. 347.
48. Eyerman and Jamison, *Social Movements,* p. 161.
49. Robert Fisher, *Let the People Decide: Neighborhood Organizing in America* (New York: Twayne, 1994), p. 217.
50. Alberto Melluci, "A Strange Kind of Newness" in *New Social Movements: From Ideology to Identity,* ed. Enrique Larana,

Hank Johnston, and Joseph R. Gusfield (Philadelphia: Temple University Press, 1994), p.127.
51. Flacks, "The Party's Over," p. 348.
52. Eyerman and Jamison, *Social Movements,* p. 27.
53. Ibid., pp. 164–165.
54. Ibid., pp. 165–166.
55. Michel Foucault, "The Subject and Power," in *Michel Foucault: Beyond Structuralism and Hermeneutics,* ed. Hubert I. Dreyfus and Paul Rabinow (Chicago: University of Chicago Press, 1983), p. 211.
56. This section is adapted and summarized from Eyerman and Jamison, *Social Movements,* pp. 26–27, 43–59, 93, 161.
57. Except where noted, this section is adapted and summarized from Carol Mueller, "Conflict Networks and the Origins of Women's Liberation," in *New Social Movements: From Ideology to Identity,* ed. Enrique Larana, Hank Johnston, and Joseph R. Gusfield (Philadelphia: Temple University Press, 1994), pp. 234–239.
58. Eyerman and Jamison, *Social Movements,* p. 55.
59. Melluci, "Strange kind of Newness," p. 127.

Chapter 15: Social Work at the Global Level

1. Abraham Kaplan, "Perspectives on the Theme" in *Individuality and the New Society,* ed. Abraham Kaplan (Seattle: University of Washington Press, 1970), pp. 19–20.
2. Peter Block, *Stewardship: Choosing Service Over Self-Interest* (San Francisco: Berrett-Koehler, 1993), p. 17.
3. Doug McAdam, "Culture and Social Movements," in *Social Movements: Perspectives and Issues,* ed. Steven M. Buechler and F. Kurt Cylke Jr. (Mountain View, CA: Mayfield, 1997), p. 481.
4. Julie Fisher, *The Road From Rio: Sustainable Development and the Nongovernmental Movement in the Third World* (Westport, CT: Praeger, 1993), p. 15.
5. Ponna Wignaraja, ed., "Introduction" and "Rethinking Development and Democracy," *New Social Movements in the South: Empowering People* (London: Zed Books, 1993), pp. xv, 3, 10.
6. Ruth Leger Sivard, *World Military and Social Expenditures, 1991* (Washington, DC: World Priorities, 1991), p. 33.
7. Julian Bond, Commencement Address, Washington University, St. Louis, reported in *New York Times,* May 29, 2000, p. A11.
8. Robert C. Linthicum, *Empowering the Poor: Community Organization Among the City's 'Rag, Tag and Bobtail'* (Monrovia, CA: MARC, 1991), p. 6.
9. John Daniszewski, "Severe Famine in Sudan Surpassing Relief Efforts," *Fresno Bee,* July 15, 1998, p. A7.
10. Linthicum, *Empowering the Poor,* p. 6.
11. Peter R. Baehr and Leon Gordenker, *The United Nations in the 1990s,* 2d ed. (New York: St. Martin's, 1994), p. 133.
12. Hubert Campfens, *Community Development Around the World* (Toronto: University of Toronto Press, 1997), p. 15.
13. Mansour Fakih, *NGOs in Indonesia* (Amherst, MA: Center for International Education, University of Massachusetts, 1991), p. 10.
14. Anisur Rahman, *People's Self-Development: Perspectives on Participatory Action Research* (London: Zed Books, 1993), p. 180.
15. Daniel Comacho, "Latin America: A Society in Motion," in *New Social Movements in the South: Empowering People,* ed. Ponna Wignaraja (London: Zed Books, 1993), p. 36.
16. Richard Flacks, "Think Globally, Act Politically," in *Social Movements: Perspectives and Issues,* ed. Steven M. Buech-

ler and F. Kurt Cylke Jr. (Mountain View, CA: Mayfield, 1997), p. 56.

17. Rahman, *People's Self-Development,* p. 162.

18. Wignaraja,"Rethinking Development and Democracy," p. 12.

19. Campfens, *Community Development,* pp.16–17.

20. Walt Whitman Rostow, *The Stages of Economic Growth: A Non-Communist Manifesto* (Cambridge: Cambridge University Press, 1960). See also David McClelland, *The Achieving Society* (New York: Van Nostrand, 1961), and Charles Inkeles and David Smith, *Becoming Modern* (Cambridge, MA: Harvard University Press, 1974).

21. Thomas Bender, *Community and Social Change in America* (New Brunswick, NJ: Rutgers University Press, 1978), pp. 23–24, 28–29.

22. Wignaraja, "Rethinking Development and Democracy," p.8.

23. Campfens, *Community Development,* p. 17.

24. Fakih, *NGOs in Indonesia,* p. 3.

25. Wignaraja, "Rethinking Development and Democracy," p. 8.

26. Rahman, *People's Self-Development,* pp. 181, 168.

27. Fakih, *NGOs in Indonesia,* p. 11.

28. Steven Buechler and F. Kurt Cylke, "The Centrality of Social Movements," in *Social Movements: Perspectives and Issues,* ed. Steven M. Buechler and F. Kurt Cylke Jr. (Mountain View, CA: Mayfield, 1997), p. 577.

29. Wignaraja, "Rethinking Development and Democracy," p. 6.

30. Comacho, "Latin America: A Society," p. 39.

31. Rahman, *People's Self-Development,* pp. 168, 181.

32. John Paul Vandenakker, *Small Christian Communities and the Parish: An Ecclesiological Analysis of the North American Experience* (Kansas City, MO: Sheed and Ward, 1994), p. 98.

33. Camacho, "Latin America: A Society," p. 50.

34. Leilah Landim, "Brazilian Crossroads: Peoples Groups, Walls and Bridges," in *New Social Movements in the South,* ed. Ponna Wignaraja (London: Zed Books, 1993), p. 219.

35. Sara M. Evans and Harry C. Boyte, *Free Spaces* (New York: Harper and Row, 1986), p. 20.

36. Guillermo Cook, *The Expectation of the Poor: Latin American Basic Ecclesial Communities in Protestant Perspective* (Maryknoll, NY: Orbis, 1985), p. 91.

37. Rahman, *People's Self-Development,* p. 26.

38. Vandenakker, *Small Christian Communities,* p. 103.

39. Alan Durning, "Action at the Grassroots: Fighting Poverty and Environmental Decline," *Worldwatch Paper, 88* (Jan. 1989): p. 5.

40. Sidney Tarrow, "A Movement Society," in *Social Movements: Perspectives and Issues,* ed. Steven M. Buechler and F. Kurt Cylke Jr. (Mountain View, CA: Mayfield, 1997), p. 570.

41. Fakih, *NGOs in Indonesia,* p. 2.

42. Sidney Tarrow, "A Movement Society,"p. 578.

43. Fakih, *NGOs in Indonesia,* pp. 1, 6–7.

44. Robert Fisher, *Let the People Decide: A History of Neighborhood Organizing* (Boston: G. K. Hall, 1984), p. xiii.

45. Fisher, *Road From Rio,* p. 81.

46. Ibid.

47. Landim, "Brazilian Crossroads," p. 224.

48. Rahman, *People's Self-Development,* p. 162.

49. Harsh Sethi, "Action Groups in the New Politics," in *New Social Movements in the South: Empowering People,* ed. Ponna Wignaraja (London: Zed Books, 1993), p. 231.

50. Landim, "Brazilian Crossroads," p. 222.

51. Fisher, *Road From Rio,* p. 216.

52. Rahman, *People's Self-Development,* p. 128.

53. Ibid.

54. Fisher, *Road From Rio,* p. 64.

55. Ibid., p. 164.

56. Rahman, *People's Self-Development,* p. 128.

57. Fisher, *Road From Rio,* pp.21, 23, 30.

58. Fakih, *NGOs in Indonesia,* p. 11.

59. Vandenakker, *Small Christian Communities,* p. xii.

60. Comacho, "Latin America: A Society in Motion," p. 47.

61. Ibid., pp. 46–47.

62. Wignaraja, "Rethinking Development and Democracy," pp. 6, 19.

63. Rahman, *People's Self-Development,* p. 68.

64. Ibid., p. 182.

65. Camacho, "Latin America: A Society in Motion," pp. 47–48.

66. Ibid.

67. Jeff Dumtra, "Power to the People," *World View* (Winter 1991/1992): pp. 8–13.

68. Campfens, *Community Development,* p. 4.

69. Ibid., p. 544.

70. Jackie Smith, "Transnational Political Processes and the Human Rights Movement," in *Social Movements: Perspectives and Issues,* ed. Buecher and Cylke (Mountain View, CA: Mayfield, 1997), p. 541.

71. Campfens, *Community Development,* p. 32.

72. Ibid., p. 16.

73. Peter R. Baehr and Leon Gordenker, *The United Nations in the 1990s,* 2d ed. (New York: St. Martin's, 1994), pp. 130–131.

74. Ibid., 133–136, 142.

75. Evan Luard, *The United Nations: How It Works and What It Does* (New York: St. Martin's, 1979), p. 57.

76. Many of the ideas in this section have been obtained from Anisur Rahman, People's Self-Development, pp. 46–48, 68–72, 195.

77. Antonia Pantoja and Wilhelmina Perry, "Community Development and Restoration: A Perspective," in *Community Organizing in a Diverse Society,* ed. Felix G. Rivera and John L. Erlich (Boston: Allyn and Bacon, 1992), pp. 224–225. Used with permission.

78. Paulo Freire, *Pedagogy of the Oppressed* (New York: Herder and Herder, 1970), p. 73.

79. William A. Smith, "Concientizacao and Simulation Games," Technical Note 2 (Amherst, MA: Center for International Education, University of Massachusetts, 1972), p. 9.

80. Si Kahn, *How People Get Power: Organizing Oppressed Communities for Action* (New York: McGraw-Hill, 1972), pp. 48–49.

81. Wignaraja, "Rethinking Development and Democracy," p. 7.

82. Timothy Luke, *Social Theory and Modernity: Critique, Dissent, and Revolution* (Newbury Park: Sage, 1990), p. 191.

Epilogue

1. Robert Bellah et al., *Habits of the Heart: Individualism and Commitment in American Life* (New York: Harper and Row, 1985), p. 138.

2. This section is summarized and adapted from *U.S. News and World Report,* March 21, 1994, p. 58.

3. Noam Chomsky, *Problems of Knowledge and Freedom: The Russell Lectures* (New York: Vintage Books, 1971), in Rivera and Erlich, p. 64.

4. Harry Specht and Mark Courtney, *Unfaithful Angels: How Social Work Has Abandoned Its Mission* (New York: Free Press, 1994), p. 27.

5. Ibid.

NAME INDEX

SUBJECT INDEX